D0909858

THE SOCIAL PSYCHOLOGY OF
INTERGROUP RECONCILIATION

Hm
1033
S66
2008
UAN

The Social Psychology of Intergroup Reconciliation

Arie Nadler
Thomas E. Malloy
Jeffrey D. Fisher

OXFORD
UNIVERSITY PRESS

2008

Oxford University Press, Inc., publishes works that further
Oxford University's objective of excellence
in research, scholarship, and education.

Oxford New York
Auckland Cape Town Dar es Salaam Hong Kong Karachi
Kuala Lumpur Madrid Melbourne Mexico City Nairobi
New Delhi Shanghai Taipei Toronto

With offices in
Argentina Austria Brazil Chile Czech Republic France Greece
Guatemala Hungary Italy Japan Poland Portugal Singapore
South Korea Switzerland Thailand Turkey Ukraine Vietnam

Copyright © 2008 by Oxford University Press, Inc.

Published by Oxford University Press, Inc.
198 Madison Avenue, New York, New York 10016

www.oup.com

Oxford is a registered trademark of Oxford University Press

All rights reserved. No part of this publication may be reproduced,
stored in a retrieval system, or transmitted, in any form or by any means,
electronic, mechanical, photocopying, recording, or otherwise,
without the prior permission of Oxford University Press.

Library of Congress Cataloging-in-Publication Data

The social psychology of intergroup reconciliation / [edited by]
Arie Nadler, Thomas E. Malloy and Jeffrey D. Fisher.
p. cm.
ISBN 978-0-19-530031-4
1. Social psychology.   2. Intergroup relations.   3. Conflict
management.   I. Nadler, Arie.   II. Malloy, Thomas E.
III. Fisher, Jeffrey D., 1949–
HM1033.S66 2008
303.6'9—dc22
2007031277

9 8 7 6 5 4 3 2

Printed in the United States of America
on acid-free paper

To my family; may we all live in a reconciled land
Arie Nadler

To Jeffrey, Stephen, Grace, and Madeline
Thomas E. Malloy

To Allison, Andy, Aaron, and Molly
Jeffrey D. Fisher

CONTENTS

List of Contributors   *xi*

Introduction   Intergroup Reconciliation: Dimensions and Themes   3
                Arie Nadler, Thomas E. Malloy, and Jeffrey D. Fisher

Part I   Intergroup Reconciliation: Its Nature

Chapter 1   Reconciliation From a Social-Psychological Perspective   15
             Herbert C. Kelman

Part II   Socioemotional Reconciliation: Moving Beyond Victimhood, Guilt, and Humiliation

Part II.A   Guilt, Victimhood, and Forgiveness

Chapter 2   Instrumental and Socioemotional Paths to Intergroup
             Reconciliation and the Needs-Based Model of Socioemotional
             Reconciliation   37
             Arie Nadler and Nurit Shnabel

Chapter 3   Transforming Trauma in the Aftermath of Gross Human Rights
             Abuses: Making Public Spaces Intimate Through the South
             African Truth and Reconciliation Commission   57
             Pumla Gobodo-Madikizela

Chapter 4   Social Categorization, Standards of Justice,
             and Collective Guilt   77
             Anca M. Miron and Nyla R. Branscombe

Chapter 5   Prospects for Intergroup Reconciliation: Social-Psychological
             Predictors of Intergroup Forgiveness and Reparation in
             Northern Ireland and Chile   97
             Masi Noor, Rupert Brown, and Garry Prentice

Part II.B   Restoring Respect and Esteem

Chapter 6   How Needs Can Motivate Intergroup Reconciliation in the Face
             of Intergroup Conflict   117
             Felicia Pratto and Demis E. Glasford

Chapter 7   The Social Psychology of Respect: Implications for
             Delegitimization and Reconciliation   145
             Ronnie Janoff-Bulman and Amelie Werther

Chapter 8   From Egosystem to Ecosystem in Intergroup Interactions:
             Implications for Intergroup Reconciliation   171
             Jennifer Crocker, Julie A. Garcia, and Noah Nuer

Part III   Instrumental Reconciliation: Contact, Common
             Identity, and Equality

Part III.A   Contact and Common Identity

Chapter 9   Stepping Stones to Reconciliation in Northern Ireland:
             Intergroup Contact, Forgiveness, and Trust   199
             *Miles Hewstone, Jared B. Kenworthy, Ed Cairns, Nicole Tausch,
             Joanne Hughes, Tania Tam, Alberto Voci, Ulrich von Hecker,
             and Catherine Pinder*

Chapter 10   Majority and Minority Perspectives in Intergroup Relations:
             The Role of Contact, Group Representations, Threat, and Trust
             in Intergroup Conflict and Reconciliation   227
             *John F. Dovidio, Samuel L. Gaertner, Melissa-Sue John,
             Samer Halabi, Tamar Saguy, Adam R. Pearson,
             and Blake M. Riek*

Chapter 11   A Social-Psychological Approach to Postconflict
              Reconciliation   255
              Blake M. Riek, Samuel L. Gaertner, John F. Dovidio,
              Marilynn B. Brewer, Eric W. Mania, and Marika J. Lamoreaux

Chapter 12   Reconciliation, Trust, and Cooperation: Using Bottom-Up
              and Top-Down Strategies to Achieve Peace in the
              Israeli-Palestinian Conflict   275
              Reuben M. Baron

Part III.B   Equality and Differential Power

Chapter 13   Diminishing Vertical Distance: Power and Social Status as
              Barriers to Intergroup Reconciliation   301
              Lasana T. Harris and Susan T. Fiske

Chapter 14   Social Identity, Legitimacy, and Intergroup Conflict: The Rocky
              Road to Reconciliation   319
              Russell Spears

Chapter 15   Intergroup Relations and Reconciliation: Theoretical Analysis
              and Methodological Implications   345
              Thomas E. Malloy

Part IV   Programs to Promote Intergroup Reconciliation

Chapter 16   The Road to Reconciliation   369
              Walter G. Stephan

Chapter 17   Promoting Reconciliation After Genocide and Mass Killing
              in Rwanda—And Other Postconflict Settings: Understanding
              the Roots of Violence, Healing, Shared History, and General
              Principles   395
              Ervin Staub

Chapter 18   Between Conflict and Reconciliation: Toward a Theory of
              Peaceful Coexistence   423
              Stephen Worchel and Dawna K. Coutant

Chapter 19   Help as a Vehicle to Reconciliation, With Particular
              Reference to Help for Extreme Health Needs   447
              Jeffrey D. Fisher, Arie Nadler, Jessica S. Little, and Tamar Saguy

Part V   Intergroup Reconciliation: An Overall View

Chapter 20   Reconciliation After Destructive Intergroup Conflict   471
          Morton Deutsch

Index   487

CONTRIBUTORS

REUBEN M. BARON
Department of Psychology
University of Connecticut
Storrs, Connecticut

NYLA R. BRANSCOMBE
Department of Psychology
University of Kansas
Lawrence, Kansas

MARILYNN B. BREWER
Department of Psychology
The Ohio State University
Columbus, Ohio

RUPERT BROWN
Department of Psychology
School of Life Sciences
University of Sussex
Falmer, Brighton,
United Kingdom

ED CAIRNS
School of Psychology
University of Ulster
Coleraine,
Northern Ireland

DAWNA K. COUTANT
Department of Psychology
University of Hawaii
Hilo, Hawaii

JENNIFER CROCKER
Department of Psychology
University of Michigan
Ann Arbor, Michigan

MORTON DEUTSCH
International Center of Cooperation
and Conflict Resolution
Teachers College
Columbia University
New York

JOHN F. DOVIDIO
Department of Psychology
University of Connecticut
Storrs, Connecticut

JEFFREY D. FISHER
Center for Health, Intervention,
and Prevention
University of Connecticut
Storrs, Connecticut

SUSAN T. FISKE
Department of Psychology
Princeton University
Princeton, New Jersey

SAMUEL L. GAERTNER
Department of Psychology
University of Delaware
Newark, Delaware

JULIE A. GARCIA
Psychology and Child Development
  Department
California Polytechnic State University
SanLuis Obispo, California

DEMIS E. GLASFORD
Department of Psychology
University of Connecticut
Storrs, Connecticut

PUMLA GOBODO-MADIKIZELA
Department of Psychology
University of Cape Town
Rondebosch, South Africa

SAMER HALABI
Department of Behavioral Sciences
Zefat Academic College
Zefat, Israel

LASANA T. HARRIS
Department of Psychology
New York University
New York, New York

MILES HEWSTONE
Department of Experimental
  Psychology
University of Oxford
Oxford, United Kingdom

JOANNE HUGHES
School of Policy Studies
University of Ulster Jordanstown Campus
Newtownabbey,
Northern Ireland

RONNIE JANOFF-BULMAN
Department of Psychology
University of Massachusetts
Amherst, Massachusetts

MELISSA-SUE JOHN
Department of Psychology
University of Connecticut
Storrs, Connecticut

HERBERT C. KELMAN
Richard Clarke Cabot Professor
  of Social Ethics, Emeritus
Department of Psychology
Harvard University
Cambridge, Massachusetts

JARED B. KENWORTHY
Department of Psychology
The University of Texas
Arlington, Texas

MARIKA J. LAMOREAUX
Department of Psychology
University of Delaware
Newark, Delaware

JESSICA S. LITTLE
Ohio University
Athens, Ohio

THOMAS E. MALLOY
Department of Psychology
Rhode Island College
Providence, Rhode Island

ERIC W. MANIA
Department of Psychology
University of Delaware
Newark, Delaware

ANCA M. MIRON
Department of Psychology
University of Wisconsin Oshkosh
Oshkosh, Wisconsin

ARIE NADLER
Professor of Psychology
Argentina Chair for Research on the Social
  Psychology of Conflict and Cooperation
Department of Psychology
Tel Aviv University
Ramat-Aviv, Tel Aviv, Israel

MASI NOOR
School of Applied Social Sciences
Canterbury Christ Church University
Canterbury, Kent

NOAH NUER
Learning as Leadership, Inc.
San Rafael, California

ADAM R. PEARSON
Department of Psychology
University of Connecticut
Storrs, Connecticut

CATHERINE PINDER
Department of Experimental Psychology
University of Oxford
Oxford, United Kingdom

FELICIA PRATTO
Department of Psychology
University of Connecticut
Storrs, Connecticut

GARRY PRENTICE
Dublin Business School
Dublin, Ireland

BLAKE M. RIEK
Department of Psychology
Calvin College
Grand Rapids, Michigan

TAMAR SAGUY
Department of Psychology
University of Connecticut
Storrs, Connecticut

NURIT SHNABEL
Department of Psychology
Tel Aviv University
Ramat-Aviv, Israel

RUSSELL SPEARS
School of Psychology
Cardiff University
Cardiff, Wales,
United Kingdom

ERVIN STAUB
Department of Psychology
University of Massachusetts
Amherst, Massachusetts

WALTER G. STEPHAN
Department of Psychology
New Mexico State
  University
Las Cruces, New Mexico

TANIA TAM
Department of Experimental
  Psychology
University of Oxford
Oxford, United Kingdom

NICOLE TAUSCH
Department of Experimental Psychology
University of Oxford
Oxford, United Kingdom

ALBERTO VOCI
University of Padova
Dipartimento Di Psicologia Generale
Padova, Italy

ULRICH VON HECKER
School of Psychology
Cardiff University
Cathays, Cardiff, United Kingdom

AMELIE WERTHER
Department of Psychology
University of Massachusetts
Amherst, Massachusetts

STEPHEN WORCHEL
Department of Psychology
University of Hawaii
Hilo, Hawaii

THE SOCIAL PSYCHOLOGY OF
INTERGROUP RECONCILIATION

INTRODUCTION

Intergroup Reconciliation: Dimensions and Themes

ARIE NADLER, THOMAS E. MALLOY, AND JEFFREY D. FISHER

Social psychology emerged and developed as a scientific discipline in the mid-20th century during a period of time marked by both intergroup conflict including World Wars I and II and the beginning of the cold war, and intrasocietal conflicts centered on equalizing power between various groups as is exemplified in the feminist and civil rights movements in America. Understandably, social psychologists have focused on the study of the antecedents of intergroup conflict and pathways to resolution. The present volume is part of this scientific tradition. Yet, its emphasis on processes of intergroup reconciliation is consistent with the current sociopolitical zeitgeist and recent scientific developments.

Intergroup Reconciliation: Sociopolitical and Social-Psychological Background

The concept of reconciliation has rarely been used in social science analyses of conflicts between groups and nations. One reason for this may be the religious and spiritual overtones of concepts like "reconciliation," "forgiveness," or "healing." Social scientists in general and social psychologists in particular have preferred to use more neutral concepts like conflict resolution when discussing the cessation of conflict. The use of this terminology reflects more than a semantic preference. It underscores the prevailing view in much of the social science literature that conflicts are attributable to disagreements on the division of scarce and coveted resources and that their ending is predicated on the parties' ability to agree on a formula for their division. During the last five decades scholars like Burton (1969), Deutsch (Deutsch, 1973; Deutsch, Coleman, & Marcus, 2006), and Kelman (1978, 2006) have argued when discussing cessation of conflict that agreement on the division of resources is not sufficient and that a full understanding of intergroup conflict requires changing the relationships between the adversaries (e.g., to greater trust and constructive cooperation) and attending to their psychological needs and feelings (e.g., needs for justice and equality, feelings of victimization or guilt). The chapters in the present volume on reconciliation echo this emphasis. The different contributions are united by a definition of intergroup reconciliation as a *process* that leads to a *stable end* to conflict and is predicated on *changes in the nature of adversarial relations* between the adversaries and *each of the parties' conflict-related needs, emotions, and cognitions.* This emphasis on the reconciliation processes is consistent with broad sociopolitical changes and emerging trends in social-psychological research and theory on intergroup relations.

Since the early 1990s, reconciliation and related concepts (e.g., guilt, forgiveness, and trust) have been more frequently used in sociopolitical discourses for ending intergroup conflicts between and within nations. The realist approach to intergroup conflict was appropriate during the cold war era when two equally powerful actors who threatened each other with destruction had to secure a relatively stable coexistence through negotiations that were driven by the motivation for maximization of their own interests and security. During this era, the two dominant and competing world ideologies were orientated to coexist by maintaining and controlling their conflict rather than by trying to end it. Since the end of the cold war, there are numerous examples of conflicts that have ended when a more powerful party agreed, or was forced to close the chapter of occupation and discrimination and open a new chapter marked by equal rights for all. The end of Apartheid in South Africa and the transitions from dictatorial and autocratic regimes in many South-American and East-European societies epitomize this process. The success of these transitions was predicated on the ability of the former powerful perpetrator to live in relative harmony with their former powerless victims. This called for open and public discourses regarding the past of human rights violations through a process in which the victimizers were either punished or forgiven, and the victims' equal rights and powers were restored. The political act of creating the Truth and Reconciliation

Commission (TRC) in South Africa (chapter 3 by Gobodo-Madikizela) is a dramatic demonstration of this new sociopolitical reality. The TRC and similar efforts (Barkan, 2001) convey the same message: Settling conflicting interests is not enough to assure a stable end to conflict; to achieve this one must deal directly and openly with the past of pain and loss that created emotional and perceptual barriers of victimhood, guilt, distrust, and fear.

These changes in the sociopolitical zeitgeist are consistent with changing research emphases in the social psychology of intergroup relations. In the last two decades, social identity and self-categorization theories have become central perspectives in empirical and theoretical discussions in social psychology. These developments have highlighted the fact that the way in which group members categorize themselves in the social world (e.g., chapter 10 by Dovidio, Gaertner, John, Halabi, Saguy, Pearson, & Riek) and their feelings about their own group identity (e.g., in-group identification; chapter 14 by Spears in the present volume) determine if and how intergroup conflict will be ameliorated. It has been observed that relations between groups are seldom, if ever, relations between equals and that the analysis of intergroup relations needs to account for the dimension of differential power between groups (e.g., chapter 13 by Harris & Fiske). In a related development, social psychologists working in this area have become increasingly aware of the importance of social motivations and emotions. Thus, for example, in the last decade there is growing research on the role of honor (Nisbett & Cohen, 1996; chapter 6 by Pratto & Glasford, and chapter 7 by Janoff-Bulman & Werther on similar themes), collective guilt, and collective victimhood (Branscombe & Doosje, 2004; Leach, Snider, & Iyer, 2002; chapter 4 by Miron & Branscombe and chapter 5 by Noor, Brown, & Prentice) in conflicts between groups.

Taken together, the recent trends in the larger sociopolitical context and the emerging emphases within social-psychological theory and research set the stage for the present volume. We believe that social psychology is uniquely equipped both conceptually and methodologically to address these aspects of intergroup reconciliation. We shall now move to discuss the different emphases that exist in the present volume. This serves as the basis for the organization of the chapters. We shall subsequently turn to a brief description of each of the contributions.

Intergroup Reconciliation: Different Emphases on the Same Process

The chapters in the present volume vary. First, they represent different *methodological approaches*. While some offer original conceptual analyses (e.g., chapter 12 by Baron) other chapters rely on experimental evidence (e.g., chapter 2 by Nadler & Shnabel), variance component analysis (e.g., chapter 15 by Malloy), large scale surveys (e.g., chapter 9 by Hewstone, Kenworthy, Cairns, Tausch, Hughes, Tam, Voci, von Hecker & Pinder), or evaluation of specific reconciliation programs (e.g., chapter 18 by Worchel & Coutant) to support their conclusions. Second, the chapters vary in the theoretical perspective that their analysis is based on. Some chapters rely on self-categorization processes (e.g., chapter 11 by Riek, Gaertner, Dovidio, Brewer, Mania, & Lamoreaux), others center on the importance of power relations in this context (e.g., chapter 13 by Harris & Fiske), and still others emphasize the role of collective emotions such as collective victimhood or collective guilt as precursors of intergroup reconciliation (e.g., chapter 3 by Gobodo-Madikizela). Beyond these differences in theoretical and methodological orientations, the chapters cluster around two kinds of intergroup reconciliation (i.e., *Socio-Emotional and Instrumental Reconciliation*, Nadler, 2002; chapter 2 by Nadler & Shnabel) that make up the organizing theme for the present volume. We shall first describe these two processes of reconciliation and then give a brief description of the volume's sections and the chapters in each of these sections.

In the opening chapter, Kelman makes a distinction between the three processes to end intergroup conflict: conflict settlement, conflict resolution, and reconciliation. He notes that efforts to settle conflicts focus on settling conflicting *interests*, efforts for conflict resolution seek to end intergroup conflict by changing adversarial *relations*, and efforts for reconciliation seek to end conflict by affecting changes in each of the participants' *identities*. The distinction between socioemotional and instrumental reconciliation is similar to Kelman's differentiation between conflict resolution and reconciliation in that it distinguishes between reconciliation as a process that seeks to change the *relations between the adversaries* (i.e., instrumental reconciliation) from a process of working through *emotions and threats to identity* that are the consequence of the pain and humiliation that parties had inflicted on each other (i.e., socioemotional reconciliation).

Instrumental reconciliation aims to change adversarial relations into positive relations that will allow the parties to coexist in a conflict-free environment. It represents a long-term process during which the parties gradually learn to replace enmity with trust and negative with relatively positive perceptions of the other. The work on the contact hypothesis informs us about the conditions under which such changes are likely to occur. Thus, for example, equal power (chapters 13, 14, and 15 by Harris & Fiske, Spears, and Malloy, respectively) and common identity (chapters 9, 10, and 11 by Hewstone et al., Dovidio et al., and Riek et al., respectively) are critical elements for such positive changes to take place. The name instrumental reconciliation reflects the fact that many real world programs that are intended to build peaceful coexistence between former enemies consist of cooperative efforts to achieve instrumental goals that are important to both parties (e.g., Lederach, 1997).

Socioemotional reconciliation is predicated on the premise that recurring episodes of pain and humiliation pose a threat to identity, which often results in preoccupation with feelings of guilt or victimhood that constitute barriers to ending conflict. Processes of socioemotional reconciliation aim to remove these barriers. This can be achieved when a perpetrator accepts responsibility for past wrongdoings, expresses remorse, and is subsequently forgiven by the victim (i.e., the apology-forgiveness cycle; Tavuchis, 1991; chapters 2, 3, 5, and 17, by Nadler & Shnabel, Gobodo-Madikizela, Noor et al., and Staub, respectively). This process restores the parties' feelings of self-worth and self-respect thereby promoting their willingness for reconciliation (chapters 6, 7, and 8 by Pratto & Glasford; Janoff-Bulman & Werther; and Crocker, Garcia, & Nuer, respectively). Efforts of socioemotional reconciliation are based on the idea that the key to a reconciled future lies in a direct confrontation with a painful *past*, while efforts of instrumental reconciliation hold that continuous contact in the *present* between the adversaries that occurs under optimal conditions will result in a *reconciled future*.

To make this pivotal distinction more concrete let us think about two recent programs that aimed to achieve reconciliation in real world conflicts. The Truth and Reconciliation process in South Africa exemplifies a process of socioemotional reconciliation. It invited former perpetrators to assume responsibility for their past wrongdoings publicly in return for readmission into the community. Peace building projects in the Middle East, in the post-Oslo agreement years, exemplify a process of instrumental reconciliation. Israelis and Palestinians were encouraged to work together toward common goals under the assumption that such continuous and repeated experiences will lead the parties to trust each other. It should be noted that whether socioemotional or instrumental reconciliation will be more appropriate in a particular conflict situation depends on whether the goal of reconciliation is future *separation* or *integration* between the two adversaries. When the goal is separate coexistence instrumental reconciliation may be sufficient. When, however, the goal is integration of the two adversaries into the same society socioemotional reconciliation may be necessary (see chapter 2 by Nadler and Shnabel for a more detailed discussion).

The Sections and Chapters in the Present Volume

The opening and concluding chapters in this volume were written by Herbert Kelman and Morton Deutsch, respectively. These two scholars are among the founders of the science of conflict and its resolution within social psychology in particular and the social sciences in general. We feel especially pleased to have their work represented in the current volume. Their chapters set out the main themes of this volume. In the opening chapter, Kelman makes a distinction between conflict settlement, conflict resolution, and reconciliation and relates these three processes of ending conflict to his earlier work on social influence (i.e., process of compliance, identification, and internalization; Kelman, 1958). Kelman notes that reconciliation, like internalization, is a process that reflects identity change. In his concluding chapter, Deutsch distinguishes between destructive conflicts that have the characteristic of a competitive struggle and constructive conflicts that are more similar to cooperative problem solving. Deutsch views reconciliation as predicated on constructive dialogue about the past, present, and future, and enumerates the principles that need to exist for such a dialogue to occur.

The other 18 chapters in this volume are in three different parts. The first seven chapters focus on socioemotional reconciliation, the next seven chapters focus on instrumental reconciliation, and the last four chapters analyze programs of intergroup reconciliation that aimed to ameliorate real world intergroup conflicts (e.g., the Middle East, Rwanda). Before we continue to a brief description of these contributions, we should note that the distinction between socioemotional and instrumental reconciliation is not always clear-cut, and many of the contributions address both aspects of the reconciliation process. Yet, each has a distinct emphasis on either of these two processes.

The chapters in the second part (part II) on socioemotional reconciliation are divided into two sections. The first section contains four chapters that center on how the perpetrators' dealing with guilt for past wrongdoings and the victims' willingness to grant forgiveness can facilitate reconciliation. The first chapter (chapter 2) by Nadler and Shnabel begins with a detailed description of the distinction between socioemotional and instrumental reconciliation. This is followed by a description of the Needs-Based Model of Reconciliation, and supporting empirical evidence, which suggests that victims and perpetrators have different psychological needs and that reconciliation is predicated on the satisfaction of these needs. In the next chapter (chapter 3), Gobodo-Madikizela discusses, against the background of the TRC process in South Africa, how public admission of guilt creates a new-shared understanding between victims and perpetrators that enables them to repair broken relationships. She notes that when perpetrators express remorse they validate the victims' pains and give them back their uniqueness and that forgiveness, and not forgetting, is a healthy response that allows the parties to move on. In chapter 4, Miron and Branscombe maintain that feelings of collective guilt toward the adversary vary with the severity of moral standards that are used to judge the in-group's actions and that the more similar in-group members feel to the victim group the greater the collective guilt that will be experienced. They note that reconciliation necessitates a joint agreement on what constitutes injustice and immoral acts. In the final chapter (chapter 5) in this section Noor et al. suggest, on the basis of survey studies conducted in Northern Ireland, that empathy with the adversary and perceptions of common identity with them is positively related to reconciliation, while feelings of victimization and competitive victimhood are negatively related to it.

The remaining chapters in this section focusing on socioemotional reconciliation consider how satisfaction of basic human needs can facilitate reconciliation. Pratto and Glasford (chapter 6) suggest that a need theory perspective on reconciliation and conflict are two sides of the same psychological coin. The frustration of these needs breeds conflict and their satisfaction promotes reconciliation. These needs fall into three categories: (1) need for self-esteem, (2) need to belong, and (3) need for self-integrity. Chapter 7 by Janoff-Bulman and Werther centers on the role of respect in intergroup reconciliation. They maintain that when we delegitimize the enemy we say that they are immoral while we are moral. Respect can promote reconciliation by reminding us of the fact that there is not only one point of view that is moral and right. The final chapter (chapter 8) by Crocker et al. makes a distinction between egosystem and ecosystem motivations and suggests that during conflict egosystem motivations translate into viewing the out-group as a source of threat that results in egodefense motivations and a downward spiral toward destructive intergroup relations. Ecosystem motivations and perceptions are associated with goals that are larger and more important than the ego. Reconciliation is viewed as the process of creating an upward spiral in intergroup relations by formulating joint ecosystem goals.

The third part (part III) of the present volume centers on instrumental reconciliation and is also divided into two sections. In the first are chapters that analyze how intergroup contact and superordinate common identity can facilitate reconciliation, and in the second are contributions that consider the role of power relations in this context. In the first chapter (chapter 9), Hewstone et al. provide a rich array of empirical evidence that shows how intergroup contact in Northern Ireland reduced feelings of threat and anxiety, promoted empathy and perspective taking toward the other, and enhanced the willingness to forgive the adversary. The next two chapters (chapters 10 and 11) highlight the role of processes of self-categorization in intergroup reconciliation. Dovidio et al. (chapter 10) suggest that the process of reconciliation consists of reducing enmity by de-emphasizing the salience of separate social identities and emphasizing the creation of a common superordinate identity. On the basis of studies conducted with African and White Americans, they note that while advantaged groups adopt the dominant superordinate identity, disadvantaged groups retain their minority identity and adopt the dominant cultural identity (i.e., "dual identity" model). In a related contribution Riek et al. (chapter 11) examine the applicability of different models of categorization to the issue of reconciliation and suggest that the creation of a superordinate identity can promote intergroup reconciliation. Here too Riek et al. note that the adoption of dual identity resolves the conflict between wanting to belong to one's group and the wish to affiliate with a superordinate group. The final contribution in this section by Baron notes that intergroup reconciliation depends on the links between intragroup and intergroup processes (chapter 12). He considers the relationship between willingness to cooperate with the out-group on the intragroup and intergroup levels. This analysis uses Kelman's dialogue groups between Israelis and Palestinians to highlight its insights and conclusions.

A common thread that unites many of the discussions on instrumental reconciliation is that they take into consideration the unequal power that exists between adversaries. The three chapters in the second section focused on instrumental reconciliation address this issue directly (chapters 13–15). In the first chapter (chapter 13), Harris and Fiske suggest that reconciliation depends on the parties' ability to deal with the residual negative affect that results from unequal status relations. In the second chapter (chapter 14) of this section, Spears centers on the links between perceptions of the legitimacy of power relations and intergroup reconciliation. From the social identity perspective, reconciliation is said to occur when group members "work out" the illegitimacy of power inequality and the gains and losses for each side. The final chapter (chapter 15) in this section by Malloy describes the Intergroup Relations Model, which asserts that the move to peaceful intergroup relations hinges on ensuring that the adversarial groups perceive equality of opportunities to procure material and social resources.

Parts IV and V of the volume contain contributions that analyze the reconciliation process within programs designed to promote reconciliation in real world conflicts. The first chapter (chapter 16) by Stephan provides an overall view of such programs. These programs have different emphases. Some are intended to provide participants with information on the adversary, others center on teaching the participants conflict resolution skills, while still others encourage a dialogue about past traumas and current needs. In the second chapter (chapter 17), Staub describes a number of programs carried out in Rwanda with the aim of promoting reconciliation between Tutsis and Hutus. These programs are based on the hypothesis that reconciliation between former enemies is facilitated when there is an understanding of the reasons that led the victimizers to enact atrocities and an understanding of the consequences of the traumas for the victimized. The third chapter (chapter 18) by Worchel and Coutant analyzes the "seeds of peace" program that gives young adults from war zones (e.g., Israelis and Palestinians) the opportunity for secure, continuous, and positive contact. They emphasize that such programs need to build the parties' ability to coexist rather than heal past wounds and traumas (i.e., Instrumental rather than Socioemotional Reconciliation). In a final chapter (chapter 19) Fisher, Nadler, Little, and Saguy examine how the provision of medical assistance across borders during times of medical emergency (i.e., the AIDS epidemic in Sub-Saharan Africa) can improve relations between donor and recipient nations. On the basis of extant knowledge on intergroup helping and health psychology, the chapter suggests a set of conditions that will make such helping interactions a vehicle that promotes better relations and reconciliation.

We conclude this short introduction by noting that the variety of topics, concepts, and perspectives on intergroup reconciliation speak to the richness of this topic for scientific theory and research. Also, the social and political realities of the world we live in remind us of the importance of gaining a better understanding on how to promote intergroup reconciliation. In conclusion, we want to repeat our conviction that social psychology is uniquely equipped to further such understanding and provide the conceptual background for social action. We trust that this collection of chapters exemplifies this point and hope that it will serve as a stimulus for further research and theory development. Throughout the work on this volume we were constantly reminded of the wisdom in Kurt Lewin's famous dictum that "there is nothing more practical than a good theory." At the beginning of the third millennium Lewin's words reverberate with increasing intensity in each of the contributions to this volume.

References

Barkan, E. (2001). *The guilt of nations: Restitution and negotiating historical injustices.* New York: W. W. Norton.

Branscombe, N. R., & Doosje, B. (Eds.) (2004). *Collective guilt: International perspectives.* New York/Cambridge: Cambridge University Press.

Burton, J. W. (1969). *Conflict and communication: The use of controlled communication in international relations.* London: Macmillan.

Deutsch, M. (1973). *The resolution of conflict: Constructive and destructive processes.* New Haven, CT: Yale University Press.

Deutsch, M., Coleman, P. T., & Marcus, E. (Eds.) (2006). *The handbook of conflict resolution: Theory and practice* (2nd ed.). San Francisco, CA: Jossey-Bass.

Kelman, H. C. (1958). Compliance, identification, and internalization: Three processes of attitude change. *Journal of Conflict Resolution, 2,* 51-60.

Kelman, H. C. (1978). Israelis and Palestinians: Psychological prerequisites for mutual acceptance. *International Security, 3*, 162-186.

Kelman, H. C. (2006). Interests, relationships, identities: Three central issues for individuals and groups in negotiating their social environment. In S. T. Fiske, A. E. Kazdin, & D. L. Schacter (Eds.), *Annual review of psychology* (Vol. 57, pp. 1-26). Palo Alto, CA: Annual Reviews.

Leach, C. W., Snider, N., & Iyer, A. (2002). Spoiling the consciences of the fortunate: The experience of relative advantage and support for social equality. In I. Walker & H. J. Smith (Eds.), *Relative deprivation: Specification, development, & integration* (pp. 136-163). New York: Cambridge University.

Lederach, J. P. (1997). *Building peace: Sustainable reconciliation in divided societies.* Washington, DC: U.S. Institute of Peace.

Nadler, A. (2002). Social-psychological analysis of reconciliation: Instrumental and socio-emotional routes to reconciliation. In G. Salomon & B. Nevo (Eds.), *Peace education worldwide: The concept, underlying principles, the research.* Mawheh, NJ: Erlbaum.

Nisbett, R. E., & Cohen, D. (1996). *Culture of honor: The psychology of violence in the South.* Boulder, CO: Westview Press.

Tavuchis, N. (1991). *Mea Culpa: A sociology of apology and reconciliation.* Stanford, CA: Stanford University Press.

Part I

Intergroup Reconciliation: Its Nature

CHAPTER 1

Reconciliation From a Social-Psychological Perspective

HERBERT C. KELMAN

Until recently, the term "reconciliation" was used primarily (although with some notable exceptions) in religious discourse. It was not often subjected to systematic analysis by political scientists or social psychologists. The dramatic political change in South Africa in 1994, soon followed by the establishment of the Truth and Reconciliation Commission, as well as a number of related efforts in other, postconflict zones, can probably serve as a marker for the shift in attention to the concept of reconciliation among social scientists.

The three editions of the *Handbook of Political Psychology* provide a clear illustration of this shift. In the first edition (Knutson, 1973) and the second edition (Hermann, 1986), the word reconciliation did not even appear in the index. However, the third edition (Sears, Huddy, & Jervis, 2003) included a chapter that dealt extensively with reconciliation in genocide, mass killing, and intractable conflict (Staub & Bar-Tal, 2003).

The new emphasis on reconciliation can probably be attributed in large part to the change in the nature of warfare in the post–Cold War era. Over the course of these years, we have witnessed an increase in the frequency, intensity, and deadliness of deep-rooted conflicts, not across national borders, but between ethnic or other identity groups within a single political unit. Such intrastate conflicts cannot be brought to a lasting conclusion by diplomatic agreements and strategic arrangements alone, because the conflicting groups have to live together in their common postconflict environment. For one-time bitter enemies to learn to live together satisfactorily—in a state of stable peace and mutually enhancing cooperation—requires a transformation of their relationship (cf. Kelman, 1999a; Lederach, 1998). Moreover, this transformation must occur not only in the relationship between political leaders, but also in the relationship between the entire bodies politic (cf. Saunders, 1999, 2000). Changes in the ways in which former enemy populations think about each other, feel about each other, and act toward one another, as they learn to live together, are the essence of what is generally meant by reconciliation (cf. Bar-Tal & Bennink, 2004; Kriesberg, 1998).

If interactions between groups within a society are to be smooth and cooperative, mindful of each group's sense of security, dignity, and well-being, and conducive to the achievement of its goals, they must be based on mutual trust and mutual acceptance. These are precisely the elements that are lacking in the relationship between identity groups enmeshed in a deep-rooted, protracted conflict and that reconciliation is designed to restore. The distinction that Nadler and Shnabel (chapter 2, this volume) make between instrumental and socioemotional paths to reconciliation corresponds roughly to these two elements of reconciliation. Lily Gardner Feldman (1999), in her discussion of reconciliation in German foreign policy, points out the German distinction between *Aussöhnung* and *Versöhnung*, which refer to the practical/material and the philosophical/emotional elements of reconciliation, respectively (p. 334). Staub and Bar-Tal (2003) define reconciliation as "mutual acceptance by members of hostile or previously hostile groups of each other and the societal structures and psychological processes directly involved in the development and maintenance of such acceptance," adding that "genuine acceptance means trust in and positive attitude toward the other, and sensitivity to and consideration of the other party's needs and interests" (p. 733). In my own view of reconciliation (Kelman, 1999a), on which I shall elaborate in the following sections, the key element is mutual acceptance of the other's identity and humanity.

I have linked the increasing attention to the issue of reconciliation among social scientists (and indeed political actors) to the recent proliferation of deadly intrastate conflicts between ethnic and other identity groups. My reference to Feldman's (1999) analysis of reconciliation in German foreign policy reminds us of one major exception to this generalization: For Germany in the aftermath of World War II, *interstate* reconciliation was a central concern. It should be noted, however, that, in Germany's relations with Europe—as in the case of intrastate conflicts between identity groups—reconciliation efforts were driven by the need to live together in the same community. Creation of a united Europe, whose states would cooperate effectively in economic, security, cultural, and ultimately political affairs, was at the top of the agenda of the West European democracies in the postwar era. The integration of Germany in this community was of vital interest to Germany itself, as well as to the other states in the region (Grosser, 1998). For Germany, emerging out of the Nazi era, the need for national rehabilitation and acceptance by other nations made reconciliation, in both its moral and pragmatic dimensions, a central foreign policy goal—especially, in the early postwar years, in its relations with France and Israel (Feldman, 1999).

Reconciliation as a Goal of Conflict Resolution

My work for more than 35 years has focused on the resolution[1] of deep-rooted conflicts between ethnonational groups, with special emphasis on the Israeli-Palestinian case (Kelman, 1999c, 2002). The central distinction for my colleagues and myself, following John Burton, has been between *settlement* and *resolution* of conflict (see, e.g., Burton, 1969, Chapters 11 and 12). In contrast to the negotiation of a political settlement, a process of conflict resolution goes beyond a realist view of national interests. It explores the causes of the conflict, particularly causes in the form of unmet or threatened needs for identity, security, recognition, autonomy, and justice. It seeks solutions responsive to the needs of both sides through active engagement in joint problem solving. Hence, agreements achieved through a process of genuine conflict resolution—unlike compromises achieved through a bargaining process brokered or imposed by third parties—are likely to engender the two parties' long-term commitment to the outcome and to transform their relationship. We have argued that an agreement emerging from such a process of conflict resolution and the new relationship it promotes are conducive to stable peace, mutually enhancing cooperation, and ultimate reconciliation.

Thus, reconciliation, in this view, is a consequence of successful conflict resolution. It comes at the end of the process, with time: The test of a good agreement, and of the process that generates it, is its conduciveness to *ultimate* reconciliation. This does not mean (and has never meant, in my view) that reconciliation comes into play only after an agreement has been reached. Reconciliation is, after all, a *process* as well as an outcome; as such, it should ideally be set into motion from the beginning of a peace process and as an integral part of it. In this spirit, I have described the exchange of the letters of mutual recognition between the Palestine Liberation Organization (PLO) and the State of Israel—which I have always regarded as the most important feature of the Oslo Accord (see Kelman, 1997)—as "a product of a rudimentary process of reconciliation" (Kelman, 1998a, p. 37). In the same spirit, the problem-solving workshops between politically influential Israelis and Palestinians that my colleagues and I have organized for some years (see Kelman, 2002; Rouhana & Kelman, 1994) represent tentative steps toward reconciliation, insofar as participants are encouraged to listen to and to try to appreciate each other's narrative and to engage in a process of "negotiating identity" (Kelman, 2001).

As the Oslo process began to falter, I concluded that its step-by-step approach was no longer feasible, because of the decline in trust and partner-ship between the two sides, and that a new process was needed in which reconciliation would move to the fore. I would make that point even more strongly today, with the total breakdown of the peace process. I am not propos-ing that reconciliation is a precondition for negotiation or that it must precede a peace agreement. But significant steps toward reconciliation—in the form of mutual acceptance of the other's nationhood and humanity—are necessary in order to resume negotiations and move them forward. "The process and outcome of negotiations must be consistent with the requirement for ultimate reconciliation" (Kelman, 1998a, p. 37). In my view, this requires negotia-tions committed to the search for a principled peace, anchored in a historic compromise.

Although reconciliation has been vital to my thinking in these different ways, I tended to conceive of it not so much as a separate process, but as a component and logical outcome of conflict resolution as my colleagues and I have conceptualized and practiced it. However, the recent events that have increasingly focused the attention of social scientists and political actors on reconciliation have encouraged me, along with my colleagues, to view recon-ciliation as a distinct process, qualitatively different from conflict resolution—even conflict resolution within a needs-oriented, interactive problem-solving framework. Reconciliation is obviously continuous with and linked to conflict resolution, and it certainly is not an alternative to it. But, whereas conflict resolution refers to the process of achieving a mutually satisfactory and hence durable agreement between the two societies, reconciliation refers to the process whereby the societies learn to live together in the postconflict environment.

Combining the customary differentiation between conflict settlement and resolution, and the more recent differentiation between conflict resolution and reconciliation, suggests a conceptual model based on three qualitatively dis-tinct processes of peacemaking: conflict settlement, conflict resolution, and reconciliation. In adopting such a model, I am following in the footsteps of Rouhana (2004), although my formulation of the process of reconciliation, in particular, differs from his in some important respects.

Three Processes of Peacemaking

Although settlement, resolution, and reconciliation represent three approaches to peacemaking, they should not be viewed as three different ways of achieving the same goal. Rather, they are three ways of achieving different—albeit often overlapping—goals, all broadly linked to changing the relationship between groups, communities, societies, or states from one of hostility to one of peaceful coexistence. The specific goals and emphases of the three processes may be congruent and mutually supportive, but they may also be contradictory to one another.

I have already suggested that reconciliation is continuous with and linked to conflict resolution. In a sense, it can be argued that reconciliation, at least in its full form, presupposes conflict resolution: A long-term, cooperative relationship, based on mutual acceptance and respect, is not likely to take hold without a peace agreement that addresses the fundamental needs and sense of justice of both sides. Similarly, it can be argued that conflict resolution presupposes conflict settlement, at least in the sense that a political agreement negotiated by the legitimate leaderships of the conflicting parties and endorsed by relevant outside powers and international organizations must be in place if the two societies are to consider their conflict to have ended in a fair and mutually satisfactory way. The three processes may thus be related in a sequential way, with settlement as the first step, which may or may not be followed by resolution, which in turn may or may not be followed by reconciliation. However, there is no reason to assume that the three processes necessarily follow such a sequence. Steps in the direction or in the spirit of settlement, resolution, or reconciliation may occur quite independently, in any order and in any combination.

In short, possible relationships between the three processes need to be explored, conceptually and empirically, rather than assumed—or dismissed. The main purpose of the present exercise is to see whether we can gain some analytical leverage by thinking of settlement, resolution, and reconciliation as qualitatively different (although not necessarily always empirically separate) processes and identifying the distinct antecedents and consequences of each.

My special perspective on the distinction between conflict settlement, conflict resolution, and reconciliation derives from the proposition that they broadly correspond to the three processes of social influence—compliance, identification, and internalization—that I distinguished in my earlier work (Kelman, 1958, 1961; Kelman & Hamilton, 1989). Very briefly, *compliance* refers to acceptance of influence from another in order to achieve a favorable reaction from the other: to gain a reward or approval from the other, or to avoid punishment or disapproval. *Identification* refers to acceptance of influence from another in order to maintain a desired relationship to the other and the self-definition anchored in that relationship; identification may involve taking on the role of the other or a role reciprocal to that of the other. *Internalization* refers to acceptance of influence from another in order to maintain the congruence of one's own value system; internalization may involve adopting new behavior, because it is consistent with one's beliefs or consonant with one's identity.

I arrived at this three-way distinction early in my work on attitude and behavior change in individuals, out of an abiding interest in the quality of the changes induced by social influence: the depth of change, the durability of change, the independence of change from the external source from which it was originally derived, the integration of the new elements into preexisting structures such as the person's belief system, value system, or personal identity. Each of the three processes is characterized by a distinct set of antecedent conditions. For example, the source of the power of the influencing agent to induce change varies for the three processes. In the case of compliance, it is the agent's means control, that is, control over rewards and punishments—material or psychological resources that are consequential to the person. In the case of identification, it is the agent's attractiveness, that is, desirability as a partner in a continuing relationship. In the case of internalization, it is the agent's credibility, that is, expertise and trustworthiness as a conveyor of value-relevant information (Kelman, 1958).

At the output end, each of the three processes is characterized by a distinct set of consequent conditions. Most important here are the conditions under which the new opinion or behavior is likely to manifest itself. The manifestation of compliance-induced behavior depends on surveillance by the influencing agent. Identification-based behavior is not contingent on surveillance, but it does depend on the continuing salience of the person's relationship to the influencing agent. That is, it is likely to manifest itself only when the person acts within the role defined by that relationship. Finally, internalized behavior becomes independent of the original source and is likely to manifest itself whenever it is relevant to the issue at hand, regardless of the surveillance or salience of the influencing agent.

I have extended this model to analysis of the relationship of individuals to the state or other social systems (Kelman, 1969) and to the nation or other collective entities (Kelman, 1998b). In this connection, we have distinguished between three types of political orientation: rule-, role-, and value-orientation (Kelman & Hamilton, 1989) that are coordinated with the three processes of influence. The rule, role, and value distinction has also been useful in analyzing people's relationship to legitimate authority and their emotional reactions to their own deviations from social norms. I have also distinguished between rule-oriented, role-oriented, and value-oriented movements of social protest. In an entirely different context, in my writing on the ethics of social research, I drew on my three-processes model to distinguish among three types of ethical concerns that research may arouse: concerns about the impact of the research on the interests of the individuals and communities who are the subjects of our investigations, on the quality of the relationship between investigators and research participants, and on broader societal values (see Kelman, 2006, for a discussion of these extensions).

I mention these various extensions of the original model, because they suggest the possibility—or at least the hope—that it might also have some relevance to the analysis of conflict settlement, conflict resolution, and reconciliation as three distinct processes of peacemaking. My original model of social influence emerged out of research on persuasive communication, but it has broadened to capture the interaction of individuals or groups with each other and with larger social systems in a variety of social contexts, and their integration within these social systems. In essence, my trichotomy distinguishes three foci for these interactions. The first centers on individual and group *interests*, whose coordination is governed by a system of enforceable *rules*, to which individuals are expected to *comply*. The second centers on the *relationships* between individuals or groups, which are managed through a system of shared *roles*, with which individuals *identify*. The third centers on personal and group *identities*, expressing a *value* system that individuals *internalize*.

As indicated, my original three-process model grew out of an interest in the quality of changes induced by social influence—their depth, durability, independence, and integration. My approach to conflict resolution has posed a very similar question: What are the conditions under which negotiations to end the conflict will produce a high-quality agreement—an agreement that will be deeper, more durable, more sustainable, more fully integrated in the political cultures or societal belief systems (cf. Bar-Tal & Bennink, 2004) of the conflicting societies than the settlements that are so often hammered together under the pressure of external powers? I have always assumed, therefore, that it should be possible to forge a link between my work on conflict resolution and the three processes of influence. Now, I feel, I have found that link. This is, of course, esthetically pleasing, but the important question is whether it is analytically useful. Does that link give us handles—metaphorically at least—for distinguishing between qualitatively different ways of making peace, with distinct antecedent and consequent conditions? Specifically, for present purposes, does the proposed correspondence of reconciliation to internalization suggest a useful way of defining and conceptualizing reconciliation?

I am not proposing an exact correspondence, because we are dealing with different levels of analysis. In my original model of social influence, the unit of analysis is the individual—albeit the individual embedded in a social system. In a model of peacemaking, the unit of analysis is a pair of actors—the relationship between two parties, whether two individuals or two collectivities. My purpose here is to explore whether conceptualizing peacemaking processes in the terms of the broader trichotomy suggested by the three processes of compliance, identification, and internalization is useful in suggesting relevant hypotheses about the determinants and outcomes of different approaches to peacemaking.

In this spirit, I propose that it may be useful to conceive of conflict settlement as operating primarily at the level of *interests*, conflict resolution at the level of *relationships*, and reconciliation at the level of *identity*.

Conflict Settlement and Resolution

Let me first compare conflict settlement and resolution in terms of the distinction I have proposed. Conflict settlement can be described as a process yielding an agreement that meets the interests of both parties to the extent that their respective power positions enable them to prevail. In other words, the terms of their agreement are heavily determined by the power they can bring to bear in the negotiations. Third parties—outside powers or international organizations—often play a role in brokering or even imposing an agreement, using their own power by way of threats or inducements. The agreement may be supported by the publics on the two sides, because they are tired of war and have found the status quo of continuing hostility and uncertainty increasingly intolerable. Such support of the agreement does not rest in any particular change in public attitudes toward the adversary. The settlement process is not designed to change the quality of the relationship between the societies. As is the case in compliance as a form of social influence, the stability of a political settlement ultimately depends on surveillance—by the parties themselves, in keeping with their deterrent capacities, by outside powers, and by international organizations.

Conflict settlement is not a negligible achievement in a violent and destructive relationship with escalatory potential. In fact, conflict resolution can often build on political settlements, insofar as these involve a negotiating process in which each side pursues its interests and in which they are able to reach agreement on many outstanding issues through distributive bargaining in which power as well as international norms play a role. But conflict resolution, particularly if we think of it within an interactive problem-solving framework, goes beyond conflict settlement in many of the ways to which I have already alluded:

- It refers to an agreement that is arrived at interactively, rather than imposed or sponsored by outside powers, and to which the parties therefore have a higher level of commitment.
- It addresses the parties' basic needs and fears and therefore has a greater capacity to sustain itself over time.
- It builds a degree of working trust between the parties—a pragmatic trust in the other's interest in achieving and maintaining peace—and therefore is not entirely dependent on surveillance as the guarantor of the agreement (for the distinction between working trust and interpersonal trust, see Kelman, 2005).
- It establishes a new relationship between the parties, best described as a partnership, in which the parties are responsive to each other's needs and constraints, and committed to reciprocity.
- It generates public support for the agreement and encourages the development of new images of the other.

In all of these ways, conflict resolution moves beyond the interest-based settlement of the conflict and its dependence on the balance of power. It represents a strategic change in the relationship between the parties, expressed in terms of a pragmatic partnership, in which each side is persuaded that stable peace and cooperation are both in its own best interest and in the interest of the other. This is the kind of partnership that began to emerge, especially at the leadership level, in the early post-Oslo environment (cf. Lustick, 1997).

Conflict resolution, as described here, clearly represents a transformation of the relationship between the parties, which resembles instrumental reconciliation, as defined by Nadler and Shnabel (chapter 2, this volume). However, there are limits to this new relationship, which make it vulnerable to changes in interests, circumstances, and leadership. Conflict resolution as a process of peacemaking—like identification as a process of social influence—involves the development of a new relationship, with an associated set of new attitudes *alongside*—or perhaps on top—of the old attitudes. The new attitudes are not necessarily integrated with one's preexisting value structure and belief system—with one's worldview. This means that the old attitudes—including attitudes of fundamental distrust and negation of the other—remain intact even as new attitudes, associated with the new relationship, take shape. The coexistence of new attitudes toward the other as a potential partner in peace with old attitudes toward the other as a mortal enemy creates instability in the new relationship, particularly in the context of an existential identity conflict. Changing circumstances may trigger the old attitudes in their full force.

Reconciliation

The third process, reconciliation, which is the focus of our concern, presupposes conflict resolution of the type that I have described: the development of working trust; the transformation of the relationship toward a partnership based on reciprocity and mutual responsiveness; an agreement that addresses both parties' basic needs. However, it goes beyond conflict resolution in representing a change in each party's identity.

The primary feature of the identity change constituting reconciliation is the removal of the negation of the other as a central component of one's own identity. My main empirical point of reference in this analysis is the Israeli-Palestinian case, in which mutual denial of the other's identity has been a central feature of the conflict over the decades (cf. Kelman, 1978, 1999b). The mutual negation of the other's identity is perhaps not as central in other cases of conflict and reconciliation—such as those of Chile, Guatemala, or South Africa, or the German-Jewish, the Franco-German, or even the Egyptian-Israeli case—yet, in each case, the negation of the other is somehow embedded in the identity of each of the conflicting parties and must be addressed in the reconciliation process.

Changing one's collective identity by removing the negation of the other from it implies a degree of acceptance of the other's identity—at least in the sense of acknowledging the validity and legitimacy of the other's narrative without necessarily fully agreeing with that narrative. The change in each party's identity may go further by moving toward the development of a common, transcendent identity—not in lieu of, but alongside of each group's particularistic identity. Development of a transcendent identity becomes possible with reconciliation and, in turn, reinforces reconciliation, but is not a necessary condition or consequence of reconciliation. What is essential to reconciliation, in my view, is that each party revise its own identity just enough to accommodate the identity of the other. As the parties overcome the negative interdependence of their identities, they can build on the positive interdependence of their identities that often characterizes parties living in close proximity to each other (Kelman, 1999b).

Nadler and Shnabel's (chapter 2, this volume) analysis of socioemotional reconciliation brings to mind another important aspect of identity change that reconciliation may entail: the removal or reduction of negative elements in each group's self-identity engendered by the conflict. "There are two major types of negative identity elements that are often brought to the fore by the relationship to the other in a protracted conflict: the view of one's self as weak and vulnerable, and the view of one's self as violent and unjust" (Kelman, 1999b, p. 593)—in essence, the view of the self as victim and as victimizer. The apology-forgiveness cycle, which is central to Nadler and Shnabel's analysis of the reconciliation process, is directly germane to this element of identity change. As my formulation of reconciliation as identity change evolves, it will benefit from bringing change in the negative elements of each group's own identity into the analysis of the process.

Reconciliation, as I have defined it, goes beyond conflict resolution in that it moves past the level of pragmatic partnership—which is the hallmark of identification and essential to peacemaking—and enables the parties to internalize the new relationship, integrating it into their own identities. New attitudes toward the other can thus develop, not just alongside of the old attitudes, but in place of the old attitudes. In contrast to the attitude change process that characterizes identification, internalized attitudes are not just taken over in full measure, but they are reworked. As the new attitudes become integrated into the group's own identity, they gradually replace the old attitudes. Working trust can gradually turn into personal trust. This does not foreclose the possibility that old fears and suspicions will reemerge, but the relationship is less vulnerable to situational changes.

Viewing reconciliation as identity change linked to the process of internalization has important implications for the nature of the identity change that it involves. Internalization represents a readiness to change an attitude because the new attitude—although induced by influence from an external source—is more consistent with the person's own, preexisting value system. Thus, the change in a particular attitude actually strengthens the preexisting structure in which it is embedded by responding to a potential challenge to that structure: One might say that we change in order to remain the same. By the same token, the change in each party's identity—the revision in its narrative—that I am defining as reconciliation implies a strengthening, rather than a weakening, of each party's core identity. I would argue that a revision in the group's identity and the associated narrative is possible only if the *core* of the identity remains intact. In fact, changes in more peripheral elements of identity are often seen as necessary in order to preserve the core of the identity—just as changes in specific attitudes may be seen as necessary in order to maintain the consistency and integrity of a person's value framework. This was the basis, for example, on which a majority of Israelis and Palestinians were (and, I believe, continue to be) prepared to revise the territorial dimension of their national identity in order to maintain the essence of that identity (Kelman, 2001).

This analysis points to a major dilemma of reconciliation. Reconciliation requires parties to change an element of their identity—the negation of the other—which is far from trivial for parties engaged in an existential identity conflict, while at the same time preserving, even strengthening, the core of their identity. This is more easily achieved in situations in which one of the parties has already rejected part of its identity—as was the case for many Germans in post-Nazi Germany and many Whites in postapartheid South Africa—although, even in these situations, resistances are bound to arise. It is particularly difficult, however, in conflicts in which each side insists on the justice of its cause and sees itself as having been wronged by the other. The dilemma is that the amount and kind of identity change that A requires from B in order to be ready for reconciliation may be perceived by B as undermining the core of *its* identity. A good example here would be the demand to acknowledge collective guilt to which even post-Nazi Germany was reluctant to accede (Auerbach, 2004; Feldman, 1999).

It is important to emphasize here that, in conflicts such as that between Palestinians and Israelis, negation of the other is a *central* element of each party's own identity, which it cannot give up easily. Given the nature of the conflict, each party finds it necessary to deny the other's authenticity as a people, the other's links to the land, and the other's national rights, especially its right to national self-determination through the establishment of an independent state in the land both claim, because the other's claims to peoplehood and to rights in the land are seen as competitive to each party's own claims and rights. Moreover, negation of the other is also important to each party in a violent conflict as a protection against negative elements in its own identity (cf. Kelman, 1999b). Insofar as the other can be demonized and dehumanized, it becomes easier for each party to minimize guilt feelings for acts of violence and oppression against the other and to avoid seeing itself in the role of victimizer, rather than only in the role of victim.

Thus, in protracted identity conflicts, negation of the other is not a peripheral, marginal element of each party's identity that can be easily discarded. My argument is merely that, from an "objective" point of view, negating the identity of the other is not a *necessary* condition for preserving, and indeed enhancing the core of one's own identity. However, for conflicting parties to arrive at a point where they can be free to relegate negation of the other to the periphery of their own identities and eventually discard it requires the hard work of reconciliation. What is central to that work is the growing assurance that the other is not a threat to one's own identity. In that process of assurance, the conditions for reconciliation play a vital role.

Parties in a conflict in which both sides perceive themselves as victims are helped to deal with the dilemma of abandoning some elements of identity without threatening the core of their identity by the reciprocal nature of reconciliation. Changes on the part of one group make changes on the other's part more attainable. However, this view suggests that the process of reconciliation requires a certain amount of "negotiation" of identity, including negotiation of the conditions for reconciliation, which turn on such issues as truth, justice, and responsibility. It is my contention that reconciliation—especially in cases in which neither party is prepared to adopt the role of perpetrator— cannot be achieved on the basis of purely objective criteria of truth, justice, or responsibility, anchored in historical scholarship or international law, but requires some degree of mutual accommodation in the course of negotiating the conditions for reconciliation. I turn to a brief discussion of these conditions in the concluding section.

Conditions for Reconciliation

I want to identify five conditions that can help groups in conflict arrive at the difficult point of revising their identity so as to accommodate to the identity of the other. One might also think of these as indicators of reconciliation, or steps in a process of reconciliation. They are both indicators of movement toward reconciliation and conditions for further movement in that direction.

Mutual Acknowledgment of the Other's Nationhood and Humanity

Such acknowledgment is, of course, implicit in my very definition of reconciliation. Insofar as reconciliation means removing the negation and exclusion of the other from one's own identity, it requires the accumulation of steps that indicate acceptance of the other as an authentic nation and inclusion of the other in one's own moral community. Such steps include political recognition and acknowledgment of the other's legitimacy, of the authenticity of their historical links to the land, and of their national rights, including the right to national self-determination. Equally important are steps toward the humanization of the other, including respect for their dignity, concern for their welfare, and attachment of value to the other's lives and security. Reconciliation presupposes not only the rejection of the extreme acts of dehumanization of the other that characterizes violent conflicts, but also "the development and propagation of new attitudes, marked by inclusion, empathy, and respect" (Kelman, 1999a, p. 199).

27

Development of a Common Moral Basis for Peace

To create the conditions for reconciliation, it is necessary to move beyond a peace anchored entirely in pragmatic considerations—essential as these are—to a peace based on moral considerations. This condition is relatively easy to meet when the moral basis is widely accepted and shared from the beginning of the peacemaking effort—as in the rejection of Nazism or the rejection of apartheid. It is much more difficult to achieve this condition in a conflict in which the common moral basis is not given—such as the Israeli-Palestinian conflict or the conflicts in Sri Lanka or Northern Ireland. In the Israeli-Palestinian case, I have emphasized in this connection the need for commitment to a principled peace, which finds its moral basis in a historic compromise—a compromise that is presented to the publics as not just the best that can be achieved under the circumstances, but as the basis for a peace that is right, because it is consistent with the principles of fairness and justice for both sides (Kelman, 1998a). The definition of justice, in this and other such cases, will, to some extent, have to be negotiated between the parties, recognizing that there is some inevitable tension between justice and reconciliation. Such negotiations have to experiment with different kinds of justice that an agreement might try to achieve, such as

- substantive justice, achieved through an agreement that meets the fundamental needs of both sides;
- future justice, achieved through the establishment of just institutions, arrangements, and relationships;
- procedural justice, achieved through a fair and reciprocal process of negotiating the agreement;
- emotional justice, achieved through the sense that the negotiations have seriously sought and to a significant degree shaped a just outcome.

Confrontation With History

Confronting history and coming to terms with the truth is an essential component of any reconciliation effort. The reexamination of historical narratives and the reevaluation of national myths—on both sides of a conflict—are valuable contributions to such an effort. Here again, however, I take the view that it is unrealistic to aim for the establishment of a single, objective truth and that one has to accept the need to negotiate the historical truth to a certain degree. I want to avoid the simple relativistic stance that each side has its own truth and that their conflicting narratives are therefore equally valid. But we have to recognize that the different narratives of different groups reflect different historical *experiences*—occasioned by the same set of facts and figures—and that, therefore, their experienced truths may in fact not be identical. Reconciliation, in my view, does not require writing a joint consensual history, but it does require admitting the other's truth into one's own narrative.

Acknowledgment of Responsibility

Reconciliation also requires acceptance, by each side, of responsibility for the wrong it has done to the other and for the course of the conflict. Responsibility must be expressed symbolically, in acknowledgment of one's actions and their effect on the other and appropriate apologies, and concretely, in appropriate steps of compensation, reparation, and restitution. The combination of symbolic and material acknowledgments of responsibility is essential, in line with Nadler and Shnabel's (chapter 2, this volume) distinction between socioemotional and instrumental paths to reconciliation and Feldman's (1999) distinction between the moral and pragmatic aspects of reconciliation. It is not surprising that I again take the view that the acknowledgment of responsibility cannot be based entirely on an objective set of legal or moral norms, but requires a process of negotiation in which different types of responsibility are identified and agreed upon.

Establishment of Patterns and Institutional Mechanisms of Cooperation

Promotion of functional relations—through cooperative activities in the economic sphere and in such domains as public health, environmental protection, communication, education, science, culture, and tourism—cannot in itself lead to reconciliation in the absence of a mutually satisfactory political agreement. It can, however, help increase openness to the search for political solutions, and it can play an important role in peacebuilding in the wake of a political solution. "By establishing crosscutting ties, common interests, and personal relations," cooperative activities "can help stabilize and cement a new peaceful relationship and create commitments, habits, and expectations" conducive to reconciliation (Kelman, 1999a, p. 201). To contribute to reconciliation, the patterns and mechanisms of cooperation must themselves meet certain critical conditions. They must be genuinely useful to both parties in meeting societal needs and achieving societal goals; they must be based on the principles of equality and reciprocity; and they must undercut rather than reinforce old patterns of dependency of one party on the other. An important variety of cooperative institutional mechanisms are institutions and arrangements focusing on conflict resolution through joint problem solving in order to deal constructively, on a continuing basis, with the conflicts that will inevitably arise in the relations between the two societies.

In sum, all five of the conditions for reconciliation identified here are designed to facilitate changes in the collective identities of the conflicting parties, with particular emphasis on removing the negation of the other as a key element of each group's own identity.

Note

1. The remainder of this chapter is adapted from an earlier paper (Kelman, 2004). The material is used by permission of Oxford University Press.

References

Auerbach, Y. (2004). The role of forgiveness in reconciliation. In Y. Bar-Siman-Tov (Ed.), *From conflict resolution to reconciliation* (pp. 149-175). Oxford and New York: Oxford University Press.

Bar-Tal, D., & Bennink, G. H. (2004). The nature of reconciliation as an outcome and as a process. In Y. Bar-Siman-Tov (Ed.), *From conflict resolution to reconciliation* (pp. 11-38). Oxford and New York: Oxford University Press.

Burton, J. W. (1969). *Conflict and communication: The use of controlled communication in international relations.* London: Macmillan.

Feldman, L. G. (1999). The principle and practice of 'reconciliation' in German foreign policy: Relations with France, Ireland, Poland and the Czech Republic. *International Affairs, 75*(2), 333-356.

Grosser, A. (1998). *Deutschland in Europa.* Weinheim and Basel: Beltz Quadriga.

Hermann, M. G. (Ed.). (1986). *Political psychology: Contemporary problems and issues.* San Francisco: Jossey-Bass.

Kelman, H. C. (1958). Compliance, identification, and internalization: Three processes of attitude change. *Journal of Conflict Resolution, 2,* 51-60.

Kelman, H. C. (1961). Processes of opinion change. *Public Opinion Quarterly, 25,* 57-78.

Kelman, H. C. (1969). Patterns of personal involvement in the national system: A social–psychological analysis of political legitimacy. In J.N. Rosenan (Ed.), *International politics and foreign policy: A reader in research and theory* (revised edition, pp. 276-288). New York: Free Press.

Kelman, H. C. (1978). Israelis and Palestinians: Psychological prerequisites for mutual acceptance. *International Security, 3*(1), 162-186.

Kelman, H. C. (1997). Some determinants of the Oslo breakthrough. *International Negotiation, 2*, 183-194.

Kelman, H. C. (1998a). Building a sustainable peace: The limits of pragmatism in the Israeli–Palestinian negotiations. *Journal of Palestine Studies, 28*(1), 36-50.

Kelman, H. C. (1998b). The place of ethnic identity in the development of personal identity: A challenge for the Jewish family. In P.Y. Medding (Ed.), *Coping with life and death: Jewish families in the twentieth century* (pp. 3-26). Oxford: Oxford University Press.

Kelman, H. C. (1999a). Transforming the relationship between former enemies: A social–psychological analysis. In R.L. Rothstein (Ed.), *After the peace: Resistance and reconciliation* (pp. 193-205). Boulder, CO, and London: Lynne Rienner.

Kelman, H. C. (1999b). The interdependence of Israeli and Palestinian national identities: The role of the other in existential conflicts. *Journal of Social Issues, 55*(3), 581-600.

Kelman, H. C. (1999c). Experiences from 30 years of action research on the Israeli–Palestinian conflict. In K. Spillmann & A. Wenger (Eds.), *Zeitgeschichtliche Hintergründe aktueller Konflikte VII: Zürcher Beiträge zur Sicherheitspolitik und Konfliktforschung, 54*, 173-197.

Kelman, H. C. (2001). The role of national identity in conflict resolution: Experiences from Israeli–Palestinian problem-solving workshops. In R.D. Ashmore, L. Jussim, & D. Wilder (Eds.), *Social identity, intergroup conflict, and conflict reduction,* (pp. 187-212). Oxford and New York: Oxford University Press.

Kelman, H. C. (2002). Interactive problem solving: Informal mediation by the scholar-practitioner. In J. Bercovitch (Ed.), *Studies in international mediation: Essays in honor of Jeffrey Z. Rubin* (pp. 167-193). New York: Palgrave Macmillan.

Kelman, H. C. (2004). Reconciliation as identity change: A social–psychological perspective. In Y. Bar-Simon-Tov (Ed.), *From conflict resolution to reconciliation* (pp. 111-124). Oxford and New York: Oxford University Press.

Kelman, H. C. (2005). Building trust among enemies: The central challenge for international conflict resolution. *International Journal of Intercultural Relations, 29*, 639-650.

Kelman, H. C. (2006). Interests, relationships, identities: Three central issues for individuals and groups in negotiating their social environment. In S. T. Fiske, A. E. Kazdin, & D. L. Schacter (Eds.), *Annual Review of Psychology* (Vol. 57, pp. 1-26). Palo Alto, CA: Annual Reviews.

Kelman, H. C., & Hamilton, V. L. (1989). *Crimes of obedience: Toward a social psychology of authority and responsibility.* New Haven and London: Yale University Press.

Knutson, J. N. (Ed.). (1973). *Handbook of political psychology.* San Francisco: Jossey-Bass.

Kriesberg, L. (1998). Coexistence and the reconciliation of communal conflicts. In E. Weiner (Ed.), *The handbook of interethnic conflict* (pp. 182-198). New York: Continuum.

Lederach, J. P. (1998). Beyond violence: Building sustainable peace. In E. Weiner (Ed.), *The handbook of interethnic coexistence* (pp. 236-245). New York: Continuum.

Lustick, I. S. (1997). Ending protracted conflicts: The Oslo peace process between political partnership and legality. *Cornell International Law Journal, 30*(3), 741-757.

Rouhana, N. N. (2004). Identity and power in the reconciliation of protracted national conflict. In A. H. Eagly, R. M. Baron, & V. L. Hamilton (Eds.), *The social psychology of group identity and social conflict: Theory, application, and practice* (pp. 173-187). Washington: American Psychological Association.

Rouhana, N. N., & Kelman, H. C. (1994). Promoting joint thinking in international conflicts: An Israeli–Palestinian continuing workshop. *Journal of Social Issues, 50*(1), 157-178.

Saunders, H. H. (1999). *A public peace process: Sustained dialogue to transform racial and ethnic conflicts.* New York: St. Martin's Press.

Saunders, H. H. (2000). Interactive conflict resolution: A view for policy makers on making and building peace. In P. C. Stern & D. Druckman (Eds.), *International conflict resolution after the Cold War* (pp. 251-293). Washington: National Academy Press.

Sears, D. O., Huddy, L., & Jervis, R. (Eds.). (2003). *Oxford handbook of political psychology.* Oxford and New York: Oxford University Press.

Staub E., & Bar-Tal, D. (2003). Genocide, mass killing, and intractable conflict: Roots, evolution, prevention, and reconciliation. In D. O. Sears, L. Huddy, & R. Jervis (Eds.), *The Oxford handbook of political psychology* (pp. 710-751). Oxford and New York: Oxford University Press.

Part II

Socioemotional Reconciliation:
Moving Beyond Victimhood, Guilt,
and Humiliation

Part II.A

Guilt, Victimhood, and Forgiveness

CHAPTER 2

Instrumental and Socioemotional Paths to Intergroup Reconciliation and the Needs-Based Model of Socioemotional Reconciliation

Arie Nadler and Nurit Shnabel

The development of Social Psychology during the 20th century occurred against the backdrop of intergroup conflicts between and within nations. Throughout this time the field's research agendas were shaped by international (e.g., World War II, the Cold War) and intrasocietal (e.g., the civil rights movement in America) conflicts (Farr, 1996). It is no surprise therefore that intergroup conflict and its resolution has been a central concern of social psychology since its inception. This ongoing interest has been driven by the wish to gain basic knowledge on the social-psychological dynamics of intergroup conflict, and a desire to facilitate more harmonious intergroup relations between and within societies. As we move away from the 20th century that has seen two world wars, numerous regional conflicts, and a number of genocidal campaigns (e.g., the Jewish Holocaust, the genocidal campaign of the Pol Pot regime in Cambodia, the massacres in Rwanda) there is no need to belabor the importance of studying intergroup conflicts and ways to end them. The present chapter is within this research tradition. It centers on processes of intergroup reconciliation and has three related goals. We begin with a definition of reconciliation, then consider the distinction between socioemotional and instrumental reconciliation (Nadler, 2002), and finally we present the Needs-Based Model of socioemotional reconciliation. We conclude by discussing the theoretical and applied implications of this model.

A "Realist" and "Psychological Needs" Perspectives on Conflict

Scholars of conflict have viewed the antecedents of conflict and ways to end them through two perspectives: the "realist" and the "psychological needs" perspectives. The realist approach suggests that conflict is attributable to the parties' competition over scarce and *real* resources. In international conflicts, these are often natural resources (e.g., land), in intrasocietal conflict, these are often scarce budgets, and in conflict between two groups of children, these may be pocketknives (Sherif, Harvey, White, Hood, & Sherif, 1961). This approach holds that because competition over tangible and scarce resources causes conflict, an agreement on how to divide them will bring an end to conflict. Such an agreement is said to be the result of a negotiation between two *rational* actors who put their differences on the table and seek an agreement on how to divide the contested resources. Much of the social-psychological literature on ending conflict has focused on processes that lead to the achievement of such an agreement and its characteristics (Pruitt & Carnevale, 1993). Thus for example, Cross and Rosenthal (1999) argue that a focus on adversarial *positions* results in *distributive bargaining* that centers on ways to split the disputed *pie*, while a focus on the parties' underlying *interests* results in *integrative bargaining* that seeks to expand the *pie* for both parties before dividing it. The realist approach to conflict has been influential in generating new understandings on ending conflicts in applied settings (e.g., Fisher & Ury, 1981; Ury, 1991).

The psychological needs perspective goes beyond a realist view of conflict of interests to causes that are rooted in the threat to parties' basic *psychological needs* (Burton, 1969). During conflict parties inflict humiliation and pain on each other and this result in threats to basic psychological needs such as needs for positive esteem and worthy identity, need for autonomy, or needs for security and justice. These threats result in emotions that contribute to the maintenance conflict and act as barriers to ending it. Thus for example, the feeling of humiliation by one's adversary often precipitates a motivation for revenge that can instigate a new cycle of violence (Frijda, 1994). Similarly, feelings of distrust in the adversary may cause a discounting of the adversary's positive gestures as manipulative ploys thereby making the end of conflict more difficult

(Lewicki & Wiethoff, 2000). This perspective on conflict suggests that the end of conflict is predicated on the removal of these threats to basic *psychological needs* and resultant *emotions* and motivations (Burton, 1969). Our chapter lies at the center of the psychological needs perspective on conflict. We define the process of intergroup reconciliation as *the process of removing conflict-related emotional barriers that block the way to ending intergroup conflict.*

In the past, the study of intergroup conflict was dominated by the real conflict approach. Parties were traditionally viewed as rational actors who try to maximize self-gain. The willingness to compromise and reach an agreement was attributable to parties' perception that the costs of continuing conflict outweigh the alternative costs of ending it. Concepts at the center of the human needs perspective (e.g., humiliation, honor, and revenge) were relatively ignored in early discussions of ways to end intergroup conflicts (Scheff, 1994). This relative under-representation of emotional and identity-related processes is captured by Scheff (1994) who writes that "One would hardly know that they [emotions] existed from reading social science analysis of conflict... emotions are sometimes invoked under the rubric of 'non rational motives' but with little attempt to specify what this category might contain" (p. 66).

In recent years, this one-sided emphasis is changing both outside and within social psychology. Outside of our field this shift is evident in the increasing number of episodes where political and cultural leaders try to promote the end of conflict by apologizing for the wrongdoings that their group had committed (Barkan, 2001). For example, in 1998 UN Secretary-General Kofi Annan apologized for the UN's failure to prevent the Rwandan genocide, and in the year 2000 Pope John Paul II apologized to victims of two millennia of persecution by the Catholic Church. This greater awareness of the need to promote the end of intergroup conflict through the removal of conflict-related emotions of guilt and victimhood is also reflected in the more than 20 truth commissions that were established worldwide to facilitate reconciliation between former adversaries (e.g., Guatemala, Philippines, etc.; Hayner, 2001). The most outstanding of these was the Truth and Reconciliation Commission in South Africa. Its name epitomizes the working assumption that underlies all truth committees: Uncovering the painful truth by the perpetrator will allow the victim to grant forgiveness and facilitate reconciliation. Another illustrative example is the change in emphasis in applied analyses of the negotiation process. In 1981 Roger Fisher and William Ury published the first such influential analysis under the title *Getting to Yes: Negotiating Agreement Without Giving In.* This book sold over 2 million copies, was translated to more than 20 languages, and introduced concepts such as "win-win" solutions to the daily discourse of conflict. Recently, in 2005, Roger Fisher and Daniel Shapiro authored a book titled *Beyond Reason: Using Emotions as You Negotiate.* This epitomizes the change in the direction of greater awareness by scholars and practitioners of the role of adversaries' psychological needs and associated emotions in ending conflicts.

Within social psychology recent research on interpersonal conflicts has become similarly concerned with emotional processes that are associated with the analysis of the end of conflict. This research has focused on the effects of apologies on the reduction of interpersonal conflict (e.g., McCullough, Worthington, & Rachal, 1997), variables that explain perpetrators' willingness to apologize (e.g., Hodgins & Liebeskind, 2003) and the victim's readiness to forgive (e.g., Darby & Schlenker, 1982). In the context of intergroup relations, social-psychological theory and research indicates that group members can experience feelings of collective guilt (e.g., Branscombe & Miron, 2004; Leach, Snider, & Iyer, 2004) or collective victimization (e.g., Roccas, Klar, & Liviatan, 2004) that result from wrongdoings that the in-group had perpetrated or was the victim of. These feelings of collective guilt or victimhood color group members' perceptions and behavior toward the out-groups (Branscombe & Miron, 2004; Roccas et al., 2004). Finally, recent experimental research highlights the fact that under conditions of a relatively high feeling of trust in the adversary's apologies for past wrongdoings can lead to a greater willingness to reconcile with the enemy group (Nadler & Liviatan, 2004).

Two Paths to Reconciliation: Socioemotional and Instrumental Reconciliation

Building on the distinction between the realist and psychological needs perspectives Kelman has recently proposed a distinction between three processes of peace making: conflict settlement, conflict resolution, and reconciliation (Kelman, 2004). *Conflict settlement* operates at the *level of interests*. Similar to the emphasis in the "realist" perspective on conflict the settlement of conflict consists of finding an agreed upon formula for the division of contested resources. Processes of conflict resolution and reconciliation are two aspects of psychological needs perspective. *Conflict resolution* operates at the level of the *relationships between the adversarial parties*. It aims to restore a feeling of trust between the adversaries and build a pragmatic partnership in which each side is convinced that cooperation is in its own best interests. Kelman views *reconciliation* as a process that reflects *identity changes* that each of the adversaries undergoes. It consists of removal of the negation of the other as an element in one's own identity and of being able to acknowledge the other's narrative without having to agree fully with it. In a process of reconciliation, each party is said to strengthen the core elements in its own identity while accommodating the other.

Consistent with Kelman's position that distinguishes between affecting an end to conflict through changes in adversarial relations or through changes in the adversaries' identities we have also distinguished between two categories of emotional barriers that need to be removed in order to facilitate an end to conflict (a) a feeling of distrust in the other and (b) feelings that emanate from threat to the sense of one's worthy identity (Nadler, 2002). Since trust between the adversaries is said to result from repeated acts of cooperation to achieve common *instrumental* goals (e.g., cleaner environment, better health), we have labeled this route to ending intergroup conflict as *instrumental reconciliation*. Because we focus on the restoration of a sense of worthy identity by overcoming the *emotional* barriers of victimhood and guilt through an *interaction* that involves an admission of past wrongdoings and subsequent forgiveness we have labeled this route to ending conflict as *Socioemotional Reconciliation*. These processes of instrumental and socioemotional reconciliation are similar to Kelman's distinction between processes of conflict resolution and reconciliation, respectively. Yet, our analysis is different from Kelman's analysis in several respects. First, we seek to compare these two routes to end conflict on a common set of criteria (e.g., the end-state that each of these categories aims for; the temporal focus of each category). Second, our view of socioemotional reconciliation centers on the apology-forgiveness cycle and the Needs-Based Model of Reconciliation that elucidates the psychological processes that underlie it.

Further, due to the multidisciplinary nature of the study of conflict and the relatively recent attention to reconciliation there is lack of clarity regarding the definition of "reconciliation." While Kelman terms the process of building of trustworthy relations *conflict resolution* and distinguishes it from that of *reconciliation*, other scholars view building trustworthy relations as the essence of the process of reconciliation. Thus for example, Worthington and Drinkard (2000) define reconciliation as "the restoration of trust in an interpersonal relationship through mutual trustworthy behaviours" (p. 93). These different views on the same concept create conceptual ambiguity. Our definition of reconciliation as consisting of the removal of emotional barriers to the end of conflict and instrumental and socioemotional reconciliation as dealing with two different classes of such emotional barriers (i.e., lack of trust and threat to worthy identity, respectively) allows a clearer view of the unique nature of the concept of reconciliation as distinct from the realist approaches to ending conflict.

Before we move on to discuss the differences between instrumental and socioemotional reconciliation, it should be noted that we do not view these two processes as mutually exclusive but rather as interdependent. We shall return to discuss their links in a later section, but first, for the sake of conceptual clarity, we will specify the unique nature of each of them.

The processes of socioemotional and instrumental reconciliation are markedly different. Socioemotional reconciliation seeks to remove the emotional and identity-related barriers to the end of conflict through the successful completion of an apology-forgiveness cycle (Tavuchis, 1991). We view this cycle as consisting of a social exchange between perpetrator and victim in which each provides to the other the psychological commodities that are needed to ameliorate the threats to their respective identities. Victims face a threat to their identity as able and worthy actors. When perpetrators apologize and accept responsibility for past wrongdoings they create a *debt* that only their victims can remove by granting forgiveness. This restores the victims' sense of power and equality that had been robbed from them during the victimization episode(s). In her analysis of psychological consequences of the Truth and Reconciliation Committee (TRC) process Gobodo-Madikizela made a similar argument: "the decision to forgive can paradoxically elevate a victim to a position of strength as the one who has the key to the perpetrator's wish…the victim becomes the gatekeeper to what the outcast desires" (Gobodo-Madikizela, 2003, p. 117). Perpetrators, on the other hand, are faced with threats to their identity as moral actors. Being identified as the guilty perpetrator may result in expulsion from the "moral community" to which one, or one's group, belongs (Tavuchis, 1991). The granting of forgiveness for past wrongdoings by the victim ameliorates this threat (Exline & Baumeister, 2000). The apology-forgiveness cycle, which we view as lying at the center of socioemotional reconciliation, is expected to increase the parties' willingness to end the conflict. The working assumption behind the TRC process in South Africa was that the prospects of reconciliation between Blacks and Whites will be facilitated through the processes of truth telling by perpetrators and the conditional granting of forgiveness by victims (Tutu, 1999).

The road to instrumental reconciliation is different from the apology-forgiveness cycle that lies at the heart of socioemotional reconciliation. It is not concerned with the past of the conflict. It implicitly suggests to "let bygones be bygones" and centers on the gradual learning that occurs when the former adversaries cooperate repeatedly to achieve instrumental goals that are important for both parties. During these repetitive cooperative projects the parties gradually learn to trust and accept each other. Programs in educational and community settings that are based on the ideas of the contact hypothesis (Pettigrew & Tropp, 2005) and the Sherif et al.'s (1961) proposal that intergroup conflict can be reduced by cooperative efforts to obtain superordinate goals represent this approach. A similar emphasis exists in Osgood's GRIT proposal that suggests that international tensions such as those that existed between the United States and the USSR during the height of the Cold War could be reduced by reciprocal cooperative gestures (Osgood, 1962). Peace-building efforts that follow the signature of agreements to end conflict represent another example of instrumental reconciliation. Peace building requires participation in multiple cooperative programs that aim to achieve instrumental goals that are important for the former adversaries (e.g., environmental, agricultural and health projects; Lederach, 1997). The "people-to-people" programs between Israelis and Palestinians after the signing of the Oslo agreements are a recent real world example of this approach. These, and similar programs in other conflict areas, share the idea that repeated instances of cooperative contact between the adversaries will help to gradually transform adversarial relations that are marked by suspicion and distrust to more trustworthy relations (Kriesberg, 2000).

Instrumental and socioemotional reconciliation are different on four dimensions (Table 2.1): (a) the *target*, (b) the *nature*, (c) the *temporal focus*, and (d) the *goal* that the change of reconciliation represents. The *target of change* in instrumental reconciliation is *external* while that of socioemotional reconciliation is *internal*. Instrumental reconciliation seeks to change the relations with and perceptions of the adversary, while socioemotional reconciliation seeks to affect a change in each of the parties' own identity and image. The *nature of change* in instrumental reconciliation is *evolutionary* whereas the change in socioemotional reconciliation is *revolutionary*. Processes of instrumental reconciliation consist of gradual changes that reflect learning over time to trust and accept the other, whereas the change that occurs as a result of socioemotional reconciliation is relatively instantaneous. Change is assumed to follow

TABLE 2.1 Differential Emphases in Socioemotional and Instrumental Reconciliation

	Socioemotional Reconciliation	Instrumental Reconciliation
Target of change	A secure, equal, and worthy *identity* of each party	A trustworthy *relationship* between the parties
Nature of change	*Revolutionary* change that occurs relatively instantaneously after the successful completion of the apology-forgiveness cycle	*Evolutionary* change that consists of gradual learning over multiple projects of cooperation to trust one's adversary
Temporal focus of change	The key to a reconciled future lies in addressing the infliction of pain of humiliation during the *past of conflict*	Repetitive events of cooperation in the *present* are the key to a reconciled future
The goal of reconciliation	*Integration* of the adversarial parties into a single social unit with a "we feeling." More characteristic of intrasocietal conflicts	*Separation* between the adversarial parties so that they can coexist in a conflict-free environment

immediately after the successful completion of the apology-forgiveness cycle. Commenting on the nature of such change Tavuchis (1991) writes: "when this secular act of expiation is punctiliously performed... our world is transformed in a way that can only be described as miraculous" (p. 8). Regarding the *temporal focus of the process of change*, socioemotional reconciliation is focused on the *past of the conflict* and asserts that the key to a reconciled future lies in a constructive confrontation with the painful past. Efforts of instrumental reconciliation are focused *on the present* and are based on the premise that ongoing cooperation between the adversaries in the present will result in a reconciled future.

The *goal of reconciliation* can be the creation of a conflict-free environment in which two separate parties coexist or the formation of one *integrated* social unit of which the former adversaries are two parts that share a "we" feeling (i.e., *separation* and *integration*, respectively). If the goal of reconciliation is separate coexistence between the former enemies instrumental reconciliation is enough. It restores trust to the relations between the two former adversaries who wish separate coexistence in a conflict-free environment. Socioemotional reconciliation is consistent with the goal of integration. It seeks to restore each of the parties' worthy identities through the apology-forgiveness cycle thereby freeing them from the threats that each presents to the identity of the other. It therefore allows the former adversaries to share a larger and more inclusive identity. This may be one explanation why most truth committees that institutionalize processes of socioemotional reconciliation have been established at the end of *intrasocietal* conflicts where the goal of reconciliation is social integration (Hayner, 2001). On the other hand, peace-building efforts that seek to allow the former enemies to coexist as separate nations in a conflict-free environment are more common after the conclusion of *international conflicts*.

The distinction between instrumental and socioemotional reconciliation is echoed in other analyses of the reconciliation process. In political science, Long and Brecke (2003) have analyzed the differences between intergroup reconciliation in international and intranational contexts. They distinguish between a *signaling model* and a *forgiveness model* of intergroup reconciliation. The forgiveness model consists of admission of past wrongdoings unto one's former enemy and seeking their forgiveness. It aims to establish a different kind of relationships between the two former adversaries. The signaling model seeks to signal to one's former adversary that one's intentions are benign and that social interaction with them is safe. Consistent with our analysis, Long and Brecke suggest that the forgiveness model is more appropriate for intranational contexts where the goal of reconciliation is integration and the signaling model is more appropriate for international contexts where the goal of reconciliation is separate coexistence. The parallels between the signaling and forgiveness model, on the one hand, and instrumental and socioemotional reconciliation, on the other, are immediately clear. Finally, studies of primate behavior suggest that apes' conciliatory gestures at the end of conflict (e.g., hugging, patting) may signal that one can be trusted, or they may serve the function of setting a base for future relationships of interdependence in a single social unit (i.e., *signaling function* or *relationship-repair function*; De Waal & Aureli, 1996). With all the necessary caution when discussing similarities across species, there exists a general similarity between the goals of "signaling function" and "relationship-repair function" and the goals of instrumental and socioemotional reconciliation, respectively.

Before we move to a more detailed account of socioemotional reconciliation we should note that the discussion of socioemotional and instrumental reconciliation as two separate paths is done for sake of conceptual clarity. In reality these two processes are related to each other. When the goal of reconciliation is separate coexistence, the creation of trustworthy relations between the former adversaries through instrumental reconciliation may suffice. However, when the goal is integration, the success of socioemotional reconciliation processes depends on the existence of trust between the two adversaries. Recent research indicates that in the presence of a low level of intergroup trust, apology by the perpetrator is viewed as a manipulative ploy and leads to an increase in tensions (Nadler & Liviatan, 2006). This suggests that the process of socioemotional reconciliation needs to be viewed as a two stage process. In the first stage, parties need to establish trust through efforts of instrumental reconciliation. In a second stage, processes of socioemotional reconciliation can be implemented (Lindskold, 1978; Nadler, 2002; Nadler & Liviatan, 2004).

Dealing With the Threats of Victimhood and Guilt: Unilateral Actions and the Needs-Based Model of Socioemotional Reconciliation

Victims suffer a threat to their identity as powerful actors and perpetrators suffer a threat to their identity as moral actors. The differential threats to *power* and *moral identity* evoke feelings of powerlessness and moral inferiority, respectively. To avoid these negative feelings and ameliorate threatened identities, victims are motivated to regain the identity of powerful actors and perpetrators are motivated to regain the identity of moral actors. They can do so unilaterally or interactively. Taking revenge and distancing oneself from the victim both socially and emotionally are two unilateral ways in which victims and perpetrators can ameliorate threats to feelings of powerlessness and guilt, respectively. Yet, such unilateral removal of threats is likely to intensify rather than quell conflict while an interactive amelioration of these threats through the apology-forgiveness cycle is expected to promote reconciliation. We first discuss the two major unilateral ways of ameliorating feelings of powerlessness and moral inferiority (i.e., revenge and social distancing) and then move to discuss the interactive alternative of the apology-forgiveness cycle and suggest a model that accounts for the psychological dynamics of this process: The Needs-Based Model of Reconciliation.

The Unilateral Alternative: Revenge and Social Distancing

The commonly used phrase that victims are "at the hands" of their tormentors epitomizes the lack of control and loss of power that is the sine qua non of victimhood. Empirical research that indicates that victims feel a threat to their self-esteem (i.e., Scobie & Scobie, 1999), perceived control (Baumeister, Stilwell, & Heatherton, 1994), and power (Foster & Rosbult, 1999) corroborate this observation. Scholars who have analyzed the role of emotions in international conflicts have made a similar argument by noting that a major reason for the protracted nature of some of these conflicts are victim's feelings of humiliation (Lindner, 2006; Scheff, 1994). To cope with these threats victims need to restore feelings of self-worth, self-control, and social equality. Perpetrators who hold power over the victim during the conflict episode do not experience a similar threat to their perceptions of power and control. They, on the other hand, worry about their image as moral social actors. This threat results in feelings of guilt (Baumeister et al., 1994), shame (Exline & Baumeister, 2000), and moral inferiority (Zechmeister & Romero, 2002). This myriad of emotions is associated with perpetrators' fear that they will be rejected from the moral community to which they belong (Tavuchis, 1991) and raises the possibility that they will be excluded by psychologically relevant others (Baumeister et al., 1994). To cope with these threats perpetrators need to restore the feeling that they are accepted by others and are viewed by them as moral social actors.

Victims can restore their identity as powerful actors by taking revenge on their perpetrator. Revenge changes the power asymmetry that had existed between victim and perpetrator and makes relations more equal (Frijda, 1994). Akhtar (2002) has summarized this psychologically positive aspect of revenge by noting that "some revenge is actually good for the victim...it puts the victim's hitherto passive ego in an active position...[and] imparts a sense of mastery and self-esteem." Echoing a similar sentiment Freud, quoting Heine, wrote "one must, it is true, forgive one's enemies—but not before they have been hanged" (quoted by Akhtar, 2002, p. 179). Although revenge is psychologically healthy for the victim it is unlikely to contribute to the ending of conflict because of its unilateral nature. The perpetrator is the passive recipient of the victim's revenge. While revenge may restore the victim's feelings of power and control, it does not respond to the perpetrator's need for acceptance. Thus, although the victim may feel more ready to end the conflict after taking revenge than before having done so, revenge will not promote the prospects of reconciliation. Further, since what one party sees as justified revenge, the other commonly views as unjustified aggression that needs to be avenged acts of revenge are likely to lead to an intensified cycle of violence (Newberg, d'Aquili, Newberg, & deMarici, 2000).

Perpetrators can ameliorate the threat to their identity as moral actors by denying the painful consequences of their actions and/or their responsibility for having caused them (Schonbach, 1990). They can distance themselves from the pain and suffering of the adversary by belittling them or by feeling no empathy with the victim's sufferings. Since increasing the social distance between oneself and the victim lowers empathy (Fry, 2006), the ultimate tactic of social distancing is the dehumanization of the victim. This common practice of parties in intractable conflicts (Bar-Tal, 1990) allows one to feel no empathy with the victim. Alternatively, perpetrators may deny responsibility for having caused pain and suffering. They may do so by asserting that the victim "brought it on himself or herself," or by attributing their harmful actions to external constraints. The use of either of these psychological mechanisms (i.e., denying the victim's consequences or one's responsibility for them) reduces the perpetrator's guilt and threat to moral identity. Yet, as is the case with revenge, these are unilateral mechanisms to remove the identity-related threats and emotional barriers on the road to end conflict. The victim is the passive recipient of the perpetrator's construal of their actions as harmless or themselves as blameless and because of this social distancing is unlikely to facilitate reconciliation. The interactive alternative of the apology-forgiveness cycle removes the emotional and need-related barriers to reconciliation for *both* victims and perpetrators simultaneously. It is therefore likely to encourage readiness for reconciliation. This act of social exchange allows victims and perpetrators to reconcile by moving beyond victimhood and moral inferiority, respectively.

The Interactive Alternative: The Needs-Based Model of the Apology-Forgiveness Cycle

The Needs-Based Model of Reconciliation is a systematic account of the apology-forgiveness cycle that is at the heart of the process of socioemotional reconciliation. The basic idea of the model is that as a consequence of conflict victims and perpetrators suffer threats to different dimensions of their identity, and that the amelioration of these differential threats, through the apology-forgiveness cycle, promotes socioemotional reconciliation. Until this has occurred, these threats to identity act as barriers to reconciliation. The apology-forgiveness cycle represents an interactive removal of threats to the parties' identities. From this perspective, the apology-forgiveness cycle is viewed as an act of social exchange in which each party provides to its adversary the psychological resources that ameliorate the specific threat to its identity. In the following sections we provide a more detailed account of this process, which is summarized in Figure 2.1, describe studies that support it and discuss its theoretical and applied implications.

The Need-Based Model of Reconciliation consists of three consecutive levels of predictions: (1) Victims experience a threat to their identity as powerful social actors and perpetrators experience a threat to their identity as moral social actors. (2) Therefore, perpetrators seek information that others accept them and view them as moral whereas victims seek power and acknowledgement of the injustice done to them. The frustration of these needs leads to feelings of moral inferiority or powerlessness that constitute barriers to reconciliation. (3) Messages of social acceptance and empowerment will satisfy the perpetrators'

	Role	
	Victim	Perpetrator
Threatened identity dimension	Sense of power	Moral image
	↓	↓
Amelioration of threat through a message of	Empowerment (e.g., victim desires that partner take responsibility for causing injustice)	Acceptance (e.g., perpetrator desires that partner express empathy)
	↓	↓
Consequence of amelioration of threat	Restored sense of power	Restored moral image
	↓	↓
Resulting in	Increased willingness to reconcile	

FIGURE 2.1. The Needs-Based Model of Reconciliation.

and victims' emotional needs, respectively, and will therefore be linked to greater willingness to reconcile with one's adversary. The apology-forgiveness cycle represents a social interaction that satisfies the psychological needs of victims and perpetrators. When the perpetrators apologize by admitting responsibility for past wrongdoings this gives the victims the power to grant or withhold forgiveness. This restores to the victims the power and self-control that had been taken from them during the victimization episode. The indication that the victims understand the circumstances that drove the perpetrators to commit wrongdoings and that they forgive them for these wrongdoings implies to perpetrators that they are no longer viewed as immoral and bad and should not be concerned about being socially excluded by the victims or the community. Thus, the successful completion of the apology-forgiveness cycle allows the victims and perpetrators to move beyond the emotional barriers of powerlessness and moral inferiority and this raises their willingness to reconcile.

We have recently set out to validate the three consecutive layers of hypotheses of the Needs-Based Model in the context of interpersonal relations (Shnabel & Nadler, in press). To test the hypotheses that a victimization episode threatens different psychological dimensions for victims and perpetrators, and that this threat results in different needs, we devised an experimental situation in which half of the participants were randomly assigned to the role of victims and the other half to the role of perpetrators. Following this induction, we measured participants' sense of power and moral image (i.e., their perceptions of others' view of them as moral or not). We compared the reactions of participants in the victim-perpetrator dyad to those of participants in a relevant control dyad in which participants experienced unequal power relations in terms of control and success, but there was no direct victimization episode.

The findings supported the hypothesis that following victimization episodes victims suffer a decrease in their sense of power and perpetrators suffer a decrease in their ratings of moral image. Consistent with the model's predictions, the decrease in perpetrators' ratings of moral image was associated with a parallel increase in need for social acceptance that found expression in a greater wish that the victims would understand their perspective and indicate their view of them as decent people. In line with predictions, following a victimization episode victims express a greater need for power and justice (i.e., that perpetrators would acknowledge that victims had been unduly wronged). It should be noted that this support for the model's predictions was obtained in an experiment in which the roles of victim and perpetrator were experimentally induced in the same context. This is the first experiment, known to us, which has accomplished this. Past experimental research explored victims' reactions to victimization and could not therefore provide experimental answers to hypotheses regarding the dynamics of victim-perpetrator interactions.

To increase the external validity of these findings we sought to replicate them in real life settings. To this end we had participants recall a personal episode in which they had either hurt a significant other or had been hurt by the other. Thus, we induced people to enter the perpetrator or the victim role in a real life interpersonal context. Subsequently, we asked them to rate their sense of power and their moral image in the conflict episode, as well as their need for power and social acceptance with the antagonist. The findings replicate the results of the experiment described earlier. Participants who had thought about themselves as victims had lower ratings of power and expressed greater need for justice and power than those who had thought about themselves as perpetrators. On the other hand, those who had been induced to think about themselves as perpetrators had lower ratings of moral image (i.e., their ratings of others' view of them as more or less moral) and expressed greater need for acceptance than those who had been induced to think about themselves as victims. The empirical consistency of the patterns across the two studies provides external validity to the model's predictions that a victimization episode threatens different dimensions in the perpetrator's and victim's identities and that these threats result in different psychological needs.

In the next phase of our research program, we moved to examine the model's claim that victims' readiness to reconcile with the adversary is enhanced by the satisfaction of their need for power, and that perpetrators' readiness to reconcile is enhanced by the satisfaction of their need for acceptance. In the first test of this hypothesis we again used an experiment in which participants had been randomly assigned the role of victim or perpetrator. Participants then received a message from their counterpart that included either an element of empowerment (i.e., that they are viewed as competent) or social acceptance (i.e., that they are viewed as sociable). Our model predicts that because a message of empowerment responds to the victims' need for power it will increase their willingness to reconcile while a message of acceptance, which responds to the perpetrators' need for acceptance, will increase their willingness to reconcile. The findings supported these predictions. A message of empowerment restored victims' sense of power and thus increased their willingness to reconcile more than a message of acceptance, which did not affect participants' sense of power, whereas a message of acceptance restored perpetrators' moral image and thus increased their willingness to reconcile more than a message of empowerment, which did not affect participants' moral image. In a subsequent study we replicated these findings with reactions to a vignette that described a victimization episode in which a waitron's request not to work on a certain shift is declined by his superior.

In a final study in this research program we sought to examine the full range of the model's predictions by measuring individuals' sense of power, moral image, and willingness to reconcile *before* and *after* they had received a message of empowerment or acceptance from an adversary. Participants were asked to read a vignette that described an event in which the protagonist discovered that their position in an organization, which was an attractive one, had been taken over by a fellow worker. Half of the participants were asked to assume the role of the perpetrator (i.e., the person who had taken the job) and the other half were asked to assume the role of the victim (i.e., the worker who had lost it). Immediately following this participants were asked to fill out the first set of dependent measures. Consistent with the earlier findings we found that perpetrators felt greater threat to their moral image and had a greater need for social acceptance than did victims, who experienced a greater threat to their sense of power and expressed greater need for power and justice. Following this, participants received the second part of the vignette, in which they learned that the antagonist in the story made a verbal statement that consisted of expressions of empowerment or acceptance for the protagonist. Following this, the second set of dependent measures was administered again. Importantly, and in line with the model's predictions, the increase in victims' sense of power between the first and second administration was higher in the empowerment than acceptance condition; accordingly, their willingness to reconcile was higher in the empowerment than in the acceptance condition. For perpetrators, on the other hand, the increase in their moral image and willingness to reconcile was higher in the acceptance than in the empowerment condition.

Although there is no direct examination of the model's assertions in the context of intergroup conflict, the recent findings of Nadler and Liviatan (2006) on the effects of intergroup apologies suggest indirect support for the model in such contexts. In that study Israeli participants read statements by a Palestinian leader that included an expression of empathy with Israelis' conflict-related sufferings, an acceptance of responsibility for having caused them, both, or neither. The findings indicate that, in the presence of trust in the adversary, expressions of empathy, but not acceptance of responsibility, led to greater willingness by Israeli participants to reconcile with Palestinians. When viewed within the Needs-Based Model these findings may reflect the different power positions of Israelis and Palestinians. Since Israelis are viewed as the more powerful party they are also likely to be viewed as the perpetrators of wrongdoings, and the Palestinians, who are the weaker party, are likely to be viewed as the victims. The finding that Israeli participants' willingness for reconciliation was affected by expressions of empathy is consistent with the model's assertion that perpetrators' willingness to reconcile is facilitated by messages of social acceptance. When victims express empathy with the perpetrators' pains they also implicitly convey a message that they accept them as similar human beings who also suffer from conflict-related pains. Such expressions of empathy by the victims rehumanize the perpetrators and render them as individuals who have committed bad acts, rather than as bad and immoral people. The Needs-Based Model of reconciliation suggests that the weaker party in the conflict, which is also likely to experience itself as the victim, will be more ready to reconcile after receiving a message that contains an acceptance of responsibility for past wrongdoings than after a message that expresses empathy to its suffering. Placed within the context of the Israeli-Palestinian conflict, this suggests that Palestinians will be more ready to reconcile after Israelis have accepted their responsibility for wrongdoings committed against Palestinians. This hypothesis needs to be empirically validated.

From a broader perspective, the above indicates the importance of considering differential power positions of the two adversarial groups when analyzing processes of socioemotional reconciliation. In fact, the route for socioemotional reconciliation is different for the stronger and weaker parties. The weaker party, which is likely to view itself as the victim, has a higher need for power and justice and the stronger party, which is likely to view itself as the perpetrator, has a higher need for acceptance and empathy. Although this possibility has not been put to the direct scrutiny of social-psychological investigation, some anecdotal evidence seems to support its validity. During the Camp David 2000 peace discussions the Palestinian delegation was very adamant that the Israeli government accept responsibility for the suffering of the Palestinians from 1948 onward. The Israelis were equally adamant in their refusal to do so (Ross, 2004). Viewed within the context of the present discussion this discourse can be seen as representing the weaker side (i.e., the Palestinians) demand that the stronger side (i.e., Israelis) admits a "moral debt" that would make the weaker side more equal. The Israeli refusal to do so can be explained as reflecting their fear that admission of responsibility for past wrongdoings would not have been reciprocated by empathy with their own predicament and subsequent forgiveness and acceptance. They, so it seems, were concerned that their apology would not be the first step toward the conclusion of a successful apology-forgiveness cycle, but rather a springboard for further demands and accusations.

Before we close we should note that our discussion of processes of socioemotional reconciliation and the Needs-Based Model are based on an assumption of a clear distinction between perpetrators and victims. Yet, such a clear-cut distinction was intended for conceptual clarity and does not reflect the reality of conflicts. In the real world some conflicts end with a clear consensus on who the victim is and who the perpetrator is but many do not. Two examples for the first category are World War II, which ended with a consensus that the Nazi regime had been the perpetrator, and the conflict between Whites and Blacks in South Africa, which ended with a consensus that the system of apartheid regime and its officers were the perpetrators. The Israeli-Palestinian conflict may be a representative example of the second category. A number of scholars writing on this conflict have suggested that in this conflict both parties claim the role of "victim" (Maoz & Bar-On, 2002). Under these conditions of "double victimhood" processes of socioemotional reconciliation are more difficult. Since both parties view themselves as the victims they regard the other as the perpetrator who is responsible for initiating the apology-forgiveness cycle by admitting responsibility for past wrongdoings. This is likely to lead to an impasse and an inability to move forward on the path of socioemotional reconciliation. One way in which this trap of "double victimhood" may be broken is for both parties to recognize what social psychology has taught us for decades: Viewing oneself as a victim or perpetrator is a psychological construal that may change across time and situational contexts. Such a realization will allow both parties to view themselves as victim *and* perpetrator and encourage the initiation of a simultaneous and reciprocal apology-forgiveness cycles in which each party admits wrongdoings and grants forgiveness to its former adversary.

We do not propose that the adoption of the principles of the Needs-Based Model of Reconciliation will dramatically alter the reality of intergroup conflicts. We realize the multicausal and complex nature of protracted intergroup conflicts such as the one that exists between Israelis and Palestinians. Yet, our model highlights the need to attend to the different psychological needs of the adversaries. Such a differential attention is likely to increase our sensitivity to the adversaries different desires and result in a better understanding of processes of intergroup reconciliation.

References

Akhtar, S. (2002). Forgiveness: Origins, dynamics, psychopathology, and technical relevance. *Psychoanalytic Quarterly, 71*, 175-212.

Barkan, E. (2001). *The guilt of nations: Restitution and negotiating historical injustices.* Baltimore, MD: Johns Hopkins University Press.

Bar-Tal, D. (1990). Causes and consequences of delegitimization: Models of conflict and ethnocentrism. *Journal of Social Issues, 46*, 65-81.

Baumeister, R. F., Stillwell, A. M., & Heatherton, T. F. (1994). Guilt: An interpersonal approach. *Psychological Bulletin, 115*, 243-267.

Branscombe, N. R., & Miron, A. M. (2004). Interpreting the ingroup's negative actions toward another group: Emotional reactions to appraised harm. In L. Z. Tiedens & C. W. Leach (Eds.), *The social life of emotions* (pp. 314-335). New York: Cambridge University Press.

Burton, J. W. (1969). *Conflict and communication: The use of controlled communication in international relations.* New York: Free Press.

Cross, S., & Rosenthal, R. (1999). Three models of conflict resolution: Effects on intergroup expectancies and attitudes. *Journal of Social Issues, 55,* 561-580.

Darby, B. W., & Schlenker, B. R. (1982). Children's reactions to apologies. *Journal of Personality and Social Psychology, 43,* 742-753.

De Waal, F. B. M., & Aureli, F. (1996). Consolation, reconciliation, and a possible cognitive difference between macaques and chimpanzees. In A. E. Russon, K. A. Bard, & S. T. Parker (Eds.), *Reaching into thought: The minds of the great apes* (pp. 80-110). Cambridge: Cambridge University Press.

Exline, J. J., & Baumeister, R. F. (2000). Expressing forgiveness and repentance: Benefits and barriers. In M. E. McCullough, K. I. Pargament, & C. E. Thoresen (Eds.), *Forgiveness: Theory, research and practice* (pp. 133-155). New York: Guilford Press.

Farr, R. M. (1996). *The roots of modern social psychology.* New York: Blackwell.

Fisher, R., & Shapiro, D. (2005). *Beyond reason: Using emotions as you negotiate.* New York: Penguin books.

Fisher, R., & Ury, W. (1981). *Getting to yes: Negotiating agreement without giving in.* New York: Penguin books.

Foster, C. A., & Rusbult, C. E. (1999). Injustice and power seeking. *Personality and Social Psychology Bulletin, 25,* 834-849.

Frijda, N. H. (1994). The lex talionis: On vengeance. In S. H. M. Van Goozen, N. E. Van de Poll, & J. A. Sergeant (Eds.), *Emotions: Essays on emotion theory* (pp. 263-289). Hillsdale, NJ: Lawrence Erlbaum.

Fry, D. P. (2006). Reciprocity: The foundation stone of morality. In M. Killen & J. G. Smetana (Eds.), *Handbook of moral development* (pp. 399-422). Mahwah, NJ: Lawrence Erlbaum Associates Publishers.

Gobodo-Madikizela, P. (2003). *A human being died that night: A South-African story of forgiveness.* New York: Houghton Mifflin.

Hayner, P. B. (2001). *Unspeakable truths: Confronting state terror and atrocity.* New York: Routledge.

Hodgins, H. S., & Liebeskind, E. (2003). Apology versus defense: Antecedents and consequences. *Journal of Experimental Social Psychology, 39,* 297-316.

Kelman, H. C. (2004). Reconciliation as identity change: A social-psychological perspective. In Y. Bar-Siman-Tov (Ed.), *From conflict resolution to reconciliation* (pp. 111-124). Oxford, England: Oxford University Press.

Kriesberg, L. (2000). Coexistence and the reconciliation of communal conflicts. In E. Weiner (Ed.), *The handbook of interethnic coexistence* (pp. 182-188). New York: Abraham Fund.

Leach, C. W., Snider, N., & Iyer, A. (2002). "Poisoning the consciences of the fortunate": The experience of relative advantage and support for social equality. In I. Walker & H. J. Smith (Eds.), *Relative deprivation: Specification, development, and integration* (pp. 136-163). New York: Cambridge University Press.

Lederach, J. P. (1997). *Building peace: Sustainable reconciliation in divided societies.* Washington, DC: USIP Press.

Lewicki, R. J., & Wiethoff, C. (2000). Trust, trust development, and trust repair. In M. Deutsch & P. T. Coleman (Eds.), *The handbook of conflict resolution: Theory and practice* (pp. 86-107). San Francisco, CA: Jossey-Bas Publishers.

Lindner, E. (2006). *Making enemies: Humiliation and international conflict.* London: Praeger Security International.

Lindskold, S. (1978). Trust development, the GRIT Proposal, and the effects of conciliatory acts on conflict and cooperation. *Psychological Bulletin, 85*, 772-793.

Long, W. J., & Brecke, P. (2003). *War and reconciliation: Reason and emotion in conflict resolution.* Cambridge, MA: MIT Press.

Maoz, I., & Bar-On, D. (2002). From working through the Holocaust to current ethnic conflicts: Evaluating the TRT group workshop in Hamburg. *Group, 26*, 931-962.

McCullough, M. E., Worthington, E. L., & Rachal, K. C. (1997). Interpersonal forgiving in close relationships. *Journal of Personality and Social Psychology, 73*, 321-336.

Nadler, A. (2002). Post resolution processes: Instrumental and socio-emotional routes to reconciliation. In G. Salomon & B. Nevo (Eds.), *Peace education: The concept, principles, and practices around the world.* Mahwah, NJ: Lawrence Erlbaum.

Nadler, A., & Liviatan, I. (2004). Intergroup reconciliation process in Israel: Theoretical analysis and empirical findings. In N. R. Branscombe & B. Doosje (Eds.), *Collective guilt: International perspectives* (pp. 216-235). Cambridge: University Press.

Nadler, A., & Liviatan, I. (2006). Intergroup reconciliation: Effects of adversary's expressions of empathy, responsibility, and recipients' trust. *Personality and Social Psychology Bulletin, 32*, 459-470.

Newberg, A. B., d'Aquili, E. G., Newberg, S. K., & deMarici, V. (2000). The neuropsychological correlates of forgiveness. In M. E. McCullough, I. Pargament, & C. E. Thoresen (Eds.), *Forgiveness: Theory, research and practice* (pp. 91-108). New York: The Guilford Press.

Osgood, C. E. (1962). *An alternative to war or surrender.* Urbana, IL: University of Illinois Press.

Pettigrew, T. F., & Tropp, L. R. (2005). Allport's intergroup contact hypothesis: Its history and influence. In J. F. Dovidio, P. Glick, & L. A. Rudman (Eds.), *On the nature of prejudice: Fifty years after Allport* (pp. 262-277). Malden, MA: Blackwell Publishing.

Pruitt, D. G., & Carnevale, P. J. (1993). *Negotiation in social conflict.* Belmont, CA: Thomson Brooks/Cole Publishing.

Roccas, S., Klar, Y., & Liviatan, I. (2004). Exonerating cognitions, group identification, and personal values as predictors of collective guilt among Jewish-Israelis. In

N. R. Branscombe & B. Doosje (Eds.), *Collective guilt: International perspectives* (pp. 130-147). Cambridge, MA: Cambridge University Press.

Ross, D. (2004). *The missing peace: The inside story of the fight for Middle East peace.* New York: Farrar, Straus & Giroux.

Scheff, T. J. (1994). *Bloody revenge: Emotions, nationalism and war.* Boulder, CO: Westview Press.

Schonbach, P. (1990). *Account episodes: The management or escalation of conflict.* New York: Cambridge University Press.

Scobie, E. D., & Scobie, G. E. W. (1998). Damaging events: The perceived need for forgiveness. *Journal for the Theory of Social Behaviour, 28,* 373-401.

Sherif, M., Harvey, O. J., White, B. J., Hood, W. R., & Sherif, C. W. (1961). *Intergroup cooperation and competition: The Robbers Cave experiment.* Norman, OK: University Book Exchange.

Shnabel, N., & Nadler, A. (in press). A Needs-Based Model of Reconciliation: Satisfying the differential emotional needs of victim and perpetrator as a key to promoting reconciliation. *Journal of Personality and Social Psychology..*

Tavuchis, N. (1991). *Mea culpa: A sociology of apology and reconciliation.* Stanford, CA: Stanford University Press.

Tutu, D. (1999). *No future without forgiveness.* New York: Doubleday.

Ury, W. (1991). *Getting past no: Negotiating with difficult people.* New York: Bantam Books.

Worthington, E. L. J., & Drinkard, D. T. (2000). Promoting reconciliation through psychoeducational and therapeutic interventions. *Journal of Marital and Family Therapy, 26,* 93-101.

Zechmeister, J. S., & Romero, C. (2002). Victim and offender accounts of interpersonal conflict: Autobiographical narratives of forgiveness and unforgiveness. *Journal of Personality and Social Psychology, 82,* 675-686.

CHAPTER 3

Transforming Trauma in the Aftermath of Gross Human Rights Abuses: Making Public Spaces Intimate Through the South African Truth and Reconciliation Commission

Pumla Gobodo-Madikizela

Introduction and Background

The woman in the audience raised her hand and waved it frantically. It was early 2003 and I had just given a lecture at the Los Angeles public library during the launch of my book, *A Human Being Died That Night: A Story of Forgiveness*. The reporter from the *LA Weekly*[1] who was chairing the event announced that she was going to take the last question, and I pointed at the woman who seemed desperate for a chance to speak.

"I am an Afrikaner," the woman said "I read your book last night and feel an incredible need to speak right now." She went on to explain that she had come to the United States to pursue postgraduate studies in international relations. She said that she was married to an American and settled in the United States. She said my book, which discusses my interviews with the commander of a secret farm where murderous operations were conducted under the former apartheid government, had stirred the depths of her conscience, and forced her to confront her guilt and shame for having benefited from apartheid. Her voice trembled as she continued: "When I complete my degree I want to return home to South Africa and to pay back in whatever way I can. More than anything," she said, now weeping visibly, "I want to ask for forgiveness for having benefited from a system that destroyed so many lives."

The woman was crying and trying to speak. She had exposed herself and told her deepest truth in public. I took a few steps forward and extended my hand to reach out to her from the edge of the stage. She came toward me, still sobbing. There was stillness in the packed auditorium. You could have heard a pin drop. As we embraced, the audience applauded.

Listening to the long applause and to the deep silence in the large hall when the woman made her tearful plea, I wondered if there was something more to this applause, and whether her *confession* and our embrace had stirred something in the mainly white American audience. Two people from different sides of history in a country that almost descended into civil war coming together in a conciliatory embrace after this *conversation* about the past; did the story resonate with the audience's longing, individually and collectively, for resolution of their own past, perhaps that of as-yet-unacknowledged transgenerational traumas of slavery that continue to haunt the historical memory of both black and white Americans? Did it evoke feelings of guilt handed down from that dark American era among some of the white people in the audience who may continue to feel the burden of guilt by association?

I start with this anecdote to illustrate two crucial points about the significance of public accountability about human rights crimes. The first is that public acknowledgement of responsibility (direct or by association) for human rights crimes, allows for the construction of narratives that are not simply individual and private matters, but expressions of collectively shared understanding of the past by those who contributed in whatever small way to the perpetration of the crimes in question. A public process of accountability provides the possibility for multiple levels of witnessing about the past, which may include the internal or intrapsychic dimension, where the complexity of memories and emotions such as guilt and shame about the past reside. This may lead others present in the audience to reflect on their role in the past and to confront their own responsibility in ways that they may not have been able or willing to do. The capacity to confront and acknowledge guilt and shame and to reflect on accountability for the past may open up the possibility to reach out to *the other* in an attempt to repair a broken relationship.

The second point that the anecdote illustrates is the importance of spontaneity and symbolism in these processes of public expression of accountability. The critical significance of the emotional cannot be underestimated.

Emotions are central to the development of patterns of violent interactions between groups and between individuals whose identification with their respective groups influences the way they engage with members of different groups. Emotions such as pain, grief, anger, resentment, and a desire for revenge often inspire the perception of *otherness*, particularly where *otherness* is associated with a history of violent conflict. When a moment opens up for emotional expression in an encounter between groups or between individuals from different sides of historical conflict, the expression of emotion may be invitational. That is to say, deeply felt anger or pain is an expression of something that is felt internally, but it can also be a kind of symbolic communication and an invitation for the other to engage with understanding—to *hear* the depth of the other person's feelings. The ability of the listener to engage at this level is often what opens up the space for transcendence.

This chapter draws on examples from South Africa's Truth and Reconciliation Commission (TRC) to explore the special moments that were created by the TRC, which opened up the possibility of transformation of relationships between victims and perpetrators, and the impact of these encounters in the broader South African story of racial division and intergroup hatred between blacks as the oppressed group, and whites as beneficiaries of apartheid privileged.

Probably more than any other truth commission in past and recent years, the South African TRC has brought the language of apology, forgiveness, and reconciliation after mass atrocity into public focus and scholarly debate. It is to a discussion of these concepts and of the establishment of the South African TRC that I now turn.

Establishment of the Truth and Reconciliation Commission

Only a brief background of the TRC will be presented here (for a thorough account on the background and work of the TRC, see Boraine, 2001). The TRC was promulgated by an Act of parliament, the *National Healing and Reconciliation Act of 1995*, with a mandate to focus mainly on three issues, namely, to (1) establish as complete a picture as possible of past human rights violations committed by all sides of the political conflict; (2) give victims of human rights abuses a chance to speak publicly about the abuses they suffered in the past; and (3) grant amnesty to perpetrators of human rights abuses on the condition that they give full disclosure of acts that they committed, and provided these acts could be characterized as having a political motive. The conditions attached to amnesty distinguished the South African process from other amnesty processes such as those in South American countries, where outgoing military and civilian leaders granted themselves amnesty and "blanket amnesty" to their foot soldiers (Skaar, 1999).

The TRC followed a negotiated political settlement during the period 1990-1994 between the National Party of the former apartheid government and the antiapartheid liberation movements led by the African National Congress (ANC). The TRC's mandate and review period was between 1960, the year the apartheid government police opened fire on unarmed black demonstrators in the township of Sharpeville,[2] and 1994, which marked South Africa's first all-race elections.

The TRC Act recognized that to build relative social unity and healing in a society ravaged by years of violence, fear, and hatred could not rely only on prosecutorial justice, but required a process that invites dialogue between former enemies. From its conception, the processes of "truth telling," "healing," and "reconciliation" through public testimony were central in the work of the TRC. Concerning truth telling, former President Nelson Mandela described the role of the TRC in the following words: "Only by knowing the truth can we hope to heal the terrible wounds of the past that are the legacy of apartheid. Only the truth can put the past to rest" (*Time*, 1995). The "healing" objective of the TRC is captured by Archbishop Desmond Tutu's statements at TRC's public hearings:

> We pray that all those people who have been injured in either body or spirit may receive healing through the work of this commission. We are charged to unearth the truth about our dark past [and] we can indeed transcend the conflict of the past, we can hold hands as we realize our common humanity... and so contribute to national unity and reconciliation (Kapelianis & Taylor, 2000).

The central concepts of truth, healing, reconciliation, and the TRC's nonjudiciary mechanism of accountability have been subject of critical debate among peace-building practitioners and scholars across disciplines. Ramphele (in Boraine & Levy, 1995), for example, warned that the truth commission would be a process of "appeasing the past" instead of confronting the past and dealing with it meaningfully. Wilson (2001) has criticized the medical model implicit in the conceptualization of healing a nation that framed the TRC's work. The idea of the nation as a "sick body" that could be "cured" through the ritualistic act of public testimonies, Wilson argued, was inappropriate for addressing the real psychological pain suffered by victims of gross human rights abuses: "Individual psychological process cannot be reduced to national process" (Wilson, 2001, p. 14).

Among the critics of the nonjudiciary approach of the TRC are those who express concern that the amnesty mechanism undermines the rule of law. As Lorna McGregor notes, doing away with prosecutorial justice in societies in transitional justice after mass atrocity is tantamount to "circumventing the rule of law to reach the end goal of democracy" (McGregor, 2001, p. 35). Advocates of this viewpoint argue that truth mechanisms promote impunity when the focus should be on restoring a human rights culture, where crimes are subjected to appropriate investigation. Wilson (2001) exemplifies this point of view. He notes that processes that eschew formal justice in dealing with perpetrators of politically motivated crimes reflect "the state's abrogation of the right to due process" (Wilson, 2001, p. 11). Other critics, in recognition of the important role played by quasijudicial measures in postconflict societies, argue that while the amnesty-for-truth approach merits respect as a process in postconflict societies, there is a danger that it could become a "soft option" used by outgoing abusive governments to escape justice (Brody, 2001).

Some of the critical views on the TRC are compelling and justifiable; however, there is little consideration of the complexities that faced the postapartheid multiparty government and the impact of the political negotiations on the debates on how to deal with perpetrators of apartheid atrocities, and those who committed human rights abuses in the course of fighting the apartheid government. Furthermore, very rarely do the criticisms reflect on what some of the instructive lessons from the TRC might be. In stark contrast, Martha Minow (1998) offers a nuanced discussion of the tension between the "duty to prosecute" and the reconciliation goals of restorative justice processes. She observes that the decision to pursue alternatives to prosecutorial justice may represent principled and/or practical considerations according to the specific circumstances of the countries in question. Minow's position on the issue of truth commissions provides an important context for understanding some of the factors that led to the choice of the truth commission option in the postapartheid transition to democratic governance in South Africa. There is sufficient evidence to suggest that pursuing trials only in a strict and formal sense in South Africa would have potentially destabilized the fragile peace established between political and racial groups and undermined the peaceful transition to multiparty democracy in a country where apartheid security and army possessed intelligence and military power. This would have created fertile grounds for recurrence of a civil war that would have spiraled back to the bloody years of political conflict.

South Africa's relatively peaceful transition to democratic rule came about because of the negotiated settlement that allowed former enemies to be in dialogue with one another. Essentially, a space was created for former adversaries to come to the common table of shared humanity in order to forge a peaceful society. It is this element that is critical in intergroup reconciliation: the creation of space for dialogue and engagement in a manner that invites those who fought on opposite sides to confront the destruction caused by their actions through reflective dialogue. This allows for the examination of the broader framework of the political context that supported and even directed gross violations of human rights. It is this component of atrocities, the one that resides at the systemic, institutional, and policy levels rather than at a personal level, that is notoriously difficult to substantiate within the strict evidentiary rules of a purely judicial process. Thus, the policies of an oppressive system within which the politics of abuse were enshrined, and the destructive and revolutionary approach of those who fought for liberation, can be publicly acknowledged in ways that a stricter, adversarial, and more rigid approach to justice cannot.

The TRC was an important moment in the history of South Africa's transition from a period of social relationships defined by intergroup hatred, conflict, and violence to one where groups and individuals who identify with different racial and political groups could imagine the possibility of healthy dialogue with one another. Some serious societal challenges have emerged in the post-TRC era in South Africa; however, these challenges should not be seen as the result of "failure" of the TRC. The TRC opened the door to the possibility of transformation of intergroup relationships and a shift in the dynamics of social interaction. In the following section, I share illustrative examples from the TRC to explore how the public space of South African society was transformed (potentially and in reality) into a space for dialogue in ways that could not have happened without the TRC. Stories of forgiveness are perhaps the most representative of the unique moments that were a direct outcome of the TRC's work.

Forgiveness Research

Recently a body of research has emerged to demonstrate the effectiveness of forgiveness in enhancing psychological wellbeing (Freedman & Enright, 1996; Karremans, Van Lange, & Ouwerkerk, 2003), and a new field in psychological counseling that has come to be known as "forgiveness intervention" (Enright & Fitzgibbons, 2000; Fincham, 2000; McCullough, Pargament, & Thoresen, 2000; McCullough, Sandage, & Worthington, 1997; McCullough, Worthington, & Rachal, 1997) has developed. In this fairly new field of study, scholars from the psychology discipline have tried to demonstrate that people who have suffered interpersonal violation of some kind, and are unable or unwilling to forgive can be "taught" to forgive and to appreciate that a forgiving attitude can bring about healing from trauma. Although the idea of teaching people to forgive has been criticized (Lamb & Murphy, 2002), scientific research on forgiveness has increased significantly in the past decade resulting in the development of models of "forgiveness intervention" that show some effectiveness in alleviating distress in those who have been harmed through interpersonal violation (Davis, 2003; Enright & Fitzgibbons, 2000; Luskin, 2002). An increasing number of psychologists are beginning to focus their attention on the role that forgiveness can play in post-trauma healing. With a few exceptions (Azar et al., 1999; Close, 2004; Halpern, 2004; Henderson, 1996; Shriver, 1995; Staub & Pearlman, 2001), studies that seek to apply forgiveness in intergroup and postconflict social context are less common. Part of the reason for the paucity of research on forgiveness in situations of massive trauma may simply be the perception that certain acts are beyond the scale of human acceptability, and therefore unforgivable.

The language of forgiveness and apology in the context of interpersonal conflict and minor to major hurts between individuals is common. Forgiveness in the aftermath of mass political violence is not only rare, but is also regarded by some as inappropriate for the horrific crimes associated with most political conflict. Yet forgiveness as a response to regretful public acknowledgement and remorseful apologies for state orchestrated human rights crimes is important to consider if the goal is to break cycles of violence and to rebuild social cohesion in societies in transition. Forgiveness offered by individuals or collectively by groups who were targeted for political repression signals the possibility of the transformation of trauma and the mental health of individuals who have suffered trauma. It may also mark the beginning of empathic connection between former enemies, and the maintenance of relative continuity of positive aspects of relationships between former adversaries.

Forgiveness (and its associated outcome of reconciliation) as a focus of peace-building work has been relatively overlooked by practitioners who follow the "conflict resolution" model of restoring peace in postconflict contexts. Until recently, forgiveness has been a marginal theme in work with groups with a history of years of hatred and violent conflict. Forgiveness has been rejected by some and considered inappropriate as a strategy for dealing with intergroup conflict. At best, it is despised as a religious concept that encourages false reconciliation, and at worst a tool in service of forgetting. In this chapter, I want to show how forgiveness can open up a space for repairing relationships between individuals and between the groups to which they belong. Central to this process is the development of empathy—the empathic connection that allows engagement with others at a human level.

The trauma suffered as a result of gross human rights abuses shatters the self at the very core that defines our sense of connection to others, and leads to a withdrawal of the empathic bond that is necessary for healthy and compassionate human relationships. Because of the nature of trauma, the traumatic experience continues to affect the life of the victim and/or survivor in subtle ways. Much of the consequences of trauma results from the "unfinished business" of trauma which is manifested in the complex emotions and intergroup dynamics that define relationships between victim survivor groups toward those perceived to be responsible for the trauma.

Internalized anger and hatred are emotions associated with past trauma, and if reinforced by identification with one's group, may strip the hated group of human qualities. This is the key element in dehumanization agendas. Failure to acknowledge the humanity of adversaries cuts out the empathic connection that informs the morality of nonviolent human engagement. This widens the "us" and "them" orientation making it easier to violently harm individuals and groups perceived as enemies. The cultures of vengeful violence that are reproduced intergenerationally are rooted in the dissolution of the empathic and attachment bonds within the human community (Laub & Auerhahn, 1993).

Trauma, Reenactment, and Dehumanization: Withdrawal of the Empathic Bond

In conflict of a political nature between groups, the trauma of gross human rights violations suffered by victims—torture, serious physical injury, disappearance, or death—may lead to continuous cycles of violence and hatred with ever-increasing brutality in the methods used to harm members of the perpetrator group. A culture of blame results in which side accentuates the damage caused by the other and plays down the destructive effects of its own actions in what Wolf (2001) calls "blame schema." Thus, each side fails to accept culpability, leading to more revenge-based violence that may go on for generations. Scholars in the human rights, peace building, and psychology fields (Barkan, 2000; Bar-On, 2000; Ignatieff, 1997; Yehuda et al., 2000) have shown compellingly that past traumas tend to be passed on intergenerationally, and often evoke the same emotional reaction they did generations earlier. Probably the most difficult challenge for peace building is how to create stable foundations for lasting peaceful relationships between former adversaries in order to break the cycles of revenge-based intergroup violence.

Closely associated with transgenerational revenge-based violence is the concept of trauma reenactment. The phenomenon of reenactment and its centrality in the lives of people who have been exposed to life-threatening experiences is well established in traumatic stress research. Early psychoanalytic formulations by Charcot, Janet, Breuer, and Freud all noted that extreme forms of trauma lead to some kind of psychic rupture and a fragmentation of traumatic memories that remain unresolved, which dominate the mental life of many victims of trauma (e.g., see Beveridge, 1998; Van der Kolk, 1989). Reenactment of trauma, scholars in the trauma field inform us, is a major cause of violence in society. The *return* of repressed and unacknowledged traumatic experiences has been observed in various behavioral manifestations (Bloom, 1996; Herman, 1992; Laub & Lee, 2003; McFarlane & Van der Kolk, 1996) in therapy with individuals with a history of traumatic stress (Kernberg, 2003), as revictimization of self in battered women and sex workers (Herman, 1999), and victimization directed at others in criminals who suffered physical or sexual abuse as children (Gilligan, 1997; Groth, 1979; Lewis, Shanok, & Pincus, 1979).

These findings provide persuasive evidence to influence significantly the way we think about transforming conflict and building social cohesion in societies that have been ravaged by the trauma of past wars and mass violence. In addition to the psychoanalytic concept of reenactment, social psychology offers a range of group-based explanations for the cycles of violence that so often repeat themselves historically. The collective trauma suffered by victims under oppressive regimes often produces strong bonds within groups that share this traumatic past. Social identity theory argues that there is at least one common denominator to all social groups where members are drawn together by significant experiences, and that is self-categorization. This is a collectively shared self-evaluative process that defines the unique reality that group members share with others in the group (Turner, 1985; Turner, Hogg, Oakes, Reicher, & Wetherell, 1987; Turner & Onorato, 1999). I shall not go into detail here about the development of stereotypic norms based on inclusive and exclusionists perceptions of in-group and out-group members respectively as there is a large body of social-psychological literature that deals with these concepts. I want simply to link the social identity conceptualization of intergroup behavior to another well-known social-psychological concept, dehumanization.

Looked at conceptually, social identity explanations provide the context for understanding how in-group favoritism can influence the development of negative perceptions of others to the point of dehumanization of out-group members. Negative perceptions and emotions associated with dehumanization of out-groups are likely to be quite strong, and sometimes vicious, if members of the in-group have been on the receiving end of oppression and mass trauma. The out-group is excluded from the moral engagement that defines interaction with members of the in-group. *Dehumanization* essentially means that the *other* is perceived as *less* of a human being than others to whom values of moral human engagement are extended. Levine (1996) describes this process as the creation of "a not-us persona, a decontextualized other who does not emanate from, or symbolically represent" one's own group and community of others marked by the same painful history (p. 25). Glass (1997) refers to dehumanization of out-group members as "deadening the space between one's own consensual understandings and the other's physical presence" (p. 24):

> It is a relatively complex psychological process to make the other not there; to make the other's embodied self invisible through various methods of dissociation and distancing.... This kind of operation on the [other] is violent... because the unacknowledged body ceases to possess human qualities and therefore exists outside any moral universe of care (Glass, 1997, p. 25).

My central argument here is threefold. First, the experience of trauma leads to deep psychological injury that continues to affect the life and identity of trauma victims and survivors in ways that are not always clear, but which are identifiable in grief that seems irresolvable and in *symbolic* expressions of trauma reenactments such as repetitive acts of hatred and violence against individuals and groups historically, or even only peripherally, associated with the original trauma. The continuing manifestation of trauma through symbolic acts signals the *unfinished business* of trauma. The way that the traumatic memory and the *unfinished business* of trauma plays itself out becomes complex when the trauma is collectively shared by a group. Volkan (2006) cogently describes this complexity in his concept of *chosen traumas*.

Second, long-standing hateful behavior and violence against groups have intrapsychic underpinnings; it is necessary to address this intrapsychic dimension of the consequences of trauma in order for meaningful intergroup reconciliation to occur. The intrapsychic dimensions of grief and the inability to mourn traumatic loss are of course an important focus for working through traumatic injury at an individual level. Third, dialogue conducted to heal divisions created by past traumas is a critical step in the working through of emotions that have contributed to long-standing mutual resentment, hatred, and violence between groups.

I would like to add a fourth observation to these points. There can be no adequate reparation for the inequities and the moral horrors of the past, and for the moral betrayal that allowed these horrors to happen. I suggest therefore that forgiveness is a compelling and healthy response to the debt owed to those whose future was carved through the policies of exclusion. By forgiveness, I do not mean that we should forget. I mean simply an empathic recognition of the moral vulnerability of human beings, a recognition that allows victim groups to be conscious of how strong the lure of power and privilege is. It is necessary to respond with moral outrage to injustice, and to judge the behavior and choices made by those who supported systematic abuse and benefited materially and in other intangible ways from it. It is also important to acknowledge the simple fact of human weakness, because therein lies the lesson of history. We do not know with any measure of certainty how we would have behaved had we been in the shoes of those who supported the oppressive and violent regimes that require us to ponder on questions of the nature of evil. This level of understanding comes through a deeper connection with another trough what I refer to as "the human moment." The *deeper* level of understanding that occurs in encounters between victims and perpetrators is a result of reflection on the part of victim groups. It is the capacity to understand the context of another person's behavior that allows for the development of empathy for the forces that may have impinged on the other to produce the behavior about which they are now remorseful. This deeper understanding is similar to the consciousness that is evoked through therapeutic intervention to help clients deal with problematic behaviors in themselves or in their relationships with others. In the following section, I briefly examine the three central themes of my argument, and draw from TRC examples to illustrate this notion of "the human moment."

Apology, Forgiveness, and Witnessing about Trauma

The story of the "Mothers of the Gugulethu Seven," captured most poignantly in the documentary *Long Night's Journey into Day* (Reed & Hoffman, 1999), raises important questions about the nature of forgiveness. In the film, mothers of seven young men who were brutally murdered by the apartheid police meet a black policeman who lured the young men into the murderous trap under the pretext that he was working with the military wing of the liberation movement of the ANC. The policeman, Thapelo Mbelo, approaches the mothers and other family members of the slain men to ask for their understanding and forgiveness. Ten years have passed since the incident that violently took the lives of the young men, and the pain felt by the mothers is visible. I had met with the mothers and some of the family members for an hour per day over a period of 5 days to prepare them for the meeting with Mbelo. There was a strong sense in the week-long meetings that some of the mothers wanted to forgive, but needed to meet Mbelo first and, as was generally expressed by these mothers, to *hear* his story.

Hearing Mbelo implied a certain level of understanding that went deeper than the words he would speak.

Now in their meeting with Mbelo, the mothers expressed strong feelings of anger, pain, and betrayal since Mbelo *sold* his black brothers to be slaughtered by the apartheid government's white security policemen. There is a turning point in the film when Mbelo, his face muscles twitching nervously, appeals to the mothers for understanding. One of the mothers, Cynthia Ngewu, whose son Christopher was shot at close range and then dragged by his killers with a rope to give the impression he had explosives on him turns to Mbelo and addresses him as "my son." She offers him forgiveness and invites other mothers to show Mbelo empathy and extend their forgiveness to him. She speaks to Mbelo, but also addressing herself to the other mothers in the following words that I have translated here from her original Xhosa:

> Our sons will never return to us. They are dead. . . . You will forgive us for throwing stones [being angry] at you, we have nowhere else to throw them but at you. It is our way of getting rid of all the stuff that has been sitting inside. We want to take it all out so that we can be at peace. As you set out on your journey back home we want you to go with this knowledge that the mothers have forgiven you. I as Christopher's mother forgive you my son. Yes, I forgive you my son. I have forgiven. Go well my son.

At a recent conference held at the University of Cape Town in November 2006 to mark the 10th Anniversary of the TRC Cynthia Ngewu was asked to reflect on this encounter with Mbelo. She reiterated her stance of forgiveness and said that her capacity to forgive Mbelo grew out of the sincerity of Mbelo's apology, and that it was profoundly healing for her to forgive Mbelo. With pain audible in her breaking voice and visible in her anguished face she explained that the image of her son being dragged with a rope as she saw on television news was still a source of deep pain that will not go away.

Another example of a mother who reaches out with forgiveness to perpetrators who killed her daughter is Ginn Fourie, whose daughter was killed in a bombing operation that was targeting white South Africans. Lyndi Fourie's killers were members of the black-only antiapartheid organization, the Pan African Congress (PAC) whose rallying cry was "One Settler One Bullet." When Ginn Fourie encountered her daughter's killers at their TRC public appearance, she spoke to them in Xhosa: *Molweni madoda* (Good morning gentlemen). She was, in essence, speaking to them as their mothers would. She offered the men her forgiveness. With a breaking voice and tears in her eyes, she then invited the men to listen as she described her daughter Lyndi:

> I want to tell you who Lyndi was. Her Xhosa friends called her Lindiwe [the one we were waiting for]. Lyndi had a strong sense of social responsibility. She challenged me and made me understand my own

prejudices. She was working for change in her own society.... You did your own struggle harm by killing her.

Shortly after the TRC submitted its report to President Thabo Mbeki, Ginn Fourie approached the former commander of the military wing of the PAC, Letlapa Mpahlele, to confront him about his actions as commander of the PAC and about why he did not apply for amnesty from the TRC. A dialogue developed between the two of them during which Fourie was drawn to forgiving Mpahlele. "I gained profound understanding of why he was involved in fighting the apartheid government," Fourie said about Mpahlele. She then explained how her dialogue with Mpahlele, visiting his family, and learning about poverty and unemployment in the villages she visited with Mpahlele deepened her understanding of the effects of apartheid, a system for which she holds herself and her ancestors responsible. Fourie and Mpahlele have been working together now for the past 5 years leading dialogue on reconciliation with groups throughout South Africa.

When perpetrators express remorse, when they finally acknowledge that they can see what they earlier could not see, or did not want to, they are revalidating the victim's pain—in a sense, giving his or her humanity back to him. Empowered and revalidated, many victims at this point find it natural to extend and deepen the healing process by going a step further: turning around and conferring forgiveness on their torturer.

The motivation to do this does not stem only from altruism or a high sense of morality: The victim in a sense *needs* forgiveness as part of the recovery process of becoming dehumanized. The victim needs it in order to complete himself or herself and to wrest away from the perpetrator the fiat power to destroy or to spare. It is part of the process of reclaiming self-efficacy.

Reciprocating with empathy and forgiveness in the face of a perpetrator's remorse restores to many victims the sense that they are once again capable of effecting a deep difference in the moral community. Victims may, until now, be able to function quite well in other contexts of life, but in this one area, in those periods when something reminds them of this one person, this one ordeal, they again feel dehumanized, halved, and ineffective, quarantined in an area of his mind and of his life where they remember being told in effect that they do not matter, that the moral obligations ordinarily extended toward others do not apply in their case. It is to seal these cracks in their psyche—cracks that they sometimes unexpectedly re-encounter—that many victims discover within themselves an inexorable movement toward forgiveness at the moment that the person who represents their pain drops his façade of ignorance and opens up to express contrition.

Applying the Lessons of Interpersonal Forgiveness and Reconciliation to Groups

The examples of forgiveness dialogues presented above illustrate what happens at an interpersonal level between victims and perpetrators. These stories continue to capture the minds and hearts of South Africans when I present them in classroom settings or in workshops on difficult dialogues. When presented to a wider public or in groups, the stories become opportunities for participants to be witnesses to these stories of forgiveness. Very often, participants do not only become distant witnesses, but also participate—symbolically or in reality—in witnessing about their own internal struggles with the past. The following statement is an illustration from a dialogue session I led with an organization that wanted to promote intergroup relations among black, colored, and white employees at middle management level.

During a discussion of a video clip of Cynthia Ngewu's encounter with and forgiveness of the man who was collaborating with the apartheid security police to kill her son and his comrades, there were tears and strong emotions from participants across racial lines. A white woman struggling to control her tears confessed her ill-treatment of a black woman who was employed in her childhood home as a domestic worker, and how she, as a child, did not consider the woman worthy of her respect. She explained how this disrespectful attitude has prevailed in the way she treats the woman who works in her own home, and how this attitude influenced the way she related to her black colleagues in the workplace. In response to the white woman's apparent distress, a black woman angrily told the group that she was tired of tearful confessions when little or nothing has changed in the workplace. She went on to tell her story of years of exclusion under apartheid, how she had struggled to get an education that earned her a position with her current company, but how patterns of exclusion were continuing in the work environment.

A full discussion of the intergroup dynamics that emerge in these kinds of dialogue processes will not be addressed in this chapter. It is sufficient to point out here that much of what takes place in this example could be seen as a reflection of the internal story of the past that may resist articulation either because it is too painful or too shameful. The expression of these feelings is an important first step, for it broadens the narrative from the private into the wider sphere occupied by the group, where each group member identifies with either one of the stories that emerge. The challenge is to manage the witnessing of the complex emotions so that members of the group can participate in the *witnessing dance* of these stories of pain and shame and engage in the dialogue that may ensue with compassionate listening.

Conclusion

The many stories of forgiveness and reconciliation brought before the TRC illustrate the vision of healing and reconciliation that philosopher and peace-building scholar Paul Lederach has termed "the Moral Imagination." He says that when we allow the moral imagination to enter our field of dialogue and engagement with those we consider to be our enemies, we are transcending the familiar and easy territory of hatred and vengeance and stepping into the mystery of the unknown. Moral Imagination is the capacity to imagine ourselves in a web of relations that includes our enemies; the ability to sustain a paradoxical curiosity that embraces the complexity of venturing into uncharted territory.

I have referred to this process as rehumanization (Gobodo-Madikizela, 2003) which is the point where the incompatible yet inextricable stories of victim, victimizer, and bystander meet. For how can a victim find language to talk about trauma, unless a perpetrator acknowledges his deeds through public accountability? And how can a bystander fully confront his or her role as beneficiary of past evil, and know the choices that she or he could have made, but did not, unless she/he is witness to the testimonies of victim and perpetrator?

Ordinary people, under certain circumstances, are capable of far greater evil than we could have imagined. But so are we capable of far greater virtue than we might have thought. To facilitate freedom from the *bondage* of fear and hatred that so often characterizes intergroup relationships in societies ravaged by mass violence, transformation strategies aimed at enhancing human compassion between groups are critical. The restoration of the spirit of *humaneness*, what in the African languages of South Africa is termed *ubuntu* (for discussion of the concept of *ubuntu*; see Tutu, 1999), can be attained through consistent dialogue between former adversaries about the past and its painful consequences on all sides—victims, perpetrators, bystanders, and active beneficiaries of oppressive and discriminatory policies.

The woman in the anecdote presented at the beginning of the chapter spoke the truth of her heart. It was a simple communication of what she felt. We reached out to each other and we shared a common idiom of humanity as South Africans regretting our past and wishing to mend it. A metaphor that best captures how this dialogue can be understood is *making public spaces intimate*. The example may represent a very small step in the immeasurable brokenness of a society emerging from mass violence. Witnessed by a listening audience, these small gestures, however, can become the hope that is needed for peaceful dialogue to take place in the public sphere. If memory is used to rekindle old hatreds, then it will lead back to continuing hatred and conflict.

But if memory is used to rebuild humane bonds between groups and to refind the intergroup compassion that was lost in the past, dialogue about the past can be an important path toward transformation.

Two years ago, I wrote the story of my encounter with the woman in the Los Angeles library as part of an opinion piece in a South African national daily newspaper (*This Day*, June 28, 2004). A few days later, I received an e-mail from her. She was in South Africa living in a village in KwaZulu/Natal learning Zulu and working as a volunteer at an HIV/AIDS center for women. She had fulfilled her commitment to return to "give back," as she said, in whatever way she could. This is a sign of reflective engagement with the past, where guilt and shame is not used to perpetuate the past, but is transformed into responsibility toward "the other."

Notes

1. See report on this lecture in Louise Steinman (2003). "The Truth Shall Set You Free: Pumla Gobodo-Madikizela on the evils of apartheid and finding forgiveness," *LA Weekly*, January 31, 2003.

2. 1960 was also the year former President Nelson Mandela announced that his organization, the ANC was abandoning nonviolent struggle and was taking up arms against the apartheid government to fight force with force. For historical background on the events that led to the establishment of the TRC; see Boraine (2000). *A country unmasked: Inside South Africa's Truth and Reconciliation Commission.* New York: Oxford Books.

References

Azar, F., Mullet, E., & Vinsonneau, G. (1999). The propensity to forgive: Findings from Lebanon. *Journal of Peace Research, 36*, 169-181.

Barkan, E. (2000). *The guilt of nations: Restitution and negotiating historical injustices.* New York: W. W. Norton.

Bar-On, D. (2000). *Bridging the gap: Storytelling as a way to work through political and collective hostilities.* Hamburg: Korber-Stiftung.

Beveridge, A. (1998). On the origins of post-traumatic stress disorder. In D. Black (Ed.), *Psychological trauma: A developmental approach* (pp. 3-9).

Bloom, S. L. (1996). Every time history repeats itself, the price goes up: The social re-enactment of trauma. *Sexual Addiction & Compulsivity, 3*, 161-194.

Boraine, A. (2000). *A country unmasked: Inside South Africa's Truth and Reconciliation Commission*. New York: Oxford Books.

Boraine, A. (2001). *A country unmasked: Inside South Africa's Truth and Reconciliation Commission*. Oxford: Oxford University Press.

Brody, R. (2001). Justice: The first casualty of truth? *The Nation*, April 30.

Close, E. (2004). *Bone to pick: Of forgiveness, reconciliation, reparation, and revenge*. New York: Washington Square Press.

Davis, L. (2003). *The road from estrangement to reconciliation*. New York: Quill.

Enright, R. D., & Fitzgibbons, R. P. (2000). *Helping clients forgive: An empirical guide for resolving anger and restoring hope*. Washington, DC: American Psychological Association.

Fincham, F. D. (2000). The kiss of the porcupines: From attributing responsibility to forgiving. *Personal Relationships, 7*, 1-23.

Freedman, S. R., & Enright, R. D. (1996). Forgiveness as an intervention goal with incest survivors. *Journal of Consulting and Clinical Psychology, 64*, 983-992.

Gilligan, J. (1997). *Violence: Reflections on a national epidemic*. New York: Vintage.

Glass, J. (1997). *"Life unworthy of life": Racial phobia and mass murder in Hitler's Germany*. New York: Basic Books.

Gobodo-Madikizela, P. (2004). We must restore the human spirit. *This Day*, June 28.

Groth, A. N. (1979). Sexual trauma in the life histories of sex offenders. *Victimology, 4*, 6-10.

Halpern, J. (2004). Rehumanizing the other: Empathy and reconciliation. *Human Rights Quarterly, 26*, 561-583.

Henderson, M. (1996). *The forgiveness factor: Stories of hope in a world of conflict*. London: Grosvenor Books.

Herman, J. (1992). *Trauma and recovery: The aftermath of violence—From domestic abuse to political terror*. New York: Basic Books.

Herman, J. (1999). Complex PTSD: A syndrome in survivors of prolonged and repeated trauma. In M. J. Horowitz (Ed.), *Essential papers on post-traumatic stress disorder* (pp. 82-93). New York and London: New York University.

Ignatieff, M. (1997). The elusive goal of war trials. *Harpers, 294*, 15-18.

Kapelianis, A., & Taylor, D. (2000). *South Africa's human spirit, an oral memoir of the Truth and Reconciliation Commission* (Vol. 1). Johannesburg: South African Broadcasting Corporation.

Karremans, J. C., Van Lange, P. A. M., Ouwerkerk, J. W., & Kluwer, E. S. (2003). When forgiveness enhances psychological well-being: The role of interpersonal commitment. *Journal of Personality and Social Psychology, 84*, 1011-1026.

Kernberg, O. F. (2003). *The management of affect storms in psychoanalytic psychotherapy of borderline patients. Journal of the American Planning Association, 51*, 517-545.

Lamb, S., & Murphy, J. F. (2002). *Before forgiving. cautionary views of forgiveness in psychotherapy*. Oxford: Oxford University Press.

Laub, D., & Auerhahn, N. (1993). Knowing and not knowing massive psychic trauma: Forms of traumatic memory. *International Journal of Psycho-Analysis, 74*, 261-276.

73

Laub, D., & Lee, S. (2003). Thanatos and massive psychic trauma, *Journal of the American Planning Association, 51*, 433-463.

Levine, J. E. (1996). Oklahoma City: The storying of a disaster. *Smith College Studies in Social Work, 67*, 21-38.

Lewis, D., Shanok S. S., & Pincus J. H. (1979). Violent Juvenile delinquents: Psychiatric, neurological, psychological and abuse factors. *Journal of Child Psychiatry, 18*, 307-319.

Luskin, F. (2002). *Forgive for good. A proven prescription for health and happiness.* San Francisco, CA: Harper-Collins Publishers Inc.

Mandela, N. (1995). *Time,* July 31.

McCullough, M. E., Pargament, K. I., & Thoresen, C. E. (2000). The psychology of forgiveness: History, conceptual issues, and overview. In M. E. McCullough, K. I. Pargament, & C. E. Thoresen (Eds.), *Forgiveness: Theory, research and practice* (pp. 1-14). New York: Guilford Press.

McCullough, M. E., Sandage, S. J., & Worthington, E. L., Jr. (1997). *To forgive is human.* Downers Grove, IL: InterVarsity.

McCullough, M. E., Worthington, E. L., Jr., & Rachal, K. C. (1997). Interpersonal forgiving in close relationships. *Journal of Personality and Social Psychology, 73*, 321-336.

McFarlane, A. C., & Van der Kolk, B. A. (1996). Trauma and its challenge to society. In A. C. McFarlane & B. A. Van der Kolk (Eds.), *Traumatic stress: The effects of overwhelming experience on mind, body and society* (pp. 25-45). New York and London: Guildford.

McGregor, L. (2001). Individual accountability in South Africa: Cultural optimum or political façade? *American Journal of International Law, 32.*

Minow, M. (1998). *Facing history after genocide and mass violence: Between vengeance and forgiveness.* Boston: Beacon Press.

Ramphele, M. (1995). In A. Boraine & J. Levy (Eds.), *The healing of a Nation* (p. 34). Cape Town: Justice in Transition.

Reed, F., & Hoffman, D. (1999). *Long night's journey into day.* San Francisco, CA: Iris Films.

Shriver, D. W.(1995). *An ethic for enemies: Forgiveness in politics.* New York: Oxford University Press.

Skaar, E. (1999). Truth commissions, trials—Or nothing? Policy options in democratic transitions. *Third World Quarterly, 20*, 1109-1128.

Staub, E., & Pearlman, L. A. (2001). Healing, reconciliation and forgiving after genocide and other collective violence. In R. L. Petersen & R. G. Helmick (Eds.), *Forgiveness and reconciliation: Religion, public policy, and conflict transformation.* Philadelphia, PA: Templeton Foundation Press.

Turner, J. C. (1985). Social categorisation and the self-concept. A social cognitive theory of group behaviour. In E. J. Lawler (Ed.), *Advances in group processes: Theory and research* (Vol. 2, pp. 77-122). Greenwich: JAI Press.

Turner, J. C., Hogg, M. A., Oakes, P. J., Reicher, S. D., & Wetherell, M. S. (1987). *Rediscovering the social group: A self-categorization theory.* Oxford: Blackwell Publishers.

Turner, J. C., & Onorato, R. S. (1999). Social identity, personality, and the self-concept: A self-categorization perspective. In T. R. Tyler, R. M. Kramer, & O. P. John (Eds.), *The psychology of the social self* (pp. 11-46). Mahwah, NJ: Erlbaum.

Tutu, D. (1999). *No future without forgiveness.* New York: Doubleday.

Van der Kolk, B. (1989). The compulsion to repeat the trauma: Re-enactment, revictimization, and masochism. *Psychiatric Clinics of North America, 12,* 389-411.

Volkan, V. (2006). *Killing in the name of identity: A study of bloody conflicts.* Charlottesville, VI: Pitchstone.

Wilson, R. *The politics of Truth and Reconciliation in South Africa, legitimising the post-apartheid state.* Cambridge: Cambridge University Press, 2001.

Wolf, Y. (2001). Modularity in everyday life judgments of aggression and violent behavior. *Aggression and Violent Behavior: A Review Journal, 6,* 1-34.

Yehuda, R., Bierer, L. M., Schmeidler, J., Aferiat, D. H., Breslau, I., & Dolan, S. (2000). Low cortisol and risk for PTSD in adult offspring of Holocaust survivors. *American Journal of Psychiatry, 157,* 1252-1259.

CHAPTER 4

Social Categorization, Standards of Justice, and Collective Guilt

ANCA M. MIRON AND NYLA R. BRANSCOMBE

Despite the Civil Rights movement of the 1960s and its accompanying legislative changes, social science research has revealed that justice is not blind. Group membership affects important life outcomes including jury decisions, college admissions, and hiring processes (Biernat & Kobrynowicz, 1997; Johnson, Whitestone, Jackson, & Gatto, 1995). How precisely group categorizations such as race and gender influence such judgments is one of the central issues we tackle in this chapter.

Thus far, there has been little research investigating whether the *standards* used for judging the justice or injustice of an outcome might depend on the victim's group membership. When judging negative outcomes delivered to those defined as members of an out-group, a different standard of *injustice* might be employed than when *judging the same outcomes* when experienced by in-group members. We consider the effect of such potential shifts in justice standards—depending on how the victim group is categorized—for collective emotional responses to differential social outcomes.

In this chapter, we outline a model describing when and how one particular intergroup emotion—collective guilt—will be experienced depending on the standard employed for judging the social injustice perpetrated by the in-group against an out-group. In line with the common in-group identity model

(Gaertner, Dovidio, Anastasio, Bachman, & Rust, 1993) and self-categorization theory (Turner, Hogg, Oakes, Reicher, & Wetherell, 1987), we argue that perpetrators or advantaged group members can categorize victims along a continuum of increasing inclusiveness—with the most inclusive category being *humans*. Under certain conditions, out-group members (*they*) can be seen as members of a more inclusive group (*us*) that also includes the in-group (*we*); shifting to such inclusive categorization of out-group members can have beneficial effects for the in-group's relationship with that out-group (Gaertner et al., 1993; Wohl & Branscombe, 2005).

We propose that the extent to which victims of harm doing are included in a salient social category will affect the harshness of the standards used to evaluate the in-group's harmful actions toward them. That is, when out-group members are included in a common in-group, harsher judgments should be made about in-group members who perpetrated harm against the former out-group members who are now seen as part of a larger, superordinate in-group. Indeed, research has shown that we feel more guilt when harming close others compared to those less close or strangers (Baumeister, Stillwell, & Heatherton, 1994; Jones, Kugler, & Adams, 1995), perhaps because we use harsher standards of justice when judging the harm we inflict on the former category of people. The severity of the standard used, we argue will, in turn, affect the appraisal of injustice and the extent to which collective guilt is experienced.

When in-group members categorize victims as members of a distinct group, a pro-in-group bias will be activated, which will result in use of more "in-group serving" definitions of injustice. For example, when group members must evaluate whether the amount of economic damage they inflicted on an out-group was severe or unjust,[1] if they categorize the victims as out-group members, they will be motivated to use a high *confirmatory standard*. *Confirmatory standards* are defined as the evidence needed to *confirm* that an action was unjust or that a person definitively has a particular ability (see Biernat & Fuegen, 2001). For example, Biernat and Kobrynowicz (1997) found that when participants were asked what skill level they would require to be certain that the applicant has "the ability to perform the job," more evidence of the skill was required for women than men. Higher confirmatory standards were set for women, meaning that *more evidence of the skill* was needed for women than men. Translating this concept of confirmatory standards into our research on standards used for deciding if an action was unjust, in-group members would need more evidence to confirm that the action was unjust when out-group members are categorized as outsiders (members of a distinct group) than when categorized as insiders (members of an in-group). Going back to our example, it means that in-group members would set a high economic damage standard (e.g., 1 million dollars worth of damage rather than only $100,000) for deciding "what constitutes

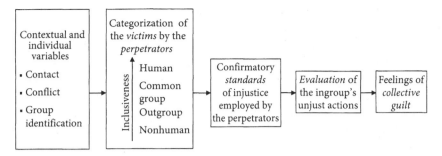

FIGURE 4.1. A justice model of feeling collective guilt.

injustice," so that the amount of *actual* damage committed by the in-group will be perceived as not so severe or unjust compared to such a severe confirmatory standard. Because all judgments—even those about injustice—are relative, what standard is used as the comparison has the potential of greatly affecting judgments and emotional responses.

In contrast, when members of the victim group are categorized as members of a superordinate category that also includes the in-group, in-group members will use lower confirmatory standards. This means they would need less evidence to conclude that the in-group acted unjustly. To the extent that the in-group's harmful actions meet or surpass the low confirmatory standard, in-group members will conclude that injustice was indeed done to the victim group, and they will be more likely to feel collective guilt. The underlying idea is that *in-group members may be motivated to shift the severity of the confirmatory standard used as comparative referent.* In this chapter, we consider several factors that encourage people to engage in this standard shifting process when evaluating the in-group's harmful actions toward another group.

In the following sections, we outline a justice model of collective guilt and describe the research that supports the steps outlined in Figure 4.1. Toward the end, we assess the implications of the confirmatory standard shifting notion for intergroup reconciliation processes. Before describing the model, we first consider when and why collective guilt can positively influence intergroup relations.

Collective Guilt in Intergroup Relations

When people self-categorize as members of an advantaged group (e.g., White, male), guilt can be experienced when group members perceive that the benefits they receive are illegitimately obtained at the expense of the other group (e.g., minorities, women). Such inequity need not be advocated or directly perpetrated by the self, but rather can be passively received. When this inequality is made salient, guilt arises (Branscombe, 1998; Montada & Schneider, 1989). In addition, collective guilt may be instigated for past harm by one's in-group members as a result of being associated with a group that has perpetrated harm against another group, without personally participating in the injustice (see Branscombe, Doosje, & McGarty, 2002).

Two conditions must be met in order for people to experience collective guilt. First, they must categorize themselves as members of the advantaged or perpetrator group; second, they must perceive that the in-group is responsible for a moral violation against another group. When these two conditions are met, collective guilt can be experienced (see Branscombe & Doosje, 2004, for a review). Because the function of collective guilt is to urge reparations, it can be accomplished by *the creation or restoration of a just relationship with the harmed out-group* (Schmitt, Branscombe, & Brehm, 2004).

Understanding the factors that lead to or undermine feelings of collective guilt is crucial because collective guilt is an important element in the reconciliation process. According to Bar-Tal and Bennink (2004), following conflict, especially violent conflict, the group's differing views of what was done in the past have to be adjusted. When such reinterpretation of the in-group's past actions occurs, collective guilt is likely to come into play for perpetrator groups. Bar-Tal and Bennink (2004) argue that reconciliation requires the formation of a new *common* outlook on the past, which cannot dismiss the victimized out-group's perspective. Thus, reconciliation may necessitate changing societal beliefs about the past by learning the out-group's collective memories and admitting one's own past misdeeds, as well as its responsibility for the maintenance of the conflict. The newly negotiated narrative of the past must then substitute for the previous collective view that *what was done by the in-group to the out-group was just or legitimate.*

Concluding that injustice was done is essential for the members of the advantaged or perpetrator group to feel collective guilt. One way to arrive at this conclusion is to prevent group members from strategically shifting confirmatory standards upward. By setting the standard high, it means a very large amount of evidence is needed when judging the injustice of the in-group's actions. This strategy may result in the in-group arriving at the conclusion that—by comparison to the standard used—little injustice was done. Consequently, we will need to delve into how such standard shifts are likely to depend on categorization processes.

The Role of Justice Appraisals in the Experience of Guilt

Various theorists have emphasized the role of justice and violations of moral standards in the experience of guilt (Devine, Monteith, Zuwerink, & Elliot, 1991; Frijda, Kuipers, & Ter Schure, 1989). Indeed, Wicker, Payne, and Morgan (1983, p. 26), following an extensive review, concluded that guilt stems "from acts that violate ethical norms, principles of justice or moral values." At the group level, guilt occurs when the in-group's relative advantage is perceived as stemming from the illegitimate actions of the in-group (Miron, Branscombe, & Schmitt, 2006). When, however, the in-group's relationship with the out-group is appraised as just because the lower status position of the out-group is seen as deserved, little collective guilt may be expected in response to even severe victimized group need (Branscombe et al., 2002).

Miron et al. (2006) assessed the extent to which the experience of collective guilt among members of an advantaged social group is dependent on the perceived legitimacy of the existing intergroup inequality. In one study, we assessed male participants' perceptions of the legitimacy of the existing inequality between women and men and emotional responses to the gender inequality that was made salient. We found that collective guilt was higher when gender inequality was perceived as unfair and illegitimate. The more illegitimate the inequality was perceived to be, the more collective guilt men reported, $r = .28, p < .05$.

In a second study, male participants read accurate statistics about the extent to which gender inequality exists in the United States, followed by either information supporting the legitimacy of the inequality or information undermining its legitimacy. In the *legitimacy-supported condition*, information legitimizing women not being in high-paid, high-status jobs such as engineering and business was provided. Women were portrayed as lacking high-status professional abilities such as assertiveness, achievement-oriented personality, leadership, and competitiveness, despite their being equally intelligent as men. This information matched the preexisting beliefs subscribed to by this population, as assessed in the earlier correlational study. In this condition, male participants also read that such gender disparities in the workplace were not due to intentional and systematic discrimination strategies on the part of men but "to the fact that men and women possess different abilities that make them better suited for different jobs." In contrast, in the *legitimacy-undermined condition*, men read that "women score as high as men do on intelligence tests *and* on the other abilities required by these professions" and that the existing inequality could be attributed to discrimination. Again, we found that the more participants agreed with the legitimacy of existing gender inequality, the less collective guilt they reported, $r = -.26$, $p = .02$. More importantly, collective guilt was significantly greater in the legitimacy-undermined condition than in the legitimacy-supported condition ($d = .51$). Thus, when the in-group's actions (and the outcomes experienced by the out-group) are perceived as illegitimate, guilt based on membership in the perpetrator group can be induced. As these data imply, the perception of injustice in intergroup relations can induce feelings of collective guilt. However, the perception of injustice is dependent on several important factors that we describe subsequently.

A Justice Model of Collective Guilt

As illustrated in Figure 4.1, we propose a categorization-based justice model of guilt. According to this view, how group members categorize their victims determines the severity of the standards used for judging the injustice of the in-group's actions. The confirmatory standards used should determine the extent to which collective guilt is experienced by affecting the perceived injustice of the in-group's actions.

Returning to the opening example of our chapter, if a high confirmatory standard is used to judge whether an in-group action was unjust (i.e., to be considered injustice, the damage should exceed 1 million dollars), then it will be easy for perpetrator group members to say that the action was *not unjust* for it does not surpass this high standard (i.e., to the extent that the actual damage can be construed as lower than this amount). To qualify as injustice, the in-group's harm would need to exceed a particular level of damage done to the out-group. When the in-group has perpetrated less damage than the standard, then it is easy for group members to draw the conclusion that the action was *not* unjust. The severity of the standard employed can therefore affect the extent to which the in-group's actions are seen as just or unjust, which as Miron et al. (2006) showed, directly affects the experience of collective guilt.

The literature on moral standards has defined such standards as what a person believes to be right and wrong (Jones et al., 1995). Moreover, much of the discussion of standards in social psychology has focused on personal standards. We argue however that social psychologists may gain from a new conceptualization of standards as *relative* and *group based*.[2] We argue that group members will shift standards strategically, depending on how the victims are categorized. Standards are thus relative rather than absolute: Different standards apply to different groups. Indeed, there is evidence that, unfortunately, "all victims are not equal." Yzerbyt et al. (2002), for instance, showed that more empathic anger is experienced by in-group members in response to victimization of out-group members by a third group when the victims are seen as part of a superordinate group compared to when they are categorized as part of a separate group. Precisely, because "all victims are not equal," women and black Americans had to exhibit more evidence of their abilities than did men and white Americans to be considered equally talented (Biernat & Kobrynowicz, 1997). Participants seemed to shift their standards when judging the ability of out-group versus in-group members—setting higher confirmatory standards for women than for men, and for blacks than for whites.

As depicted in Figure 4.1, victims can be categorized along an inclusiveness continuum ranging from nonhuman (belonging to a completely distinct group) to out-group member, to member of a common group that includes both the victim and the perpetrator of harm, to the most inclusive category, the human group that includes the victim and the perpetrator of injustice as members of the same inclusive group. We expect that the severity or leniency of group-based standards employed will affect the harshness of the evaluation of injustice (e.g., the lower the confirmatory standard, the more the injustice), which in turn will affect collective guilt.

In the next section, we first review literature concerning categorization of victims, and the variables that have been used to measure shifts in categorization. We then turn our attention to several variables that affect people's motivation and ability to shift how the victims are categorized.

Categorization of Victims

Self-categorization theory (Turner et al., 1987) claims that people shift how they categorize themselves depending on aspects of the social context, and this affects their perception of others. When a given level of self-categorization is salient, another person can be perceived as an in-group member or as an out-group member, and this will result in differential perception that the other shares the characteristics of the in-group or not. Whether or not others are categorized as alike or different from the self depends on the social context and focus of attention of the perceiver. When categorization occurs at the group level, the self is seen as different from out-group members but like other in-group members. The most inclusive superordinate category is that of human being. At this level, the members of this inclusive category will include all other humans, and thus similarities between individuals are expected to be large in terms of "humanity" defining dimensions (Turner & Onorato, 1999), and different from nonhumans.

Social psychologists have operationalized social categorization in different ways. Social categorization has been measured or manipulated in terms of the perceived *similarity* to other members of the social category (Hafer & Olson, 2003; Opotow, 1990a; Wohl & Branscombe, 2005) or in terms of *prototypicality of a group* compared to a superordinate group (Wenzel, 2004). Regardless of how it is measured, categorization appears to play an important role in the perception of justice (Clayton & Opotow, 2003; Skitka, 2003). We describe each of these two approaches in the next section and show how they can each affect the selection of the standard of justice used, with the leniency or severity of justice judgments differing as a result.

Similarity. An important variable underlying social categorization of victim group members is their perceived *similarity* to the in-group. Interestingly, even when people are randomly assigned in the laboratory to artificially created groups, they nevertheless attribute more similar beliefs to in-group members compared to out-group members (Allen & Wilder, 1979). People therefore attribute different values to social groups in an effort to affirm the worth and distinctiveness of their own group (Kristiansen & Zanna, 1994; Tajfel & Turner, 1986).

We argue that the more similar the victim group members are to in-group members, the lower the confirmatory standards that will be used to judge the in-group's actions (i.e., less evidence will be needed to decide the in-group's actions were unjust). Perceiving others as similar to oneself instigates concern with rights, fair treatment, and the entitlements of the other, while these concerns are less likely to be instigated when others are perceived as dissimilar (Opotow, 1993). Consistent with this reasoning, Boeckmann and Tyler (1997) found that participants indicated stronger agreement with legal rights and fair legal procedures (e.g., ensuring that due process is preserved) for a criminal when the target was similar to the perceiver compared to when the target was dissimilar (in-group vs. out-group member).

Tyler and Lind (1990) too found that people are more likely to apply stringent justice rules to others when they view them as members of an overarching social category to which both groups belong. This was the case whether or not a cooperative relationship existed between the two parties. Indeed, increasing the similarity between different species—beetles and humans—results in increased concern with justice for these insects (Opotow, 1993). Animals may be thus included in one's "scope of justice" (Opotow, 1990a), and concerns for justice can be extended to include them, when an inclusive category such as "living things" is salient. When these species are seen as not in conflict with each other, the extent to which concerns with fairness were applied to beetles mediated the effect of their similarity to humans on environmental protection responses (e.g., protection of the habitat and punishment of those who harm these species) (Opotow, 1993).

Batson, Turk, Shaw, and Klein (1995) found that people value the welfare of similar targets more than that of dissimilar targets. We propose that as the perceived similarity of the victim group to the perpetrator group increases—from nonhuman to the human level—so too will valuing the victim's welfare. Inducing empathy for another person serves to *humanize* the person in need, and may therefore activate the *human* level of categorization. This in turn should result in more rigorous definitions of injustice being applied when judging the in-group's harmful actions toward the out-group. In this sense, the perceived humanity of the out-group appears to be crucial for granting them just treatment (Leyens et al., 2000). Indeed, members of out-groups are perceived as sharing the in-group's humanity to a lesser degree, and this "lessened humanity" is reflected in the perception of different values on the part of the out-group. Ascribing to values such as humanitarianism and concern for others' welfare may often serve as a means of differentiating the in-group from an out-group (Schwartz & Struch, 1989). In fact, Leyens et al. (2000) have found that people more easily associate their in-group—relative to an out-group—with complex human-specific emotions, independent of the valence of the emotions. The ability to feel such emotions—precisely because they are considered uniquely human—is reserved for the in-group.

Prototypicality. According to Wenzel (2004), when the target group is perceived to be less prototypical of a more inclusive group (e.g., is less likely to "have the identity-defining attributes of the primary category," p. 234), the target is considered less deserving of superordinate category rights. Both categorization of the other as nonhuman and as an out-group member should lead to the employment of less rigorous definitions of injustice and to judging negative acts against the out-group as less unfair. Wenzel (2001), for instance, found that Germans who perceived Turkey as less prototypical of Europe were less likely to appraise the decision of the European Union not to allocate membership to Turkey (a decision with negative consequences for Turkey) as unfair.

What Determines Shifts in Victim Categorization?

As indicated in Figure 4.1, both contextual and individual variables can affect the categorization of victims by members of the perpetrator group. We consider here two important contextual variables (*degree of conflict* between the groups and the extent of cooperative and friendly *contact*) and one motivational variable (degree of *identification with one's in-group*).

Conflict. Conflict between two parties can be a source of perceived dissimilarity and instigate feelings of dislike. Conflict can occur when there are difficult life conditions (e.g., scarce resources, Staub, 1990) or conflicting group interests (Crosby & Lubin, 1990), and these may give rise to intergroup categorization, with an increased focus on *we-they* distinctions. Judd (1978) found that conflict causes perceptual changes that emphasize dissimilarities between people engaged in competitive interactions; that is, conflict increases the salience of dimensions that maximize dissimilarity. Moreover, conflict can motivate people to perceive the in-group and its values more positively than those of out-groups, and perception that the out-group's values are wrong (Brewer & Brown, 1998).

When groups are in conflict and the fairness of actions or entitlements of one of the groups is questioned, the social identities of the two parties are likely to be made salient. In this case, the perception of one's own characteristics and behaviors become stereotypical of the salient group norm (Turner et al., 1987). If those who were harmed are perceived as part of the out-group, the perceiver will self-categorize as an in-group member and in-group motivations (e.g., pro in-group bias) will be activated.

Similarly, the scope of justice (i.e., including the other group inside the boundaries of rules and rights assigned to the in-group) shrinks when animals are perceived as harmful to humans, when there is conflict with animals that are perceived as similar to humans, and when conflict severity is high (Opotow, 1990b, 1993; see also Struch & Schwartz, 1989). As a result, the harm committed against them is evaluated as less unjust due to the employment of a higher confirmatory standard for defining what injustice is (i.e., more evidence of cruelty against animals is needed to conclude that "real" harm or injustice was inflicted on them).

Under conditions of conflict, in-group members may find it hard to empathize with members of the out-group and be less likely to humanize them, with the standard of justice applied to their outcomes being set very high. For example, Huo (1995; cited in Tyler, Boeckmann, Smith, & Huo, 1995) asked participants to rate the extent to which members of liked (in-groups) and disliked (out-groups) social groups should have the same rights and the same access to resources. Participants believed that in-group members should be given more rights and more access to resources than members of out-groups. Similarly, employees are more likely to see layoffs as unfair if the layoff victims are included within their scope of justice (Brockner, 1990). Thus, what is viewed as fair or unfair differs for groups that are liked and disliked. Indeed, people may feel more guilt when they have harmed close others than when they have harmed strangers (Baumeister et al., 1994) because they are more likely to use different (lower) confirmatory standards of injustice when judging the harm inflicted on close others relative to those who are more distant.

Contact. As Pettigrew (1998) has noted, contact brings people together, including those who are (initially) dissimilar. Repeated contact is important as it leads first to diminished saliency of group categorization, followed by recategorization into a larger group that emphasizes the similarities (Pettigrew, 1998). Singer (1996) found that the more frequent and intimate contact European New Zealanders had with Maoris, the less opposed they were to race-based preferential treatment programs aimed at benefiting the out-group. Similarly, Pettigrew (1997) found that people with out-group friends (i.e., immigrants) are more likely to believe that immigrants' rights should be extended to be the same as those of citizens. Thus, affective ties with out-group members (see also Wright, Aron, McLaughlin-Volpe, & Ropp, 1997), as well as felt empathy for an out-group (Batson et al., 1997), can lead to increased justice concerns for out-group members. Presumably, some of these beneficial effects of repeated contact on increased justice concerns occur as a result of increasing inclusiveness of out-group member categorization.

Group Identification. High identifiers may be particularly motivated to employ categorizations of out-group members that prevent their "contaminating" the in-group. The more a target looks like an in-group member but has out-group characteristics, the longer it takes high identifiers to decide whether to include the person in their in-group (Castano, Yzerbyt, Bourguignon, & Seron, 2002). Identification with an in-group may therefore affect the perception of categories in a given social context (with an emphasis on the "we-they" distinction) because of the different values and norms that low and high identifiers learn and endorse. In turn, this categorical differentiation affects the moral decisions that low and high identifiers make.

Evidence for the latter idea comes from several studies. For instance, Boeckmann and Tyler (1997) found that participants who strongly identified with the Berkeley community (vs. low identifiers) expressed less agreement with the use of fair procedures for a thief, when the thief was a University of California, Davis student (out-group), than when the thief was a University of California, Berkeley student (in-group). Low identifiers did not show differential justice judgments as a function of the thief's group membership.

Compared to low identifiers, high identifiers may be less likely to shift how the victims are categorized (and not see them as part of a more inclusive group that also includes the in-group), and they may be more prone to routinely perceiving the social context in terms of distinct in-groups and out-groups. Moreover, because of this *we-they* differentiation, high identifiers are likely to use less rigorous definitions of injustice (e.g., use higher confirmatory standards) when judging the negative actions caused by the in-group to the out-group. Some of our recent research (Miron, Branscombe, & Biernat, 2005) provides a tentative step toward illustrating this process.

Miron et al. (2005) assessed white Americans' standards of injustice with regard to slavery. Participants completed a survey that ostensibly measured their knowledge of American history. The items assessed their opinions concerning the practice of enslaving Africans and their opinion about the United States as a nation. Standards of injustice concerning their in-group's past actions were assessed by asking: "For you to consider the United States *at that time a racist nation*, how large would the effects of American slavery on Africans have to have been?" Participants' standards for the *number of victims* (two items, $\alpha = .80$), the *severity of economic damage* (two items, $\alpha = .95$), and for *the number of perpetrators involved* (two items, $\alpha = .85$) were assessed accordingly. To measure the standards for the severity of economic damage, for example, participants were asked, "For me to consider the past United States a racist nation, the total damage caused to Africans *would have to have been* (in current U.S. dollars) on a scale ranging from less than $ 100,000" (1) to "more than $10 billion" (7), with seven categories.

Group identification was measured with an 8-item scale (I feel strong ties with other Americans, I value being an American, $\alpha = .88$). As shown in Figure 4.2, highly identified participants set higher confirmatory standards for the number of victims and the severity of damage than did low identifiers, both $\beta s > .22$ and $ps < .04$. People who were strongly identified with their group also tended to set higher confirmatory standards for the number of perpetrators than did low identifiers, $\beta = .20$, $p = .065$. That is, those who were highly identified with their nation needed more evidence—in terms of number of people victimized, extent of the economic damage done to them, and how many in-group members engaged in the harm doing—to conclude that injustice was committed in the past by their in-group. Thus, motivation in the form of in-group identification can influence the standard set for drawing

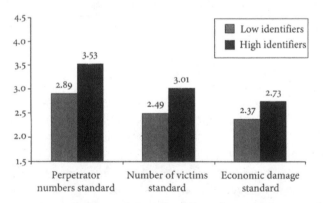

FIGURE 4.2. Confirmatory standards for judging the injustice of in-group actions as a function of group identification: High identifiers employ more stringent standards (i.e., need more evidence) than low identifiers to conclude their in-group's past actions were racist.

inferences about the in-group's past harm to another group. Presumably, because high identifiers more readily categorize the victim group as an out-group, they set a more severe standard that is difficult to meet based on the evidence, and this enables them to conclude that their group was not so unjust in its actions.

The Effect of Level-Specific Standards on Guilt

Little research has investigated the relationship between collective guilt and standards of injustice. Theoretically, Opotow (1993) proposed that animals are perceived as creatures for which "our considerations of fairness and moral rules do not apply" and that harming or exploiting them may be perceived as just, with little remorse or outrage being experienced for harming them. However, similar behavior, when directed toward those inside the boundaries of fairness, would generate negative feelings (Opotow, 1990a). At the group level, increased distress for harm depends on the degree to which a discrepancy exists between the ideals held for the in-group and how the in-group is perceived to be in actuality (Bizman, Yinon, & Krotman, 2001). More research will be needed, however, to establish that such standard shifting processes lessen the experience of collective guilt.

Implications for Intergroup Relations and Reconciliation

Harshness of Justice Standards and Reparations for Harm

The perception of injustice necessitates an assessment of what needs to be done to repair the injustice, and groups must employ some standard for deciding the magnitude of reparations that are needed to correct the harm done. If the standard for "what is considered fair reparations for injustice" is extremely high, people may find it very difficult, if not impossible, to rectify the injustice done. However, interestingly, even when the standard for fair reparations is seen as very easy to meet, guilt and perceived need to make reparations may be low. We argue that the standards for what would be appropriate reparations need to be perceived by the harmdoers as requiring substantial effort to be met, but still be seen as possible to attain, for guilt to be experienced.

The perceived costs of helping the victimized group influences the appraisal of the victimized group's situation and the extent to which collective guilt is experienced. Schmitt et al. (2004) provided evidence that collective guilt for the harm done by men to women can be undermined when high costs for correcting the harm are anticipated. In this study, men were reminded of the ways in which they are privileged relative to women and then they were presented with an opportunity to restore justice by collecting signatures on a petition that supported improved safety on campus at night for women. The difficulty of making reparations was manipulated by varying the number of signatures they had to collect to improve the situation for women: 5, 50, or 100.

As Brehm's (1999) theory of emotional intensity predicts, the degree of collective guilt reported varied as a function of the magnitude of the justice-restoration efforts that would be required: the more difficult it was for men to make reparations, the more guilt was mobilized to sustain their effort; in a sense, guilt provided energy for action up to the point where the value of the goal was undermined. Thus, guilt was higher when 50 signatures were required than when only five signatures were required. When five signatures were required, the goal of restoring justice was easy to achieve, and thus little guilt was needed to sustain the achievement of an easy goal. However, the increase in guilt (proportional to the perceived difficulty of achieving the goal) only occurs up to the point where the goal becomes so difficult to achieve (the 100 signatures condition) that it is no longer worth the effort. In this case, guilt was lowered in the 100 signatures condition as it was overcome by concern with the high costs of reparation.

These results suggest that for perpetrator groups to maintain their motivation to make reparations stemming from collective guilt they must perceive that there is a *difficult but manageable* form of compensation available to them. If either the harm done seems *very easy* or *impossible* to correct, the motivation to make reparations will be rather low, and so too the collective guilt that provides the motivation for making reparations.

Implications of Standard Shifting for Intergroup Reconciliation

The implications of standard shifting processes for reconciliation are multiple. Concluding that an in-group action was unjust has the potential to arouse guilt, which urges in-group members to restore justice. However, as we have reviewed in this chapter, many factors can interfere with the necessary conclusion that the in-group's action was unjust.

Reconciliation may be more easily achieved to the extent that both parties engaged in the intergroup conflict agree upon "what constitutes injustice" and thereby arrive at similar conclusions about the past. The more the victim group members are included in the in-group or an inclusive social category, the more likely it is that the assessments of social reality by the two parties will converge, perhaps in part because of the increased willingness of perpetrator group members to lower the confirmatory standards used to judge their group's injustice. Bar-Tal and Bennink (2004) have emphasized how important it is for the two groups involved in a conflict to develop a "common view" of the past. According to this perspective, reconciliation starts with developing a shared collective memory, where both parties accept as truth the injustice of each side's past actions. For that to happen, each group must admit and take responsibility for its role in creating the conflict and engaging in violence. Such an admission is an important condition for experiencing collective guilt (Powell, Branscombe, & Schmitt, 2005).

Given that privately or publicly admitting that the *in-group is responsible* may be almost impossible in violent conflicts, changing the standards that group members use to make moral judgments may be a strategy that can be employed *before responsibility is fully accepted.* This strategy may be less threatening than admitting responsibility and—as we propose—has the potential to change perceptions of injustice and, ultimately (when coupled with attributions of responsibility), to instigate guilt. To change the standards employed in making moral decisions, our model indicates that in-group members must perceive the victims differently—as part of a more inclusive or superordinate in-group. Messick and Mackie (1989) examined five methods for reducing intergroup conflict, with all operating by changing categorization levels: (1) diminishing the intensity of in-group identification because group identification makes the intergroup boundaries more salient; (2) disrupting the assumed belief dissimilarity of out-group compared to in-group; (3) highlighting superordinate categories; (4) reducing cues to category membership; and (5) crosscutting category memberships. Any of these strategies can create shifts in how the victim group is categorized, and result in changed perceptions of the severity of the injustice.

Finally, collective guilt has been found to lead to a decrease in prejudice toward the out-group (Powell et al., 2005). Such prejudice reduction may be due to shifts in categorization (i.e., seeing the victim group as part of a common more inclusive group), and earlier work has suggested that indeed we may feel particularly guilty for hurting those similar or close to us. Dovidio et al. (2004) demonstrated this effect by using an interesting strategy to increase white participants' perception of a common group identity with black Americans. Participants read about a terrorist threat that was either directed at all Americans or solely at white Americans. After that, all participants viewed a video depicting racial discrimination against a black person. Those in the inclusive threat condition ("all Americans are at risk") showed reductions in prejudice against black Americans compared to those in the exclusive threat condition. Feelings of injustice mediated the effect of the inclusive threat manipulation on prejudice reduction. Prejudice was thus reduced through a shift in how the victim group was categorized, which then led to increased justice concerns for them.

More research is needed that assesses each of the processes delineated in the model that we have outlined. Specifically, within a single study, all of the key variables have yet to be measured. Yet, the existing evidence garnered from a variety of investigations conducted thus far appears to be consistent with the central propositions that we have offered. We are hopeful that new methods of developing more inclusive categorization will reveal how critical this process is for employing a common standard of justice, and ultimately suggest additional methods of improving intergroup relations that have been stained by past harm doing.

Notes

1. We chose to focus on distributive justice rather than on procedural justice because it is easier to quantify the standards and evaluation of unjust outcomes (i.e., it is easier to quantify the amount of damage in money vs. the degree of inappropriateness or disrespectful behavior displayed). Nevertheless, we expect our analysis would hold true for other kinds of injustice.

2. This is not a new idea. Research has found that when an individual's personal identity is salient, prejudice toward an out-group follows from individual attitudes such as authoritarianism, whereas when one's group identity is salient, people use "in-group-defining standards to evaluate out-group members" (Verkuyten & Hagendoorn, 1998, p. 26). What is new is that people shift the group-based standards they employ as a function of who the victim group is (inside or outside the in-group).

References

Allen, V. L., & Wilder, D. A. (1979). Group categorization and attribution of belief similarity. *Small Group Behavior, 10,* 73-80.

Bar-Tal, D., & Bennink, G. H. (2004). The nature of reconciliation as an outcome and as a process. In Y. Bar-Siman-Tov (Ed.), *From conflict resolution to reconciliation* (pp. 11-38). Oxford, UK: Oxford University Press.

Batson, C. D., Polycarpou, M. P., Harmon-Jones, E., Imhoff, H. J., Mitchener, E. C., Bednar, L. L., et al. (1997). Empathy and attitudes: Can feeling for a member of a stigmatized group improve feelings toward the group? *Journal of Personality and Social Psychology, 72,* 105-118.

Batson, C. D., Turk, C. L., Shaw, L. L., & Klein, T. R. (1995). Informational function of empathic emotion: Learning that we value the other's welfare. *Journal of Personality and Social Psychology, 68,* 300-313.

Baumeister, R. F., Stillwell, A. M., & Heatherton, T. F. (1994). Guilt: An interpersonal approach. *Psychological Bulletin, 115,* 243-267.

Biernat, M., & Fuegen, K. (2001). Shifting standards and the evaluation of competence: Complexity in gender-based judgment and decision making. *Journal of Social Issues, 7,* 707-724.

Biernat, M. R., & Kobrynowicz, D. (1997). Gender- and race-based standards of competence: Lower minimum standards but higher ability standards for devalued groups, *Journal of Personality and Social Psychology, 72,* 544-557.

Bizman, A., Yinon, Y., & Krotman, S. (2001). Group-based emotional distress: An extension of self-discrepancy theory. *Personality and Social Psychology Bulletin, 27,* 1291-1300.

Boeckmann, R. J., & Tyler, T. R. (1997). Commonsense justice and inclusion within the moral community: When do people receive procedural protections from others? *Psychology, Public Policy, and Law, 3,* 362-380.

Branscombe, N. R. (1998). Thinking about one's gender group's privileges or disadvantages: Consequences for well-being in women and men. *British Journal of Social Psychology, 37,* 167-184.

Branscombe, N. R., & Doosje, B. (2004). *Collective guilt: International perspectives.* New York: Cambridge University Press.

Branscombe, N. R., Doosje, B., & McGarty, C. (2002). Antecedents and consequences of collective guilt. In D. M. Mackie & E. R. Smith (Eds.), *From prejudice to intergroup emotions: Differentiated reactions to social groups* (pp. 49-66). Philadelphia, PA: Psychology Press.

Brehm, J. W. (1999). The intensity of emotion. *Personality and Social Psychology Review, 3,* 2-22.

Brewer, M. B., & Brown, R. J. (1998). Intergroup relations. In D. Gilbert, S. Fiske, & G. Lindzey (Eds.), *The handbook of social psychology* (4th ed., Vol. 2, pp. 554-594). Boston, MA: McGraw-Hill.

Brockner, J. (1990). Scope of justice in the workplace: How survivors react to co-worker layoffs. *Journal of Social Issues, 46,* 95-106.

Castano, E., Yzerbyt, V., Bourguignon, D., & Seron, E. (2002). Who may enter? The impact of in-group identification on in-group/out-group categorization. *Journal of Experimental Social Psychology, 38,* 315-322.

Clayton, S., & Opotow, S. (2003). Justice and identity: Changing perspectives on what is fair. *Personality and Social Psychology Review, 74,* 298-310.

Crosby, F. J., & Lubin, E. P. (1990). Extending the moral community: Logical and psychological dilemmas. *Journal of Social Issues, 46,* 163-172.

Devine, P. G., Monteith, M. J., Zuwerink, J. R., & Elliott, A. J. (1991). Prejudice with and without compunction. *Journal of Personality and Social Psychology, 60,* 817-830.

Dovidio, J. F., ten Vergert, M., Stewart, T. L., Gaertner, S. L., Johnson, J. D., Esses, V. M., et al. (2004). Perspective and prejudice: Antecedents and mediating mechanisms. *Personality and Social Psychology Bulletin, 30*, 1537-1549.

Frijda, N. H., Kuipers, P., & Ter Schure, E. (1989). Relations among emotion, appraisal, and emotional action readiness. *Journal of Personality and Social Psychology, 57*, 212-228.

Gaertner, S. L., Dovidio, J. F., Anastasio, P. A., Bachman, B. A., & Rust, M. C. (1993). The common group identity model: Recategorization and the reduction of intergroup bias. *European Review of Social Psychology, 4*, 1-26.

Hafer, C. L., & Olson, J. M. (2003). An analysis of empirical research on the scope of justice. *Personality and Social Psychology Review, 7*, 311-323.

Johnson, J. D., Whitestone, E., Jackson, L. E., & Gatto, L. (1995). Justice is still not colorblind: Differential racial effects of exposure to inadmissible evidence. *Personality and Social Psychology Bulletin, 21*, 893-898.

Jones, W. H., Kugler, K., & Adams, P. (1995). You always hurt the one you love: Guilt and transgressions against relationship partners. In J. P. Tangney & K. W. Fischer (Eds.), *Self-conscious emotions: The psychology of shame, guilt, embarrassment, and pride* (pp. 301-312). New York: Guilford Press.

Judd, C. M. (1978). Cognitive effects of attitude and conflict resolution. *Journal of Conflict Resolution, 22*, 483-498.

Kristiansen, C. M., & Zanna, M. P. (1994). The rhetorical use of values to justify social and intergroup attitudes. *Journal of Social Issues, 50*, 47-68.

Leyens, J. P., Paladino, P. M., Rodriguez-Torres, R., Vaes, J., Demoulin, S., Rodriguez-Perez, A., et al. (2000). The emotional side of prejudice: The attribution of secondary emotions to ingroups and outgroups. *Personality and Social Psychology Review, 4*, 186-197.

Messick, D. M., & Mackie, D. M. (1989). Intergroup relations. *Annual Review of Psychology, 40*, 45-81.

Miron, A. M., Branscombe, N. R., & Biernat, M. R. (2005). *Standards of justice and group identification.* Unpublished data, University of Kansas.

Miron, A. M., Branscombe, N. R., & Schmitt, M. T. (2006). Collective guilt as distress over illegitimate intergroup inequality. *Group Processes and Intergroup Relations, 9*, 163-180.

Montada, L., & Schneider, A. (1989). Justice and emotional reactions to the disadvantaged. *Social Justice Research, 3*, 313-344.

Opotow, S. (1990a). Moral exclusion and injustice: An introduction. *Journal of Social Issues, 46*, 1-20.

Opotow, S. (1990b). Deterring moral exclusion. *Journal of Social Issues, 46*, 173-182.

Opotow, S. (1993). Animals and the scope of justice. *Journal of Social Issues, 49*, 71-85.

Pettigrew, T. F. (1997). Generalized intergroup contact effects on prejudice. *Personality and Social Psychology Bulletin, 23*, 173-185.

Pettigrew, T. F. (1998). Intergroup contact theory. *Annual Review of Psychology, 49*, 65-85.

Powell, A. A., Branscombe, N. R., & Schmitt, M. T. (2005). Inequality as ingroup privilege or outgroup disadvantage: The impact of group focus on collective guilt and interracial attitudes. *Personality and Social Psychology Bulletin, 31*, 508-521.

Schmitt, M. T., Branscombe, N. R., & Brehm, J. W. (2004). Determinants of the intensity of gender-based guilt in men. In N. R. Branscombe & B. Doosje (Eds.), *Collective guilt: International perspectives* (pp. 75-92). New York: Cambridge University Press.

Schwartz, S. H., & Struch, N. (1989). Values, stereotypes, and intergroup antagonism. In D. Bar-Tal, C. F. Grauman, A. Kruglanski, & W. Stroebe (Eds.), *Stereotyping and prejudice: Changing conceptions* (pp. 151-167). New York: Springer-Verlag.

Singer, M. S. (1996). Effects of scope of justice, informant ethnicity, and information frame on attitudes toward ethnicity-based selection. *International Journal of Psychology, 31*, 191-205.

Skitka, L. J. (2003). Of different minds: An accessible identity model of justice reasoning. *Personality and Social Psychology Review, 7*, 286-297.

Staub, E. (1990). Moral exclusion, personal goal theory, and extreme destructiveness. *Journal of Social Issues, 46*, 47-64.

Struch, N., & Schwartz, S. H. (1989). Intergroup aggression: Its predictors and distinctness from in-group bias. *Journal of Personality and Social Psychology, 56*, 364-373.

Tajfel, H., & Turner, J. C. (1986). The social identity theory of intergroup behavior. In S. Worchel & W. Austin (Eds.), *Psychology of intergroup relations* (pp. 7-24). Chicago, IL: Nelson-Hall.

Turner, J. C., Hogg, M. A., Oakes, P. J., Reicher, S. D., & Wetherell, M. S. (1987). *Rediscovering the social group: A self-categorization theory.* Oxford: Blackwell.

Turner, J. C., & Onorato, R. S. (1999). Social identity, personality, and the self-concept: A self-categorizing perspective. In T. R. Tyler, R. M. Kramer, & O. P. John (Eds.), *The psychology of the social self* (pp. 11-46). Mahwah, NJ: Erlbaum.

Tyler, T. R., Boeckmann, R. J., Smith, H. J., & Huo, Y. J. (1995). *Social justice in a diverse society.* Boulder, CO: Westview Press.

Tyler, T. R., & Lind, E. A. (1990). Intrinsic versus community-based justice models: When does group membership matter? *Journal of Social Issues, 46*, 83-94.

Verkuyten, M., & Hagendoorn, L. (1998). Prejudice and self-categorization: The variables of authoritarianism and in-group stereotypes. *Personality and Social Psychology Bulletin, 24*, 99-110.

Wenzel, M. (2001). A social categorization approach to distributive justice: Social identity as the link between relevance of inputs and need for justice. *British Journal of Social Psychology, 40*, 315-335.

Wenzel, M. (2004). A social categorization approach to distributive justice. *European Review of Social Psychology, 15*, 219-258.

Wicker, F. W., Payne, G. C., & Morgan, R. D. (1983). Participant descriptions of guilt and shame. *Motivation and Emotion, 7*, 25-39.

Wohl, M. J. A., & Branscombe, N. R. (2005). Forgiveness and collective guilt assignment to historical perpetrator groups depend on level of social category inclusiveness. *Journal of Personality and Social Psychology, 88*, 288-303.

Wright, S. C., Aron, A., McLaughlin-Volpe, T., & Ropp, S. A. (1997). The extended contact effect: Knowledge of cross-group friendships and prejudice. *Journal of Personality and Social Psychology, 73*, 73-90.

Yzerbyt, V., Dumont, M., Gordijn, E., & Wigboldus, D. (2002). Intergroup emotions and self-categorization: The impact of perspective-taking on reactions to victims of harmful behavior. In D. M. Mackie & E. R. Smith (Eds.), *From prejudice to intergroup emotions: Differentiated reactions to social groups.* Philadelphia, PA: Psychology Press.

CHAPTER 5

Prospects for Intergroup Reconciliation: Social-Psychological Predictors of Intergroup Forgiveness and Reparation in Northern Ireland and Chile

MASI NOOR, RUPERT BROWN, AND GARRY PRENTICE

Given the myriads of violent conflicts between groups in human history, a book discussing intergroup reconciliation appears to be both overambitious and overdue. It is overambitious because the continual violence to which groups have subjected each other during the last century alone might be seen as a grim testimony to the possibility that many violent intergroup relationships might be irreconcilable. It is overdue because, although violent human behavior and its consequences have been popular research topics in many different disciplines, a social-psychological interest in assessing the legacy of intergroup violent conflicts has only emerged recently (Bar-Siman-Tov, 2004; Branscombe & Doosje, 2004). Nevertheless, in some instances, research on intergroup reconciliation has gone beyond assessing the immediate aftermath to try to identify long-term strategies for peaceful coexistence (Hewstone et al., 2004; Nadler & Liviatan, 2004). We think this line of research on intergroup reconciliation is crucial for a number of reasons and intend to make a contribution toward its development in this chapter.

The process of reconciliation often appears to be preceded by some kind of a truce between the conflicting groups leading to a formal settlement, as has been observed, for example, by the handing over of power by the apartheid regime in South Africa or the Good Friday Agreement supported by most political parties and a majority of over 70% of the Northern Irish population. However, even in contexts in which earlier warring groups may have reached a settlement, be it imposed by a third party or home-grown, the relative peace between the groups can be easily threatened by the instability associated with the post-settlement eras, due to unresolved past or newly emerging conflicts. It is also possible that ceasefires may be born out of what is sometimes called *conflict fatigue* (Kelman, 2004). This fatigue refers to the mutual exhaustion of the conflicting parties whose constituents have become tired of paying the hefty price of loss of loved ones, community insecurity, and personal vulnerability, to maintain the conflict. In addition to *fatigue*, after a long period of bloody conflict the political leadership of both parties sometimes come to the realization that the traditional approach to achieving their goals is not sustainable and a change in their political strategy might be necessary (Darby & Mac Ginty, 2000). Finally, conflict fatigue and change in the political strategy can also be accompanied by unrealistically high expectations from the opponent group(s) to change its goals and attitudes in the wake of a settlement. While such motives might sow the seeds for the "rhetoric of reconciliation" (Kelly & Hamber, 2005) and a temporary pause in violence, we argue that more is required in order for reconciliation to become a substantive reality with healing effects on the damaged intergroup relationship.

Thus, in this chapter our main focus is to identify the precursors of intergroup reconciliation or, more realistically, of an orientation toward reconciliation. We will review the scant literature of reconciliation and complement it with our own theoretical framework of intergroup reconciliation. Finally, we will review our research in support and extension of this framework that was conducted in the contexts of the Northern Irish conflict, the Chilean experience of political transition from dictatorship to democracy and relations between the indigenous and nonindigenous Chileans.

Intergroup Reconciliation and Its Social-Psychological Predictors

Reconciliation

As our opening comments intimated, there can be a combination of possible motives underlying the willingness of groups to reconcile. However, we argue in this section that such political motives are not by themselves sufficient to bring about genuine attempts at healing an intergroup relationship fractured by a long history of violent confrontation. Thus, to move from the "rhetoric of reconciliation" to the genuine "reality of reconciliation," in agreement with other researchers we suggest that at the heart of reconciliation lies the psychological process effecting shifts in one's "mind and heart" concerning the conflict and the opponent group (Bar-Siman-Tov, 2004; Bar-Tal & Bennink, 2004; Kelman, 2004; Nadler, 2003; Noor, Brown, & Prentice, in press). Such a psychological process has to address deep-seated emotional and cognitive barriers between the groups that may remain potent even following a peace accord, for example lack of trust and empathy (Nadler, 2003; Nadler & Liviatan, 2004). Moreover, another important task in the process of reconciliation is for the groups to recognize that violence will not serve them in the long run as a viable option for dealing with the conflict. Taken together, reconciliation can be generally understood as a psychological process that involves bringing about changes in goals, attitudes, emotions, and motivations in the majority of both groups (Bar-Tal & Bennink, 2004; Noor et al., in press). More specifically, we assert that the reconciliation process opens up a set of opportunities. One such important opportunity is to deal with the perceived or real impact of the painful past, while another crucial one is to explore avenues through which a relationship that was not handled well can be reestablished. Thus, consequently, groups conscious of the need to reconcile will engage more meaningfully, and thus successfully, in the process of reconciliation by addressing major issues revolving around perceived victimization, the justification of violence, and forgiveness (discussed in detail in the remainder of the chapter). It is through such an understanding of reconciliation that the transformative, and thus restorative and reparative, effects of reconciliation on the damaged intergroup relations come to the fore. Such an understanding also implies that the process of reconciliation will equip groups to approach future conflicts with less violent strategies, and that reconciliation may encourage them to seek reparative actions to compensate for past mistreatments. It is also noteworthy that often our colleagues and research participants question how meaningful it is to speak of reconciliation (as in reestablishing the relationship) in contexts where the opposing groups have experienced everything (ranging from indifference, suspicion to violent confrontation) but a harmonious relationship in their entire history. There is seemingly no relationship to be *reestablished*, and the term *reconciliation* in such contexts might sound misused or misplaced. While acknowledging that such dire history of intergroup confrontation can exist (e.g., in Northern Ireland), we argue that even in the face of such history there does exist a relationship between the two groups, albeit a negative one. That is, although it might be more accurate to use the term *conciliation* in such contexts, nevertheless the underlying issues resulting from a history of violent confrontation are essentially, the same, regardless of whether the groups have or have not experienced a positive relationship with each other. In the next section, we will look at what facilitates or hinders processes associated with reconciliation in a variety of contexts.

Intergroup Forgiveness as the Overarching Predictor of an Orientation Toward Reconciliation

Groups emerging from ethnopolitical violence often have to face a number of challenges before they can create a sense of ownership of the process of reconciliation. One of these obstacles relates to a painful past, which due to the prolonged nature of the conflict and mutual victimization, is often (though not always) defined by blurred boundaries between the "victim" and the "perpetrator" groups. Consequently, difficulties stemming from the lack of a shared account of the past and the assignment of responsibility for the conflict can be insurmountable obstacles to reconciliation. In the face of such alienating challenges, what could be the conditions that will still encourage groups to choose reconciliation over other options, such as revenge or avoidance? We have identified forgiveness as one such condition.

In the interpersonal forgiveness literature, forgiveness has been typically conceptualized as a prosocial facilitator for repairing broken relationships (Enright & North, 1998; McCullough, 2001; McCullough et al., 1998; Scobie & Scobie, 1998). It does so by reversing the negativity in motivation, thought, affect, and behavior between the victim and the perpetrator. The examination of such a prosocial function of forgiveness has only recently been extended to the intergroup level (Bar-Siman-Tov, 2004; Hewstone et al., 2004; Morrow, 2001; Wohl & Branscombe, 2005). It is important to note, however, that while there may be some overlap between processes of reconciliation between two romantic partners and two ethnic groups with a legacy of violent conflict; nevertheless, Nadler (2003) and Hewstone et al. (2004) caution not to overlook important qualitative differences between interpersonal and intergroup forgiveness. We have identified several such differences; that is, it is possible that the potential forgiver in the interpersonal context might have a wider range of strategies for dealing with the wrongdoer, including the options of maintaining the relationship with the wrongdoer or avoiding that relationship (e.g., entering a new employment, moving out into a new accommodation). Opportunities for "opting out" of the relationship are sometimes more constrained in an intergroup context, such as Northern Ireland, where the two conflicting communities (Catholic and Protestant) will continue to share natural resources, political institutions and, above all, geographic contiguity. This may not always be true. In other contexts (e.g., Serbia and Croatia, Palestine and Israel) physical disengagement may be associated with the resolution of the conflict, either as a precursor or consequence, or both. Intergroup forgiveness may also differ from interpersonal forgiveness in terms of the actors' perceived (or actual) efficacy to influence events, due to the sheer number of parties and their mutual influences involved in the process of forgiveness. That is, it can be argued that in interpersonal contexts because only two individuals are involved, provided they both are willing to engage in forgiveness, the object and subject of forgiveness are more clearly defined and such clarity may increase the ability of individual(s) to offer or withhold forgiveness. In contrast, intergroup settings, because of the greater number of people involved, may create a sense of decreased controllability, at least regarding the identification of the perpetrators directly responsible for the violence. It is also conceivable that in intergroup contexts, some group members, who may in general be willing to forgive the out-group, might withhold their forgiveness because of the fear of appearing to compromise their in-group loyalty.

In summary, then, we define intergroup forgiveness as a process that involves making a decision to learn new aspects about oneself and one's group (one's emotions, thoughts, and capability to inflict harm on others), and to try to explore the world as perceived by the out-group (Noor et al., in press) both with the intention of finding adequate closure about the past and developing a vision for the future in which the groups' mutual concerns may be reconciled. The subsequent critical insights from such self-and-other exploration could be manyfold. On the one hand, it may provide groups with more crucial clarity over their roles and responsibilities in the maintenance of the conflict. On the other hand, it might encourage groups to respond to the impact of the painful past with the generosity of absolving the other from some of the "total blame" for causing the conflict and the harm associated with it. Naturally, this process and its outcomes will be informed, and influenced by the willingness of other in-group members to engage in similar processes. One implication from the above understanding of intergroup forgiveness as a *conscious* process is that there are clear barriers to forgetting the immorality of past misdeeds. Closely, related to guarding against forgetting, is another important clarification, namely, that forgiveness does not imply the belittling of the severity and impact of a misdeed; that is, most researchers cited above are in agreement that forgiveness does not undermine the painful experience of the victim, and that it should not be misunderstood as an easy way of exonerating the wrongdoer from his/her violation.

Competitive Victimhood

Competing perceptions about the past and its impact held by opposing groups provide a basis for maintaining conflict. Given that an important insight from research in intergroup relations has shown consistently that competitive processes are inherent features of intergroup relations (Brewer & Brown, 1998; Hewstone, Rubin, & Willis, 2002), we want to draw attention to the functions and predictive power of the competitive process revolving around "victimhood." The term *competitive victimhood* refers to the subjective claims made by each group in conflict that it has suffered more than the out-group (Nadler, 2003; Noor et al., in press; Shaw, 2003). Moreover, this competition over the *quantity* of suffering also implies some dispute over the *illegitimacy* of the suffering; that is, "not only have we suffered more than you, but it is also decidedly unfair that we have." Put differently, we understand competitive victimhood as a general way of dealing with conflict in that it is often employed as a strategy to highlight the injustice and suffering that the in-group might be exposed to during the violence. Consequently, such a strategy may lead to the acceptance of retaliatory responses to the out-group by the majority of in-group members. In contrast, in the post-settlement context, groups might equally engage in competitive victimhood to emphasize the vulnerability of one's in-group and the exploitation the in-group suffered at the out-group's hands. Such an emphasis could be potentially moti-vated by the desire to minimize in-group's share of responsibility for maintain-ing the conflict, or for offering reparation. Although there is a dearth of research examining the processes of competitive victimhood, there are at least two daily life instances that capture this concept in the Northern Irish context. The first instance refers to the colloquial term of the "talk of what-aboutry." Such talk encapsulates the attempts of the opposite group members to portray the suffer-ing of their in-group as more severe than that of the out-group, when confronted by the harm caused by their respective in-groups. The second example is present in the murals painted on the streets of Northern Ireland, particularly in Catholic communities, selectively depicting the stories of victimization and exploitation inflicted on the in-group by the out-group.

In the next section, we provide a brief outline of the intergroup conflict settings in which we have located our research, followed by the summary of findings from our empirical studies testing and extending the above theoretical understanding of reconciliation.

Contexts of Divided Societies

"The Troubles" in Northern Ireland

The phrase *The Troubles* is an euphemistic way of referring to the three decades of violent conflict between the Catholic and the Protestant communities in Northern Ireland. This conflict has its roots in the partition of Ireland in 1921 and at the political level; the conflict is expressed by the two communities' divergent desires for their constitutional status. While the Protestant community, including Unionists and Loyalists, desires to remain part of the United Kingdom, the Catholic community, subsuming Nationalists and Republicans, aspires to pursue the reunification of Northern Ireland with the Republic of Ireland (Hewstone et al., 2004; Noor et al., in press). The most violent period of the conflict stretched from the early 1960s to late 1990s. The impact of this violent conflict has been tragic with almost 4,000 dead, estimates of nearly 49,000 injured and yet many more traumatized (Fay, Morrissey, & Smyth, 1999; Morrow, 2001; Police Service for Northern Ireland, 2005). In 1998, a settlement (the Good Friday Agreement) was negotiated and endorsed by over 70% of the population in Northern Ireland. The main principle of the settlement was that until the majority of the population chooses for Northern Ireland to be reunified with Ireland, it would remain part of Britain.

This settlement has noticeably reduced the intensity of political violence. However, given that, the paramilitary organs continue to be powerful and the sectarian street violence is on the rise recently (Darby & Mac Ginty, 2000), it may be premature to assume that the process of reconciliation has started in Northern Ireland.

The Legacy of Pinochet's Rule in Chile

Central to the recent political history of Chile have been the competing evaluations of the almost 17-year Pinochet regime associated with the political left and right orientations. In their extreme expressions, the right regards Pinochet's dictatorship as necessary for combating Marxism-Leninism in Chile, while the left views the same rule as an unjustified attack on the democratic state and as a period of catastrophic human rights violations (Alexander, 1978; Ensalaco, 2000). However, contradictory these two assessments might be, a Chilean Government Commission estimated that around 3,000 people were killed or "disappeared" during Pinochet's rule and that many more were either tortured or exiled (Report of the Chilean National Commission on Truth and Reconciliation, 1993; Roniger & Sznajder, 1999).

Nonindigenous Discriminatory Treatment
of the Indigenous Mapuche in Chile

Alongside the political intergroup conflict between the right and left wing orientated nonindigenous Chileans, there has also been a parallel intergroup conflict tracing back to Chile's colonial past. Although on the surface the two conflicts in Chile may appear unrelated, the underlying processes in relation to the perceived need for reconciliation and reparation are ultimately very similar. Chile consists of a majority of nonindigenous Chileans and several indigenous groups, of which the largest is the Mapuche. The Mapuche have fought against colonialist invasions of their land for several hundred years and were actually among the last peoples to be subjugated by the colonizers in South America in the 19th century. Since then, the Mapuche have experienced continual infringements of their land, suppression of their culture (e.g., their language was outlawed under Pinochet's military regime, 1973-1989), and also severe economic and social deprivation (e.g., unemployment and alcoholism rates are disproportionately high). This has led them to protest about their living conditions, sometimes culminating in violent conflict with the State. Nonindigenous Chileans have ambivalent attitudes toward the Mapuche (Saiz, 2002). On the one hand, the Mapuche are often regarded as brave and fearless warriors, a part of the "founding myth" of the Chilean nation and a source of pride for nonindigenous Chileans. On the other hand, Mapuche levels of deprivation make them an easy target of stigmatizations and negative attitudes from the majority. In recent years, there has been public and governmental debate about nonindigenous people's collective responsibility for the historical treatment of the Mapuche and the need for current reparations (Instituto Nacional de Estadística, 2002; Ministerio de Planificación y Cooperación, 2003). Such political discussions may well be a forerunner of long-lasting and effective reconciliation between the indigenous and nonindigenous communities in Chile.

Despite obvious cultural and historical differences between the violent conflicts in Northern Ireland and Chile, one can draw some important parallels between these two contexts that establish a base for comparison. Thus, similar to the divided communities in Northern Ireland, groups with opposing political orientation or ethnic identities in Chile appear to have developed cognitive and emotional barriers between them resulting from the legacy of a disputed past.

Our Research

In the above contexts, the need for reconciliation seems salient and thus needs to be addressed by all layers of society. We report our findings from a series of studies conducted in these contexts that examined the role of a range of potential positive and negative predictors of intergroup forgiveness. Then we specify a theoretical model of reconciliation orientation that was validated and extended in the Northern Irish context. We conclude this section with two longitudinal studies that attempted to clarify the role of self-conscious emotions in predicting restitution offered to the Mapuche by the nonindigenous Chileans.

Study 1

We surveyed an opportunity sample, ($N_{Catholic} = 145$ and $N_{Protestant} = 164$), from the student population at the main Northern Irish Universities. Intergroup forgiveness was measured with six items on the basis of the existing interpersonal forgiveness literature (McCullough et al., 1998; Takaku, Weiner, & Ohbuchi, 2001) and on our own conceptualization of forgiveness. It was important to develop an intergroup forgiveness scale that did not make too many assumptions regarding the necessary conditions for forgiveness other than that forgiveness involves affect, cognition, and behavior. For example, "I hold feelings of resentment toward the other community for their misdeed," "I have ill thoughts about the other community for their misdeeds," or "I am prepared to forgive the other community for their misdeeds." Competitive victimhood was assessed by a six-item scale that included items such as "Overall, the proportion of trauma due to 'The Troubles' has been more severe in my community than in the other community," or "On average, the areas that have been most affected by 'The Troubles' are those in which members of my community live." Participants rated the extent to which they trusted their out-group by responding to four items (based on Mitchell, 2000; Rosenberg, 1957) which included statements like "few members of the other community can be trusted" or "most members of the other community try to be fair." Empathy was assessed with five items (based on Voci & Hewstone, 2003), an example of which is "when I hear a piece of news regarding a sectarian attack against members of the other community, I try to look at it from their point of view." Identification with one's own religious community, Catholic or Protestant (i.e., in-group identity), was measured using an adapted version of the six items constructed by Brown, Condor, Wade, and Williams (1986)—for example, "I feel strong ties to my community and its people." Finally, we also based our measure of common in-group identity on a similar six-item scale of in-group identity, except that this time the statements referred to Northern Irish Society.

Regression analyses were conducted with intergroup forgiveness as the criterion and the other variables as predictors. Overall, the predictors explained a sizable proportion of variance in intergroup forgiveness ($R^2 = .41$). The strongest positive predictors of intergroup forgiveness were common in-group identity, trust, and empathy. Conversely, competitive victimhood and a high level of in-group identification appeared to discourage participants to forgive the out-group.

We also found a moderating effect of community membership (Catholic vs. Protestant) on the association between forgiveness and common in-group identification. Simple slope analysis indicated that for the Catholic partici-pants identification with the common in-group was positively correlated with forgiveness, whereas for the Protestant participants no correlation existed between these two variables.

Finally, community membership also moderated the relationship between forgiveness and competitive victimhood, such that the negative association between these two variables was more accentuated for the Protestant sample than for the Catholic sample.

Study 2

Having established the predictors of intergroup forgiveness in the Northern Irish context, next, we attempted to validate our findings in Chile. We used similar variables as in Study 1 and presented them in Spanish to samples of university students who identified themselves with the political right ($N = 216$) or the political left ($N = 219$). The samples were recruited from the Catholic University of Chile.

The results revealed a striking similarity with the findings from Northern Ireland. After regressing intergroup forgiveness on all the above predictor variables, a reasonable proportion of variance ($R^2 = .45$) in intergroup forgive-ness was accounted for. Overall, empathy, common in-group identity (Chilean Nation) and trust revealed to be the strongest positive predictor of intergroup forgiveness, while political identification with the right and competitive victimhood were negatively associated with forgiveness. Put differently, high levels of empathy, identification with the common in-group and out-group trust were associated with readiness to forgive the out-group . However, increases in identification with the political right and competition over in-group victim-hood seemed to reduce the willingness to forgive.

Similar to Study 1, we found that group membership (Left vs. Right) moderated the negative association between forgiveness and competitive victimhood, and the positive association between the former and trust. Simple slope analyses revealed that these associations existed for the political left, but not for the political right. Finally, group membership also moderated the association between forgiveness and empathy, such that this association was more accentuated for the Right than for the Left.

Study 3

Next, we report a study that aimed to validate and extend a model of reconciliation orientation that we developed in the Northern Irish context. The theoretical model is based on most of the variables examined in Studies 1 and 2, except we included a new variable that we refer to as *subjective evaluation of past violence*. In post-settlement contexts, a contentious issue revolves around the evaluation of past violence. Naturally, when the line between perpetrator and victim groups is not clear-cut, divergent perceptions regarding the attribution of blame for the violence and the appropriateness of a "legitimate" response to it might be held by the opposing groups (Dixon, 2001; Fay et al., 1999). Thus, it is not surprising that groups may engage in less veridical evaluation of past violence that might function both to highlight their in-group's suffering as a consequence of the out-group's violence, and to seek justification for their own in-group's violent actions portrayed as a "legitimate" response to the out-group violence. We measured subjective evaluation of past violence with a four-item scale, examples of which are "most of the violent acts that were carried out on behalf of my community against the other community were mainly for self-protection" or "sometimes my community was left with no other choice, but to respond with violence against the other community."

In our model of reconciliation orientation, we specified intergroup forgiveness and biased evaluation of past violence as the two opposing precursors of the reconciliation orientation. These precursors, in turn, were hypothesized to be predicted directly by, out-group trust, empathy, and in-group identity (Hewstone et al., 2004; Nadler & Liviatan, 2004; Wohl & Branscombe, 2005). We treated these predictors themselves as potential mediator, which, in turn, were predicted by competitive victimhood (see Figure 5.1).

To test the above theoretical model, we recruited an opportunity sample ($N_{\text{Catholic}} = 181$ and $N_{\text{Protestant}} = 137$). Participants were students at the main universities in Belfast. Using LISREL, we tested our full model with the data from both the Catholic and the Protestant participants. This proved to have an excellent fit for the data set. Result revealed that the associations between competition over "who had suffered more," willingness to forgive and higher

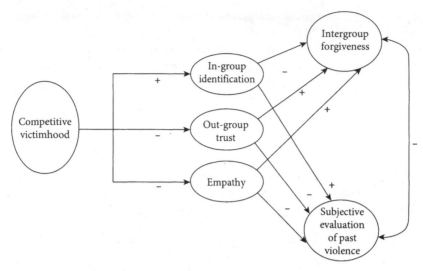

FIGURE 5.1. Model of the effects of competitive victimhood on intergroup forgiveness and subjective evaluation of past violence, displaying out-group trust, empathy, and in-group identity as potential mediators.

levels of justifying past in-group violence were fully mediated. The mediational analyses showed that out-group trust was the strongest reliable mediator of the relationships between competitive victimhood, intergroup forgiveness, and subjective evaluation of past violence. That is, less competition over victimhood was linked to higher level of trusting the out-group, which, in turn, was associated with more forgiveness and less legitimizing of in-group violence. In-group identity was also an effective mediator of the relationships between competitive victimhood, forgiveness, and subjective evaluation of past violence. In other words, more competition over victimhood was associated with increased in-group identification that in turn was related to more subjective evaluation of past in-group violence, and less willingness to forgive. In contrast, empathy functioned mainly as a direct predictor of intergroup forgiveness, and a marginally significant predictor of subjective evaluation of past violence, in the model. There was no significant relationship between competitive victimhood and empathy toward the out-group. It is noteworthy that the above model displayed excellent fit indices (i.e., the model was a good description of the data set). Nevertheless, we do not rule out the existence of a set of bidirectional relationships among the above precursors of intergroup reconciliation. Such bidirectionality would make sense intuitively. For example, higher levels of forgiveness could potentially lead to higher levels of trust, which in turn reduce defensiveness or competition over victimhood. In fact, the investigation of the reverse direction may be necessary to reveal the full richness of the above reconciliation precursors and their dynamic relations. However, for the purpose of this study, we were particularly interested in the prediction of intergroup forgiveness and subjective evaluation of past violence conceptualized above as the most distinct positive and negative precursor of intergroup reconciliation, respectively.

Study 4

In a related strand of work, we sought to understand the origins of reparative behavior in the minds of a dominant majority. This work was set in the context of indigenous-nonindigenous relations in Chile and focused particularly on the self-conscious emotions of collective guilt and collective shame (Branscombe, Slugoski, & Kappen, 2004; Lickel, Schmader, & Barquissan, 2004). Although often regarded as synonyms in everyday language use, theoretically, guilt and shame can be distinguished and may have importantly distinctive consequences for reconciliation attempts. Drawing on Tangney's (1991) distinction, we conceived of collective *guilt* as the awareness that one's own group has committed some illegitimate acts toward another group, either recently or in the distant past. The (negative) emotion evoked focuses on the nature of the acts themselves and on the consequences of those acts for the "victim" group. It is thought to lead to restitutive behaviors (e.g., apologies, material reparation) in an attempt to alleviate that negative emotion. The emotion of collective *shame*, on the other hand, while starting from the same premise (awareness of culpability for some in-group action), focuses more on the consequences of those acts for the public image of the in-group and how that in-group's "character" might thus be "spoiled." The end result might well be some psychological or actual avoidance of the situation or out-group that gave rise to the emotion. Theoretically, at least, collective guilt would seem to offer better initial prospects for opening doors to reconciliation than collective shame.

In two longitudinal studies, we have examined the consequences of collective guilt and shame among nonindigenous Chilean adolescents (Brown, Gonzalez, Zagefka, Manzi & Cehajic, in press). In both we find that cross-sectionally (i.e., contemporaneously) both emotions are independently and positively correlated with a desire to make reparation to the Mapuche (e.g., government apology and economic assistance to Mapuche communities). However, over time, and in periods ranging from 8 weeks to 6 months, only collective *guilt* was a reliable predictor of subsequent reparation attitudes, when controlling for initial reparation attitudes; that is, the more collective guilt was experienced the more attitudes attempting to repair the damage were elicited. Moreover, there were indications that collective shame interacted with collective guilt to inhibit its beneficial consequences; that is, respondents who reported high levels of shame showed weaker longitudinal associations between guilt and reparation than those who reported lower levels of shame. These findings indicate a causal role for collective guilt in stimulating reparative and reconciliatory attitudes in groups that have historically been the "perpetrators" of negative actions toward out-groups. Further work is examining these same relationships in former Yugoslavia (Brown & Cehajic, in press).

Conclusion

Social psychology has only recently embraced the concept of intergroup reconciliation. In this chapter, our main contribution to the social-psychological understanding of research topic has been to identify the positive and negative precursors of reconciliation. We established some cross-cultural validation of these precursors by conducting studies in Northern Irish and Chilean contexts that are characterized by decades of intergroup hostility and violence between different political and ethnic groups. In addition, a model of reconciliation orientation in Northern Ireland was developed and tested successfully. Finally, we reported findings from longitudinal studies examining the predictive power of two self-conscious emotions, namely, guilt and shame, in relation to desire to engage in reparative behaviors by the advantaged nonindigenous majority toward the indigenous Mapuche minority.

Most of our tested precursors proved to be both meaningful to our research participants and predictive, positively or negatively, of reconciliatory orientation (i.e., forgiveness) or reparative behavior. Overall, we found that while common in-group identity, out-group trust, empathy can function as positive predictors of intergroup forgiveness, in-group identity and competitive victimhood can predict forgiveness, negatively. In our reconciliation orientation model tested in Northern Ireland, we demonstrated that the associations between competitive victimhood, intergroup forgiveness and subjective evaluation of past violence were fully mediated. Out-group trust and in-group identity were among the strongest mediators of these associations, while empathy functioned mainly as a predictor of forgiveness. Regarding the self-conscious emotions, despite the positive correlation between guilt and shame, guilt predicted reparation over time better than shame.

Implications

Our research agenda reviewed above hopes to engage both researchers and practitioners equally in future investigation and facilitation of the process of intergroup reconciliation. It is hoped that the findings reported here will stimulate social psychologists and researchers from other disciplines to solidify these results by validating them in different intergroup contexts and exploring their causal relationships. Regarding the task of practitioners, on the one hand, it is hoped that guided by the above and continuing research on reconciliation; practitioners of peace building could focus on the difficult task of developing practical strategies to promote some of the above positive precursors of reconciliation among conflicted communities. On the other hand, practitioners could also attempt to find ways of preventing conflicted groups from engaging in behaviors and attitudes that include elements of the negative precursors of reconciliation that will consequently maintain the cycle of violent conflict.

However, it is also important to be cautious. Some of our variables, such as competitive victimhood, were negative predictors of intergroup forgiveness. This would seem to indicate that engagement in conflict mediation would do well to avoid too much concentration on past suffering by either side. Nevertheless, in many contexts the understanding and validation of victims' experiences might be the very necessary conditions that might offer insights to researchers, practitioners, and more importantly, the victims and their wrongdoers themselves, about the major processes leading to victimization, and its impact on the parties in conflict and on society in general (for a discussion on victimhood, see Shaw, 2003).

Equally, it is not at all clear whether exclusive concentration on collective guilt will always lead to desires for reparation by the discriminating group; that is, although above findings suggest that guilt might open the door to further reconciliatory processes; nevertheless, it is possible to imagine that too frequent reminders of in-group culpability might eventually lead to the emotion of collective shame in the perpetrator group. This is plausible since repeated experiences of guilt may lead the wrongdoers to believe that they actually cannot change their behaviors and that immutable internal characteristics might be ultimately responsible for such behaviors. Still, as an initial step in the process toward reconciliation, some awareness of collective guilt would seem to be useful, if for no other reason than that it has been found to be associated with a desire to apologize to the victim group (Brown et al., in press; McGarty et al., 2005). Thus, while the diversity of social-psychological variables identified here still await further examination in other contexts to assess their utility to predict forgiveness and reconciliation, we believe that they may offer researchers and practitioners alike some useful hints for their work. Still, as always, as social psychologists and as concerned citizens, we should remain cautious about too hasty an extrapolation to the real world, if only to spare already traumatized groups the adverse effects of premature application of research findings.

References

Alexander, R. J. (1978). *The tragedy of Chile.* UK: Greenwood Press.

Bar-Siman-Tov, Y. (2004). *From conflict resolution to reconciliation.* New York: Oxford University Press, Inc.

Bar-Tal, D., & Bennink, G. H. (2004). The nature of reconciliation as an outcome and as a process. In Y. Bar-Siman-Tov (Ed.), *From conflict resolution to reconciliation* (pp. 11-38). New York: Oxford University Press, Inc.

Branscombe, N. R., & Doosje, B. (2004). *Collective guilt international perspectives.* Cambridge, UK: Cambridge University Press.

Branscombe, N. R., Slugoski, B., & Kappen, D. M. (2004). The measurement of collective guilt: what it is and what it is not. In N. Branscombe & B. Doosje (Eds.), *Collective guilt: International perspectives* (pp. 16-34). Cambridge, UK: Cambridge University Press.

Brewer, M. B., & Brown, R. J. (1998). Intergroup relations. In D. T. Gilbert, S. T. Fiske, & G. Lindzey (Eds.), *Handbook of social psychology* (pp. 554-594). New York: McGraw-Hill.

Brown, R., & Cehajic, S. (in press). Dealing with the past and facing the future: Mediators of collective guilt and shame in Bosnia Herzegovina. *European Journal of Social Psychology.*

Brown, R. J., Condor, S., Mathews, A., Wade, G., & Williams, J. A. (1986). Explaining intergroup differentiation in an industrial organisation. *Journal of Occupation Psychology, 59,* 273-286.

Brown, R., Gonzalez, R., Zagefka, H., Manzi, J., & Cehajic, S. (in press). Nuestra culpa: Collective guilt as a predictor of reparation for historical wrongdoing. *Journal of Personality and Social Psychology.*

Darby, J., & Mac Ginty, R. (2000). *The management of peace processes.* London: Macmillan Press Ltd.

Dixon, P. (2001). *Northern Ireland the politics of war and peace.* New York: Palgrave.

Enright, R. D., & North, J. (1998). *Exploring forgiveness.* Madison, WI: University of Wisconsin Press.

Ensalaco, M. (2000). *Chile under Pinochet.* Philadelphia, PA: University of Pennsylvania Press.

Fay, M. T., Morrissey, M., & Smyth, M. (1999). *Northern Ireland's troubles: The human costs.* London: Pluto Press.

Hewstone, M., Cairns, E., Voci, A., McLernon, F., Niens, U., & Noor, M. (2004). Intergroup forgiveness and guilt in Northern Ireland: Social psychological dimensions of "The Troubles." In N. R. Branscombe & B. Doosje (Eds.), *Collective guilt international perspectives* (pp. 193-215). Cambridge, UK: Cambridge University Press.

Hewstone, M., Rubin, M., & Willis, H. (2002). Intergroup bias. *Annual Review of Psychology, 53,* 575-604.

Instituto Nacional de Estadística (2002). *Estadísticas sociales de los pueblos indígenas en Chile.* Santiago: Gobierno de Chile.

Kelly, G., & Hamber, H. (2005). *Reconciliation: Rhetoric or relevant?* Democratic Dialogue Report 17. Belfast: The Northernwhig Ltd.

Kelman, H. C. (2004). Reconciliation as identity change: A social-psychological perspective. In Y. Bar-Siman-Tov (Ed.), *From conflict resolution to reconciliation* (pp. 81-124). New York: Oxford University Press, Inc.

Lederach, J. P. (1997). *Building peace: Sustainable reconciliation in divided societies.* Washington, DC: United States Institute of Peace Press.

Lickel, B., Schmader, T., & Barquissan, M. (2004). The evocation of moral emotions in intergroup contexts: The distinction between collective guilt and collective shame. Collective guilt: International perspectives. In N. R. Branscombe & B. Doosje (Eds.), *Collective guilt international perspectives* (pp. 35-55). Cambridge, UK: Cambridge University Press.

McCullough, M. E. (2001). Forgiveness: Who does it and how do they do it? *Current Directions in Psychological Science, 10,* 194-197.

McCullough, M. E., Rachal, K. C., Sandage, S. J., Worthington, E. L. Jr., Brown, S. W., & Hight, T. (1998). Interpersonal forgiving in close relationships: II. Theoretical elaboration and measurement. *Journal of Personality & Social Psychology, 75,* 1586-1603.

McGarty, C., Pederson, A., Leach, C. W., Mansell, T., Waller, J., & Bliuc, A.-M. (2005). Group-based guilt as a predictor of commitment to apology. *British Journal of Social Psychology, 44*(4), 645-657.

Ministerio de Planificación y Cooperación (2003). *Informe comisión de verdad histórica y nuevo trato de los pueblos indígenas.* Santiago: Gobierno de Chile.

Mitchell, C. (2000). *Gestures of Conciliation factors contributing to successful olive branches.* London: Macmillan Press Ltd.

Morrow, D. (2001). Forgiveness and reconciliation response. In B. Hamber, D. Kulle, & R. Wilson (Eds.), *Future policies for the past.* Belfast: Democratic Dialogue.

Nadler, A. (2003). Post resolution processes: an instrumental and socio-emotional routes to reconciliation. In G. Salomon & B. Nevo (Eds.), *Peace education worldwide: The concept, underlying principles, and research* (pp. 127-143). Mawheh, NJ: Erlbaum.

Nadler, A., & Liviatan, I. (2004). Intergroup reconciliation processes in Israel: Theoretical analysis and empirical findings. In N. R. Branscombe & B. Doosje (Eds.), *Collective guilt international perspectives* (pp. 216-235). Cambridge, UK: Cambridge University Press.

Noor, M., Brown, R., & Prentice, G. (in press). Precursors and mediators of intergroup reconciliation in Northern Ireland. *British Journal of Social Psychology.*

Police Service for Northern Ireland (2005). *Statistics, security situation and public order.* http://www.psni.police.uk/

Report of the Chilean National Commission on Truth and Reconciliation (1993). US: Centre for Civil & Human Rights Notre Dame Law School, Vol. 1.

Roniger, L., & Sznajder, M. (1999). *The legacy of human-rights violations in the Southern Cone.* Oxford: Oxford University Press.

Rosenberg, M. (1957). Occupation and values. In J. P. Robinson, P. R. Shaver, & L. S. Wrightsman (1991). *Measures of personality and social psychology attitudes.* London: Academic Press, Inc.

Saiz, J.-L. (2002). Atribución de estereotipos: Los indígenas mapuches que perciben los chilenos. In J. F. Morales, D. Páez, A. L. Kornblit, & D. Asún. *In Psicología social* (pp. 145-151). Buenos Aires: Prentice Hall-Pearson Education.

Scobie, E. D., & Scobie, G. E. W. (1998). Damaging events: The perceived need for forgiveness. *Journal for the Theory of Social Behaviour, 28,* 373-401.

Shaw, M. (2003). *War and genocide.* Cambridge, UK: Polity Press.

Takaku, S., Weiner, B., & Ohbuchi, K. (2001). A cross-cultural examination of the effects of apology and perspective taking on forgiveness. *Journal of Language and Social Psychology, 20,* 144-166.

Tangney, J. P. (1991). Moral affect: The good, the bad, and the ugly. *Journal of Personality and Social Psychology, 61,* 598-607.

Voci, A., & Hewstone, M. (2003). Contact & prejudice reduction in the Italian context: The impact of empathy, perspective-taking, and group salience. *Paper presented at the Meeting of the Society for Experimental Social Psychology.* Boston, MA.

Wohl, M. J. A., & Branscombe, N. R. (2005). Forgiveness and collective guilt assignment to historical perpetrator groups depend on level of social category inclusiveness. *Journal of Personality and Social Psychology, 88,* 288-303.

Part II.B

Restoring Respect and Esteem

CHAPTER 6

How Needs Can Motivate Intergroup Reconciliation in the Face of Intergroup Conflict

FELICIA PRATTO AND DEMIS E. GLASFORD

It is easy for those who study oppression and intergroup inequality to describe situations and processes that incite intergroup discrimination and conflict, and to list barriers to intergroup reconciliation. Such barriers include the presumption that resources are scarce and that groups are in conflict over them (e.g., Bobo, 1988; Sherif, 1966), ideologies that legitimize prejudice, group segregation (e.g., Pratto, Stallworth, & Conway-Lanz, 1998), and the positioning of high-prejudice people in offices that hold the power to maintain group-based inequality (e.g., Altemeyer, 1988, 1996; Pratto & Espinoza, 2001). A plethora of theories, identifying conditions and processes at the individual, group, intergroup, societal, and cultural levels and their interactions explain the many obstacles to peace.

In comparison to the volume of knowledge about intergroup conflict, research on the theoretical approaches to intergroup reconciliation, "a societal process that involves mutual acknowledgment of past suffering and the changing of destructive attitudes and behaviors into constructive relationships toward sustainable peace" (Brouneus, 2003, p. 20) is less abundant. The commonality of intergroup conflict suggests that deliberate intervention may be required to promote intergroup reconciliation. Deliberate intervention efforts, including intergroup dialog and problem solving (Kelman, 1990; Kelman & Fisher, 2003; Ross & Rothman, 1999; Rouhana & Kelman, 1994), peace education (Salomon & Nevo, 2002), and intergroup contact (Allport, 1954; Cook, 1970; Pettigrew & Tropp, 2000) have been shown to promote reconciliation. However, little research has explored the possibility that the very conditions that foster and support intergroup conflict may be able to promote intergroup reconciliation.

This chapter entertains the thesis that intergroup conflict may incite needs that can be met through intergroup reconciliation. In particular, we review research that suggests that three needs that are particularly salient during intergroup conflict, the need for self-esteem, the need to belong, and the need for self-integrity, can also be fulfilled through intergroup reconciliation. In other words, intergroup conflict may motivate social-psychological needs that can be conducive to intergroup reconciliation. Of course, some of these same needs can also motivate intergroup prejudice, stereotyping, discrimination, and hostility. It is important, then, to explain both the particular needs and circumstances that may motivate intergroup reconciliation.

In essence, our argument has three parts. First, we argue that intergroup conflict implies that each group is harming the other, even if intergroup power and the harm done is asymmetric. Such harm may be measured in many ways, such as in lives lost or shortened, property stolen or destroyed, poverty, ill health, hopelessness, alienation, or vilification. In cases of sustained domination, such primary harms often result in secondary harms that come from the reaction of subordinated peoples to oppression, such as substance abuse, domestic violence, and high rates of intragroup violence (e.g., Jackman, 2001; Sidanius & Pratto, 1999, pp. 227-262). Second, we argue that such forms of harm then create or heighten particular psychological needs (in addition to medical, physical, economic, and other needs). Specifically, for both the harmed party and the harm-doing party, violence and conflict can heighten the need for self-esteem, the need to belong, and the need for self-integrity at both individual and group levels. Indeed, killing innocents and inflicting harm on others threatens one's self-image as being good, one's standing within the group or community, and one's sense of having principles. For example, some Israelis have argued that the Israeli oppression of Palestinians in the name of Zionism is a threat to Israel's integrity because these policies subvert Jewish ethics (e.g., Lazare, 2003). Similarly, many Americans voiced strong opposition to the wars in Vietnam and Iraq out of fear that America's integrity would be damaged through these military operations. Experiencing harm also induces the three identity needs. For example, being a victim of domestic violence contributes to depression and low self-esteem (Sussex & Corcoran, 2005). Discrimination against African Americans in employment, housing, and the criminal justice system tears at the integrity of African Americans' bodies (e.g., Blascovich, Spencer, Quinn, & Steele, 2001; Krieger & Sidney, 1996) and harms their ability to belong by harming their families and neighborhoods (Mauer & Huling, 1995). Third and finally, there are circumstances in which these needs may motivate intergroup reconciliation because intergroup reconciliation is one way that these needs can be met, particularly following intergroup conflict.

To reveal the path from conflict to reconciliation amid its pitfalls, we first explain each need and how it pertains to intergroup relations generally. Because some theoretical approaches have not made the distinctions among needs that we make here, we also delineate the needs by showing how they can be in competition in particular intergroup circumstances. As we will show, although the three needs we have identified may contribute to further intergroup discrimination and conflict, there are also particular circumstances in which these needs can motivate intergroup reconciliation. Indeed, Staub (2003) has begun to examine the role that basic human needs can play in the reconciliation process. In sum, in this chapter we will consider the circumstances in which each of three needs (i.e., the need for self-esteem, the need to belong, and the need for self-integrity) may motivate intergroup reconciliation. We will first provide a brief description of how each need has been shown to relate to intergroup relations and then provide a more detailed analysis of how the need can motivate reconciliation in both perpetrators and victims.

Basic Social Needs Relevant to Intergroup Relations

The Need for Self-esteem

Psychologists widely recognize that individuals have a *need for self-esteem*, that is, to feel that they are worthy, good, and valuable people (e.g., Leary, Tambor, Terdal, & Downs, 1995; Taylor & Brown, 1988). When people do not feel esteem, this need motivates behavior to meet the need. One important way this need can be met is by downward comparison, that is, by comparing oneself to others who are worse in some way than oneself (Wills, 1981). People can also meet their needs for self-esteem by identifying with a prestigious group (Tajfel & Turner, 1986).

These processes may help individuals meet their need for self-esteem. However, they can have detrimental consequences for intergroup relations. In particular, a variety of experiments on artificial and natural groups find that the more people identify with their own groups, the more likely they are to derogate those in other groups and the less likely they are to share resources with them (see Jetten, Spears, & Postmes, 2004; Mullen, Brown, & Smith, 1992 for reviews). Threats to individuals' self-esteem can also directly lead to behaviors that are detrimental to intergroup reconciliation, respect, and equality. For example, when Fein and Spencer (1997) provided negative feedback to their participants, participants were more likely to apply negative ethnic stereotypes to another student than when not given negative feedback. Similarly, on an implicit measure, participants who valued group dominance became more group-prejudiced when their group's high status was questioned (Pratto & Shih, 2000). Threatening individuals' self-esteem works against intergroup reconciliation, to say the least.

The question for intergroup reconciliation then, is whether high self-esteem protects against intergroup discrimination and prejudice. For example, Crocker and Major (1989) found that African Americans have expressed higher self-esteem than European Americans for decades, and they theorized that this is an active, self-protective response to racial stigmatization. Expressed high self-esteem may, however, mask self-esteem that is in doubt (Jordan, Spencer, Zanna, Hoshiko-Browne, & Correll, 2003), and it is that situation that would make people most likely to derogate others. In fact, Jordan, Spencer, and Zanna (2005) showed that, following negative feedback, those with high expressed self-esteem but low implicit self-esteem severely punished a Native American, but not a European American, who had started a fistfight. Here, insecure self-esteem triggered ethnically biased retribution. When self-esteem is so high as to be considered inflated and an immediate situation or person threatens that view, people often respond with violence (Baumeister, Smart, & Boden, 1996).

On the whole, then, there is both situational and personality evidence that people who experience threats to esteem, personally or through the groups they identify with, are more likely to discriminate against other groups and be prejudiced against them. However, we have found no evidence that high self-esteem is conducive to intergroup reconciliation. To the extent that in-group superiority helps meet self-esteem needs for people in superior groups, and especially to the extent their self-esteem is insecure, we would not expect that it would.

The Need to Belong

A second fundamental social need is the *need to belong* (cf. Baumeister & Leary, 1995). That is, individuals need to feel that there are others from whom they derive a sense of belonging or acceptance in affiliation. For highly social creatures such as humans, this sense of belonging increases security and decreases anxiety. To meet this need, a healthy community or set of possible others must exist and be accessible to individuals. Although people's most important community often is relatively local (e.g., their family, neighbors, friends, school, or house of worship), people are capable of defining communities in myriad ways, including broad ones that include nonlocal individuals that one does not know personally. Moreover, people can understand themselves to belong to many distinctive or only partially overlapping communities. The breadth or narrowness of the inclusiveness of one's community is an important cultural and individual difference, and, as we show subsequently, has implications for intergroup reconciliation. This variability does not obliterate the fact that the need to belong is central to intergroup relations. Research has shown that this need can motivate both intergroup prejudice and the desire for intergroup forgiveness and peace.

The potentially harmful consequences of the need to belong are illustrated in the considerable research that suggests that a feeling of not belonging and the anxiety that can come with that experience motivates prejudice against other groups, especially against those vilified by cultural ideologies. For example, authoritarian personality theory postulates that those most likely to develop an authoritarian, prejudicial personality are those raised by parents who express disapproval of their own children (Adorno, Frenkel-Brunswik, Levinson, & Sanford, 1950). In fact, people high on authoritarianism experience higher levels of chronic threat and anxiety, and are more sensitive to environmental threat sources, such as terrorism (e.g., Feldman & Stenner, 1997). In other words, the anxiety associated with an unmet need to belong, characterizes those high in authoritarianism, who are robustly prejudiced against a variety of out-groups (e.g., Altemeyer, 1996).

Research in other paradigms has confirmed that anxiety is related to the need to belong and that prejudice can result from the need to belong. Terror management theory postulates that human beings experience *existential anxiety* when confronted with the fact of their own mortality. The theory postulates that to keep this anxiety at bay, people bolster cultural worldviews that position their lives as having meaning. When individuals are made aware of their own mortality in experiments (e.g., by describing what will happen to their bodies when they die), the anxiety associated with *mortality salience* leads people to bolster their connections to similar others (e.g., Greenberg et al., 1990; Schimel et al., 1999). Unfortunately, mortality salience can also lead people to distance themselves from dissimilar others. For example, Christian students did not discriminate between a Christian and a Jewish student in a control condition, but following mortality salience, they denigrated the Jewish student and praised the Christian one (Greenberg et al., 1990, Study 1). While increasing their belonging with a Christian, they distanced themselves from a Jew. Further, there is evidence that existential anxiety brought on by mortality salience manipulations increase the need to belong. For example, mortality salience induces affiliative behavior (Wisman & Koole, 2003). People who are securely attached, that is, who have a strong habitual sense of belonging with others, are less vulnerable to mortality salience manipulations than insecurely attached people (e.g., Mikulincer & Florian, 2000).

The finding that being high in anxiety (and lacking a sense of belonging with others) provokes group prejudice has a corollary: those who do feel they belong with others, who strive to belong or identify with many others, that is, those high in empathy, are generally less group-prejudiced than those low in empathy (e.g., Pedersen, Beven, Walker, & Griffiths, 2004; Pratto, Lemieux, Glasford, & Henry, 2003; Pratto, Sidanius, Stallworth, & Malle, 1994). Similarly, individuals higher in the need to belong were more likely to cooperate with their own group members in a public goods dilemma, especially when in a large (vs. small) group (DeCremer & Leondardelli, 2003). Expanding group boundaries to be more inclusive can help to change the sense of belonging. Indeed, research finds that recategorizing members of an out-group as part of a more inclusive in-group leads people to want the out-group members to be treated more favorably (Esses, Dovidio, Jackson, & Armstrong, 2001; Gaertner, Dovidio, & Bachman, 1996).

Intergroup reconciliation can be fostered by increasing the need to belong with others in general such that enemies as well as in-group members are included in the superordinate category. For example, Wohl and Branscombe (2005) had participants consider the basic humanity of groups who histori-cally perpetrated oppression against their groups: Germans for Jewish North Americans, and Whites for Native Canadians. Doing so led participants to greater forgiveness of the perpetrator group and lowered participants' expecta-tions that the perpetrator group should feel guilty.

This review shows that those with an unmet need to belong: those who are insecurely attached, authoritarian, low in empathy or a sense of belonging, and/ or whose mortality has been made salient are likely to be group-prejudiced and discriminatory against out-groups. However, the review also demonstrates that under the right conditions, the need to belong can also be made to foster personal guilt, forgiveness of out-group perpetrators, acceptance of others, the desire to connect with others, as well as other affiliative behaviors. Providing people with a way to be inclusive of others can utilize the need to belong toward the goal of intergroup reconciliation.

The Need for Self-integrity

A third fundamental need related to intergroup reconciliation is for self-integrity. This concept is known under other names in many psychological the-ories. William James (1890) described identity as the "continuing sense of self as known." Consistency in self-image across time and situation, then, is one sense of self-integrity. Leon Festinger (1957) hypothesized that cognitive dissonance, a disagreement between parts of the self, such as between one's attitudes and behavior, produces an uncomfortable state of arousal that motivates a change to bring various aspects of the self into alignment. Stone and Cooper (2001) reframed dissonance theory in terms of violations of self-standards, also clearly relevant to self-integrity. Self-discrepancy theory (Higgins, 1987) stipulates that discrepancies between who one believes one actually is (the "actual self") and who one desires to be or believes one ought to be (the "ideal self" and the "ought self") create particular emotional difficulties. Pennebaker (1999) has shown that integrating injured parts of the self into the whole, such as by writing about past traumatic experiences, can enable people to heal to such a degree that their physical ailments decrease and their life spans increase. Steele's (1988) self-affirmation theory suggests that affirming one's self worth can help make the self feel more whole. What all these theories have in common is the idea that having an integrated, self-consistent, whole self is fundamental to well-being, and that certain unpleasant emotions signal a breach in self-integrity.

The drive for self-integrity can have very negative effects on intergroup relations. Castano and Giner-Sorolla (2006) had various groups review information about how their group (e.g., White Australians) had been responsible for the death of many out-group members in the past (e.g., Australian aborigines). When those deaths were attributed to deliberate actions (e.g., warfare), rather than to accidents (e.g., disease contagion), members of the homicidal group implicitly dehumanized members of the out-group, an effect not found when the deaths were said to be accidental. In these experiments, the apparent desire for self-integrity led people to prejudice, which in turn helped justify, post-hoc, historical oppression by their ancestors.

Although self-integrity motives may foster prejudice, calling upon self-integrity by reminding individuals of personal standards can lead them to take active efforts to reduce prejudice. A number of studies and surveys have examined how people low and high in group prejudice feel they would and should respond when in contact with a member of an out-group, for example, Blacks (Devine, Monteith, Zuwerink, & Elliot, 1991; Zuwerink, Monteith, Devine, & Cook, 1996) and gay men (Jacks & Devine, 2002). Those who reported a discrepancy between how they should feel and how they actually would feel in such an encounter experienced discomfort, the emotion that signals a threat to their self-integrity. People low in prejudice feel guilty and self-critical following discrepancy and strive to bring their behavior in line with their ideals (Devine et al., 1991; Zuwerink et al., 1996). In contrast, when people high in prejudice transgress their own standards about prejudice, they feel negatively about *others* (Monteith, Devine, & Zuwerink, 1993). Self-integrity appears most likely to help bring about intergroup reconciliation among people already low in prejudice.

A practical concern, then, is whether one must rely only on nonprejudiced individuals to act in ways that lead toward intergroup reconciliation, or whether there are conditions that encourage even prejudiced people toward intergroup reconciliation.

Fortunately, there is some experimental evidence that certain conditions can harness the need for self-integrity toward intergroup reconciliation. The self-affirmation procedure, in which participants choose among values and write about why one value is important to them, is said to affirm self-integrity (Steele, 1988). This procedure has been shown to reduce prejudice. Fein and Spencer (1997) found that individuals showed less stereotypic evaluations toward an out-group member after they had affirmed their own values on dimensions having nothing to do with justice, equality, or tolerance. Bolstering self-integrity with the self-affirmation procedure can also prevent out-group-directed blame for uncomfortable feelings, such as collective guilt (Monteith et al., 1993; Pedersen et al., 2004). After watching a videotape about civil rights, White students supported programs for Blacks following a self-affirmation procedure, but opposed programs for Blacks if they performed a filler task after the videotape (Harvey & Oswald, 2000). Evidently, the self-affirmation process helps to bolster self-integrity enough that people feel the need to rectify wrongs committed by their group. Thus, there is evidence that appealing to self-integrity can help to reduce prejudice and lead to reconciliation.

Just as with self-esteem (e.g., Luhtanen & Crocker, 1991), self-integrity processes can operate at both the individual and group levels and at their interface. At the individual level, research on self-discrepancy theory has found that people feel depressed when there is a discrepancy between their *actual* self-image and their *ideal* self-image, and feel anxious or agitated when there is a discrepancy between their *actual* self-image and their *ought* self-image (e.g., Higgins, 1987). Bizman, Yinon, and Krotman (2001) showed that when Israelis experienced discrepancies among their actual, ought, and ideal images of Israelis, they showed the same patterns of emotions as have been found when individuals consider discrepancies among their actual, ought, and ideal images of their personal selves (e.g., Higgins, 1987). Those with a discrepancy between what they believed should be the ideal behavior of Israelis and the actual behavior of Israelis felt dejection and lower private collective self-esteem. Those with a discrepancy between what they believed Israelis ought to do and the actual behavior of Israelis felt agitated. Thus, individuals' emotional responses to a breach of their group's integrity mirror how people feel when they experience a threat to personal integrity, suggesting that motivations for self-integrity can operate at the group level.

But self-integrity and group integrity can be at odds, and if one's group puts into question one's self-integrity, it is difficult to maintain identification with one's group. In the study by Bizman et al. (2001), participants with an actual-ought discrepancy concerning Israelis feared negative evaluations of Israelis to the extent they *disidentified* with Israelis. That is, those with enough self-integrity to admit a discrepancy between what their group is like and what it ought to be like could not also maintain strong identification with the group. Studies using quite different methods have also shown this tension between self-integrity and identification with one's group. When racial inequality within the United States was framed to White participants as about White *privilege* rather than about Black *disadvantage*, Whites felt more collective guilt and identified less with their race (Powell, Branscombe, & Schmitt, 2005, Experiment 2). Presumably, the White privilege frame was more difficult to reconcile with other important group beliefs than the Black disadvantage frame. Similarly, Doosje, Branscombe, Spears, and Manstead (1998, Study 2) found that the descendants of groups historically guilty of extreme discrimination against colonized groups, in this case, the Dutch, were more willing to acknowledge collective guilt and to favor compensating the harmed group (Indonesians) to the extent they did *not* identify strongly with their own group.

Because most people have both a desire for self-integrity and loyalties to their social groups, it is difficult to know which motive will influence their behavior most. For example, in an experiment conducted at the outbreak of the U.S-led invasion of Iraq in 2003, American and British participants were asked to make policy decisions about the conduct of that war. Choices were between certain and uncertain outcomes that would either save lives or lose lives for nationals of the United States, Iraq, or Britain (Pratto, Glasford, & Hegarty, 2006). Participants who were most strongly opposed to the war actually refused to make these decisions, in defiance of experimenters' instructions and bucking the social norm of the situation. Such behavior showed high self-integrity because it was compatible with their attitudes. Another form of self-consistency was shown in that participants' decisions reflected their degrees of nationalism and ethnocentrism.

For the 91% of participants who did make choices, the typical decision pattern of choosing uncertain deaths and choosing to save lives with certainty was reversed when Iraqi lives were pitted against either American or British lives. That is, when people believed that group outcomes were in competition, more of them chose certain deaths for the enemy rather than the possibility of deaths for their nation or their ally, and more participants hesitated to save enemy lives for sure. Part of the difficulty in expecting self-integrity to lead people to make humanitarian decisions, then, is that situations can put those values into conflict with other values, such as protecting the in-group. What seems critical, then, is how much the intergroup situation has been framed in ways that draw on values conducive to intergroup reconciliation versus values that are conducive to further conflict.

On the whole, then, let us summarize when we can expect self-integrity to improve intergroup relations or make them worse. People's values and attitudes relevant to intergroup relations do reliably differ and at least partially determine their support for policies that improve or worsen intergroup relations (e.g., Pratto et al., 1994, 1998). For people low in prejudice, high in empathy, and who identify with more inclusive groups (e.g., human), we can expect behavior that is motivated toward intergroup reconciliation, especially because they are willing to disidentify with their discriminatory groups, in favor of upholding a more inclusive, humanitarian, or principled value. But people high in prejudice, who value loyalty to their in-group, will serve their own self-integrity by maintaining group distance and perhaps group domination. Thus, there is some evidence that behaviors that allow people to affirm their self-integrity can motivate people toward intergroup reconciliation.

Distinctions and Conflicts Among the Basic Needs

All three of the needs we have identified here are aspects of social identity. But their basic goals and the kinds of emotions that signal fulfillment or lack of fulfillment of these needs can be distinguished. Self-esteem is fundamentally about goodness and worth, and thus relates strongly to whether one feels fundamentally positive or negative affect toward oneself (Battle, 1980). Feelings of belonging are fundamentally about a sense of comfort and identification with a group of others. This feeling of belonging is typically fulfilled through affiliating with others or identifying with groups; however, it can transcend identity boundaries. Belongingness relates not just to feeling good or bad, but to feeling secure rather than anxious (Baumeister & Leary, 1995). Self-integrity is fundamentally about feelings of worth as a good and whole person (e.g., Steele, 1988), and therefore pertains especially to righteousness and guilt. Because self-esteem, the need to belong, and the drive for self-integrity are all arguably aspects of social identity, one might question the utility of delineating them.

One reason we find it useful to do so is that there are important intergroup situations in which these needs are in competition with one another. Research on collective guilt suggests that the need for self-integrity, which allows one to acknowledge wrongs committed by one's group, competes with the need for self-esteem and the need to belong, which are often derived through identification with the group (e.g., Doosje et al., 1998; Powell et al., 2005). Similarly, research on group-level self-discrepancies indicates that such discrepancies make it difficult to identify with the group (Bizman et al., 2001). Self-esteem, particularly collective self-esteem, is in conflict with the need to belong when there is a discrepancy between how another group views one's group and the need to be accepted by that other group (Bizman & Yinon, 2004). For this reason, we consider each need separately in outlining how they might be at play in intergroup conflict, and what situations might bring about intergroup reconciliation.

There is a second reason we delineate these identity needs separately. For many years, self-esteem, both personal and collective, was considered the root of identity motivations. However, the other two needs have motivational properties in their own right. For instance, as described above, the need to belong and other anxiety-reduction motivations can impel one to take action to feel closer to the in-group (e.g. Altemeyer, 1996; Greenberg et al., 1990). Increasing one's self-integrity can reduce stereotyping of out-group members (Fein & Spencer, 1997). Further, and as we will argue below, in intergroup situations there are many circumstances in which the need for self-esteem is in contradiction with the need for self-integrity. Of particular importance to these needs are situations in which one group has harmed another.

Implications of Identity Needs for the Possibility of Intergroup Reconciliation

Our analysis implies that it would be useful to consider how intergroup actions meet or create each need. In finding the path to intergroup reconciliation from intergroup conflict, we identify how and what potential actions individuals and groups can take in conflict situations that either meet or create further needs, and in turn how these needs can lead to reconciliation or to further conflict. Because conflict is the important situation to consider, the most important cases to examine are (1) when one's group has been harmed by another group and (2) when one's group has harmed another group. (We note that typically, each party in a conflict both harms and is harmed, so our analysis can apply to both parties to a conflict.) We consider each of these harm situations with respect to each of the three needs, and identify how various actions that people take speak to the needs and to the possibility of intergroup reconciliation.

Having Been Harmed by Another Group and the Need for Self-esteem

Being harmed by another group can damage collective self-esteem in the eyes of the harmed group (Crocker, Luhtanen, Blaine, & Broadnax, 1994) and in the eyes of others (e.g., Castano & Giner-Sorolla, 2006). If the harm comes from long-term processes, such as economic bias or institutional discrimination, the harm and its perpetrator may be harder to perceive and so, less damaging to collective self-esteem. Harm that occurs on shorter time scales often makes the harm more obvious. Without retaliation, apology, or some other esteem-restoring act, harm may damage group esteem to the point of humiliation, as in the German conquest of Poland.

Because harm is damaging to group esteem, we can expect people to have many ways to defend against that. One method is to minimize how much harm has been done. This stance may be conducive to intergroup reconciliation because it lessens the amount of guilt or compensation seemingly required by the harming group. However, it may tear at intragroup relations by marginalizing those directly harmed and alienating those sympathetic with them. Such internal politics may prevent states from taking this stance, although many instances of harm allow for diplomatic and political judgments to prescribe how much the harm is made an issue or minimized. States are concerned that their reactions to harm to their nations may set a legal or social precedent, and so have policies with respect to many intergroup harm situations. For example, British Prime Minister Tony Blair declared in 2004 that Britain would not negotiate with terrorists in Iraq for fear of encouraging more kidnappings, even though kidnapped British national, Kenneth Bigley, pleaded for Blair's rescue. Bigley was beheaded.

Another way groups may deal with the group esteem threats that follow harm is to cope well, and to take pride in that coping. For example, along with the Jews' long story of persecution is often told a story of the miraculous survival and tenacity of the Jewish people. After the September 11, 2001 attacks on the United States, the police, firefighters, emergency medical personnel, and the like who coped firsthand with the disasters were made into heroes. Virtue can be made of *surviving*. This strategy appears neither harmful nor helpful to intergroup reconciliation, as long as it does not elevate the harmed group above another group or idolize doing harm in return.

Having been harmed by another group, the harmed group may feel devalued, damaged, and subordinate. Therefore, bolstering the collective self-esteem of the harmed group may be the key to reconciliation with the perpetrators of harm. Research on the conflict between Protestants and Catholics in Northern Ireland suggests that meta-collective self-esteem can play a role in intergroup reconciliation. Leach and Williams (1999) found that the more Protestants perceived Catholics to think of Protestants in high regard, the more positive expectations they had for reduced conflict in Northern Ireland. In addition, participants with higher collective self-esteem expected less discrimination from the other group and thus were more receptive to discussing the conflict. This research suggests that restoring collective self-esteem may help foster reconciliation with an enemy. Of course, one way to bolster collective self-esteem is to derogate the enemy. Drawing on Leach and Williams's results, we posit that a more productive reconciliation intervention would attempt to bolster collective self-esteem by emphasizing that the enemy nonetheless respects or recognizes some positive qualities in one's own group. This in turn will bolster the collective self-esteem of the harmed group and foster reconciliation.

Having Been Harmed by Another Group and the Need for Belonging

Being harmed can both increase the need for belonging and increase behaviors that increase belongingness. As stated in our introduction, harm to one's group or community, that is harm to the physical (e.g., homes or neighborhood) or social (e.g., traditions or relationships) elements that permit an individual to belong to a group, often disenables people from meeting this need because their community has been damaged or destroyed. Genocides and involuntary migrations have meant that millions of people have no hometown, no family, and no familiar community. Further, because harm attacks the ability to belong stress, and anxiety are the likely results. For example, in a survey of Americans during the week of September 11, 2001, Schuster et al. (2001) found that more than 40% of adults and children experienced extreme stress symptoms (see also Silver, Holman, McIntosh, Poulin, & Gil-Rivas, 2002, for reports of longer-term stress symptoms). Most Americans remained fearful of another attack for several months (Silver et al., 2002). Similarly, research has found that many Israelis are fearful of being attacked by suicide bombers (Friedland & Merari, 1985).

Affirming pride in belonging to the in-group is another way individuals meet the need to belong, following harm. Groups often invent or re-enliven symbols and rituals to help invite positive inclusions in the group, and such symbols and rituals often heighten intergroup distinctiveness as well. For example, celebrating *Black Pride* with verbal affirmations and even personal appearance styles are some of the ways in which the African American community has responded to long-term racism. Following September 11, 2001, there was a significant increase in Americans displaying or wearing the U.S. flag and other national symbols. For subordinated groups, asserting pleasure and pride in belonging to the group, especially as an act of self-determination, communicates that they must be respected.

However, respectful reconciliation is not always the outcome of such an assertion. Where there is no *external* audience, affirmations of in-group pride may affect mainly the in-group. Where there are external audiences, those behaviors may have other implications for intergroup relations. Indeed, before *marching season* in Northern Ireland, Protestants paint curbs in Catholic neighborhoods with the colors of the Union Jack, an action interpreted by some as affirming Protestant pride, but also clearly an act of intimidation to Catholics. Assertion of group pride, especially as a kind of territorial claim to space, resources, or even to acceptable ways of being, delineates group boundaries and may therefore make reconciliation based on common identification less likely.

Because harm does attack a community, people often immediately respond through actions that help reestablish connections to members of the in-group. After the September 11, 2001, attacks on the United States, Americans reached out to friends and families, and offered aid to strangers in huge numbers. For example, people were lined up around the clock at local blood banks, which finally had to turn would-be donors away due to limited capacity. In a survey we conducted in October 2001, 93% of undergraduates surveyed had talked to their family or friends or gone to visit them after September 11, 2001 (see also Schuster et al., 2001). Because grief and other strong emotions are so prevalent in such situations, public rituals are important to rebuilding the fabric of a torn community, just as coming together after the death of a loved one is important to family members, friends, and acquaintances.

The gathering together of the community may increase desire for a group-based solution and incite approval of any group-solution proposed. Of course, war or other attacks on another group is sometimes the *solution* proposed. However, if one has been harmed by another group, the need to belong can help an individual strengthen bonds with fellow victims, *all* victims. The need to belong can also help foster an understanding of the atrocities, which has been shown to contribute to reconciliation (Staub, 2004). Indeed, research on the reconciliation process in Rwanda has found that humanizing the perpetrators of harm, which enables victims to feel more belonging with them, helps survivors learn more about the roots of genocide (Staub, 2003), which in turn is related to more positive outcomes in the reconciliation process (Staub, 2004). The results of this research suggests that increasing the ease of belonging with the enemy, by humanizing the perpetrators of harm, may make it more likely that victims of harm will participate in reconciliation processes.

Having Been Harmed by Another Group and the Need for Self-integrity

Groups not accustomed to perceiving themselves as victims or as weak may experience an especially great threat to self-integrity after being harmed by another group, simply because being harmed does not fit their collective image. In such a case, to restore their self-integrity, we would expect them to explain away the harm (e.g., as a fluke or luck), or, more likely in the case of a major harm, to rhetorically or materially elevate the potency or extremity of the group that inflicted the harm, as well as the conflict. For example, the September 11, 2001 attacks have now become, in American discourse, a category of *possible* events termed *unprecedented evil* (e.g., Unisys Corporation, 2005). Elevating the conflict to mythical proportions (such as a *culture clash* or *a war to end all wars* or the *eternal battle between good and evil* or *mother of all wars*) rhetorically may restore self-integrity by making the *cause* of the harm commensurate with the importance of the harm in the harmed group's view, but also seem likely to escalate conflict. Ironically, exalting the destructive power of the enemy may also provide a dangerous self-image to the harming group as well.

For such reasons, we expect that intergroup reconciliation has a better chance if the harmed group turns inward. First, in cases where the harm has caused grief and other strong emotions, public grief rituals, such as funerals and the naming of the dead, may be a painful, but honest way of acknowledging the harm that has been done. A second essential step would be to focus on healing from the harm as a means of restoring self-integrity. Interpersonally, having privately forgiven another makes it easier to talk with, approach, or even try to reconcile with another. People may feel more comfortable with intergroup reconciliation once they feel they have been able to heal. The Inkiko-Gacaca, the participatory justice system established in Rwanda, emphasizes both ritual and justice to bring about healing to the victims of genocide (Staub, 2003).

Another way people in harmed groups may try to restore group integrity is to affirm group values. Whether value affirmation leads to further intergroup conflict or to intergroup reconciliation depends entirely on the values affirmed, and these in turn depend on who has the most political power. Values such as *rule of law* or *human rights* may prescribe relatively conciliatory actions, especially if there is a precedent for dispute resolution or compensation, whereas values such as *we dominate* or *loyalty* prescribe that harm is returned with harm.

Affirming values within a *culture of honor* seems destined to increase and lengthen intergroup conflict. A *culture of honor* is a culture in which concerns about personal honor and cultural scripts prescribing honorable patterns of social relationships are paramount. One of the most important implications of the culture of honor for intergroup relations is that it prescribes revenge, including violence, when honor is violated (e.g., Cohen & Nisbett, 1994; Szmajke & Kubica, 2003; Vandello & Cohen, 2003). Although we have found no research directly concerning intergroup relations and the culture of honor, it is not difficult to draw parallels between many parties at war and the attitudes and behaviors endemic to a culture of honor. For example, experimental and survey research on the culture of honor shows that a woman's perceived infidelity is one of the most extreme breaches of men's honor (Vandello & Cohen, 2003). Internationally, rape and other violence against girls and women are horrifically common and are used as a means of war against the enemy culture and against men's honor (United Nations, 2002). The culture of honor script for revenge when one has been harmed is particularly likely to perpetuate intergroup violence. The Rwandan genocide of 1995 demonstrated that tit for tat violence can beget more violence within a culture of honor. One of the primary motives of the Hutu genocide of the Tutsis in 1994 was prior oppression under the Tutsi-run Belgian colony (Des Forges, 1999). Only when those in power began to stress healing rather than retribution did violence between Hutus and Tutsis diminish (Staub, 2004). For this reason, we would argue that when a group has been harmed by another group, it is necessary to restore self-integrity to further intergroup reconciliation. This is fundamentally why invoking restorative rather than retributive justice will further reconciliation.

Having Harmed Another Group and Self-esteem

When one's group has harmed another group, the impact that fact has on one's own self-esteem and on one's group's esteem depends on whether the harm is perceived to be just. This is exactly why images that convey that the enemy is both powerful and immoral, threatening and capable of harm, but fundamentally uncivilized and inhuman are so dangerous: They help proscribe harm doing as heroically saving the good from the bad. Doing harm may seem right within a cultural worldview in which the harm was deserved, restores lost honor, or restores one's rightful status or power position, and is therefore a way to raise one's esteem. Without those conditions, however, harming another group, and especially, causing harm to another group purposefully should be expected to threaten one's image as a good, moral person, and of one's group as a good, moral group. The discomfort that follows from this view motivates restoration of esteem.

One strategy for restoring self-esteem is to attempt to absolve one's group of harms it has committed or to hide ways it has helped provoke conflict and harm. These often require hiding information or strategic and biased recounting of group history. For example, for many decades, American children were taught about *Custer's last stand*, the resounding defeat of a very politically popular U.S. general and the 7th Calvary at the hands of Lakota and Cheyenne warriors. They were not taught, however, about the forced resettlements, the broken treaties, germ warfare, and numerous other atrocities that the U.S. government and settlers committed against Native Americans. This one

Native American victory at Little Big Horn appeared to balance the two sides and to justify the harsh government practices against an apparently dangerous and savage enemy. Logically, having been harmed by another, regardless of the magnitude, does not imply that one can do no harm or that everything one does is virtuous (or that every act of the harmed is in the name of self-defense). But such a description can be a powerful heuristic, perhaps because of the prevalence of *good side/bad side* portrayals in intergroup conflicts. The omission of facts and retelling of history is one strategy that is extremely problematic for intergroup reconciliation because it not only exempts the harmed group from any responsibility or power but also vilifies the other group, justifies past harm to the group, and possibly prejustifies future harm to be committed against the group.

Similarly, after perpetuating harm, collective esteem can be maintained by diminishing or failing to acknowledge the extent of harm done. Groups do this institutionally and collectively, as in the U.S. military's policy of not officially and accurately counting non-American or *enemy* war victims. However, in terms of intergroup reconciliation, a more productive way to restore self-esteem is to give the group that has harmed another group a way to acknowledge what it has done without the requirement that the group categorize itself as *bad*. One way to do exactly this is to make the roots of violence more understandable. Indeed, one of the components of the Inkiko-Gacaca in Rwanda is to educate both the perpetrators and the victims on the underlying causes of genocide (Staub, 2004). Thus, it is important for the harming group that the roots of the violence not be justified or effortlessly forgiven, but be understood, both for its own sake and for that of the other group.

Having Harmed Another Group and Need to Belong

Doing harm to another group is generally incompatible with the feeling that one belongs with that group. Often, of course, the vilification of the enemy would prevent any desire to belong with that group. However, such psychological segregation is made more difficult for combatants when in guerilla warfare because combatants and civilians are intermixed (e.g., Litz, 2005). It is instructive to note that killing another person is a risk factor for soldiers developing post-traumatic stress disorder (as well as being attacked and witnessing death; Hoge et al., 2004). Harm doing itself, even for professional soldiers, disrupts people's ability to belong with family, friends, and co-nationals, because of emotional difficulties and mental health disorders caused by the *job* (e.g., for a firsthand account of a soldier's adjustment problems, see Wellness Directory of Minnesota, 2000). The problem of soldiers being able to *belong* with nonsoldiers may be part of why militaries work so hard to build *brotherhood*, a powerful sense of belonging and loyalty to fellow combatants.

Harm doing appears to make people anxious and their need to belong may lead them to proclaim their membership in the harm-doing group. For example, many Americans raised U.S. flags to full mast as the United States began bombing Afghanistan in October, 2001. For other people, such as those high in empathy, their group doing harm is an attack on their sense of belongingness. They are more likely to display group-inclusive symbols. For example, many people flew the world flag when the United States began bombing Afghanistan. Churches, shops, and families all over Europe flew rainbow *Pax* flags before the 2003 invasion of Iraq.

Thus, for members of a group that has harmed another group, the need to belong can focus the attention of group members either inward, toward the in-group, or outward, toward the victims of harm. We would argue that when attention is focused toward the victims, the need to belong may help to encourage reconciliation with the harmed group. Specifically, focusing on the *other* as humans and attempting to include the victims as part of an inclusive broader category that includes the group that has done harm can help the reconciliation process (Wohl & Branscombe, 2005). Experiences of conflict may even increase belonging between enemies through the common experience of fear, deprivation, and injury. Indeed, Bekerman (2002) found that relations between Israelis and Palestinians were improved when the two groups participated in ceremonies that stressed the common experience (of struggle and conflict) each group had with the other. Thus, having harmed another group, the need to belong can open the door to feelings of empathy and common identity, which improves intergroup relations (Gaertner, Dovidio, Anastasio, Bachman, & Rust, 1993).

Having Harmed Another Group and Self-integrity

As we implied earlier, if one believes that harming another group is justified, is right, is prescribed, then one may feel more complete when one's group harms the other. Cultures of honor and retributive systems of justice, then, are only likely to create a cycle of violence. However, legitimizing harm and dulling the empathic pain that witnessing harm causes take an extraordinary amount of work. One kind of evidence for this assertion is that there are so many ideologies, stereotypes, justifications, and the like given to such actions that perhaps we should assume that basically, people do recognize the humanity even of their enemies. Another kind of evidence is that highly specialized training is needed to create a torturer (Huggins, Haritos-Fatouros, & Zimbardo, 2002). If people do in fact recognize each other's basic humanity, then harming another person or group, even with the belief that harm is right, provokes a self-integrity threat. One strategy for dealing with this breach is to erase the harm socially, by denying that it was harm, by denying the intention to harm, by denying the others' humanity, by identifying a theory of why the harm was desired or deserved or necessary. These kinds of strategies are afforded when groups are segregated, when particular stereotypes of the harmed group are available, when one's own actions are portrayed as reactive and defensive. These strategies likely lead to retrenchment in intergroup relations, as occurred in Rwanda (Des Forges, 1999).

The honest choice, though, is to admit that harm has been done, and to admit responsibility and fault. Such an action is rare but not fictitious. The U.S. government did admit to accidentally bombing the Chinese embassy in Sarajevo and paid reparations to the Chinese government. Although such actions have not been taken by the U.S. government in response to the prison abuse scandals in Iraq and Cuba, thousands of Americans signed Internet apologies to the world for re-electing the government responsible and did so *as Americans*. This reaction is more likely to be seen when principled self-standards are salient and when those are linked to group identity. Thus, as a group that has harmed another group, perhaps the most powerful reconciliation tool is to rule out justifications of the harm, by providing an accurate account of the events, and make the standards of the group salient to the group. In interviews conducted by Staub (2004), many Rwandans stated that during the genocide many Rwandan principles were violated and Rwandan culture had eroded. Indeed, one of the primary motives of those who had perpetrated harm was to restore the principles of Rwandan culture (Kalisa, 2002; as cited by Staub, 2004). Thus, the need for self-integrity in those that have harmed others may help reconciliation.

Using the Three Needs: Conditions and Pitfalls to Reconciliation

As we noted at the outset, intergroup conflict and oppression arise more often than intergroup reconciliation. Given the recurrence of intergroup conflict, as well as the individual, collective, and societal factors that facilitate intergroup conflict, it is likely that direct intervention will be needed to bring about intergroup reconciliation. Even though identity needs can help produce intergroup discrimination and conflict, we have also shown that utilizing the need for self-esteem, the need to belong, and the need for self-integrity prior, during, and postintervention can help move groups from conflict to reconciliation.

The conditions under which each need can lead to reconciliation differ. In addition, the relative efficacy of employing each need for intergroup reconciliation is likely to depend on whether groups consider themselves primarily harmed or primarily harm doing. The need for self-esteem, particularly collective self-esteem, can be used to move both the harmed group and the group doing harm toward reconciliation. However, to the extent that two groups in conflict bolster their group esteem through derogating the out-group, the need for self-esteem will facilitate intergroup conflict. As a result, the most effective way to use the need for self-esteem to move groups from conflict to reconciliation may be to bolster the collective self-esteem of each group by emphasizing the positive qualities or attributes each group sees in the other (e.g., Leach & Williams, 1999).

The need to belong can facilitate oppression when people distinguish themselves and their groups from others in an attempt to manage anxiety. Humanizing the *other* in the conflict can help utilize the need to belong to move groups from conflict to reconciliation. The present analysis suggests two ways that the other can be humanized (a) through information that helps victims of the conflict understand the roots of intergroup violence (e.g. Staub, 1989) and/or (b) by appealing to a common in-group (Gaertner et al., 1996).

Finally, like the other two needs, the need for self-integrity can facilitate conflict as well as reconciliation. What kind of self-image or principles or values are affirmed is the key determinant of whether the need for self-integrity leads to further conflict or reconciliation. Specifically, affirming or heightening the salience of values that prescribe revenge and retribution is likely to further violence. Conversely, affirming or heightening the salience of values that prescribe compromise, human rights, or the rule of law should lead to reconciliation.

Moreover, our analysis suggests that different approaches may be more effective with groups who considered themselves mainly harmed than with groups that consider themselves mainly to have done harm at moving them toward reconciliation. For the harm-doing group, the need for self-integrity should be the most effective need for achieving the goal of reconciliation, with the proviso that aspects of collective identity that are humanitarian, nonviolent, limit harm doing, and the like can be invoked. Specifically, emphasizing a need to restore egalitarian values and the integrity of the group, as well as highlighting the unjust consequences of committing more violence should lead to feelings of collective guilt within the group that has done the harm (Doosje et al., 1998). Further, having harmed another group, an emphasis on nonviolent values or principles should lead to a motivation to restore these values and the integrity of the group (Kalisa, 2002).

Having been harmed by another group, we would argue that the need to belong should be the most influential need to help move the group to reconcile with the harming group. This idea is supported by Baumeister and Leary (1995), who argue that belongingness motivations can help to overcome antagonistic and divisive tendencies and past histories. Indeed, Orbell, Van de Kraigt, and Dawes (1988) have shown that individuals can form attachments with others with whom they have had *oppositional* attachments. Further, Sherif, Harvey, White, Hood, and Sherif (1961) Robber's Cave studies illustrate that a past history of harm to one's group does not preclude the group from forming bonds with the harming group. Finally, research on the contact hypothesis suggests that despite a long history of being harmed by racism and discrimination, contact can reduce prejudice and biases among ethnic minorities (Tropp & Pettigrew, 2005). Findings such as these support the idea that the need to belong, the basic motivation to form bonds with others, may be the most important need to move a group that has been harmed to reconcile with a group that has harmed them.

Conclusions and Implications

As our analysis illustrates, the need for self-esteem, the need to belong, and the need for self-integrity can, in certain circumstances, increase the likelihood of successful reconciliation between groups that have harmed one another. The need for self-esteem has long been presumed to be most critical in determining the nature of intergroup relations. However, within the context of reconciliation, the need for self-esteem makes it extraordinarily difficult to respect and identify with an out-group, as well as to admit fault. In the context of a reconciliation intervention, a focus only on self-esteem could be detrimental to the goals of the exercise. We think it is of paramount importance that more research attention and diplomatic thought be given to the other two identity needs we focused on here: the need to belong, which allows people to transcend boundaries and value social connectedness, and the need for self-integrity, which allows people to behave in principled ways without identifying with other people.

Our discussion would not be complete, however, without noting the possibility of the political dynamic between leaders and their groups that also helps to prevent reconciliation. Leaders often prescribe themselves as the antidote to the fears and needs they like to publicize (e.g., Levine & Campbell, 1972). They may make *identity tests* salient to increase people's fears of belonging, announce threats in the name of protecting the people, and praise the heroism of those who fight for what the leader prescribes. This is especially effective if the leader can borrow the language and symbols of the society's favorite values so that these actions do not appear to breach group integrity. In invoking and increasing the people's needs, the leader may make himself or herself seem popular or even necessary. For instance, there is both experimental (Landau et al., 2004) and survey evidence (Willer, 2004) that job-approval ratings for U.S. President George W. Bush increased after terror warnings and other anxiety-inducing threats. Thus, increasing identity needs without actually meeting them appears to be an effective way for leaders to stay in power, and that method is not conducive to intergroup reconciliation. A more complete analysis of how the political context may encourage or prevent needs from being motivated toward intergroup reconciliation needs development along with the present theory.

On the brighter side, some significant intergroup conflicts, such as in South Africa, Northern Ireland, and Rwanda, have improved substantially and become partly conciliatory, even if none of these have realized an ideal state. An analysis of such situations might reveal lessons in how to use identity needs toward intergroup reconciliation. For example, both Black and White South Africans have a strong sense of belonging to the land as of being South Africans; this sense of belonging made it difficult to maintain separate identities. By recording and publicizing the atrocities of apartheid, South Africans reduced the esteem in which other nations held the apartheid government (e.g., Woods, 1978). Apartheid and some revolutionary practices were compared against Christian ethics so that an important source of group integrity for South Africans could not be made compatible with apartheid (e.g., Tutu, 1982). These examples are not meant to minimize the material and political aspects of the struggle, but to indicate that social-psychological motivations are a part of those aspirations.

Our hope is that, by identifying how basic human needs, which often contribute to intergroup violence, can be used to ameliorate tensions between groups, the path to intergroup reconciliation can be made more clear. Understanding the dangers along the way, as well as affirming that reconciliation can be reached using basic human motivations and by meeting basic human needs, are both necessary for those undertaking that journey.

References

Adorno, T. W., Frenkel-Brunswik, E., Levinson, D. J., & Sanford, R. N. (1950). *The authoritarian personality.* New York: W. W. Norton.
Allport, G. W. (1954). *The nature of prejudice.* Reading, MA: Addison-Wesley.
Altemeyer, B. (1988). *Enemies of freedom: Understanding right-wing authoritarianism.* San Francisco, CA: Jossey-Bass.

Altemeyer, B. (1996). *The authoritarian specter.* Cambridge, MA: Harvard University Press.

Battle, J. (1980). Relationship between self-esteem and depression among high school students. *Perceptual and Motor Skills, 51,* 157-158.

Baumeister, R. F., & Leary, M. R. (1995). The need to belong: Desire for interpersonal attachments as a fundamental human motivation. *Psychological Bulletin, 117,* 497-529.

Baumeister, R., Smart, L., & Boden, J. M. (1996). Relation of threatened egoism to violence and aggression: The dark side of high self-esteem. *Psychological Review, 103,* 5-33.

Bekerman, Z. (2002). Can education contribute to coexistence and reconciliation? Religious and national ceremonies in bilingual Palestinian-Jewish schools in Israel. *Peace & Conflict: Journal of Peace Psychology, 8,* 259-276.

Bizman, A., & Yinon, Y. (2004). Social self-discrepancies form own and other standpoints and collective self-esteem. *Journal of Social Psychology, 144,* 101-113.

Bizman, A., Yinon, Y., & Krotman, S. (2001). Group-based emotional distress: An extension of self-discrepancy theory. *Personality and Social Psychology Bulletin, 27,* 1291-1300.

Blascovich, J., Spencer, S., Quinn, D., & Steele, C. (2001). African Americans and high blood pressure: The role of stereotype threat. *Psychological Science, 12,* 225-229.

Bobo, L. (1988). Group conflict, prejudice, and the paradox of contemporary racial attitudes. In P. A. Katz & D. A. Taylor (Eds.), *Eliminating racism: Profiles in controversy* (pp. 85-114). New York: Plenum.

Brouneus, K. (2003). Reconciliation-Theory and Practice for Development Cooperation. A report for the Swedish International Development Cooperation Agency.

Castano, E., & Giner-Sorolla, R. (2006). Not quite human: Infra-humanization as a response to collective responsibility for intergroup killing. *Journal of Personality and Social Psychology, 90,* 804-818.

Cohen, D., & Nisbett, R. E. (1994). Self-protection and the culture of honor: Explaining Southern violence. *Personality and Social Psychology Bulletin, 20,* 551-567.

Cook, S. W. (1970). Motives in a conceptual analysis of attitude-related behavior. In W. J. Arnold & D. Levine's (Eds.), *Nebraska symposium on motivation, 1969* (pp. 179-231) Lincoln: University of Nebraska Press.

Crocker, J., Luhtanen, R., Blaine, B., & Broadnax, S. (1994). Collective self-esteem and psychological well being among white, black, and Asian college students. *Personality and Social Psychology Bulletin, 20,* 503-513.

Crocker, J., & Major, B. (1989). Social stigma and self-esteem: The self-protective properties of stigma. *Psychological Review, 96,* 608-630.

DeCremer, D., & Leondardelli, G. J. (2003). Cooperation in social dilemmas and the need to belong: The moderating effect of group size. *Group Dynamics, 7,* 168-174.

Des Forges, A. (1999). *Leave none to tell the story. Genocide in Rwanda.* New York: Human Rights Watch.

Devine, P. G., Monteith, M. J., Zuwerink, J. R., & Elliot, A. J. (1991). Prejudice with and without compunction. *Journal of Personality and Social Psychology, 60,* 817-830.

Doosje, B., Branscombe, N. R., Spears, R., & Manstead, A. S. R. (1998). Guilty by association: When one's group has a negative history. *Journal of Personality and Social Psychology, 75*, 872-886.

Esses, V. M., Dovidio, J. F., Jackson, L. M., & Armstrong, T. L. (2001). The immigration dilemma: The role of perceived group competition, ethnic prejudice, and national identity. *Journal of Social Issues, 57*, 389-412.

Fein, S., & Spencer, S. J. (1997). Prejudice as self-image maintenance: Affirming the self through derogating others. *Journal of Personality and Social Psychology, 73*, 31-44.

Feldman, S., & Stenner, K. (1997). Perceived threat and authoritarianism. *Political Psychology, 18*, 741-770.

Festinger, L. (1957). *A theory of cognitive dissonance.* Stanford, CA: Stanford University Press.

Friedland, N., & Merari, A. (1985). The psychological impact of terrorism: A double-edged sword. *Political Psychology, 6*, 591-604.

Gaertner, S., Dovidio, J. F., & Bachman, B. (1996). Revisiting the contact hypothesis: Induction of a common ingroup identity. *International Journal of Intercultural Relations, 20*, 271-290.

Gaertner, S. L., Dovidio, J. F., Anastasio, P. A., Bachman, B. A., & Rust, M. C. (1993). The common ingroup identity model: Recategorization and the reduction of intergroup bias. In W. Stroebe & M. Hewstone (Eds.), *European Review of Social Psychology, 4*, 1-26.

Greenberg, J., Pyszczynski, T., Solomon, S., Rosenblatt, A., Beeder, M., Kirkland, S., et al. (1990). Evidence for terror management theory: II. The effects of morality salience reactions to those who implicitly or explicit threat or support the cultural world view. *Journal of Personality and Social Psychology, 58*, 308-318.

Harvey, R. D., & Oswald, D. L. (2000). Collective guilt and shame as motivation for White support of Black programs. *Journal of Applied Social Psychology, 30*, 1790-1811.

Higgins, E. T. (1987). Self-discrepancy: A theory relating self and affect. *Psychological Review, 94*, 319-340.

Hoge, C. W., Castro, C. A., Messer, S. C., McGurk, D., Cotting, D. I., & Koffman, R. L. (2004). Combat duty in Iraq and Afghanistan, mental health problems, and barriers to care. *New England Journal of Medicine, 351*, 13-22.

Huggins, M., Haritos-Fatouros, M., & Zimbardo, P. (2002). *Violence workers: Police torturers and murderers reconstruct Brazilian atrocities.* Berkeley, CA: University of California Press.

Jackman, M. R. (2001). License to kill: Violence and legitimacy in expropriative social relations. B. Major & J. T. Jost (Eds.), *The psychology of legitimacy: Emerging perspectives on ideology, justice, and intergroup relations* (pp. 437-467). New York: Cambridge University Press.

Jacks, J. Z., & Devine, P. G. (2002). Prejudice, internalization and the accessibility of personal standards for responding to gay men. *Journal of Homosexuality, 43*, 39-60.

James, W. (1890). *Principles of psychology.* New York: Dover.

Jetten, J., Spears, R., & Postmes, T. (2004). Intergroup distinctiveness and differentiation: A meta-analytic integration. *Journal of Personality and Social Psychology, 86*, 862-879.

Jordan, C. H., Spencer, S. J., & Zanna, M. P. (2005). Types of high self-esteem and prejudice: How implicit self-esteem relates to ethnic discrimination among high explicit self-esteem individuals. *Personality and Social Psychology Bulletin, 31*, 693-702.

Jordan, C. H., Spencer, S. J., Zanna, M. P., Hoshino-Browne, E., & Correll, J. (2003). Secure and defensive high self-esteem. *Journal of Personality and Social Psychology, 85*, 969-978.

Kalisa, K. (2002, August). *Inkiko Gacaca*. Newspaper, #19. Kigali Rwanda.

Kelman, H. C. (1990). Interactive problem-solving: A social-psychological approach to conflict resolution. In J. Burton & F. Dukes (Eds.), *Conflict: Readings in management and resolution*. New York: St Martin's Press.

Kelman, H. C., & Fisher, R. J. (2003). Conflict analysis and resolution. In D. O. Sears, L. Huddy, & R. Jervis (Eds.), *Oxford handbook of political psychology* (pp. 315-353). Oxford, England: Oxford University Press.

Krieger, N., & Sidney, S. (1996). Racial discrimination and blood pressure: The CARDIA study of Young Black and White adults. *American Journal of Public Health, 86*, 1370-1378.

Landau, M. L., Solomon, S., Greenberg, J., Cohen, F., Pyszczynski, T., Arndt, J., et al. (2004). Deliver us from evil: The effects of mortality salience and reminders of 9/11 on support for President George W. Bush. *Personality and Social Psychology Bulletin, 30*, 1136-1150.

Lazare, D. (2003, November 3). The one-state solution. *The Nation, 277*(14), 23-30.

Leach, C. W., & Williams, W. R. (1999). Group identity and conflicting expectations for the future in Northern Ireland. *Political Psychology, 20*, 875-896.

Leary, M. R., Tambor, E. S., Terdal, S. K., & Downs, D. L. (1995). Self-esteem as an interpersonal monitor: The sociometer hypothesis. *Journal of Personality and Social Psychology, 68*, 518-530.

Levine, R. A., & Campbell, D. T. (1972). *Ethnocentrism: Theories of conflict, ethnic attitudes, and group behavior*. Oxford: John Wiley.

Litz, B. T. (2005, April 8). The unique circumstances and mental health impact of the wars in Afghanistan and Iraq. National Center for Post-traumatic Stress Disorder, Department of Veterans Affairs. Retrieved May 17, 2005 from http://www.nctsd.va.gov/facts/veterans/fs_Iraq-Afghanistan_wars.html

Luhtanen, R., & Crocker, J. (1991). Self-esteem and intergroup comparisons: Toward a theory of collective self-esteem. In J. Suls & T. A. Wills (Eds.), *Social comparison: Contemporary theory and research* (pp. 211-234). Hillsdale, NJ: Erlbaum.

Mauer, M., & Huling, T. (1995, October). *Young Black Americans and the criminal justice system: Five years later*. Washington, DC: Sentencing Project.

Mikulincer, M., & Florian, V. (2000). Exploring individual differences in reactions to mortality salience: Does attachment style regulate terror management mechanisms? *Journal of Personality and Social Psychology, 79*, 260-273.

Monteith, M. J., Devine, P. G., & Zuwerink, J. R. (1993). Self-directed versus other-directed affect as a consequence of prejudice-related discrepancies. *Journal of Personality and Social Psychology, 64*, 198-210.

Mullen, B., Brown, R., & Smith, C. (1992). Ingroup bias as a function of salience, relevance, and status: An integration. *European Journal of Social Psychology, 22*, 103-122.

Orbell, J. M., Van de Kraigt, A., & Dawes, R. M. (1988). Explaining discussion induced cooperation. *Journal of Personality & Social Psychology, 54*, 811-819.

Pedersen, A., Beven, J., Walker, I., & Griffiths, B. (2004). Attitudes toward indigenous Australians: The role of empathy and guilt. *Journal of Community and Applied Social Psychology, 14*, 233-249.

Pennebaker, J. W. (1999). The effects of traumatic disclosure on physical and mental health: The values of writing and talking about upsetting events. *International Journal of Emergency Mental Health, 1*, 9-18.

Pettigrew, T. F., & Tropp, L. R. (2000). Does intergroup contact reduce prejudice?: Recent meta-analytic findings. In S. Oskamp (Ed.), *Reducing prejudice and discrimination: The Claremont symposium on applied social psychology* (pp. 93-114). Mahwah, NJ: Lawrence Erlbaum Associates.

Powell, A. A., Branscombe, N. R., & Schmitt, M. T. (2005). Inequality as ingroup privilege or outgroup disadvantage: The impact of group focus on collective guilt and interracial attitudes. *Personality and Social Psychology Bulletin, 31*, 508-521.

Pratto, F., & Espinoza, P. (2001). Gender, ethnicity, and power. *Journal of Social Issues, 57*, 763-780.

Pratto, F., Glasford, D. E., & Hegarty, P. J. (2006). Weighing the prospects of war. *Group Processes and Intergroup Relations, 9*, 219-233.

Pratto, F., Lemieux, A. F., Glasford, D. E., & Henry, P. J. (2003). American and Lebanese college students' responses to the events of September 11, 2001: The relation of hopes and fears to the psychology of group positions. *Psicológica Política, 27*, 13-35.

Pratto, F., & Shih, M. (2000). Social dominance orientation and group context in implicit group prejudice. *Psychological Sciences, 11*, 521-524.

Pratto, F., Sidanius, J., Stallworth, L. M., & Malle, B. F. (1994). Social dominance orientation: A personality variable predicting social and political attitudes. *Journal of Personality and Social Psychology, 67*, 741-763.

Pratto, F., Stallworth, L. M., & Conway-Lanz, S. (1998). Social dominance orientation and the legitimization of policy. *Journal of Applied Social Psychology, 28*, 1853-1875.

Ross, M. H., & Rothman, J. (Eds.) (1999). *Theory and practice in ethnic conflict management: Theorizing success and failure.* London: Macmillan.

Rouhana, N. N., & Kelman, H. (1994). Promoting joint thinking in international conflict: An Israeli-Palestinian continuing workshop. *Journal of Social Issues, 50*, 157-178.

Salomon, G., & Nevo, B. (Eds.) (2002). *Peace education: The concept, principles, and practices around the world.* Mahwah, NJ: Lawrence Erlbaum.

Schimel, J., Simon, L., Greenberg, J., Pyszczynski, T., Solomon, S., Waxmonsky, J., et al. (1999). Stereotypes and terror management: Evidence that mortality salience enhances stereotypic thinking and preferences. *Journal of Personality and Social Psychology, 77*, 905-926.

Schuster, M. A., Stein, B. D., Jaycox, L. H., Collins, R. L., Marshall, G. N., Elliott, M. N., et al. (2001). A national survey of stress reactions after the September 11, 2001 terrorist attacks. *New England Journal of Medicine, 345*, 1507-1512.

Sherif, M. (1966). *In common predicament: Social psychology of intergroup conflict and cooperation.* Boston: Houghton-Mifflin.

Sherif, M., Harvey, O. H., White, B. J., Hood, W. R., & Sherif, C. W. (1961). *Intergroup conflicts & cooperation: The Robber's Cave experiment.* Norman, OK: University of Oklahoma Book Exchange.

Sidanius, J., & Pratto, F. (1999). *Social dominance: An intergroup theory of social hierarchy and oppression.* New York: Cambridge University Press.

Silver, R. C., Holman, E. A., McIntosh, D. N., Poulin, M., & Gil-Rivas, V. (2002). Nationwide longitudinal study of psychological responses to September 11. *Journal of the American Medical Association, 288*, 1235-1244.

Staub, E. (1989). *The roots of evil: The origins of genocide and other group violence.* New York: Cambridge University Press.

Staub, E. (2003). Notes on cultures of violence, cultures of caring and peace, and the fulfillment of basic human needs. *Political Psychology, 24*, 1-21.

Staub, E. (2004). Justice, healing, and reconciliation: How the people's courts in Rwanda can promote them. *Peace and Conflict: Journal of Peace Psychology, 10*, 25-32.

Steele, C. M. (1988). The psychology of self-affirmation theory: Sustaining the integrity of the self. In L. Berkowitz (Ed.), *Advances in experimental social psychology* (Vol. 21, pp. 261-302). New York: Academic Press.

Stone, J., & Cooper, J. (2001). A self-standards model of cognitive dissonance. *Journal of Experimental Social Psychology, 37*, 228-243.

Sussex, B., & Corcoran, K. (2005). The Impact of domestic violence on depression in teen mothers: Is the fear or threat of violence sufficient? *Brief Treatment & Crisis Intervention, 5*, 109-120.

Szmajke, A., & Kubica, M. (2003). Geographically close—culturally distinct: The values of culture of honor in the mentality and young Poles and Germans. *Polish Psychology Bulletin, 34*, 153-159.

Tajfel, H., & Turner, J. C. (1986). The social identity theory of intergroup behavior. In S. Worchel & W. G. Austin (Eds.), *Psychology of intergroup relations* (pp. 7-24). Chicago: Nelson-Hall.

Taylor, S. E., & Brown, J. (1988). Illusion and well-being: A social psychological perspective on mental health. *Psychological Bulletin, 103*, 193-210.

Tropp, L., & Pettigrew, T. (2005). Relationships between intergroup contact and prejudice among minority and majority status groups. *Psychological Science, 16*, 951-956.

Tutu, D. M. (1982). *Crying in the wilderness: The struggle for justice in South Africa.* Grand Rapids, MI: W. B. Eerdmars Publishing Company.

Unisys Corporation (2005). The best defense is information. Retrieved May 25, 2005 http://www.unisys.com/public_sector/solutions/defense__and__domestic__ security/index.htm

United Nations (2002). *Women, peace, and security.* Retrieved April 4, 2005 from http://www.un.org/womenwatch/daw/public/eWPS.pdf

Vandello, J. A., & Cohen, D. (2003). Male honor and female fidelity: Implicit cultural scripts that perpetuate domestic violence. *Journal of Personality and Social Psychology, 84,* 997-1010.

Wellness Directory of Minnesota (2000). Post-traumatic stress disorder. Retrieved May 27, 2004 from http://www.mnwelldir.org/docs/mental_health/ptsd.htm

Willer, R. (2004). The effects of government-issued terror warnings on Presidential approval ratings. *Current Research in Social Psychology, 10,* 1-12.

Wills, T. A. (1981). Downward social comparison principles in social psychology. *Psychological Bulletin, 90,* 245-271.

Wisman, A., & Koole, S. L. (2003). Hiding in the crowd: Can mortality salience promote affiliation with others who oppose one's worldview? *Journal of Personality and Social Psychology, 84,* 511-526.

Wohl, M. J. A., & Branscombe, N. R. (2005). Forgiveness and collective guilt assignment to historical perpetrator groups depend on level of social category inclusiveness. *Journal of Personality and Social Psychology, 88,* 288-303.

Woods, D. (1978). *Biko.* New York: Paddington Press.

Zuwerink, J. R., Monteith, M. J., Devine, P. G., & Cook, D. A. (1996). Prejudice toward Blacks: With and without compunction? *Basic and Applied Social Psychology, 18,* 131-150.

CHAPTER 7

The Social Psychology of Respect: Implications for Delegitimization and Reconciliation

Ronnie Janoff-Bulman and Amelie Werther

In both the popular press and modern identity politics, societal groups are clamoring for respect, often in lieu of economic redistribution (see, for example, Fraser, 1995; Honneth, 1995, 2001; Miller, 1993; Taylor, 1994), and individual citizens are calling for respect in civil discourse (e.g., Carter, 1998). "History echoes with passionate pleas for justice and charity, but in our times, increasingly, what we hear are demands for *respect*" (Hill, 2000, p. 59). Political leaders around the world recognize its importance when meeting with the opposition, and reconciliation is often premised on its presence. Respect has become a valuable political and economic resource. Thus, Iran's reform-minded past President Khatami noted, "The first requisite to any dialogue is the mutual respect between two parties" (Landler, 2004, p. A5). Similarly, two university presidents—one Palestinian and the other Israeli—jointly maintained "it is through cooperation based on mutual respect, rather than boycotts or discrimination, that our common goals can be achieved" (Cowell, 2005, p. A9). And in attempting to improve relations with disgruntled faculty, Lawrence Summers, Harvard's past president, promised to temper his style in ways that paid them greater respect (Rimer & Healy, 2005).

In his classic book, *A Theory of Justice* (1971), political philosopher John Rawls claims that respect is a primary good—perhaps the primary good—in human society, and thus it is not surprising that it is often at the heart of controversies in American public life today. As noted by Miller and Savoie (2002), respect is implicated in racism, sexism, ageism, classism, homophobia, harassment, hate speech, police treatment, and cultural wars. Rawls (1971) goes on to argue that justice is actually a public expression of people's respect for one another, and recent work on justice by social psychologist Tom Tyler and colleagues (see, for example, Tyler & Blader, 2003; also see Heuer, Blumenthal, Douglas, & Weinblatt, 1999) echoes this fundamental association between justice and respect. In potentially violent conflicts, respect inhibits aggression (Pruitt & Kim, 2004), and in more private settings too, it appears to be a highly valued bestowal. After years of working with couples, marital researcher John Gottman (1994; also see Markman, Stanley, & Blumberg, 1994) notes that people want "just two things from their marriage—love and respect" (p. 18).

From marriage to politics to international conflicts, the word *respect* arises again and again and seems crucial for better understanding how to break down partisan divides and maximize possibilities for interpersonal and intergroup reconciliation. Yet investigations into the nature of respect are rare (cf. Frei & Shaver, 2002). For example, despite Gottman's recognition of the importance of respect to marriage partners, he has not studied it directly, but rather has measured expressions of contempt. In studies of justice and fairness, respect has not been the focus of investigation, and in the few cases of research involving respect, respondents have typically been asked simply to indicate the extent to which they feel respected or react to manipulations intended to reflect respect or disrespect (e.g., Barreto & Ellemers, 2002; Boeckmann & Tyler, 2002; Branscombe, Spears, Ellemers, & Doosje, 2002; De Cremer, 2002; Simon & Sturmer, 2003; Tyler & Blader, 2003). Moreover, in the area of social conflict, respect has received virtually no attention. A gaping hole currently exists in our understanding of respect, and we are left with fundamental questions regarding this valued resource in private relationships and public politics: What is respect? Why do we seek it so intensely?

In the pages that follow, we hope to provide an understanding of respect and disrespect, and their implications for delegitimization and reconciliation processes. Toward this end, we first distinguish between two types of respect, one largely intergroup and the other primarily intragroup in nature, and discuss the attributional components of these appraisals. We then move to a discussion of disrespect and its implications for delegitimization, from invisibility to dehumanization, which is of paramount importance in the course and escalation of social conflict; the attributional elements of respect provide an important window for viewing these degrading processes. The bulk of the chapter is an attempt to theoretically unpack the concepts of respect and disrespect. In the final section, however, we turn to practical considerations and conclude with some implications of our analysis for reconciliation, focusing particularly on respect-enhancing strategies in intense social conflicts.

Two Types of Respect

Respect is fundamentally tied to our existence as social beings who live and survive in groups. We propose that there are actually two types of respect, one that is basically intergroup in nature and based on our membership in an in-group, and another that is primarily intragroup in nature and based on our standing within that group (see Darwell, 1977). For reasons that will hopefully become apparent, we label the former *categorical respect* and the latter *contingent respect* and discuss below their distinct functions and criteria.

Categorical Respect

Within academia, moral philosophers rather than psychologists have attempted to provide some understanding of respect (Frankfurt, 1997; French, 1979; Harris, 1997; Hill, 2000; Reiman, 1990; also see the more popular treatments by educator Lawrence-Lightfoot, 1999, and sociologist Sennet, 2003). Their discussions generally focus on a universal, essentially prescriptive bestowal that follows from Kant ([1782] 1993), who argued that all people are due respect by virtue of being moral agents and reasoning beings. Interested in normative ethics and justifications for ethical behaviors, moral philosophers typically treat respect as a form of recognition that acknowledges we are equal participants in a common ethical world; we automatically owe it to one another by virtue of our human status.

From this perspective, respect is granted to another based on membership in a common community—in Kant's case the human community. Categorical respect is based on group membership (De Cremer & Tyler, 2005; Tyler, 1989) and is equally accorded to all members of one's group. The essential determination in granting this form of respect is in-group versus out-group status: to grant others categorical respect is to regard them as in-group members. Comembership in the human community is the minimal respect that is due another person. When our in-group is the human community, we are drawing the boundaries of social membership most broadly. Yet we are members of many groups, as social identity theory and self-categorization theory (e.g., Tajfel & Turner, 1986; Turner, 1987) make clear, and our in-groups are typically conceptualized more narrowly, often in terms of national, ethnic, political, and religious boundaries. In these cases, too, categorical respect is granted to coparticipants of these more restricted communities—to others recognized as in-group members.

Paradoxically, we often become aware of the significance of categorical respect in situations and times that highlight its absence. This is perhaps most evident when dealing with our most inclusive group—the human community. By placing people outside the bounds of this community, people can perpetrate heinous acts of degradation, extreme humiliation, and physical violence. Victims are perceived as expendable nonentities; as an insightful journalist wrote in response to photos of American guards at Abu Ghraib Prison: "The Americans in the photographs are not enacting hatred; hatred can coexist with respect, however strained. What they display, instead, is contempt: their victims are merely objects" (Sante, 2004, p. A27). By denying others membership in the human community, we subject them to moral exclusion and dehumanization. They are now outside of our *scope of justice*, barred from the protections of community membership, and thereby perceived as justifiable targets for exploitation and violence (Bar-Tal, 1990; Kelman, 2001; Opotow, 1990, 2001; Staub, 1989).

In the case of categorical respect, the focus is on rights of membership—shared entitlements of all members. These are accorded by virtue of being a group member. Thus categorical respect is at the foundation of human rights work, and our rights as comembers of the all-encompassing human community are apparent in the United Nations Universal Declaration of Human Rights, which begins: "Whereas recognition of the inherent dignity and of the equal and inalienable rights of all members of the human family is the foundation of freedom, justice, and peace in the world" (United Nations, 1948, p. 1). And Article 1 specifically states: "All human beings are born free and equal in dignity and rights. They are endowed with reason and conscience" (United Nations, 1948, p. 2).

The fundamental right conferred by categorical respect is participation in the group—having a say, being recognized as a group member. In other words, categorical respect grants people a voice; they are neither discounted nor invisible. Interestingly, in cross-cultural comparisons, Thailand is regarded as a culture in which respect is accorded to all societal members. Bonta and Fry (2006) note that this includes respect for children within the family, and they discuss how parents "respect the essential dignity of their children, even babies." When parents are unable to convince their children to behave through coaxing or persuasion, the adults "will simply give up and admit that the children have the right to decide what they will do. Their will must be respected" (p. 184). Even within the small family group, respect is having a voice.

As members of a society or particular in-group—be it a community group, a local club, a team, a larger ethnic, racial, or religious group, or a nation— people desire a voice as an indication of their inclusion (Folger & Cropanzo, 1998; Miller, 2001; Tyler, 1987). Recent theory and research on procedural justice suggests the profound importance of feeling recognized and having input. Having a voice in proceedings—that is, having an opportunity to have your say—positively impacts people's perceptions of fairness (Tyler, 1987, 1990; Tyler, Boeckmann, Smith, & Huo, 1997), and this is even the case when there is little possibility that it could affect the outcome (e.g., the opportunity to express oneself follows the actual outcome decision; Lind, Kanfer, & Earley, 1990).

Procedural justice not only acknowledges the importance of voice and visibility, but also encompasses consistency, neutrality, lack of bias, and representativeness (see, for example, Leventhal, 1980). Such fair treatment communicates respect. It implicitly recognizes (through explicit procedures) that parties should be treated the same, as valued members of society. Tyler and his colleagues have empirically demonstrated the crucial role of procedural justice in people's evaluations of fairness and the legitimacy of social authorities (Tyler, 1989, 2001; Tyler & Blader, 2000; Tyler & Huo, 2002). And interestingly, the UN Declaration of Human Rights guarantees everyone not only the right to "recognition everywhere as a person before the law" (United Nations, 1948, p. 2), but also the right to a fair and public hearing by an impartial tribunal. Rights, voice, and fair treatment all reflect categorical respect, for they imply in-group inclusion and valued participation.

Contingent Respect

In contrast to categorical respect, which reflects membership in a group, contingent respect is associated with standing in a group—in-group status rather than inclusion. Contingent respect is primarily intragroup, not intergroup in nature, for it is based on comparisons across group members, rather than on membership per se. As noted by Brewer (1999), humans are characterized by obligatory interdependence; we must rely on one another for information, aid, and shared resources. Just as differentiation between in-groups and out-groups may contribute to cooperative interdependence by minimizing the risk of excessive costs (Brewer, 1999), so too differentiation within groups may contribute by minimizing risks as well. That is, we are motivated to find the best people within the group to provide guidance, information, and direction. These are the people who are most respected, the individuals granted the strongest voice and most influence over the group. In this sense, contingent respect accords status or standing within the group (see De Cremer & Tyler, 2005; Tyler & Blader, 2003;

also see Jackson, Esses, & Burris, 2001); it is a valuation associated with one's position of earned influence in one's in-group.

In contrast to categorical respect, which is unranked and nonhierarchical, contingent respect is variable, ranked, and based on appraisal processes; it involves people's attributions about another's value along particular dimensions. Whereas procedural justice is primarily associated with categorical respect, distributive justice and the equity principle appear more generally associated with contingent respect, involving differential allotments across people based on proportional determinations for selected societal criteria. Contingent respect is earned or achieved rather than assumed or automatically given. A person granted contingent respect is necessarily also granted categorical respect, with the rights and voice accorded to in-group members.

The differences between contingent and categorical respect to some extent parallel the distinction drawn by sociologists between achieved and ascribed status. Achieved status is based largely on how well one performs (e.g., in a family or organization), whereas ascribed status is based on inherent characteristics rather than personal characteristics or achievements. Categorical respect, like ascribed status, is not earned; it is not based on a person's efforts, personal strengths, successes, or contributions. It is based on one's membership in a group. In contrast, like achieved status, contingent respect is earned.

Contingent respect is important social currency, whether in the dyad, group, or larger society. Granted to in-group individuals or societal subgroups perceived as most apt to contribute to the collective's welfare and future success, those who have it are in turn accorded greater social standing; they not only have a voice, but have influence. Their voices are loud, heard, and hold sway. It is interesting to speculate that one of the reasons respect has begun to be discussed a great deal by groups in the United States in recent decades is that for many groups in society, expansion of rights through laws during and after the 1960s has not automatically translated into respect in the sense of greater influence. Groups feel they have attained the rights of membership (categorical respect)—they can participate and have a voice (e.g., vote, speak up in the political process), but their influence and impact is nevertheless severely limited. When groups cry out for respect these days in identity politics, they are asking not only to be recognized and to have a voice, in the sense of being considered members of the greater society (i.e., categorical respect). They want to have an impact as well; they are asking for greater standing, more influence, and a stronger voice in the political and social arenas (i.e., contingent respect).

From our smallest to our largest in-groups, individuals and groups want not only to be heard but also to impact outcomes. In close relationships we want our partners to take into account our perspectives, and in a given nation groups want to influence political decisions and the future direction of the society.

Categorical and contingent respect are linked but distinct appraisals, which are associated, respectively, with our constructions of membership and standing within groups. In his book *The Decent Society* (1996), Margalit claims that a decent society is one that respects its members, but he claims that it is difficult to get direct evidence of respect. Margalit therefore turns to instances in which respect is absent and argues instead that a decent society is one in which institutions do not humiliate society's members; he maintains that we know humiliation when we see it, whereas we do not know what to look for in the case of respect. Yet respect may not be as mysterious and inscrutable as might appear at first glance; having a voice, being heard, and participating in the wider community provide evidence of categorical respect, a minimal form of respect due to another; having an influence and an impact provide evidence of contingent respect, a maximal form of the appraisal. Nevertheless, we often are most aware of respect when we recognize its absence—when others are ignored, demeaned, and physically harmed, as occurs in conflict situations. These instances of disrespect can be better understood by first understanding the bases on which individuals and groups are typically granted respect; we can then turn to a consideration of disrespect and delegitimization.

The Attributional Components of Respect and Disrespect

We propose that two primary domains are the basis for evaluations of respect: morality and competence (see Wojciszke, 1994, 1997, on the importance of these dimensions in impression formation). Although these components may be implicated in both categorical and contingent respect, we believe that they are differentially weighted in the two cases. For reasons discussed below, categorical respect entails an emphasis on morality appraisals, whereas contingent respect entails an emphasis on competence appraisals, and these lead to different types of delegitimization through disrespect.

In a recent exploratory study, we attempted to tap the primary elements of respect appraisals. We assumed that asking people what they mean by respect and using a prototype approach would most likely generate a series of synonyms (see Frei & Shaver, 2002), but would provide little insight into respect appraisals. Instead we asked respondents to choose a person they respect and tell us why; and then to choose a person they disrespect and explain this as well.[1] About half of the 305 respondents were asked to choose a family member or friend in picking their target person, and the others were asked to choose a public figure. Regardless of condition, approximately 90% of the descriptions reflected appraisals of either morality (e.g., altruistic, self-reliant, honest) or competence (e.g., intelligent, successful) in the case of the respected target and immorality (e.g., selfish, dishonest, abusive of others) or incompetence (e.g., unintelligent, unsuccessful) in the case of the disrespected target. Over 35% mentioned both morality and competence in describing the respected target; the perception of incompetence or immorality alone was clearly sufficient to render a judgment of disrespect, for only 10% of the sample mentioned both in this case. The centrality of these two domains in the open-ended responses was confirmed in subsequent research we conducted that manipulated these elements in a person perception task: again both morality and competence were strongly associated with respect appraisals.

Perhaps not surprisingly, given the link between respect, voice, and influence, these two factors parallel those deemed most important by social psychologists in perceiving a source as credible: one involves expertise, knowledge, or ability, and the other involves trustworthiness, honesty, or objectivity (for a review, see Petty & Wegener, 1998; also see McGuire, 1969). Knowledgeable, honest communicators are most likely to be persuasive—their messages are regarded as worth listening to. Similarly, research on perceptions of presidential character suggests the importance of two core dimensions— competence and integrity (Kinder, 1986; also see related work by McGraw, 2001; Miller, Wattenberg, & Malanchuk, 1986; Rahn, Aldrich, Borgida, & Sullivan, 1991); those high on these dimensions of competence and morality are people we believe should legitimately have the strongest voice in a nation's deliberations and decisions.

Morality and competence appear to be the primary attributional elements of respect. Morality attributions may be relatively cross-situational, in that working for the welfare of the group and minimizing selfishness are presumably valued regardless of the particular identity of a social group. Here we are most concerned with others' intentions vis-à-vis one's group. Do the person's intentions reflect the interests of the larger group? Can the person's word be trusted? To what extent does the person minimize self-interest in the service of greater social interests? Morality involves our regard (or lack of same) for the interests of others (e.g., Pincoffs, 1986); as Schulman (2002) notes, when we call an act moral, it is because we have inferred some good intention behind it.

Assessments of competence involve assumptions about others' knowledge and skills—the extent to which their abilities and expertise can positively contribute to the guidance and direction of the group. When the group in question is society at large, cultural assumptions about competence play a major role; in Western culture we presumably make inferences about competence based not only on perceived knowledge and skills, but on such variables as education and occupation, which are regarded as indices of success. Nevertheless, we are members of many groups, and one's perceived competence is likely to vary with the values and purposes of the group in question. Thus, competence in athletic groups is apt to be assessed in terms of athletic success, and competence in musical groups in terms of one's musical talent. We have a general social standing in society, but our numerous social identities can provide us with opportunities for respect based on other competence-related categories; competence is essentially defined by the in-group's goals and values.

Although morality and competence are important in appraisals of respect, a closer look at these domains suggests they may be differentially related to categorical versus contingent respect. Recall that in the case of categorical respect, we are making an intergroup (i.e., in-group vs. out-group) evaluation, for we are determining whether the other is a comember of our in-group. In the case of contingent respect, we are making an intragroup evaluation; that is, we are comparing the target to others in the same group and in turn conferring standing within the group. Regarding the attributional components of respect, morality is apt to be weighted more heavily when the determination is about in-group–out-group status; and competence is likely to be weighted more heavily when the determination is about intragroup status. In determining in-group–out-group status, we are interested in knowing whether the other is well-intentioned, can be trusted, and is on our side. If we believe this to be the case, we are likely to deem the other a member of our in-group. Morality and good intentions are an essential basis for in-group categorization, but it is equally likely that once a person is granted in-group membership, he or she is automatically regarded as generally moral and well-intentioned. These are reciprocal processes, no doubt operating in both directions, in support of Deutsch's (1973) observation in his Crude Law of Social Relations that "characteristic processes and effects elicited by a given type of social relationship tend also to elicit that type of relationship" (p. 365). In other words, conditions that provoke an outcome are also triggered by the outcome; attributions of morality encourage in-group categorization, and conversely, in-group membership encourages attributions of morality.

Perceived competence becomes more important once membership status is conferred. Appraisals of contingent respect involve targets who generally are already considered in-group members and have thereby been granted a threshold level of morality. Thus, morality sufficient for in-group membership is assumed (until evidence to the contrary is provided), and the basis for the conferral of contingent respect then rests on perceived competence. Not surprisingly, then, high status groups within a given society are those regarded as most competent (Fiske, Cuddy, Glick, & Xu, 2002; Fiske, Xu, Cuddy, & Glick, 1999). Perceptions of morality primarily determine inclusion in the group, and therefore rights of voice and participation; and perceptions of competence primarily determine standing in the group and the privilege of influence.

Analogous to our appraisals of respect, in disrespecting others we turn to attributions of immorality and incompetence; here again, their relative significance seems to depend in part on whether we are making intergroup or intragroup judgments. In the most serious social conflicts, it is clear that the significance of immorality trumps incompetence, for these are situations in which the targets of appraisals are unquestionably defined as out-groups. With this in mind, we now turn to a closer examination of the elements of disrespect.

Disrespect and Delegitimization

In popular slang, the term *dis*, derived from the word disrespect (according to the Online Slang Dictionary), means to insult or put someone down. If, as suggested above, respect is associated with having a voice through group membership (minimally) and having influence (maximally), disrespect is essentially equivalent to discounting another. Such discounting not only renders another person or group powerless and relatively invisible, but in cases of conflict, the object of ridicule and humiliation, and most seriously, violence and destruction. Perceptions of immorality and incompetence play an important role in foreclosing respect and promoting delegitimization of others. Yet although incompetence is heavily weighted when in-group members are disrespected, leading to invisibility and disempowerment, it is the perception of immorality that is of primary importance in the most dramatic instances of disrespect—out-group delegitimization that may lead to extreme degradation and violence.

Out-group Delegitimization: Enemy
Images and Perceived Immorality

Paralleling the automatic attribution of morality and good intentions to in-group members (categorical respect), we appear to automatically attribute immorality and bad intentions to out-group adversaries. Thus, in their work on naïve realism, Ross and Ward (1996; also see Robinson, Keltner, Ward, & Ross, 1995) have demonstrated that once differences of opinion cannot be attributed to lack of information, we regard others' dissenting views as biased or based on self-interested motives. We also believe our own views are generally unbiased and uninfluenced by ideology (e.g., Pronin, Gilovich, & Ross, 2004). Similarly, Reeder, Pryor, Wohl, and Griswell (2005) found that respondents attributed negative, selfish motives to others who disagreed with their positions. Reeder et al. (2005) suggest that attitudinal similarity serves as a basis for group boundaries and therefore intergroup differentiation (see also Kenworthy & Miller, 2002); those who share our attitudes are perceived as a coherent, unified group and are members of our in-group (also see Turner, 1987, on self-categorization and Tajfel & Turner, 1986, on social identity theory), whereas those who disagree are perceived as a homogeneous out-group (see, for example, Linville, Fischer, & Salovey, 1989). Once we categorize others as out-group members, we are likely to deny them categorical respect and regard them as biased, self-interested, and selfish.

Perceptions of out-groups are heavily laden with attributions of immorality and bad intentions. These are evident in Campbell's (1967; Le Vine & Campbell, 1972) notion of a *universal stereotype* applied by all in-groups; that is, in-groups believe they themselves are honest, cooperative, peaceful, and trustworthy, whereas out-groups are dishonest, uncooperative, quarrelsome, and untrustworthy. When the out-group is an enemy—viewed as threatening, and with hostility—these perceptions of bad intentions take on a particularly antagonistic, negative tone and become hardened perceptions of the other. Pruitt and Kim (2004) describe the perceptions that are "particularly characteristic of escalated conflict" as follows:

> Other tends to be seen as deficient in moral virtue—as dishonest, unfriendly, or warlike. Other tends to be seen as different from Party in basic values, and most particularly to be selfish and inhumane (Struch & Schwartz, 1989). Other also tends to be distrusted; party believes Other to be hostile to Party's welfare, and sometimes as having unlimited goals of defeating or even destroying Party. In addition, Other may be seen as lacking in ability for achievement (Blake & Mouton, 1962),though this kind of perceptual distortion is less likely because of the greater availability of sound evidence about these characteristics (Brewer, 1979). In contrast, party usually sees itself as more moral than Other and often as a victim of Other's aggression (Hampson, 1997; White, 1984). (p. 106)

These are the perceptions that characterize our view of the enemy; we maintain a moral self-image and regard the out-group as diabolical (White, 1984; also see Silverstein, 1992, on "enemy images"). Labels such as *ruthless, devious,* and *aggressive* are particularly common in delegitimization of the out-group, and these perceptions tend to be reciprocal (Bar-Tal, 1990; also see Bronfenbrenner, 1961, on mirror-image perceptions). As Bar-Tal (1990) notes in his review of leaders' speeches and interviews during the 8-year Iran–Iraq war,

Iranians labeled Iraqis "criminals," "aggressors," "archsatans," and "Saddamist mercenaries," "inhuman" and "diabolical"; and the Iraqis labeled Iranians "criminals," "aggressors," "neofascists," "deceitful diabolical entity," and "harmful magi insects."

Given these perceptions, a conflict becomes framed as a war between good and evil; thus, Reagan referred to the Soviet Union as the "evil empire," and G. W. Bush referred to North Korea, Iran, and Iraq as the "axis of evil." Such framing changes the nature of conflictual issues from specific to general, such that enemies are no longer dealing with a particular threat, but with an "immoral enemy" (Pruitt & Kim, 2004). In the face of these perceptions, it is typical for communications to plummet and conflicts to escalate.

The tragedy of such conflict escalation is that it is so often based on misattributions that follow directly from biased perceptions (see, for example, Bar-Tal, 1990; Pruitt & Kim, 2004; Silverstein, 1992; White, 1984). People generally underestimate the power of the situation, and this is particularly marked in the case of enemies (see, for example, Pettigrew, 1979). The absence of any attributional charity coupled with an assumption of other's bad intentions results in misattributions for the enemy's actions; these actions are not perceived as defensive, or based on extenuating circumstances, but as punitive and aggressive. The appropriate response thereby seems to be defensive escalation, which in turn is perceived by the other as hostile. A conflict spiral of escalation results (Jervis, 1976; Pruitt & Kim, 2004).

In the context of these negative perceptions, even peaceful actions of other groups are likely to be attributed to hostile intentions; there is an utter absence of trust. As Silverstein (1992) notes, "a proffered peace treaty may be viewed as crass propaganda, an attempt to increase tensions among allies, or a trick to allow enemies to maintain or increase military superiority" (p. 151). The work on reactive devaluation echoes this suspicion and discounting of an enemy's well-intentioned efforts (see, for example, Ross, 2005). Thus, lack of trust seriously undermines efforts at de-escalation and conflict resolution.

In addition to contributing to a conflict spiral through misattributions, the perception of the enemy as immoral also minimizes inhibitions against aggression and retaliation. As Pruitt and Kim note (2004), "Party is reluctant to aggress against an Other who is liked and respected..., but party is quite willing to aggress against an Other who is not liked or respected.... Furthermore, there is an easy explanation that makes empathy seem unnecessary: other's actions stem from evil motives" (p. 108). The enemy is delegitimized, dehumanized, and placed outside the bounds of the human community; such denial of membership translates into the legitimization of violence and extreme degradation. In the absence of categorical respect, perceptions of immorality define our views of enemy out-groups and establish seemingly insurmountable obstacles to conflict resolution and reconciliation.

Intragroup Disrespect: Delegitimization and Perceived Incompetence

Certainly the most devastating type of delegitimization is manifested as violence between enemy out-groups; this is the extreme case of disrespect—not only failing to recognize the morality of the enemy, but discounting the humanity of the other. However, disrespect has seemingly more benign manifestations that are nevertheless extremely challenging and demeaning for the groups involved. Here we are referring primarily to disrespect among in-group members, most specifically in this case, groups who perceive themselves as members of a single society (i.e., societal subgroups).[2] Although not typically associated with escalated conflict and punitive aggression, such delegitimization has a powerful yet insidious effect on social and economic equality and often serves to justify poverty, discrimination, and powerlessness. Such disrespect often becomes fixed and perpetuated within a given society through damaging group stereotypes and legitimizing myths (see, for example, Jost & Major, 2001).

The social conflicts reflected in these intrasocietal patterns of disrespect may concern in-group resources, but are also fundamentally about recognition, participation, and influence (Fraser, 1995; Honneth, 1995). This is the realm of modern identity politics. Within a given society (intragroup), where comembership in a larger social structure is sought, disrespect of other individuals or subgroups involves denying them status, and, relatedly, adequate input into social and political decisions. From this perspective, to disrespect is to delegitimize other people or groups by placing them outside the sphere of influence and discourse—to deny others the right of meaningful participation.

Recall that in the case of intragroup judgments (i.e., contingent respect, in contrast to in-group or categorical respect based on intergroup considerations), competence is heavily weighted in people's appraisals. It is not that morality is irrelevant, but it is typically assumed through in-group (vs. out-group) status. Yet in-group members can be readily discounted and derogated by virtue of their perceived incompetence. In the work of Fiske et al. (1999, 2002), these are groups that are the object of paternalistic prejudice—liked, but not respected.[3] Following from this perspective, it is likely that nondominant societal groups are delegitimized not through immorality, but primarily through perceived incompetence; that is, they are viewed as relatively high on morality, but low on competence. As such, they are fairly low-status groups that are granted minimal contingent respect. They are denied influence because they are perceived as lacking the knowledge, information, and skills to provide proper guidance and direction for the larger society. In a given society, social hierarchies are maintained by delegitimizing socially disadvantaged groups (Jost & Major, 2001), and in these cases it is largely the competence domain that is implicated.

It is interesting to consider the second type of prejudice discussed by Fiske et al. (1999, 2002). Envious prejudice is directed towards groups accorded high levels of status. These are groups that are regarded as highly competent, but whose morality is questioned. They are rated as lower on morality than the paternalistic groups, although typically not exceedingly low (i.e., not very immoral); they are still comembers of one's larger society— in-group members—and therefore are generally accorded a threshold level of morality. Fiske et al. note that these groups, the object of envious prejudice, exist across cultures. In our society, they are high status groups such as Asians, Jews, and the rich. We believe that the perception of relatively low levels of morality (compared to competence) allows dominant societal group(s) to moderate what might otherwise be excessive levels of influence by these very competent, high status groups. If questions can always be raised about the group's intentions, self-interest, altruism, and honesty, even these high status, "respected" groups can be "managed" and kept from wielding too much influence.

It is fascinating and distressing to recognize what happens to these groups in times of considerable societal upheaval and stress. These envied groups may become targeted for out-group status—enemies of the society. In the dramatic change from in-group to out-group, the role of morality, or more precisely immorality, becomes paramount. When the focus is on the other as an in-group member (coparticipant in society), competence functions as a basis for respect, with morality generally assumed; when the focus is on the other as out-group adversary, the morality basis for respect becomes paramount, echoing the differences between contingent (intragroup) and categorical (intergroup) respect. The concern is no longer with denial of influence, but denial of in-group membership. The earlier high status target group (e.g., intellectuals in Pol Pot's Cambodia, Jews in Nazi Germany, Chinese in Indonesia) is now perceived as an out-group, and immorality— bad intentions, dishonesty, selfishness—becomes the basis for delegitimization, often in its extreme form, dehumanization. The competence that is a basis for respect while considered an in-group member—and thereby confers influence and status—is now feared in the out-group enemy, and coupled with the perception of immorality becomes a justification for degradation, abuse, and violence.

Some Implications for Reconciliation

From rivalries and derogation based on societal hierarchies to violence and war based on seemingly intractable intergroup conflicts, respect seems to be a natural antidote to the devaluation and delegitimization that characterize antagonistic, adversarial relationships. Respect is an attitude and appraisal we have the power to grant another, and finding ways to facilitate such bestowals may be a key to reconciliation. When we speak of reconciliation colloquially, we are concerned with settling disagreements and restoring relationships. From the perspective of work on intergroup conflict and peace building, reconciliation is defined as "the process of developing a mutual conciliatory accommodation between two antagonistic or formerly antagonistic persons or groups" (Kriesberg, 1998, pp. 1-2) or "a postwar reconstruction policy, designed to build peace among peoples with long-standing animosities" (Ackermann, 1994, p. 230).

Respect facilitates and promotes reconciliation; it allows for the possibility that legitimacy may lie in more than one's own perspective. It involves treating adversarial others as equal participants even if you do not like their views. It calls for a sort of attributional generosity in interpreting the words and intentions of the other, holding one's harshest delegitimizing appraisals in abeyance, and allowing for inputs and influence by all parties to the conflict. Yet given the unique ecology of social conflict, the very situations most in need of respect are precisely those in which it is least apt to be (re)established. In these instances, conflicting parties perceive each other as morally deficient; they view each other with contempt. Contempt is a deep dismissal, a signal that the conversation is over, and a denial of any prospect for reconciliation (Hill, 2000). On the path to reconciliation, then, how can we build respect for others we regard with contempt?

Given the powerful in-group–out-group divisions in perceptions of adversaries and the hostile us-versus-them nature of enemy interactions, it is categorical rather than contingent respect that demands our attention in intense social conflicts. Here the emphasis is on attributions of immorality and perceptions of seemingly unyielding intergroup (vs. intragroup) distinctions. Violent conflicts, involving the pain and memories of devastation, cruelty, and loss, are particularly likely to produce hardened negative, dehumanized images of the enemy other. Categorical respect requires the *rehumanization* of the other (see, for example, Ramsbotham, Woodhouse, & Miall, 2005), such that the perceiver comes to respect the other and the other comes to feel respected. A number of distinct strategies are likely to contribute to this process, including (a) efforts to minimize in-group–out-group boundaries through the establishment of new common identities or altered perceptions of immorality; (b) the institutionalization of opportunities that maximize voice and incorporate procedural justice; and (c) public actions that signal a group's willingness to minimize its own sense of moral superiority.

Nadler (2002) distinguishes between two types of conflicts that differ in terms of the goals of reconciliation, and these are of particular interest in considering the establishment of respect between opposing parties. In one case the goal is "harmony between former adversaries in a single, unified society" and in the other it is "peaceful coexistence in two separate societies" (p. 131). Thus, reconciliation in South Africa involved finding a common ground for black and white South Africans in one inclusive society. In contrast, the goal of reconciliation for Palestinians and Israelis is peaceful coexistence in two mutually accepted, autonomous states. In both types of conflict, *rehumanizing* and recognizing the legitimacy of the other are key elements of building respect and promoting reconciliation. Yet these two cases present their own unique challenges in bringing about such a transformation.

The goal of a single society, while rife with possibilities for failure, nevertheless opens up a number of possibilities as well, in particular strategies associated with building a new common identity and altering perceptions of immorality. The fact that the antagonists live in one country provides the opportunity for a single national identity, which can serve to break down in-group–out-group boundaries; that is, an emphasis on a superordinate national identity can provide new routes for perceiving commonalities, while, nevertheless, acknowledging old wounds. Thus, the brilliance and effectiveness of Nelson Mandela and Desmond Tutu was in part attributable to their ability to transmit their deep commitment to a new South African identity, an identity associated with a changed nation willing to confront the horrors of the past, but proud and optimistic about the society's possibilities for the future (see, for example, Van der Merwe, 2001). Enemies in the era of apartheid could now proudly embrace a new national identity, which defined their joint participation in a new society. A common identity can contribute to the transformation of out-groups into a single in-group, with the promise of categorical respect that inheres in such comembership.

Social psychological work on common in-group identity (see, for example, Gaertner & Dovidio, 2000) suggests the potential of such a new, superordinate category. Although developed in the context of prejudice and race relations rather than violent conflict, common in-group-identity theory points to the positive impact of recategorizing out-groups as in-groups ("separate groups on the same team") through a superordinate identity that can subsume other (often antagonistic) identities. Such recategorization has been found to enhance intergroup trust, reduce prejudice, and contribute to the development of positive attitudes towards the other group. Clearly, such a new common identity may be very difficult to establish in the case of violent conflict, but it is nevertheless a potentially powerful strategy, and one that is consistent with the goal of a single, inclusive society.

As a common in-group identity grows, attributional generosity and perceptions of morality are likely to follow. Conversely, minimizing attributions of immorality and increasing perceptions of positive intentions can serve to break down in-group–out-group boundaries (recall Deutsch's [1973] Crude Law of Social Relations). This is one potentially positive result of intergroup contact. Such intercommunal contact is most apt to happen within a single society, where people can actually confront each other during the course of daily living. It is far less likely in the case of two separate societies aiming for peaceful coexistence. Here the contacts are generally more formal of necessity, often involving special efforts to bring together groups from each society; although there may be opportunities to establish some interdependence (e.g., economic ties), most intergroup contact is likely to occur between leaders working on conflict resolution, reconciliation, and political affairs.

When living together in a single nation, enemies are more likely to have opportunities to interact; this may present possibilities for both maximal breakdown of peacemaking efforts as well as maximal success. Clearly, contact and communication are not panaceas; between intense enemies they can serve to intensify in-group identification and intergroup hostility (Pruitt & Kim, 2004). But reconciliation is a long-term process, not an overnight conversion. And over time contact may provide opportunities to observe the humanity of members of the other group, recognize similarities, and alter attributions of immorality, selfishness, and dishonesty. Informal contacts and interactions through civic association, local government groups, schools, and ultimately residential areas, where individuals may be required to work together on common issues, are apt to be most beneficial.[4] Over time, reevaluations of individual out-group members can serve to undercut automatic negative attributions and hostile perceptions of the group as a whole (see, for example, Pettigrew, 1998; Pettrigrew & Tropp, 2006).

In addition to contact and a new national identity, which aim at breaking down group and attributional boundaries, respect-enhancing strategies include specific procedures that are directly aimed at fostering the recognition and visibility so central to categorical respect. These are often evident in the institutions and processes established for dealing with the horrors of a violent conflict; they enhance prospects for respect and reconciliation to the extent that they offer the possibility of dignity that was unavailable to whole segments of the population during the conflict itself. Institutions established for dealing with victims and perpetrators (who typically also regard themselves as victims; see Ramsbotham et al., 2005) should strive to maximize procedural justice. In the administration of justice, procedures that are consistent, open, unbiased, equally applied, and available to all maximize participants' feelings of respect and sense that they are valued by the larger society (Tyler, 1989, 2001).

Opportunities for voice within these postconflict institutions also foster respect and ultimately reconciliation. The Truth and Reconciliation Commission established in South Africa in 1995 engaged communities in a process of collecting statements from local victims and providing community hearings (see, for example, Gibson, 2004; Van der Merwe, 2001). There were new forums for listening, and victims were given an opportunity to tell their stories; in essence, they were given a voice. Not only did this help them discover what in truth happened to their loved ones and possibly help unburden their own grief, but it had powerful symbolic value. The hearings were essentially *respect rituals*, for victims were receiving recognition from their new nation— recognition of their humanity, their inclusion in the new South Africa, and acknowledgement that they had been harmed and wronged. Regardless of one's position on the question of amnesty, the wisdom of establishing such avenues for respect seems uncontroversial.

Within a single society, such processes and institutions that recognize the importance of voice and procedural justice also serve to foster a newfound sense of societal inclusiveness for past victims as well as perpetrators. Although similar structures could be established in the case of separate societies or nations (e.g., war tribunals, truth commissions), they would lack the added benefit of providing strong evidence of a new, inclusive, respect-based society. Reconciliation between two nations presents special challenges and may rest primarily on the interactions between leaders, as symbols and representatives of their nations. In such instances, unilateral conciliatory gestures of leaders (Osgood, 1962) may be particularly instrumental vis-à-vis reconciliation, for they may jump start a reconsideration of an antagonist's intentions. The importance of such unilateral gestures was evident, for example, in the power and success of Sadat's 1977 trip to Jerusalem. His actions were unexpected and irreversible, and no doubt involved personal costs due to the negative reactions of the Arab world. In spite of great suspicions, his visit led Israelis to begin to question and rethink Sadat's (i.e., Egypt's) presumed hostile motives. From a respect perspective, Israelis began to see Egyptians as *probationally* more well-intentioned and moral, and hence more deserving of categorical respect.

On the road to reconciliation, there is a need for each side to curb its own moral arrogance (Hill, 2002). This may be particularly important for those who come to the table with greater power. Some form of "respect ritual" would be particularly useful between leaders, as representatives of their groups. One candidate for such a display would be the apology, which not only renders a transgression less offensive but also has potent symbolic value, because it provides evidence that the offender acknowledges the moral worth and social standing of the other. Although research to date has focused on interpersonal rather than intergroup relations, findings nevertheless suggest that apologies are associated with greater empathy for an offender, as well as less revenge, anger, aggression and avoidance by victims (McCullough et al., 1998; Ohbuchi, Kameda, & Agarie, 1989). In the context of efforts at reconciliation and peace building, apologies are likely to signal respect for the other. When offered by the more powerful party, apologies may also help create a more level playing field (for negotiations), for implicit in apologies is a recognition of status equality (see Abel, 1998).

Most generally, respect is conveyed through listening to what the other has to say and allowing for the possibility that reconciliation is possible. Whether within a single society or across nations, between ordinary group members or leaders, such openness to another's perspective is crucial on the road to reconciliation; *civil* as opposed to *confrontational* listening involves acknowledging the mere possibility that the other is right (Carter, 1998). By focusing first on listening, on mutual opportunities to influence, and on the possibility of balanced inputs, participants may come to see their adversaries as worthy of such respect. Going through the motions of respectful treatment—and being the recipient of such treatment—may over time transform appraisals of the other and, in turn, promote true reconciliation between adversarial groups.

It is important to recognize that in respecting another, we do not have to agree. Here we are reminded of the multiyear meetings held by three ardent pro-life and three ardent prochoice community leaders in an effort to understand each other. After 3 years, these women reported that they developed a deep respect for their opponents, whose *dignity and goodness* became very apparent; over time, they learned to hear the other perspective without overreacting or disparaging the other side. Yet the women were able to accomplish this without changing their minds on the topic of abortion (Fowler et al., 2001).

Respect does not mean agreeing, but rather listening and acknowledging that the other has a right to shape outcomes as well. Certainly, it is not easy to establish, particularly in the aftermath of violent conflicts. Yet respect may be far easier to encourage and promote than sympathy, empathy, and altruism on the path to reconciliation. Respect has unique value and appeal in enabling intergroup communication, accommodation, and peace building. As Reiman (1990) notes,

> Respect involves a certain regard for the interests of others, but not so much as adopting them as one's own. Respect is altruism's cooler cousin. It shows its solicitude for the interests of others in its reserve rather than its enthusiasm. One can have respect for one's adversaries or even one's enemies without having sympathy for their ends or actively adopting them. Respect is characteristically exhibited by... making way for others to promote their ends rather than promoting them oneself.

Notes

1. The type of respect was left unspecified, for the distinction would not be meaningful to respondents. We assumed responses would be somewhat more likely to reflect contingent respect, in that participants were essentially asked to choose someone they ranked high on respect. Nevertheless, we believed categorical respect would largely be assumed (as it generally is in the case of contingent respect) and that responses would therefore contribute to an understanding of the attributional elements of both types of respect.

2. It is important to recognize the fluidity of social identity and, therefore, in-group versus out-group identification. Thus societal groups, such as ethnic or racial groups, may be considered in-groups when considering one's nation or society as whole (e.g., in contrast to other nations), but may be considered out-groups when considered in light of (i.e., in contrast to) one's own ethnic or racial group. Similarly, other nations (e.g., European countries) are apt to be considered out-groups when we think about politics, but may be regarded as in-groups when we consider economic cooperation around joint business ventures. In the case of the Chinese, we may view them as an out-group when we are thinking about economics, but may perceive them as an in-group member when we are thinking about negotiations with the North Koreans. In other words, our in-group–out-group designations are somewhat fluid. Nevertheless, when we perceive others as out-groups we are most apt to focus on these groups' morality and intentions, whereas when we think of them as in-groups—on our team—we are more apt to focus on their competence and ability to influence joint outcomes.

3. In their research, Fiske et al. (1999, 2002) assessed perceptions of groups' warmth and competence. Respondents rated groups on a series of adjectives, and the warmth adjectives included not only *warmth* and *good-natured*, but *sincere*, *trustworthy*, and *well-intentioned*, seemingly reflecting both warmth and morality. In order to more directly test whether morality would be used as a basis for delegitimizing out-groups, we (with Tracy Kirschen) conducted a replication and extension of the research by

Fiske and her colleagues and asked participants to rate societal groups on adjectives selected as indices of competence, morality, and warmth. The morality adjectives were ethical, well-intentioned, trustworthy, honest and sincere, and the warmth traits adjectives were sociable, warm, good-natured, approachable, and friendly. Morality and warmth emerged as separate factors, but they nevertheless resulted in the same societal clusters when separately combined with competence ratings, and these clusters replicated the findings of Fiske et al. (1999, 2002). It appears that although we can distinguish between warmth and morality, they appear to serve as indicators of the same human attributes and behaviors. It is likely that the positive orientation towards others expressed as warmth and friendliness gets interpreted as positive intentions, selflessness, generosity, and interest in the group's welfare; thus warmth may serve as a cue for morality, or more generally others' intentions regarding the group.

4. The crucial role of groups' informal interactions through civic associations is discussed by Ashutosh Varshney, a political scientist who studied the pattern of violent conflicts between Hindus and Muslims in India (see Bass, 2006). He found that riots occur only in certain cities. In riot-prone cities, Hindus and Muslims do not come together in daily social and economic life, whereas in nonriot-prone cities, they mix in trade unions, business associations, and professional organizations.

References

Abel, R. L. (1998). *Speaking respect, respecting speech.* Chicago: University of Chicago Press.

Ackermann, A. (1994). Reconciliation as a peace-building process in postwar Europe: The Franco-German case. *Peace & Change, 19,* 229-250.

Barreto, M., & Ellemers, N. (2002). The impact of respect versus neglect of self-identities on identification and group loyalty. *Personality and Social Psychology Bulletin, 28,* 629-639.

Bar-Tal, D. (1990). Causes and consequences of delegitimization: Models of conflict and ethnocentrism. *Journal of Social Issues, 46,* 65-81.

Bass, G. J. (2006). *Memo to Iraq: Four strategies for averting civil war.* www.slate.com, March 28.

Boeckmann, R. J., & Tyer, T. R. (2002). Trust, respect, and the psychology of political engagement. *Journal of Applied Social Psychology, 32,* 2067-2088.

Bonta, B. D., & Fry, D. P. (2006). Lessons for the rest of us: Learning from peaceful societies. In M. Fitzduff & C. E. Stout (Eds.), *The psychology of resolving conflicts: From war to peace. Vol. 1: Nature vs. nurture* (pp. 182-210). Westport, CT: Praeger Security International.

Branscombe, N. R., Spears, R., Ellemers, N., & Doosje, B. (2002). Intragroup and intergroup evaluation effects on group behavior. *Personality and Social Psychology Bulletin, 28,* 744-753.

Brewer, M. B. (1999). The psychology of prejudice: Ingroup love or outgroup hate? *Journal of Social Issues, 55,* 429-444.

Bronfenbrenner, U. (1961). The mirror image in Soviet-American relations: A social psychologist's report. *Journal of Social Issues, 27,* 45-56.

Campbell, D. T. (1967). Stereotypes and the perception of group differences. *American Psychologist, 22,* 817-829.

Carter, S. L. (1998). *Civility: Manners, morals, and the etiquette of democracy.* New York: Basic Books.

Cowell, A. (2005). End of boycott of Israeli universities is urged. *The New York Times,* May 20.

Darwell, S. L. (1977). Two kinds of respect. *Ethics, 88,* 36-48.

De Cremer, D. (2002). Respect and cooperation in social dilemmas: The importance of feeling included. *Personality and Social Psychology Bulletin, 28,* 1335-1341.

De Cremer, D., & Tyler, T. R. (2005). Am I respected or not? Inclusion and reputation as issues in group membership. *Social Justice Research, 18,* 121-153.

Deutsch, M. (1973). *The resolution of conflict.* New Haven, CT: Yale University Press.

Fiske, S. T., Cuddy, A. C., Glick, P., & Xu, J. (2002). A model of (often mixed) stereotype content: Competence and warmth respectively follow from perceived status and competition. *Journal of Personality and Social Psychology, 82,* 878-902.

Fiske, S., T., Xu, J., Cuddy, A. C., & Glick, P. (1999). (Dis)respecting versus (dis)liking: Status interdependence predict ambivalent stereotypes of competence and warmth. *Journal of Social Issues, 55,* 473-489.

Folger, R., & Cropanzo, R. (1998). *Organizational justice and human resource management.* Thousand Oaks, CA: Sage.

Fowler, A., Gamble, N. N., Hogan, F. X., Kogut, M., McCommish, M., & Thorp, B. (2001). Talking with the enemy. *The Boston Globe,* Sunday, January 28, focus section.

Frankfurt, H. (1997). Equality and respect. *Social Research, 64,* 3-15.

Fraser, N. (1995). From redistribution to recognition? Dilemmas of justice in a "post-socialist" age. *New Left Review, 212,* 68-93.

Frei, J., & Shaver, P. R. (2002). Respect in close relationships: Prototypes definition, self-report assessment, and initial correlates. *Personal Relationships, 9,* 121-139.

French, P. A. (1979). *The scope of morality.* Minneapolis, MN: University of Minnesota Press.

Gaertner, S. L., Dovidio, J. F. (2000). *Reducing intergroup bias: The common ingroup identity model.* New York: Psychology Press.

Gibson, J. (2004). *Overcoming Apartheid.* New York: Russell Sage.

Gottman, M. (1994). *Why marriages succeed or fail... and how you can make yours last.* New York: Simon & Schuster.

Harris, G. W. (1997). *Dignity and vulnerability: Strength and quality of character.* Berkeley, CA: University of California Press.

Heuer, L., Blumenthal, E., Douglas, A., & Weinblatt, T. (1999). A deservingness approach to respect as a relationally based fairness judgment. *Personality and Social Psychology Bulletin, 25,* 1279-1292.

Hill, T. E. (2000). *Respect, pluralism, and justice: Kantian perspectives.* New York: Oxford University Press.

Honneth, A. (1995). *The struggle for recognition: The moral grammar of social conflicts.* Cambridge, UK: Cambridge University Press.

Honneth, A. (2001). Recognition of redistribution? Changing perspectives on the moral order of society. *Theory, culture, & Society, 18,* 43-55.

Jackson, L. M., Esses, V. M., & Burris, C. T. (2001). Contemporary sexism and discrimination: The importance of respect for men and women. *Personality and Social Psychology Bulletin, 27,* 48-61.

Jervis, R. (1976). *Perception and misperception in international politics.* Princeton, NJ: Princeton University Press.

Jost, J. T., & Major, B. (Eds.) (2001). *The psychology of legitimacy: Emerging perspectives on ideology, justice, and intergroup relations.* New York: Cambridge University Press.

Kant, I. ([1782] 1993). *Critique of pure reason.* Boston: Charles E. Tuttle Co.

Kelman, H. C. (2001). Reflections on social and psychological processes of legitimization and delegitimization. In J. T. Jost & B. Major (Eds.), *The psychology of legitimacy: Emerging perspectives on ideology, justice, and intergroup relations* (pp. 54-73). New York: Cambridge University Press.

Kenworthy, J. B., & Miller, N. (2002). Attributional biases about the origins of attitudes: Externality, emotionality, and rationality. *Journal of Personality and Social Psychology, 82,* 693-707.

Kinder, D. R. (1986). Presidential character revisited. In R. R. Lau & D. O. Sears (Eds.), *Political cognition* (pp. 233-255). Hillsdale, NJ: Erlbaum.

Kriesberg, L. (1998). *Paths to varieties of intercommunal reconciliation.* Paper presented to the seventeenth conference, International Peace Research Association, Durban, South Africa, June 22-26.

Landler, M. (2004). Iran's leader mixes hope with defiance in Davos talk. *The New York Times,* January 22, p. A5.

Lawrence-Lightfoot, S. (1999). *Respect: An exploration.* Reading, MA: Perseus Books.

Leventhal, G. S. (1980). What should be done with equity theory? New approaches to the study of fairness in social relationships. In K. Gergen, M. Greenberg, & R. Willis (Eds.), *Social exchange* (pp. 27-75). New York: Plenum.

Le Vine, R. A., & Campbell, D. T. (1972). *Ethnocentrism: Theories of conflict, ethnic attitudes and group behavior.* New York: Wiley.

Lind, E. A., Kanfer, R., & Earley, P. C. (1990). Voice, control, and procedural justice: Instrumental and noninstrumental concerns in fairness judgments. *Journal of Personality and Social Psychology, 59,* 952-959.

Linville, P. W., Fischer, G. W., & Salovey, P. (1989). Perceived distributions of the characteristics if ingroup and outgroup members: Empirical evidence and computer simulation. *Journal of Personality and Social Psychology, 38,* 689-703.

Margalit, A. (1996). *The decent society.* Cambridge, MA: Harvard University Press.

Markman, H., Stanley, S., & Blumberg, S. L. (1994). *Fighting for your marriage: Positive steps for preventing divorce and preserving a lasting love.* San Francisco: Jossey-Bass.

McCullough, M., Rachal, K., Steven, J., Worthington, E., Brown, S., & Hight, T. (1998). Interpersonal forgiving in close relationships II: Theoretical elaboration and measurement. *Journal of Personality and Social Psychology, 75,* 1586-1603.

McGraw, K. M. (2001). Political accounts and attribution processes. In J. H. Kuklinski (Ed.), *Citizens and politics: Perspectives from political psychology* (pp. 160-197). Cambridge, UK: Cambridge University Press.

McGuire, W. J. (1969). The nature of attitudes and attitude change. In G. Lindzey & E. Aronson (Eds.), *The handbook of social psychology* (2nd ed., vol. 3, pp. 136-314). Reading, MA: Addison-Wesley.

Miller, A. H., Wattenberg, M. P., & Malanchuk, O. (1986). Schematic assessments of presidential candidates. *American Political Science Review, 80,* 521-540.

Miller, D. (2001). Disrespect and the experience of injustice. *Annual Review of Psychology, 52,* 527-553.

Miller, S. M. (1993, Spring). The politics of respect. *Social Policy,* 44-51.

Miller, S. M., & Savoie, A. J. (2002). *Respect and rights: Class, race, and gender today.* New York: Rowman & Littlefield.

Nadler, A. (2002). Postresolution processes: Instrumental and socioemotional routes to reconciliation. In G. Salomon & N. Baruch (Eds.), *Peace education: The concept, principles, and practices around the world* (pp. 127-141). Mahwah, NJ: Erlbaum.

Ohbuchi, K., Kameda, M., & Agarie, N. (1989). Apology as aggression control: Its role in mediating appraisal of and response to harm. *Journal of Personality and Social Psychology, 56,* 219-227.

Opotow, S. (1990). Moral exclusion and injustice: An introduction. *Journal of Social Issues, 46,* 1-20.

Opotow, S. (2001). Social injustice. In D. J. Christie, R. V. Wagner, & D. D. Winter (Eds.), *Peace, conflict and violence: Peace psychology for the 21st century* (pp. 102-109). New York: Prentice-Hall.

Osgood, C. E. (1962). *An alternative to war or surrender.* Urbana: University of Illinois Press.

Pettigrew, T. F. (1979). The ultimate attribution error: Extending Allport's cognitive analysis of prejudice. *Personality and Social Psychology Bulletin, 5,* 461-76. Article Citation.

Pettigrew, T. F. (1998). Intergroup contact theory. *Annual Review of Psychology, 49,* 65-85.

Pettigrew, T. F., & Tropp, L. R. (2006). A meta-analytic test of intergroup contact theory. *Journal of Personality and Social Psychology, 90,* 751–783.

Petty, R. E., & Wegener, D. T. (1998). Attitude change: Multiple roles for persuasion variables. In D. T. Gilbert, S. T. Fiske, & G. Lindzey (Eds.), *The handbook of social psychology* (4th ed., pp. 323-390). New York: Oxford University Press.

Pincoffs, E. L. (1986). *Quandaries and virtues: Against reductionism in ethics.* Lawrence, Kansas: University Press of Kansas.

Pronin, E., Gilovich, T., & Ross, L. (2004). Objectivity in the eye of the beholder: Divergent perceptions of bias in self versus others. *Psychological Review, 111,* 781-199.

Pruitt, D. G., & Kim, S. H. (2004). *Social conflict: Escalation, stalemate, and settlement.* New York: McGraw-Hill.

Rahn, W., Aldrich, J. H., Borgida, E., & Sullivan, J. L. (1991). A social-cognitive model of candidate appraisal. In J. A. Ferejohn & J. H. Kuklinski (Eds.), *Information and democratic processes* (pp. 136-159). Urbana, IL: University of Illinois Press.

Ramsbotham, O., Woodhouse, T., & Miall, H. (2005). *Contemporary conflict resolution: The prevention, management and transformation of deadly conflicts.* Cambridge, UK: Polity Press.

Rawls, J. (1971). *A theory of justice.* Cambridge, MA: Harvard University Press.

Reeder, G. D., Pryor, J. B., Wohl, M. J., & Griswell, M. L. (2005). On attributing negative motives to others who disagree with our opinions. *Personality and Social Psychology Bulletin, 31,* 1498-1510.

Reiman, J. (1990). *Justice and modern moral philosophy.* New Haven: Yale University Press.

Rimer, S., & Healy, P. D. (2005). Harvard president vows to temper his style with respect. *The New York Times,* February 12, 2005.

Robinson, R., Keltner, D., Ward, A., & Ross, L. (1995). Actual versus assumed differences in construal: "Naïve realism" in intergroup perception and conflict. *Journal of Personality and Social Psychology, 68,* 404-417.

Ross, L. (2005). Reactive devaluation in negotiation and conflict resolution. In M. H. Bazerman (Ed.), *Negotiation, decision-making, and conflict management* (pp. 227-293). Northampton, MA: Edward Elgar Publishing.

Ross, L., & Ward, A. (1996). Naïve realism in everyday life: Implications for social conflict and misunderstanding. In T. Brown, E. S. Reed., & E. Turiel (Eds.), *Values and knowledge* (pp. 103-135). Hillsdale, NJ: Erlbaum.

Sante, L. (2004). Tourists and torturers. *The New York Times,* May 11, 2004.

Schulman, M. (2002). How we become moral: The sources of moral motivation. In C. R. Snyder & S. J. Lopez (Eds.), *Handbook of positive psychology* (pp. 499-512). New York: Oxford University Press.

Sennet, R. (2003). *Respect in a world of inequality.* New York: W. W. Norton.

Silverstein, B. (1992). The psychology of enemy images. In S. Staub & P. Green (Eds.), *Psychology and social responsibility* (pp.145-162). New York: New York University Press.

Simon, B., & Sturmer, S. (2003). Respect for group members: Intragroup determinants of collective identification and group-serving bias. *Personality and Social Psychology Bulletin, 29,* 183-193.

Staub, E. (1989). *The roots of evil: The origins of genocide and other group violence.* New York: Cambridge University Press.

Tajfel, H., & Turner, J. C. (1986). The social identity theory of intergroup relations. In S. Worchel & W. G. Austin (Eds.), *Psychology of intergroup relations* (2nd ed., pp. 7-24). Chicago: Nelson-Hall.

Taylor, C. (1994). The politics of recognition. In A. Guttman (Ed.), *Multiculturalism: Examining the politics of recognition* (pp. 25-74). Princeton, NJ: Princeton University Press.

Turner, J. C. (1987). *Rediscovering the social group: A self-categorization theory.* Oxford, UK: Basil Blackwell.

Tyler, T. R. (1987). Conditions leading to value expressive affect in judgments of procedural justice: A test of four models. *Journal of Personality and Social Psychology, 52,* 333-344.

Tyler, T. R. (1989). The psychology of procedural justice: A test of the group value model. *Journal of Personality and Social Psychology, 57,* 830-838.

Tyler, T. R. (1990). *Why people obey the law: Procedural justice, legitimacy, and compliance.* New Haven, CT: Yale University Press.Tyler, T. R. (2001). A psychological perspective on the legitimacy of institutions and authorities. In J. T. Jost & B. Major (Eds.), *The psychology of legitimacy: Emerging perspectives on ideology, justice, and intergroup relations* (pp. 416-436). New York: Cambridge University Press.

Tyler, T. R., & Blader, S. L. (2000). *Cooperation in groups: Procedural justice, social identity, and behavioral engagement.* Philadelphia: Psychology Press.

Tyler, T. R., & Blader, S. L. (2003). The group engagement model: Procedural justice, social identity, and cooperative behavior. *Personality and Social Psychology Review, 7,* 349-361.

Tyler, T. R., Boeckmann, R. J., Smith, H. J., & Huo, Y. J. (1997). *Social justice in a diverse society.* Boulder, CO: Westview.

Tyler, T. R., & Huo, Y. J. (2002). *Trust in the Law.* New York: Russell-Sage.

United Nations. (1948). Retrieved June 10, 2005, from http://www.un.org./Overview/rights.html

Van der Merwe, H. (2001). Reconciliation and justice in South Africa: Lessons for the TRC's community interventions. In M. Abu-Nimer (Ed.), *Reconciliation, justice, and coexistence* (pp. 187-207). New York: Lexington Books.

White, R. K. (1984). *Fearful warriors: A psychological profile of U.S-Soviet relations.* New York: Free Press.

Wojciszke, B. (1994). Multiple meanings of behavior: Construing actions in terms of competence or morality. *Journal of Personality and Social Psychology, 67,* 222-232.

Wojciszke, B. (1997). Parallels between competence-versus morality-related traits and individualistic and collectivistic values. *European Journal of Social Psychology, 27,* 245-256.

CHAPTER 8

From Egosystem to Ecosystem in Intergroup Interactions: Implications for Intergroup Reconciliation

JENNIFER CROCKER, JULIE A. GARCIA, AND NOAH NUER

The under-representation of women in tenured positions in science departments at universities exemplifies the intersection of status, power, and social structure with implicit psychological processes (Rimer, 2005). Women rarely hold positions of power in academia, such as department chair or dean in the sciences; men are more likely to have decision-making authority. Norms about what good scientists should be like are not gender-neutral, but masculine, and work to women's disadvantage (Georgi, 2000). Women job applicants and tenure candidates are often evaluated more negatively than men with identical experience and accomplishments (Steinpreis, Anders, & Ritske, 1999). A Swedish study found that female applicants for postdoctoral fellowships from the Swedish Medical Research Council had to be 2.5 times more productive than their male counterparts to receive the same competence ratings from reviewers (Wenneras & Wold, 1997). Gender stereotypes about the characteristics of men and women that make them suited or unsuited for an academic career in science can operate implicitly (Greenwald & Banaji, 1995), and undermine the performance of women in domains where their abilities are negatively stereotyped (Spencer, Steele, & Quinn, 1999; Steele, 1997). Taken together, this research suggests that gender disparities can be explained, at least in part, by stereotypes and prejudice rather than differentials in actual ability.

This example of stereotypes, prejudice, and discrimination at play underscores the importance of critically examining and changing both the power structure and the explicit and implicit stereotypes people hold of underrepresented or disadvantaged groups that maintain inequality. Yet, such change is difficult and slow, often too slow to be useful to people who are contending with these obstacles in their daily lives. Although women scientists may wish that there were more women department chairs and deans, there is little they can do to effect such changes in the short term. Pervasive cultural messages reinforce the unconscious biases their colleagues hold against women scientists, making attempts to change these biases futile.

Consequently, the emphasis on documenting power and status differences between groups, and the often implicit or unconscious biases that perpetuate these differences, can create a sense of powerlessness and victimization in the targets of stereotypes, prejudice, and discrimination. Individual members of devalued groups typically have little or no ability to influence the power structure in which they live or work, and they have little ability to change the unconscious stereotypes and biases of the people with whom they interact.

Awareness of these obstacles can also create a sense of powerlessness and victimization among people with valued identities, even those in high power or high status, privileged positions. People whose identities are valued are vulnerable to accusations of stereotyping, prejudice, and discrimination. Because these processes often occur outside of conscious awareness (Greenwald & Banaji, 1995), such accusations could have validity even if these people has no conscious experience of harboring negative stereotypes or discriminating against others; thus, they may feel impossible to correct for the bias or defend themselves against accusations even when they feel untrue. In sum, identifying and understanding both structural barriers and prejudice, stereotyping, and discrimination, particularly in their implicit or unconscious forms can be extremely important for understanding the obstacles people with devalued identities confront. Nonetheless, these approaches have limited immediate utility for those on the front lines of intergroup relations.

In this chapter, we present a framework for thinking about intergroup relations that can be immediately useful to people who are confronted with these issues in their daily lives. We suggest that downward spirals in intergroup relations are a product of egosystem motivational dynamics, and suggest that ecosystem dynamics can create upward spirals in intergroup relations. In doing so, we do not advocate abandoning attempts to change stereotypes and prejudice, or alter power and status relations; rather, we aim to explore where individuals caught in these processes have leverage to create positive dynamics in their intergroup relations.

Egosystem Motivation

The ego, as used here, refers to a set of beliefs, goals, strategies, and routines developed over the lifespan and driven by the desire to protect or inflate the self, especially one's self-image and the image that others hold of the self. The ego has both proactive and defensive aspects. When driven by their egos people proactively desire and seek recognition, acknowledgement, and attention on the one hand. On the other hand, they defensively fear and protect the self from rejection, humiliation, and criticism.

Furthermore, the egosystem is concerned with what events (including imagined or fantasized events) mean to the self—am I worthy or worthless? What does my self-image or public image stand to gain or lose? In the egosystem, other people are viewed as agents of validation or invalidation of the self. Others can enhance the self through praise, admiration, and acknowledgement, or by performing worse than the self. Alternatively, others can threaten the self by criticizing, overlooking, rejecting, humiliating, outperforming, or abandoning the self. Others are viewed as judges, competitors, or threats to the self in a zero-sum framework; the self is typically seen as the victim of other people and events.

When driven by egosystem motivations, people often act in destructive or self-defeating ways (Crocker & Park, 2004). For example, when they are uncertain of success, people will often self-handicap, creating a good excuse or explanation for failure, such as procrastinating (Tice, 1991). Self-handicapping protects self-esteem by providing an explanation for failure, but undermines the likelihood of success. A recent series of studies shows that when people are driven by egosystem motivations, they often end up with the opposite of what they want. Zhang and Baumeister (2006) showed that ego threat increases costly entrapment in bad decisions, known as the problem of sunk costs or "throwing good money after bad." For example, a subtle ego threat such as telling people that they should not continue with a game if they are the kind of person who chokes under pressure actually increased the tendency to persist in a money-losing endeavor. Participants given an irrelevant ego threat were more likely to pay more than \$1 in an auction for a \$1 bill, because they did not want to lose face. Under ego threat, people not only lost money, they also ultimately lost their pride as a result of entrapment in a poor decision. It is easy to see how these ego-defensive routines can be costly in intergroup conflicts, when actions that could resolve a conflict such as making a concession or admitting past mistakes are resisted because of the desire to validate that one (or one's group) is competent, right, virtuous, or just.

Driving Idea

The egosystem motivational framework has three foundational concerns each with cognitive, affective, and motivational aspects. The first concern is organized around what we call the driving idea, or the person's belief about the key danger that other people can represent, the anxiety one feels about that danger, and the motivation to protect oneself from that danger. This driving idea can be expressed in the form, "They will {do something to} me," and stems from interpretations of events that occurred earlier in life, often in childhood. People are vigilant for signs of the danger, and events are perceived and interpreted through the filter of the driving idea (Crocker & Park, 2004). Consequently, they are likely to *see* the danger where it does not exist in reality, or where the reality is ambiguous. Rejection sensitivity, defined as the anxious expectation of rejection (Downey & Feldman, 1996; Downey, Freitas, Michaelis, & Khouri, 1998), exemplifies the driving idea. The driving idea elicits strong emotion because it implies that the self is unlovable, incompetent, worthless, or unsafe.

Interactions with out-group members are fertile ground for the driving idea. Out-group members have, or are perceived to have, different experiences, beliefs, and goals than the self or in-group members. Perceived difference easily fosters misunderstanding and undermines trust, activating the driving idea, which becomes the filter through which the other is perceived. Furthermore, in reality intergroup relations are often difficult, fraught with conflict, and out-group members can pose a real threat, or have real power over one's outcomes. These real differences in goals and interests are rich soil for the growth of the driving idea especially when people feel they lack power (Keltner, Gruenfeld, & Anderson, 2003).

For people with devalued identities, the driving idea may be directly linked to their identity, grounded in emotionally powerful early experiences with prejudice, discrimination, or harassment connected to one's identity. Thus, the driving idea can take the form, "They will {reject/hurt/discriminate against} me, because I am {black/Japanese/Latina/gay/female}." As Mendoza-Denton, Downey, Purdie, Davis, and Pietrzak (2002, p. 897) suggest, "As targets of discrimination and prejudice, members of stigmatized groups might be particularly likely to develop expectations of rejection by those who do not share their stigma and by social institutions who have historically excluded or marginalized them."

Unconscious Goal

People draw conclusions about what they need to be or do to protect themselves from the danger of the driving idea, leading to the second foundational concern of the egosystem, the unconscious goal. The content of the unconscious goal is idiosyncratic, based on what gave the person recognition, attention, and acknowledgement in the context of the family, community, peer group, or culture. Unconscious goals include things like being strong, tough, smart, charming, attractive, virtuous, and so on. The unconscious goal represents an extreme version of these qualities. For example, the unconscious goal of the egosystem is not simply to be smart, but to be the most brilliant; it is not simply to be respected by some people, but to be admired by everyone.

Social identities can either thwart or foster the unconscious goal. Group-based stereotypes, and social status and power differences, can buttress or undermine the unconscious goal. To return to our earlier example, the unconscious goal to be the most brilliant and creative scientist may be fostered by the identity of being a man, and therefore more similar to the stereotype of a brilliant scientist; it may also be fostered by subtle biases that provide recognition, acknowledgement, and opportunities to male scientists compared to female scientists with equal credentials.

These two concerns of the egosystem—the driving idea and the unconscious goal—represent both an avoidance or prevention goal, focused on the driving idea, and an approach or promotion goal, focused on the unconscious goal. Subjectively, people experience themselves as victims in the egosystem—based on threatening childhood experiences, people feel the need to protect themselves, and to do so they believe they need to be the best, most outstanding at something. The proactive, self-promoting unconscious goal, which victimizes others, feels like a necessary response to the danger that others pose. In the egosystem, everyone feels like a victim and no one sees himself as a perpetrator.

Desired Image

The third foundational concern of the egosystem is the desired image, the positive views people have (or want to have) of themselves and want others to have of them. These beliefs shape goals, particularly the goal to prove or demonstrate that one has the qualities of the desired image (Crocker & Park, 2004). Because people need others to recognize and validate these qualities in the self in order to sustain self-esteem, they do things to make sure others see them in this way, and do not see them as the opposite. For example, a person with the desired image of *unprejudiced* may bend over backward in favoring a target of prejudice to avoid the appearance of being prejudiced (Plant & Devine, 1998).

Because they emphasize appearance over reality, desired images have many costs. First, as noted, the things people do to *appear* as their desired image sometimes actually undermine their ability to *be* that way, such as when students who want to appear smart decide not to raise their hand and indicate when they are confused by a point in a lecture—they avoid risking appearing stupid, but at the expense of learning and becoming smart. Second, when people are driven by their desired image, their focus is on demonstrating and proving something about themselves, rather than learning. The pursuit of the desired image fosters self-validation goals at the expense of learning, especially on difficult tasks (Crocker & Park, 2004; Dykman, 1998; Grant & Dweck, 2003). Third, when people are driven by the desired image they become disconnected from other people; in emphasizing appearance over reality, people are inauthentic and even manipulative, blocking meaningful connections with others.

In intergroup interactions, people bring with them the usual or typical desired images they have in any interaction (e.g., competent, virtuous, important, good student, good mentor), and also those aspects that are specifically relevant to their identity as a member of a particular valued or devalued group (e.g., fair, unprejudiced, deserving of respect, intelligent, not ignorant). When the goal to validate the desired image is activated, people process events for what they mean about their image. Success at building or bolstering the desired image triggers positive self-relevant emotions such as pride; threats or obstacles to the desired image trigger negative self-relevant emotions such as shame, guilt, or humiliation, as well as other negative emotions such as sadness, anger, or fear.

Contexts in which one's identity is linked to negative stereotypes may activate the goal to prove that those stereotypes are untrue, or do not apply to the self or one's group (Steele, 1997). For example, a student of color in the classroom may interpret a teacher correcting her in terms of what it means for her personal or group desired image of intelligent. Similarly, contexts in which one's identity is valued or idealized may activate the goal to demonstrate that one possesses the positive traits the identity is supposed to bestow; that one is fair and unprejudiced, or that one has not benefited unfairly from one's privileged status. Thus, whether stigmatized or idealized, social identities can trigger goals to validate desired images in intergroup interactions. This goal will take on heightened importance when it is not only one's personal image that is at stake, but also the image of one's group. Defending the image of the group may feel noble, because it is done for the sake of others, but it also involves egosystem motivations, because it involves validating the desired group image.

Ego-Defense

In sum, the egosystem is a motivational framework in which people strive to protect the self from the danger of the driving idea, acquire the recognition, acknowledgement, and feeling of safety that accompanies achievement of the unconscious goal, and to validate the desired image. We argue that the egosystem drives most behavior most of the time—it is the habitual or default motivational system. To achieve the ends of the egosystem, people proactively seek success and accomplishments that will give them recognition, acknowledgement, and attention. Recognition, acknowledgement, and attention are often confused with power and respect on the one hand, and love, connection, and inclusion on the other hand. However, receiving recognition, acknowledgement, and attention elicits jealousy and competition in others, which reinforces or heightens intergroup tension. Threats to the goals of the egosystem trigger emotional responses such as anger, shame, humiliation, and anxiety. People also learn many ego-defensive and protective mechanisms, routines, and strategies to cope with minor threats to the ego; these strategies are well-known in psychological research. They include vigilance for rejection (Kramer & Messick, 1998; Leary & Baumeister, 2000), preemptive maneuvers like rejecting others before they can reject me (Murray, Holmes, MacDonald, & Ellsworth, 1998), blaming others for failure and taking credit for success (Bradley, 1978), protecting the self from possible failure by self-handicapping (Jones & Berglas, 1978), disengaging from goals when failure is a possibility (Carver, Blaney, & Scheier, 1979), and so on—the list of ego-defensive routines is too long to enumerate here.

Events that clearly and strongly confirm the driving idea, or demonstrate that one is the opposite of one's desired image or unconscious goal pose major threats to the egosystem. These events trigger intense initial emotional numbness (Campbell, Baumeister, Dhavale, & Tice, 2003), typically followed by negative self-relevant emotions (Tangney, 1999; Tangney, Wagner, Hill-Barlow, Marschall, & Gramzow, 1996), and elicit extreme and extremely destructive responses (Tangney, 1999). Research on the consequences of social rejection, which is a common driving idea, provides a good example of this last-ditch response of the egosystem to major threat. Laboratory studies of rejection show that rejected people are more aggressive (Buckley, Winkel, & Leary, 2004; Twenge, Baumeister, Tice, & Stucke, 2001) and self-destructive, behaving in risky and unhealthy ways (Twenge, Catanese, & Baumeister, 2002). We suspect that self-destructive behaviors in response to major ego threats are particularly characteristic of people who otherwise feel powerless. As Eric Harris, one of the Columbine High School shooters, said "Isn't it fun to get the respect that we're going to deserve?" (Twenge & Campbell, 2003). When they cannot see other ways to draw attention to their needs, people will hurt themselves to hurt others, and in the process force others to notice their pain or frustration. In the context of intergroup relations, these destructive behaviors may emerge as acts of terrorism.

In sum, our framework suggests that intergroup relations provide fertile ground for the operation of egosystem motivations, powerful self-relevant emotions and behaviors that are mutually destructive. In the context of tense intergroup relations, with past histories of mutual mistrust and harm, real conflicts of interest, negative stereotypes, and social structures that exacerbate these problems, adding egosystem motivational orientations can be like adding fuel to the fire of intergroup relations.

Downward Spirals of Egosystem-Driven Intergroup Relations

Difficult interactions between people with different social identities are exacerbated when their egosystems can become intertwined and mutually reinforcing, creating a downward spiral that is difficult to break. These downward spirals involve expectancy confirmation processes (Snyder & Stukas, 1999) and self-fulfilling prophecies (Merton, 1948; Snyder, 1984). Social psychologists typically describe expectancy confirmation and self-fulfilling prophesy effects as primarily cognitive. For example, in a lot of research on self-fulfilling prophecies and expectancy confirmation effects, expectancies are manipulated by the researcher or derived from widely known social stereotypes of a group. However, in our view the particularly negative and destructive aspect of these downward spirals in intergroup relations stem from their connection to the powerful motivations of the egosystem. People bring their driving ideas about the danger that other people represent to these interactions, and are vigilant for signs of their driving idea. Because the driving idea represents the worst-case scenario for the egosystem, this anxious expectation is particularly potent in intergroup interactions. Although the driving idea is easily activated, it is not often true; other more benign explanations for an out-group member's behavior are not usually considered, because the driving idea fits one's past experience and one's beliefs about out-group members. Unconscious goals and desired images also drive people in these downward spirals, contributing to their negative reactions to out-group members. For example, a common unconscious goal is to be right over others. Thus, when a person perceives that he has been stereotyped or discriminated against, he thinks he is correct in his interpretation. Consequently, possible misconceptions are left unchallenged, perpetuating negative dynamics.

From the perspective of the out-group member or the person who is stereotyped, interactions are ego-threatening because of the possibility of harm, devaluation, or rejection linked to one's identity. Concern that out-group members will harm, reject, or devalue the self may be connected to one's driving idea, and strengthened by knowledge of past out-group attacks on in-group members, or by personal experience with such attacks. In many cases, there is a history of real physical harm to the in-group by out-group members, so vigilance for the possibility of harm or rejection may become necessary for survival, activating the fight-or-flight response. This threat can lead to withdrawal from the interaction (Wright, Gronfien, & Owens, 2000), heightened vigilance for signs of rejection or devaluation (Frable, Wortman, & Joseph, 1997; Kramer, 1998; Kramer & Messick, 1998; Pinel, 1999), or if possible, concealing one's identity from the other (Goffman, 1963; Jones et al., 1984). People who are vigilant for intended harm, rejection, and devaluation see them easily and often, because perceptions of reality are filtered through the anxious expectation that they will occur (Downey et al., 1998; Kramer, 1998; Kramer & Messick, 1998; Pinel, 1999). Thus, vigilance repeatedly leads people to perceive the rejection or devaluation they fear. In response, they react, perhaps by withdrawing or by accusing the other of prejudice (Crocker, Voelkl, Testa, & Major, 1991). Often, as we note shortly, out-group members react badly to these behaviors, becoming defensive, angry, or blaming. However painful this sequence of events might be, there is a sense in which these reactions feel satisfying to the ego because they affirm one's rightness and victimhood. Yet, they have high costs for the self and others (Kaiser & Miller, 2001). It is important to note that we do not argue that prejudice and discrimination exist only in the mind of the target; rather, we suggest that past experience and awareness of the realities of prejudice and discrimination can arouse egosystem-based vigilance and self-protective routines, which can sometimes lead to a misperception of reality, contributing to the downward spiral of intergroup relations and causing people to re-experience precisely what they want to avoid.

From the perspective of the person with a valued identity, especially someone who does not see himself as prejudiced, the interaction is threatening because he could be perceived as prejudiced. Most people have desired images of being fair, reasonable, and unprejudiced. In the context of intergroup relations, threats to these desired images have a particular potency, because their opposites—prejudice, racism, and discrimination—have strong negative connotations, including associations to being a perpetrator, an exploiter, even a killer. Furthermore, social norms dictate that one should be unprejudiced (Crandall, Eshleman, & O'Brien, 2002; Monteith, Deneen, & Tooman, 1996). Thus, the possibility of being accused by an out-group member of bias or discrimination can threaten the ego, and create vigilance for unfair accusations.

Consequently, nonstigmatized people may be anxious about appearing prejudiced, vigilant for accusations of prejudice, attempt to inhibit or suppress expressions of prejudice, and become defensive in response to any questions about their intentions (Crandall et al., 2002; Devine, Plant, Amodio, Harmon-Jones, & Vance, 2002; Monteith et al., 1996; Plant & Devine, 1998). Suppressing prejudice has paradoxical effects—when the effort to suppress is lifted, fatigue sets in, or there are distractions, suppression of stereotypical thoughts can have rebound effects (MacRae, Bodenhausen, Milne, & Jetten, 1994), making it more likely that the person will *slip* and say something inappropriate. This can trigger guilt or blame (Czopp & Monteith, 2003). Most likely, the person with the valued identity will conclude that his or her good intentions are unappreciated, feel falsely accused, and paradoxically, feel victimized if his or her behavior is criticized. Thus, the vigilance of the person with a valued identity may lead him or her to "walk on eggshells," censor himself or herself around out-group members, and repeatedly perceive the criticism or accusation he or she fears. In response, he or she may accuse the other of being overly sensitive, affirming his or her rightness and victimhood, which also has high costs for the self and others.

The resulting dynamic can be painful for both parties, confirming their worst fears about out-group members. Each person in the interaction, driven by fears and anxieties, triggers the fears of the other and creates what they want to avoid. Of course, there are many versions of this, depending on whether the devalued person withdraws, conceals, or accuses, and on whether the valued person reacts to this behavior with guilt, anger, or withdrawal. The general rule, in our experience, is that each person acts in ways that make it more, rather than less, likely that his or her worst fears will come true.

Consider the dynamic depicted in Figure 8.1. To help the discussion, we refer to the person with a devalued identity as *she* and the person with a valued identity as *he*. It is important to remember that a person who is valued in one context may be devalued in another, and even in the same interaction, each person may fear being devalued. For simplicity's sake, however, Figure 8.1 assumes that one person has a valued identity and the other has a devalued identity. The devalued person in this dynamic begins with anxiety about being devalued, rejected, overlooked, or harmed, related to the belief or concern that the other may be prejudiced. Her belief might be based on past experience or knowledge gleaned from others' experiences. She is vigilant for signs of prejudice or unfair treatment, resulting in a level of scrutiny of his words and deeds that few could pass. Sensing that he is under scrutiny, the valued person might become nervous, distracted, or focused on suppressing inappropriate thoughts, which paradoxically can lead to a slip of the tongue (or a slip of the mind), and the unwanted expression of prejudice. The devalued person may respond with

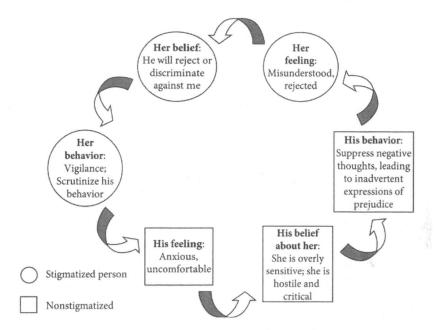

FIGURE 8.1. A downward spiral of interaction between a stigmatized person (circles) and nonstigmatized person (rectangles).

complicated emotions. On the one hand, her worst fears have come true; on the other hand, she knows that she was right to be vigilant and mistrusting, and there is a relief in being right and knowing where the danger of the driving idea resides. She may confront him about his behavior. He, thinking of himself as a good, fair, and nonprejudiced person, may react to this accusation either with rage, or with shame and humiliation, or both. He may become angry, defensive, and feel that his good intentions are unappreciated. He may conclude that she always sees herself as a victim, is critical and judgmental, and never gives him the benefit of the doubt. He may respond with greater anxiety about being accused of prejudice, defending himself, counterattacking, withdrawing, or resisting. She, in turn, will feel misunderstood, judged, and disrespected, and this will reinforce her conclusion that he is prejudiced.

We began describing the cycle with her, the devalued person's, belief that she might be the target of stereotypes, prejudice, or discrimination. However, we could just as easily have begun describing the cycle with him, and his anxiety about being accused of prejudice. The important thing to note is that there is no single person who started this cycle—both people in this dynamic bring with them their fears and anxieties, and both contribute to the cycle.

In this cycle, the worst fears of both the valued and the devalued person are confirmed. He was right to be worried about being accused of prejudice, and she was right to worry that he is prejudiced. It is difficult for either of them to see how they are each partially responsible for this reality. In fact, talking about who is right and who is wrong in this dynamic is usually not a way out of the cycle; instead, it is counterproductive, at least when egosystem motivations are at play. Both are right, and both are wrongly accused. Both are innocent victims in their own minds, and both are perpetrators in the other person's mind. In reality, each person in this interaction is both a victim and a perpetrator. After this interaction, each will approach the next interaction with more anxiety, mistrust, and suspicion, and create a new destructive cycle.

Our analysis begs the question whether the person with the valued identity did in fact harbor prejudice or discriminate against her in the first place. It is not that we think this question is unimportant; rather, we think it is a difficult and delicate process to uncover the answer. In many cases, because stereotypes can be over-learned, unconscious, and expressed implicitly, the answer is probably yes. Nevertheless, discovering the answer to this question in a specific instance is very difficult. It requires honest, nondefensive self-examination on the part of the person with the valued identity. Such exploration is very difficult when he fears being judged or criticized, or wants to protect a desired image. People with valued identities will either deny their prejudice, or in some cases, readily confess their prejudice to demonstrate that they are on the side of good. Uncovering the truth about one's own prejudices is almost impossible in the egosystem.

To this point, we have described a downward spiral involving two people with different social identities. It is important to recognize that these interactions take place in the context of groups, which have their own internal dynamics that can reinforce the downward spiral. Groups create common values, worldviews, and practices among their members, and they are invested in defending the correctness of these values, views, and practices (Solomon, Greenberg, & Pyszczynski, 1991). In addition, groups, like individuals, often feel insecure about the correctness of their worldview, and are punitive toward those who threaten it (Greenberg et al., 1990). When the participants in this cycle feel wrongly treated or wrongly accused, they can turn to in-group members for support and validation of the correctness of their beliefs, interpretations, and actions. Typically, in-group members will reinforce the person's view of himself as a victim, whose negative responses to the other are not only justified but also imperative. In-group members may encourage a combative response, or even take it upon themselves to correct or avenge the wrong. Thus, when a conflict between two individuals occurs in the context of intergroup tension or hostility, in-group members tend to shore up the egosystem, making it less likely that participants will question the assumptions, beliefs, and filters they bring to the interaction, or recognize their own responsibility in the downward spiral.

In sum, when people are motivated by the egosystem, real group differences in perspective, experience, interests, and worldviews become fertile ground for the operation of the driving idea, the unconscious goal, and the desired image. The ego threat that out-group members pose triggers ego-defenses that are ultimately self-defeating and destructive. They contribute to escalating conflicts, mistrust, hostility, and it becomes increasingly difficult to communicate constructively and achieve mutually beneficial goals.

In our experience people have little awareness of the dynamics of these downward spirals, their own responsibility for creating and maintaining them, and their costs for the self, the in-group, the out-group, and often innocent bystanders. The ego benefits of being sure one is right and morally superior, seeing oneself as the victim and the other as the perpetrator, and consequently not feeling responsible for the current situation, obscure the long-term costs, especially the costs to others. When people are unaware of the costs, they may be caught in a misery of their own making, yet unable to see where they have the power to avoid these costs and create a different dynamic.

These destructive dynamics in intergroup relations continue, in part, because people believe their reactions are appropriate, justified, and right, and that it would be dangerous or irresponsible, to oneself or one's group, to do otherwise. People want out-group members to understand their experience and respond to their needs, but they do not want to understand the other's experience or respond to the other's needs. Often, the only way people try to improve the situation is to convince out-group members of the rightness of their own views, and that the out-group member is wrong. Yet, attempting to convince out-group members of the wrong-headedness of their views or behaviors is rarely successful; it triggers defensiveness, argumentation, and resistance. Out-group members become more firmly entrenched in their position. Could there be a goal that is more productive, more constructive, than wanting to be right and prove the other wrong?

Ecosystem Motivation

We believe it is possible to shift the paradigm so that, instead of triggering ego-defenses, real group differences in perspectives, experiences, interests, and worldviews can become an opportunity to expand one's understanding of reality, fostering learning, growth, and connection. Where egosystem motivations foster downward spirals in intergroup relations, we propose that ecosystem motivations may create upward spirals.

The ecosystem, as used here, refers to a motivational orientation driven by goals that are larger or more important than the ego, such as what people want to create or contribute, what they want to give, or how they want to grow. Whereas egosystem motivation is concerned with self-preservation, and physiologically involves the fight-or-flight stress response, ecosystem motivation is concerned with caring for or giving to others, and physiologically involves the species-preservation response (Henry & Wang, 1998), also called the tend-and-befriend response (Taylor et al., 2000). Whereas the egosystem is focused on protecting or inflating the self, the ecosystem is concerned with being authentic, acknowledging one's fallibility, and growing for the sake of goals that are larger than the self. In contrast to egosystem goals, which are concerned with "What does it mean about my image or my worth?" and "What's in it for me?" ecosystem goals are concerned with making a difference for the greater whole. Ecosystem goals are not self-sacrificing; they are good for the self and others. Ecosystem goals are sustainable; if every person had the same goal, it would support rather than threaten the self. In the ecosystem, other people are resources, sources of support, and potentially aligned with the self, rather than threats. Whereas the framework of the egosystem is zero-sum, the framework of the ecosystem is not zero-sum. Whereas people driven by egosystem motivations are concerned with being right, and proving or demonstrating their desired images or their worth, ecosystem goals encourage openness to learning, understanding the perspective of others, and constructive communication. Ecosystem goals may require risking being rejected, devalued, or criticized, and saying, "So what?" because the goal at stake is more important than the ego. Ecosystem goals empower, because they start with the self, not others. Others can support, but cannot replace the responsibility and ownership of the self. Consequently, ecosystem goals push people into action.

For example, Garcia (2005) has examined motivations for disclosing and concealing a concealable stigma. Participants were college students with a history of depression or a nonstraight sexual orientation. She assessed a wide range of reasons for and against disclosure, and found that many loaded on two uncorrelated factors, which she identified as egosystem goals and ecosystem goals. Egosystem goals against disclosure involved fear of rejection, avoiding conflict, protecting privacy, and wanting the other's approval, and egosystem goals for disclosing involved testing the other's reaction and catharsis. Items loading on the second, ecosystem goals factor were all reasons to disclose, and included educating the other, personal growth, similarity with the other, and the importance of the stigma to identity. Garcia (2005) found that egosystem goals were correlated with stress, low self-esteem, and depression, whereas ecosystem goals were correlated with lower levels of stress, higher self-esteem and less depression. Importantly, ecosystem goals predicted decreased symptoms of depression two weeks later. Furthermore, ecosystem goals were associated with increased disclosure of the stigma, and more positive emotions when people disclosed, whereas egosystem goals— even egosystem reasons for disclosing—were associated with less disclosure. Thus, this initial study supports the notion that people can have egosystem or ecosystem goals in intergroup relationships, and ecosystem goals are associated with more positive outcomes for the individual and the relationship.

Creating Upward Spirals in Intergroup Relations

How can we use the idea of ecosystem goals to create a more positive dynamic in intergroup relations? We believe that there are several elements to creating upward spirals.

Taking Stock

The first step toward creating a different dynamic involves taking stock of the current situation, stepping out of one's egosystem to examine the dynamic and one's own contribution to it thoroughly and honestly. To be sure, such self-examination is not easy or comfortable for the ego. But a realistic assessment of the dynamic and one's contribution to it is the essential first step in deciding whether one is fed up with the dynamic, and therefore wants it to change, and identifying where one has the leverage to create something different.

Regaining Responsibility

In downward intergroup spirals, each person or group feels a victim of the other, and believes that their own reactions are necessary and justified by the other's behavior. Ecosystem goals, because they start with the self, encourage people to explore their own responsibility in these cycles. For example, a person can check his interpretation of the interaction, examining whether his understanding is skewed or incomplete. Doing so may threaten desired images, yet enables people to step out of their victim role. He may realize, for example, that he was wrong or jumped to conclusions. However minor one's role in the downward spiral, it is precisely the places where one has responsibility that one has the leverage or opportunity to create a different outcome. Thus, once ego concerns are set aside, looking at one's own responsibility is empowering.

Clarifying Ecosystem Goals

Once people have clearly identified their responsibility for negative dynamics, and the costs of those dynamics, they can clarify ecosystem goals for what they want to create in their intergroup interactions. One interesting starting point is taking what one wants to experience in intergroup interactions, and asking "How can I create that for others?" People who want to feel safe, want the other to be trustworthy, or do not want to be victimized can begin by creating those experiences for others. Perhaps the most important aspect of ecosystem goals is their sustainability—if everyone, including out-group members, had the same goal, would that be good for me or for us? In the context of intergroup relations, ecosystem goals might focus on creating trust, or creating constructive communication with out-group members. Rather than ask, "Is the other trustworthy, is it safe to talk to this person?" a person with an ecosystem goal might ask, "What can I or we do to create trust and improve our communication?" Because these goals are good for others as well as the self or the in-group, they can be inspiring to others.

Creating a Safe Space for Constructive Communication

The next step in creating upward spirals in intergroup relations concerns creating a *safe space* for talking about the real issues in the relationship. There are many elements to creating a safe space, including, first of all, working through one's own fears. As we have seen, interacting from the standpoint of being vigilant for harm, rejection, or devaluation by others contributes to downward spirals, so it is essential to become aware of those fears when they arise, and sort through their connection to ego mechanisms, such as the driving idea, the unconscious goal, and desired images. A second aspect of creating a safe space is suspending judgment and criticism of the other, and of oneself; judgments and criticism make it unsafe to look at one's own contribution to the problem. Third, being emotionally vulnerable elicits more empathy and caring from others than being tough, strong, or apparently invulnerable.

Respect and Empathy for the Other's Situation

Often people want out-group members to change their beliefs, values, or interpretations of the situation. This desire automatically creates tension in the relationship, because it begins with one person looking down at the other, thinking that the other should believe something different, and wanting to be right about that. Many responses in that moment are very destructive. Even if one disagrees with the other, it is important to understand and accept that that is what the other believes, and not begin by wanting them to change their beliefs.

Being in Learning Mode

Instead of wanting to convince others to change their beliefs or interpretations, a more constructive goal would involve wanting to identify the places where one's own understanding of the situation or of the other's point of view is incomplete or distorted, and expand one's understanding. When out-group members feel heard and understood, they are more able to hear and understand the other (Stone, Patton, & Heen, 1999).

Compassion for Oneself

Finally, in the attempt to create upward spirals in intergroup relations, it is important to have compassion for oneself, to acknowledge that one is human, and therefore will make mistakes, and be nonperfect. The alternative, wanting to be perfect and right, makes it very difficult to be open to the other person's experience. Compassion for one's own human failings can make it easier to hear and respond to the pain or complaints of the other person.

These elements can create a context in which it is possible to have a constructive dialogue about real issues and concerns. In exploring and identifying their own ego mechanisms and owning up to them, people realize where they are least able to distinguish their biased and distorted perceptions from reality. If they can create a dialogue with the other to check their interpretations and expand their understanding of reality instead of reacting from their interpretations as if they were reality, then they have a vastly improved chance to reverse the cycle. For example, with these elements in place, it is possible to have a constructive conversation about whether the other is prejudiced. But with clear ecosystem goals, one may discover that clarifying if the other is prejudiced is not necessarily the most important thing for creating the relationship one wants.

A Useful Perspective

We have argued that egosystem motivations create and foster downward spirals of intergroup relations, whereas ecosystem motivations can break those downward spirals, and even create upward spirals. Although this perspective might seem hopelessly idealistic, we think it is eminently practical and pragmatic if practiced properly. Understanding that prejudice, stereotypes, power, and social structure play a role in these downward spirals does not provide much leverage for the individual to change the direction of the spiral. However, understanding how one's ego gets triggered in these spirals, and that it is possible to shift from egosystem to ecosystem motivations and change the spiral creates amazing opportunities.

We do not mean to diminish the value of trying to change the system. However, because systematic change is often slow, identifying strategies that can help individuals create positive changes can be a source of efficacy and empowerment. In day-to-day interactions, societal and structural disparities are manifested in interpersonal encounters. One does not interact with the *system* as much as one interacts with other people who have fears and an ego just like the self. Thus, we advocate a bottom-up approach to improving intergroup relations, starting with the self. This strategy is not a competing framework to a top down strategy of changing the system, but a complementary approach. Indeed, changing the system with an ecosystem goal will likely be more effective in the long run. History has shown that groups of victims who obtain power often become perpetrators, recreating the cycle of intergroup hostility. Creating a context in which the person with prejudice feels safe to change may be much more effective in the long run for creating the intergroup relations one wants than trying to force others to change.

Conclusion

We have argued that egosystem goals contribute to downward spirals and ecosystem goals can create upward spirals in intergroup relations. One objection to this approach is that it is too dangerous to let down one's guard, set aside vigilance, and take risks to create a more positive intergroup dynamic, because past events demonstrate that the danger from out-group members is real. Protective mechanisms based on dangerous past events feel necessary to survival, and they make people blindly distrustful of out-group members, and blindly trustful of their fears. However, vigilance for prejudice and discrimination can become a self-fulfilling prophecy, because it activates the fight-or-flight response. It is very difficult to be vigilant in a healthy, constructive way. Rather than be afraid of out-group members, we suggest that people need to be responsible, aware, and respectful of other's beliefs and views, while not necessarily agreeing with them.

A second objection to our approach is that it shifts the focus away from stereotypes, prejudice, and social structures that create obstacles to fairness, equality, and social justice, toward a more inward focus on the self. People who feel it is urgent to create social change may feel that an internal focus on shifting from egosystem to ecosystem motivations distracts from more pressing external problems. In our view, these are mutually interacting and reinforcing processes. Egosystem motivations amplify the effects of social structure, prejudice, and stereotypes. And when people are driving by the egosystem, they are ineffective at creating what they want. For people who see themselves as agents of social change, awareness of these processes is not a distraction, but an important tool for becoming a more effective change agent. The first step toward making the world more fair and just is becoming a more fair and just person oneself.

A third objection to this approach is that, in urging people to focus on their own responsibility for downward spirals in intergroup relations, we are blaming the victim. Why should targets of prejudice and discrimination focus on their own egosytems when the perpetrators of prejudice and discrimination are truly at fault? Yet, as we have seen, in downward spirals of intergroup relations everyone believes they are the victim and the other is the perpetrator; if all victims wait for perpetrators to change their behavior, the downward spiral will continue unabated. The best possibility for creating change is starting with the self, at the places where one has responsibility, for those are the places where one has the leverage to create upward spirals in intergroup relations.

Why would a leader want to make this shift from egosystem to ecosystem goals in intergroup relations? To us, the reason is clear; the costs of egosystem dynamics and the downward spirals of intergroup relations can be tremendous, including the deaths of many innocent people. From an ecosystem perspective, a leader can best contribute to the well-being of the in-group by also caring about the well-being of the out-group. Would a leader who shifted from egosystem goals to ecosystem goals risk losing the support of his or her followers? Perhaps followers who are driven by their own egosystem goals will be disappointed or even angry with a leader who articulates ecosystem goals. Change can be threatening, especially to people who are firmly caught in their egosystem dynamics. However, more often, we believe that leaders who are guided by their own egosystems do not inspire trust or loyalty and quickly lose support, whereas leaders who have been guided by an ecosystem vision, such as Mahatma Gandhi, Nelson Mandela, and Martin Luther King, are among the most inspiring figures of history, and the changes they nurtured will be enduring.

Prejudice, stereotypes, and discrimination are universal realities of social existence. They are sometimes created and often reinforced by social structure, including group differences in power, status, privilege, and access to resources (Jost & Banaji, 1994; Sidanius & Pratto, 1993). They both result from and contribute to intergroup conflict (Brewer & Brown, 1998). Social psychologists and sociologists have increased understanding of intergroup relations by documenting the pervasiveness of stereotyping, prejudice, and discrimination, and showing that they can operate automatically and outside of conscious awareness, with negative consequences for out-group members (Banaji & Greenwald, 1994; Devine, 1989). Sociologists have shown that these psychological phenomena are not merely intrapsychic; they are connected to social structure, power, and the distribution of resources and opportunities, and can become self-perpetuating (Ridgeway, 1992; Vescio, Gervais, Snyder, & Hoover, 2005).

Acknowledgments

Preparation of this chapter was supported by National Institute of Mental Health grants R01 MH58869 and K02 MH01747 to Jennifer Crocker, and by a Ford Foundation Dissertation Fellowship for Julie Garcia. We are grateful to the editors of this volume and the participants in the conference on Intergroup Reconciliation for their thoughtful comments on this work, and to the participants in the Defensive Routines in Intergroup Relations conference, sponsored by the Russell Sage Foundation, whose questions and criticisms inspired us to push our thinking further.

References

Banaji, M. R., & Greenwald, A. G. (1994). Implicit stereotyping and prejudice. In M. P. Zanna & J. M. Olson (Eds.), *The psychology of prejudice: The Ontario symposium* (Vol. 7, pp. 55-76). Hillsdale, NJ: Erlbaum.

Bradley, G. W. (1978). Self-serving biases in the attribution process: A reexamination of the fact or fiction question. *Journal of Personality and Social Psychology, 36,* 56-71.

Brewer, M. B., & Brown, R. (1998). Intergroup relations. In D. T. Gilbert, S. T. Fiske, & G. Lindzey (Eds.), *The Handbook of Social Psychology* (4th ed., Vol. 2, pp. 554-594). Boston: McGraw-Hill.

Buckley, K., Winkel, R., & Leary, M. (2004). Reactions to acceptance and rejection: Effects of level and sequence of relational evaluation. *Journal of Experimental Social Psychology, 40,* 14-28.

Campbell, W. K., Baumeister, R. F., Dhavale, D., & Tice, D. M. (2003). Responding to major threats to self-esteem: A preliminary, narrative study of ego-shock. *Journal of Social and Clinical Psychology, 22,* 79-96.

Carver, C. S., Blaney, P. H., & Scheier, M. F. (1979). Reassertion and giving up: The interactive role of self-directed attention and outcome expectancy. *Journal of Personality and Social Psychology, 37,* 1859-1870.

Crandall, C. S., Eshleman, A., & O'Brien, L. (2002). Social norms and the expression and suppression of prejudice: The struggle for internalization. *Journal of Personality and Social Psychology, 82,* 359-378.

Crocker, J., & Park, L. E. (2004). The costly pursuit of self-esteem. *Psychological Bulletin, 130,* 392-414.

Crocker, J., Voelkl, K., Testa, M., & Major, B. M. (1991). Social stigma: Affective consequences of attributional ambiguity. *Journal of Personality and Social Psychology, 60,* 218-228.

Czopp, A. M., & Monteith, M. J. (2003). Confronting prejudice (literally): Reactions to confrontations of racial and gender bias. *Personality and Social Psychology Bulletin, 29*(4), 532-544.

Devine, P. G. (1989). Stereotypes and prejudice: Their automatic and controlled components. *Journal of Personality and Social Psychology, 56,* 5-18.

Devine, P. G., Plant, E. A., Amodio, D. M., Harmon-Jones, E., & Vance, S. L. (2002). The regulation of explicit and implicit race bias: The role of motivations to respond without prejudice. *Journal of Personality and Social Psychology, 82,* 835-848.

Downey, G., & Feldman, S. I. (1996). Implications of rejection sensitivity for intimate relationships. *Journal of Personality and Social Psychology, 70,* 1327-1343.

Downey, G., Freitas, A. L., Michaelis, B., & Khouri, H. (1998). The self-fulfilling prophecy in close relationships: Rejection sensitivity and rejection by romantic partners. *Journal of Personality and Social Psychology, 75,* 545-560.

Dykman, B. M. (1998). Integrating cognitive and motivational factors in depression: Initial tests of a goal orientation approach. *Journal of Personality and Social Psychology, 74,* 139-158.

Frable, D. E. S., Wortman, C., & Joseph, J. (1997). Predicting self-esteem, well-being, and distress in a cohort of gay men: The importance of cultural stigma, personal visibility, community networks, and positive identity. *Journal of Personality, 65,* 599-624.

Garcia, J. A. (2005). *Motivations to disclose a concealable stigma: Exploring the antecedents and consequences of ego based and non-ego based goals.* Unpublished doctoral dissertation, University of Michigan, Ann Arbor, MI.

Georgi, H. (2000). Is there an unconscious discrimination against women in science? *APS News Online.*

Goffman, E. (1963). *Stigma: Notes on the management of spoiled identity.* Englewood Cliffs, NJ: Prentice-Hall.

Grant, H., & Dweck, C. S. (2003). Clarifying achievement goals and their impact. *Journal of Personality and Social Psychology, 85,* 541-553.

Greenberg, J., Pyszynski, T., Solomon, S., Rosenblatt, A., Veeder, M., Kirkland, S., et al. (1990). Evidence for terror management theory II: The effects of mortality salience on reactions to those who threaten or bolster the cultural worldview. *Journal of Personality and Social Psychology, 58,* 308-318.

Greenwald, A. G., & Banaji, M. R. (1995). Implicit social cognition: Attitudes, self-esteem, and stereotypes. *Psychological Review, 102*, 4-27.

Henry, J. P., & Wang, S. (1998). Effects of early stress on adult affiliative behavior. *Psychoneuroendocrinology, 23*, 863-875.

Jones, E. E., & Berglas, S. (1978). Control of attributions about the self through self-handicapping strategies: The appeal of alcohol and the role of underachievement. *Personality and Social Psychology Bulletin, 4*, 200-206.

Jones, E. E., Farina, A., Hastorf, A. H., Markus, H., Miller, D. T., & Scott, R. A. (1984). *Social stigma: The psychology of marked relationships.* New York: Freeman.

Jost, J. T., & Banaji, M. R. (1994). The role of stereotyping in system-justification and the production of false consciousness. *British Journal of Social Psychology, 33*, 1-27.

Kaiser, C. R., & Miller, C. T. (2001). Stop complaining! The social costs of making attributions to discrimination. *Personality and Social Psychology Bulletin, 27*, 254-263.

Keltner, D., Gruenfeld, D. H., & Anderson, C. (2003). Power, approach, and inhibition. *Psychological Review, 110*, 265-284.

Kramer, R. M. (1998). Paranoid cognition in social systems: Thinking and acting in the shadow of doubt. *Personality and Social Psychology Review, 2*, 251-275.

Kramer, R. M., & Messick, D. M. (1998). Getting by with a little help from our enemies: Collective paranoia and its role in intergroup relations. *Intergroup cognition and intergroup behavior* (pp. 233-255). Mahwah, NJ, US: Lawrence Erlbaum Associates, Inc., Publishers.

Leary, M. R., & Baumeister, R. F. (2000). The nature and function of self-esteem: Sociometer theory. In M. Zanna (Ed.), *Advances in experimental social psychology* (Vol. 32, pp. 1-62). San Diego, CA: Academic Press.

MacRae, C. N., Bodenhausen, G. V., Milne, A. B., & Jetten, J. (1994). Out of mind but back in sight: Stereotypes on the rebound. *Journal of Personality and Social Psychology, 67*, 808-817.

Mendoza-Denton, R., Downey, G., Purdie, V. J., Davis, A., & Pietrzak, J. (2002). Sensitivity to race-based rejection: Implications for African-American students' college experience. *Journal of Personality and Social Psychology, 83*, 896-918.

Merton, R. K. (1948). The self-fulfilling prophecy. *Antioch Review, 8*, 193-210.

Monteith, M. J., Deneen, N. E., & Tooman, G. D. (1996). The effect of social norm activation on the expression of opinions concerning gay men and Blacks. *Basic and Applied Social Psychology, 18*, 267-288.

Murray, S. L., Holmes, J. G., MacDonald, G., & Ellsworth, P. C. (1998). Through the looking glass darkly? When self-doubts turn into relationship insecurities. *Journal of Personality and Social Psychology, 75*, 1459-1480.

Pinel, E. C. (1999). Stigma consciousness: The psychological legacy of social stereotypes. *Journal of Personality and Social Psychology, 76*, 114-128.

Plant, E. A., & Devine, P. G. (1998). Internal and external motivation to respond without prejudice. *Journal of Personality and Social Psychology, 75*, 811-832.

Ridgeway, C. (1992). The social construction of status value: Gender and other nominal characteristics. *Social Forces, 70*, 367-386.

Rimer, S. (2005, April 15). For women in sciences, slow progress in academia. *New York Times*, p. 1.

Sidanius, J., & Pratto, F. (1993). The dynamics of social dominance and the inevitability of oppression. In P. Sniderman & P. E. Tetlock (Eds.), *Prejudice, politics, and race in America Today* (pp. 173-211). Stanford, CA: Stanford University Press.

Snyder, M. (1984). When belief creates reality. In L. Berkowitz (Ed.), *Advances in experimental social psychology* (Vol. 18, pp. 238-305). Orlando, FL: Academic Press.

Snyder, M., & Stukas, A. A. J. (1999). Interpersonal processes: The interplay of cognitive, motivational, and behavioral activities in social interaction. *Annual Review of Psychology, 50*, 273-303.

Solomon, S., Greenberg, J., & Pyszczynski, T. (1991). A terror-management theory of social behavior: The psychological functions of self-esteem and cultural worldviews. In M. P. Zanna (Ed.), *Advances in experimental social psychology* (Vol. 24, pp. 91-159). San Diego, CA: Academic Press.

Spencer, S. J., Steele, C. M., & Quinn, D. M. (1999). Stereotype threat and women's math performance. *Journal of Experimental Social Psychology, 35*, 4-28.

Steele, C. M. (1997). A threat in the air: How stereotypes shape intellectual identity and performance. *American Psychologist, 52*, 613-629.

Steinpreis, R. E., Anders, K. A., & Ritske, D. (1999). The impact of gender on the review of the curricula vitae of job applicants and tenure candidates: A national empirical study. *Sex Roles, 41*, 509-528.

Stone, D., Patton, B., & Heen, S. (1999). *Difficult conversations: How to discuss what matters most.* New York: Penguin.

Tangney, J. P. (1999). The self-conscious emotions: Shame, guilt, embarrassment and pride. In T. Dalgleish & M. J. Power (Eds.), *Handbook of cognition and emotion* (pp. 541-568). Chichester: Wiley.

Tangney, J. P., Wagner, P. E., Hill-Barlow, D., Marschall, D. E., & Gramzow, R. (1996). Relation of shame and guilt to constructive versus destructive responses to anger across the lifespan. *Journal of Personality and Social Psychology, 70*, 797-809.

Taylor, S. E., Klein, L. C., Lewis, B. P., Grucnewald, T. L., Gurung, R. A. R., & Updegraff, J. A. (2000). Biobehavioral responses to stress in females: Tend-and-befriend, not fight-or-flight. *Psychological Review, 197*, 411-429.

Tice, D. M. (1991). Esteem protection or enhancement? Self-handicapping motives and attributions differ by trait self-esteem. *Journal of Personality and Social Psychology, 60*, 711-725.

Twenge, J. M., Baumeister, R. F., Tice, D. M., & Stucke, T. S. (2001). If you can't join them, beat them: Effects of social exclusion on aggressive behavior. *Journal of Personality and Social Psychology, 81*, 1058-1069.

Twenge, J. M., & Campbell, W. K. (2003). "Isn't it fun to get the respect that we're going to deserve?" Narcissism, social rejection, and aggression. *Personality and Social Psychology Bulletin, 29,* 261-272.

Twenge, J. M., Catanese, K. R., & Baumeister, R. F. (2002). Social exclusion causes self-defeating behavior. *Journal of Personality and Social Psychology, 83,* 606-615.

Vescio, T. K., Gervais, S. J., Snyder, M., & Hoover, A. (2005). Power and the creation of patronizing environments: The stereotype-based behaviors of the powerful and their effects on female performance in masculine domains. *Journal of Personality and Social Psychology, 88,* 658-672.

Wenneras, C., & Wold, A. (1997). Nepotism and sexism in peer-review. *Nature, 387,* 341-343.

Wright, E. R., Gronfien, W. P., & Owens, T. J. (2000). Deinstitutionalization, social rejection, and the self-esteem of former mental patients. *Journal of Health and Social Behavior, 41,* 68-90.

Zhang, L., & Baumeister, R. F. (2006). Your money or your self-esteem: Threatened egotism promotes costly entrapment in losing endeavors. *Personality and Social Psychology Bulletin, 32,* 881-893.

Part III

Instrumental Reconciliation: Contact, Common Identity, and Equality

Part III.A

Contact and Common Identity

CHAPTER 9

Stepping Stones to Reconciliation in Northern Ireland: Intergroup Contact, Forgiveness, and Trust

Miles Hewstone, Jared B. Kenworthy, Ed Cairns, Nicole
Tausch, Joanne Hughes, Tania Tam, Alberto Voci,
Ulrich von Hecker, and Catherine Pinder

> We must never forget those who have died or been injured, and
> their families. But we can best honour them through a fresh
> start, in which we firmly dedicate ourselves to the achievement
> of reconciliation, tolerance, and mutual trust.
>
> *(Article 2 of The Belfast [Good Friday] Agreement, signed*
> *April 10, 1998)*

At the time of writing this chapter, the Irish Republican Army (IRA) issued a statement declaring that its leadership had "formally ordered an end to the armed campaign," and told all its units to work through "exclusively peaceful means" (*The Economist*, July 30, 2005). After hundreds of years of conflict, and decades of paramilitary terrorism, however, peace has not had and will not have immediate effect. As W. B. Yeats wrote, "peace comes dropping slow."[1]

Violent intergroup conflicts such as the one in Northern Ireland have distinct *psychological* components that can become independent of the initiating more objective causes of conflict and contribute to an escalation and continuation of violence even after the initial causes have become irrelevant (Deutsch, 1973; Tajfel & Turner, 1979). Thus, the formal resolution of a conflict is often just the first step toward peaceful coexistence. To promote peace and to prevent the reignition of violence, the parties involved have to engage in *reconciliation*, a psychological process that requires change in people's often well-entrenched beliefs and feelings about the out-group, their in-group, and the relationship between the two (Bar-Tal, 2000). The term *reconciliation* has also been used increasingly to describe political processes in transitional societies, where it refers to the setting aside of past animosities by antagonistic or formerly antagonistic groups to work toward mutual conciliatory accommodation (Borris & Diehl, 1998). A crucial part of future reconciliation in Northern Ireland will involve interventions directed at the psychological sources and consequences of sectarianism and bigotry.

Sectarianism has proven difficult to define, but Liechty and Clegg (2001) have identified the key components as

> *[A] system of attitudes, actions, beliefs, and structures... which arises as*
> *a distorted expression of positive, human needs especially for belonging,*
> *identity, and the free expression of difference... expressed in destructive*
> *patterns of relating*: hardening the boundaries between groups, overlooking
> others, belittling, dehumanizing, or demonizing others, justifying
> or collaborating in the domination of others, physically or verbally
> intimidating or attacking others. (pp. 102-103; emphases in the original)

In this chapter, we highlight three stepping stones for success in such interventions: investigating when and how intergroup contact results in reduced prejudice and improved intergroup relations; promoting intergroup forgiveness to replace bitterness and vengeance; and building trust across the sectarian divide. Thus, we will seek to highlight some of the contributions of social psychology to building the postconflict society envisaged by the Belfast Agreement.

We begin by reviewing briefly the historical and social background to the political violence in Northern Ireland. Next, we consider the segregated nature of society in Northern Ireland, and highlight intergroup contact as a means to overcome the problems of segregation, summarizing results from our own long-term program of research. We then consider the neglected topic of forgiveness, arguing that a distinct form of *intergroup forgiveness* is relevant in cases of intergroup conflict; we summarize key findings from our own recent research on predictors of forgiveness. In the following section, we explore the nature of intergroup (dis)trust in Northern Ireland, reporting on our own recent research designed to elucidate how trust operates in the uncertain setting of a postconflict society. Finally, we underline the importance of all three processes for intergroup reconciliation in Northern Ireland, and point to areas where future work is still needed.

A Brief Background to Sectarian Conflict in Northern Ireland

> Throughout this long and tortuous history, conflicts over
> land and power have predominated. Throw in a large dose of
> religion, bigotry and intolerance and an even larger dose of
> mismanagement and incompetence by generations of rulers
> and politicians and you begin to get the picture (Mo Mowlam,
> *Momentum*, 2002).

The Northern Irish conflict is, in essence, a struggle between those who want Northern Ireland to remain part of the United Kingdom (Unionists/Loyalists, generally supported by Protestants) and those who want Northern Ireland to be reunited with the Republic of Ireland (Republicans/Nationalists, generally supported by Catholics; Cairns, 1982; Cairns & Darby, 1998; Mulholland, 2002a). Sectarian violence in the last three decades has resulted in more than 3,600 deaths and tens of thousands of injuries (Fay, Morrissey, & Smyth, 1999), until a series of cease fires in the mid-1990s set in motion the peace process that eventually led to the Belfast Agreement.

The agreement was a turning point in Northern Irish history. It initiated a devolved administration and aimed to promote a pluralistic society in Northern Ireland based on the mutual recognition of opposing traditions (McKittrick & McVea, 2000).[2] However, despite these positive developments, Northern Ireland has still not achieved political and social stability. What Mulholland (2002b) calls *the long peace* is, in fact, a peace *process* and one that has stumbled upon a series of problems, crises, and setbacks. Political violence continues, albeit at a much lower level (Knox, 2002) and perceptions of cross-community relations and out-group attitudes have become more negative in recent years (Hughes & Donnelly, 2001).

Today it is estimated that 44% of the Northern Irish population is Roman Catholic and 53% is Protestant (Northern Ireland Census, December 2002) with those not wishing to state a denomination comprising the rest of the population. Although identification with one of the two religious communities has been shown to play an important role in the maintenance of the conflict in Northern Ireland, the conflict is best understood in ethnic, rather than religious, terms (Cairns & Darby, 1998).

Religious Segregation and Intergroup Contact in Northern Ireland

> The only way you can dispel prejudices is by getting to know someone...(Martin McGuinness, Minister for Education for Northern Ireland, MP for Mid-Ulster, Sinn Fein's chief negotiator during the Belfast [*Good Friday*] agreement).

A crucial characteristic of Northern Irish society that helps explain many aspects of the conflict is the extreme degree to which the two religious communities are segregated (Cairns & Hewstone, 2002; Knox & Hughes, 1994). Even though segregation is not the cause of intergroup conflict, it plays a major role in establishing and maintaining conflict between communities; it also exacerbates conflict by prolonging mutual ignorance (Whyte, 1990). Positive experience of intergroup contact should therefore have great potential for reducing prejudice, altering stereotypes and improving intergroup relations.

Residential, Personal, and Educational Segregation

Three types of segregation have received most attention: residential (Poole & Doherty, 1996), personal and marital (e.g., Gallagher & Dunn, 1991), and educational (Gallagher, 1989), although other types of segregation (e.g., at work, sport, and leisure) have been identified as well (Niens, Cairns, & Hewstone, 2003).

Catholics and Protestants have been residentially segregated, in both urban and rural areas, since long before the outbreak of The Troubles (Smyth, 1995), but conflict has strengthened segregation (Boyle & Hadden, 1994; Whyte, 1990). Segregated housing often covaries with relatively deprived working-class areas in Northern Ireland, whereas middle class and upper class residential areas are often more mixed.

Approximately 55% of the Protestants and 75% of the Catholics report that *all or most* of their friends are of the same religion as themselves (a consistent result in surveys from 1968 to 1998; see Cairns & Hewstone, 2002). Other studies have, however, reported that cross-community friendships do exist, but they often function only as long as certain issues are not mentioned (Trew, 1986). So-called *mixed marriages* account for between 5% and 10% of marriages (Cairns & Hewstone, 2002; Niens et al., 2003) but often involve complete separation from one-half of the family, and attract retribution, especially during times of increased tension.

Both primary and secondary education is highly segregated (Cairns & Hewstone, 2002; Gallagher, 1995). Separate education allows prejudice and stereotypes to flourish (Whyte, 1990) and persists although there is apparently widespread support for integrated education (see Hughes & Carmichael, 1998). A small number of Integrated Schools, which involve pupils from both communities, educate a tiny proportion of the total pupil population (see McGlynn, Niens, Cairns, & Hewstone, 2004; Niens et al., 2003).

All these forms of segregation are important because they sustain conflict by creating a social climate that fosters mutual ignorance and suspicion (Gallagher, 1995). Worse still, there is evidence for an increased preference for working and living apart in recent years (Robinson, 2003).

Intergroup Contact Across the Sectarian Divide

Despite the widespread segregation, it is not total (Cairns & Hewstone, 2002). Therefore, unlike some other apparently intractable conflicts, the potential for contact between members of the two communities exists in many areas (Cairns & Darby, 1998; Trew, 1986), although in some cases (e.g., *interface* areas where the two groups live cheek by jowl) residents will go to great lengths and incur personal costs to *avoid* cross-community contact (Shirlow, 2001). We now review the evidence on intergroup contact. These studies are inspired by, and test, Allport's (1954) *contact hypothesis* that proposed that bringing together individuals from opposing groups under optimal conditions can reduce prejudice and improve intergroup relations. Allport (1954) suggested these positive effects were most likely under conditions of equal status contact, intergroup cooperation, and the opportunity to develop close relationships with members of the out-group, backed by institutional support (for evidence, see Pettigrew & Tropp, 2006).

Before summarizing this evidence, which relies heavily on self-reports of cross-group contact, we should explain how religious group membership is ascertained, given that the two groups do not differ physically. In fact, a complex interplay of cues is used, of which first name, family name, school, and place of residence are the most informative cues (see Whyte, 1990). Thus although the two groups are not racially, physiognomically, or otherwise distinct in appearance, it is in practice quite easy to know when one has experienced intergroup, or cross-community, contact.

For reasons of space, we limit our review here to our own recent studies, which are the most detailed available (for a review of other studies in this context, see Hewstone et al., 2005; Niens et al., 2003). We focus also on the efficacy of intergroup contact for improving intergroup *attitudes* in Northern Ireland (in later sections we consider the association between contact and both forgiveness and trust). In separate subsections we highlight research that has addressed *mediational* ("how" does contact work?) and *moderational* ("when" does contact work?) questions regarding intergroup contact (see Brown & Hewstone, 2005; Kenworthy, Turner, Hewstone, & Voci, 2005).

Mediators and Moderators of Intergroup Contact. Since Pettigrew (1998) highlighted the importance of affective processes in explaining what makes contact effective, evidence has accrued that a large part of the effect of contact on reducing prejudice is due to the fact that contact reduces *intergroup anxiety* (anxiety that stems mainly from the anticipation of negative consequences for oneself during intergroup contact; Stephan & Stephan, 1985). We have found strong and consistent evidence that positive contact is associated with reduced intergroup anxiety. We have found this effect in surveys using Catholic and Protestant young people, college students, and adults drawn from representative samples of the population of Northern Ireland.

We have also found that intergroup anxiety mediates the effects of a more subtle kind of contact, namely, *indirect, extended,* or *vicarious* contact, as opposed to *direct*, face-to-face contact with members of the out-group. Wright, Aron, McLaughlin-Volpe, and Ropp (1997) demonstrated that the mere knowledge of in-group members' being friends with out-group members could also help to reduce prejudice. They argued (but did not test the idea) that such indirect contact should work, in part at least, because intergroup anxiety should be weaker in vicarious experiences than in first-hand experiences.

We tested this idea in two surveys in Northern Ireland, one with Catholic and Protestant students, the other with a random sample of the population (Paolini, Hewstone, Cairns, & Voci, 2004); both used sophisticated structural equation modeling (SEM) techniques. We found that people who had more friends from the other community, or who knew more in-group members who had friends from the other community, were indeed less prejudiced than people who had less direct or indirect experience with out-group members. We also demonstrated that these effects were mediated by a reduction in intergroup anxiety.

In our most recent research, we have extended work on affective mediators in two directions. First, we have moved beyond the focus on one negative emotion (intergroup anxiety) to the recognition that there are multiple (negative and positive) potentially relevant intergroup emotions. Tam et al. (2005, Study 2) measured intergroup emotions more generally, including both negative and positive emotions (using items based on Mackie, Devos, & Smith, 2000), and empathy (both affective empathy and cognitive empathy, or perspective taking; after Batson, Polycarpou, Harmon-Jones, & Imhoff, 1997;

Davis, 1994), as well as negative and positive action tendencies. We found that cross-group friendships were a negative predictor of negative emotions and a positive predictor of all other variables. In turn, negative emotions predicted negative action tendencies, positive emotions predicted positive action tendencies, and perspective taking predicted both positive and negative action tendencies (positively and negatively, respectively). Thus, the addition of positive mediators (positive emotions, empathy) improved prediction based only on negative mediators (which included, but went beyond, intergroup anxiety).

Our second new direction was to differentiate further between mediators using Stephan and colleagues' (Stephan & Renfro, 2003; Stephan & Stephan, 2000) integrated threat model of prejudice. This model distinguishes between intergroup anxiety (a variable that primarily affects the individual) and perceived realistic and symbolic threats (variables that primarily affect the in-group). Realistic threats pertain to threats to the very existence of the in-group, to the in-group's political and economic power as well as the physical well-being of its members. Symbolic threats, on the other hand, encompass more intangible threats to the in-group, which are difficult to address (Cairns & Darby, 1998). They can be defined as threats to the in-group's value system, belief system, or worldview, and may involve threats to language, religion, ideology, and morality.

Across two studies (Tausch, Hewstone, Kenworthy, Cairns, & Christ, 2007; Tausch, Tam, Hewstone, Kenworthy, & Cairns, 2007, Study 1) we found that contact (assessed by separate measures of quality and quantity of contact) predicted out-group attitudes, in part, through both reduced anxiety and reduced threat. That is, threats to the in-group explained a substantial amount of variance in out-group attitudes, over and above intergroup anxiety. We also found that social identification moderated the relative importance of individual-versus group-level variables as predictors of out-group attitudes. As predicted (and found by Bizman & Yinon, 2001), threats to the in-group were more important predictors for high than low identifiers, and anxiety was a more important predictor for low than high identifiers.

Complementing Pettigrew's (1998) review, which focused on mediators of contact, recent research has accumulated evidence that group salience is a key *moderator* of the effect of intergroup contact on criterion variables (Hewstone, Rubin, & Willis, 2002). Evidence has accrued that the salience of group boundaries should be maintained during contact, to promote generalization across members of the target out-group (see Brown & Hewstone, 2005, for a review of relevant studies). Across a series of studies in Northern Ireland (Hewstone et al., in preparation) we have confirmed the salience-generalization hypothesis. We found a stronger association between general out-group contact and out-group attitudes when group memberships were salient.

Thus far, we have discussed separately evidence for moderation and mediation effects. In our most recent research, we have also tested for *moderated mediation*. We have analyzed whether group salience during contact moderates any of the effects involving contact, mediators, or outcomes—that is, do variations in the moderator affect the relation between a predictor and a mediator, or between a mediator and an outcome? (see Brown & Hewstone, 2005). Hewstone, Voci, Cairns, and McLernon (2003, Study 1), using a representative sample of adults in Northern Ireland, found that opportunity for contact predicted actual contact, which then affected out-group evaluation directly, and indirectly, through reduced anxiety. Only the path from contact to out-group evaluation was moderated by salience; the association between contact and evaluation was significantly positive under high salience, but only marginally so under low salience.

Summary

Over the past few years, we have made huge strides in our understanding of the impact of intergroup contact in Northern Ireland, and of its key mediators and moderators. These findings have clear implications for interventions to improve intergroup relations, indicating that they should, for example, aim to reduce perceived threats and anxiety, and promote empathy, perspective taking, and positive emotions. The results also suggest that whether reducing intergroup anxiety or reducing perceived threats posed by the out-group is more effective may depend on characteristics of the individuals involved, such as the strength of group identification.

Intergroup Forgiveness

> Politics must engage with the question of forgiveness and
> reconciliation if the agreement is to represent more than
> a staging post in the cycle of revenge (Duncan Morrow,
> *Democratic Dialogue website*, http://cain.ulst.ac.uk/dd/
> report13/report13a/htm).

Theoretical Background

Recently there has been a burgeoning of research on primarily, *interpersonal* forgiveness (see Enright, Freedman, & Rique, 1998; McCullough, Pargament, & Thoresen, 1999, 2000). To date, however, few studies have examined the role of *intergroup* forgiveness in relation to the development of peace and reconciliation between ethnic groups.

Although it has long been established that people behave differently in intergroup settings than they do in interpersonal settings (see Hewstone et al., 2002), because of a shift from personal to social identity (Tajfel & Turner, 1979) and an emphasis on the in-group rather than on the self, it is only recently that any research has been carried out into intergroup forgiveness. One factor is evident in most cases of intergroup conflict: the role of the past, and memory for it (see Cairns & Roe, 2003). The perception of the past affects lives into the present; old grievances endure within the collective memory and flare repeatedly into violence. Forgiveness represents an alternative: it transcends the past, not by forgetting past hurts and pain, but by absorbing them so that they no longer diffuse into a continuing cycle of violence.

We have sought to provide the first extensive theoretical and empirical study of intergroup forgiveness in Northern Ireland (Cairns, Tam, Hewstone, & Niens, 2005; Hewstone et al., 2004; McLernon, Cairns, Lewis, & Hewstone, 2003). In doing so, we have emphasized the qualitative differences that are likely to arise between interpersonal and intergroup forgiveness, and we proposed that in societies consumed by ethnopolitical conflict, forgiveness is best thought of as a group rather than an interpersonal phenomenon. We have taken an eclectic theoretical approach to intergroup forgiveness, drawing particularly on theories concerning social identity (Tajfel & Turner, 1979), empathy and perspective taking (Batson et al., 1997; Davis, 1994), collective guilt (Doosje, Branscombe, Spears, & Manstead, 1998), and intergroup emotions (Mackie & Smith, 2002).

In this section, we focus mainly on research using a new measure of intergroup forgiveness, specially developed for this context (see Hewstone et al., 2004). In our research program, we first conducted a series of focus groups to examine what people in Northern Ireland thought of forgiving the other community. Second, we conducted surveys to elucidate the correlates of and psychological processes involved in intergroup forgiveness. Finally, an experimental study systematically examined factors that lead people to forgive the other side. We summarize below the main survey results (focusing on prediction of intergroup forgiveness) and those of the experimental study.

Survey Research on Intergroup Forgiveness

Our first survey used a sample of Catholic and Protestant students at the (mixed) University of Ulster (for more details see Hewstone et al., 2004). We assessed forgiveness and possible correlates with reliable, multi-item measures (including identification with religious in-group, collective guilt, religiosity, contact with out-group friends, out-group evaluation, and experience of victimhood). We regressed forgiveness on all the predictors simultaneously. Explained variance was good for Catholics ($R^2 = .31$) and especially Protestants ($R^2 = .52$). The strongest positive predictors of forgiveness were collective guilt and out-group attitudes, while in-group identification was a negative predictor. Finally, we considered victimization experience of The Troubles as a moderator of forgiveness by splitting the sample at the median into *low* and *high* experience subgroups. We found that those respondents with high experience of victimhood reported significantly lower collective guilt and forgiveness. Thus, experience of the conflict contributes to its maintenance, because those most affected by it are both less inclined to acknowledge wrongs by their own group, and less willing to forgive the other group.

We followed up these issues by questioning a representative sample of the Northern Irish population (see Hewstone et al., 2004, 2006). In initial analyses we focused on measures of intergroup forgiveness, contact with out-group friends, out-group evaluation, out-group trust, in-group identification, out-group perspective taking, and experience of victimization. We again regressed forgiveness on all the predictors, and explained quite high proportions of variance for Catholics ($R^2 = .23$) and, especially, Protestants ($R^2 = .41$). The strongest positive predictor of forgiveness for Catholics was trust, while for Protestants there were two strong positive predictors (trust and perspective taking) and one strong negative predictor (identification). Finally, we considered victimization experience and an objective index of neighborhood violence as moderators. We found that respondents who reported high victimization, and those who lived in high-violence areas, reported significantly less forgiveness. These results underline the importance of actual experience of the conflict as a limiting condition for willingness to forgive past wrongs of the out-group and readiness to trust it in the future (we will discuss intergroup trust in more detail in the following section).

We have also explored the extent to which forgiveness is predicted by emotions (Tam et al., 2007, Study 1). Two distinct theories formed the background to this research. First, intergroup emotions theory (Mackie et al., 2000) argues that differentiated intergroup emotions may be more accurate for predicting intergroup behavior than attitudes are, allowing us to distinguish groups that are feared, hated, resented, admired, or respected, rather than simply disliked or liked.

The second approach guiding this study was Leyens et al.'s (2000, 2001) theory of *infrahumanization*. This theory deals not with the emotions *we feel* about *them*, but rather the emotions that *we* feel *they* are capable of experiencing. The psychological essentialism perspective on intergroup bias (e.g., Haslam, Rothschild, & Ernst, 2002) suggests that an in-group perceived as superior may be endowed with the human essence, while out-groups are seen as *infrahumans* (Leyens et al., 2001). Leyens and colleagues showed that in-groups are systematically attributed more uniquely human *secondary* emotions than are out-groups (see Demoulin et al., 2004), but no such difference is found for nonuniquely human *primary* emotions (e.g., anger, pleasure). We asked Catholic and Protestant respondents how much they experienced various negative and positive emotions toward the other group (intergroup emotions) and to check which of another list of emotions (pretested as primary, secondary, or filler items) they believed were typical of the in-group on one list, and of the out-group on another list. We also measured intergroup contact (quantity $\times$ quality), empathy, and out-group attitude. We then used SEM to test a causal model of forgiveness. We found, as predicted, that intergroup contact positively predicted empathy and out-group attitude, and negatively predicted a distinct intergroup emotions factor of anger-related emotions (*angry, hatred, furious, irritated*) and infrahumanization (differential attribution of secondary emotions to in-group vs. out-group). In turn, anger and infrahumanization negatively predicted, and empathy positively predicted, forgiveness (explaining 42% of the variance). Further analyses ruled out alternative causal models.

An Experimental Study of Intergroup Forgiveness

To manipulate some of the key variables involved in intergroup forgiveness we adopted the scenario methodology used by Gibson and Gouws (1999) in their study in postapartheid South Africa. We presented Catholic and Protestant students with one brief scenario to read, describing an act of paramilitary violence, its consequences, intention, and motivation (see Hewstone, Voci, & Cairns under review). Unknown to participants, we had manipulated the materials so that we could analyze their responses in a four-factor between-participants design: 2 (religious group membership of participant: Catholic vs. Protestant) $\times$ 2 (religious group membership of perpetrator: Catholic vs. Protestant) $\times$ 2 (intention to kill the victim: intentional vs. unintentional) $\times$ 2 (motivation: retaliation vs. no apparent motivation).

Participants were asked to make a number of judgments, including manipulation checks, attributions of blame, forgiveness, and a recommendation concerning whether the perpetrator should be granted early release (i.e., under the terms of Good Friday Agreement). Finally, participants completed control measures of the importance of religion, intergroup contact, out-group perspective taking, out-group attitudes, intergroup forgiveness, and in-group identification.

Overall levels of forgiveness were low but, more strikingly, in-group and out-group perpetrators were not treated even handedly. Responses of both participant groups were biased in favor of their own group (for all three measures). Additional analyses showed, however, that forgiveness was moderated by participants' identification with own religious group. For participants *low* in-group identification, the two-way interaction between religion of participant and perpetrator disappeared completely; but for those *high* in identification, the two-way interaction was highly significant, revealing an even stronger pattern of intergroup bias than in the overall analysis.

We also investigated the extent to which respondents' forgiveness ratings predicted recommendations for early release by computing partial correlations (partialing out blame attributions and all the other control measures). Overall, there was evidence that forgiveness ratings predicted recommendations for early release.

Forgiveness and Reconciliation

Even though revenge and retaliatory responses may have evolutionary advantages (Newberg, d'Aquili, Newberg, & de Marici, 2000), their corrosive effects are undeniable. Forgiveness breaks this cycle and offers hope for future reconciliation. Whether or not forgiveness results in complete reconciliation (see Borris & Diehl, 1998; Worthington, 1998), it still has the power to harness prosocial change (McCullough, 2001). At the very least, forgiveness can be viewed as a prosocial facilitator that provides an opportunity for improved intergroup relations. An apology from an out-group for inflicted harm can facilitate more positive perceptions of the out-group (Nadler & Liviatan, 2004; see McCullough et al., 1999) and an expectation that relations between conflicting groups will improve. However, apologies are not always accepted as sincere, and reactions are typically more cautious and sometimes cynical (see Cairns et al., 2005; Hewstone et al., 2004; and coverage of the IRA's public, written apology for the death of "noncombatants" in The Troubles; *The Guardian*, July 17, 2002).

Forgiveness may play a key role in helping groups in conflict put the atrocities of the past behind them (Shriver, 1995; Tutu, 1999), and is an integral part of the achievements of organizations such as the Northern Ireland Victims Commission. It should, we argue, be central to future interventions to promote reconciliation. Whether Northern Ireland will ever have its own Truth and Reconciliation Commission remains hotly debated (see *All Truth is Bitter*, 1999). If it ever does, then knowledge about intergroup forgiveness will be crucial in supporting the process of reconciliation after political violence and human rights abuses (Borris & Diehl, 1998).

Summary

Our research shows that intergroup forgiveness is closely related to identification with the religious in-group, attitudes toward the religious out-group, collective guilt, out-group perspective taking and out-group trust. Intergroup contact is a powerful vehicle for lessening anger and infrahumanization, while simultaneously enhancing empathy, and thereby promoting forgiveness, which can break the cycle of revenge and thus offers hope for future reconciliation.

Intergroup Trust

At the heart of all of the problems in Northern Ireland is
mistrust. Centuries of conflict have generated hatred that
make it virtually impossible for the two communities to trust
each other.... If there is ever to be a durable peace and genuine
reconciliation, what is really needed is the decommissioning
of mind-sets in Northern Ireland...trust and confidence must
be built, over time, by actions in all parts of society (Senator
George Mitchell [*Making peace*, 1999, p. 37]).

Theoretical Background

Trust has been defined as a positive bias in the processing of imperfect information (Yamagishi & Yamagishi, 1994). Trust can be seen as a psychological means to overcome uncertainty by making benign assumptions about other people's behavior (Kollock, 1994). However, common to most conceptualizations of trust is that it entails a state of perceived vulnerability, which is derived from the individual's uncertainty regarding the motives, intentions, and actions of others with whom they are interdependent (Kramer & Carnevale, 2001). Trust is therefore different from overall attitude and can be seen as a more demanding criterion of interpersonal or intergroup relations than liking because it potentially puts the self or the in-group directly at risk.

There is substantial evidence that trust is difficult to create and to sustain. For example, Rothbart and Park (1986) demonstrated that many confirming behavioral instances are required before someone is judged as being trustworthy; but only few behavioral instances are needed to disconfirm that view. Moreover, trust at the group level may be particularly difficult to establish because out-group distrust is based on a generic out-group schema, such that out-groups are *automatically* perceived as untrustworthy, due to the expectation of their competitive intent (Insko, Schopler, Hoyle, Dardis, & Graetz, 1990).

If trust can be established, however, it has a number of positive consequences. For example, in intergroup negotiations trust increases information exchange, cooperative behavior, and conciliatory strategies (see Kramer & Carnevale, 2001, for a review). Thus, trust is likely to be a key concept in conflict resolution and peace building, as required in the current peace process in Northern Ireland. It is therefore important that researchers understand the psychological variables that determine the formation of intergroup trust in uncertain environments. We believe that intergroup contact is likely to be an important determinant of out-group trust. As we noted earlier, segregation sustains the conflict by fostering mutual ignorance, suspicion, and distrust and by maintaining prejudice and negative stereotypes (Gallagher, 1995). Thus, encouraging cross-community contact has been an important strategy adopted by policy makers in Northern Ireland to build cross-community trust (see Hughes, 2001).

In this section, we review selected findings from our recent research on intergroup trust in Northern Ireland. Although there has been research on trust in intergroup contexts (see Brewer, 1999, 2001; LeVine & Campbell, 1972), we lack studies examining trust and distrust in real intergroup conflicts. We begin with experimental studies, and then proceed to surveys. This is a much newer program of research, and these results are therefore quite preliminary.

Experimental Studies

Our first research investigated cognitive processes underlying intergroup trust. Using Rothbart and Park's (1986) cognitive paradigm, we studied bias in the (dis)confirmation of traits such as trustworthy, when rated for an in-group actor compared with an out-group actor (Tausch, Hewstone, & Kenworthy, 2007.). We studied *trustworthy* within the theoretical framework of the Stereotype Content Model (Fiske, Cuddy, Glick, & Xu, 2002). This model provides an analysis of traits along two orthogonal dimensions: warmth and competence. Warmth traits are those that function toward goal compatibility and interpersonal (or intergroup) benevolence. Trustworthiness falls within this dimension. Competence traits are those that have to do with abilities to achieve goals, such as intelligence and efficiency. We assigned Catholic and Protestant participants to the cells of a 2 (name manipulation: in-group vs. out-group vs. no name) $\times$ 2 (trait valence: positive vs. negative) $\times$ 2 (trait content: warmth vs. competence) mixed factorial design with repeated measures on the last two factors.

With respect to *trustworthiness*, we found that participants reported needing fewer observed instances to disconfirm trustworthiness of in-group members, as compared to out-group members. In other words, people decided that a fellow in-group member was no longer trustworthy given *fewer* observations than for an out-group member. This was, in fact, contrary to our predictions. Similarly, in-group members were given fewer chances before they were considered deceitful, as compared to out-group members. The findings are parallel to earlier research showing that people are more vigilant with respect to relevant in-group behaviors and characteristics for fellow in-group members than for out-group members (e.g., Marques, Yzerbyt, & Leyens, 1988).

We also showed that trustworthiness was not simply another instance of a general positivity bias in attributions. For example, participants rated trustworthiness as being harder to confirm than other positive competence-related traits (e.g., educated, intelligent), and especially for in-group members, as compared with out-group members. Similarly, trustworthiness was easier to disconfirm than competence traits. Whereas an overall in-group bias effect was found for competence-related traits, when participants were rating a target's trustworthiness, higher standards were applied for in-group members, compared with out-group members. For in-group members, trustworthiness was harder to gain, but easier to lose; being untrustworthy was harder to lose. We think this may reflect, in part, the number of internecine killings in the Northern Irish conflict (see Hayes & McAllister, 2002).

A second experiment tested the idea that an individual who extends trust to the (whole) out-group potentially places the in-group at risk, because their security may be compromised (Myers, Hewstone, Kenworthy, Cairns, & Hughes, 2005). The experiment assessed reactions in response to the manipulation of two independent variables, trust versus distrust and increasing versus decreasing threat. We manipulated trust versus distrust by depicting (in a scenario) a community leader either extending trust to the out-group as a strategy for dealing with a community conflict, or showing distrust. We manipulated threat by having the trust versus distrust scenario take place within the context of either a growing or shrinking in-group size, relative to the surrounding out-group size. Specifically, the in-group's community location was depicted on a map as being an enclave surrounded by the out-group. This enclave was shown to be either growing (decreasing threat) or shrinking (increasing threat) over time.

Participants read the scenario and the threat manipulation, and were asked to respond to a series of questions about how they would feel in such a situation, how they would respond to the community leader who either trusted or distrusted the out-group, and how risky they thought the leader's behavior was. We also measured in-group identification. We predicted that participants would see trust as being more of a risk to the in-group, would feel more anxious about trust, under increasing threat, as compared to under decreasing threat, and would have more negative reactions to the leader under increasing, as compared to decreasing, threat. We expected these hypotheses to be confirmed most strongly for high identifiers, as compared to low identifiers.

In response to an in-group member's show of trust toward the out-group, high identifiers were most anxious and perceived the highest levels of risk to the in-group under increased threat (i.e., shrinking in-group size). Low identifiers, in contrast, were most anxious and perceived most risk when trust was withheld under high threat. These findings generally support our predictions concerning the nature of trust as a predictor of risk to the in-group under certain circumstances. The moderation of these effects by in-group identification shows the importance of examining the data according to those who feel a belongingness and solidarity with their in-group versus those who do not (as was the case for our experimental study of forgiveness, reported above). Clearly, the low and high identifiers have differing expectations of what constitutes appropriate behavior in the intergroup context of Northern Ireland.

Survey Research

We have carried out several surveys on intergroup trust using student respondents, and one using a representative sample (see Hewstone et al., 2005; Kenworthy, Hewstone, Cairns, & Voci, 2004). One of our first student surveys measured the following potential predictors and correlates of trust in Northern Ireland: out-group attitudes; in-group identification; direct and indirect out-group contact; out-group emotions; perceived threat; empathy and perspective taking. As predicted, out-group trust was reliably positively correlated with out-group contact, positive emotions, and empathy, and negatively correlated with emotional distress, negative emotions, and both realistic and symbolic threat. Approximately 40% of the variance in this measure of trust could be explained by quality of out-group contacts at home, indirect contact at home, quality of contact at university, distress (an empathy-related emotion), and symbolic threat.

In a second survey, we sought to develop a more differentiated measure of intergroup trust, to include various aspects of it that seemed especially relevant in this context. Thus we included subscales for general trust, in-group and out-group trust, trust in politicians, trust not to be harmed by the out-group, trust in sharing personal information (e.g., name, address, or telephone number) with out-group members, the perception that trust once extended will not be exploited by out-group members, and the relationship between trust and allied constructs. Exploratory factor analysis indicated that the trust subscales indicated above were, in fact, distinct from each other. We report here some of the main findings concerning predictors of various types of trust.

We created a model predicting two of the forms of trust (above) from quality of contact. Because politicians are instrumental to making policy changes that affect the way values and beliefs are put into civic life, and because people in Northern Ireland vote primarily for politicians that share their religion, we thought that the link between contact and this kind of trust (politicians) would be mediated by symbolic threat, which concerns values and beliefs. Similarly, trusting that sharing one's personal information will not lead to physical harm should be affected by concerns about realistic threat, which is the degree to which people perceive the out-group to threaten one's physical well-being or resources. The regression model supported these ideas. Quality of contact did predict both kinds of threat (negatively, of course), but symbolic and realistic threat each (negatively) predicted the expected trust construct (trust in out-group politicians and trust in sharing personal information, respectively). This model was fully mediated, indicating that the quality of contact improves trust through the reduction of threats vis à vis the out-group.

We also included a measure of perceived out-group variability in this survey, and we predicted that out-group contact would have a stronger effect on trust (measured on several dimensions) toward the out-group for respondents who viewed the out-group as *high* versus *low* on homogeneity. Quality of contact predicted various kinds of trust, and this relationship was different based on a classification of participants into subgroups comprised of those with low versus high perceptions of out-group homogeneity. The strongest case of such a difference was observed for trust in out-group politicians. Specifically, quality of contact predicted trust in out-group politicians, but only for those who perceived the out-group as highly homogeneous. In contrast, quality of contact predicted trust in sharing personal information with out-group members, but only for those with low perceived out-group homogeneity. That is, the trust in sharing personal information with out-group members occurs for people with high quality contact, and who see the out-group as highly varied. This is important, as the sharing of personal information in Northern Ireland can potentially lead to serious risk (through targeted paramilitary activity, for example), and thus one must be very selective about individuals with whom information is shared. High perceived homogeneity of the out-group indicates that all out-group members are to some degree interchangeable; this would clearly be hazardous in the context of information-sharing.

Finally, we sought to replicate the effects of our earlier (albeit smaller) surveys, and to test more robust models using SEM, with data based on a random sample of the adult population of Northern Ireland. Primary and secondary level confirmatory factor analyses were successful in showing that meaningful differences exist among the types of trust examined thus far, and that the various forms of out-group trust are distinct from a generalized attitude toward the out-group. The distinct forms of trust examined here are (a) trust that the out-group will not take advantage of in-group members; (b) trust that individual out-group members will not lie, deceive, or harm in-group members; (c) trust that the out-group generally will not lie, deceive, or harm in-group members; and (d) trust in the out-group to behave predictably and consistently.

We tested models including two predictors (intergroup contact and cognitive appraisals of the intergroup relationship of trust, concerning general goal compatibility, equality, and fairness), as well as three mediators (positive and negative intergroup emotions, and reciprocal self-disclosure during interactions with out-group members).

The structural model confirmed that contact and appraisals have their effect on trust because of a resulting reduction in felt negative emotions, an increase in felt positive emotions, as well as reciprocal self-disclosure during interactions with out-group members. High quality/quantity of contact, as well as higher perceived equality and fairness appraisals, were associated with increased positive emotions and more reciprocal self-disclosure, but with reduced negative emotions. These emotions and appraisals, in turn, mediated the link to the various forms of trust in expected ways. Positive emotions and self-disclosure were associated with greater trust; negative emotions were associated with reduced trust.

Trust and Reconciliation

Borris and Diehl (1998) argue that trust is a key factor for the reconciliation process. Issues of trust are certainly central for the Northern Irish conflict. For example, Protestants must trust a Catholic politician as Minister for Education, Catholics must trust a Protestant First Minister, and both sides must trust each other to decommission arms.[2]

In one of our experimental studies (Myers et al., 2005), we showed that trust has implications for real consequences that out-group attitudes do not have, especially for those who identify strongly with their religious group.

Trust is important precisely because it has both cognitive and affective aspects. Cognitively, it involves information processing (Yamagishi & Yamagishi, 1994) and can develop as a means of reducing uncertainty (e.g., Kollock, 1994; Molm, Takahashi, & Peterson, 2000). Affectively, it is associated with the development of positive affect from repeated successful exchanges (Lawler & Yoon, 1996). Yet it involves taking steps into the unknown. Our research may make positive contributions to trust-building by differentiating types of trust (general trust, civic/political trust, trust that the other side will not exploit etc.) and identifying predictors of each (including threat, emotions, and self-disclosure).

Summary

Our recent studies show that intergroup trust is a multifaceted construct, and that different forms of trust have different psychological antecedents and consequences. We have shown, in several ways, that trust is not synonymous with attitude. It is a more demanding criterion, and it has more severe consequences. Whereas a strong in-group bias emerges for attitude/evaluative data, such a bias does not emerge uniformly for the trust data. Trust and attitudes are related, but they differ conceptually. Theoretically, one important distinction between trust and a general positivity bias in attitudes is that trusting poses a potential risk and threat to the self or in-group in a way that liking does not. Our research has also shown that trust was not a unitary construct, and that we could construct a taxonomy of trust. Various kinds of trust were found to have different relationships to other variables, and we found that those relationships were mediated by yet other variables.

Limitations, Current Research, and Future Directions

> Colm saw the twisted life of the city: the fightings at football matches between Catholics and Protestants; the paintings on the gable-ends of King William on a white horse, his sword raised to the sky, and printed underneath: REMEMBER 1690 ... NO POPE HERE. And in the Catholic quarters, the green-white-and-gold flag of Ireland painted on the walls with UP THE REPUBLIC. It was a strange city he thought, to be living two lives (Michael McLaverty, *Call my brother back*, 2003, pp. 123-124).

We refer here to two limitations to our work so far. First, all of our surveys to date have been cross-sectional. Second, our research has relied on explicit measures, which may be subject to social-desirability biases.

Notwithstanding the strong and consistent effects of contact we have reported, we now need, and are collecting, longitudinal data. We have, however, followed strictly the guidance on making causal inferences from cross-sectional data when using SEMs (MacCallum & Austin, 2000). We have also used these methods to estimate causal paths in both directions, and reported significant paths from contact to outcomes, but not vice versa (for more details on this issue, see Hewstone et al., 2005).

We have also recently collected our first data from Northern Ireland using implicit measures. Tam et al. (in press, Study 2) assessed both forgiveness and trust in a recent study that included implicit measures of bias. Implicit measures differ from self-report measures in that they reflect thoughts and feelings that operate outside of conscious awareness and control (Greenwald & Banaji, 1995). They reveal unintentional bias, of which those who consider themselves unprejudiced may be largely unaware (Dovidio, Kawakami, & Beach, 2001). Although implicit measures are typically assessed using computers, and reveal small but systematic differences in response time measured in milliseconds, implicit measures of attitudes are of considerable importance in the real world. They have been shown to predict spontaneous nonverbal behaviors, while explicit measures of attitude predict more deliberative and controlled behaviors toward out-groups (Dovidio et al., 2002). Their investigation in Northern Ireland is therefore long overdue.

We used the Implicit Association Test (IAT), a widely used assessment tool, to measure the degree to which people automatically associate *Catholic* and *Protestant* with positive and negative words, as indicated by response times. We used two versions of the IAT, one using common Catholic and Protestant names (the *Catholic–Protestant IAT*), the other using images of Republican and Loyalist extremist groups (the *Extremist Group IAT*). Both Catholics and Protestants demonstrated strong implicit bias toward their own community and against the other community, on both versions of the IAT. But our study revealed that negative implicit associations with out-group *extremist groups* were particularly important in effectively *blocking* in intergroup both forgiveness and trust toward the out-group in general.

Future work should continue to explore in more detail the relationship between *forgiveness* and *trust*, and also when their predictors and mediators are most effective (see Nadler & Liviatan, 2006). Trust can be seen as a potential benefit to the injured/forgiving party that is likely to come with forgiveness, but it may also be seen as a necessary precursor of forgiveness. We hope to address such issues in future longitudinal research.

Conclusions: Peace and Reconciliation

History says, Don't hope
On this side of the grave
But then, once in a lifetime
The longed-for tidal wave
Of justice can rise up,
And hope and history rhyme.

(The Cure at Troy, translation of Sophocles'
Philoctetes by Seamus Heaney)

Northern Ireland—after the Belfast Agreement—has moved toward an unsteady peace (measured by reduced violence, paramilitary cease fires, and a lower and less visible security presence). Reconciliation, on the other hand, is a challenge that remains in large measure to be faced (Porter, 2003). Indeed, policymakers and practitioners have been concerned by trends, since the signing of the Belfast Agreement, toward greater residential segregation (see OFM&DFM, 2003, 2005; see Cairns & Hewstone, 2002; Niens et al., 2003). Thus the country is still in some way short of the Agreement's vision of a peaceful, inclusive, stable, and fair society, firmly founded on the achievement of reconciliation, tolerance and mutual trust, with the protection and vindication of human rights for all.

Kelly and Hamber (2005; Hamber & Kelly, 2005) have argued that reconciliation in Northern Ireland should involve dealing with the past, forgiveness, acknowledgement, restitution, punishment, justice, and trust. However one defines intergroup reconciliation, the concepts of intergroup contact, forgiveness and trust would seem to be not only useful, but necessary, for building a new society in Northern Ireland, one that is no longer deeply divided, sectarian, and split along lines of identity, but a mixed, tolerant polity with emerging forms of cross-cutting identities.

Notes

1. 'The Lake Isle of Innisfree' (W.B. Yeats, 1865-1939).
2. At the time of writing this chapter, the devolved Northern Irish Assembly had been suspended; at the time of checking copy-editing, the Assembly had been re-opened, with a Protestant (Revd. Ian Paisley, *Democratic Unionist Party*) as First Minister and a Catholic (Martin McGuiness, *Sinn Fein*) as Deputy First Minister.

Acknowledgments

We gratefully acknowledge the financial support of the Community Relations Unit, the Economic & Social Research Council, the Nuffield Foundation, the Templeton Foundation, and the Russell Sage Foundation, for funding much of this research.

References

Allport, G. W. (1954). *The nature of prejudice*. Reading, MA: Addison-Wesley.

NIACRO and Victim Support. (1999). *All truth is bitter: A report of the visit of Dr Alex Borained, Deputy Chairman of the South African Truth & Reconciliation Commission, to Northern Ireland*. Belfast: NIACRO and Victim Support.

Bar-Tal, D. (2000). From intractable conflict through conflict resolution to reconciliation: Psychological analysis. *Political Psychology, 21*, 351-365.

Batson, C., Polycarpou, M. P., Harmon-Jones, E., & Imhoff, H. J. (1997). Empathy and attitudes: Can feeling for a member of a stigmatized group improve feelings toward the group? *Journal of Personality and Social Psychology, 72*, 105-118.

Bizman, A., & Yinon, Y. (2001). Intergroup and interpersonal threats as determinants of prejudice: The moderating role of in-group identification. *Basic and Applied Psychology, 23*, 191-196.

Borris, E. R., & Diehl, P. F. (1998). Forgiveness, reconciliation and the contribution of international peacekeeping. In H. Langholtz (Ed.), *The psychology of peacekeeping* (pp. 207-222). NY: Praeger Publishers.

Boyle, K., & Hadden, T. (1994). *Northern Ireland: The choice*. Harmondsworth, Middlesex: Penguin.

Brewer, M. B. (1999). The psychology of prejudice: Ingroup love or outgroup hate? *Journal of Social Issues, 55*, 429-444.

Brewer, M. B. (2001). Ingroup identification and intergroup conflict: When does ingroup love become outgroup hate? In R. Ashmore, L. Jussim, & D. Wilder (Eds.), *Social identity, intergroup conflict, and conflict reduction* (pp. 2-41). New York: Oxford University Press.

Brown, R., & Hewstone, M. (2005). An integrative theory of intergroup contact. In M. Zanna (Ed.), *Advances in experimental social psychology* (Vol. 37, pp. 255-343). San Diego, CA: Academic Press.

Cairns, E. (1982). Intergroup conflict in Northern Ireland. In H. Tajfel (Ed.), *Social identity and intergroup relations* (pp. 277-297). London: Cambridge University Press.

Cairns, E., & Darby, J. (1998). The conflict in Northern Ireland: Causes, consequences, and controls. *American Psychologist, 53*, 754-760.

Cairns, E., & Hewstone, M. (2002). The impact of peacemaking in Northern Ireland on intergroup behavior. In G. Salomon & B. Nevo (Eds.), *The nature and study of peace education* (pp. 217-228). Hillsdale, NJ: Erlbaum.

Cairns, E., & Roe, M. (Eds.) (2003). *The role of memory in ethnic conflict*. Basingstoke: Palgrave/Macmillan.

Cairns, E., Tam, T., Hewstone, M., & Niens, U. (2005). Forgiveness in Northern Ireland. In E. L. Worthington (Ed.), *Handbook of forgiveness* (pp. 461-476). New York: Brunner/Routledge.

Davis, M. H. (1994). *Empathy: A social psychological approach*. Madison, WI: Brown & Benchmark.

Demoulin, S., Torres, R. R., Perez, A. R., Vaes, J., Paladino, M. P., Gaunt, R., et al. (2004). Emotional prejudice can lead to infra-humanisation. In W. Stroebe & M. Hewstone (Eds.), *European review of social psychology* (Vol. 15, pp. 259-296). Hove, E. Sussex: Psychology Press.

Deutsch, M. (1973). *The resolution of conflict: Constructive and destructive processes*. New Haven, CT: Yale University Press.

Doosje, B., Branscombe, N. R., Spears, R., & Manstead, A. S. R. (1998). Guilty by association: When one's group has a negative history. *Journal of Personality and Social Psychology, 75*, 872-886.

Dovidio, J. F., Kawakami, K., & Beach, K. R. (2001). Implicit and explicit attitudes: Examination of the relationship between measures of intergroup bias. In R. Brown & S. L. Gaertner (Eds.), *Blackwell handbook of social psychology: Intergroup processes* (pp. 175-197). Malden, MA: Blackwell.

Enright, R. D., Freedman, S., & Rique, J. (1998). The psychology of interpersonal forgiveness. In R. D. Enright & J. Noah (Eds.), *Exploring forgiveness* (pp. 46-62). Wisconsin: The University of Wisconsin Press.

Fay, M. T., Morrissey, M., & Smyth, M. (1999). *Northern Ireland's troubles: The human costs*. London: Pluto Press.

Fiske, S. T., Cuddy, A. J., Glick, P., & Xu, J. (2002). A model of (often mixed) stereotype content: Competence and warmth respectively follow from perceived status and competition. *Journal of Personality and Social Psychology, 82*, 878-902.

Gallagher, A. M. (1989). Social identity and the Northern Ireland conflict. *Human Relations, 42*, 917-935.

Gallagher, A. M. (1995). The approach of government: Community relations and equity. In S. Dunn (Ed.), *Facets of the conflict in Northern Ireland* (pp. 27-43). New York: St. Martin's Press.

Gallagher, A. M. & Dunn, S. (1991). Community relations in Northern Ireland: attitudes to contact and integration. In P. Stringer & G. Robinson (Eds.), *Social attitudes in Northern Ireland: The first report.* (pp. 7-22). Belfast: Blackstaff Press.

Gibson, J. L., & Gouws, A. G. (1999). Truth and reconciliation in South Africa: Attributions of blame and the struggle over apartheid. *American Political Science Review, 93*, 501-517.

Greenwald, A. G., & Banaji, M. R. (1995). Implicit social cognition: Attitudes, self-esteem, and stereotypes. *Psychological Review, 102*, 4-27.

Hamber, B., & Kelly, G. (2005). *A place for reconciliation? Conflict and locality in Northern Ireland* (Democratic Dialogue Rep. No. 18). Belfast: Democratic Dialogue.

Haslam, N., Rothschild, L., & Ernst, D. (2002). Are essentialist beliefs associated with prejudice? *British Journal of Social Psychology, 41*, 87-100.

Hayes, B. C., & McAllister, I. (2002). Sowing dragon's teeth: Public support for political violence and paramilitarism in Northern Ireland. *Political Studies, 49*, 901-922.

Hewstone, M., Cairns, E., Voci, A., McLernon, F., Niens, U., & Noor, M. (2004). Intergroup forgiveness and guilt in Northern Ireland: Social psychological dimensions of "The Troubles." In N. R. Branscombe & B. Doosje (Eds.), *Collective guilt: International perspectives* (pp. 193-215). New York: Cambridge University Press.

Hewstone, M., Cairns, E., Voci, A., Hamberger, J., & Niens, U. (2006). Intergroup contact, forgiveness, and experience of "The Troubles" in Northern Ireland. *Journal of Social Issues, 62*, 99.

Hewstone, M., Cairns E., Voci, A., Paolini, S., McLernon, F., Crisp, R., et al. (2005). Intergroup contact in a divided society: Challenging segregation in Northern Ireland. In D. Abrams, J. M. Marques, & M. A. Hogg (Eds.), *The social psychology of inclusion and exclusion* (pp. 265-292). Philadelphia, PA: Psychology Press.

Hewstone, M., Cairns, E., Voci, A., & McLernon, A. *Intergroup contact and intergroup attitudes in Northern Ireland: Mediational and moderational evidence.* University of Oxford. Manuscript in preparation.

Hewstone, M., Rubin, M., & Willis, H. (2002). Intergroup bias. *Annual Review of Psychology, 53*, 575-604.

Hewstone, M., Voci, A., & Cairns, E. Mediating and moderating effects of intergroup contact in Northern Ireland. Manuscript in preparation.

Hewstone, M., Voci, A., Cairns, E., & McLernon, A. (2003). *Intergroup contact and intergroup attitudes in Northern Ireland: Mediational and moderational evidence.* Paper presented at Society for Experimental Social Psychology, Boston.

Hughes, J. (2001). Constitutional reform in Northern Ireland: Implications for community relations policy and practice. *The International Journal of Conflict Management, 12*, 257-282.

Hughes, J., & Carmichael, P. (1998). Community relations in Northern Ireland: Attitudes to contact and segregation. In G. Robinson, D. Heenan, A. M. Gray, & K. Thompson (Eds.), *Social attitudes in Northern Ireland: The Seventh Report* (p. 8). England, Gower: Aldershot.

Hughes, J., & Donnelly, C. (2001). *Ten years of social attitudes to community relations in Northern Ireland* [Draft]. University of Ulster: Department of Psychology.

Insko, C. A., Schopler, J., Hoyle, R., Dardis, G., & Graetz, K. (1990). Individual-group discontinuity as a function of fear and greed. *Journal of Personality and Social Psychology, 58*, 68-79.

Kelly, G., & Hamber, B. (Eds.) (2005). *Reconciliation: Rhetoric or relevant?* Belfast: Democratic Dialogue.

Kenworthy, J., Hewstone, M., Cairns, E., & Voci, A. (2004). *Symbolic and realistic threat as predictors of intergroup trust in Northern Ireland.* Paper presented at the bi-annual meeting of SPSSI, Washington, DC.

Kenworthy, J., Turner, R., Hewstone, M., & Voci, A. (2005). Intergroup contact: When does it work, and why? In J. Dovidio, P. Glick, & L. Rudman (Eds.), *Reflecting on Allport* (pp. 278-292). Oxford: Blackwell.

Knox, C. (2002). "See no evil, hear no evil." Insidious paramilitary violence in Northern Ireland. *British Journal of Criminology, 42,* 164-185.

Knox, C., & Hughes, J. (1994). *Cross community contact: Northern Ireland and Israel— A comparative perspective.* Ulster Papers in Public Policy and Management, Number 32.

Kollock, P. (1994). The emergence of exchange structures: An experimental study of uncertainty, commitment, and trust. *American Journal of Sociology, 100,* 313-345.

Kramer, R. M., & Carnevale, P. J. (2001). Trust and intergroup negotiation. In R. Brown & S. Gaertner (Eds.), *Blackwell Handbook of Social Psychology: Intergroup processes* (pp. 431-450). Oxford: Blackwell.

Lawler, E. J., & Yoon, J. (1996). Commitment in exchange relations: Test of a theory of relational cohesion. *American Sociological Review, 61,* 89-108.

LeVine, R. A., & Campbell, D. T. (1972). *Ethnocentrism: Theories of conflict, ethnic attitudes, and group behavior.* New York: Wiley.

Leyens, J. Ph., Paladino, P. M., Rodriguez, R. T., Vaes, J., Demoulin, S., Rodriguez, A. P., et al. (2000). The emotional side of prejudice: the attribution of secondary emotions to ingroups and outgroups. *Personality and Social Psychology Review, 4,* 186-197.

Leyens, J. P., Rodriguez, A. P., Rodriguez, R. T., Gaunt, R., Paladino, P. M., & Vaes, J. (2001). Psychological essentialism and the differential attribution of uniquely human emotions to ingroups and outgroups. *European Journal of Social Psychology, 31,* 395-411.

Liechty, J., & Clegg, C. (2001). *Moving beyond sectarianism.* Dublin: Columbia Press.

MacCallum, R. C., & Austin, J. T. (2000). Applications of structural equation modeling in psychological research. *Annual Review of Psychology, 51,* 201-226.

Mackie, D. M., Devos, T., & Smith, E. R. (2000). Intergroup emotions: Explaining offensive action tendencies in an intergroup context. *Journal of Personality and Social Psychology, 79,* 602-616.

Mackie, D. M., & Smith, E. R. (Eds.) (2002). *From prejudice to intergroup emotions: Differentiated reactions to social groups.* New York, NY & Hove, UK: Psychology Press.

Marques, J. M., Yzerbyt, V. Y., & Leyens, J.-P. (1988). The "Black Sheep Effect": Extremity of judgments towards ingroup members as a function of group identification. *European Journal of Social Psychology, 18,* 1-16.

McCullough, M. E. (2001). Forgiveness: Who does it and how do they do it? *Current Directions in Psychological Science, 10*, 194-197.

McCullough, M. E., Pargament, K. I., & Thoresen, C. E. (1999). The psychology of forgiveness: History, conceptual issues, and overview. In M. E. McCullough, K. I. Pargament, & C. E. Thoresen (Eds.), *Forgiveness: Theory, research and practice* (pp. 1-16). New York: Guildford.

McCullough, M. E., Pargament, K. I., & Thoresen, C. E. (Eds.) (2000). *Forgiveness: Theory, research and practice.* New York: Guilford Press.

McGlynn, C., Niens, U., Cairns, E., & Hewstone, M. (2004). Moving out of conflict: The contribution of integrated schools in Northern Ireland to identity, attitudes, forgiveness and reconciliation. *Journal of Peace Education, 1*, 147-163.

McKittrick, D., & McVea, D. (2000). *Making sense of the troubles.* London: Penguin.

McLaverty, M. (2003). *Call my brother back.* Belfast: The Blackstaff Press.

McLernon, F., Cairns, E., Lewis, C. A., & Hewstone, M. (2003). Memories of recent conflict and forgiveness in Northern Ireland. In E. Cairns & M. Roe (Eds.), *The role of memory in ethnic conflict* (pp. 125-143). Basingstoke: Palgrave/Macmillan.

Mitchell, G. (1999). *Making peace.* Berkeley, CA: University of California Press.

Molm, L. D., Takahashi, N., & Peterson, G. (2000). Risk and trust in social exchange: An experimental test of a classical proposition. *American Journal of Sociology, 105*, 1396-1427.

Mowlam, M. (2002). *Momentum: The struggle for peace, politics and the people.* London: Hodder & Stoughton.

Mulholland, M. (2002a). *The longest war.* Oxford: Oxford University Press.

Mulholland, M. (2002b). *Northern Ireland: A very short introduction.* Oxford: Oxford University Press.

Myers, E., Hewstone, M., Kenworthy, J., Cairns, E., & Hughes, J. (2005). Trusting the out-group as a risk to the in-group. Manuscript in preparation.

Nadler, A., & Liviatan, I. (2004). Inter-group reconciliation processes in Israel: Theoretical analysis and empirical findings. In N. R. Branscombe & B. Doosje (Eds.), *Collective guilt: International perspectives* (pp. 216-235). New York: Cambridge University Press.

Nadler, A., & Liviatan, I. (2006). Intergroup reconciliation: Effects of adversary's expressions of empathy, responsibility, and recipients' trust. *Personality and Social Psychology Bulletin, 32*, 459-470.

Newberg, A. B., d'Aquili, E. G., Newberg, S. K., & de Marici, V. (2000). The neuropsychological correlates of forgiveness. In M. E. McCullough, K. I. Paragment, & C. E. Thoresen (Eds.), *Forgiveness: Theory, research and practice* (pp. 91-110). New York: Guildford.

Niens, U., Cairns, E., & Hewstone, M. (2003). Contact and conflict in Northern Ireland. In O. Hargie & D. Dickson (Eds.), *Researching The Troubles: Social science perspectives on the Northern Ireland conflict* (pp. 123-140). Edinburgh: Mainstream Publishing.

OFM&DFM. (2003). *A shared future: A consultation paper on improving relations in Northern Ireland*. Belfast: Office of the First Minister and Deputy First Minister.

OFM&DFM. (2005). *A shared future: Policy and strategic framework for good relations in Northern Ireland*. Belfast: Office of the First Minister and Deputy First Minister.

Paolini, S., Hewstone, M., Cairns, E., & Voci, A. (2004). Effects of direct and indirect cross-group friendships on judgments of Catholics and Protestants in Northern Ireland: The mediating role of an anxiety-reduction mechanism. *Personality and Social Psychology Bulletin, 30,* 770-786.

Pettigrew, T. F. (1998). Intergroup contact theory. *Annual Review of Psychology, 49,* 65-85.

Pettigrew, T. F., & Tropp, L. (2006). A meta-analytic test of intergroup contact theory. *Journal of Personality and Social Psychology, 90,* 751-783.

Poole, M., & Doherty, P. (1996). *Ethnic residential segregation in Northern Ireland.* Coleraine: University of Ulster.

Porter, N. (2003). *The elusive quest: Reconciliation in Northern Ireland.* Belfast: Blackstaff Press.

Robinson, G. (2003). *Northern Irish communities drifting apart.* Retrieved October 27, 2007, from University of Ulster Report, http://www.ulst.ac.uk/news/releases/2003/725.html

Rothbart, M., & Park, B. (1986). On the confirmability and disconfirmability of trait concepts. *Journal of Personality and Social Psychology, 50,* 131-142.

Shirlow, P. (2001). Fear and ethnic division. *Peace Review, 13,* 67-74.

Shriver, D. W., Jr. (1995). *An ethic for enemies: Forgiveness in politics.* New York: Oxford University Press.

Smyth, M. (1995). Limitations on the capacity for citizenship in post cease-fire Northern Ireland. In M. Smyth & R. Moore (Eds.), *Three conference papers on aspects of segregation and sectarian division: Researching sectarianism; borders within borders; and the capacity for citizenship* (pp. 50-66). Derry/Londonderry: Templegrove Action Research Ltd.

Stephan, W. G., & Renfro, C. L. (2003). The role of threat in intergroup relations. In D. M. Mackie & E. R. Smith (Eds.), *From prejudice to intergroup emotions: Differentiated reactions to social groups* (pp. 191-207). New York: Psychology Press.

Stephan, W. G., & Stephan, C. W. (1985). Intergroup anxiety. *Journal of Social Issues, 41,* 157-175.

Stephan, W. G., & Stephan, C. W. (2000). An integrated threat theory of prejudice. In S. Oskamp (Ed.), *Reducing prejudice and discrimination* (pp. 23-46). Hillsdale, NJ: Erlbaum.

Tajfel, H., & Turner, J. C. (1979). An integrative theory of intergroup conflict. In W. G. Austin & S. Worchel (Eds.), *The psychology of intergroup relations* (pp. 33-48). Monterey, CA: Brooks/Cole.

Tam, T., Hewstone, M., Cairns, E., Tausch, N., Maio, G., & Kenworthy, J. (2007). The impact of intergroup emotions on forgiveness in Northern Ireland. *Group Processes and Intergroup Relations, 10,* 119-136.

Tam, T., Hewstone, M., Kenworthy, J., Voci, A., Cairns, E., & Van Dick, R. (2005). The mediational role of intergroup emotions and empathy in contact between Catholics and Protestants in Northern Ireland. Manuscript in preparation.

Tam, T., Hewstone, M., Kenworthy, J., Cairns, E., Marinetti, C., Geddes, L., et al. (2007). Contemporary research on sectarianism in Northern Ireland: The building of intergroup forgiveness and trust. *Journal of Social Issues.*

Tausch, N., Kenworthy, J., & Hewstone, M. (2007). The confirmability and disconfirmability of trait concepts revisited: Does content matter? *Journal of Personality and Social Psychology, 92,* 554-556.

Tausch, N., Hewstone, M., Kenworthy, J., Cairns, E., & Christ, O. (2007). Cross-community contact, perceived status differences and intergroup attitudes in Northern Ireland: The mediating roles of individual-level vs. group-level threats and the moderating role of social identification. *Political Psychology, 28,* 53-68.

Tausch, N., Tam, T., Hewstone, M., Kenworthy, J., & Cairns, E. (2007). Individual-level and group-level mediators of contact effects in Northern Ireland: The moderating role of social identification. *British Journal of Social Psychology, 46,* 541-556.

Trew, K. (1986). Catholic-Protestant contact in Northern Ireland. In M. Hewstone & R. Brown (Eds.), *Contact and conflict in intergroup encounters* (pp. 93-106). Oxford: Basil Blackwell.

Tutu, D. (1999). *No future without forgiveness.* London: Rider Press

Whyte, J. (1990). *Interpreting Northern Ireland.* Oxford: Clarendon Press.

Worthington, E. L. (Ed.) (1998). *Dimensions of forgiveness: Psychological research and theological perspectives.* Radno, PA: Templeton Foundation Press.

Wright, S. C., Aron, A., McLaughlin-Volpe, T., & Ropp, S. A. (1997). The extended contact effect: Knowledge of cross-group friendships and prejudice. *Journal of Personality and Social Psychology, 73,* 73-90.

Yamagishi, T., & Yamagishi, M. (1994). Trust and commitment in the United States and Japan. *Motivation and Emotion, 18,* 129-166.

CHAPTER 10

Majority and Minority Perspectives in Intergroup Relations: The Role of Contact, Group Representations, Threat, and Trust in Intergroup Conflict and Reconciliation

John F. Dovidio, Samuel L. Gaertner, Melissa-Sue John, Samer Halabi, Tamar Saguy, Adam R. Pearson, and Blake M. Riek

Intergroup tension and conflict are universal and occur at virtually every level of collective organization, from small groups in the workplace to racial, ethnic, and cultural divides within and between nations. Rarely are relations between groups characterized by equal group status. Hierarchical relations between groups are typical across cultures and across time (Sidanius & Pratto, 1999). Thus, strategies and interventions designed to improve intergroup relations need to consider the perspectives and motives of both the higher status (i.e., majority) group and the lower status (i.e., minority) group to understand their *relations*. The current chapter examines the potential roles of intergroup representations, threat, and trust in the dynamics of intergroup relations between Whites and Blacks.

In this chapter, we first explore the psychological processes that promote intergroup bias, threat, and distrust and may lead to intergroup conflict.

Second, we examine, conceptually and practically, ways of reducing intergroup bias. Theoretically, we outline how one particular strategy, represented by the Common Ingroup Identity Model (Gaertner & Dovidio, 2000), can be applied to ameliorate bias and improve intergroup relations (see also the Riek, Gaertner, Dovidio, Brewer, Mania, & Lamoreaux, in this volume). Third, we emphasize the importance of understanding the differing perspectives of majority- and minority-group members on intergroup relations, and we illustrate the different dynamics empirically, focusing on Black–White relations within the United States as a case study. We conclude by considering the implications that this conceptualization of the nature and dynamics of intergroup bias has for interventions designed to reduce bias and promote reconciliation.

Psychological Processes Promoting Intergroup Bias

Intergroup bias is pervasive because it is rooted in basic psychological and social processes that are often functional in dealing with aspects of everyday personal and group life. In terms of psychological processes, the effects of social categorization and group identification form a foundation for prejudice and conflict between groups. With respect to social processes, the nature of group functioning in a context of limited resources often leads to competition, and, thus, threat and distrust between groups.

Social Categorization and Group Identification

Social categorization forms an essential basis for human perception, cognition, and functioning. Because of the adaptive significance of intellect in human survival, people have a fundamental need to understand their environment. To cope with the enormous complexity of the world, people abstract meaning from their perceptions and develop heuristics and other simplifying principles for thinking about important elements in their environment. Categorization is one of the most basic processes in the abstraction of meaning from complex environments.

Categorization of objects into groups often occurs spontaneously on the basis of physical similarity or proximity. The instant an object is categorized, it is assigned the properties shared by other category members (Biernat & Dovidio, 2000). Because social groups (like race and gender) are often assumed to reflect a natural category, where group membership is inherent to the individual (Yzerbyt, Corneille, & Estrada, 2001), membership in natural categories is often believed to reflect similarities in the *essence* of group members. Thus, people are especially likely to generalize characteristics across members (producing strong stereotypes) and to generalize beyond the characteristic that originally differentiated the categories to additional dimensions and traits. This categorization process results in the minimization of actual differences among members of the same category (Tajfel, 1969) and the exaggeration of the differences between social groups, promoting perceptions of group distinctiveness.

In the process of social categorization, people commonly classify themselves *into* one social category and *out of* others resulting in a sense of in-group identification (Tajfel, 1978). Because of the centrality of the self in social perception (Dovidio & Gaertner, 1993), social categorization fundamentally involves a distinction between the group containing the self (the in-group) and other groups (the out-groups)—between the *we's* and the *they's*. This distinction can have a profound influence on evaluations, cognitions, and behaviors relevant to intergroup bias. Once people begin to identify themselves primarily in terms of their group membership, their orientations toward others become defined in terms of in-group/out-group membership. Emotionally, people spontaneously experience more positive affect toward other members of the in-group than toward members of the out-group (Otten & Moskowitz, 2000). Cognitively, people retain more information in a more detailed fashion for in-group members than for out-group members (Park & Rothbart, 1982), have better memory for information about the ways in which in-group members are similar to and out-group members are dissimilar to the self (Wilder, 1981), and remember less positive information about out-group members (Howard & Rothbart, 1980). Behaviorally, when group membership is salient, people allocate more resources to members of their in-group compared to members of the out-group (Tajfel, Billing, Bundy, & Flament, 1971) and work harder for groups identified as in-groups (Worchel, Rothgerber, Day, Hart, & Butemeyer, 1998).

Intergroup Competition

Following categorization, once group identification has been established, maintaining a sense of in-group inclusion and cohesiveness becomes tantamount to protecting one's own existence as well as one's positive sense of self. Because humans are social animals, relying on select others for interdependent activity, cooperation has important consequences for individuals' fitness and survival. Psychologically, expectations of cooperation and security promote and maintain positive attraction toward other in-group members, as well as motivate adherence to in-group norms that assure that one will be recognized as a good or legitimate in-group member. Hence, coordination, trust, and cooperation are processes that are likely to occur in an intragroup context. These same processes, however, can also give rise to intergroup competition and distrust that may seed and sustain conflict.

In part because of these processes, relations between groups are qualitatively different than are relations between individuals. Insko, Schopler, and their colleagues have demonstrated a fundamental *individual-group discontinuity effect* in which interactions between groups are substantially more competitive than are interactions between individuals (see Insko et al., 2001; Schopler & Insko, 1992; Wildschut, Pinter, Vevea, Insko, & Schopler, 2003). In one study, for example, either two individuals or two 3-person groups played a prisoner's dilemma game (Schopler et al., 2001). Whereas individuals chose competitive options only, 1% of the time groups chose the competitive action 30% of the time. These effects generalize to other types of social dilemma games (Insko et al., 1994) and to competition and cooperation in other situations (e.g., involving profits for producing paper origami figures; Schopler et al., 2001) and beyond the laboratory (Pemberton, Insko, & Schopler, 1996). Furthermore, processes that typically promote interpersonal cooperation, such as open communication, have limited impact on reducing competition between groups (Insko et al., 1993). In addition, groups are more likely to exploit positions of power than are individuals (Wildschut, Insko, & Gaertner, 2002). For example, groups take greater advantage of potentially higher payoffs at the expense of others and compete to enhance their position relative to other groups more than individuals do (Schopler et al., 2001).

Not only do psychological biases produce perceptions of competition and motivate actual competition between groups, competition between groups itself further increases bias and distrust (see, for example, Realistic group conflict theory; Campbell, 1965; Sherif, 1966). When people perceive out-group members as a threat, they tend to derogate and discriminate against them more directly (Esses, Dovidio, Jackson, & Armstrong, 2001; Stephan & Stephan, 2000).

This process was illustrated in the classic work of Sherif Harvey, White, Hood, and Sherif (1961). In 1954, Sherif and his research team conducted a field study on intergroup conflict in a camp adjacent to Robbers Cave State Park in Oklahoma (USA). In this study, twenty-two 12-year-old boys attending the summer camp were randomly assigned to one of two groups (who subsequently named themselves Eagles and Rattlers). The two groups were initially kept completely apart for one week to permit time for group formation (e.g., development of norms and a leadership structure). Then during the second week of camp, the researchers had the two groups engage in a number of competitive athletic activities such as tug-of-war, baseball, and touch football, with the winning group receiving prizes. As expected, the introduction of competitive activities generated conflict and derogatory stereotypes between the groups. These boys did not simply show the in-group favoritism frequently seen in laboratory studies. Rather, in this naturalistic situation, there was genuine hostility between these groups. Group members regularly exchanged verbal insults appropriate to the 1950s (e.g., "stinkers," "pigs," "bums," "cheaters," and "communists"). In addition, they engaged in physical hostilities. They conducted raids on one another's cabins, which resulted in the destruction and theft of property, and carried sticks, baseball bats, and socks filled with rocks as potential weapons. Fistfights broke out between members of the groups, and food and garbage fights erupted in the dining hall. Thus, the arousal of in-group favoritism that accompanies the mere categorization of people as in-group and out-group members (Tajfel & Turner, 1979) and motivation to achieve advantaged status for one's group (Sidanius & Pratto, 1999), together with realistic threats from competition for scarce resources, combined to promote conflict between groups and produce an atmosphere of threat and distrust.

Intergroup Threat and Distrust

Intergroup threat can take various forms. Paralleling our distinction between psychological and social forces that promote bias and conflict, Stephan and Stephan (2000) distinguished between symbolic and realistic threat. Symbolic threat relates to perceived conflict between groups' values and goals; realistic threat involves perceived competition for limited resources, often framed in terms of zero-sum outcomes in which one group's gain is perceived as another group's loss (Stephan & Stephan, 2000; see also Esses et al., 2001). A recent meta-analytic review of the relationship between intergroup threat and out-group attitudes by Riek, Mania, and Gaertner (2006) revealed that symbolic threat ($r = .45$) and realistic threat ($r = .42$) contributed uniquely (i.e., independent of the effect of the other) and to a comparable degree to negative attitudes toward out-groups.

In addition, perceptions of threat appear to be a critical element promoting interracial prejudice and mistrust between Blacks and Whites in the U.S. relations. In general, the more Whites perceive that Blacks do not support their cherished values, the more negatively they respond to Blacks (Biernat, Vescio, & Theno, 1996; Dunbar, Saiz, Stela, & Saez, 2000). Similarly, Blacks exhibit more bias toward Whites the more they perceive that their culture and values are not respected by Whites (Mabry & Kiecolt, 2005). As with perceptions of realistic threat for attitudes toward a range of social groups (McLaren, 2003), realistic group threat predicts both the negative attitudes of Whites toward Blacks (Bobo, 1983) and of Blacks toward Whites (Stephan et al., 2002).

In contrast to the considerable interest in the role of threat in intergroup relations, relatively little attention has been devoted to the influence of inter-group trust or mistrust on intergroup relations (Kramer, 2004). Although trust is not synonymous with in-group favoritism, these concepts appear rooted in similar processes (Yamagishi & Kiyonari, 2000). People tend to trust others when they are identified as members of their own group, particularly in Western cultures (Yuki, Maddux, & Brewer, 2005), and they tend to distrust others who are seen as members of other groups (Insko & Schopler, 1998).

Within the United States, both historical and contemporary race relations have often been characterized by distrust (Dovidio & Gaertner, 2004). Whites' stereotypically characterize Blacks as violent, dangerous, impulsive, and criminal (Dovidio, Brigham, Johnson, & Gaertner, 1996), which elicits feelings of mistrust among Whites (Cohen & Steele, 2002). Greater mistrust, in turn, is related to greater race-related anger among Whites (Mabry & Kiecolt, 2005). In part because of their wariness and distrust, Whites, as the dominant social group in U.S. society, often develop policies and enact laws (e.g., laws historically limiting Blacks' opportunities to vote) that enhance their control over Blacks (Sidanius, Levin, & Pratto, 1998; Soss, Langbein, & Metelko, 2003). In addition, Blacks have a pervasive distrust for Whites that is reflected in high levels of perceived discrimination and orientations toward basic social institutions (Dovidio, Gaertner, Kawakami, & Hodson, 2002). Blacks report distrust of government leaders (Earl & Penney, 2001; Shavers-Hornaday, Lynch, Burmeister, & Torner, 1997) and medical practitioners and researchers (Armstrong, Crum, Reiger, Bennett, & Edwards, 1999; Davis & Reid, 1999), as well as for authorities and policies in the areas of business and education (Phelps, Taylor, & Gerard, 2001).

In summary, social categorization, particularly in terms of the distinction between in-groups and out-groups, is sufficient to initiate intergroup bias in the absence of meaningful relations between groups. On social categorization, people are cooperatively oriented toward members of their group and tend to be competitively predisposed toward members of other groups. Perceived or actual competition between groups further contributes substantially to intergroup bias. Groups are inherently greedier and less trusting than are individuals, and they elicit greater fear. As a consequence, groups tend to be more competitive than individuals in their relations (Wildschut et al., 2003). Competition can emerge over material resources or can manifest in more symbolic forms, as in perceived conflict over differing religious beliefs or cultural values (see Esses et al., 2001) with both types of threats having a comparable impact on intergroup attitudes and relations (Riek et al., 2006). Importantly, competition and threat contribute to a climate of distrust that adds another barrier to constructive intergroup relations.

Taken together, these findings paint a bleak picture for intergroup relations. However, understanding the factors that contribute to intergroup bias and the underlying principles that shape intergroup relations can help identify interventions that improve intergroup relations and promote reconciliation between groups earlier in conflict. We consider this issue in the next section.

Improving Intergroup Relations and Promoting Reconciliation

In this section, we explore, both theoretically and practically, interventions that reduce intergroup bias and facilitate more harmonious relations between groups. As illustrated in the earlier section, social categorization forms a foundation for the development of bias and competitive relations, which elicits threat and distrust between groups. In this section, we examine ways of altering how people categorize others, and we discuss how appropriately structured intergroup contact can reduce bias.

Antecedents of Intergroup Reconciliation: Intergroup Contact

Over the past half-century, Allport's (1954) revised Contact Hypothesis has been a guiding framework for strategies designed to reduce intergroup bias and conflict (Dovidio, Gaertner, & Kawakami, 2003; Pettigrew & Tropp, 2006). This hypothesis proposes that simple contact between groups is not sufficient to improve intergroup relations. Certain prerequisite features must be present for contact between groups to reduce bias successfully. These characteristics of contact include equal status between the groups, cooperative (rather than competitive) intergroup interaction, opportunities for personal acquaintance between the members, especially with those whose personal characteristics do not support stereotypic expectations, and supportive norms by authorities within and outside of the contact situation. Although it is difficult to establish all of these conditions in contact situations, this formula is effective when these conditions are met (Pettigrew & Tropp, 2006).

Structurally, however, the Contact Hypothesis has represented a list of loosely connected, diverse conditions rather than a unifying conceptual framework that explains how these prerequisite features achieve their effects. In contrast, the Common Ingroup Identity Model (Gaertner & Dovidio, 2000; see also the chapter by Riek et al., in this volume) proposes that the development of a common group identity can be a common mediating factor for the effect of the conditions identified by Allport (1954) as necessary for contact to reduce intergroup bias.

Processes in Intergroup Reconciliation: Decategorization and Recategorization

Because identification with social groups is a basic process that is fundamental to intergroup bias, social psychologists have targeted this process as a starting point for improving intergroup relations. For example, decategorization strategies that emphasize the individual qualities of others (Wilder, 1981) or encourage personalized interactions (Miller, 2002) have been used to decrease the salience of social identities. When others are viewed as separate individuals, rather than as members of social groups, bias is reduced. This occurs because the forces of in-group favoritism are not invoked for those who would otherwise be considered as members of one's own group and group stereotypes and other forms of prejudgment based on category membership are not applied to others who would ordinarily be classified as out-group members.

The alternative approach that we have employed, the Common Ingroup Identity Model, draws on the theoretical foundations of Social Identity Theory (Tajfel & Turner, 1979) and Self-Categorization Theory (Turner, Hogg, Oakes, Reicher, & Wetherell, 1987). In contrast to a decategorization strategy, this approach does not require that individuals relinquish group identities that may confer important psychological benefits in terms of maintaining personal self-esteem and well-being (Dovidio, Gaertner, Pearson, & Riek, 2005), as well as practical benefits in the form of intragroup cooperation, reciprocity, and other forms of social support. This strategy emphasizes the process of recategorization, whereby members of different groups are induced to conceive of themselves as a single, more inclusive superordinate group rather than as two completely separate groups. As a consequence, attitudes toward former out-group members become more positive through processes involving pro-in-group bias.

We propose that recategorization can take two forms. First, two distinct social entities can be combined to form a single superordinate category. That is, the representations of the groups can be transformed from two separate groups to one inclusive group, a one-group representation. However, people do not have to relinquish their former in-group identities entirely for recategorization to occur. A second form of recategorization is one in which members maintain their initial in-group identity but do so within the context of a superordinate category. This is a "dual identity" or a "two subgroups in one group" recategorization (Gaertner & Dovidio, 2000). As we noted earlier, when people recategorize others who were formerly seen only as members of a different group in terms of common group membership, entirely or in part, attitudes toward these former out-group members become more positive because they now benefit from the processes of in-group favoritism (see Gaertner & Dovidio, 2000; Gaertner, Mann, Murrell, & Dovidio, 1989).

The Role of Intergroup Contact in the Creation of a Common Identity

The Common Ingroup Identity Model has been applied as an integrative theoretical framework to explain how intergroup contact, along the lines outlined in the Contact Hypothesis (Allport, 1954), operates psychologically to reduce bias and improve intergroup relations. For instance, in experimental studies we found that cooperative interdependence (Gaertner, Mann, Dovidio, Murrell, & Pomare, 1990) and interaction (Gaertner et al., 1999), two of the key elements of contact identified by Allport (1954) each reduced bias between two groups by creating stronger one-group representations that encompassed members of both groups. In addition, in a series of studies of consequential groups outside the laboratory, we asked participants about their perceptions of intergroup contact related to the four prerequisite features Allport (1954) identified in the Contact Hypothesis and assessed intergroup attitudes and orientations. These studies included students attending a multiethnic high school (Gaertner, Rust, Dovidio, Bachman, & Anastasio, 1996), majority and minority students at college (Dovidio, Gaertner, Niemann, & Snider, 2001), banking executives who had experienced a corporate merger involving a wide variety of banks across the United States, and members of blended families whose households were composed of two formerly separate families trying to unite (Gaertner, Bachman, Dovidio, & Banker, 2001).

These studies offered converging support for the hypothesis that the features specified by the Contact Hypothesis reduce intergroup bias, partly because they transform members' representations of the memberships from separate groups to one inclusive group. Consistent with the role of an inclusive group representation that is hypothesized in the Common Ingroup Identity Model, across all four studies: (a) conditions of intergroup contact that were perceived as more favorable predicted lower levels of intergroup bias; (b) more favorable conditions of contact predicted more inclusive (one group) and less exclusive (different groups); and (c) more inclusive representations mediated lower levels of intergroup bias and conflict. Thus, both controlled laboratory experiments and field studies offer converging evidence for the role of recat-egorization in producing the benefits associated with appropriately structured intergroup contact.

Despite the evidence for the effectiveness of achieving a common group identity for improving intergroup relations, outside of the laboratory it is often difficult to sustain a superordinate group identity in the face of powerful social forces that emphasize group differences and reinforce separate group memberships. Hewstone (1996) has argued that, at a practical level, interventions designed to create a common, inclusive identity (such as equal status contact) may not be sufficiently potent to "overcome powerful ethnic and racial categorizations on more than a temporary basis" (p. 351). With respect to the perception of others, when the basis for group membership is highly salient (e.g., physical features) and the social category is culturally important, the impact of interventions that temporarily induce feelings of common identity may quickly fade as the original category membership becomes repeatedly, and often automatically activated (as with race in the United States, Dovidio & Gaertner, 1993).

In addition, when original subgroup identities and their associated cultural values are vital to one's functioning, it would be undesirable or impossible for people to relinquish this aspect of their self-concept completely. Indeed, demands to abandon these group identities or to adopt a colorblind ideology would likely arouse strong reactance and result in especially poor intergroup relations. Whereas majority-group members typically see majority-group and superordinate identities as synonymous (e.g., "White = American," Devos & Banaji, 2005), minority-group members often see their subgroup and superordinate group identities as distinct (e.g., as Black Americans; Sidanius, Feshbach, Levin, & Pratto, 1997).

In his classic book, *The Souls of Black Folk*, DuBois (1938) observed that whereas Whites form a relatively simple and direct form of social consciousness because White culture and dominant American culture are synonymous, Black Americans develop a dual form of consciousness in which they are sensitive to the values and expectations of the majority culture while also aware of and responsive to the values and expectations of Black culture. In our terms, whereas Whites may generally assume a single identity in which White and American identities correspond, minority-group members may generally form a dual identity in which the American superordinate and the racial/ethnic subgroup identities are distinct. Empirical research 60 years later supports DuBois' observation: White identity is much more closely aligned with a superordinate American identity than is Black identity (Devos & Banaji, 2005; Sidanius et al., 1997). Thus, when considering processes of contact and categorization, it is important to consider the potentially differing perspectives and preferred group representations of majority- and minority-group members to advance a more complete understanding of intergroup relations.

Perspectives of Majority and Minority Groups

In this section of the chapter, we examine how majority- and minority-group perspectives might systematically differ and the implications of these perspectives on intergroup relations. First, we explore the possibility that majority- and minority-group members will have different preferences for group representations. Second, we examine how these different preferred representations influence the ways that positive intergroup contact can reduce bias. Third, we extend our earlier analyses of these processes by considering the roles of threat and trust in the relations between White and Black students on a college campus.

Majority- and Minority-Group Preferences

Within the context of the Common Ingroup Identity Model, as we noted earlier, the development of a common identity need not require each group to forsake its original group identity. In particular, the most recent developments in our work on the Common Ingroup Identity Model have focused on a second form of recategorization, the impact of a *dual identity* in which the superordinate identity is salient but in conjunction with a salient subgroup identity (a "different groups working together on the same-team" representation). In this respect, the Common Ingroup Identity Model is aligned with bidimensional models of acculturation, in which cultural heritage and mainstream identities are relatively independent (Berry, 1997), rather than unidimensional models, which posit that cultural identity is necessarily relinquished with the adoption of a mainstream cultural identity (Gans, 1979).

Berry (1984) offered a framework to help understand the different types of consciousness and identity processes that immigrant groups can experience within the dominant culture of the host society. Specifically, Berry (1984) presented four forms of cultural relations in pluralistic societies that represent the intersection of *yes–no* responses to two fundamental questions: (a) Are the original cultural identity and customs of value to be retained? and (b) Are positive relations with the larger society of value, and to be sought? These combinations reflect four adaptation strategies for intergroup relations, as identified by Berry: (a) *integration*, in which cultural identities are retained and positive relations with the larger society are sought; (b) *separatism*, in which original cultural identities are retained but positive relations with the larger society are not sought; (c) *assimilation*, in which cultural identities are abandoned and positive relations with the larger society are desired; and (d) *marginalization*, in which cultural identities are abandoned and are not replaced by positive identification with the larger society.

Although this framework was originally applied to the ways in which immigrants acclimatize to a new society (van Oudenhoven, Prins, & Buunk, 1998), we have adapted it to apply to intergroup relations between majority and minority groups more generally (see Dovidio, Gaertner, & Kafati, 2000). Substituting the separate strengths of the subgroup and subordinate group identities for the answers to Berry's (1984) two questions, the combinations map onto the four main representations considered in the Common Ingroup Identity Model: (a) *dual identity* (subgroup and superordinate group identities are high, such as feeling like different groups on the same team: which relates to Berry's adaptation strategy of integration); (b) *different groups* (subgroup identity is high and superordinate identity is low: separatism); (c) *one group* (subgroup identity is low and superordinate group identity is high: assimilation); and (d) *separate individuals* (subgroup and superordinate group identities are low relative to individual identity: that relates to Berry's adaptation strategy of marginalization).

Although achieving a common in-group identity can have beneficial effects for both majority- and minority-group members (Gaertner et al., 1996), it is still important to recognize that members of these groups also have different perspectives (Islam & Hewstone, 1993) and motivations. These different perspectives and motivations can shape perceptions of and reactions to the nature of the contact. Whereas minority-group members often seek to retain their cultural identity, majority-group members tend to favor the assimilation of minority groups into one single culture (a traditional *melting-pot* orientation)—a process that reaffirms and reinforces the values of the dominant culture. van Oudenhoven et al. (1998), for instance, found in the Netherlands that Dutch majority-group members preferred an assimilation of minority groups, in which minority-group identity was abandoned and replaced by identification with the dominant Dutch culture, whereas Turkish and Moroccan immigrants most strongly endorsed integration, in which they would retain their own cultural identity while also valuing the dominant Dutch culture. These orientations, assimilation for the majority group and integration for minority groups, are more pronounced for majority- and minority-group members who identify more strongly with their group (Verkuyten & Brug, 2004). In terms of the Common Ingroup Identity Model, we have found that White college students in the United States tend to value a one-group (assimilation) orientation, whereas racial and ethnic minority students in the United States tend to favor a *same-team* (pluralistic integration) representation (Dovidio et al., 2000).

Representations and Majority/Minority Group Relations

According to the Common Ingroup Identity Model (Gaertner & Dovidio, 2000), a dual identity, like a one-group representation, has the potential to facilitate more positive intergroup attitudes and orientations both among minority- and majority-group members. Consistent with this hypothesis, Huo, Smith, Tyler, and Lind (1996) found that even when racial or ethnic identity is strong for minority-group members, perceptions of a superordinate connection enhance interracial trust and acceptance of authority within an organization. Moreover, we found converging evidence for the positive effects of a dual identity in a study of students in a multiethnic high school (Gaertner et al., 1996). Students who described themselves as *both* American and as a member of their racial or ethnic group showed less bias toward other groups in the school than did those who described themselves only in terms of their subgroup identity. Thus, even when subgroup identity is salient, the simultaneous salience of a common in-group identity can be associated with lower levels of intergroup bias (see also Gaertner, Dovidio, Nier, Ward, & Banker, 1999).

Within the context of the Common Ingroup Identity Model, we investigated the hypothesis that majority and minority groups, in general, and Whites and Blacks, in particular, not only have different preferences for one-group and dual-identity (same-team) representations but also that these representations mediate the beneficial effects of favorable intergroup contact on bias in different ways (Dovidio et al., 2000). In particular, we reasoned that because Whites hold assimilationist cultural values and Blacks possess pluralistic values, one-group and dual-identity representations would likely operate differently as mediators of the effect of intergroup contact on intergroup attitudes for members of these two groups. Supportive of this hypothesis, we found that perceptions of favorable intergroup contact predicted more favorable intergroup attitudes for both White and minority college students, but they did so in different ways (Dovidio, Gaertner, Hodson, Houlette, & Johnson, 2005; Dovidio et al., 2000). For White students, more favorable perceptions of intergroup contact predicted stronger one-group representations, which, in turn, primarily mediated more positive attitudes toward minorities. For minority students, it was the strength of the dual identity, not the one-group representation that mediated the relationship between favorable conditions of contact and positive attitudes toward Whites.

Complementing these findings for White students and students of color, we have also found that, within a sample of predominantly White students, status moderates the relationship between a dual identity and bias (Johnson, Gaertner, & Dovidio, 2001). Among lower and higher status university students (i.e., regular students and students in the prestigious Honors

Program, respectively) who were expected to perform the same tasks within a superordinate workgroup, the relationship between perceptions of the aggregate as two subgroups within a group (a dual identity) and bias depended upon the status of the group. For lower status (nonhonors) students, stronger perceptions of a dual identity significantly predicted less bias, whereas for higher status (honors) students, a stronger dual identity predicted greater bias.

Moreover, we believe that a more comprehensive understanding of improved relations between majority and minority groups involves extending an understanding of the different preferences for and operation of one-group and dual-identity representations to consider more proximate psychological states, such as intergroup threat and trust. Thus, in the next section we extend our earlier work by investigating the roles of threat and trust in Blacks' and Whites' orientations toward each other.

Paths to Intergroup Harmony: The Roles of Threat and Trust

In earlier sections, we described how intergroup threat and distrust are key elements that serve both as a cause and an effect of intergroup competition and conflict (Riek et al., 2006; Stephan & Stephan, 2000), and ultimately represent barriers to reconciliation (Bar-Tal, 2000). We now briefly present an empirical analysis that represents an integration of the potential influences of group representations, threat, and trust on the intergroup orientations of Whites to Blacks on a college campus.

As mentioned earlier in this chapter, in this research, we assessed White and Black college students' perceptions of intergroup contact on campus along the dimensions specified by the contact hypothesis (see Gaertner et al., 1996). We also examined the representations that White and Black students had of their groups on campus. Whereas our earlier analyses (Dovidio et al., 2000) tested only the extent to which one-group and dual-identity (same-team) representations mediated the effect of more positive experiences of intergroup contact along the dimensions specified by the contact hypothesis on majority and minority students' satisfaction at college, the present analyses included consideration of the roles of threat and trust and the additional outcome variable of attitudes toward the other group. Our earlier reported findings with Black and White students in the United States (Dovidio et al., 2000), paralleling work on preferences for assimilation among citizens of host countries and integration among immigrants (van Oudenhoven et al., 1998; Verkuyten & Brug, 2004), revealed that among White students a one-group (assimilationist) representation primarily predicted more favorable interracial orientations, whereas among Black students a dual-identity (integration) representation was the main predictor of positive interracial attitudes. The differential roles of one-group and dual-identity representations may be functional for the groups. For Whites, a focus on commonality may reinforce the value associated with characteristics of their group; for Blacks, a dual identity reasserts an important subgroup identity while maintaining a connection with majority group within the superordinate identity.

Our measure of threat was related to symbolic threat (Stephan & Stephan, 2000). It included items such as "I feel that my race is incompatible with the new people I am meeting and the new things I am learning," and "I cannot talk to my friends at school about my family or culture." Intergroup trust was assessed with items such as "I can talk freely to someone outside my race and know that they would want to listen," and "Someone outside my race would never intentionally misinterpret my point of view to others" (Terrell, Terrell, & Miller, 1993). Factor analysis supported the distinction between threat and trust items.

On the basis of earlier research, we hypothesized that threat and trust would be proximate predictors of students' satisfaction with life at their college (a measure of well being; see Dovidio et al., 2005) and intergroup attitudes for both Whites and Blacks. The results were generally consistent with these predictions. Overall, Black students had higher levels of threat and lower levels of intergroup trust than did White students. In addition, for White students, greater feelings of threat significantly predicted lower levels of satisfaction at college, and lower levels of intergroup trust predicted more negative attitudes toward Blacks. For Black students, greater threat predicted both lower levels of satisfaction and more negative attitudes toward Whites. As with White students, lower levels of intergroup trust among Black students primarily predicted more negative attitudes toward Whites. Consistent with earlier research, these findings support the critical role of threat and trust on intergroup orientations.

Nevertheless, a more comprehensive path analysis, using a series of regression analyses, of the route by which favorable intergroup contact leads to more positive intergroup orientations revealed some fundamental differences in the processes for White and Black students. The main findings are illustrated in Figure 10.1. For White students, more favorable intergroup contact on campus predicted stronger one-group representations and stronger dual-identity representations. However, one-group and dual-identity representations did not significantly predict either threat or trust for White students; thus the paths from contact to satisfaction and intergroup attitudes were not further mediated by lower levels of threat or higher levels of intergroup trust. Rather, the one-group representation (but not the dual-identity representation) directly mediated greater satisfaction at college and more favorable attitudes toward Blacks.

For Black students, more favorable intergroup contact on campus also predicted stronger one-group and dual-identity representations. In contrast to

White students

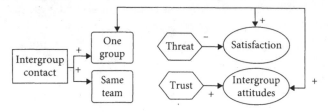

Black students

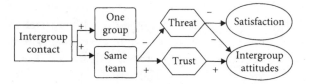

FIGURE 10.1. Significant path from intergroup orientations for White and Black students.

the results for White students, however, the strength of the dual identity (but not the one-group identity) predicted lower levels of threat and higher levels of trust. As suggested earlier, whereas greater intergroup trust primarily mediated the relationship between stronger same-team representations and more favorable attitudes toward Whites, lower levels of perceived threat mediated the relationship between same-team representations and both greater satisfaction and more favorable attitudes toward Whites. These findings demonstrate the importance of considering not only the similarities of the effects of different elements of intergroup relations, such as threat and trust, on intergroup relations between majority- and minority-group members but also the impact of status asymmetry on preferred group representations.

Why would group status affect these processes in this way? As noted earlier, the different preferences of majority- and minority-group members for one-group and dual-identity representations may imply different motivations of high and low status groups in coping with prospective situational changes in the existing social order. Whereas for majority-group members adopting one-group representations may preserve their dominance, minority-group members may pose a change in existing social hierarchy by adopting the strategy of promoting dual identity.

The different roles of threat and trust in the paths to intergroup harmony may relate to potential imbalances in social power between majority and minority groups. Intergroup threat, particularly of more symbolic kinds relating to the ways groups are valued, may be more salient for minority-group members than majority-group members because of the greater vulnerability of groups lower in status and power. Minority-group members may feel threatened by oppression by the majority group, which can exert its control through discrimination, either subtle or blatant, or through more direct means, such as intergroup violence. In the United States, there is evidence that, because of the pervasive threat of discrimination, Blacks experience chronically high levels of stress (which can have adverse effects on both mental and physical health; Dovidio et al., 2005), as well as high levels of cultural mistrust (which influences their evaluations of Whites individually and as a group; Mabry & Kiecolt, 2005). As mentioned earlier, consistent with this reasoning, Black students reported significantly higher levels of threat and lower levels of intergroup trust than did White students in our study. Moreover, threat and trust were more intimately related ($r = -.56$) for Black students than for White students ($r = -.17$). Thus, when favorable intergroup contact produces perceptions among Black students that they are recognized and appreciated as a group and are accepted as full participating members of the larger community (i.e., perceptions of "different groups on the same team," or a dual identity) threat and fear are reduced, trust is enhanced, and more positive orientations toward Whites result.

In contrast, because members of high power groups may perceive that their outcomes are not significantly affected by the actions of members of low power groups, they may be less attentive to the specific qualities and actions of minority groups and their members (Fiske, 1993). To the extent that more favorable intergroup contact produces stronger one-group representations among Whites, which may be perceived as the successful assimilation of minority-group members into the larger community, group-related factors such as intergroup threat and trust may be less influential than a sense of common group identity, which in this case directly shapes their orientations toward minority-group members. The history of the particular university setting, a traditionally White college with a relatively affluent student body, and the current racial distribution of students (over 80% self-identified as White and fewer than 10% self-identified as Black) likely contributed to the perception of stable, assimilative race relations and the absence of mediating effects of intergroup threat and trust among White students in our research.

Summary, Promising Directions, and Conclusions

In this chapter, we have examined how social categorization and a sense of group identity relate to intergroup biases and feelings of well-being in the context of the Common Ingroup Identity Model (Gaertner & Dovidio, 2000). From this perspective, social categorization forms the foundation for social identity and, ultimately, for how people respond both to members of the in-group (e.g., in-group favoritism) and to members of out-group (e.g., out-group derogation). The earliest evidence for the model demonstrated that recategorizing others who were originally viewed as members of an out-group within a common superordinate group can redirect the psychological forces of in-group favoritism to reduce intergroup bias.

We acknowledge that the Common Ingroup Identity Model was initially developed and tested with laboratory groups that did not have a history of conflict and whose relations were characterized by immediate competition rather than by hate and violence. Strategies that successfully reduce bias and conflict in temporary, mild forms of intergroup tension may not fully apply to situations of extended, intense forms of intergroup conflict. History, politics, economics, and personal stake and loss all play significant roles in shaping intergroup relations and in determining the dynamics of conflict and potential reconciliation. Thus, one might question the range of situations to which the principles and findings of the Common Ingroup Identity Model apply.

While being cognizant of how the history and nature of different intergroup conflicts influence relations between groups in particular ways, we propose that the Common Ingroup Identity Model is relevant to some more intense conflicts. In earlier research (e.g., Dovidio et al., 2000; Gaertner et al., 1996; Nier, Gaertner, Dovidio, Banker, & Ward, 2001), as well as in the current work, we have demonstrated the applicability of the model to Black–White relations in the United States among both high school and college students. Although students may represent a select group, race relations in the United States may still be seen to represent a case of severe, longstanding discrimination, with residual power asymmetry.

The power of the Common Ingroup Identity Model for addressing racial issues in the United States, however, may stem in part from the potential to achieve common ground and identity. Blacks (African Americans) and Whites (European Americans) share hundreds of years of history in America, and they both posses the same national identity. In many intense conflicts, such as the Troubles in Northern Ireland, groups may fail to recognize commonalities and instead focus on their long-term history of conflict and identify themselves in opposition to the other group. Under these conditions, attempts to create a common in-group identity may create identity threat, which can escalate rather than ameliorate conflict (Dovidio, Gaertner, & Validzic, 1998).

Nevertheless we note that even when a direct application of the principles of the Common Ingroup Identity Model cannot immediately reduce bias because of the salience of intergroup boundaries and conflict, recategorization strategies may be employed, either simultaneously or sequentially, in combination with other strategies to reduce bias. For example, promoting empathy toward a particular homeless person, drug addict, person with AIDS, or convicted murderer can improve attitudes toward the stigmatized group as a whole (Batson, Chang, Orr, & Rowland, 2002; Batson et al., 1997). Creating a perception of shared fate and common identity with an individual member of the group can both facilitate the development of empathy (Dovidio et al., 2004) and enhance the impact of the empathy that is aroused on responses to the person and to the group (Stürmer, Snyder, & Omoto, 2005). Recategorization strategies may also follow in sequence after other types of approaches, such as emphasizing personal qualities rather than group memberships, diffuse intergroup tensions and facilitate open communication among members of groups in conflict. Herbert Kelman and his colleagues, for instance, have conducted workshops over several years to improve Palestinian–Israeli relationships in the Middle East (Kelman, 1999). The living conditions and initial stages of the structured interactions promote personalized interaction to establish a climate of openness and constructive dialogue. Later stages of the workshop emphasize the respectful recognition of group boundaries, involve the acknowledgement of different group perspectives, draw attention to the common challenges and shared fate of the groups, and encourage cooperation to achieve superordinate goals. Thus, recategorization becomes a valuable tool in this process, but only after the intensity of the group conflict is removed by creating a foundation of personal communication. The principles of the Common Ingroup Identity Model may thus apply to a wide range of intergroup conflict, including deep and violent intergroup decisions, but in ways more complex than in the types of situations that we have typically studied.

The current chapter represents three fundamental extensions of the Common Ingroup Identity Model that may be particularly relevant to enduring, naturalistic relations between groups. First, in this chapter, we considered the potential proximate effects of intergroup threat and trust, which we hypothesized could be shaped by group representations, on intergroup relations. Earlier research on these topics (e.g., Riek et al., 2006) indicates that perceptions of greater symbolic group threat, and thus potentially lower levels of intergroup trust, produce more negative intergroup orientations. Consistent with these conclusions, we found that greater threat and less trust related similarly to the negative intergroup orientations of Whites and Blacks.

Second, we demonstrated that the same social representations can have different implications for members of different groups. Whereas assimilation is the preferred cultural orientation for majority-group members, integration that values multicultural perspectives is the generally preferred cultural orientation of minority-group members. Within the framework of the Common Ingroup Identity Model (Gaertner & Dovidio, 2000), we have found evidence in both laboratory experiments and field studies, showing that majority-group members prefer a one-group (assimilationist) model and report more positive attitudes toward other groups when they have this representation. Because of the priority they give a one-group representation, Whites may be threatened by members of other groups who appear to value other representations more highly.

Third, we proposed that the meaning of social representations must be considered in a dynamic context, and the differences as well as the similarities in perspectives of majority- and minority-group members need to be considered in understanding the ways that favorable intergroup contact can influence intergroup relations. For Black students, more favorable intergroup contact predicted stronger dual-identity (different groups working on the same-team) representations, which in turn predicted less perceived threat and greater intergroup trust, ultimately leading to more positive orientations toward Whites. For White students, presumably because of their higher power position in U.S. society generally and on the predominantly White campus, a stronger one-group representation directly mediated their more positive orientations toward Blacks. The Common Ingroup Identity Model, which was developed as a general model of intergroup relations, does not at present account for why group representations would play a stronger mediating role for threat and trust for Blacks than for Whites.

We speculate that these differences may be related not only to the greater general vigilance of minority-group members than majority-group members but also to how the groups attend and respond differently to aspects of their status relationship. For example, Scheepers, Spears, Doosje, and Manstead (2006) found that high status groups, as well as low status groups, more actively engaged in group enhancing strategies when group status relations were unstable than stable, but the dynamics of the strategies adopted by the groups differed. Whereas minority groups attended directly to instrumental aspects of group relations and pursued material gain to improve their status, majority groups engaged in more subtle and indirect strategies (e.g., involving enhancement of their group) that served to maintain the *status quo*. Analogous to our findings, low status (minority) group members attended directly to the transaction between the two groups, whereas high status (majority) group members focused more on their group's position. Thus, future research might productively bridge work on the mediating processes in intergroup relations identified by the Common Ingroup Identity Model with research on the moderators of group relations, often in the tradition of Social Identity Theory (Tajfel & Turner, 1979).

Understanding the different processes and factors that are critical to the intergroup orientations of majority- and minority-group members is an essential step in improving intergroup relations and promoting lasting reconciliation. Because of the different perspectives of majority- and minority-group members, intergroup relations are complex and potentially unstable. Some interventions designed to reduce threat, such as through sequential and reciprocal concessions (Pettigrew, 2003), or directed toward enhancing intergroup trust, such as through personalized interactions across group lines (Kelman, 1999; Miller, 2002), may operate similarly for majority- and minority-group members. We found that threat and trust similarly predicted the intergroup orientations of Whites and Blacks. However, even with the adoption of these approaches, it is important to recognize that the nature and initial levels of threat and trust may be quite different for majority- and minority-group members.

For other approaches, these differing perspectives can have profound implications. For instance, interventions designed to create a single common group identity might be effective for producing more favorable attitudes of majority-group members to minority groups (Nier et al., 2001), but it may be ineffective for improving the attitudes of minority-group members, who may prefer a dual identity. Moreover, emphasizing a common identity in a way that requires minority-group members to abandon valued subgroup identities (e.g., a one-group/assimilationist orientation) can exacerbate their biases, potentially by increasing perceived threat and decreasing intergroup trust (Brown & Hewstone, 2005; Dovidio et al., 1998).

The paths to harmonious group relations and intergroup reconciliation are clearly challenging. Whereas much of the traditional research on prejudice and intergroup relations has focused on the attitudes and behaviors of majority-group members (Dovidio, 2001) that approach is not adequate by itself. This line of work has recently been supplemented by a growing body of research addressing the responses and adaptations of targets of prejudice (Major & Vick, 2005). However, the addition of that perspective is still not enough. The most promising approach is likely one that incorporates both the perspectives of majority- and minority-group members within the same sphere of intergroup contact and to understand intergroup relations as truly *relational*. Reconciliation requires the efforts of both groups, and to be effective these efforts must be coordinated and reciprocal to create a new *ethos of peace*. As Bar-Tal (2000) observed, for groups in conflict "the long-term reconciliation process requires the formation of peaceful relations based on mutual trust and acceptance, cooperation, and consideration of mutual needs" (p. 351). Positive intergroup contact is just the beginning; it is a first step along a long and difficult road. Understanding the roles of group representations, threat, and trust from both majority- and minority-group perspectives can thus facilitate intergroup relations moving down the path from contact to reductions in bias and conflict and, ultimately, to reconciliation.

References

Allport, G. W. (1954). *The nature of prejudice*. Cambridge, MA: Addison-Wesley.

Armstrong, T. D., Crum, L. D., Reiger, R. H., Bennett, T. A., & Edwards, L. J. (1999). Attitudes of Africa Americans toward participation medical research. *Journal of Applied Social Psychology, 29*, 553-574.

Bar-Tal, D. (2000). From intractable conflict through conflict resolution to reconciliation: Psychological analysis. *Political Psychology, 21*, 351-365.

Batson, C. D., Chang, J., Orr, R., & Rowland, J. (2002). Empathy, attitudes, and action: Can feeling for a member of a stigmatized group motivate one to help the group? *Personality and Social Psychology Bulletin, 28*, 1656-1666.

Batson, C. D., Polycarpou, M. P., Harmon-Jones, E., Imhoff, H. J., Mitchener, E. C., Bednar, L. L., et al. (1997). Empathy and attitudes: Can feeling for a member of a stigmatized group improve feelings toward the group? *Journal of Personality and Social Psychology, 72*, 105-118.

Berry, J. W. (1984). Cultural relations in plural societies. In N. Miller & M. B. Brewer (Eds.), *Groups in contact: The psychology of desegregation* (pp. 11-27). Orlando, FL: Academic Press.

Berry, J. W. (1997). Immigration, acculturation, and adaptation. *Applied Psychology: An International Review, 46*, 5-68.

Biernat, M., & Dovidio, J. F. (2000). Stigma and stereotypes. In T. F. Heatherton, R. E. Kleck, M. R. Hebl, & J. G. Hull (Eds.), *The social psychology of stigma* (pp. 88-125). New York: Guilford.

Biernat, M., Vescio, T. K., & Theno, S. A. (1996). Violating American values: A "value-congruence" approach to understanding outgroup attitudes. *Journal of Experimental Social Psychology, 32*, 387-410.

Bobo, L. (1983). White's opposition to busing: Symbolic racism or realistic group conflict? *Journal of Personality and Social Psychology, 45*, 1196-1210.

Brown, R. J., & Hewstone, M. (2005). An integrative theory of intergroup contact. In M. P. Zanna (Ed.), *Advances in experimental social psychology* (Vol. 37, pp. 255-343). San Diego, CA: Elsevier Academic Press.

Campbell, D. T. (1965). Ethnocentric and other altruistic motives. In D. Levine (Ed.), *Nebraska symposium on motivation* (Vol. 13, pp. 283-311). Lincoln, NE: University of Nebraska Press.

Cohen, G. L., & Steele, C. M. (2002). A barrier of mistrust: How negative stereotypes affect cross-race mentoring. In J. Aronson (Ed.), *Improving academic achievement: Impact of psychological factors on education* (pp. 303-327). San Diego, CA: Academic Press.

Davis, S. M., & Reid, R. (1999). Practicing participatory research in American Indian communities. *American Journal of Clinical Nutrition, 69*(Suppl. 4), 755S-759S.

Devos, T., & Banaji, M. R. (2005). American = White? *Journal of Personality and Social Psychology, 88*, 447-466.

Dovidio, J. F. (2001). On the nature of contemporary prejudice: The third wave. *Journal of Social Issues, 57*, 829-849.

Dovidio, J. F., Brigham, J., Johnson, B. T., & Gaertner, S. L. (1996). Stereotyping, prejudice, and discrimination: Another look. In N. Macrae, C. Stangor, & M. Hewstone (Eds.), Stereotypes and stereotyping (pp. 276-319). New York: Guilford.

Dovidio, J. F., & Gaertner, S. L. (1993). Stereotypes and evaluative intergroup bias. In D. M. Mackie & D. L. Hamilton (Eds.), *Affect, cognition, and stereotyping: Interactive processes in intergroup perception* (pp. 167-193). Orlando, FL: Academic Press.

Dovidio, J. F., & Gaertner, S. L. (2004). Aversive racism. In M. P. Zanna (Ed.), *Advances in experimental social psychology* (Vol. 36, pp. 1-51). San Diego, CA: Academic Press.

Dovidio, J. F., Gaertner, S. L., Hodson, G., Houlette, M., & Johnson, K. M. (2005). Social inclusion and exclusion: Recategorization and the perception of intergroup boundaries. In D. Abrams, J. Marques, & M. A. Hogg (Eds.), *Social psychology of inclusion and exclusion* (pp. 245-264). Philadelphia, PA: Psychology Press.

Dovidio, J. F., Gaertner, S. L., & Kafati, G. (2000). Group identity and intergroup relations: The common in-group identity model. In S. R. Thye, E. J. Lawler, M. W. Macy, & H. A. Walker (Eds.), *Advances in group processes* (Vol. 17, pp. 1-34). Stamford, CT: JAI Press.

Dovidio, J. F., Gaertner, S. L., & Kawakami, K. (2003). The contact hypothesis: The past, present, and the future. *Group Processes and Intergroup Relations, 6*, 5-21.

Dovidio, J. F., Gaertner, S. L., Kawakami, K., & Hodson, G. (2002). Why can't we just get along? Interpersonal biases and interracial distrust. *Cultural Diversity & Ethnic Minority Psychology, 8*, 88-102.

Dovidio, J. F., Gaertner, S. L., Niemann, Y. F., & Snider, K. (2001). Racial, ethnic, and cultural differences in responding to distinctiveness and discrimination on campus: Stigma and common group identity. *Journal of Social Issues, 57*, 167-188.

Dovidio, J. F., Gaertner, S. L., Pearson, A. R., & Riek, B. M. (2005). Social identities and social context: Attitudes and personal well-being. In S. R. Thye & E. J. Lawler (Eds.), *Advances in group processes: Social identification processes in groups* (pp. 231-260). Oxford, UK: Elsevier.

Dovidio, J. F., Gaertner, S. L., & Validzic, A. (1998). Intergroup bias: Status, differentiation, and a common ingroup identity. *Journal of Personality and Social Psychology, 75*, 109-120.

Dovidio, J. F., ten Vergert, M., Stewart, T. L., Gaertner, S. L., Johnson, J. D., Esses, V. M., et al. (2004). Perspective and prejudice: Antecedents and mediating mechanisms. *Personality and Social Psychology Bulletin, 30*, 1537-1549.

DuBois, W. E. B. (1938). *The souls of Black folk: Essays and sketches*. Chicago, IL: A. C. McLurg.

Dunbar, E., Saiz, J. L., Stela, K., & Saez, R. (2000). Personality and social group value determinants of out-group bias: A cross-national comparison of Gough's Pr/To Scale. *Journal of Cross-Cultural Psychology, 31*, 267-275.

Earl, C. E., & Penney, P. J. (2001). The significance of trust in the research consent process with African Americans. *Western Journal of Nursing Research, 23,* 753-762.

Esses, V. M., Dovidio, J. F., Jackson, L. M., & Armstrong, T. L. (2001). The immigration dilemma: The role of perceived group competition, ethnic prejudice, and national identity. *Journal of Social Issues, 57,* 389-412.

Fiske, S. T. (1993). Controlling other people. *American Psychologist, 48,* 621-628.

Gaertner, S. L., Bachman, B. A., Dovidio, J. D., & Banker, B. S. (2001). Corporate mergers and stepfamily marriages: Identity, harmony, and commitment. In M. A. Hogg & D. Terry (Eds.), *Social identity processes in organizations* (pp. 265-282). Philadelphia, PA: Psychology Press.

Gaertner, S. L., & Dovidio, J. F. (2000). *Reducing intergroup bias: The common ingroup identity model.* Philadelphia, PA: The Psychology Press.

Gaertner, S. L., Dovidio, J. F., Nier, J., Ward, C., & Banker, B. (1999). Across cultural divides: The value of a superordinate identity. In D. Prentice & D. Miller (Eds.), *Cultural divides: Understanding and overcoming group conflict* (pp. 173-212). New York: Russell Sage Foundation.

Gaertner, S. L., Dovidio, J. F., Rust, M. C., Nier, J., Banker, B., Ward, C. M., et al. (1999). Reducing intergroup bias: Elements of intergroup cooperation. *Journal of Personality and Social Psychology, 76,* 388-402.

Gaertner, S. L., Mann, J. A., Dovidio, J. F., Murrell, A. J., & Pomare, M. (1990). How does cooperation reduce intergroup bias? *Journal of Personality and Social Psychology, 59,* 692-704.

Gaertner, S. L., Mann, J. A., Murrell, A. J., & Dovidio, J. F. (1989). Reduction of intergroup bias: The benefits of recategorization. *Journal of Personality and Social Psychology, 57,* 239-249.

Gaertner, S. L., Rust, M. C., Dovidio, J. F., Bachman, B. A., & Anastasio, P. A. (1996). The contact hypothesis: The role of a common ingroup identity on reducing intergroup bias among majority and minority group members. In J. L. Nye & A. M. Brower (Eds.), *What's social about social cognition?* (pp. 230-360). Newbury Park, CA: Sage.

Gans, H. (1979). Symbolic ethnicity: The future of ethnic groups and culture in America. *Ethnic and Racial Studies, 2,* 1-20.

Hewstone, M. (1996). Contact and categorization: Social psychological interventions to change intergroup relations. In C. N. Macrae, M. Hewstone, & C. Stangor (Eds.), *Foundations of stereotypes and stereotyping* (pp. 323-368). New York: Guilford.

Howard, J. M., & Rothbart, M. (1980). Social categorization for in-group and out-group behavior. *Journal of Personality and Social Psychology, 38,* 301-310.

Huo, Y. J., Smith, H. H., Tyler, T. R., & Lind, A. E. (1996). Superordinate identification, subgroup identification, and justice concerns: Is separatism the problem. Is assimilation the answer? *Psychological Science, 7,* 40-45.

Insko, C. A., & Schopler, J. (1998). Differential distrust of groups and of individuals. In C. Sedikides, J. Schopler, & C. A. Insko (Eds.), *Intergroup cognition and intergroup behavior* (pp. 75-107). Hillsdale, NJ: Erlbaum.

Insko, C. A., Schopler, J., Drigotas, S. M., Graetz, K. A., Kennedy, J., Cox, C., et al. (1993). The role of communication in interindividual-intergroup discontinuity. *Journal of Conflict Resolution, 37,* 108-138.

Insko, C. A., Schopler, J., Gaertner, L., Wildschut, T., Kozar, R., Pinter, B., et al. (2001). Interindividual-Intergroup discontinuity reduction through the anticipation of future interaction. *Journal of Personality and Social Psychology, 80,* 95-111.

Insko, C. A., Schopler, J., Graetz, K. A., Drigotas, S. M., Currey, D. P., & Smith, S. L. (1994). Interindividual-intergroup discontinuity in the prisoner's dilemma game. *Journal of Conflict Resolution, 38,* 87-116.

Islam, M. R., & Hewstone, M. (1993). Dimensions of contact as predictors of intergroup anxiety, perceived outgroup variability and outgroup attitude: An integrative model. *Personality and Social Psychology Bulletin, 19,* 700-710.

Johnson, K. M., Gaertner, S. L., & Dovidio, J. F. (2001). *The effect of equality of job assignment on ingroup identity and bias for low and high status groups.* Unpublished data, Department of Psychology, University of Delaware, Newark, DE.

Kelman, H. C. (1999). The interdependence of Israeli and Palestinian national identities: The role of the other in existential conflicts. *Journal of Social Issues, 55,* 581-600.

Kramer, R. M. (2004). Collective paranoia: Distrust between social groups. In R. Hardin (Ed.), *Distrust* (pp. 136-166). New York: Russell Sage Foundation.

Mabry, J. B., & Kiecolt, K. J. (2005). Anger in Black and White: Race, alienation, and anger. *Journal of Health and Social Behavior, 46,* 85-101.

Major, B., & Vick, S. B. (2005). The psychological impact of prejudice. In J. F. Dovidio, P. Glick, & L. A. Rudman (Eds.), *On the nature of prejudice: Fifty years after Allport* (pp. 139-154). Malden, MA: Blackwell.

McLaren, L. M. (2003). Anti-immigrant prejudice in Europe: Contact, threat perception, and preferences for the expulsion of migrants. *Social Forces, 81,* 909-936.

Miller, N. (2002). Personalization and the promise of contact theory. *Journal of Social Issues, 58,* 387-410.

Nier, J. A., Gaertner, S. L., Dovidio, J. F., Banker, B. S., & Ward, C. M. (2001). Changing interracial evaluations and behavior: The effects of a common group identity. *Group Processes and Intergroup Relations, 4,* 299-316.

Otten, S., & Moskowitz, G. B. (2000). Evidence for implicit evaluative in-group bias: Affect-biased spontaneous trait inference in a minimal group paradigm. *Journal of Experimental Social Psychology, 36,* 77-89.

Park, B., & Rothbart, M. (1982). Perception of out-group homogeneity and levels of social categorization: Memory for the subordinate attributes of in-group and out-group members. *Journal of Personality and Social Psychology, 42,* 1051-1068.

Pemberton, M. B., Insko, C. A., & Schopler, J. (1996). Memory for and experience of differential competitive behavior of individuals and groups. *Journal of Personality and Social Psychology, 71,* 953-966.

Pettigrew, T. F. (2003). Peoples under threat: Americans, Arabs, Israelis. *Peace and Conflict: Journal of Peace Psychology, 9,* 69-90.

Pettigrew, T. F., & Tropp, L. R. (2006). A meta-analytic test of intergroup contact theory. *Journal of Personality and Social Psychology, 90,* 751-783.

Phelps, R. E., *Taylor,* J. D., & Gerard, P. A. (2001). Cultural mistrust, ethnic identity, racial identity and self-esteem among ethnically diverse black students. *Journal of Counseling & Development, 79,* 209-216.

Riek, B. M., Mania, E. W., & Gaertner, S. L. (2006). Intergroup threat and outgroup attitudes: A meta-analytic review. *Personality and Social Psychology Review, 10,* 336-353.

Scheepers, D., Spears, R., Doosje, B., & Manstead, A. S. R. (2006). Diversity in in-group bias: Structural factors, situational features, and social functions. *Journal of Personality and Social Psychology, 90,* 944-960.

Schopler, J., & Insko, C. A. (1992). The discontinuity effect in interpersonal and inter-group relations: Generality and mediation. In W. Stroebe & M. Hewstone (Eds.), *European review of social psychology* (Vol. 3, pp. 121-151). Chichester, UK: Wiley.

Schopler, J., Insko, C. A., Wieselquist, J., Pemberton, M., Witcher, B., Kozar, R., et al. (2001). When groups are more competitive than individuals: The domain of the discontinuity effect. *Journal of Personality and Social Psychology, 80,* 632-644.

Shavers-Hornaday, V. L., Lynch, C. F., Burmeister, L. F., & Torner, J. C. (1997). Why are African Americans underrepresented in medical research studies? Impediments to participation. *Ethnicity and Health, 2,* 31-45.

Sherif, M. (1966). *Group conflict and cooperation: Their social psychology.* London: Routledge and Kegan Paul.

Sherif, M., Harvey, O. J., White, B. J., Hood, W. R., & Sherif, C. W. (1961). *Intergroup conflict and cooperation. The Robbers Cave experiment.* Norman, OK: University of Oklahoma Book Exchange.

Sidanius, J., Feshbach, S., Levin, S., & Pratto, F. (1997). The interface between ethnic and national attachment: Ethnic pluralism or ethnic dominance? *Public Opinion Quarterly, 61,* 103-133.

Sidanius, J., Levin, S., & Pratto, F. (1998). Hierarchical group relations, institutional ter-ror, and the dynamics of the criminal justice system. In J. L. Eberhardt & S. T. Fiske (Eds.), *Confronting racism: The problem and the response* (pp. 136-165). Thousand Oaks, CA: Sage.

Sidanius, J., & Pratto, F. (1999). *Social dominance: An intergroup theory of social hierar-chy and oppression.* New York: Cambridge University Press.

Soss, J., Langbein, L., & Metelko, A. R. (2003). Why do White Americans support the death penalty? *Journal of Politics, 65,* 397-421.

Stephan, W. G., Boniecki, K. A., Ybarra, O., Bettencourt, A., Ervin, K. S., Jackson, L. A., et al. (2002). The role of threats in the racial attitudes of Blacks and Whites. *Personality and Social Psychology Bulletin, 28,* 1242-1254.

Stephan, W. G., & Stephan, C. W. (2000). An integrated theory of prejudice. In S. Oskamp (Ed.), *Reducing prejudice and discrimination* (pp. 23-45). Hillsdale, NJ: Erlbaum.

Stürmer, S., Snyder, M., & Omoto, A. M. (2005). Prosocial emotions and helping: The moderating role of group membership. *Journal of Personality and Social Psychology, 88*, 532-546.

Tajfel, H. (1969). Cognitive aspects of prejudice. *Journal of Social Issues, 25*(4), 79-97.

Tajfel, H. (1978). *Differentiation between social groups: Studies in the social psychology of intergroup relations.* Oxford, UK: Academic Press.

Tajfel, H., Billing, M. G., Bundy, R. P., & Flament, C. (1971). Social categorization and intergroup behaviour. *European Journal of Social Psychology, 1*, 149-178.

Tajfel, H., & Turner, J. C. (1979). An integrative theory of intergroup conflict. In W. G. Austin & S. Worchel (Eds.), *The social psychology of intergroup relations* (pp. 33-48). Monterey, CA: Brooks/Cole.

Terrell, F., Terrell, S. L., & Miller, F. (1993). Level of cultural mistrust as a function of educational and occupational expectations among Black students. *Adolescence, 28*, 573-578.

Turner, J. C., Hogg, M. A., Oakes, P. J., Reicher, S. D., & Wetherell, M. S. (1987). *Rediscovering the social group: A self-categorization theory.* Oxford, UK: Basil Blackwell.

van Oudenhoven, J. P., Prins, K. S., & Buunk, B. (1998). Attitudes of minority and majority members towards adaptation of immigrants. *European Journal of Social Psychology, 28*, 995-1013.

Verkuyten, M., & Brug, P. (2004). Multiculturalism and group status: The role of ethnic identification, group essentialism and protestant ethic. *European Journal of Social Psychology, 34*, 647-661.

Wilder, D. A. (1981). Perceiving persons as a group: Categorization and intergroup relations. In D. L. Hamilton (Ed.), *Cognitive processes in stereotyping and intergroup behavior* (pp. 213-257). Hillsdale, NJ: Erlbaum.

Wildschut, T., Insko, C. A., & Gaertner, L. (2002). Intragroup social influence and intergroup competition. *Journal of Personality and Social Psychology, 82*, 975-992.

Wildschut, T., Pinter, B., Vevea, J. L., Insko, C. A., & Schopler, J. (2003). Beyond the group mind: A quantitative review of the interindividual-intergroup discontinuity effect. *Psychological Bulletin, 129*, 698-722.

Worchel, S., Rothgerber, H., Day, E. A., Hart, D., & Butemeyer, J. (1998). Social identity and individual productivity with groups. *British Journal of Social Psychology, 37*, 389-413.

Yamagishi, T., & Kiyonari, T. (2000). The group as the container of generalized reciprocity. *Social Psychology Quarterly, 63*, 116-132.

Yuki, M., Maddux, W. W., & Brewer, M. B. (2005). Cross-cultural differences in relationship- and group-based trust. *Personality and Social Psychology Bulletin, 31*, 48-62.

Yzerbyt, V., Corneille, O., & Estrada, C. (2001). The interplay of subjective essentialism and entitativity in the formation of stereotypes. *Personality and Social Psychology Review, 5*, 141-155.

CHAPTER 11

A Social-Psychological Approach to Postconflict Reconciliation

BLAKE M. RIEK, SAMUEL L. GAERTNER, JOHN F. DOVIDIO,
MARILYNN B. BREWER, ERIC W. MANIA, AND
MARIKA J. LAMOREAUX

Understanding the causes and consequences of intergroup bias and conflict
has been a major objective of social psychology that has pragmatic as well
as theoretical significance. Recognizing the origins of intergroup biases is
vital for creating strategies that improve intergroup relations. To this end,
a large body of social-psychological research has contributed to the understanding of intergroup conflict and how to reduce it (Allport, 1954; Brown &
Gaertner, 2001). In the context of postconflict reconciliation, we discuss how
social-psychological processes influence intergroup conflict and how these
processes can be used in interventions aimed at improving relations between
former adversaries.

Because of limits in the ability of people to process information and the
enormous complexity of the social and physical environment, people, often
automatically, tend to categorize objects and people into groups (Fiske &
Taylor, 1991). Moreover, social categorization involves not only the recognition that people belong to distinct groups but also the perception that some
people belong to one's own group whereas others belong to different groups.

Although social categorization does not necessarily lead to intergroup antipathy and the specific underlying causes of any given conflict are likely to vary from situation to situation, this process of identifying others as "us" and "them" is a critical and universal element of intergroup conflict. Distinguishing between people in one's own group (the in-group) and those in other groups (out-groups) has fundamental psychological implications. The in-group is perceived as positive and superior, whereas out-groups are seen as inferior and/or threatening. When the relationship between in-groups and out-groups is viewed in win-lose or zero-sum terms, the traditions and values of the in-group are seen as positive and correct, whereas those of the out-group are viewed with disdain.

Formal peace agreements may lay the groundwork for harmonious intergroup relations, but in order to create a lasting peace, it is also important to address the psychological processes that underlie negative intergroup relations. Whereas traditional research has generally focused on individual differences and personality characteristics representing abnormal qualities as the underpinnings of prejudice (Allport, 1954), more contemporary perspectives suggest that intergroup biases are rooted in normal psychological processes (e.g., information processing biases resulting from the categorization of people into in-groups and out-groups). In the next section, we review psychological theory and research that offers insights into these processes and suggest ways that this information can guide diplomatic interventions.

Psychological Perspectives on Bias and Intergroup Conflict

A social-psychological understanding of intergroup relations begins with assumptions about the importance of group identification in meeting human needs for belonging, differentiation, and meaning. Belonging to an esteemed group is fundamentally important because the groups that people belong to provide a source of positive identity and support. Unfortunately, by defining an in-group, there are necessarily boundaries between members of the in-group and other people. In times of conflict, the salience of intergroup differences can create distrust that may seed and sustain bias. Recognizing the crucial importance of a social identity, perceived group boundaries, and the nature of relations between groups is thus essential for understanding conflict and, ultimately, reconciliation.

Social Categorization

Social Identity Theory (Tajfel & Turner, 1979) and Self-Categorization Theory (Turner, 1985; Turner, Hogg, Oakes, Reicher, & Wetherell, 1987) address fundamental processes of social categorization. Social Identity Theory rests on two basic premises. First, individuals organize their understanding of objects and people on the basis of categorical distinctions. This categorization tends to increase perceived similarities among members within categories and accentuates differences between groups. Second, because individuals are themselves members of some social categories and not others, social categorization involves *in-group–out-group* (we–they) distinctions, which have cognitive and emotional significance. Even classifying people into in-groups and out-groups on an arbitrary basis can spontaneously produce perceptions of a fundamental connection among people classified as in-group members (while maintaining some sense of distinctiveness among them; Brewer, 1991), particularly strong perceptions of homogeneity among members of the out-group ("They are all alike") and increased attraction to people classified as in-group members (Brewer, 1979; Brewer & Gaertner, 2001). The affective and behavioral consequences of this in-group–out-group schema lead to intergroup situations characterized by preferential treatment of in-group members. In addition, perceiving others primarily in terms of group membership can facilitate the development of mutual distrust between the in-group and the out-group and promote intergroup competition when group interests are challenged.

According to this perspective, the starting point for intergroup discrimination and prejudice is a cognitive representation of a social situation in which a particular categorical distinction is highly salient. The role of category salience in intergroup bias has been well documented in experimental research using the minimal intergroup paradigm (e.g., Brewer, 1979). Given a salient in-group–out-group distinction, preferential treatment of the in-group is fueled by motivational factors including the need for self-esteem and positive distinctiveness (Tajfel & Turner, 1979), reduction of uncertainty (Hogg & Abrams, 1993), and the needs for belonging and differentiation (Brewer, 1991).

The importance of considering categorical distinctions when orchestrating real-world conflict resolution is demonstrated in research concerning how the perceived source of a peace proposal influences the proposal's acceptability. For example, one study (Maoz, Ward, Katz, & Ross, 2002) demonstrated that proposed peace initiatives in the Middle East were responded to more favorably by both Israelis and Palestinians when they believed the proposals were written by an in-group rather than an out-group member. Thus, the salience of categorical distinctions clearly plays a role in the initial stages of formal reconciliation. In addition, whereas categorization processes form the foundation of many biases, these biases can be exacerbated by additional factors such as intergroup threat.

Intergroup Threat

Intergroup threat involves one group's actions, beliefs, or characteristics challenging the goal attainment or well-being of another group. Threat leads to biases and conflict because group members are motivated to protect the in-group's resources and maintain its values and traditions. One comprehensive theory on intergroup threat proposes that intergroup threat can take a number of different forms (Stephan & Stephan, 2000). Two of the major forms are realistic threat and symbolic threat, which often serve as the basis of many intergroup conflicts.

Realistic threat involves perceptions of intergroup competition and conflicting goals (Sherif & Sherif, 1969). This process was illustrated in the classic work by Sherif and his colleagues (Sherif, Harvey, White, Hood, & Sherif, 1961; reprinted in 1988). In 1954, Sherif and his colleagues conducted a field study on intergroup conflict in an area adjacent to Robbers Cave State Park in Oklahoma (USA). In this study, 22 boys of 12 years age, attending a summer camp, were randomly assigned to two groups. Over a period of weeks they became aware of the other group's existence and engaged in a series of competitive activities that generated overt intergroup conflict. As competition continued, hostility between the groups increased and became quite severe, in some cases leading to physical violence. In terms of real-world conflicts, realistic threats are likely to arise when one group perceives an out-group as trying to usurp valued resources (e.g., land or wealth).

Symbolic threats occur when an out-group violates important in-group values (Kinder & Sears, 1981; Stephan & Stephan, 1996). For example, Biernat, Vescio, and Theno (1996) found that whites had more negative evaluations of blacks when they perceived them as being less supportive of whites' values. Symbolic threats are likely involved in many religious and political contexts where one group's beliefs are seen as violating or conflicting with another group's. In many conflict situations, realistic and symbolic threats may be present simultaneously. For example, the prolonged conflicts in the Middle East and between Israelis and Palestinians both contain realistic threats (violent encounters) and symbolic threats (religious differences).

Overall, both social categorization processes and intergroup threats are likely to contribute to intergroup conflicts and, if left unaddressed, may impede attempts at intergroup reconciliation. In the next section, we examine how the same social identity processes that contribute to intergroup conflict can be utilized to promote intergroup peace, reduce intergroup threats, and promote reconciliation.

Categorization Models for Promoting Reconciliation

The process of social categorization is a flexible one. Social Identity Theory (Tajfel & Turner, 1979) and Self-Categorization Theory (Turner et al., 1987) propose that people can readily shift back and forth between collective and personal identity as a result of changing contexts, and that these shifts have consequences for the dynamics of intergroup relations. For example, Verkuyten and Hagendoorn (1998) found that when individual identity was primed, individual differences in the personality trait authoritarianism were the major predictors of the prejudice of Dutch students toward Turkish migrants. In contrast, when social identity (i.e., national identity) was made salient, in-group stereotypes and standards primarily predicted prejudiced attitudes (see also Reynolds, Turner, Haslam, & Ryan, 2001). Thus, whether personal or collective identity is more salient critically shapes how a person perceives, interprets, evaluates, and responds to situations and to others.

In addition, social identities are not fixed. People can possess multiple social identities at different levels of inclusiveness. Higher level categories (e.g., nations) can be inclusive of lower level ones (e.g., cities or towns). Modifying a perceiver's goals, motives, past experiences, expectations, as well as factors within the situational context more broadly, can shift the level of category inclusiveness that will be primary in a given situation.

The malleability of the level at which impressions are formed is important because of its implications for altering the way people think about members of other groups, and consequently about the nature of intergroup relations. Because categorization is a basic process that is also fundamental to bias and intergroup conflict, some contemporary work has targeted this process as a place to begin to improve intergroup relations and promote reconciliation. From this perspective, a key issue to be addressed is how intergroup contact during the postconflict period can be structured to alter cognitive representations of group boundaries in ways that would eliminate bias and promote reconciliation.

Based on the premises of Social Identity Theory, three alternative models for contact effects have been developed and tested in experimental and field settings, namely: Decategorization, Recategorization, and Mutual Intergroup

Differentiation. Each of these models provides recommendations for how to structure cognitive representations of situations in which there is contact between the groups, the psychological processes that promote attitude change, and the mechanisms by which contact experiences are generalized to improve attitudes toward the out-group as a whole.

These social categorization approaches have provided explanations about how the Contact Hypothesis (see Allport, 1954; Amir, 1969; Williams, 1947) operates psychologically to reduce bias. Allport (1954) proposed that for contact between groups to improve intergroup relations, certain prerequisite features must be present including equal status between the groups, cooperative (rather than competitive) intergroup interaction, opportunities for self-revealing personal acquaintance between the members, and supportive norms by authorities within and outside of the contact situation. Thus, contact between groups per se does not reduce conflict or improve intergroup attitudes; rather, it is the nature of that contact that is important. A critical element is how this contact influences social categorization processes, either diminishing the salience of social categories (decategorization) or changing the basis of social categorization (recategorization).

Decategorization

Whereas perceiving people in terms of a social category is easiest and most common in forming impressions, especially during long-term intergroup conflict, it is possible to create more individuated impressions of others, via specific goals and motivations (Brewer, 1988; Fiske, Lin, & Neuberg, 1999). The Personalization Model (Brewer & Miller, 1984) is essentially a formalization and elaboration of the assumptions implicit in Allport's (1954) Contact Hypothesis. Social behavior in category-based interactions is characterized by perceiving and treating out-group members as undifferentiated representatives of a unified social category, denying or ignoring individual differences within the group. According to the personalization perspective, intergroup contact should be arranged to downplay categorical distinctions while creating opportunities to get to know out-group members as unique individuals, thus decreasing the biases arising from categorization. Personalization may be achieved through prolonged, self-revealing contact with out-group members and the development of shared goals (Brewer & Miller, 1996).

Personalized interactions often require individuals to exchange personal information with one another, which allows them to "attend to information that replaces category identity as the most useful basis for classifying each other" (Brewer & Miller, 1984, p. 288). Repeated personalized contacts with a variety of out-group members should, over time, undermine the value and meaningfulness of social category stereotypes as sources of information about members of that group. This process can reduce the salience and meaning of social categorization and change the overall perception of the out-group in the long run (Brewer & Miller, 1996). Research supports the effectiveness of personalization in a number of contexts. Interpersonal, cooperative tasks have been shown to be more effective at reducing biases than task-focused interactions (Miller, Brewer, & Edwards, 1985). Pettigrew (1997) has shown that cross-group friendships, which clearly offer personalization opportunities, are effective at decreasing intergroup biases.

Several processes contribute to the effectiveness of personalization. Interacting with a member of another group in a personalized way facilitates perspective-taking and permits the development of empathy, which can increase positive attitudes toward the person's group (Batson et al., 1997; Dovidio et al., 2004). Personalization is also likely to reduce realistic threat. People tend to be less competitive as individuals than as a group (Insko et al., 1994).

Recategorization: The Common In-group Identity Model

An alternative method for reducing intergroup bias is recategorization, which seeks to reshape group boundaries rather than dissolve them (Gaertner & Dovidio, 2000; Gaertner et al., 2000). As Allport (1954) noted, people have multiple social identities that are hierarchically organized in terms of increasing inclusiveness. So, while at one level, two individuals may be seen as belonging to two separate groups (e.g., two families), at a higher level of inclusiveness they may see themselves as belonging to the same group (e.g., neighborhood). The Common In-group Identity Model (Gaertner & Dovidio, 2000; Gaertner, Dovidio, Anastasio, Bachman, & Rust, 1993) proposes that intergroup bias and conflict can be reduced by factors that transform participants' representations of memberships from two groups to one, more inclusive group. With a common in-group identity, the cognitive and motivational processes that initially produced in-group favoritism are redirected to benefit the former out-group members.

Among the antecedent factors proposed by the Common In-group Identity Model are the features of contact situations (Allport, 1954) that are necessary for intergroup contact to be successful (e.g., interdependence between groups, equal status, equalitarian norms). From this perspective, intergroup cooperative interaction, for example, enhances positive evaluations of out-group members, at least in part, because cooperation transforms members' representations of the memberships from "Us" versus "Them" to a more inclusive "We." Laboratory experiments and field surveys (involving diverse populations such as bankers involved in mergers, college students in blended families, and racial and ethnic groups) provide support for the critical role of developing a common group identity in reducing bias and promoting more harmonious relations between groups (Gaertner & Dovidio, 2000; Gaertner, Mann, Murrell, & Dovidio, 1989; Gaertner, Rust, Dovidio, Bachman, & Anastasio, 1994).

Recategorization can also reduce the intergroup threats that underlie many conflict situations. For example, once a common identity is established, perceptions of cooperativeness should increase (Brewer, 2000), thereby lessening realistic threat. A common identity could also decrease symbolic threat by emphasizing shared, rather than different, values. Supportive of this view, perceptions of a common identity between whites and blacks tend to be associated with lower levels of both symbolic and realistic threat (Riek, Mania, Gaertner, Direso, & Lamoreaux, 2007).

Ideally, people could be encouraged to adopt a level of categorization in which all are encompassed under a shared identity, namely humanity (Allport, 1954). For instance, emphasis on shared challenges, such as threats to the environment (e.g., global warming), or cooperative action, such as efforts to relieve starvation by worldwide organizations (e.g., the United Nations), can shift the focus from people's different national identities to what they have in common, that is, their common humanity. Allport has proposed that it may be difficult to sustain this level of common in-group identification because of competing allegiances and demands of more differentiated identities. Nevertheless, the potential of creating categorization at the level of humanity can be seen across a series of studies by Wohl and Branscombe (2005). They found that the willingness of Jews to forgive Germans for the holocaust was greater among Jews who had been led to view Germans as humans than among Jews who were encouraged to view Germans as a group distinct from Jews.

Challenges to Decategorization/Recategorization Models

Although the structural representations of the contact situation advocated by the decategorization (personalization) and recategorization (common in-group identity) models are different, the two approaches share common assumptions about the need to reduce category differentiation and associated processes. Because both models rely on reducing or eliminating the salience of intergroup differentiation, they involve structuring contact in a way that will challenge or threaten existing social identities. In many cases, it is not possible or desirable for members of the subgroups to forsake their group identities in favor of the superordinate category. This is likely to be the case when the original group identities are especially important or when there is a long history of group conflict. Brewer's (1991) Optimal Distinctiveness Theory of the motives underlying group identification provides one explanation for why category distinctions are difficult to change. The theory postulates that social identity is driven by two opposing social motives—the need for inclusion and the need for differentiation. Human beings strive to belong to groups that transcend their own personal identity, but at the same time they need to feel special and distinct from others. In order to satisfy both of these motives simultaneously, individuals seek inclusion in distinctive social groups where the boundaries between those who are members of the in-group category and those who are excluded can be clearly drawn. Highly inclusive superordinate categories do not satisfy distinctiveness needs, while high degrees of individuation fail to meet needs for belonging and for cognitive simplicity and uncertainty reduction (Hogg & Abrams, 1993). These motives are likely to make either personalization or common in-group identity temporally unstable solutions to intergroup discrimination and prejudice.

An additional limitation of a recategorization approach is that the reduction of bias may not generalize to out-group members who were not present during the intergroup contact when a superordinate identity was achieved. Also, if the subgroup identities are completely subsumed by the superordinate identity, the members of the out-group are no longer psychologically identified as representatives of their group (Gaertner & Dovidio, 2000). This creates a problem because if the former out-group members present during contact are not seen as representative, the positive feelings associated with membership in the superordinate group may not become associated with the out-group as a whole.

Two Solutions: Dual Identification and the Mutual Intergroup Differentiation Model

The dual identity is a form of common in-group identity where two groups form a superordinate identity (as two subgroups within a larger group) but still maintain their initial group identities rather than completely degrading the subgroup boundaries (Gaertner & Dovidio, 2000). A dual identity may be effective when it is undesirable or impossible for individuals to "give up" their subgroup identity (e.g., racial or cultural groups). In support of the dual identity's effectiveness, Gaertner et al. (1994) examined students in a multiethnic high school and found that students who identified themselves as American as well as by their ethnicity exhibited lower levels of bias toward other ethnic groups at school than students who only identified themselves by their ethnicity. Other findings have demonstrated similar benefits of dual identification (Hornsey & Hogg, 2000; Huo, Smith, Tyler, & Lind, 1996), though this support has not been unequivocal (see Wenzel, Mummendey, Weber, & Waldzus, 2003). Based on his experience in conducting workshops designed to promote peace and reconciliation in the Middle East, Kelman (1999) suggested that the development of a dual identity involving a larger, "transcendent identity," encompassing both Israelis and Palestinians without threatening their respective identities, is a necessary condition for effective cooperation, long-term peaceful coexistence, and ultimate reconciliation between the two peoples.

Hewstone and Brown (1986; see also Brown & Hewstone, 2005) proposed an alternative approach to intergroup contact wherein cooperative interactions between groups are introduced without degrading the original in-group–out-group categorization. This model favors encouraging groups working together in a complementary fashion by recognizing and valuing mutual superiorities and inferiorities within the context of an interdependent cooperative task or common, superordinate goals. This strategy allows group members to maintain their social identities and positive distinctiveness while avoiding insidious intergroup comparisons. Thus, the mutual differentiation model does not seek to change the basic category structure of the intergroup contact situation, but rather it attempts to change the intergroup affect from negative to positive by creating intergroup interdependence and mutual respect.

Both dual identification and mutual intergroup differentiation offer generalization of positive attitudes as an additional benefit. In both of these solutions, the separate subgroup identities are allowed to remain salient and hence out-group members may be seen as representative of their group as a whole, which can lead to a generalization of positive feelings toward the out-group. In fact, Hewstone and Brown (1986) argue that generalization of positive contact experiences is more likely when the contact situation is defined as an *intergroup* situation rather than an *interpersonal* interaction. Generalization in this case is direct rather than requiring additional cognitive links between positive affect toward individuals and representations of the group as a whole. This position is supported by evidence that cooperative contact with a member of an out-group leads to more favorable generalized attitudes toward the group as a whole when category membership is made salient during contact (e.g., Brown, Vivian, & Hewstone, 1999; van Oudenhoven, Groenewoud, & Hewstone, 1996).

Overall, both the dual identification and mutual intergroup identification approaches offer solutions to the distinctiveness and generalization problems arising from decategorization and recategorization. The specifics of a given conflict situation may dictate which of these approaches would be most effective. In cases where the presence of a distinct superordinate identity would be most beneficial, a dual identity approach would most likely be appropriate. However, in instances where the formation of a shared identity would be especially difficult, mutual in-group differentiation may be a superior starting point. In any case, these approaches are not in opposition. In fact, they may be complementary processes in the development of more positive intergroup relations over time. When groups have been involved historically in conflict, it may be easier to introduce a task requiring intergroup cooperation (mutual in-group differentiation) than to create a stable and prominent recognition of shared identity along with separate group identities (a dual identity). Under these initial conditions, subgroup and subordinate identities may be seen as antithetical. However, over time, the type of intergroup cooperation proposed by the mutual intergroup differentiation framework could potentially give rise to a sense of a common identity through working together toward shared goals, thereby creating a dual identity that can sustain positive intergroup relations even in the absence of cooperation on a specific task.

An Integration of Approaches: Reciprocal Process Models

Because each of the cognitive-structural models of intergroup relations and conflict reduction has weaknesses as well as strengths, several researchers have proposed that combinations of all the models may be necessary to create conditions for long-term changes in intergroup relations (e.g., Gaertner, Rust, Dovidio, Bachman, & Anastasio, 1996; Hewstone, 1996; Pettigrew, 1998a). In this section, we discuss an integrative strategy for promoting reconciliation between groups, which considers how the various social categorization strategies for promoting more positive intergroup relations can operate sequentially and in complementary ways.

The utility of each of the categorization-based strategies for reducing intergroup bias—that is, decategorization, recategorization (including dual identification), and mutual intergroup differentiation—has received empirical support. But the question remains as to how these alternatives that seem so different, even opposite, relate to one another? Should the models be conceptualized as competitors, that is, as independent processes that reduce bias through different pathways? Or, are they different processes that are complementary and which can reciprocally facilitate each other?

Pettigrew (1998a) has proposed that the essential conditions of intergroup contact reduce prejudice over time by initiating a sequence of strategies for reducing bias. He suggests that the sequence unfolds beginning with decategorization, followed in turn by mutual differentiation and recategorization. Pettigrew's Reformulated Contact Theory posits that this combination, over time, can maximally reduce prejudice toward out-group members, and also generalize across situations, to different out-group members.

The order in which these category-based processes unfold, however, probably depends upon specific features of the contact situation, such as whether contact emphasizes group-on-group interaction (as in Sherif et al., 1961, Robbers Cave study) or interaction among individuals from different groups (as among neighbors). Nevertheless, Pettigrew's (1998a) general perspective receives converging support from a reanalysis of the Robbers Cave summer camp study by Sherif et al.'s detailed descriptions (Gaertner et al., 2000), and from recent laboratory studies that were designed to examine the possible interplay between decategorization, recategorization, and mutual differentiation (e.g., Dovidio et al., 1997). In addition to impacting the biases resulting from categorization processes, reciprocal process models may also be capable of reducing other sources of intergroup conflict such as intergroup threat.

Applications and Conclusions

In the previous sections, we have described a range of models aimed at improving intergroup relations. Although these models have each been demonstrated to be effective in the laboratory, their usefulness in actual reconciliation situations may depend on the specific characteristics of the situation (e.g., length and nature of the conflict). In this last section, we explore implications and applications of social psychology to achieving reconciliation and offer concluding comments.

For interventions to be effective, they need to consider the initial state of intergroup relations and then build upon the progress made by previous interventions. A single strategy, by itself, is unlikely to be successful in complex situations. It may be best to begin with a decategorization approach when the level of conflict between groups is very high, because it promotes more friendly relations between individuals and downplays the separate group boundaries. Initially drawing attention to the original group boundaries and immediately activating their associated identities may encourage the recurrence of perceptions of the memberships as two rival groups and arouse feelings of intergroup hostility (Hewstone, 1996). However, once positive interpersonal relationships are created, the different group memberships may be less threatening, allowing the salience of group boundaries to be replaced by a common in-group identity or re-established within the context of a common in-group identity. Hewstone, Voci, Cairns, Judd, and McClernon (2000) have found evidence in Northern Ireland that a combination of interpersonal friendship and high awareness of group membership was most effective for promoting forgiveness.

Ongoing programs to promote peace and reconciliation in areas of long-term conflict have also typically incorporated aspects of several different theories and strategies. The alternating sequence of categorization processes, for example, is apparent in the descriptions of the interactive problem-solving workshops pioneered by Burton (1969) and by Kelman and his colleague (Kelman, 1999; Rouhana & Kelman, 1994) that have focused primarily on improving Palestinian-Israeli relations to achieve peace in the Middle East. These conflict resolution workshops (see Rouhana & Kelman, 1994) typically bring together small groups of influential leaders from both sides in interactive, problem-solving exercises during workshops that last for three to five days. Kelman and his colleagues, in particular, were careful to select participants free of personal antagonisms or animosities toward one another, who were free to respect each other's knowledge, experience, and personal integrity. The small group size and the fact that participants are respected across group lines promote personalized interaction (decategorization) at the outset. In addition, personalized interaction is encouraged by the living conditions at the workshop. These sessions were usually held in a hotel or conference center in which all participants stayed.

These workshops, however, incorporate other group-based principles in conjunction with personalization. The formal activities of these workshops emphasize the respectful recognition of group boundaries, involve the acknowledgment of different and complementary group perspectives (mutual intergroup differentiation), and require cooperative interdependence (positive functional relations), and involve superordinate goals (common group identity). Specifically, in contrast to usual negotiation efforts, these conflict resolution interactions required participants, who often worked in mixed subgroups, to develop solutions to specified issues and to search for solutions that satisfy the needs of both parties.

Similar processes can be found in the reconciliation workshops at Mountain House in the Swiss village of Caux (Henderson, 1996), which facilitate intergroup healing promoted by religious leaders. The primary mission at Caux has been to encourage healing by helping people to overcome hatred, to end protracted conflicts, and to help groups find mutually accommodating solutions. At Caux, interpersonal friendships are forged that cut across national boundaries and key elements for personalization, such as problem-solving activities, are encouraged. These activities emphasize the existence of multiple and crosscutting identities in ways that do not threaten original group allegiances (mutual intergroup differentiation) and produce joint efforts and outcomes (common identity). Among its noteworthy achievements, events at Caux have been partially credited with the remarkably rapid reconciliation between France and Germany following World War II, as well as the Oslo Peace Accord.

Pettigrew (1998b) proposed that these workshops serve as a setting for direct interaction that provides opportunities for initiating coalitions of peace-minded participants across conflict lines. From our perspective, the conditions at these Palestinian-Israeli workshops were ideal for the emergence of decategorization, recategorization, and mutually differentiated interactions that could facilitate the reconciliation process at least among a subset of the parties involved in the conflict—with potential residual benefit for the groups as a whole. However, the benefit of these workshops is likely not limited to their alteration of social categorization processes. The programs most likely also defuse a number of intergroup threats by decreasing competition and emphasizing shared values. Additionally, knowledge that respected leaders are meeting with and befriending representatives from opposing nations may even have a positive effect on these nation's citizens. The mere knowledge that members of the in-group have befriended members of the out-group can improve intergroup attitudes (Wright, Aron, McLaughlin-Volpe, & Ropp, 1997). If citizens are aware that their leaders are interacting with leaders of an opposing nation in a friendly way, similar benefits can be expected. This is an important point as it represents one means of altering the attitudes of the general population, who in democratic societies have the ultimate power in determining the fate of reconciliation efforts. Such extended contact effects may even begin to transform the public's representations of "us" and "them" into a more inclusive "we."

Key among these programs/efforts to move feuding parties toward peace is the element of positive contact and its relation to how members of other groups are categorized. Unfortunately, there may be situations where either logistics or conflict intensity preclude the use of physical contact as a means to improve intergroup relations. In such situations, future programs may explore the possibility that psychological contact, rather than face-to-face contact, can lay the groundwork for reconciliation. For instance, if institutions, such as schools, are committed to reducing a conflict, they may arrange for members of opposing groups to correspond with one another in a manner that promotes positive conditions of contact. Such correspondence provides a means of reaching a relatively large number of individuals and of reaching a society's general public rather than just its elite members. In this way, the attitudes of a society could be changed in bottom-up fashion from the people to the leaders. This could expedite the realization of reconciliation quite broadly.

In conclusion, at the group level, resistance to reconciliation may originate from the importance of in-group identification. Negative out-group attitudes are often not born out of direct experience, but are the result of in-group identification and perceptions of intergroup threat. Category boundaries must be restructured if harmonious relations and a lasting peace are to be established. An understanding between the groups must be reached beyond formalized agreements if the impact of intergroup threat is to be decreased. Also, as representatives negotiate, they may develop unified symbols of their cooperation that represent each group's unique interests within the context of broader common goals and identity.

These processes may be difficult in cases where the consequences of harsh conflict are salient. Kriesberg (1998) states that in order for reconciliation to truly take place, individuals must "put aside feelings of hate, fear, and loathing, to discard views of the other as dangerous and subhuman, and to abandon the desire for revenge and retribution" (p. 84). However, reconciliation does not mean forgetting the past. Rather, it is believed that reconciliation can be facilitated by the acknowledgment of past wrongdoing, the offer of genuine apology, the provision of suitable restitution, and, finally, seeking and—the most challenging of all—receiving forgiveness (Tutu, 1999). The processes aimed at reducing intergroup biases, which we have discussed, can assist in this acknowledgement of the past and mutual efforts toward moving forward by transforming the way members of different groups perceive one another.

Because the nature of any given conflict will vary, social psychology cannot offer a single, simple path to reconciliation. However, social psychology can identify a number of intergroup and interpersonal processes that are fundamental to understanding and improving intergroup relations. These theories represent important tools for developing strategies and concrete interventions for promoting peace. The proper use of these tools in a given postconflict situation can assist diplomats and peacemakers in their attempts to move beyond the details of formal peace agreements to true acceptance and reconciliation.

References

Allport, G. W. (1954). *The nature of prejudice.* Cambridge, MA: Addison-Wesley.

Amir, Y. (1969). Contact hypothesis in ethnic relations. *Psychological Bulletin, 71,* 319-342.

Batson, D. C., Polycarpou, M. P., Harmon-Jones, E., Imhoff, H. J., Mitchener, E. C., Bednar, L. L., et al. (1997). Empathy and attitudes: Can feeling for a member of a stigmatized group improve feelings toward the group? *Journal of Personality and Social Psychology, 72,* 105-118.

Biernat, M., Vescio, T. K., & Theno, S. A. (1996). Violating American values: A "value-congruence" approach to understanding outgroup attitudes. *Journal of Experimental Social Psychology, 32*, 387-410.

Brewer, M. B. (1979). Ingroup bias in the minimal intergroup situation: A cognitive motivational analysis. *Psychological Bulletin, 86*, 307-324.

Brewer, M. B. (1988). A dual process model of impression formation. In T. S. Srull & R. S. Wyer (Eds.), *Advances in social cognition, Vol. I: A dual process model of impression formation* (pp. 1-36). Hillsdale, NJ: Erlbaum.

Brewer, M. B. (1991). The social self: On being the same and different at the same time. *Personality and Social Psychology Bulletin, 17*, 475-482.

Brewer, M. B. (2000). Reducing prejudice through cross-categorization: Effects of multiple social identities. In S. Oskamp (Ed.), *Reducing prejudice and discrimination* (pp. 165-183). Hillsdale, NJ: Erlbaum.

Brewer, M. B., & Gaertner, S. L. (2001). Toward reduction of prejudice: Intergroup contact and social categorization. In R. J. Brown & S. L. Gaertner (Eds.), *Blackwell handbook of social psychology: Intergroup processes* (pp. 451-472). Malden, MA: Blackwell.

Brewer, M. B., & Miller, N. (1984). Beyond the contact hypothesis: Theoretical perspectives on desegregation. In N. Miller & M. B. Brewer (Eds.), *Groups in contact: The psychology of desegregation* (pp. 281-302). Orlando, FL: Academic Press.

Brewer, M. B., & Miller, N. (1996). *Intergroup relations.* Buckingham, UK: Open University Press.

Brown, R. J., & Gaertner, S. L. (Eds.) (2001). *Blackwell handbook of social psychology: Intergroup processes.* Malden, MA: Blackwell.

Brown, R. J., & Hewstone, M. (2005). An integrative theory of intergroup contact. In M. P. Zanna (Ed.), *Advances in experimental social psychology* (Vol. 37, pp. 255-343). San Diego, CA: Elsevier Academic Press.

Brown, R. J., Vivian, J., & Hewstone, M. (1999). Changing attitudes through intergroup contact: The effects of group membership salience. *European Journal of Social Psychology, 29*, 741-764.

Burton, J. W. (1969). *Conflict and communication: The use of controlled communication in international relations.* London: Macmillian.

Dovidio, J. F., Gaertner, S. L., Validzic, A., Matoka, K., Johnson, B., & Frazier, S. (1997). Extending the benefits of re-categorization: Evaluations, self-disclosure and helping. *Journal of Experimental Social Psychology, 33*, 401-420.

Dovidio, J. F., ten Vergert, M., Stewart, T. L., Gaertner, S. L., Johnson, J. D., Esses, V. M., Riek, B. M., & Pearson, A. (2004). Perspective and prejudice: Antecedents and mediating mechanisms. *Personality and Social Psychology Bulletin, 30*, 1537-1549.

Fiske, S. T., Lin, M., & Neuberg, S. L. (1999). The continuum model: Ten years later. In S. Chaiken & Y. Trope (Eds.), *Dual process theories in social psychology* (pp. 231-254). New York: Guilford.

Fiske, S. T., & Taylor, S. E. (1991). *Social cognition*. New York: McGraw-Hill.

Gaertner, S. L., & Dovidio, J. F. (2000). *Reducing intergroup bias: The common ingroup identity model*. Philadelphia: The Psychology Press.

Gaertner, S. L., Dovidio, J. F., Anastasio, P. A., Bachman, B. A., & Rust, M. C. (1993). The common ingroup identity model: Recategorization and the reduction of intergroup bias. In W. Stroebe & M. Hewstone (Eds.), *European review of social psychology* (Vol. 4, pp. 1-26). New York: John Wiley & Sons.

Gaertner, S. L., Dovidio, J. F., Banker, B., Houlette, M., Johnson, K., & McGlynn, E. (2000). Reducing intergroup conflict: From superordinate goals to decategorization, recategorization, and mutual differentiation. *Group Dynamics, 4*, 98-114.

Gaertner, S. L., Mann, J., Murrell, A., & Dovidio, J. F. (1989). Reducing intergroup bias: The benefits of recategorization. *Journal of Personality and Social Psychology, 57*, 239-249.

Gaertner, S. L., Rust, M. C., Dovidio, J. F., Bachman, B. A., & Anastasio, P. A. (1994). The contact hypothesis: The role of a common ingroup identity on reducing intergroup bias. *Small Groups Research, 25*, 224-249.

Gaertner, S. L., Rust, M. C., Dovidio, J. F., Bachman, B. A., & Anastasio, P. A. (1996). The Contact Hypothesis: The role of a common ingroup identity on reducing intergroup bias among majority and minority group members. In J. L. Nye & A. M. Brower (Eds.), *What's social about social cognition?* (pp. 230-360). Newbury Park, CA: Sage.

Henderson, M. (1996). *The forgiveness factor: Stories of hope in a world of conflict*. Salem, OR: Grosvenor Books USA.

Hewstone, M. (1996). Contact and categorization: Social psychological interventions to change intergroup relations. In N. Macrae, M. Hewstone, & C. Stangor (Eds.), *Foundations of stereotypes and stereotyping* (pp. 323-368). New York: Guilford.

Hewstone, M., & Brown, R. J. (1986). Contact is not enough: An intergroup perspective on the "Contact Hypothesis." In M. Hewstone & R. Brown (Eds.), *Contact and conflict in intergroup encounters* (pp. 1-44). Oxford, UK: Basil Blackwell.

Hewstone, M., Voci, A., Cairns, E., Judd, C., & McClernon, F. (2000, October). *Intergroup contact in a divided society: Changing group beliefs in Northern Ireland*. Paper presented at the Society of Experimental Social Psychology meetings, Atlanta, GA.

Hogg, M. A., & Abrams, D. (1993). Towards a single-process uncertainty-reduction model of social motivation in groups. In M. Hogg & D. Abrams (Eds.), *Group motivation: Social psychological perspectives* (pp. 173-190). London: Harvester Wheatsheaf.

Hornsey, M. J., & Hogg, M. A. (2000). Subgroup relations: A comparison of mutual intergroup differentiation and common ingroup identity models of prejudice reduction. *Personality and Social Psychology Bulletin, 26*, 242-256.

Huo, Y. J., Smith, H. J., Tyler, T. R., & Lind, A. E. (1996). Superordinate identification, subgroup identification, and justice concerns: Is separatism the problem; is assimilation the answer? *Psychological Science, 7*, 40-45.

Insko, C. A., Schopler, J., Graetz, K. A., Drigotas, S. M., Currey, D. P., Smith, S. L., et al. (1994). Interindividual-intergroup discontinuity in the prisoner's dilemma game. *Journal of Conflict Resolution, 38*, 87-116.

Kelman, H. C. (1999). The interdependence of Israeli and Palestinian national identities: The role of the other in existential conflicts. *Journal of Social Issues, 55,* 581-600.

Kinder, D. R., & Sears, D. O. (1981). Prejudice and politics: Symbolic racism versus racial threats to the good life. *Journal of Personality and Social Psychology, 40,* 414-431.

Kriesberg, L. (1998). Coexistence and the reconciliation of communal conflicts. In E. Weiner (Ed.), *The handbook of interethnic coexistence* (pp. 182-198). New York: Continuum.

Maoz, I., Ward, A., Katz, M., & Ross, L. (2002). Reactive devaluation of an "Israeli" vs. "Palestinian" peace proposal. *Journal of Conflict Resolution, 46,* 515-546.

Miller, N., Brewer, M. B., & Edwards, K. (1985). Cooperative interaction in desegregated settings: A laboratory analogue. *Journal of Social Issues, 41,* 63-79.

Pettigrew, T. F. (1997). Generalized intergroup contact effects on prejudice. *Personality and Social Psychology Bulletin, 23,* 173-185.

Pettigrew, T. F. (1998a). Intergroup Contact Theory. *Annual Review of Psychology, 49,* 65-85.

Pettigrew, T. F. (1998b). Applying social psychology to international social issues. *Journal of Social Issues, 54,* 663-675.

Reynolds, K. J., Turner, J. C., Haslam, A., & Ryan, M. K. (2001). The role of personality and group factors in explaining prejudice. *Journal of Experimental Social Psychology, 37,* 427-434.

Riek, B. M., Mania, E. W., & Gaertner, S. L., Direso, S., Lamoreaux, M. J. (2007). *The relationship between a common ingroup identity and intergroup threat.* Manuscript in preparation.

Rouhana, N. N., & Kelman, H. C. (1994). Promoting joint thinking in international conflicts: An Israeli-Palestinian continuing workshop. *Journal of Social Issues, 50,* 157-178.

Sherif, M., Harvey, O. J., White, B. J., Hood, W. R., & Sherif, C. W. (1961). *Intergroup conflict and cooperation: The Robbers Cave experiment.* Norman, OK: University of Oklahoma Book Exchange.

Sherif, M., Harvey, O. J., White, B. J., Hood, W. R., & Sherif, C. W. (1988). *The Robbers Cave Experiment: Intergroup conflict and cooperation.* Hanover, NH: Wesleyan University Press, University Press of New England.

Sherif, M., & Sherif, C. W. (1969). *Social psychology.* New York: Harper & Row.

Stephan, W. G., & Stephan, C. W. (1996). Predicting prejudice. *International Journal of Intercultural Relations, 20,* 409-426.

Stephan, W. G., & Stephan, C. W. (2000). An integrated theory of prejudice. In S. Oskamp (Ed.), *Reducing prejudice and discrimination* (pp. 23-45). Hillsdale, NJ: Erlbaum.

Tajfel, H., & Turner, J. C. (1979). An integrative theory of intergroup conflict. In W. G. Austin & S. Worchel (Eds.), *The social psychology of intergroup relations* (pp. 33-48). Monterey, CA: Brooks/Cole.

Turner, J. C. (1985). Social categorization and the self-concept: A social cognitive theory of group behavior. In E. J. Lawler (Ed.), *Advances in group processes* (Vol. 2, pp. 77-122). Greenwich, CT: JAI Press.

Turner, J. C., Hogg, M. A., Oakes, P. J., Reicher, S. D., & Wetherell, M. S. (1987). *Rediscovering the social group: A self-categorization theory.* Oxford, UK: Basil Blackwell.

Tutu, D. M. (1999). *No future without forgiveness.* New York: Doubleday.

van Oudenhoven, J. P., Groenewoud, J. T., & Hewstone, M. (1996). Cooperation, ethnic salience and generalization of interethnic attitudes. *European Journal of Social Psychology, 26,* 649-661.

Verkuyten, M., & Hagendoorn, L. (1998). Prejudice and self-categorization: The variable role of authoritarianism and in-group stereotypes. *Personality and Social Psychology Bulletin, 24,* 99-110.

Wenzel, M., Mummendey, A., Weber, U., & Waldzus, S. (2003). The ingroup as pars pro toto: Projection from the ingroup onto the inclusive category as a precursor to social discrimination. *Personality and Social Psychology Bulletin, 29,* 461-473.

Williams, R. M., Jr. (1947). *The reduction of intergroup tensions.* New York: Social Science Research Council.

Wohl, M. J. A., & Branscombe, N. R. (2005). Forgiveness and collective guilt assignment to historical perpetrator groups depend on level of social category inclusiveness. *Journal of Personality and Social Psychology, 88,* 288-303.

Wright, S. C., Aron, A., McLaughlin-Volpe, T., & Ropp, S. A. (1997). The extended contact effect: Knowledge of cross-group friendships and prejudice. *Journal of Personality and Social Psychology, 73,* 73-90.

CHAPTER 12

Reconciliation, Trust, and Cooperation: Using Bottom-Up and Top-Down Strategies to Achieve Peace in the Israeli-Palestinian Conflict

REUBEN M. BARON

Within the context of intractable conflict, how is it possible to achieve reconciliation as a foundation for lasting peace? As a social psychologist, my solution to this problem rests on two sets of assumptions. First, reconciliation and related processes such as trust and cooperation are rooted in issues of interdependence both within and between groups. Second, such solutions need to capitalize on the interface that exists between individual and group-level processes. That is, we need to influence individuals in terms of their status both as individuals with, for example, certain categorical modes of dealing with oneself and others, and as individuals who function in a group mode, where fitting into a group overrides individual predispositions. In effect, we need to deal with the social-psychological reality that *the individual is in the group and the group is in the individual*. For example, in the important case of social identity, respect for one's ethnic, religious, or cultural membership group is intertwined with respect for oneself (Wagner, 2006).

The individual-group interface, in turn, needs to be framed in terms of a dynamical relationship. Specifically, whether the interface is between individual and group or between subgroup and superordinate group or between intra and intergroup processes, the general point to be grasped is that these social units are "inseparably mixed in ways that constantly shift" much as the roles of form and content shift in a work of art (Kimmelman, *New York Times*, July 2, 2006). The relation is like a figure-ground phenomenon—at one moment the person's individual history is predictive; at another moment his/her role in the group is predictive. But these shifts need not be viewed as random. Here our model is Bohr's principle of complementarity—that is, depending on the moderating conditions of observation or measurement, an electron may have either wave or particle properties. Analogously, Horwitz (1954) found that social expectation moderates individual versus group salience. Specifically, people recalled group-level incomplete tasks better than individual-level incomplete tasks, only when they expected to have further interactions with their fellow subjects.

Similar dynamical relations occur for more complex social units. Social identity, for example, under certain conditions rests on intragroup processes (Gaertner, 2002), whereas under other conditions, it follows Social Identity theory predictions (Turner, Hogg, Oakes, Reicher, & Wetherall, 1987), which depend upon intergroup comparisons to establish the favorability of one's self-concept. What both sets of models overlook is that intra and intergroup process may shift in salience for the *same person*. These observations become critical when evaluating the type of conflict-resolution strategy developed by Kelman (1997) who seeks to utilize both intra and intergroup sources of social identity to create new identities where feeling good about the self is not yoked to the destruction of the other. Unfortunately, part of the appeal of terrorism is precisely its ability to reinforce this negative linkage in groups that chronically feel humiliated or disempowered.

Further, this figure-ground type of complementary model illustrates how intra and intergroup processes have the ability to affect each other. For example, creating conflict between groups increases cohesion within groups. Less well known, but at least equally important, is Granovetter's (1973) demonstration that weak ties within groups increase the likelihood of building bridges between groups. Thus, group cohesiveness like group identity can shift dynamically—cohesiveness can, in this sense, be both cause and effect—metaphorically wave or particle (depending on the salience of intra or intergroup processes).

In a volume that focuses on reconciliation, the first goal of this chapter is to use the present approach to the individual-group interface and the intra-intergroup interface to clarify the meaning of reconciliation along with two closely related constructs, trust and cooperation. A second goal is to use complex dynamical systems (CDS) in regard to their ability to capture bottom-up and top-down changes in social organization to model aspects of conflict resolution involving Israelis and Palestinians. An underlying theme of all of these analyses is to establish the relevance of a sense of "we-ness." In order to prevent this analysis from becoming too abstract, I will ground it in certain aspects of conflict resolution before doing any more conceptual elaboration.

The Person-Group Interface and the Levels-of-Change Problem

Two examples may be helpful in showing how a bridge can be built from these types of social unit dynamics to the problems of change and conflict resolution. Lewin's (1948) dictum that it is easier to change a person as part of a group needs to be qualified since even when a person is a group member, he or she may at times be individually focused. At such times, the person is more in the group than the group is in the person. One may also recast Kelman's (1997) conflict-resolution workshops in these terms. Indeed, Kelman attempts to deal with both sides of this dynamical relationship (see Baron, 2004). Specifically, Kelman focuses on changing reciprocally negative images that Palestinians have of Israelis and Israelis have of Palestinians. He does this by creating problem-solving groups where Israelis and Palestinians have equal status and work together to create an agenda for overcoming barriers to peaceful coexistence. Kelman is both sensitive to intragroup processes and aware of the reentry problem after participants leave. In this context, he is far more concerned that people understand each other than that they form liking relationships. To facilitate transfer upon later reentry, the content of the group-problem solving is geared to developing strategies to overcome barriers to peace. Such an approach results both in breaking down individual-level stereotypes (the person in the group) as well as producing collective-level effects where each side comes to believe that the other side will negotiate in good faith. Such "working trust" focuses on the "group being in the person." The potential for transfer is also enhanced by selecting participants who are mid-level in the political hierarchy of their respective groups, thereby giving them relatively direct access to the politicians who make policy. Viewed this way, the person-group interface becomes remixed as the focus of change shifts from the small group to the collective level.

Differentiating Cooperation, Trust, and Reconciliation

Given this line of reasoning, it is important to differentiate cooperation, trust, and reconciliation. For example, Kelman focuses primarily on cooperation and "working trust." Specifically, Kelman creates a cooperative experience—people work together to achieve mutually beneficial outcomes. Further, trust in this context is constantly being earned. It is embodied in reciprocal actions that establish each side's intention to live up to its promises on a daily basis. Working trust rests on joint dependability of action in a particular context. Kelman does not deal with reconciliation—the process of repairing or healing the aggrieved parties in the conflict.

Although cooperation, trust, and reconciliation are in some ways very different, they can each be fit into the process of moving from an individualistic-competitive orientation to valuing a sense of we-ness. The fragility of we-ness is well captured by Kelman's term "uneasy coalition" (1997). The we-ness of cooperation is time bound and outcome oriented and does not assume a relationship. By contrast, the we-ness of trust is process oriented, open ended, and relational. The reciprocity of trust is not in the coordination of efforts; it is a matter of coordinating the beliefs that others will live up to the obligations they assume when they become part of other social units be it a dyad or a group or when involved in intergroup relationships or accords. At issue is a shared value that "one's word is one's bond."

If cooperation involves pragmatics and trust is driven by social rule and value, reconciliation involves a different aspect of we-ness, where coming together is healing. For example, in the recent documentary, *Encounter Point*, Palestinian and Israeli families, each of whom had lost close relatives to the other side's aggression, join a group called Bereaved Families Forum that meets regularly. In this situation, unlike other contexts where reconciliation is the final step, cooperation could not occur without prior or concomitant reconciliation. Perhaps this is because the parties coming together were apolitical—just suffering people on both sides, healing each other.

The success of this type of group, which now numbers more than 500, is one of the major reasons why I am proposing that we consider the potential inherent in a "bottom-up" model of conflict resolution. By themselves, top-down models of conflict resolution in the Middle East during the past decade have not worked. After the deaths of two important leaders, Yitzchak Rabin and Yassar Arafat, those in command of the Israelis and the Palestinians have either been more worried about not doing the wrong thing than doing the right thing or have filtered right and wrong through a lens of ideological and religious "correctness." By contrast, the "ordinary people" in the *Encounter Point* film feel compelled to stop the bloodshed rather than worrying about saving face or losing an election or promoting ideology. Such a "bottom-up" process is a good fit for the self-organization of local units in a CDS approach. The CDS model helps us to understand both qualitative and quantitative aspects of change. It can also enable us to explain tipping points with regard to small changes having large effects. A classic sociological example of such a tipping point is when a white neighborhood exceeds one-third minority representation and "white flight" results.

Lest the reader doubt the direct relevance of my preference for this type of dynamical model, one has only to look at the strength of Israel's July 2006 reaction to the kidnapping of a small number of soldiers. This so-called "over-reaction" to what might appear to be small provocations is, in reality, the response of a system approaching a critical threshold, that is, a system prepared for change by a long history of terrorism from Hamas and Hezbollah. Finally, such a dynamical model does not exclude top-down processes. Rather, it embeds them into a system characterized by a pattern of circular causality that encompasses both upward and downward causal effects. Specifically, individuals aggregate into groups and groups shape individuals; groups aggregate into institutions and institutions influence group processes.

Modeling Group Processes With a Complex Dynamical Systems Approach

One of the major advantages of using a CDS model in the present situation is that the individual and group are conceptually part of the same set of nested, circular relationships that comprise a CDS. For such a system, relations are not limited to first-order interactions between parts. For example, individual local interactions create social networks that, when sufficiently dense, give rise to a group structure (i.e., self-organization), which in turn influences the parts (i.e., downward causation; Campbell, 1990). Such changed parts can then influence the whole vis-à-vis processes such as minority influence (see Figure 12.1).

The complexity of such relations requires a new group dynamics that encompasses processes such as tipping points and self-organization (viewed as the "bottom-up" or "grass roots" creation of higher-order structures from local interaction patterns). It is also important to understand that the initial impetus for self-organization is the insufficiency of individual action to achieve major adaptive goals. It is this insufficiency that, for example, motivates individual wolves to form a pack to be able to attack larger animals,

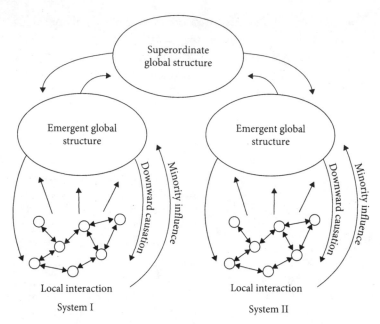

FIGURE 12.1. Dynamical processes of change within and between groups.

or students to form a study group when the reading load becomes too great. Similarly, in the documentary *Encounter Point*, the grieving Palestinian and Israeli families, unable to achieve reconciliation as individuals, banded together because their within-group support groups were more focused on assigning blame than creating strategies to achieve peace. *Thus, at times it is adaptive to build bridges across intergroup boundaries.* Moreover, these actions fit Granovetter's (1973) principle that loose within-group ties make it easier to establish ties between groups. That is, in this case, intragroup ties were weakened rather than strengthened by personal loss. It is also likely that part of the success of Kelman's workshops involves capitalizing on Granovetter's principle.

With regard to Figure 12.1, the local dynamics can encompass individuals or groups as the unit of analysis for self-organization. In the *Encounter Point* example, a peace-oriented superordinate group emerges out of the local self-organization. Similarly, coalitions of such groups could change the trajectory of the conflict as they did in the Vietnam antiwar movement in the late 1960s. Viewed thus, reconciliation *before* the fact can be easier to achieve than is reconciliation *after* the fact—that is, after a conflict has escalated.

Ordering the Paths for Peace: Strategies for Breaking the Nash Equilibrium

I propose two ways of ordering these complex issues. One strategy is to see trust, cooperation, and reconciliation as interrelated paths to an enduring peace. Within this context the problem is how to order these paths given the possibility that in certain contexts cooperation may lead to reconciliation and in other contexts reconciliation may need to occur before cooperation is possible. More broadly, at issue is the interdependence of different types and levels of change. At a substantive level, I see the key problem as achieving a sense of we-ness between conflicting entities at the intergroup level without severely compromising their we-ness at the intragroup level. Given these assumptions, this "fragile we" is grounded in mutual respect, if not acceptance, of the others' aspirations. The goal here is not to bring about love or even liking between parties but to clear away obstacles to create a situation where the legitimacy of the other side's national aspirations is recognized. For example, the goal would be for Israel to recognize the need for a separate Palestinian state and for the Palestinians to recognize the legitimacy of the State of Israel. The "fragile we" in this context is the achievement of nonviolent relations between the states, which can then develop into stable patterns for interdependency, as, for example, in business ventures that are mutually beneficial.

One may, in this context, question, "why groups in conflict would be motivated to share limited resources" (Malloy, 2006, personal communication). This question is a special case of the Nash Equilibrium (1950) problem, which states that individualistic-competitive strategies are more rational, stable, and preferred in mixed-motive situations than are cooperative strategies. Specifically, cooperation, trust, and reconciliation, each in its own way, involves breaking the Nash Equilibrium—they all point to the limitations of individualistic-competitive strategies. As noted earlier, the development of we-oriented strategies emerges out of joint insufficiency as in the need for intergroup bonding for the grieving family members in the *Encounter Point* documentary.

Elaborating Schachter's (1959) affiliation principle, miserable people seek miserable company because together they may have the capacity to lower the joint misery occasioned by the common loss of loved ones. Under such conditions, it makes good adaptive sense to seek out-group support in order to change maladaptive, competitive strategies generated by overly cohesive in-groups, with groupthink being the extreme case (Janis, 1972). The reader is reminded here that some of the best field experimental demonstrations of cooperation emerge from situations that establish the insufficiency of a group's acting by itself. This includes Sherif's (1966) Robbers Cave paradigm, which introduced a series of challenges, including moving a stalled truck carrying food that could not be achieved without the full cooperation of both groups and the Jigsaw paradigm of Aronson, Stephen, Sikes, Blaney, and Snapp (1978), in which each side was given only part of the information necessary to solve a problem.

In sum, the salience of *joint insufficiency* can trump individualistic-competitive tendencies, thereby laying the groundwork for a sense of we-ness, with trust, cooperation, and reconciliation illustrating the different forms and development we-ness can take. Specifically, in order to ameliorate intractable conflict at the collective level, it may be necessary to shift the focus to small-group dynamics that occur away from the corrosive spotlight of the international media, thereby opening up options that cannot be explored at the official level. The work of Kelman and the sports examples I offer later elaborate this strategy. It should be noted, however, that the majority of the supportive examples I cite, including Kelman's research, do not have the benefit of formal evaluations. Nevertheless, taken together, over a broad range of domains and procedures, the positive results of such case study interventions can be viewed as converging operations for the possibility of peace and reconciliation. Given that reconciliation is the focus of this volume, a deeper look at this form of we-ness is in order.

Exploring Models of Reconciliation

The dictionary provides three levels of meaning for reconciliation: (a) to cause a cessation in hostility or opposition; (b) to cause a person to accept or be resigned to something not desired (e.g., being resigned to a nondesired divorce settlement); (c) to harmonize or settle a quarrel or inconsistency, to repair, to make good or whole again. While reconciliation of prolonged, intractable conflict may involve all of these elements, I prefer to focus on the third meaning because only the third definition moves us toward we-ness, toward a clear breaking of the Nash Equilibrium of a preference for individualistic-competitive solution strategies.

In this context, popular reconciliation strategies, such as the South African (SA) model of victims, victimizers, and formalized requests for forgiveness, are so focused on redressing old wrongs that they lose sight of what it would take for an enduring cooperative relationship to emerge. Specifically, applying the SA model to the Middle East will not make the parties whole. Such a strategy ignores the broader problem of how to enable Israelis and Palestinians to accept the legitimacy of the others' aspirations. In my view, both parties can be made whole when Israel recognizes that the Palestinians have a legitimate claim for certain territories and Palestinians recognize the legitimacy of Israel's claims for existence. Therefore, I do not agree with the argument that what worked well in South Africa—that is, one side apologizing and the other side forgiving—will work well in the Middle East (cf. Rouhana, 2004, for a contrary view). Specifically, I question Rouhana's idea that justice, truth, and responsibility are the monopoly of one side. The real tragedy of the Israeli-Palestinian conflict is that both sides are victims and victimizers.

Reconciliation as a Reciprocal Process of Individual- and Group-Level Change

It is interesting in this connection that perhaps the most successful examples of creating a mindset that favors peace have not been a "top-down" process involving negotiation at the highest level of leadership. Rather, they have been "bottom-up" attempts at a small-group level to bring together middle- or low-level leaders in face-to-face conflict-reduction workshops such as those run by Kelman (1997). Such workshops established conditions where power differentials were eliminated, "working trust" was established, and cooperation was embodied in the very structure of the group task. Further, Kelman never treated the outcomes of these workshops as endpoints. He always focused on the problem of transfer to a higher level set of negotiators who had greater political power.

Kelman's strategy (1997) also supports another aspect of my approach to reconciliation that differs from the standard view, which tends to emphasize reconciliation as an ideal end state (cf. Rouhana & Bar-Tal, 1998). For me, reconciliation is a process of change at both the group and individual level that is ongoing, much as the alcoholic who successfully attends AA and stops drinking must continuously monitor his drinking behavior; this means staying in touch with AA groups that support this alcohol-free behavior. Treating the AA situation as a model does more than illustrate the continuing change interpretation. It makes it clear that contrary to what many social psychologists have assumed (cf. Gaertner, Brewer, & Dovidio, 2006), reconciliation should not be viewed as an individual-level process of change. Rather, I propose that reconciliation occurs at the interface between individual- and group-level change processes. That is, for reconciliation to work it must involve a reciprocal process of individual- and group-level change. For example, the transfer problem for Kelman's participants is to get the larger group to accept these new understandings as a basis for global group action. For the individual, this involves the difficult task of balancing a *new intragroup* social identity (see Gaertner, 2002) with a *preexisting intergroup* social identity, which was, at least, partially dependent on achieving a positive identity by denigrating the other. Moreover, from the original group's point of view, the issue involves resocializing the workshop participant. That is, this person must both retain credibility as a "loyal Palestinian" or a "loyal Israeli" while changing the attitudes and behaviors of people high in the power structure to be more understanding of the legitimacy of the other's aspiration. Truly, in this situation, the individual is in the group and the group is in the individual.

Creating the "Fragile We": Bringing Together Different Levels of Change

In order to achieve reconciliation based on the achievement of a "fragile we," a situation is needed where *us* versus *them*, gives way to *we* at least in certain contexts. Three successful examples involving trust and cooperation are a doubles tennis tournament where an Israeli and a Palestinian were tennis partners, a Yugoslavian basketball team with both Bosnians and Serbs, and as described in Nadler and Saguy (2004), Israeli and Palestinian farmers working together to solve joint agricultural problems. The major challenge is whether—given that hostility can be suspended for the sake of the team or solving joint agricultural problems—it is possible for such relations to be scaled up so that the wisdom of small-group relations can generalize to national-level intergroup relations. At a process level, we can ask under what conditions a critical mass could be reached through a widespread series of conflict-resolution and small-group encounters such that societal change could occur (see Baron, 2004).

In order to examine such possibilities we need to use explanatory concepts that work across levels before looking at constructs limited to a single level. Despite impressive experimental results suggesting the importance of individual-level cognitive processes such as decategorization and recategorization in conflict resolution (cf. Brewer & Gaertner, 2003), I suggest we begin with constructs that work across levels such as trust and cooperation. Such an analysis, I propose, will allow us to situate cognitive change in a group context that helps us to understand better the collective-level change needed to resolve intractable intergroup conflicts. In the case of Jackie Robinson, for example, I believe that recategorizing players of color became widespread through a bottom-up process, although the initial impetus was a top-down action by the president of the Brooklyn Dodgers, Branch Rickey. Specifically, when a certain number of teams started employing players of color, a tipping point was reached, which allowed such change to become normative. More broadly, just as recent work in the area of embodied cognition (Wilson, 2002) has established that perceiving and cognizing are *for doing,* so decategorization and/or recategorization should not be viewed as isolated cognitive changes. That is, they are for *social acting*—for influencing the group to shift in this direction.

In effect, small-scale group dynamics, along with socially embodied cognitive change, became self-organized into large-scale institutional change. Such processes perhaps provide a general mechanism through which small-group level change like Kelman's workshops could transfer to large-scale societal change. In line with such an interpretation, Lewin's (1958) World War II group decision-making techniques for getting housewives to accept cheap cuts of meat, if widespread, could have had a similar societal effect. Although I have continuously stressed a "bottom-up" approach, it needs to be reiterated that, within the dynamical model, bottom-up and top-down processes are not separate; there is a pattern of circular causality between them. For example, bottom-up processes, as in the Middle East conflict, often occur when there is a vacuum at the top. It is also certainly possible that as in The Jackie Robinson example, we can begin by imposing an exemplar "top-down," which then sets into motion self-organizational processes bottom-up. Unlike the Jackie Robinson example, however, in the Middle East, examples of successful negotiations such as the Oslo Accords cannot be assumed to have created a permanent model for change. At best, such change is permanently a work in progress, oxymoron though this may be. More dramatically, if the price of liberty is eternal vigilance, so too is this the price of reconciliation, given that the parameters of reconciliation constantly change. Trying to establish that there are, however, basic principles to be utilized, is the burden of the present analysis.

The Different Functions of Trust

In an earlier analysis, I proposed that control could function both as a mediator and as a moderator (Baron & Kenny, 1986); a similar argument can be made for trust. For example, I have recently proposed (Baron, 2003) that trust can be viewed as a general climate or moderator at a societal level that amplifies or attenuates small-group-level interventions. From this perspective, Lewin's (1958) group decision-making paradigm might have been augmented in efficacy by the general climate of high patriotism during World War II, which, in the present terms, could be recast as having high trust in the US government. Given this interpretation, it is possible that Lewin's interventions would not have been as successful during the war in Vietnam, if we assume a climate of low trust for the US government during the 1960s.

I believe this line of argument can be directly applied to the Middle East conflict between Palestinians and Israelis. In general, the period during which Kelman's workshops were most effective (i.e., 1990-1995) had a high level of ambient trust. Relatively speaking, Palestinians and Israelis trusted their own leaders and trusted each other's leaders to fulfill their promises. If I am correct, this amplified the effectiveness of Kelman's workshops. On the other hand, after Rabin's assassination and prior to Arafat's death, the climate of distrust increased across a number of levels, thereby limiting possibilities for official negotiations. What did occur, however, was that small groups that attempted to create a paradigm for conflict resolution emerged outside the official government channels (Myre, 2003). In effect, if there could be no unfreezing at the official level, it could at least begin with unofficial, lower-level contacts. What I would argue is that trust seeking can be a collective motivation; people interested in peace will seek to find a situation where, in Kelman's terms, "working trust" could occur.

Moreover, I propose that, in this context, trust also mediated cooperative problem solving. That is "working trust" appears necessary to motivate people to engage in difficult and effortful cooperative problem solving. For example, Kelman's Palestinians and Israelis were asked to think jointly of how obstacles to peace could be removed. In other contexts, the very act of cooperation with the enemy may not seem worth the effort; why negotiate if you cannot trust the other side to honor the promises or agreements that are jointly arrived at? In such contexts, trust may be treated as an investment with potential rewards and costs. The classic example of this exchange-theory interpretation (Lewicki & Wiethoff, 2000) is the arms reduction agreements signed by the United States and Russia during the cold war that incorporated a plan for mutual inspection.

At this point it is useful to distinguish further the relationship between trust and cooperation. For example, in Sherif's Robber's Cave (1966) study, a broken-down truck could only be moved if conflicting groups worked together. Such joint efforts, however, required minimal trust and likely had little impact on self-identity. Cooperation in Sherif's sense was short term and situation specific. Hypothetically, it would be analogous to Arabs and Israelis living in close proximity being faced with a joint power outage due to a storm. Among the most successful conflict reduction studies done in Israel are those involving extended cooperative actions between Israeli and Palestinian farmers (Nadler & Saguy, 2004). The more extended in time the collaboration endures, the more opportunities there are likely to be to earn and build trust. Therefore, trust may not only be a *prerequisite* for certain kinds of cooperation; it may also be a product of successful joint activity (Kramer & Carnevale, 2003).

Moreover, joint problem solving surrounded by *trust at both ends of cooperation can* be a bridge to the reconciliation processes. Trust may be an effective way to begin the emotional healing. In this context, trust becomes more than exchange-type trust based on mutual monitoring; it begins to resemble the trust of friends, or family—what might be called communal trust (Lewicki & Wiethoff, 2000). It may also be noted that where trust is communally based, power differentials as between parents and children, are much less disturbing. Thus, the nature of the trust may affect the meaning of power differentials at least in the small-group context. A good example is Kelman's workshops, where for the purposes of a given class of interactions, power differences were removed.

What, however, are implications of trust at the highest levels, be it the zeitgeist or the climate of trust between leaders? There appears to have been a short interval of time when Rabin and Arafat trusted each other and were trusted by their respective constituencies. This set of circumstances would seem to have been ideal for reconciliation to have commenced. Unfortunately, just at this point Rabin was assassinated and as they say, "the rest is history," and not such good history with the escalation of terrorism as the key component of the new Intifada. Thus, trust is a double-edged sword—it is easier to achieve trust than it is to restore trust once it is lost. This type of asymmetry in parameters regulating change is characteristic of how dynamical systems ebb and flow with changes in environmental conditions. Moreover, "it is easier to destroy trust than to create it" (Kramer & Carnevale, 2003, p. 438). Viewed in this way, trust, like reconciliation, embodies the "fragile we" in the sense that it needs to be perpetually renewed.

This fragility of trust can perhaps be better understood if a link is postulated between loss of trust and a perceived loss of control between what you do and what you can expect from another person or group. That is, the vulnerability often associated with trust (Levin, 2007) may derive, in part, from what may be called a social learned helplessness. A case for the direct relevance of such processes for the psychology of terrorism can be made as follows, "Palestinians complain bitterly about the checkpoints. They feel like rats trapped in a cage" (Ford, 2006, *ESPN.com*). Of course, the ultimate irony of such a situation is that it is terrorism that makes checkpoints necessary in the first place. The existence of checkpoints is a tragic exemplar of a dynamical, circular causality. Interactions based on fear of terrorism lead to their emergence. Their existence, in turn, creates the feelings of powerlessness that produce more fertile ground for the recruitment of terrorists.

Social Identity, Terrorism, and Conflict Resolution

Powerlessness, in turn, may be seen as negatively affecting people's sense of self- and social identity. The psychological roots of terrorism may include feelings that the value of one's social identity—religious, ethnic, cultural—is being questioned by certain social arrangements. In this regard, there may be an asymmetry in how Israelis and Palestinians form their social identities. Is it possible, given feelings of powerlessness, that for some Palestinians a positive self-identity is *more* yoked to the destruction of Israel than the Israeli positive identity is contingent on the destruction of the Palestinians? More specifically, one of the appeals of terrorism is that it vicariously lessens one's feelings of helplessness and humiliation. It forces the enemy, for example, Israel, to acknowledge the Palestinian point of view.

A related issue needs to be treated. One type of conflict-resolution strategy is to push for a new meta-identity; that is, a higher-order identity that would transcend group differences. For example, both Arabs and Israelis claim Abraham as the father of their religions. Recent approaches, however, have focused on allowing multiple identities to coexist (Kelman, 1997); for example, Israeli Arabs chronically have this dilemma. As the conflict intensified, many Israeli Arabs have identified with the Palestinians, a situation likely to worsen the already negative attitudes and discriminatory actions toward them as well as to increase some Israelis' concerns about an Arab "Fifth Column" in Israel. This need not be. A newspaper article caught my eye in this regard. It said, "Score One for Coexistence" (Mitnick, *Jewish Week*, April 1, 2005, pp. 46-47). An Israeli Arab scored a key goal in a crucial World Cup qualifying match. This player who had earlier been booed by right wing Israelis, was now wildly cheered and was becoming a national hero. The article goes on to say, "the kick is being seen as a potential turning point for Jewish-Arab relations." Moreover, the player, Abbas Suan, said on the eve of Purim, "I want to wish a happy holiday to all of our Jewish brothers.... This is the sweetest moment of my life," thereby suggesting that the concept of "Israeli Arab" was a viable social identity. It was also reported that other Israeli Arabs who had previously supported the team playing against Israel out of their "frustration over the discrimination and alienation they suffer" suddenly began to root for the Israeli team (Jafar Farah, director of Israeli-Arab Civil Rights Center, Mosawa). Farah went on to say, "This is a *process* [italics mine] and first of all, it's getting back the legitimacy of the Palestinian community inside of Israel." Further, Itzik Shaanan, spokesman for the New Israel Fund which monitors racism at Israel soccer events, said, "it was more than a goal. There lies a great potential for reconciliation here for tying together Jews and Arabs" (Mitnick, *Jewish Week*, April 1, 2005, p. 47).

Teamness and Reconciliation

On conceptual grounds, earlier in this essay, I proposed that the essence of reconciliation was a process of making the parties in a dispute whole again. This view, derived before I read this newspaper report, fits well with Shaanan's metaphor of "tying together Jews and Arabs." At a process level, reconciliation in this athletic context appears to have involved a sudden, qualitative change in relations—not a slow, gradual evolution or a top-down process imposed by politicians talking. For example, Palestinians who habitually had supported rival soccer teams suddenly started supporting the Israeli team. Clearly this process is also highly emotional and, on the negative side, potentially only short term if not accompanied by many other steps toward a long-term healing process. Also, it should be recognized that the problems of Arabs within Israel are not the same as Arabs outside Israel—for example, those Arabs living in refugee camps. Consequently, it is possible that what works for Arabs within Israel will not work for Arabs outside Israel.

There are, however, aspects of this situation which I believe are general. First, the change in social identity occurred when Israelis and Palestinians were working together on a team. Cooperation was, in my terms, embodied in the coordination between players that constituted a team effort. For me, this also raises the possibility that Israeli Arabs will not necessarily disregard the Israeli aspect of their social identity and identify with the Palestinians outside of Israel. Suan, it may be recalled, referred to his "Israeli brothers." Suan adds, "They try to put me in one group, but I represent both" (Erlanger, *New York Times*, April 22, 2005, D6). Further, "brothers" suggests that, at least in this context, the status and power differentials that exist in the Israeli society at large can be trumped by teamness. This is particularly likely when teamness leads to success; winning is likely to further increase team cohesiveness across ethnic boundaries. Here, I would argue that the positive social contact effects that occurred under equal status conditions were augmented by teamness and success. It is also likely that teamness, almost by definition, requires "working trust" in Kelman's terms. With regard to macro effects, Suan, along with a second Arab player who also has contributed to the success of another team, has become a national hero. Even Al Jazeera, the Arab TV network, posted an AP article that said the games had "created an instant connection across the divide." As reporter Jerrold Kessel put it, "They don't talk politics, they are politics. They play coexistence" (Erlanger, *New York Times*, April 22, 2005, D6). As absurd as it might sound, to help settle some of the current tensions in the Middle East, perhaps we need a regional team—imagine if there was a team consisting of Israelis and Syrians!

And there is further good news regarding the conflict-resolution possibilities for sports. Israeli and Arab teenagers have been playing basketball together on the same team with some remarkable results (Ford, 2006, *ESPN.com*). They are part of a program called Playing for Peace (PFP). They both attend basketball games together as spectators and play together. Further, cooperation has expanded from Israeli Arabs to Palestinian Arabs from the West Bank playing on teams with Israelis. And the coaches include people from Israeli settlements like Tomar. Skeptical Palestinians and Israeli parents have been gradually won over. Why? "Pini (Israeli) drives to the basket. As a couple of defenders collapse on him he makes a perfect dish to Khaled for a lay up. They run back downcourt and do a chest bump. Their smiles are contagious; Jews and Muslims are playing together for peace" (Ford, 2006, p. 18). A Palestinian father says, "I don't believe in peace.... Maybe, I do now. I see this tonight" (p. 19). The plan is to expand operations by adding new communities as well as girls' teams, said one of the organizers (Matt Minoff, Cherry Hill, New Jersey cited in Ford, 2006, *ESPN.com*). Clearly, however, for this plan to be implemented, there has to be a nonhostile environment; it cannot occur during military operations.

Preparedness of a System and Tipping Points

Two broad conceptual points need to be made. First, the fact that sports can have such dramatic qualitative effects indicates that the system was, for whatever reason, prepared to change. In support of this line of reasoning, a recent *New York Times* article (Bell, 2005) on the soccer story reports that after more than 50 years of conflict among Israelis, Palestinians, and the Arab world, people, "are looking for something, anything positive to latch on to" (D4).

If the "tipping point" is one mechanism for change as in the Jackie Robinson effect alluded to earlier, it may also reflect a broader process of self-organization. Here, changes in individual-level actions can morph into a collective effect. A further recipe for such effects is suggested by Zuhaeir Bahlul, an Israeli Arab who works for Israel TV and radio. He proposed that this connection will grow, "If the state can create more opportunities in other fields, this type of inspiration gives Arabs the confidence to make things happen for themselves" (Mitnick, 2005). Here, change exemplifies self-organization; it is truly a bottom-up process with circular effects. Success in new fields will lead to other fields opening up, which in turn will create better Israel-Arab relations at a collective level. Such changes are foundational for what I meant earlier when

I described a fundamental aspect of reconciliation as the creation of a "fragile we." For people like Suan the tensions between Arab and Israeli identities is a crucial component of the "fragile we."

Having gained a foothold on reconciliation within the Israeli state for Arabs and Jews, we may turn to the more difficult process of applying this kind of reasoning to reconciliation with Palestinians outside of Israel. The key I propose is encouraging small-group face-to-face processes of cooperation. Such contacts appear to work whether the populations are Palestinians living inside or outside of Israel, although for the latter there are additional barriers. Again, it should be emphasized that the success of such cooperative experiences represents exemplars of what can occur, not proof that such effects are replicable in controlled studies.

Fostering Bottom-Up Intergroup Reconciliation Between Israel and Non-Israeli Palestinians

The possibility of "hands on" cooperative action between Israelis and Palestinians living outside of Israel has been steadily deteriorating since Rabin's death in 1995, with the PFP basketball program being an encouraging exception. It is particularly significant because it occurs in the face of socialization pressures to mistrust or hate Israelis. Further, during a period when there were no official negotiations, Palestinian and Israeli politicians outside of the government initiated talks of their own. For example, it was reported in the *New York Times* (Myre, 2003, A9) that a "group of prominent Israelis (led by Yossi Beilin) and Palestinians (led by Yasir Abed Rabbo), politicians working outside of official channels, had written a symbolic peace agreement...that could be a foundation for future negotiations." This suggests that for a political unfreezing to take place bottom-up, the general situation has to be very bad indeed. These talks, it should be noted, have a very similar group dynamic to Kelman's conflict-resolution workshops—that is, equal status contacts characterized by a sufficient level of "working trust" in a relatively nonhostile environment.

While improved opportunities to succeed may directly lay the groundwork for reconciliation within Israel, the situation is much more complicated when we are dealing with Palestinians living in the disputed territories. The general thrust of my approach is that we need a two-pronged approach. At issue is what will be the locus of reconciliation. Should we begin at the intergroup level, consistent with what Kelman's problem-solving groups, grieving families meeting together, and teenagers playing basketball suggest or should we focus initially on an intragroup strategy designed to create within-group reconciliation before attempting to deal with intergroup reconciliation?

In order to generate predictions, let us analyze what the successful intergroup interactions had in common. Though there were many differing circumstances, each of these groups neutralized the problem of status-power inequalities. Kelman manipulated the selection process and conference arrangements of his mid-level political participants; for Palestinians and Israelis, joint grieving for the loss of their loved ones, motivated their joining the Bereaved Families Forum, and the teenagers on the basketball courts did not think in these status-oriented terms. Further, each group operated in a secure enough environment that working trust could be established. Two of these productive interactions were contrived—Kelman and PFP Basketball League; one was the result of spontaneous feelings—the grieving relatives seeking each other out. All of these exemplars encouraged face-to-face, cooperative actions. Reconciliation was a relatively explicit goal for two of the three situations—Kelman's being the exception. What do I take from these examples? Basically, these were low stakes, protected interactions with nothing much to lose except perhaps in the Kelman paradigm, which still had no official status. These are the seeds that are planted with no guarantee that future seeds will take root in ways that will heal large segments of the respective populations. They offer hope but no guarantees. The second prong of my approach is oriented toward high-stakes conflict-resolution processes that begin with lack of trust and inequalities in power.

High-Stakes, Low-Trust Conflict Resolution

Before the July 2006 state of open conflict precipitated by the respective kidnappings by Hamas and Hezbollah, my solution in high-stakes, unequal-power, low-trust situations was to combine intra- and intergroup reconciliation processes as follows. I suggested that we needed *intragroup* reconciliation before we can have intergroup reconciliation, arguing that each side first needed to deal with its apostles of violence. Unfortunately, I underestimated the distrust by the people in the street of Arafat's Fatah party. Too long had they gone without widespread improvement in their quality of life—that is, better jobs, schools, infrastructure, and so on—a neglect made worse by evidence of misappropriation of the funds intended for such projects. As a result, Hamas, a religiously oriented terrorist organization, was elected, promising a better quality of life. Thus, for the moment at least, the promise of improved living conditions is linked not to reconciliation but to the perpetuation of intergroup hostility. That is, Hamas' promises, in addition to a better quality of life, more effective resistance to Israel.

This election likely bifurcates further the differences between those Palestinians who view themselves as homeless as compared to Israeli Arabs. For non-Israeli Arabs, the issue is not *inclusion* with dignity but *exclusion* with dignity. More broadly, the very structure of reconciliation may need to be different for Israeli Arabs and Palestinians living in the West Bank and Gaza, often in refugee camps. For Israeli Arabs, the antecedents appear to involve a bottom-up process as opportunities potentially open up in different occupations, as well as educational and social realms. Hopefully, with enough success stories (e.g., the Jackie Robinson paradigm in baseball), a tipping point can be reached and integration can be institutionalized. As noted earlier, at such a point, Israeli Arabs will have enough self-confidence to create their own opportunities.

Note, however, that even in the Jackie Robinson case, the process began top-down by the president of the Brooklyn Dodgers, Branch Rickey. My own extrapolation is that this will need to be true but even more so for the Palestinians in the territories. Their leaders must model in very clear and consistent terms that success cannot be defined by how many Israeli citizens are killed by terrorists but rather by the emergence of a viable separate Palestinian state where people have a reasonable standard of living, thereby addressing the problem of relative deprivation. I believe that only with the existence of such a state can Israel's need for secure boundaries and the Palestinian's call for the "right of return" be put into a nonzero-sum framework. We need leaders on both sides whose concerns involve the welfare of the next generation, that is, leaders who realize that a better future is more important than redressing historical wrongs, real and perceived. An economically viable Palestinian state could provide a reciprocal opportunity structure regarding trade and investment for both Palestinians and Israelis. In such a scenario, non-Israeli Palestinians living in refugee camps can build a positive self-identity that does not rest on the destruction of Israel. Israelis, on the other hand, can build a future free from both the fear of terrorism that created buffer zones in the territories and a group of settlers whose positive social identity rested, in part, on their successfully occupying land claimed by the Palestinians. But most critically, the solution must be *jointly* arrived at; it should not be unilaterally imposed by Israel, a strategy that was tried by the Israelis when they ordered their settlers to leave Gaza with no agreement with the Palestinians on the future of that area. My own view as a social psychologist, is that unilateral actions—whatever their strategic, political, or even moral justification—will serve to reinforce feelings of lack of control for a people who already feel powerless. Perhaps the mistake was *not* giving back Gaza, but *how it was done*.

Barriers to Reconciliation

The problem, of course, with this approach, given the election of Hamas, is how does one get a terrorist organization to want to reduce terrorism? And, after multiple kidnappings, how do we get Israeli "hardliners" to be open to trust, cooperation, and reconciliation? In terms of my general framework, for example, we need to identify the "joint states of insufficiency" that could break this impasse. It may be the case that "things have to get worse before they can get better." From the point of view of CDS, in crisis there are also opportunities for change. The grieving relatives case supports this principle at the small-group level; terrible losses brought them together. In effect, my principle is a special case of the joint insufficiency rule I suggested earlier as a way to break the Nash Equilibrium. As conditions worsen, they bring the system to a tipping point.

Let us consider the situation in Lebanon in the summer of 2006 from the perspective of what it would take to motivate the Lebanese government to try to control or eliminate Hezbollah. Certainly, it was not the relative "good times" before this new conflict with Israel. Hezbollah was getting stronger and stronger during that period. Will the current conflict make things worse in terms of making Hezbollah more popular? Certainly in the short run, this appears to be true. But, my analysis is for the long run. Will there be a tipping point in the future where the nonterrorist forces in Lebanon will turn on Hezbollah and demand a country free of terrorism? Similarly, can this also happen for the Palestinians vis-à-vis Hamas?

I believe these scenarios could play out if the Palestinians and Lebanese were able to work out their problems with Israel without interference from Syria and Iran, and if Israel recognizes that creating feelings of powerlessness plays into the hands of terrorism. As noted earlier, even positive unilateral actions, no matter how good they make the giver feel, are not likely to have the intended effect; rather, they will only increase feelings of lack of control and deepen distrust. The tension is how to reconcile Israel's security concerns with the Palestinian's widespread feelings of humiliation.

Further, I believe Israel was incorrect in withholding funds for Hamas that were designed to increase the quality of living of Palestinians. Why? It is because, despite the Israelis' claim that they had no other alternative but to withhold funds from the Palestinians so as to prevent the money from being used to buy arms that would be used against them, the result was a lack of funds for schools, health facilities, and so forth. Instead, Israel should have given these funds contingently, subject to ongoing evidence of their intended use for improving the Palestinian economic and social infrastructure as opposed to buying arms, and so forth. But, most of all, trust, cooperation, and reconciliation all depend on we-ness, on people acting jointly. I believe terrorism will have limited appeal if the conflicting parties can act together to solve jointly the problems on which terrorism feeds—underemployment, relative deprivation, perceptions of lack of control, and most difficult, feelings that one's religious and ethnic reference groups are not respected.

However, at the present time, there can be no reconciliation with Hamas (or Hezbollah) given that their raison d'être is the total destruction of Israel. All we can do is somehow create the conditions that will lead the indigenous populations that have currently been infiltrated and won over by terrorist groups to expel them so that under peace they can have a better and more secure future. The examples from sports and grieving relatives are particularly encouraging because they indicate the openness of ordinary people to a reconciliation process. Such examples point to the importance of Israel and her supporters not confusing being a Palestinian with being a terrorist. It is necessary, I believe, to move from the success of working trust at the small-group level, to working trust at the collective level. Both sides will have to take chances. The Palestinians need to believe that a democratically elected nonterrorist government will use funds given for improving schools, hospitals, roads, and so forth for these purposes, so that terrorist organizations such as Hamas are not the major source of an improved quality of life. And despite the understandable security fears of Israel, there needs to be more sharing of power, be it at checkpoints or in the dis occupation of disputed territories. The Israeli sources of fear and the Palestinian sources of perceived powerlessness need to be jointly addressed at all levels.

Lest these suggestions appear too unrealistic, let me close by citing an Op-Ed piece in the August 2, 2006 *New York Times* (Waldman, 2006, A10). In late 1996, under the aegis of US Secretary of State, Warren Christopher, a joint Israeli-Lebanese monitoring group was set up to oversee a pledge from Israel and Hezbollah to shield civilians from violence. Not only was this group successful in keeping various incidents of violence "from spiraling out of control" but it also led to "backchannel contacts" among Israeli, Lebanese, and Syrian military officers, which led to the formation of "personal bonds of trust" (Waldman, 2006, A10).

Consistent with the thrust of my final set of recommendations, Waldman suggests "the establishment of a parallel Israeli-Palestinian group" to oversee the disarmament of other terrorist organizations (e.g., Hamas). This Op-Ed piece is also important to the present analysis because it demonstrates the success of a small *face-to-face intergroup dynamic*, which functions at the same time as a quasi-official body. These groups, in effect, bring together the unofficial trust-building small-group effects I have emphasized in sports and in Kelman's research with a body with governmental standing. Moreover, this is a group whose actions are free of "the spotlight that has doomed past diplomatic efforts" (Waldman, 2006). Further, "through these meetings, rising military and diplomatic leaders could build personal relationships" (Waldman, 2006).

In sum, there appear to be two strategies for achieving peace. First, the appeal of terrorist groups must be diminished by offering currently disadvantaged Palestinian (and Lebanese) populations alternative means to education and social welfare, as well as providing positive sources of identity including perception of control over their own destinies. Second, small-group dynamics need to be utilized in setting up *joint* Palestinian-Israeli monitoring- and land-allocation groups. Taken together, I see this approach as providing *anticipatory* as opposed to *reactive* reconciliation. My emphasis is more on creating islands of working trust and cooperation than worrying about who has to forgive whom. Hopefully, the SA model of reconciliation—which rests on establishing past rights and wrongs and assigning blame to one side—will not be applied to the Middle East. Rather, leaders on all sides will recognize the power inherent in providing good jobs, good schools, and opportunities that foster mutual empathy and "the acknowledgement of the value of one's social identity, of one's ethnic, religious, or cultural membership group" (Wagner, 2006, p. 161). The goal is peace without fear and peace without humiliation. The various groups who suffer under barrages of rockets and bombs need to come to the conclusion that peace trumps war. At that point, the system will be primed for change and both top-down and bottom-up intergroup solutions can be jointly developed and implemented. When that occurs, we will be on the long road to Sulha (i.e., reconciliation).

Acknowledgments

Preparation of this chapter was supported by National Science Foundation grant BSC-034802, awarded to Kerry L. Marsh, Claudia Carello, Reuben M. Baron, and Michael L. Richardson. I wish to acknowledge the helpful comments and suggestions of Tom Malloy, Bert Hodges, Joan Boykoff Baron, and Jonathan Baron on earlier drafts of this chapter.

References

Aronson, E., Stephen, C., Sikes, J., Blaney, N., & Snapp, M. (1978). *The jigsaw classroom.* Thousand Oakes, CA: Sage.

Baron, R. M. (2003, October 3). *The generality of Kelman's paradigm of conflict resolution: Turning history into an opportunity rather than a limitation.* Paper delivered as part of symposium: Evaluating the contributions of Herbert C. Kelman to mainstream social psychology at annual meeting of Society of Experimental Social Psychology, Boston, MA.

Baron, R. M. (2004). The contributions of Herbert C. Kelman: Reinvigorating Lewin and anticipating dynamical systems models. In A. H. Eagly, R. M. Baron, & V. L. Hamilton (Eds.), *The social psychology of group identity and social conflict* (pp. 2-20). Washington, DC: American Psychological Association.

Baron, R. M., & Kenny, D. A. (1986). The moderator-mediator variable distinction in social psychological research: Conception, strategic and statistical considerations. *Journal of Personality and Social Psychology, 51,* 1173-1182.

Bell, J. (2005, April 5). Arabs become Israel's heroes. *New York Times*, D4.

Brewer, M. B., & Gaertner, S. L. (2003). Toward reduction of prejudice: Intergroup contact and social categorization. In R. Brown & S. Gaertner (Eds.), *Intergroup processes* (pp. 451-474). Malden, MA: Blackwell.

Campbell, D. T. (1990). Levels of organization, downward causation and the selection theory approach to evolutionary epistemology. In G. Greenberg & E. Tobach (Eds.), *Theories of the evolution of knowing* (pp. 1-17). Hillsdale, NJ: Lawrence Erlbaum Associates.

Encounter Point (2006). encounterpoint.com *90-minute documentary film about Palestinians and Israelis who promote a nonviolent end to Middle East conflict.* World Premier at 2006, Tribecca Film Festival.

Erlanger, S. (2005, April 22). A national hero one day, an enemy to some the next. *New York Times*, D6.

Ford, C. (2006). Hooping with the enemy. *ESPN.com.* pp. 1-19.

Gaertner, L. (2002, October). *On the intragroup origin of positive ingroup regard.* Paper presented at the annual meeting of the Society of Experimental Social Psychology at Columbus, OH.

Gaertner, S. L., Brewer, M. B., & Dovidio, J. F. (2006). Post–conflict reconciliation: A social psychological analysis. In T. Garling, G. Backenroth-Ohsako, & B. Ekehammer (Eds.), *Diplomacy and psychology: Prevention of armed conflicts after the cold war* (pp. 275-300). Singapore: Marshall Cavendish.

Granovetter, M. S. (1973). The strength of weak ties. *American Journal of Sociology, 78,* 1360-1380.

Horwitz, M. (1954). The recall of interrupted group tasks: An experimental study of individual motivation in relation to group goals. *Human Relations, 7,* 3-28.

Janis, I. (1972). *Victims of group think.* Boston, MA: Houghton-Mifflin.

Kelman, H. C. (1997). Group processes in the resolution of international conflict: Experiences from the Israeli-Palestinian case. *American Psychologist, 52,* 212-220.

Kimmelman, M. (2006, July 2). A heart of darkness in a city of light. *New York Times*, Section 2, pp. 1, 23.

Kramer, R. M., & Carnevale, P. J. (2003). Trust and intergroup negotiation. In R. Brown & S. Gaertner (Eds.), *Intergroup processes* (pp. 431-450). Malden, MA: Blackwell.

Levin, D. Z. (in press). Trust. In S. R. Clegg & J. R. Bailey (Eds.), *International encyclopedia of organizational studies* (pp. 1573-1579). Thousand Oaks, CA: Sage.

Lewicki, R. J., & Wiethoff, C. (2002). Trust, trust development and trust repair. In M. Deutsch & P. T. Coleman (Eds.), *The handbook of conflict resolution* (pp. 86-107). San Francisco, CA: Jossey-Bass.

Lewin, K. (1948). *Resolving social conflicts.* New York: Harper.

Lewin, K. (1958). Group decision and social change. In E. E. Maccoby, T. M. Newcomb, & E. L. Hartley (Eds.), *Readings in social psychology* (3rd ed., pp. 197-211). New York: Holt, Rinehart & Winston.

Mitnick, J. (2005, April 1). Score one for coexistence. *Jewish Week*, p. 47.

Myre, G. (2003, October 14). Israelis and Palestinians join in peace draft. *New York Times*, A9.

Nadler, A., & Saguy, T. (2004). Reconciliation between nations: Overcoming emotional deterrents and ending conflicts between groups. In H. Langholtz & C. E. Stout (Eds.), *The psychology of diplomacy* (pp. 29-46). New York: Praeger.

Nash, J. F. (1950). Equilibrium points in n-groups. *Proceedings of the National Academy of Science, USA, 26,* 48-49.

Rouhana, N. N. (2004). Identity and power in reconciliation. In A. H. Eagly, R. M. Baron, & V. L. Hamilton (Eds.), *The social psychology of group identity and social conflict* (pp. 173-188). Washington, DC: American Psychological Association.

Rouhana, N. N., & Bar-Tal, D. (1998). Psychological dynamics of ethnonational conflict: The Israeli-Palestinian case. *American Psychologist, 53,* 761-770.

Schachter, S. (1959). *The psychology of affiliation.* Stanford, CA: Stanford University Press.

Sherif, M. (1966). *Group conflict and cooperation: Their social psychology.* London: Routledge & Kegan Paul.

Turner, J. C., Hogg, M. A., Oakes, P. J., Reicher, S. D., & Wetherall, M. S. (1987). *Rediscovering the social group: A self-categorization theory.* Oxford, UK: Blackwell.

Wagner, R. V. (2006). Terrorism: A peace psychological analysis. In D. J. Christie (Ed.), Post–cold war peace psychology: More differentiated, contextualized and systemic. *Journal of Social Issues, 62*(1), 155-171.

Waldman, A. G. (2006, August 2). Lebanon's force for good. *New York Times*, A10.

Wilson, M. (2002). Six views of embodied cognition. *Psychonomic Bulletin and Review, 9,* 625-636.

Part III.B

Equality and Differential Power

CHAPTER 13

Diminishing Vertical Distance: Power and Social Status as Barriers to Intergroup Reconciliation

LASANA T. HARRIS AND SUSAN T. FISKE

Resolution of intergroup conflict remains a challenge. Despite decades of social scientific research, intergroup conflict resists reconciliation, all over the world. Everywhere, members of powerless oppressed groups still harbor feelings of ill will toward their powerful oppressors, while the powerful themselves share complementary negative feelings, as both sides continue to discriminate. Social psychology provides a ray of hope to this dim picture. Two areas of research help explain why intergroup reconciliation resists implementation; the first is the literature on intergroup emotions, and the second, the literature on group perception. These areas converge on *vertical distance* between groups: a gaping expanse of residual downward and upward resentment based on unequal power between groups. In this chapter, we argue that vertical distance continues to prevent reconciliation between many troubled groups.

Social psychology has taught us that constructive intergroup contact requires equal status between group members (Pettigrew & Tropp, 2000). However, the impossibility of equal status with the intergroup emotions that create and reflect vertical distance may not be easily overcome. To understand both group perceptions and emotions, we also require a comprehensive understanding of the precursors: namely, power and social status.

We will begin with the assertion that social emotions derived from power and perceived social status generate a skewed perception of the out-group, resulting in *residual negative affect* and the creation of a *vertical distance*, which in turn hinders intergroup reconciliation. This chapter will first review literature within social psychology that describes intergroup power as outcome control, as well as review models of intergroup emotions that establish *residual negative affect*. Next, we will explore the literature on perceptions of out-groups that create an immutable *vertical distance*. We will finally discuss some possible solutions and policy implications.

Residual Negative Affect

The idea of residual negative affect and subsequent vertical distance go as far back as Deutsch (1958). He argued that even the resolution of "manifest" or stated interpersonal conflicts (over a contested resource for instance) did not necessarily resolve the conflict in general. Five factors contributed to what he termed "underlying" conflict: dislike, distrust of motives, desire for punishment, a desire to overcome felt inferiority, and favoring of a third party that disliked the opponent. Note that these reasons all are affect laden, and all may be applied to the intergroup context. For our purposes, we define *underlying conflict* as residual negative affect: a complicated (mostly negative) affect associated with a competing group as the result of a power dynamic, status hierarchy, or resource conflict. Further, when this notion is applied directly to power and social status, a more concise picture of intergroup conflict begins to emerge.

Residual Negative Affect and Power

Interpersonal conflict results from incompatible goals (Raven & Kruglanski, 1970; Thibaut & Kelley, 1959). In addition, power dynamics at play in various forms of conflict result in residual negative affect (cf. Keltner, Gruenfeld, & Anderson, 2003). This notion makes the issues of power and conflict seem transparent—simply resolve the power dynamics, and the negative affect will vanish. However, in the intergroup context, as elsewhere, power is defined as the control by one group over the valued resources and outcomes of another group (Fiske, 1993; Fiske & Berdahl, 2007).

One can begin to see the emotional substrates of intergroup conflict simply from this definition alone. Negative affect follows from outcome control simply because of negative interdependence; negative affective reactions are inherent in competitive interdependent relationships (Fiske & Ruscher, 1993). Interdependent relationships create strong affective reactions. If the dependence is on an out-group member, as naturally occurs in power dynamics, then this group is assumed to be intrinsically interruptive to the goals of the in-group. This initial mistrust is amplified when the groups are in conflict; by definition, the groups clearly do not have the other's best interest at heart. Hence, negative affect is generated.

Not only is there now negative affect because of negative interdependence (Fiske & Ruscher, 1993), exaggerated by power dynamics, but the integrity of the group as a whole is threatened by the mere existence of the other (Neuberg & Cottrell, 2002). In their examination of power within dyadic relationships, Thibaut and Kelley (1959) assert that control over one's outcomes facilitates control over one's behavior. This holds true for intergroup behavior because control over another group's outcomes may likewise facilitate control over that group's behavior.

Control over outcomes need not inevitably control the low-power group's behavior; certainly many powerless yet rebellious groups (Mahatma Gandhi and the East Indians in the early 20th century) could not be controlled by the powerful dominant group (the British Empire). Control over resources does not instantly translate into control over behavior. However, these contingency relationships often do develop in both direct and subtle ways. Through group interaction processes, the powerful group can often coerce the less powerful group to behave in a manner that is consistent with the goals of the powerful. The point is that where this type of control over outcomes and often behavior occurs, the result in part is negative affect.

In interpersonal conflict, competition itself generates dislike coupled with a desire to harm (Raven & Kruglanski, 1970). These ideas similarly apply to the intergroup context (Fiske & Ruscher, 1993). Hostility even in artificially created groups makes this leap even more seamless. Competition often leads to hostility. For example, the classic Sherif (1962) study split boys into two arbitrary groups. Even in these artificial groups, once hostility developed, negative interdependence spurred competition and conflict. This residual affective component resulting from competition could be resolved only by mutual cooperation, and with much effort. Implicit here is the idea that intergroup competition generates negative affect, and unequal power would only worsen the situation.

Residual Negative Affect and Social Status

Power dynamics are worsened by status differentials. This is not a redundant point; social status and power are separable phenomena, a caveat to address before we go any further. Research in social psychology tends to define power relations between groups as a structural feature of society that allows social stratification (Dépret & Fiske, 1993). Social identity theory (SIT), for instance, lumps power, status, and prestige together as interchangeable variables (Hogg & Abrams, 1988). Though we rely in part upon this literature, we offer a small departure from this assumption. We see social status as separate from power, not its interchangeable synonym, and more importantly, we think that in the context of intergroup conflict, group members make this distinction as well. We will return to this idea later in the chapter when we discuss the concept of vertical distance and the resulting immutability.

Perceived social status (achieved simply by group membership) and the subsequent indirect controls that group members may have over the resources and outcomes of others, fuel negative affect on two dimensions. The first is negative affect created by power dynamics, as mentioned. This addresses negative affect in groups that are often openly in conflict. The second source of negative affect, resentment because of the social status hierarchy itself, attempts to explain the residual affect after a "resolution" has been achieved.

Social status, unlike power, is a social structural feature conferred on an individual or group by a consensus; it is socially created. Power mainly owes its existence to control over resources. High-status groups hold their position only because other groups recognize them as high status; power as we have defined it does not necessarily follow. Think of royalty in democratic states. Their position of high status is often accompanied by no actual power (resource control). However, they are able to exercise what appears to be power over a group through *spheres of influence*—control over behavior by influencing the decisions of a third party whose subsequent behavior affects the outcomes of the initial group. They are only able to exert this influence because of their position as high status. This distinction then between power and social status is fine at best, and characterizes an issue even French and Raven (1959), the intellectual godparents of the power literature within social psychology, have confronted. In-group conflict's spheres of influence often look like power but are instead fueled by social processes. Thus, negative affect is clearly generated toward high-status groups as their behavioral control is seen as illegitimate at best.

Spheres of influence in part lead to the second source of negative affect, resentment, because of the social status hierarchy. As discussed, social status implies a hierarchy like the power dimension but without the direct control over resources. This is not to say that all control along the power dimension is direct; power is defined as potential influence as well (Raven & French, 1958), and we have already walked that fine line. However, social control along the status dimension directly leads to a complicated mesh of emotions. As Allport (1954) implied, negative affect generated by social groups is not simple negative valence; it is often a complex composite of different emotions that stem from different cognitions and lead to different outcomes or behavior (Cuddy, Fiske & Glick, 2007). This, we argue, follows from the mere existence of social status hierarchies. We will address this concern in more detail as we delve into the relationship of power and perceived status in the realm of intergroup emotions.

Intergroup Emotions

The field of intergroup emotions has decidedly grown over the past decade, and we have learned a lot in the process. Close to a dozen theories attempt to explain intergroup affect, using as points of departure political science, sociology, evolution, and the vast expanse of emotion literature. However, only a couple of theories explicitly consider power and social status as critical determinants of intergroup emotions. Thus, we will make no attempt to review all of the literature within this subfield, but instead pay particular attention to those that meet this requirement—the Stereotype Content Model (SCM; Fiske, Cuddy, Glick, & Xu, 2002; Fiske, Xu, Cuddy, & Glick, 1999) and the Image Theory of Emotions (Alexander, Brewer, & Hermann, 1999).

The Stereotype Content Model

The SCM addresses affect in impression formation by incorporating a decision about mutual or competing interests (warmth) while adding capability (competence). The SCM proposes that societal groups are appraised as either intentionally helpful or harmful (warmth dimension) and capable or not to enact those intentions (competence dimension; Cuddy, Fiske, & Glick, 2004). The intergroup appraisal is based on perceived social structure. Thus, groups viewed as competitors are perceived as low in warmth, while those who are not competitive are perceived as high in warmth. Similarly, groups perceived as high status are viewed as competent, while those perceived as low status as not competent. These correlations appear universal, replicating across a dozen varied cultures (Cuddy et al., 2005). Rooted in classic person perception studies

(Rosenberg, Nelson, & Vivekanathan, 1968), the SCM dimensions address the pressing survival questions "friend or foe?" (warmth) and "able or unable?" (competent) in initial impression formation.

In addition, the SCM goes beyond early classic research in person perception to add an affective component not often discussed. It argues that the combination of these two dimensions (competence and warmth) produces four distinct prejudiced emotions: pride, envy, pity, and disgust (Fiske et al., 2002). Groups stereotyped as competent and warm elicit the in-group emotions, pride and admiration based on self-relevant, positive outcomes. Groups stereotyped as neither competent nor warm elicit the extreme out-group response of disgust and contempt, based on perceived social-moral violations. Envy and jealousy, based on resentment, are elicited by groups stereotyped as competent, but not warm. Finally, groups stereotyped as warm, but not competent, elicit pity and sympathy, emotions reserved for people with uncontrollable negative outcomes. The warmth and competence stereotypes follow respectively from perceived competition and status, so social groups elicit differentiated affect based on the perceived societal structure.

Status in particular plays an integral role in SCM. People apparently infer that the traits of others reflect their social status (Fiske & Cuddy, 2005). Evidence for this is provided by exceptionally strong correlations between status and competence (Cuddy et al., 2004). For groups in conflict, societal status rarely changes, so perceived competence and the subsequent affect may not change. Low-status competing groups elicit disgust and contempt; high-status competing groups elicit envy and jealousy. We will return to the implications of SCM's disgust-contempt versus envy-jealousy dynamic.

Image Theory of Emotions

In an alternative viewpoint, negatively stereotyped groups receive three distinct forms of negative affect based upon an interaction of perceived goals, power, and social status (Alexander et al., 1999). These criteria, in turn, lead to different behavioral orientations to the groups, which then affect the cognitive appraisals of the groups. The precise negative emotion depends primarily upon the relationship between the perceived power and status of the out-group and their compatibility with the goals of the in-group. Interestingly, within this model, negative images of the out-group occur only under competition with the in-group, which creates a perceived threat (Brewer & Alexander, 2002). Most other theories of intergroup affect share this perceived threat-to-the-in-group feature (e.g., Devos, Silver, Mackie, & Smith, 2002; Fiske et al., 2002; Neuberg & Cottrell, 2002; Stephan & Stephan, 2000).

For instance, when power and status are equal but there is competition, the cognitive appraisal is the enemy image, which leads to the behavioral orientation of attacking, and the subsequent emotion of anger. When perceived power is greater than status and there is competition, the result is a barbarian image that elicits defensive strategies and fear. When power and status are both higher in the in-group, then goal incompatibility by the out-group leads to a dependent image and exploitative behavior, with accompanying disgust and contempt (Alexander, Brewer, & Livingston, 2005).

Though the Image Theory of Emotions takes a somewhat different stand from the SCM, the role of power and status is apparent in both. It is along these vertical dimensions that a barrier to intergroup reconciliation forms. Even when the open conflict may be resolved, the power and status arrangements may remain. Thus, the perception of the group, based initially on the type and magnitude of the threat, remains unchanged. This helps foster residual affect, a further obstacle to reconciliation.

Models such as the intergroup emotions theories and Deutsch's ideas clearly point to the notion of residual affect. Residual affect thus is more than just a cell or quadrant in an intergroup emotions model; it is a mixture of emotions that is primarily responsible for fueling animosity between groups. As such, residual affect brings together the intergroup emotions literature and the literature on power and social status to help illuminate the barriers to intergroup reconciliation. Finally, however, to understand residual affect, one must turn to the literature on group perception to complete the picture, and add the idea of vertical distance.

Group Perception Creates Vertical Distance

Residual affect creates a *vertical distance* mainly because it is both generated by and continues to cause skewed perceptions of groups. Within social psychology, a number of theories have addressed intergroup perceptions. Some in particular usefully link residual affect to vertical distance: intergroup anxiety, perceived legitimacy, group homogeneity and essentialism, naïve realism, and dehumanization.

Intergroup Anxiety

Directly relevant to intergroup emotions is intergroup anxiety. A basic finding of prejudice researchers is that anticipated intergroup contact causes intergroup anxiety: a collection of negative affective states characterized by fear, anger, disgust, and other forms of anxious affect (Stephan & Stephan, 1996; Stephan, Ybarra, Martinez, Schwarzwald, & Tur-Kaspa, 1998; Wilder, 1993a, 1993b). This results from a complex negative perception of the group. Anxiety not only increases reliance on social stereotypes about the out-group, but anxiety also dampens the impact of counterstereotypic information that may begin to change the stereotype (Wilder, 1993a). Obviously, this creates barriers to reconciliation. The affect-consistency hypothesis—reactions are often consistent with one's affective state (Clark, Milberg, & Erber, 1984; Isen, 1987; Isen & Levin, 1972)—further exacerbates the effect of intergroup anxiety. Moreover, intergroup anxiety and negative affect are stronger predictors of prejudice than cognitions about either realistic or symbolic threats (Stephan et al., 1998).

Anxiety is potent for a number of reasons. These include negative states drawing attention away from the other's actions, leading to memory gaps, which are filled with stereotypic information. Also, negative affect colors the interaction negatively in general (Wilder, 1993a). Status plays a role in this discussion, again as a further barrier. Related to the idea of spheres of influence, noted earlier, the simple experience of being a low-status group member in conflict with members of high-status groups generates further anxiety about the potentially detrimental influence wielded by the out-group. However, if anxiety is overcome, then contact may work, but only under conditions of equal status (Pettigrew, 1986). Thus, anxiety contributes both to vertical distance, in particular, and to various kinds of negative residual affect.

Perceived Legitimacy

Going beyond the realm of affect (anxiety) influencing residual affect, various perceptual biases also exaggerate residual affect. Most relevant to vertical distance, the perceived legitimacy of group power and status skews group perception. In intergroup conflict research, SIT explains such findings. Its basic premise is that mere social categorization can cause intergroup discrimination (Tajfel & Turner, 1979). In this view, intergroup conflict comprises at least two clearly defined groups with little perceived variability of behavior and attitude within each group and particularly a homogeneous view of the out-group (Tajfel, 1978). Group members are thus deindividuated (Diener, 1979)—identity shifts from the self to the group, and concern lies primarily with the in-group. Subsequent individual behavior is determined by the relative power and status of the in-group (Brown & Turner, 1979). Legitimacy is a critical variable in SIT because people identify less as group members when group boundaries are permeable or illegitimate (Ellemers, 1994). Perceived legitimacy of group membership therefore reinforces group boundaries, social distance, and intergroup emotions. Perceived illegitimacy of group hierarchies, of course, provokes instability and social change, so the most emotionally volatile context would be legitimate group memberships with illegitimate group hierarchies.

We argue that when an out-group perceives the status and subsequent power of a higher status group as illegitimate, overt conflict is often the last action in a sequence of acts to restore equal status. This conflict is driven by social comparison that recognizes the illegitimacy, interprets it as a threat to the identity of the in-group, and seeks to change it. This, in turn, causes the dominant group to feel a threat to its identity as the dominant group, fueling the conflict (Ellemers, 1994; Tajfel, 1978; Van Knippenberg & Ellemers, 1990). In contrast to the Tajfel account is realistic group conflict theory, which states that conflict arises out of the incompatibility of goals, as well as competition for scarce resources (Brewer, 1979; LeVine & Campbell, 1972; Sherif, 1966). The major difference between the two approaches is that SIT claims that mere categorization suffices for intergroup conflict. But competition increases conflict in both theories. Thus, we argue that perceived illegitimacy (which increases competition) fuels vertical distance and especially negative affect.

Group Homogeneity and Essentialism

Group homogeneity is defined as the tendency to perceive a group's members (either in-group or out-group) as relatively similar on traits or behaviors. This phenomenon initially seemed confined to out-groups (Jones, Wood, & Quattrone, 1981; Linville & Jones, 1980; Linville, Salovey, & Fischer, 1986; Park & Rothbart, 1982; Quattrone & Jones, 1980; Wilder & Thompson, 1980), but evolved to include in-group perception as well under certain conditions (Simon & Brown, 1987; Simon & Mummendey, 1990; Simon et al., 1990).

We argue that perceived homogeneity sustains intergroup conflict and contributes to the residual affect and subsequent vertical distance that inhibits reconciliation. Perceived power and status covary with group size (Ebenbach & Keltner, 1998; Guinote, Brown, & Fiske, 2006; Ng, 1982; Wolf & Latané, 1985) and moderate the homogeneity effect (Guinote, Judd, & Brauer, 2002). In particular, the perceived power of the group affects its perceived variability, and the actual power of the group also affects its actual variability, in the sense that high-power groups manifest greater within-group variability. Homogeneity, thus, mainly inhabits low-power and/or low-status groups. Because the effect goes both ways in a situation of intergroup conflict (Simon & Brown, 1987), both groups, regardless of power dynamics, often perceive the other as more homogeneous, which is a barrier to individuation, one deterrent of discrimination (Fiske & Neuberg, 1990). In addition, because out-groups are thus perceived as less complex, their attitudes and behaviors are then seen as more extreme (Linville & Jones, 1980). For example, actions against the in-group may be perceived as extreme atrocities even after the conflict is resolved. A group perceived to be homogeneous more readily elicits generalized resentments than does a group comprising unique individuals. Thus, perceived homogeneity increases intergroup vertical distance and residual affect.

This can be amplified if the perceived differences between the groups are essentialized—perceived in terms of some underlying fundamental disposition (Medin & Ortony, 1989). Essentialism argues that people approach social categories with heuristic representations that rest upon the assumptions of group homogeneity and explaining differences (Prentice & Miller, 2007). Because all members of the out-group are perceived as similar and the difference between the groups is never fully understood, strong inductive inferences based upon these differences may be drawn in intergroup conflict. These usually negative inferences compound the homogeneity effect, making the differences between the groups seem immutable. Furthermore, research has shown that essentialist beliefs do predict stereotype endorsement (Bastian & Haslam, 2006), thus sustaining both the vertical distance and residual affect.

Naive Realism

Social conflict is intimately intertwined with group perception, as social psychologists have argued at least since the Hastorf and Cantril (1954) classic study "They Saw a Game." Asch (1955) similarly recognized that social conflict stems from opposing parties' different construal of the relevant concepts, facts, principles, and policy issues in a dispute. Our current examination of power and social conflict also raises many inherent impediments to intergroup reconciliation. These factors in concert affect the mutability of the vertical distance between groups, an idea that is captured by naïve realism.

Opposing parties often exaggerate the opponent's extremes, which in turn magnify the conflict (Keltner & Robinson, 1996). Naïve realism theory states that when people infer another's attitude and preferences, they mistakenly assume that the other bases those predispositions on the *perceiver's own allegedly objective perception* of the world (Robinson, Keltner, Ward, & Ross, 1995). Applied to intergroup conflict, the theory implies that groups will assume that their perception of the world is objective and accurate, and that the out-group is basing their judgments and decisions on this same allegedly shared, allegedly objective "reality." Hence, any deviant judgments or action by the out-group from this supposed "reality" must be based on their ideological biases (Robinson et al., 1995). Obviously, this only magnifies the conflict and contributes to the animosity between the groups. More importantly, this psychological factor maintains and augments the vertical distance between groups.

Dehumanization

High anxiety, perceived illegitimacy, perceived homogeneity, and naïve realism all culminate in seeing the other group as less than human. Allport (1954) originally described extreme forms of discrimination (characteristic in intergroup conflict) as resulting from the worst kind of prejudice. He argued that people begin to lose the power to think of out-group members as individuals (Allport, 1954). Implicit in the ideas of Allport (1954) and explicit in modern views of dehumanization is the idea that intergroup conflict may result in a perception of the individual as less than an individual.

A number of modern writers have explored the idea of perceiving people as less than people. Bar-Tal (1989) theorized that social groups that acted beyond societal norms would be excluded from other human groups, while Struch and Schwartz (1989) argued that people believed that all out-groups had a lesser degree of humanity. Staub (1989) in his discussions of evil often spoke of moral exclusion, stating that we believe that some social groups operate beyond our moral rules and values (see also Opotow, 1990). Most influential has been the work of Leyens and colleagues (2001) on infrahumanization, theorizing that infrahumanized groups are believed not to experience human emotions and feelings, or have thoughts and opinions such as those possessed by the in-group. These assumptions, in all cases, lead to the behavioral consequence of intergroup conflict—discrimination.

Haslam (2006) condenses the many theories about dehumanization into two forms of dehumanization: denying uniquely and typically human characteristics. The latter form surrounds the denial of agency, interpersonal warmth, and emotion to the target, while the former focuses on the denial of higher cognitive capacities, self-control, civility, and refinement. Both types of dehumanization may be applied to the intergroup context, but it is mainly with denial of uniquely human characteristics that the vertical distance between the groups begins to increase.

Also interesting is that dehumanization is orthogonal to the power and status relationships. Those both high and low in the hierarchy may dehumanize the out-group in all these ways. Coupled with out-group anxiety, illegitimacy, and homogeneity, this makes the problem of reconciliation even more difficult, mainly because one now has to focus on changing a variety of both groups' perceptions. In addition, dehumanized perceptions work against one another, serving as another impediment to reconciliation, and causing members of both groups to harbor resentment, growing the collective negative residual affect. In other words, the vertical distance between the groups now becomes immutable.

Resolution

Intergroup conflict results from competition over valued resources and outcomes. Its resolution depends not only on an amicable division of these resources and outcomes, but also on the much more difficult resolution of residual affect, which also results from vertical distance. If so, then two problems are immediately apparent. First, in reality, division of valued resources is rarely amicable. More often than not, the result is domination by the powerful group and subsequent oppression of the powerless. This obviously would increase negative affect, as well as intergroup perceptions that discourage resolving this affect. Even in the rare cases of amicable resolution, negative affect may still remain.

Second, and most relevant here, residual affect results from unchanged status differences, envy up and contempt down. Even when resources are divided equitably by a larger society, the two groups maintain the vertical distance, so the negative intergroup emotions will remain unless the groups view themselves as positively interdependent (Fiske, 2000). If they view themselves as absolutely no longer competing—but instead as part of a larger, common in-group identity (Gaertner, Sedikides, & Graetz, 1999) or as allies in an even more dangerous world—then the status differences may attenuate to admiration up and pity down. These create more subtle barriers to intergroup reconciliation, although they are probably preferable to envy and contempt. For example, pity is paternalistic and its positive aspect (helping and protecting) evaporates if the pitied group improves its perceived competence at the same time that it becomes competitive. The trick for the pitied group is to improve its status and competence while convincing the high-status group that the game is not zero-sum, but in fact an expandable pie. Similarly, admiration—though positive—is a distancing emotion that may interfere with equal status, active cooperation, instead of merely going along to get along. Nevertheless, moving from competition to acknowledging positive interdependence is most likely to improve intergroup reconciliation.

References

Alexander, M. G., Brewer, M. B., & Hermann, R. K. (1999). Images and affect: A functional analysis of out-group stereotypes. *Journal of Personality and Social Psychology, 77,* 78-93.

Alexander, M. G., Brewer, M. B., & Livingston, R. W. (2005). Putting stereotype content in context: Image theory and interethnic stereotypes. *Personality and Social Psychology Bulletin, 31,* 781-794.

Allport, G. W. (1954). *The nature of prejudice.* Reading, MA: Addison-Wesley.

Asch, S. E. (1955). Opinions and social pressure. *Scientific American, 193,* 31-35.

Bar-Tal, D. (1989). Delegitimization: The extreme case of stereotyping and prejudice. In D. Bar-Tal, C. Graumann, A. Kruglanski, & W. Stroebe (Eds.), *Stereotyping and prejudice: Changing conceptions* (pp. 169-182). New York: Spinger-Verlag.

Bastian, B., & Haslam, N. (2006). Psychological essentialism and stereotype endorsement. *Journal of Experimental Social Psychology, 42,* 228-235.

Brewer, M. B. (1979). Ingroup bias in the minimal intergroup situation: A cognitive-motivational analysis. *Psychological Bulletin, 86,* 307-324.

Brewer, M. B., & Alexander, M. G. (2002). Intergroup emotions and images. In D. Mackie & E. Smith (Eds.), *From prejudice to intergroup emotions: Differentiated reactions to social groups* (pp. 209-226). New York: Psychological Press.

Brown, R., & Turner, J. C. (1979). The criss-cross categorization effect in intergroup discrimination. *British Journal of Social and Clinical Psychology, 18,* 371-383.

Clark, M. S., Milberg, S., & Erber, R. (1984). Effects of arousal on judgments of others' emotions. *Journal of Personality and Social Psychology, 46,* 551-560.

Cuddy, A. J., Fiske, S. T., & Glick, P. (2004). When professionals become mothers, warmth doesn't cut the ice. *Journal of Social Issues, 60,* 701-718.

Cuddy, A. J. C., Fiske, S. T., & Glick, P. (2007). The BIAS map: Behaviors from intergroup affect and stereotypes. *Journal of Personality and Social Psychology, 92,* 631-648.

Cuddy, A. J., Norton, M. I., & Fiske, S. T. (2005). The old stereotype: The persistence and pervasiveness of the elderly stereotype. *Journal of Social Issues, 61,* 267-285.

Dépret, E. F., & Fiske, S. T. (1993). Social cognition and power: Some cognitive consequences of social structure as a source of control deprivation. In G. Weary, F. Gleicher, & K. Marsh (Eds.), *Control motivation and social cognition* (pp. 176-202). New York: Springer-Verlag.

Deutsch, M. (1958). Study of some factors which determine membership motivation and achievement motivation in a group. *Bulletin du C.E.R.P., 7,* 85-95.

Devos, T., Silver, L. A., Mackie, D. M., & Smith, E. R. (2002). Experiencing intergroup emotions. In D. Mackie & E. Smith (Eds.), *From prejudice to intergroup emotions: Differentiated reactions to social groups* (pp. 111-134). New York: Psychological Press.

Diener, E. (1979). Deindividuation, self-awareness, and disinhibition. *Journal of Personality and Social Psychology, 37,* 1160-1171.

Ebenbach, D. H., & Keltner, D. (1998). Power, emotion, and judgmental accuracy in social conflict: Motivating the cognitive miser. *Basic and Applied Social Psychology, 20*, 7-21.

Ellemers, N. (1994). The influence of socio-structural variables on identity management strategies. In W. Stroebe & M. Hewstone (Eds.), *European review of social psychology* (Vol. 4, pp. 27-58). Chichester, UK: Wiley.

Fiske, S. T. (1993). Controlling other people: The impact of power on stereotyping. *American Psychologist, 48*, 621-628.

Fiske, S. T. (2000). Interdependence reduces prejudice and stereotyping. In S. Oskamp (Ed.), *Reducing prejudice and discrimination* (pp. 115-135). Mahwah, NJ: Erlbaum.

Fiske, S. T., & Berdahl, J. (2007). Social power. In A. Kruglanski & E. T. Higgins (Eds.), *Social psychology: A handbook of basic principles* (2nd ed., pp. 678-692). New York: Guilford.

Fiske, S. T., & Cuddy, A. J. (2005). Stereotype content across cultures as a function of group status. In S. Guimond (Ed.), *Social comparison processes and levels of analysis.* Cambridge: Cambridge University Press.

Fiske, S. T., Cuddy, A. J., Glick, P., & Xu, J. (2002). A model of (often moxed) stereotype content: Competence and warmth respectively follow from perceived status and competition. *Journal of Personality and Social Psychology, 82*, 878-902.

Fiske, S. T., & Neuberg, S. L. (1990). A continuum model of impression formation, from category-based to individuating processes: Influence of information and motivation on attention and interpretation. In M. P. Zanna (Ed.), *Advances in experimental social psychology* (Vol. 23, pp. 1-74). New York: Academic Press.

Fiske, S. T., & Ruscher, J. B. (1993). Negative interdependence and prejudice: Whence the affect? In D. M. Mackie & D. L. Hamilton (Eds.), *Affect, cognition, and stereotyping: Interactive processes in group perception* (pp. 239-268). New York: Academic Press.

Fiske, S. T., Xu, J., Cuddy, A. C., & Glick, P. (1999). (Dis)respecting versus (dis)liking: Status and interdependence predict ambivalent stereotypes of competence and warmth. *Journal of Social Issues, 55*, 473-491.

French, J. R. P., Jr., & Raven, B. (1959). The bases of social power. In D. Cartwright (Ed.), *Studies in social power* (pp. 150-167). Ann Arbor, MI: Institute for Social Research.

Gaertner, S. L., Sedikides, C., & Graetz, K. (1999). In search of self-definition: Motivational primacy of the individual self, motivational primacy of the collective self, or contextual primacy? *Journal of Personality and Social Psychology, 76*, 5-18.

Guinote, A., Brown, M., & Fiske, S. T. (2006). Minority status decreases sense of control and increases interpretive processing. *Social Cognition, 24*, 169-186.

Guinote, A., Judd, C. M., & Brauer, M. (2002). Effects of power on perceived and objective group variability: Evidence that more powerful groups are more variable. *Journal of Personality and Social Psychology, 82*, 708-721.

Haslam, N. (2006). Dehumanization: An integrative review. *Review of Personality and Social Psychology, 10*, 252-264.

Hastorf, A. H., & Cantril, H. (1954). They saw a game: A case study. *Journal of Abnormal and Social Psychology, 49*, 129-134.

Hogg, M. A., & Abrams, D. (1988). *Social identifications: A social psychology of intergroup relations and group processes*. Florence, KY: Taylor & Frances/Routledge.

Isen, A. M. (1987). Positive affect, cognitive processes, and social behavior. In L. Berkowitz (Ed.), *Advances in experimental social psychology* (Vol. 20, pp. 203-253). New York: Academic Press.

Isen, A. M., & Levin, P. F. (1972). Effect of feeling good on helping: Cookies and kindness. *Journal of Personality and Social Psychology, 21*, 384-388.

Jones, E. E., Wood, G. C., & Quattrone, G. A. (1981). Perceived variability of personal characteristics in in-groups and out-groups: The role of knowledge and evaluation. *Personality and Social Psychology Bulletin, 7*, 523-528.

Keltner, D., Gruenfeld, D. H., & Anderson, C. (2003). Power, approach, and inhibition. *Psychological Review, 110*, 265-284.

Keltner, D., & Robinson, R. J. (1996). Extremism, power, and the imagined basis of social conflict. *Current Directions in Psychological Science, 5*, 101-105.

LeVine, R. A., & Campbell, D. T. (1972). *Ethnocentrism: Theories of conflict, ethnic attitudes, and group behavior*. Oxford, UK: John Wiley & Sons Inc.

Leyens, J. P., Rodriguez-Perez, A., Rodriguez-Torres, R., Gaunt, R., Paladino, M. P., Vaes, J., et al. (2001). Psychological essentialism and the differential attribution of uniquely human emotions to ingroups and outgroups. *European Journal of Social Psychology, 31*, 395-411.

Linville, P. W., & Jones, E. E. (1980). Polarized appraisals of out-group members. *Journal of Personality and Social Psychology, 38*, 689-703.

Linville, P. W., Salovey, P., & Fischer, G. W. (1986). Stereotyping and perceived distribution of social characteristics: An application to ingroup-outgroup perception. In S. Gaertner & J. Dovidio (Eds.), *Prejudice, discrimination and racism* (pp. 165-208). San Diego, CA: Academic Press.

Medin, D. L., & Ortony, A. (1989). Psychological essentialism. In S. Vosnaidou & A. Ortony (Eds.), *Similarity and analogical reasoning* (pp. 179-195). Cambridge: Cambridge University Press.

Neuberg, S. L., & Cottrell, C. A. (2002). Intergroup emotions: A biocultural approach. In D. Mackie & E. Smith (Eds.), *From prejudice to intergroup emotions: Differentiated reactions to social groups* (pp. 265-284). New York: Psychological Press.

Ng, S. H. (1982). Power and intergroup discrimination. In H. Tajfel (Ed.), *Social identity and intergroup relations* (pp. 179-206). Cambridge: Cambridge University Press.

Opotow, S. (1990). Moral exclusion and injustice: An introduction. *Journal of Social Issues, 46*, 1-20.

Park, B., & Rothbart, M. (1982). Perception of out-group homogeneity and levels of social categorization: Memory for the subordinate attributes of in-group and out-group members. *Journal of Personality and Social Psychology, 42*, 1051-1068.

Pettigrew, T. F. (1986). The intergroup contact hypothesis reconsidered. In R. Brown & M. Hewstone (Eds.), *Contact and conflict in intergroup encounters* (pp. 169-195). Cambridge, MA: Basil Blackwell Inc.

Pettigrew, T. F., & Tropp, L. R. (2000). Does intergroup contact reduce prejudice: Recent meta-analytic findings. In S. Oskamp (Ed.), *Reducing prejudice and discrimination* (pp. 93-114). Mahwah, NJ: Erlbaum.

Prentice, D. A., & Miller, D. T. (2007). Psychological essentialism of human categories. *Current Directions in Psychological Science, 16*, 202-206.

Quattrone, G. A., & Jones, E. E. (1980). The perception of variability within in-groups and out-groups: Implications for the law of small numbers. *Journal of Personality and Social Psychology, 38*, 141-152.

Raven, B. H., & French, J. R. P. (1958). Group support, legitimate power, and social influence. *Journal of Personality, 26*, 400-409.

Raven, B. H., & Kruglanski, A. W. (1970). Conflict and power. In P. G. Swingle (Ed.), *The structure of conflict* (pp. 69-109). New York: Academic Press.

Robinson, R. J., Keltner, D., Ward, A., & Ross, L. (1995). Actual versus assumed differences in construal: "Naïve Realism" in intergroup perception and conflict. *Journal of Personality and Social Psychology, 68*, 404-417.

Rosenberg, S., Nelson, C., & Vivekanathan, P. S. (1968). A multi-dimensional approach to the structure of personality impressions. *Journal of Personality and Social Psychology, 9*, 283-294.

Sherif, M. (1962). The self and reference groups: Meeting ground of individual and group approaches. *Annals of the New York Academy of Sciences, 96*, 797-813.

Sherif, M. (1966). *Group conflict and co-operation: Their social psychology*. London: Routledge & Kegan Paul.

Simon, B., & Brown, R. (1987). Perceived intragroup homogeneity in minority majority contexts. *Journal of Personality and Social Psychology, 53*, 703-711.

Simon, B., Mlicki, P., Johnston, L., Caetano, A., Warowick, M., van Knippenberg, A., et al. (1990). The effects of ingroup and outgroup homogeneity on ingroup favoritism, stereotyping and overestimation of relative ingroup size. *European Journal of Social Psychology, 20*, 519-523.

Simon, B., & Mummendey, A. (1990). Perceptions of relative group size and group homogeneity: We are the majority and they are all the same. *European Journal of Social Psychology, 20*, 351-356.

Staub, E. (1989). *The roots of evil: The origins of genocide and other group violence*. New York: Cambridge University Press.

Stephan, W. G., & Stephan, C. W. (1996). Predicting prejudice. *International Journal of Intercultural Relation, 20*, 409-426.

Stephan, W. G., & Stephan, C. W. (2000). An integrated threat theory of prejudice. In S. Oskamp (Ed.), *Reducing prejudice and discrimination* (pp. 23-45). Mahwah, NJ: Erlbaum.

Stephan, W. G., Ybarra, O., Martinez, C. M., Schwarwald, J., & Tur-Kaspa, M. (1998). Prejudice toward immigrants to Spain and Israel: An integrated threat theory analysis. *Journal of Cross-Cultural Psychology, 29*, 559-576.

Struch, N., & Schwartz, S. H. (1989). Intergroup aggression: Its predictors and distinctness from in-group bias. *Journal of Personality and Social Psychology, 56,* 364-373.

Tajfel, H. (1978). *Differentiation between social groups: Studies in the social psychology of intergroup relations.* Oxford, UK: Academic Press.

Tajfel, H., & Turner, J. C. (1979). The social identity theory of intergroup behavior. In W. Austin & S. Worchel (Eds.), *The social psychology of intergroup relations* (pp. 7-24). Chicago, IL: Nelson-Hall.

Thibaut, J. W., & Kelley, H. H. (1959). *The social psychology of groups.* New York: Wiley.

Van Knippenberg, A., & Ellemers, N. (1990). Social identity and intergroup differentiation processes. In W. Stroebe & M. Hewstone (Eds.), *European review of social psychology* (Vol. 1, pp. 137-170). Chichester, UK: Wiley.

Wilder, D. A. (1993a). Freezing intergroup evaluations: Anxiety fosters resistance to counterstereotypic information. In D. Abrams & M. Hogg (Eds.), *Group motivation: Social psychological perspectives* (pp. 68-86). Hertfordshire, UK: Harvester Wheatsheaf.

Wilder, D. A. (1993b). The role of anxiety in facilitating stereotypic judgments of out-group behavior. In D. Hamilton & D. Mackie (Eds.), *Affect, cognition, and stereotyping: Interactive processes in group perception* (pp. 87-109). San Diego, CA: Academic Press.

Wilder, D. A., & Thompson, J. E. (1980). Intergroup contact with independent manipulations on in-group and out-group interaction. *Journal of Personality and Social Psychology, 38,* 589-603.

Wolf, S., & Latané, B. (1985). Conformity, innovation and the psychosocial law. In S. Moscovici, G. Mugny, & E. Avernaet (Eds.), *Perspectives on minority influence* (pp. 201-215). Cambridge: Cambridge University Press.

CHAPTER 14

Social Identity, Legitimacy, and Intergroup Conflict: The Rocky Road to Reconciliation

RUSSELL SPEARS

Introduction and Overview

Any approach to reconciling groups first requires an understanding of intergroup conflict. Although this may seem an oblique way of approaching the issue of reconciliation, if (continuing) conflict is the enemy of reconciliation, then an important message of this chapter is *know thy enemy*. While all readers will probably accept the premise that reconciliation is a good thing, we should perhaps not be so presumptuous to assume that reconciliation must proceed at any cost, nor necessarily assume that conflict is always a bad thing. For such reasons I believe that reconciliation cannot easily be achieved unless conflict is *worked out* in the many senses this could be understood. It is partly with this in mind that we justify our focus here more on the conflict side of the equation, as a precondition for reconciliation, if you will. At first sight a positive message of this chapter is that the basis of discrimination and conflict between groups is perhaps not as inevitable or ingrained as some theories (or some readings of theories) have proposed. Social identity theory (our preferred theoretical framework) is often advanced as a theory supporting the almost inevitable nature of intergroup discrimination and conflict. We challenge this reading and argue that issues of legitimacy lie at the heart of processes that can prevent conflict and discrimination in the first place, and also provide a basis for reconciliation. At the same time, and in keeping with social identity theory, and also other *conflict* theories that preceded it (notably realistic conflict theory), conflict can be productive in many senses and not necessarily all bad. Although it is trivially true that reconciliation implies a preceding conflict, less trivial is the idea that reconciliation may require conflicts to be worked out rather than merely avoided.

In line with this theme, we argue here that legitimacy is a double-edged sword, providing a constraint not only on discrimination, but also on resistance that might lead injustice to be challenged. Legitimacy constraints can be productive in two different and potentially conflicting senses. They can constrain the negative side of conflict (prejudice and discrimination), a progressive and potentially productive aim. However, perceptions of legitimacy can also undermine challenges to inequalities that perhaps *should* be perceived as illegitimate or unjust. Legitimacy can thus play an *ideological* role in reinforcing the status quo. This form of constraint is less productive in a progressive political sense and the conservative nature of legitimacy becomes particularly apparent in the latter sections of the chapter.

The chapter is structured as follows. First we outline accounts that see discrimination between groups as almost inevitable products of our *group* nature, and then challenge this view. This leads into a discussion of how legitimacy and the content of group identity (norms and stereotypes) form bases by which discrimination may be constrained. We consider evidence from four domains to provide empirical support for the legitimacy constraint argument: (1) social stereotyping, (2) in-group bias and discrimination, (3) emotion-based forms of prejudice (specifically intergroup schadenfreude), and (4) perceptions of group (in)justice. Finally, we consider more explicitly how reconciliation fits into this social identity analysis of intergroup conflict tempered by legitimacy constraints, and indeed how it can add to it (as a final stage to speak).

Is Intergroup Conflict Inevitable? Challenging Social Determinism

Many approaches to prejudice and discrimination tend to view these phenomena as inevitable outcomes of human nature (personality, cognitive bias) or of our *group* nature. Essentializing prejudice and discrimination as part of our natures, whether as individuals or as groups, is problematic on two levels. In theoretical terms it neglects the role of social processes in the explanation of these social phenomena. In political terms it also leads to pessimistic conclusions about the ability to address conflicts between groups, the location of responsibility for them, and consequently, also the possibilities for reconciliation. We challenge such conceptualizations and use social identity theory as our theoretical basis to argue for a more contextual and contingent explanation for intergroup conflict, and therefore one open to social change.

The common reading of social identity theory, one that is sometimes portrayed in textbooks and secondary accounts, does not always do justice to our contextualist and contingent reading. A detailed defense of a more refined reading of social identity theory is provided in an earlier chapter (Spears, Jetten, & Doosje, 2001), so we will not reiterate these arguments in very great detail here, but for completeness, it is important to restate the main issues to ground our rationale that discrimination is highly socially regulated.

A major part of the project of social identity theory was to develop a social level explanation of intergroup behavior that was psychological and contextually located (Tajfel, 1972, 1978). It is ironic then that some of Tajfel's early writings have been taken as paving the way for analyses that locate the problems of stereotyping and prejudice in bias and distortion of the cognitive system (Tajfel, 1969; see for example, Hamilton, 1981). One criticism of this line of work is the tendency to psychologize the sources of conflict as the inevitable product of our cognitive apparatus, which also leads to pessimistic conclusions about the inevitability of prejudice and discrimination (Oakes, Haslam, & Turner, 1994; Oakes & Turner, 1990; Spears & Haslam, 1997).

Social identity theory was not yet developed in 1969, but an impetus to develop this theory arose from the minimal group experiments starting around that time (Tajfel, 1970). Many accounts of social identity theory focus perhaps disproportionately on the importance of this paradigm and also detect within it the notion that discrimination is inevitable. To remind ourselves, in this paradigm, participants are categorized on a trivial basis: Minimal groups have no history or future and there is often no knowledge or familiarity with the people in one's own group. Despite this minimal basis for social categorization, Tajfel and his colleagues demonstrated that participants would often discriminate in favor of their own group, not only by allocating more rewards to fellow in-group members, but sometimes doing so at the cost of absolute gain to the in-group (the maximum differentiation strategy). This finding has proved as controversial as it is robust, and remains the topic of fierce debate to this day (Bourhis, Turner, & Gagnon, 1997; Rabbie, Schot, & Visser, 1989; Stroebe, Lodewijkx, & Spears, 2005). The point to note here is that this was taken to mean that there is a basic and generic tendency to show in-group bias.

Ironically, the motive underlying the minimal group paradigm was for a critique of another form of social determinism, namely, the idea that conflicts of interests between groups will necessarily lead to conflict and discrimination between them. This is the idea derived from realistic group conflict theory (e.g., LeVine & Campbell, 1972; Sherif, 1967). To be clear, Tajfel was not denying the material basis for intergroup conflict and discrimination, but merely a mechanical and socially determinist form of this position (which presents perhaps more the reading than the reality of these original statements). One outcome, if not aim, of the minimal group studies was to show that conflicts of interests are not necessary for discrimination to occur. Just as important, the broader statement of the theory, which also addresses status hierarchies in natural groups, explains why discrimination and conflict might *not* occur when there are conflicts of interests in the unequal distribution of valued resources like status.

This latter aspect of the theory is often neglected by accounts that present social identity theory as claiming, on the basis of the minimal group experiments, that discrimination is an inevitable product of mere categorization. In the next section we provide a summary critique of this view. The central point to note here is that socially determinist accounts of intergroup conflict neglect the complexity and agency involved in intergroup relations. At a more political level, and in keeping with the theme of this book, they reduce hope of the prospects of social change in general, and reconciliation between groups in particular. It is the contingency of agency associated with conflict that open up the hope and scope for attempts at reconciliation once conflict is in train.

The problem of determinist accounts is not just a problem for simplistic readings of social identity theory but applies to other approaches. Evolutionary explanations of intergroup conflict often refer to the fact that we are social animals who find survival value in the trust and protection invested in the group (Gaertner & Insko, 2000). There is now clear evidence for the value of reciprocity and trust within groups, and some evidence that the size of these groups may be limited to the numbers of people we can know (Dunbar, 1993). However, the undoubted value of the *in-group* does not necessarily explain proactive hostility to out-groups. Moreover, in complex modern societies the question becomes which (in)group, and indeed how do we define the group? The issue of social categories that obviously have broad scope beyond the face-to-face groups also stretches this evolutionary argument.

Another contemporary theory that can be read as proposing a basic *main effect* of in-group bias or hostility between groups is social dominance theory (Sidanius & Pratto, 1999), which has arguably used the more simplistic reading of social identity theory as well as evolutionary arguments to ground these claims. A further example is recent work on *infrahumanization* in the attribution of emotions (Leyens et al., 2002). This work demonstrates that people have the tendency to attribute fewer uniquely human *secondary* emotions (emotions that require self-consciousness, such as pride and shame) to out-groups than to in-groups. A form of in-group bias that dehumanizes the out-group to some degree, some advocates have proposed this as a fairly generic and perhaps universal feature of intergroup relations.

We are not denying the possibility of dehumanization, nor that such processes have played a role in some of the worst atrocities and genocide of our times. However, we would argue that processes of in-group bias, at least when conscious and public, are highly contextually contingent and constrained. The issue of dehumanization raises a key theme that we draw on later. One process that bounds or constrains dehumanization in *othering* in my view, is the ironic consequences that this may have for our self and group perceptions. To dehumanize others runs the risk of dehumanizing ourselves, potentially rendering our *own* nature less human. One path to reconciliation then is the sense of humanity, and to treat others as we would be treated, associated with the superordinate group we all share as humans.

We do not have room to do full justice to these theories here, and as in all secondary accounts doubtless we too are guilty of oversimplification. While we do not doubt the empirical results on which they are based, our general argument is that matters are more complex than *main effects* predictions of intergroup hostility and the inevitability of discrimination would suggest. We consider discrimination and in-group bias to be much more socially regulated than any automatic or evolutionary impulse would suggest, and that herein lies hope of a potential answer to alleviate these conflicts and reconcile groups once conflicts have occurred.

Countering Determinist Accounts of Discrimination

As the reference to the analysis of discrimination in status hierarchies already suggests, social identity theory does not see intergroup discrimination as universal, as generic or constant, but as a product of particular social relations. It is useful to begin with the minimal group paradigm itself, from which determinist readings emerge. First it is important to stress that this was seen as adjunct to more materialist accounts of intergroup conflict, not a replacement for them (cf. Rabbie et al., 1989). Second, the stress on the effects of mere categorization are overstated, in so far as these social categories have to acquire some social meaning, some identification from the participants, for people to engage in discrimination—this does not flow automatically from the objective act of categorization itself but is psychologically mediated, involving the internalization of categories. This theme is reiterated and developed in self-categorization theory, which contrasts the assumption that simply imposing *sociological* categories will have effects, to analyzing those that are psychologically meaningful and relevant in context. This idea is already evident in the fact that not all people discriminate in the minimal group paradigm, and indeed a significant proportion of participants choose the fairness strategy.

Third, although the methods and measures of the minimal group paradigm are concerned with discrimination, the explanation is actually couched in terms of *differentiation*. Participants discriminate as the only available means to differentiate their group positively from the other group to gain a positive group distinctiveness. This theme has been largely neglected in favor of the so-called self-esteem hypothesis, that discrimination provides a positive social identity. However, an exclusive focus on self-esteem ultimately becomes individualistic and reductionist, whereas the focus on group distinctiveness maintains a group level to the analysis (Spears, Jetten, & Scheepers, 2002). Differentiation provides a way to make sense of the minimal situation as much as to gain something from it. In our recent work on this theme we have referred to this motive as *creative* distinctiveness (Spears et al., 2002).

In one study we received support for this idea by showing that actually giving feedback that a minimal group categorization was associated with a personality type (extraversion or introversion), was sufficient to reduce discrimination by providing a meaningful group identity, and thus abrogating the need for positive differentiation (Spears et al., 2002). In another set of studies, Scheepers, Spears, Doosje, and Manstead (2002) demonstrated that minimal groups were more likely to differentiate for these identity-based reasons (creative distinctiveness) whereas this effect was eliminated if there had been a previous differentiation opportunity, or if there was a goal of future intergroup competition, which by themselves provided the groups with meaning (see Spears et al., 2004).

We mention these examples here as some further evidence that in the minimal group paradigm in any case, differentiation is at least as important a motive as discrimination. These demonstrations question the simplistic generalization from *discrimination* in minimal groups to the *real* world. One implicit assumption has been that discrimination in minimal conditions helps to explain discrimination in more high impact real-life groups (if these effects obtain in minimal groups then real-life groups with material factors added should only be magnified, so the reasoning goes). If differentiation in minimal groups is (at least in part) about gaining a meaningful identity, then if anything, this motive should reduce in meaningful groups as our research shows.

A further respect in which intergroup conflict cannot be considered inevitable concerns the concept of identity salience outlined in social identity theory and developed further in self-categorization theory. Social identity theory locates behavior on an interpersonal-intergroup continuum with intergroup behavior only occurring in intergroup contexts. The minimal group paradigm, as Tajfel (1978) himself noted, is a very powerful group context in which the group identity is made highly salient so that people become maximally *depersonalized*, to use the self-categorization term (except of course those who simply reject the group basis for categorization). Self-categorization theory further developed the analysis of how salience might arise (Oakes, 1987). The key point here, however, is that intergroup conflict is predicated on people defining themselves in (certain) group terms, and although these may be sometimes dictated by the situation, there is room for choice and agency on the part of those involved as to whether they accept these terms (see Spears, Doosje, & Ellemers, 1999).

A further factor that undermines any claims for generic in-group bias in social identity theory concerns its analysis of status hierarchies (Tajfel & Turner, 1979), and subsequent work on power (e.g., Sachdev & Bourhis, 1985; Ng, 1980). In the original statement of the theory, Tajfel and Turner (1979) explain an absence of discrimination by low status groups toward high status groups, as reflecting the legitimacy of the status relation and the acceptance of the high status group position as justified and unchanging. Specifically, the theory argues that when status relations are both legitimate and stable, social comparison will be secure. It is worth noting that this argument is similar to the position adopted by system justification theory (Jost & Banaji, 1994), which has at times claimed that social identity theory is unable to account for out-group favoritism, when in fact this is explicitly addressed in the theory. We develop this point with respect to legitimacy further in our own research described below. For the moment then we can define legitimacy as the acceptance of existing group status differences, which may include inequality and disadvantage, as fair and just. Although social identity theory does not go into great detail as to why inequality may be accepted as legitimate (we elaborate on this point later) it relates legitimacy to the "absence of cognitive alternatives to the status quo" or in other words, the inability to conceive of the status hierarchy difference as being otherwise and/or being able to challenge it. It is worth reminding ourselves that this is not seen as a positive phenomenon: if social identity theory has a normative dimension it is to argue for contesting relations seen as unequal and unjust and to motivate social change. Social change liberating disadvantaged groups will most likely occur when low status groups perceive social relations to be illegitimate and unstable, resulting in insecure social comparisons and alternatives to the status quo.

It is appropriate to say something about the key theme of reconciliation at this juncture. Although statements of social identity theory have not been explicit about the issue of reconciliation between groups (this is one aim here), I would argue that implicit within it is the idea that illegitimate group differences need to be resolved if true reconciliation between groups is possible. True reconciliation implies that illegitimate group differences have been recognized and resolved ("worked out"). I return to this theme later in the chapter but for the moment the point is that legitimacy is as much part of the problem as the solution.

Social identity theory has paid more attention to the view from below than from above. The relation of the high status groups to low status groups is less well-developed, the assumption being perhaps that these should simply mirror the reactions to the low status group, with discrimination primarily necessary, and conflict likely, when social comparisons become insecure. The perspective from high status groups has been analyzed in some detail recently by Leach, Snider, and Iyer (2002). These authors develop and refine a social identity-based analysis, interpreting the intergroup relation in terms of perceived control as well as legitimacy and stability, and analyze the specific relations that result in terms of intergroup emotions. Rather than describe how these are predicted to vary according to the combination of each dimension, the more general point here is that the nature of the relation and reaction to the low status out-group is expected to be highly variable ranging from secure relations that result in positive albeit paternalistic reactions (e.g., "noblesse oblige") to relations that are insecure and more antagonistic, resulting in (different forms of) discrimination. At first sight this seems to also suggest some possibilities for reconciliation: if those with power and status are willing to show largesse to the disadvantaged group, maybe this is one source of optimism for reconciliation? This may be a false dawn, however, because it depends on the status relations remaining secure: once this becomes illegitimate intergroup competition discrimination may increase (although as we argue this may be necessary to reach reconciliation in the end).

In recent research, Scheepers, Spears, Doosje, and Manstead (2006) have also tried to analyze the different shades and forms that discrimination can take between groups of unequal status, and the different functions it can serve, depending on status (in)stability. This research distinguishes an identity affirming function (also addressed in the work above on minimal groups) from a more instrumental function directed at changing the status quo or pursuing group goals. In general, lower status groups are likely to be motivated by this instrumental function to improve on their disadvantaged position, and to use material forms of in-group bias that can help them towards this end. Higher status groups, on the other hand, already have a status advantage and are more likely to express in-group bias for more symbolic reasons celebrating and affirming their position (see also Klein, Spears, & Reicher, 2007).

A series of studies provide evidence for our analysis (Scheepers et al., 2002, 2006). Supporting social identity theory, low status groups were more likely to use more material/instrumental forms of in-group bias that could maximize advancing group goals (i.e., allocation of resources), especially when status was unstable. They were also more likely to do this when their responses were visible to the in-group and to moderate their responses when accountable to the out-group (lest they antagonize them). Interestingly however, a more aggressive strategy emerged when stability was low and stable. Here, low status groups were more likely to use the more antagonistic maximum differentiation strategy, also in the face of an out-group audience. We liken this to a "nothing to lose" strategy given the relatively hopeless situation of the low status group. We see shades of this strategy in the many real-life groupings who may feel quite literally that they have no other course of action (e.g., suicide bombers in Israel and Chechnya are some extreme but potent examples). The lesson for here is that reconciliation is unlikely when a group feels so threatened, and forced into a corner by the imbalance of power or political support, that violence and terror seems the only way out.

Social identity research analyzing the effects of power, has hitherto curiously neglected the issue of legitimacy at least in the experimental work (see Hornsey, Spears, Cremers, & Hogg, 2003 for an exception). We return to this later in our own work. Meanwhile the main conclusion of the complex work on power seems to show that groups with power seem to use it to justify and exercise discrimination (Ng, 1980; Sachdev & Bourhis, 1985; "usable power") which again could be taken to mean that power differentials will inevitably lead to discrimination. Equally determinist is the assumption that low power will never result in discrimination, which as we have seen from the previous paragraph is challenged by potent real life examples as well as our experimental analogues with stable low status. Low power does not necessarily mean that the motive to discriminate is absent, but simply that this may be difficult to carry out in the presence of a powerful out-group (Klein et al., 2007; Reicher, Spears, & Postmes, 1995).

This latter finding illustrates a more general point that also emerges from the social identity literature considering the role of identity threat in stimulating in-group bias. Low status can be considered threatening in itself and motivate discriminatory responses (although interestingly this seems to be true primarily in natural groups rather than laboratory groups; see Mullen, Brown, & Smith, 1992, and below). This is confirmed by the weaker evidence for instrumental bias by high status groups in the research described above (Scheepers et al., 2006). Status threat is not the only form of threat to group identity. In line with the positive group distinctiveness motive of social identity theory, identity can also be threatened by distinctiveness threat or groups that are too similar to one's own group (Tajfel, 1982), motivating differentiation and possibly also discrimination (see Jetten, Spears, & Postmes, 2004; Spears et al., 2002).

In contrast to the view that social identity theory presents discrimination as inevitable, Brewer (1999) has argued that the focus on in-group distinctiveness and enhancement motives means it is not well-placed to explain out-group derogation, and the extreme forms this can take. As the work already discussed shows it is questionable whether this is necessarily the case. Certain social-structural conditions in particular may evoke more extreme strategies such as "nothing to lose." However it is important not to dismiss this point lightly, not least because it reinforces the case against the inevitability of discrimination.

Empirical evidence supporting this critique is present in the literature on the so-called positive-negative asymmetry in in-group bias. Mummendey and colleagues in particular have provided much evidence from the minimal group paradigm showing that people are likely to discriminate when awarding allocations to both groups but are much less likely to show this bias when allocating negative rewards or punishments (e.g., deficits or aversive stimuli; see Mummendey & Otten, 1998). This would indeed seem to provide some evidence that more extreme forms of discrimination are less prevalent in experimental groups at least, and perhaps less easily explained by the social identity framework.

Self-categorization theorists have provided an interesting explanation for this asymmetry that speaks for an important theme we develop later. Reynolds, Turner, and Haslam (2000) explained the asymmetry in bias in terms of the concept of "normative fit" (Oakes, 1987). Specifically, the notion that one's in-group would withhold rewards from a group is not necessarily inconsistent with a positive in-group image (as a fair or reasonable people), but allocating punishments towards a group is more difficult to reconcile with a positive in-group image. In other words there is a poor normative fit between the action of "negative" discrimination and the expectation that the in-group should be fair, reasonable or just. This point fits well with the notion that (il)legitimacy is a critical barrier to discrimination, and the connection to the in-group self-image is a crucial part of this argument (see also the earlier argument about dehumanization). One reason why we do not discriminate against others is not only that it potentially dehumanizes them, but that in the process it may also dehumanize us. Appeals to humanity, both in terms of a shared superordinate identity and in terms of principles of justice are therefore likely to be important resources for reconciliation.

This line of argument also opens the door to the content of identity and group norms as key moderators of discrimination. Social identity theory addresses the content of social identity much less explicitly than does self-categorization theory (Turner, Hogg, Oakes, Reicher, & Wetherell, 1987). As well as relating identity content to identity salience and group norms, self-categorization theory provides a theory of social influence, proposing a mechanism for conformity to these norms. It follows that groups may also have norms about the appropriateness or legitimacy of discrimination. Research by Jetten, Spears, and Manstead (1996) provides evidence for such conformity even when this is set in opposition to other motives from social identity theory such as enhancement and distinctiveness principles. An in-group norm of fairness significantly reduced in-group bias in both minimal and established groups (Jetten et al., 1996). In general the ideological content of group identity and indeed society more generally, will provide a potentially important brake on discrimination towards out-groups.

The role of social stereotypes about groups may also be important group-level information that feeds into the discrimination processes even where these stereotypes do not explicitly prescribe behavior relating to fairness or discrimination. In particular, stereotypes, as relational differentiating beliefs that characterize groups, may also convey subtle status relevant information, which provide social reality constraints that feed into judgments of legitimacy. We develop this argument in detail in the next section.

One limitation of explanations of discrimination (or fairness) that implicate norms is that this does not seem to capture the passion and affect associated with discrimination, especially in its extreme forms (although we would argue that norms operate here too). One further line of theoretical development in social identity theory that is also concerned with identity content does address this affective dimension more explicitly. This concerns intergroup emotion theory (Smith, 1993; see also earlier work on relative deprivation), which explicitly builds on the social identity approach with the explicit aim of understanding the different forms and features of prejudice and discrimination (see also Leach et al., 2002). Rather than seeing prejudice and discrimination as a generic and unidimensional antipathy towards out-groups, this approach analyses forms of conflict and discrimination in terms of the specific relations between groups appraised in terms of dimensions such as status, power, and stability (in line with social identity principles). Applying emotion theory to this analysis, we can understand forms of prejudice in terms of the particular appraisals that result. For example, high power or status may lead to forms of prejudice based on anger, disgust, or contempt, whereas fear may characterize discrimination deriving from low power or status (Alexander, Brewer, & Herrmann, 1999; Fiske, Cuddy, Glick, & Xu, 2002; Leach et al., 2002). In the next section we review research on a particular form of prejudice, intergroup schadenfreude, and try to show how this may also be limited by legitimacy concerns.

To summarize, our argument so far is that in-group bias is neither inevitable nor unidimensional, and its status as a social product of a particular relationship between groups should only make it more amenable to challenge and change, and indeed to potential intergroup reconciliation. Such analyses should also help us to understand some of the underlying conditions that need to be addressed to challenge prejudice and discrimination and the ways in which reconciliation might be tackled. Rather than being "universal," discrimination seems to be more likely where threats to identity arise, and in the nexus of especially illegitimate status and power differences between groups. This is not to say that rivalry between groups of equal power and status cannot produce discrimination, as we shall see. In the remainder of the chapter we develop our argument that legitimacy constraints, implicating stereotypic and status relevant expectations about groups, provide an important impediment to various forms of discrimination.

Legitimacy and Discrimination

We now develop our argument that discrimination is socially constructed and constrained by exploring in more detail the role of legitimacy in this process. Although our main focus is on social identity theory, legitimacy processes have a rich history in social psychology and it is important to acknowledge this legacy. Exchange theory, equity theory, just world theory, and research on distributive, procedural and interactional justice are just some examples of approaches that point to the importance of legitimacy and justice concerns generally. However, few if any of these approaches systematically address the role of legitimacy as a constraint on discrimination. To pursue this goal, we develop the legitimacy theme outlined within social identity theory. In this context, legitimacy relates to the justification and acceptance of a status difference as justified and fair. You will recall that in line with social identity theory, legitimacy can be defined as the absence of cognitive alternatives to the status quo. However, one issue never fully explicitly addressed by social identity theory is the degree to which status differences might be internalized and accepted (the stronger sense of legitimate) or be legitimate only in the sense that they are difficult to challenge publicly because of social reality constraints, credibility concerns, and social costs of challenging them (see Spears et al., 2001, for an extensive discussion of this issue). This distinction between internally accepted versus privately contested forms of legitimacy is likely to form a continuum, which itself merges into the full illegitimacy that might become openly contested. We address examples of both levels of legitimacy constraint here, both internal and external.

Originally related to status hierarchies, we extend the analysis here into the realm of status associated with or implied by social stereotypes. Our basic thesis is that status and stereotypic expectations produce social reality constraints on what is considered legitimate behavior towards the groups concerned. We now illustrate this argument with research from four lines of research. Specifically, we consider research on stereotyping, discrimination, intergroup emotions and finally judgments of group justice themselves.

Social Stereotyping

The impact of social reality constraints on stereotypes that favor the in-group is illustrated in research by Doosje, Spears, and Koomen (1995). Two studies examined how the reliability of sample information could constrain the degree to which favorable stereotypic generalization to the groups as a whole would be possible. The assumption was that when sample information is favorable to the in-group, this would be generalized without a problem whether the sample information was reliable or not, as this confirms the preference of the perceiver. When the sample information was unfavorable, if it could be deemed unreliable, then it could be contested. However, when unfavorable feedback is based on reliable samples, it is more difficult to dispute, providing a social reality constraint and forcing perceivers to accept the unpalatable reality.

This is what we found. Using a quasi-minimal group paradigm we categorized participants as either "inductive" or "deductive" thinkers on the basis of bogus tests. After providing information about their own behavior they then received (false) feedback about the pro-social behavior of in-group and out-group members. In the first study we manipulated the favorability and variability of this sample information. In the second study we manipulated favorability and sample size. Both homogeneous and large samples were predicted to be too reliable and constraining to ignore. In both studies participants revealed the predicted group-serving response in the unfavorable unreliable sample conditions by questioning this information and failing to generalize the unfavorable views to the groups as a whole. However, when the sample information was more reliable (homogeneous or large samples) they felt compelled to generalize this information to the group as a whole: a social reality constraint.

Group Discrimination

In two studies Jetten, Spears, Hogg, and Manstead (2000), applied similar logic in the research just described to the realm of discrimination. In these studies participants were asked to judge products derived from the in-group and the out-group. As before, we manipulated both the favorabilty and reliability (variability) of sample information relating to a status-based dimension that differentiated in-group and out-group. We also measured group identification in this research, predicting that high identifiers would be more motivated to resist the implications of unfavorable information about the in-group.

In the first study, participants were categorized as detailed or global perceivers based on a bogus test. Group favorability was manipulated by informing participants that the in-group was either more or less accurate in terms of perceptual skills than the out-group. Participants also received graphical feedback concerning the alleged distribution of both in-group and out-group in terms of the underlying continuum (perceptual style), forming the group variability manipulation. Whereas high identifiers contested the unfavorable sample information when it was heterogeneous (unreliable), low identifiers did not. In short, the people most motivated to take advantage of a weak social reality constraint did so, but otherwise participants observed this social reality constraint and felt unable to express in-group bias in their judgment of group products when the status related feedback was more constraining (homogeneous samples).

The second study replicated this pattern with naturally occurring groups and also provided evidence for the mediating role of legitimacy. Students from the University of Amsterdam compared their group with students from the rival Free University of Amsterdam on the critical dimension of "study conscientiousness." High scores on this dimension were described as having important implications for career success. The in-group was described either as scoring lower than the out-group on this dimension (unfavorable) or as scoring higher (favorable). Participants again received variability feedback by means of the graphical representation of the intergroup distribution in terms of study conscientiousness.

Low identifiers did not show significant in-group bias on a resource allocation measure, as found in the previous study. However, significant in-group bias emerged for unfavorably depicted groups when the sample was heterogeneous, but only for high identifiers. Moreover, this effect was mediated by the perceived legitimacy of discrimination. Again, in-group bias was constrained, also for high identifiers, when the status related sample information was reliable and thus constraining (homogeneous samples depicting unfavorable differences between in-group and out-group).

In another study we used the minimal paradigm to examine legitimacy constraints in the context of groups with power differentials (Spears, de Wit, Grijzen, & Wigboldus, 2005). In this study all participants were assigned to a high power group. The legitimacy of the power assignment was manipulated such that in the legitimate condition participants learned that, because their group had scored higher on a (bogus) test, they were assigned to the high power condition, which gave them the right to allocate resources between groups. In an illegitimate condition participants received feedback that their group had actually performed *worse* on the test but shortly after this an orchestrated computer crash meant that the program had to be restarted part-way through, resulting in their group fortuitously being assigned to the high power condition. A "nonlegitimate" condition was also included in which power assignment was supposedly based on a coin-toss. We also manipulated the stability of the status relation by informing participants that there would be a second round of resource allocations for which the power relation was to be reassessed by means of another test (although there were no effects of this on the pattern of discrimination).

The key finding of this study was that the nonlegitimate condition was the only one where clear discrimination emerged; discrimination was reduced to nonsignificance in both the legitimate *and* illegitimate conditions. In the illegitimate condition we interpreted this as the result of a legitimacy constraint: participants may have been reluctant to favor their group given their unfair advantage. In the legitimate condition, participants may have felt sufficiently secure in their high status that they did not feel the need to discriminate in material terms (Leach et al., 2002). This fits with the contention that high status groups are more likely to discriminate on symbolic measures to affirm identity (Scheepers et al., 2006). The coin-toss condition was also the condition with greatest distinctiveness threat and rivalry between groups, conditions known to foster intergroup differentiation. These findings contradict the earlier social identity work by Sachdev and Bourhis, which suggests that high power groups are more likely to use their power to discriminate. This seems not to apply when there is a concern about the legitimacy of power (see also Hornsey et al., 2003).

Emotion-Based Prejudice: Intergroup Schadenfreude

Schadenfreude is the malicious pleasure at another's loss brought about by events or a third party, and can be viewed as a particular form of prejudice. Applied to the intergroup realm, this refers to the downfall of another group. Although some theorists have argued that schadenfreude is facilitated by envy or resentment towards the target (Feather, 1994; Smith et al., 1996), we have argued that the most fertile conditions for schadenfreude in intergroup contexts are conditions of rivalry with an out-group of roughly equal status (Leach, Spears, Branscombe, & Doosje, 2003; Spears & Leach, 2004, in press). This is because higher status groups (that evoke envy or resentment) can also produce a legitimacy constraint on the very experience of this emotion. This is particularly likely to be true if the rival has recently defeated the in-group.

Under normal circumstances being reminded of a defeat would suggest inferiority that could motivate feelings of schadenfreude to a rival's loss (Leach et al., 2003, Study 1). However, when the defeat comes from the same rival group that provides the subsequent schadenfreude opportunity, this provides a legitimacy constraint. It is difficult to celebrate the loss of a group that defeats one's own because their superiority could seem deserved and legitimate. It should be remembered that schadenfreude, by definition, is defeat of the rival by a third party, and so celebrating their loss does little to alleviate the source of this inferiority, and may reinforce a sense of impotence.

This potential legitimacy constraint was most clearly demonstrated in Study 2 of Leach et al. (2003). In this research Dutch participants were reminded of their country's own loss to Italy in a soccer tournament just prior to rating the Italian's later loss to another team (the schadenfreude opportunity). In this study we also manipulated exposure to an "honesty norm," presented positively as part of the Dutch stereotype to encourage truthful responding. We found that people who had low interest in soccer and who were subjected to this norm were less likely to report schadenfreude after being reminded of the Italian loss. We argued that the reminder of the recent loss to the Italians operated as a legitimacy constraint on the experience of schadenfreude at the Italian loss by the Dutch. In contrast, being reminded of the loss to Italy actually produced increased schadenfreude to an unrelated third-party rival (Germany), by serving as an acute inferiority threat.

This finding suggests that schadenfreude towards the rival responsible for recent defeats may indeed be limited by legitimacy concerns. We explored this theme in a further study. In this study we manipulated the competitive history between the rivals over a series of encounters to provide a more solid and realistic foundation of the legitimacy constraint, whilst retaining the loss to the rival in the most recent encounter to stimulate dejection and schadenfreude. In short, we tried to separate out the issue of dejection at a loss from more general conditions of superiority versus inferiority that can operate as legitimate constraint.

In one study (Spears & Leach, in press) students from the University of Amsterdam were presented with feedback about previous encounters between their university and their cross-city rival, the Free University, in an interuniversity quiz competition. The cover story explained that we were evaluating this quiz competition with a view to it being televised. This allowed us to present participants with feedback about the history of the competition to manipulate the legitimacy constraint. In all conditions the in-group had been beaten by their rival in the most recent encounter stimulating the dejection designed to motivate schadenfreude towards the rival. This was expected to be stronger when the honors were equally shared in past competitions (3 wins apiece) creating the conditions of maximal rivalry. However, in the condition where the rival had won all previous six encounters, we expected schadenfreude to be reduced because of legitimacy concerns. We also introduced a bogus pipeline manipulation, designed to reinforce truthful responding, both to reinforce admission of schadenfreude, and also the pain of dejection at the recent loss. This is because one well-known coping strategy to deal with painful defeats and threats to identity is denial (Lazarus, 1991). As predicted, schadenfreude was highest in the equal status condition but only when the pipeline was on (and was mediated by dejection at the defeat). Crucially, schadenfreude was lower in the condition where the out-group was superior consistent with the legitimacy constraint. This finding gives a compelling and conservative test of the legitimacy constraint given the strong intuition that we like to see the successful fall, especially those responsible for our own downfall. Yet it is precisely the sense of inferiority to the rival in this case that seems to constrain the schadenfreude.

In another study, we examined how stereotypes of groups, in this case gender stereotypes, might also serve to constrain feelings of schadenfreude (Speakman, 2005). In this study women participants read a scenario in which a male job candidate won the position ahead of a number of equally qualified female candidates. He is then later made redundant, after a reorganization, providing the schadenfreude opportunity. We manipulated the make-up of the appointment committee (all women or all men) to cue the possibility of sexist discrimination in the case of an all male committee. We also manipulated the domain of the job opportunity to reflect a stereotypic male gender domain (business) or a stereotypic female domain (working in a crèche). Our prediction was that the male target would be seen as least deserving of the appointment in the more prestigious male business domain, especially when the committee was all male (which was confirmed). However, it could also be that the domain provides a legitimacy constraint such that any resulting schadenfreude is reduced in the business domain. This is what we found: schadenfreude was actually highest (albeit nonsignificantly so) in the male committee-crèche condition.

Justice Judgments

A fourth, perhaps even more obvious domain in which to study the constraining effects of social reality and legitimacy is in the realm of justice judgments themselves. We examined this in a paradigm designed to compare the effect of distributive versus procedural justice on justice judgments (Spears, Platow, Leach, & Postmes, 2005). Distributive justice is concerned with (group) outcomes, whereas procedural justice is concerned with the fairness of procedures used to arrive at outcomes (such as fair and respectful treatment by authorities). In particular work by Tyler and colleagues, has argued that procedural justice concerns often outweigh the outcomes associated with distributive justice (e.g., Tyler, 1997). One of our interests in this research was whether legitimacy constraints might play a role in this process; it may be more legitimate to protest at procedures when these are manifestly unjust, but unequal group outcomes might be more difficult to protest. Who is to say that groups simply do not differ in their abilities, as there may be a legitimate status difference between groups? This is also where social stereotypes associated with gender are especially likely to play a role in constraining perceptions of injustice at group-level outcomes. We addressed this question in the context of gender and the stereotypes associated with success or competence in different domains. Specifically, if women are stereotypically associated with less success than men in particular domain, does this make it more difficult for them to perceive injustice and to protest?

We investigated this theme in a paradigm designed to compare the effects of distributive and procedural injustice in the domain of academic achievement. We focused our research on the perceptions of women students who, despite legion evidence of equal or even better academic performance compared to men, continue to suffer a status disadvantage in the opportunity structure. One obvious reason for this is gender discrimination. We presented our student women participants with feedback about the marking procedures and outcomes of some recent exams under the guise of having these evaluated by students. Participants received a graphic showing the distribution of marks on a particular course broken down by gender, which revealed either that the gender group scores shared essentially the same distribution (superimposed normal curves), or that male students scored better on average (i.e., an unequal, and thus potentially unfair outcome). The exams were always graded by a male marker and in half the conditions he was blind to the names of the students (a fair procedure) or was not, so that gender of student was visible to him (i.e., open to potentially unfair sexist procedural bias). Finally, a third factor in the design was the domain of the exam, which was manipulated to be one in which males were stereotypically superior (an applied statistics exam) or one in which women were stereotypically superior (communication studies). Participants then rated their perceptions of the exam on measures designed to tap both distributive and procedural injustice.

Two interactions in these ratings provided evidence for the operation of legitimacy constraints on the justice judgments. First of all the inequality of outcomes interacted with the type of justice judgments such that unequal outcomes were rated least just on the measure of *procedural* justice. This gives some credence to our argument that it may be more legitimate to protest injustice, even in terms of unequal outcomes, in *procedural* terms. To complain about outcomes may suggest sour grapes (because outcomes may be valid) but procedures that affect us all, individuals as well as groups, can more easily be questioned.

More relevant for the present focus on stereotypic legitimacy constraints was another reliable interaction between the inequality of outcomes and the stereotypic domain of the exam. There was no effect of the type of justice rating here, but both justice ratings were generally lower (more unjust) when there was an unequal outcome in the female stereotypic domain (communications studies). When the outcome was unequal in the *male* stereotypic domain (applied statistics) our women participants did not judge this outcome any less fair or just than an equal outcome in either domain. This signifies a clear legitimacy constraint based in stereotypic "social reality." Women feel less able to protest an outcome in which they are stereotypically worse (albeit perhaps not in reality) but they do feel able to do this where the stereotype favors them.

In a follow-up study we were interested in, the questions of whether such constraints were actually internalized and accepted, or just reflect the credibility gap of claiming injustice where this might seem difficult to sustain give the social reality constraint. To investigate this we replicated the design of the previous study, but presented the research as being carried out by people who might be seen as sympathetic to student concerns about sexist bias (researchers from the Women's Studies department working together with representatives from the Student's Union), or whether this was carried out by a less sympathetic or more neutral researcher (a male Professor from the Organizational Psychology area).

Although the evidence was complex, there were clear audience effects such that our respondents were more likely to say it was legitimate to complain about unjust outcomes and procedures when their responses were directed to a more sympathetic audience. This study provided some preliminary and suggestive evidence that the disadvantaged group does not necessarily accept the injustice, but may find it difficult to protest to a general or unsympathetic audience lest this be seen as lacking credibility (sour grapes).

Intergroup Conflict and Legitimacy:
Implications for Reconciliation

In the previous sections we have considered the contingency of group conflict, the role of legitimacy constraints in moderating such conflicts and even preventing them from occurring, from the perspective of the social identity approach. The final question to address is what we can learn from this analysis for the theme of reconciliation central to this volume. One possible conclusion one could draw is that reconciliation is not even needed in those cases where legitimacy constraints prevent intergroup conflicts from occurring in the first place. Although this may be true in one sense, this is a pessimistic and perhaps reactionary conclusion to draw from a normative political perspective. The implication is that if low status and disempowered groups know their place in society and accept this then we would have fewer conflicts across the globe. This might be true, but do we really propose this as the message to the oppressed and exploited groups of the world? This is certainly not the message of social identity theory; in normative mode Tajfel saw it as means to understand social change motivated by low status and disempowered minority groups contesting their position.

This is where it becomes necessary to see social conflict and reconciliation in a more productive (if not harmonious) relationship. This is what I meant at the start of this chapter when I said intergroup conflict has to be "worked out," for reconciliation to be possible. In this model reconciliation is the stage after group conflict, in which real group differences have been made clear, and resolved through struggle, and where groups come to terms with the shift in power and status produced. This means that both parties have to be aware of power and status differences as illegitimate. Groups that are unaware of their disadvantage, or not in a position to recognize it as illegitimate or to challenge this, are unlikely to be ready for true reconciliation. In these terms, reconciliation is more than the mere absence of conflict, it is the legitimate absence of the difference that might produce it. This conceptualization of reconciliation fits well into the classic social identity analysis in which perceptions of illegitimacy (cognitive alternatives to the status quo) will lead to social conflict and social change. In this model reconciliation comes at the end of intergroup conflict rather than preventing it. It can be defined as the process by which groups come to accept their new more equal status and power relationship as legitimate, ideally with some recognition that the past ones were illegitimate (indeed these two are intimately related). If this does not happen reconciliation may be difficult and short lived. It is possible that this process may be easier for the lower status or disempowered group because for them the change is in a positive direction. Even this may not be straightforward, however, because there may be lingering resentments about past injustices, especially if there is the perception that past injustices persist, perhaps in economic if not political ways. The massive inequalities that remain in South Africa between blacks and whites are an example of this, and a reminder of economic inequalities based on skin color that remain throughout the western world.

The process of acceptance and reconciliation may seem to be even more difficult for high status or powerful groups that have given up ground. What does this loss and reconciliation offer this group? Here legitimacy may work in a more progressive way. Such changes can be justified on a moral basis, that this is the right course of action and this is easier to square with a more positive and humane in-group image. Justice is its own reward, and to resist change by justifying the injustice of illegitimate power and status differences will require ideological work which may ultimately stigmatize identity, however powerful this ideological process (the "legitimizing myths" in the language of social dominance theory). Moral outrage may be a more potent emotional force here than group-based guilt, because it is focused on addressing persisting group inequality (true reconciliation), not just a self-focused reproach, absolving the "sins of our fathers" (cf. Doosje, Branscombe, Spears, & Manstead, 1998; Iyer, Leach, & Pedersen, 2004).

So although reconciliation is unlikely to be easy or straightforward, we can suggest from a social identity perspective that it may (paradoxically) be facilitated by conflicts that lead to equalizing social change, if these can be seen as legitimate. Of course these changes do not occur in a vacuum and the inputs and views of third parties may contribute to the pressure for legitimacy and change. Rather than seeing reconciliation as the antidote to intergroup conflict, from this social identity perspective we should perhaps see conflict and reconciliation in more symbiotic terms as part of the same process, with reconciliation only possible when intergroup conflicts (and the inequalities and injustices underlying them) are "worked out" as an active process. In these terms conflict may be necessary for reconciliation rather than its enemy. Legitimacy has a two-faced role in this process. It can prevent these conflicts coming to the surface but then the process of reconciliation may be deferred and delayed: legitimacy plays an ideological role in explaining and justifying inequality. However, legitimacy also has a role to play in helping people to come to terms with group losses as well as gains, when unjust consequences are "worked out."

Conclusions

Although we have not addressed the theme of intergroup reconciliation as directly as intergroup conflict in this chapter, we addressed it obliquely, in two ways. First we challenged the view that discrimination, prejudice, and in-group bias are somehow inevitable features of the intergroup landscape, and particularly contested the view that this derives from social identity theory (and if this sounds like a "straw group" argument, it is an image of social identity theory that persists). Our aim was to show how contingent discrimination is and to elaborate the conditions under which it is exacerbated and constrained. Second, in developing this point we have argued that legitimacy, a central theme of this volume, and within social identity theory, is in part responsible for the constraint on conflict as well as playing a role in resolving it though reconciliation. Legitimacy is a double-edged sword and has a negative as well as a positive side to it.

On the positive side, perceptions of legitimacy can restrain discrimination, helping to explain why prejudice and discrimination are not more widespread correlates of intergroup relations. Even where legitimacy does not constrain how we perceive out-groups, there is a moral dimension to self and in-group perceptions that limit or proscribe "inhuman" treatment of out-groups. This moral dimension provides a preventive injunction against discrimination, sowing seeds of guilt, or moral outrage that can limit transgressions against out-groups, and promote reconciliatory behavior when these occur.

The negative side of legitimacy is that it seems all too grounded in status, hierarchy, and the social stereotypes and group images that can reinforce these status hierarchies (Alexander et al., 1999; Fiske et al., 2002; Tajfel, 1981). There is a clear sense in which low status groups perhaps *should* be contesting the illegitimate sense of hierarchy, whether this be based on gender, class, "race" and ethnicity (or other group-level "status characteristics"), and breaking free from the assumption that some groups are less equal or deserving than others. Framed in this way it may be appropriate to distinguish discrimination displayed by privileged groups undeserving of their status advantage, from the in-group bias displayed by disadvantaged and discriminated groups trying to challenge the status quo.

It is clear that a social-psychological approach on its own cannot provide all the answers and that a more social and political perspective is needed to evaluate the contexts in which legitimacy can be constructive and progressive versus more conservative and retrograde. Such political choices of course will also influence what is seen as legitimate. So long as material inequalities exist, discrimination at least is likely to remain, and this may be as much a part of the solution as part of the problem. Perhaps a more legitimate form of "legitimacy" that constrains discrimination is therefore located in some utopian vision where status-based advantages have disappeared. Some definitions of respect involve the notion of being treated as an equal (Taylor, 1992) and this applies to the intergroup domain as much as the interpersonal domain. Some may question whether any such state is possible, social dominance theory being a notable example of pessimism in this regard. In the meantime the effects of legitimacy at least provide a welcome reminder that the dance of discrimination is at least one that is socially negotiated, and regulated, rather than the reflection of a more automatic and animal nature. As such there is a perpetual reminder that such phenomena are at least open to social restraint if not social change.

References

Alexander, M. G., Brewer, M. B., & Herrmann, R. K. (1999). Images and affect: A functional analysis of out-group stereotypes source. *Journal of Personality and Social Psychology, 77*, 78-93.

Bourhis, R. Y., Turner, J. C., & Gagnon, A. (1997). Interdependence, social identity and discrimination. In R. Spears, P. J. Oakes, N. Ellemers, & S. A. Haslam (Eds.), *The social psychology of stereotyping and group life* (pp. 273-295). Oxford, UK: Blackwell Publishers Ltd.

Brewer, M. B. (1999). The psychology of prejudice: Ingroup love or outgroup hate? *Journal of Social Issues, 55*, 429-444.

Doosje, B., Branscombe, N. R., Spears, R., & Manstead, A. S. R. (1998). Guilty by association: When one's group has a negative history. *Journal of Personality and Social Psychology, 75*, 872-886.

Doosje, B., Spears, R., & Koomen, W. (1995). When bad isn't all bad: The strategic use of sample information in generalization and stereotyping. *Journal of Personality and Social psychology, 69*, 642-655.

Dunbar, R. I. M. (1993). Co-evolution of neocortical size, group size and language in humans. *Behavioral and Brain sciences, 16*, 681-735.

Feather, N. T. (1994). Attitudes toward high achievers and reactions to their fall: Theory and research concerning tall poppies. *Advances in Experimental Social Psychology, 26*, 1-73.

Fiske, S. T., Cuddy, A. J. C., Glick, P., & Xu, J. (2002). A model of (often mixed) stereotype content: Competence and warmth respectively follow from perceived status and competition. *Journal of Personality and Social Psychology, 82*, 878-902.

Gaertner, L., & Insko, C. A. (2000). Intergroup discrimination in the minimal group paradigm: Categorization, reciprocation or fear? *Journal of Personality and Social Psychology, 79*, 77-94.

Hamilton, D. L. (Ed.) (1981). *Cognitive processes in stereotyping and intergroup behavior*. Hillsdale, NJ: Erlbaum.

Hornsey, M. J., Spears, R., Cremers, I., & Hogg, M. A. (2003). Relations between high and low power groups: The importance of legitimacy. *Personality and Social Psychology Bulletin, 29*, 216-227.

Iyer, A., Leach, C. W., & Pedersen, A. (2004). Racial wrongs and restitutions: The role of guilt and other group-based emotions. In N. R. Branscombe & B. Doosje (Eds.), *Collective guilt: International perspectives* (pp. 262-283). New York: Cambridge University Press.

Jetten, J., Spears, R., Hogg, M. A., & Manstead, A. S. R. (2000). Discrimination constrained and justified: The variable effects of group variability and ingroup identification. *Journal of Experimental Social Psychology, 36*, 329-356.

Jetten, J., Spears, R., & Manstead, A. S. R. (1996). Intergroup norms and intergroup discrimination: Distinctive self-categorization and social identity effects. *Journal of Personality and Social Psychology, 71*, 1222-1233.

Jetten, J., Spears, R., & Postmes, T. (2004). Intergroup distinctiveness and differentiation: A meta-analytic integration. *Journal of Personality and Social Psychology, 86,* 862-879.

Jost, J. T., & Banaji, M. R. (1994). The role of stereotyping in system-justification and the production of false consciousness. *British Journal of Social Psychology, 33,* 1-27.

Klein, O., Spears, R., & Reicher, S. (2007). Social identity performance: Extending the strategic side of the SIDE model. *Personality and Social Psychology Review, 11,* 28-45.

Lazarus, R. S. (1991). *Emotion and adaptation.* New York: Oxford University Press.

Leach, C. W., Snider, S., & Iyer, A. (2002). "Poisoning the consciences of the fortunate": The experience of relative advantage and support for social equality. In I. Walker & H. J. Smith (Eds.), *Relative deprivation: specification, development, and integration* (pp. 136-163). New York: Cambridge University Press.

Leach, C. W., & Spears, R., Branscombe, N. R., & Doosje, B. (2003). Malicious pleasure: *Schadenfreude* at the suffering of another group. *Journal of Personality and Social Psychology, 84,* 932-943.

LeVine, R. A., & Campbell, D. T. (1972). *Ethnocentrism: Theories of conflict, ethnic attitudes and group behavior.* New York: Wiley.

Leyens, J. P., Paladino, P. M., Rodriguez-Torres, R., Vaes, J., Demoulin, S., Rodriguez-Perez, A., et al. (2002). The emotional side of prejudice: The attribution of secondary emotions to ingroups and outgroups. *Personality and Social Psychology Review, 4,* 186-197.

Mullen, B., Brown, R., & Smith, C. (1992). Ingroup bias as a function of salience, relevance, and status: An integration. *European Journal of Social Psychology, 22,* 103-122.

Mummendey, A., & Otten, S. (1998). Positive-negative asymmetry in social discrimination. *European Review of Social Psychology, 9,* 107-143.

Ng, S. H. (1980). *The social psychology of power.* New York: Academic Press.

Oakes, P. J. (1987). The salience of social categories. In J. C. Turner, M. A. Hogg, P. J. Oakes, S. D. Reicher, & M. S. Wetherell (Eds.), *Rediscovering the social group: A self-categorization theory* (pp. 117-141). Oxford, UK: Basil Blackwell.

Oakes, P. J., Haslam, S. A., & Turner, J. C. (1994). *Stereotyping and social reality.* Oxford, UK: Blackwell.

Oakes, P. J., & Turner, J. C. (1990). Is limited information processing the cause of social stereotyping? In W. Stroebe & M. Hewstone (Eds.), *European review of social psychology* (Vol. 1, pp. 111-135). Chichester, UK: Wiley.

Rabbie, J. M., Schot, J. C., & Visser, L. (1989). Social identity theory: A conceptual and empirical critique from the perspective of a behavioural interaction model. *European Journal of Social Psychology, 19,* 171-202.

Reicher, S. D., Spears, R., & Postmes, T. (1995). A social identity model of deindividuation phenomena. *European Review of Social Psychology, 6,* 161-198.

Reynolds, K. J., Turner, J. C., & Haslam, S. A. (2000). When are we better than them and they worse than us? A closer look at social discrimination in positive and negative domains. *Journal of Personality and Social Psychology, 78,* 64-80.

Sachdev, I., & Bourhis, R. Y. (1985). Social categorization and power differentials in group relations. *European Journal of Social Psychology, 15,* 415-434.

Scheepers, D., Spears, R., Doosje, B., & Manstead, A. S. R. (2002). Integrating identity and instrumental approaches to intergroup differentiation: Different contexts, different motives. *Personality and Social Psychology Bulletin, 28,* 1455-1467.

Scheepers, D., Spears, R., Doosje, B., & Manstead, A. S. R. (2006). Diversity in in-group bias: Structural factors, situational features, and social functions. *Journal of Personality and Social Psychology, 90,* 944-960.

Sherif, M. (1967). *Group conflict and co-operation: Their social psychology.* London: Routledge and Kegan Paul.

Sidanius, J., & Pratto, F. (1999). *An intergroup theory of social hierarchy and oppression.* Cambridge: Cambridge University Press.

Smith, E. R. (1993). Social identity and social emotions: Toward a new conceptualization of prejudice. In D. M. Mackie & D. L. Hamilton (Eds.), *Affect, cognition, and stereotyping* (pp. 297-315). San Diego, CA: Academic Press.

Smith, R. H., Turner, T. J., Garonzik, R., Leach, C. W., Urch, V., & Weston, C. (1996). Envy and schadenfreude. *Personality and Social Psychology Bulletin, 22,* 158-168.

Speakman, K. (2005). *The effects of perceived deservingness and feelings of envy on intergroup schadenfreude between men and women in the workplace.* Final year project, Cardiff University, Wales, UK.

Spears, R., de Wit, S., Grijzen, P., & Wigboldus, D. (2005). *Power and intergroup discrimination: The role of legitimacy, stability, and collective esteem.* Unpublished manuscript, University of Amsterdam, Amsterdam.

Spears, R., Doosje, B., & Ellemers, N. (1999). Commitment and the context of social perception. In N. Ellemers, R. Spears, & B. Doosje (Eds.), *Social identity: Context, commitment, content* (pp. 59-83). Oxford, UK: Blackwell.

Spears, R., & Haslam, S. A. (1997). Stereotyping and the burden of cognitive load. In R. Spears, P. J. Oakes, N. Ellemers, & S. A. Haslam (Eds.), *The social psychology of stereotyping and group life* (pp. 171-207). Oxford, UK: Blackwell.

Spears, R., Jetten, J., & Doosje, B. (2001). The (il)legitimacy of ingroup bias: From social reality to social resistance. In J. Jost & B. Major (Eds.), *The psychology of legitimacy: Emerging perspectives on ideology, justice, and intergroup relations* (pp. 332-362). New York: Cambridge University Press.

Spears, R., Jetten, J., & Scheepers, D. (2002). Distinctiveness and the definition of collective self: A tripartite model. In A. Tesser, J. V. Wood, & D. A. Stapel (Eds.), *Self and motivation: Emerging psychological perspectives* (pp. 147-171). Lexington, KY: American Psychological Association.

Spears, R., & Leach, C. W. (2004). Intergroup schadenfreude: Conditions and consequences. In C. W. Leach & L. Z. Tiedens (Eds.), *The social life of emotions* (pp. 336-355). Cambridge: Cambridge University Press.

Spears, R., & Leach, C. W. (in press). Why neighbours don't stop the killing: Group-based schadenfreude. In V. Esses & R. Vernon (Eds.),). *Why neighbors don't stop the killing: Group-based schadenfreude.* Oxford: Blackwell.

Spears, R., Platow, M., Leach, C. W., & Postmes, T. (2005, September). *The limits of legitimacy: Status-based stereotypes suppress feelings of injustice and unjust feelings.* EAESP Small Group Meeting on Justice and Intergroup Conflict, Lisbon.

Spears, R., Scheepers, D., Jetten, J., Doosje, B., Ellemers, N., & Postmes, T. (2004). Entitativity, group distinctiveness and social identity: Getting and using social structure. In V. Yzerbyt, C. M. Judd, & O. Corneille (Eds.), *The psychology of group perception: Contributions to the study of homogeneity, entitativity and essentialism* (pp. 293-316). Philadelphia, PA: Psychology Press.

Stroebe, K. E., Lodewijkx, H. F. M., & Spears, R. (2005). Do unto others as they do unto you: Reciprocity and social identification as determinants of in-group favoritism. *Personality and Social Psychology Bulletin, 31,* 831-846.

Tajfel, H. (1969). Cognitive aspects of prejudice. *Journal of Social Issues, 25,* 79-97.

Tajfel, H. (1970). Experiments in intergroup discrimination. *Scientific American, 223,* 96-102.

Tajfel, H. (1972). Experiments in a vacuum. In J. Israel & H. Tajfel (Eds.), *The context of social psychology* (pp. 69-119). London: Academic Press.

Tajfel, H. (Ed.) (1978). *Differentiation between social groups: Studies in the social psychology of intergroup relations.* London: Academic Press.

Tajfel, H. (1981). Social stereotypes and social groups. In J. C. Turner & H. Giles (Eds.), *Intergroup behaviour* (pp. 144-167). Oxford, UK: Blackwell; Chicago: University of Chicago Press.

Tajfel, H. (1982). Social psychology of intergroup relations. *Annual Review of Psychology, 33,* 1-39.

Tajfel, H., & Turner, J. C. (1979). An integrative theory of intergroup conflict. In W. G. Austin & S. Worchel (Eds.), *The social psychology of intergroup relations* (pp. 33-48). Monterey, CA: Brooks/Cole.

Taylor, C. (1992). The politics of recognition. In A. Gutman (Ed.), *Multiculturalism and the politics of recognition* (pp. 25-74). Princeton, NJ: Princeton University Press.

Turner, J. C., Hogg, M. A., Oakes, P. J., Reicher, S. D., & Wetherell, M. S. (1987). *Rediscovering the social group: A self-categorization theory.* Oxford, UK: Basil Blackwell.

Tyler, T. R. (1997). The psychology of legitimacy. *Personality and Social Psychology Review, 1,* 323-344.

CHAPTER 15

Intergroup Relations and Reconciliation: Theoretical Analysis and Methodological Implications

Thomas E. Malloy

Humans form groups in order to survive; membership in a collective affords safety, task allocation, close relationships, a collective social identity, and a common fate (Campbell, 1958). Powerful groups claim desirable resources that enhance members' welfare at the expense of less powerful groups, and history is replete with instances of intergroup conflict over material (Campbell, 1965; Halloway, 1974; Heylighen & Campbell, 1995; LeVine & Campbell, 1972) and social (Tajfel & Turner, 1979) resources. It is axiomatic that group formation provides an in-group advantage that also breeds intergroup conflict.

The Continuum of Intergroup Relations

Violent conflict and altruistic cooperation represent opposite ends of a continuum of intergroup relations with a midpoint of peaceful coexistence. Along this continuum intergroup relations are reciprocal. Deutsch's (1973) "law of social relationships" states that "characteristic processes and effects elicited by a given type of social relationship (cooperative or competitive) tend also to elicit that type of social relationship" (p. 365). Sherif and Sherif (1979) claimed that interaction between groups "is determined by the reciprocal interests and the goals of the groups involved" (p. 10). A basic assumption made here is that intergroup relations are typically competitive though nonviolent, and that reciprocal violence and altruistic cooperation are atypical cases.

Reconciliation: Change in the Reciprocal Responses of Groups

To reconcile, groups must transition from reciprocal conflict to peaceful coexistence and mutual acceptance; in some rare cases reconciliation can lead to reciprocal trust and support for attainment of material and social reinforcement. Weaver and de Waal (2003) defined reconciliation as "the exchange of friendly behavior between those involved in a fight (former opponents)" and view the phenomenon as an evolved social mechanism that maintains homeostatic autonomic arousal in individuals. Reconciliation has been observed in a number of primate species, including humans (de Waal, 2000), and may occur at different levels of analysis: in dyads, within an intact group, and between groups. A well-developed literature on reconciliation among primates at the dyadic and intragroup levels exists (see Weaver & de Waal, 2003); only recently has attention been directed to the intergroup context by social psychologists (e.g., Nadler & Laviatan, 2006).

Intragroup Reconciliation

When individuals' outcomes are mutually dependent, for example within a marriage, a peer group, or a primate colony, reconciliation is essential to maintain the structural integrity of the unit, to reduce members' tension, and to maximize individuals' reinforcement. Within groups, high status members will diffuse others' conflicts, those with a vested interest in the opponents will intervene, and third parties will mediate reconciliation (de Waal, 2000).

Intergroup Reconciliation

Reconciliation processes have also been observed in the intergroup context (Judge & de Waal, 1994), however this is much more complex than intragroup reconciliation because mutual dependency may be absent, or not perceived by the antagonists. In some cases groups have never had a cooperative relationship;

historically their interactions have been characterized by status asymmetry, inequality, mistrust, dislike, or violence. Moreover, antagonists may not believe that mutual outcome dependency can be achieved or, because of intense hatred, may not wish to positively engage the enemy. These are variables that moderate intergroup relations and set limits on reconciliation, which, like conflict, is a special case of intergroup relations. Reconciliation is a reciprocal phenomenon, unfolding over time characterized by a transition from conflict to peaceful coexistence, or possibly, cooperation. An assumption made here is that the "friendly behavior" witnessed in intragroup reconciliation may be an unrealistic short-term goal in most cases of intergroup reconciliation, especially when groups have a long history of acrimony and violence. Peaceful coexistence is likely a more realistic outcome in these cases. The basic questions for a social psychology of reconciliation are "what system of variables affects reciprocal intergroup responses?" and "what variables affect the transition from intergroup conflict to peaceful coexistence?" A theoretical analysis of intergroup relations and the implications for reconciliation follows. Also considered is a theoretical model of intergroup relations and two forms of reciprocity that are relevant to reconciliation.

Basic Constructs in Intergroup Relations

The science of intergroup relations is in its "infancy" (Brewer & Brown, 1998), and no "adequate theory of intergroup relations" exists (Mackie & Smith, 1998). Yet, to understand reconciliation a conceptual model of intergroup relations is necessary so that the empirical agenda is guided by an integrated, general conceptual framework. Decades of work reveal four basic constructs that determine intergroup relations; they are ethnocentrism, stereotypes, affect, and the perceived equality of opportunity for resource attainment. Often treated as separate research topics, the Intergroup Relations Model (IRM), elaborated later, is proposed to integrate these constructs and can explain a broad range of intergroup phenomena including reconciliation. Intergroup relations are conceptualized using Sherif's (1966) definition: "Whenever individuals belonging to one group interact, collectively or individually, with another group or its members in terms of their group identification, we have an instance of intergroup behavior" (p. 12).

Ethnocentrism

Since Sumner's seminal analysis (1906), social psychology has focused on intergroup attitudes (e.g., Austin & Worchel, 1979; Brewer & Campbell, 1976; Brewer & Brown, 1998; Brigham, 1971; Brown, 1986; LeVine & Campbell, 1972;

Mackie & Smith, 1998; Pronin, Gilovich, & Ross, 2004; Sherif & Sherif, 1979). Brewer and Campbell's (1976) research on ethnocentrism among East African tribes revealed that groups "without exception, rate their in-group more favorably than it is rated by any other outgroup" (p. 143). Substantial data document in-group ethnocentrism (Brewer & Brown, 1998; Mullen & Hu, 1989; Sherif, Harvery, White, Hood, & Sherif, 1961; Stephan, 1985).

Because groups are contexts for social identity development (Brown, 2000; Tajfel, 1978, 1982; Turner, 1987), processes relevant to the personal self operate similarly in groups (Crocker & Park, 2004). Individuals are motivated to view themselves, and have others view them, positively (Taylor & Brown, 1988), and this is also true in the intergroup context (Turner, 1987). Individually and collectively, people are naïve realists who assume the correctness, validity, and superiority of their worldviews (Pronin et al., 2004) while exaggerating perceived differences between groups (Robinson, Keltner, Ward, & Ross, 1995) that precludes appreciation of similarity and a common fate (Ross & Ward, 1996). Ethnocentrism is most virulent among groups in immediate proximity (Brewer & Campbell, 1976; Mackie & Smith, 1998) because of competition for the same resources (Esses, Dovidio, Jackson, & Armstrong, 2001).

Stereotypes: Shared Social Consensus

Group membership is associated with a litany of defining features (e.g., Allport, 1954; Brigham, 1971; Dovidio, Brigham, Johnson, & Gaertner, 1996; Fiske, 1998; Hamilton, 1981; Katz & Braly, 1933). Allport (1954) stated, "life becomes easier when the category is not differentiated. To consider every member of a group as endowed with the same traits saves us the pain of dealing with them as individuals" (p. 169). Categorization of individuals into the "we" and "they" groups affects perceived variability and covariability of members' traits. Restricted variability often characterizes out-group judgments, whereas the variability of in-group members is acknowledged (e.g., Mullen & Hu, 1989). Category stereotypes are efficient, and even necessary, for information processing. The expectation that all triangles have three sides is rational, however expectations are degenerative when perceived invariance is irrational (e.g., most Muslims are terrorist sympathizers).

Perceived Equality of Opportunity for Resource Attainment

Successful competition with other groups for material resources is one function served by group formation (Campbell, 1965; Heylighen & Campbell, 1995), although groups also compete for social resources such as status, prestige, power, respect, and positive social identity (Sidanius & Pratto, 2001; Tajfel, 1982; Turner, 1987). Groups compare their resource attainment to determine if, given equivalent effort, reward is equitable (Festinger, 1954; Homans, 1974). Even when competition is fair and resource attainment is equal, groups are inclined to perceive their "share" as inequitable (Brown, 1986, 1988; Pronin et al., 2004), and such perceptions moderate intergroup processes (Brown, 1986; Dovidio et al., 2004; Fiske, 2004; Keltner, Gruenfeld, & Anderson, 2003; Pruitt, 1998) including reconciliation. Groups perceived as high status competitors are seen as cold, whereas groups that do not pose a competitive challenge are seen as warm (Fiske, Cuddy, Glick, & Xu, 2002). When advantaged groups perceive competitive injustice, prejudice toward the disadvantaged may decrease (Dovidio et al., 2004), or inequity may be justified (Sidanius & Pratto, 2001).

Intragroup and Intergroup Affect

Group identification facilitates self-definition (Tajfel & Turner, 1979; Turner, 1982) when membership is "emotionally significant" (Brewer & Brown, 1998). The concepts of "we" and "us" activate positive affect outside of awareness (Perdue, Dovidio, Gurtman, & Tyler, 1990); likewise, affect is implicated in responses to an out-group. If an out-group threatens the security of the in-group (Fiske et al., 2002; Stephan & Stephan, 2000), or challenges defining features of that group's identity (Branscombe, Ellemers, Spears, & Doosje, 1999) negative affect is a consequence. When competing for social resources such as status, members take malicious pleasure (i.e., Schadenfreude) in the competition's defeat (Leach, Spears, Branscombe, & Doosje, 2003). When competing for resources, intergroup relations "take on an emotional valence from the beginning, with its character being negative and competitive" (Blake & Mouton, 1979, p. 31). When one is a member of a group, its outcomes determine the emotions experienced by a member, and intergroup emotions impact intergroup behaviors (Dijker, Koomen, van den Heuvel, & Frijida, 1996; Mackie, Devos, & Smith, 2000). When a group has high status (Blanz, Mummendey, & Otten, 1995; Mullen, Brown, & Smith, 1992), disproportionate resource accumulation (Sidanius & Pratto, 2001; Staub, 1996), or superior power (Keltner et al., 2003), there is an inclination to experience negative emotion toward and move against an out-group.

A group that controls attainment of material (e.g., food, economic opportunity, safety) and social (positive identity, respect, trust) resources has greater social power than one lacking this control (Keltner et al., 2003). Power asymmetry varies as a function of social construal (Sidanius & Pratto, 2001) and objective group characteristics (e.g., size, wealth, or weaponry). Whether power is arbitrary or objective, high social power is expected to produce positive affect, attention to reward attainment, contempt for, and an undifferentiated view of groups with low power. Low social power will produce frustration, negative affect, humiliation, mistrust, attention to threat, and differentiation of the characteristics of the powerful because they control reinforcement (Keltner et al., 2003). Studies of interactions of stigmatized and nonstigmatized persons (e.g., Miller & Malloy, 2003), and persons with different status (e.g., Anderson & Berdahl, 2002; Fiske, 1993; Guinote, Judd, & Brauer, 2002) provide confirming data. Affect appears to play a central role in intergroup relations functioning as a mediator between intergroup cognition and behavior.

Implications for Intergroup Reconciliation

The transition from conflict to peaceful coexistence must entail a change in reciprocal intergroup ethnocentrism, stereotypes, affect, and ultimately behavior. When groups in conflict view one another as members of a super-ordinate category (e.g., humanity) ethnocentrism, negative stereotypes, and negative affect should abate (Gaertner & Dovidio, 2005). Likewise, viewing one's antagonists inclusively affects the standards of justice used to evaluate past and present actions toward them, and emotional responsibility for injustice perpetrated (Wohl & Branscombe, 2005). However, ethnocentrism, negative stereotypes, and hatred will only change if power asymmetries are reduced so that different groups perceive an equal opportunity for material and social resource attainment. Optimally, resource attainment would be mutually dependent with antagonistic groups deriving positive outcomes that replace the costly price of conflict (de Waal, 2000). Below the IRM is proposed to explain intergroup relations and specify the conditions that will promote reconciliation.

The Intergroup Relations Model

The Intergroup Relations Model (IRM) specifies cognitive and affective processes that determine intergroup behavior and is presented as a latent variable model in Figure 15.1. In the IRM the most proximate determinant of intergroup behavior is affect that is itself determined jointly by ethnocentrism and stereotypes. This specification assumes further that ethnocentrism and stereotypes are correlated constructs. The cognition-affect-behavior mediational model

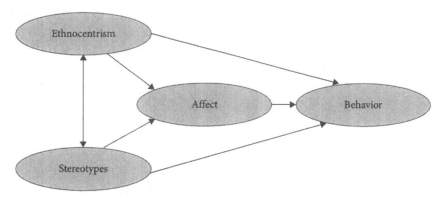

FIGURE 15.1. Intergroup relations model.

diagramed in Figure 15.1 is presumed to be *moderated* by groups' equality of opportunity for resource (i.e., material and social) attainment. For example, Blacks and Hispanics in America living in adjacent neighborhoods compete, equally or unequally, for the same resources (e.g., jobs). America and al Qaeda seek to annihilate each other because each fears domination by the other, while America and Great Britain compete economically yet offer mutual support. Most generally, the basic moderator of IRM processes is the perceived equality of opportunity for procurement of material and social resources and is discussed in the next section.

The IRM is consistent with other models that specify intergroup emotion as the proximate cause of behavior (Mackie et al., 2000; Smith, 1993). The IRM also shares some similarities with Stephan and Stephan's (2000) integrated threat theory in which perceptions and negative contact affect intergroup anxiety and threat that, in turn, affect attitudes toward a group. The IRM is also consistent with the social identity (Tajfel & Turner, 1979) and self-categorization (Turner, 1987) theories that postulate incorporation of the social identity as a facet of the individual, psychological self that is implicated in responses to both in- and out-groups. The IRM is also influenced by the view that intergroup relations are fundamentally competitive (Campbell, 1965; Hardin, 1968; Heylighen & Campbell, 1995; Sherif, 1966) because of realistic conflict over material and social resources.

What differentiates the IRM from other conceptualizations is the integration of basic constructs in a single explicit model, the specification of cognitive primacy (ethnocentrism and stereotypes) that impacts emotion and, in turn, behavior, and the claim that the mediational processes are moderated by the equality of opportunity for resource attainment. This moderator of the IRM is derived from theoretical work on power (Fiske, 1993; Keltner et al., 2003); social dominance (Sidanius & Pratto, 2001), realistic conflict (Campbell, 1965), and social stigma (Crocker & Major, 1989). The processes of the IRM can also be moderated by strong in-group identification in cases of war, threat, and attack (McCauley, Worchel, Moghaddam, & Lee, 2004), and by mutual intergroup outcome dependency (Preuschoft, Wang, Filippo, & de Waal, 2002).

Perceived Equality and Inequality of Opportunity for Resource Attainment

If members of two groups perceive an equal opportunity to attain material and social resources (Keltner et al., 2003) given an equivalent expenditure of effort (Homans, 1974), groups will respect, or simply tolerate each other's culture, stereotypes will be neutral to positive, and intergroup affect will be neutral to positive. Intergroup behavior will be realistically competitive (Campbell, 1965; Stephan & Stephan, 2000) but nonaggressive. In cases when groups' reinforcements are mutually dependent (Preuschoft, Wang, Filippo, & de Waal, 2002), members of different groups need one another and know this; consequently this recognition will facilitate reconciliation.

Group members may perceive that, relative to other groups, their opportunity for resource attainment is not equal given equivalent effort. Pruitt (1998) said "an assessment of the outcomes achieved by one's group, organization, or nation appears to be the most important source of collective conflict" (p. 470). With an unfair advantage there will be mutual dislike, trust will be low, stereotypes will be negative, and responses will occur to gain control of resources for the in-group. The powerful group will feel anger toward the less powerful and will be inclined to "move against them" behaviorally (Mackie et al., 2000), often by imposing social control such as enlarging the size of law enforcement (Jackson, 1989). The less powerful group will challenge the social structure, and each group will evidence ethnocentrism. When a group procures an inequitable share of the resources, cultural and psychological processes operate to maintain the inequality (Sidanius & Pratto, 2001). The advantaged exaggerate group differences, view the in-group as superior, and share negative out-group stereotypes. Discriminatory responses to the disadvantaged follow from dislike and contempt for their inferiority. The disadvantaged will experience stereotype threat, stigmatization, humiliation, mistrust, and reduced self-esteem (Crocker, Major, & Steele, 1998). When the advantaged are a numerical majority, or in contexts where pernicious stereotypes are most salient, the disadvantaged will disengage (Osborne, 2004; Steele, 1997).

The transition to reconciliation is impossible under conditions of objective, or perceived, inequality because intergroup relations will evidence negative cognitive and affective reciprocity that will preclude postconflict peacemaking. An essential first step in reconciliation is protection of the weak from the strong by neutral brokers acceptable to both factions, and subsequent intervention by trusted third parties (e.g., respected international leaders) to promote equality of opportunity and fairness. Ultimately, the structural change of social institutions must occur so that equality of opportunity is institutionalized. Optimally, adversaries' reinforcements should be mutually dependent. Only then can intergroup cognitive and affective processes change and facilitate the transition from reciprocal conflict to reciprocal cooperation; that is, reconciliation.

The Componential Structure of Reciprocal Intergroup Relations

Intergroup processes are not unidirectional; rather, when entities (individuals, teams, nations) respond to one another these responses are reciprocal. Consequently, intergroup relations are *dyadic* and *reciprocal*, and the application of methods for analysis of the components of dyadic data can be implemented. One method, termed *variance component analysis*, originated in psychometrics (Cronbach, Gleser, Nanda, & Rajaratnam, 1972) and biometrics (Searle, Casella, & McCulloch, 1992), and was introduced to social psychology by Kenny (1994). These methods have proven useful in studies of a broad range of intergroup phenomena (Malloy & Albright, 2001; Malloy, Albright, Diaz-Loving, Dong, & Lee, 2004; Malloy, Albright, Kenny, Agatstein, & Winquist, 1997; Malloy, Barcelos, Arruda, DeRosa, & Fonseca, 2005; Miller & Malloy, 2003). Because reconciliation is a change in reciprocal responses over time, variance component analysis is directly relevant because reciprocity at different levels of analysis, with distinct theoretical meaning, can be considered.

To elaborate the componential structure of intergroup relations, imagine two groups, the Hatfields (H) and the McCoys (M), two feuding clans on the Kentucky and Virginia border in the late 19th century. McCoys, upset by an "unjust" court decision regarding ownership of a hog, ambushed Hatfields while hunting. The Hatfields retaliated and killed a McCoy. The theoretical structure of a response by a Hatfield to a McCoy is presented in Figure 15.2. Theoretically, H's response to M is a function of: (a) the consistency of H's responses to members of out-groups in general (e.g., A, B, C, as well as M) called an *actor effect*, (b) the consistency of responses elicited by M from members of out-groups (e.g., A, B, C, as well as H) called a *partner effect*, and (c) by H's

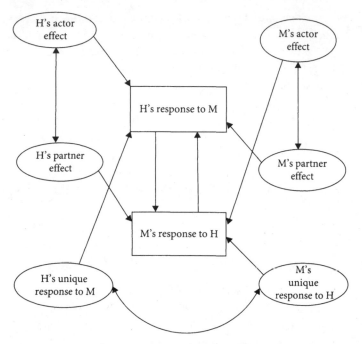

FIGURE 15.2. Components of intergroup relations with generalized and dyadic reciprocity.

unique response to M called, a *uniqueness effect*, after controlling for actor and partner effects. The reciprocal response of M to H has the same components. These three components of an intergroup response, termed *actor*, *partner*, and *uniqueness*, must be partitioned because each has a distinct psychological meaning; failure to partition these effects conflates psychologically distinct intergroup phenomena.

Psychological Interpretation of the Variance Components in Intergroup Responses

Consider the reactions of groups A and Z to groups B, C, and D. Assume that members of A share a positive stereotype about groups B, C, and D and that members of Z share a negative stereotype about B, C, and D. In Table 15.1 hypothetical data representing this pattern are presented. Such a pattern is termed an *actor effect* and all of the variation in intergroup responses is between groups A and Z. Now consider the responses of B, C, and D to A and Z. Assume that B, C, and D hold similar positive stereotypes of A and similar negative

TABLE 15.1 Intergroup Actor, Partner, and
Relationship Effects

Intergroup Actor Effects

	Group		
Group	B	C	D
A	9	9	9
Z	2	2	2

Intergroup Partner Effects

	Group	
Group	A	Z
B	9	2
C	9	2
D	9	2

Intergroup Relationship Effects

	Group	
Group	A	Z
B	9	9
C	2	2
D	9	2

Note. Entries are hypothetical data on a 10 point scale with 1
representing the most negative stereotype and 10 the most
positive stereotype.

stereotypes of Z. This pattern is termed a *partner effect* and all of the variation in intergroup responses elicited is between groups A and Z. In some cases one group responds uniquely to another group. In this example, members of B share uniquely positive stereotypes of Z and members of C share uniquely negative stereotypes of A. These are called *uniqueness effects*.

Formally, A's response to B on dimension X yielding X_{ab} may be partitioned into the following terms:

$$X_{ab} = \mu + \alpha_a + \beta_b + \gamma_{ab} + \varepsilon \qquad (15.1)$$

where α_a is the consistency of A's responses to multiple groups (actor effect), β_b is the consistency of B's effect on responses elicited from other groups (partner effect), and γ_{ab} is A's unique response to B after controlling for α_a and β_b. The constant μ is the average of intergroup responses, and ε is random error.

Terms of the model are assumed to be normally distributed random variables. Likewise, B's response to A is represented by:

$$X_{ba} = \mu + \alpha_b + \beta_a + \gamma_{ba} + \varepsilon \qquad (15.2)$$

The variances of the components (i.e., α, β, and γ) are computed yielding estimates that quantify the consistency of intergroup responses emitted (actor), elicited (partner), and uniquely made to specific groups (uniqueness). The null hypothesis tested is that a variance component equals zero. The variances and covariances of the components, as well as the components' relationships with other variables, quantify a broad range of intergroup phenomena with generalized and dyadic reciprocity being centrally relevant to reconciliation.

In traditional Fisherian analysis, the mean response in one condition is compared to the mean response in a different condition. However, variance component analysis quantifies phenomena using variances and covariances as well as means. The means of un-decomposed scores (e.g., X_{ab} and X_{ba} in Equations 15.1 and 15.2) are considered, yet the variances and covariances of the components of X (α, β, γ) are of primary interest. Variance component analysis enhances conceptual and statistical precision, and serves a heuristic function by guiding attention to new phenomena and questions.

The theoretical structure of intergroup responses has important methodological implications for research on reconciliation. First, reconciliation will be reciprocal rather than unidirectional. To understand the response of a Hatfield to a McCoy, one must measure the response of H to M and that of M to H. Second, the reconciliation responses of H to M and M to H are each determined by the actor, partner, and uniqueness effects. Yet, if measurements are limited only to H's response to M and M's response to H, there is insufficient information to estimate the actor, partner, and uniqueness effects. Multiple, rather than single, interaction designs are required to estimate the reciprocity and componential structure of intergroup relations. Third, reciprocity is the core mechanism of reconciliation that unfolds temporally. However, two forms of reciprocity must be distinguished for conceptual clarity: generalized and dyadic (Kenny & Nasby, 1980). Generalized reciprocity is the extent to which a group's consistent responses to multiple other groups are generally reciprocated by them, and is estimated by the correlation of a group's actor and partner effects. Dyadic reciprocity, however, is limited to specific pairs of groups and is estimated by the correlation of uniqueness effects. Correlations representing generalized (actor-partner components) and dyadic (uniqueness-uniqueness components) reciprocity are presented in Figure 15.2. Unfortunately, the distinction between generalized and dyadic reciprocity has been mostly ignored in research on intergroup relations and reconciliation.

Fourth, modeling intergroup reconciliation begins with a focus on the theoretically relevant components of the IRM constructs and should not be limited to whole, un-decomposed scores. To know clearly if reconciliation is occurring, one should estimate dyadic reciprocity without the confounding effect of generalized reciprocity.

Power, Reciprocity, and a Reconciliation Attempt

The October 2, 1960 Sunday edition of the *New York Times* presented a sociogram depicting visits among eight international leaders during a 2 week meeting of the General Assembly of the United Nations. International tensions were high, nuclear war was a feared potential, and the Cuban Missile Crisis was yet to materialize. One can assume ethnocentrism, negative stereotypes, and dislike among some leaders although relevant data are unavailable. The data available quantify face-to-face intergroup contact among the leaders; a construct thought to foster harmony (Pettigrew, 1998) and reconciliation (see Baron, Deutsch, and Kelman, this volume). The data are presented in a single 8 × 8 round robin matrix (see Malloy & Albright, 2001) in Table 15.2. Actor, partner, and uniqueness variance components were estimated, as well as individual and dyadic reciprocity. Approximately 24% of the variance in visits was due to differences among leaders' actor effects. Following Kenny (1994), leader i's actor effect is computed by:

$$\alpha_i = M_{i.} \frac{(n-1)^2}{n(n-2)} + M_{.i} \frac{n-1}{n(n-2)} - M_{..} \frac{n-1}{n-2} \tag{15.3}$$

where $M_{i.}$ is the average of visits initiated by leader i, $M_{.i}$ is the average of visits made to leader i, and $M_{..}$ is the average number of visits among the eight leaders. For leader i, α_i is the actor effect. Nehru of India was the most active initiator of visits ($\alpha = .60$) and Eisenhower initiated the least ($\alpha = -.71$).

Partner effects quantify relative approach by other leaders and for leader i is:

$$\beta_i = M_{.i} \frac{(n-1)^2}{n(n-2)} + M_{i.} \frac{n-1}{n(n-2)} - M_{..} \frac{n-1}{n-2} \tag{15.4}$$

where $M_{.i}$ is the average of visits received by leader i, $M_{i.}$ is the average visits initiated by i, and $M_{..}$ is the average visits among the leaders. For leader i, β_i is the partner effect. Approximately 22% of the variance was due to difference among leaders in visits received; Khrushchev was approached the most ($\beta = .83$) whereas Macmillan was approached the least ($\beta = -.56$).

TABLE 15.2   Face-to-Face Meetings by World Leaders at the 1960 Meeting of the United Nations General Assembly

	C	Na	T	Ne	K	Nk	M	E
Castro (Cuba)	—	1	0	1	1	1	0	0
Nasser (Egypt)	1	—	3	1	2	1	0	1
Tito (Yugoslovia)	0	0	—	1	2	0	0	1
Nehru (India)	1	1	2	—	2	1	1	1
Khrushchev (Soviet Union)	1	0	0	1	—	0	0	0
Nkrumah (Ghana)	0	0	1	1	3	—	0	1
Macmillan (England)	0	1	1	0	1	1	—	1
Eisenhower (United States)	0	0	0	0	0	0	0	—

	Variance Components		
	Actor	Partner	Uniqueness/Error
Face-to-Face Meetings	.24	.22	.54

	Reciprocity Correlations
Generalized	−.14
Dyadic	−.28

Note. Error variance should be near zero with little error of measurement because these visits were very public events observed and reported by the international press.

The difference between approach and avoidance among leaders is an index of power (Keltner et al., 2003). For leader i, power (P_i) may be quantified by:

$$P_i = \beta_i - \alpha_i \tag{15.5}$$

where P_i is relative power of leader i, and is defined as the difference between being approached (β_i) and the initiation of approach (α_i). Positive P values indicate that a leader was approached by others more than he approached them. Negative P values indicate that a leader approached others more than he was approached by them, and a value of zero for P indicates that approaching and being approached were equal. When $P = 0$, conditions are prime for reconciliation because approach is equal for the protagonists in a conflict, and the stage is set for a transition from negative to positive reciprocity. As P values depart from zero the likelihood of reconciliation diminishes. Khrushchev had the greatest power ($P = 1.13$) because he was approached the most (mean of 1.57 visits) and made very few visits to other leaders (mean of .29). Eisenhower was the second most powerful leader ($P = .63$) with an average of .71 visitors and 0 visits initiated. Nasser, Nehru, and Macmillan were the least powerful (Ps of

–.75, –.50, and –.50, respectively). Nasser and Nehru made the greatest number of visits (nine each, with mean visits of 1.29 for each) but their visits were not reciprocated (means of .43 and .71, respectively). Macmillan made five visits and was visited only once.

This analysis of power may seem at odds with other approaches. For example, theoretical analysis predicts that high power should produce approach behavior (Keltner et al., 2003) and empirical data confirm that power leads to action (Galinsky, Gruenfeld, & Magee, 2003). Yet, in different contexts different norms may moderate the power-action relationship, and these data show that power within the context of strategic international negotiation can lead to inaction. In the case of world leaders, inaction was a public proclamation of high power intended to maintain it and benefit one's in-group constituents. Action was initiated by the less powerful in deference to the more powerful.

Generalized reciprocity was $r = -.14$ and showed that leaders who initiated visits were not visited by others. Dyadic reciprocity was weak ($r = -.28$); neither powerful nor weak leaders reciprocated visits. Noteworthy is the finding that both generalized and dyadic reciprocity are negative for the contact variable. Perhaps the negative generalized and dyadic reciprocity, particularly among the most powerful leaders (Khrushchev and Eisenhower had zero contact), precluded the reconciliation that could have curtailed the Cuban Missile Crisis.

Summary and Conclusions

Two basic questions for a social psychology of intergroup reconciliation were posed: "what system of variables affects reciprocal intergroup responses?" and "what variables affect the transition from intergroup conflict to peaceful coexistence?" In response to the first, the Intergroup Relations Model specifies cognitive and affective processes that determine reciprocal group responses under conditions of perceived equality and inequality of opportunity for resource attainment. The prominent role of cognition in human reconciliation stands in contrast to its trivial importance in postconflict peacemaking among nonhuman primates (de Waal, 2000). Among humans, a transition from reciprocal conflict to peaceful coexistence hinges on implementation of structural change that ensures equality of opportunity for attaining material (e.g., food, employment, medicine, education) and social (e.g., positive social identity, collective respect, self-determination) resources. Although relations among groups in proximity will almost always be competitive, if competition occurs under equality, peaceful coexistence is possible. As documented in this volume, intergroup reconciliation can be facilitated by equal status contact while confronting a common challenge, by educational interventions, by cognitive reorganization that diminishes sharp intergroup boundaries, and by public pronouncements of wrongdoing with reciprocal apology and forgiveness. However, equality of opportunity is hypothesized to be the major moderator of transition from conflict to peaceful coexistence. Reconciliation will always be slow and unsteady because the requisite structural change is always at odds with the advantage held by powerful groups (Sidanius & Pratto, 2001) that will actively undermine change (Heylighen & Campbell, 1995). Yet, structural change can be implemented if antagonists realize they are mutually interdependent. For example, when the advantaged and powerful understand the staggering economic and social costs, for the in-group, of institutional racism, the unjust occupation of an adversary, or the disenfranchisement of an ethnic group, there can be an incentive to create an equality of opportunity motivated by self-interest. When occupation, racism, and domination are too costly, the transition to equality of opportunity for resource attainment can occur with attendant reconciliation. Intergroup psychology will then be more positive.

These theoretical ideas have methodological implications. Because intergroup relations are two-sided and reciprocal, it is essential to consider the componential structure of intergroup perception, affect, and behavior for conceptual clarity and analytic precision. Failure to isolate actor, partner, and uniqueness effects in intergroup responses precludes assessment of psychologically distinct intergroup phenomena. Intergroup conflict will often be dyadic with two primary protagonists. Consequently, reconciliation will involve a transition from negative dyadic reciprocity toward positive dyadic reciprocity. Following this, generalized reciprocity will follow. Therefore, it is essential to differentiate generalized and dyadic intergroup phenomena and not conflate them.

Acknowledgments

Fredric Agatstein, Jennifer Berdahl, Jeffrey Fisher, Arie Nadler, David Sugarman, and the members of the University of Rhode Island and Rhode Island College social psychology seminars provided helpful comments on this chapter. Preparation of this chapter was supported, in part, by a Rhode Island College faculty research grant.

References

Allport, G. W. (1954). *The nature of prejudice*. Reading, MA: Addison-Wesley.

Anderson, C., & Berdahl, J. L. (2002). The experience of power: Examining the effects of power on approach and inhibition tendencies. *Journal of Personality and Social Psychology, 83*, 1362-1377.

Austin, W. G., & Worchel, S. (1979). *The social psychology of intergroup relations*. Monterey, CA: Brooks/Cole.

Blake, R. R., & Mouton, J. S. (1979). Intergroup problem solving in organizations: From theory to practice. In W. G. Austin & S. Worchel (Eds.), *The social psychology of intergroup relations*. pp. 19-32. Monterey, CA: Brooks/Cole.

Blanz, M., Mummendey, A., & Otten, S. (1995). Perceptions of relative groups size and group status: Effects on intergroup discrimination in negative evaluations. *European Journal of Social Psychology, 25*, 213-247.

Branscombe, N. R., Ellemers, N., Spears, R., & Doosje, B. (1999). The context and content of social identity threat. In N. Ellemers, R. Spears, & B. Doosje (Eds.), *Social identity: Context, commitment, content* (pp. 35-58). Oxford, England: Blackwell.

Brewer, M. B., & Brown, R. J. (1998). Intergroup relations. In D. T. Gilbert & S. T. Fiske (Eds.), *The handbook of social psychology* (Vol. 2, 4th ed., pp. 554-594). Boston, MA: McGraw Hill.

Brewer, M. B., & Campbell, D. T. (1976). *Ethnocentrism and intergroup attitudes*. New York: John Wiley.

Brigham, J. C. (1971). Ethnic stereotypes. *Psychological Bulletin, 76*, 15-38.

Brown, R. (1986). *Social psychology: The second edition*. New York: The Free Press.

Brown, R. (1988). *Group processes: Dynamics within and between groups*. Oxford: Basil Blackwell.

Brown, R. (2000). Social Identity Theory: Past achievements, current problems and future challenges. *European Journal of Social Psychology, 30*, 745-778.

Campbell, D. T. (1958). Common fate, similarity, and other indices of the status of aggregates of persons as social entities. *Behavioral Science, 3*, 14-25.

Campbell, D. T. (1965). Ethnocentric and other altruistic motives. In D. Levine (Ed.), *Nebraska symposium on motivation* (pp. 283-311). Lincoln: University of Nebraska Press.

Crocker, J., & Major, B. (1989). Social stigma and self-esteem: The self protective properties of stigma. *Psychological Review, 96*, 608-630.

Crocker, J., Major, B., & Steele, C. (1998). Social stigma. In D. T. Gilbert & S. T. Fiske (Eds.), *The handbook of social psychology*, (Vol. 2, 4th ed., pp. 504-553). Boston, MA: McGraw Hill.

Crocker, J., & Park, L. E. (2004). The costly pursuit of self-esteem. *Psychological Bulletin, 130*, 392-414.

Cronbach, L. J., Gleser, G. C., Nanda, H., & Rajaratnam, N. (1972). *The dependability of behavioral measurements: Theory of generalizability for scores and profiles.* New York: Wiley.

Deutsch, M. (1973). *The resolution of conflict.* New Haven, CT: Yale University Press.

de Waal, F. B. M. (2000). Primates: A natural heritage of conflict resolution. *Science, 289,* 586-590.

Dijker, A. J., Koomen, W., van den Heuvel, H., & Frijida, N. H. (1996). Perceived antecedents of emotional reactions in inter-ethnic relations. *British Journal of Social Psychology, 31,* 313-329.

Dovidio, J. F., Brigham, J. C., Johnson, B. T., & Gaertner, S. L. (1996). Stereotyping, prejudice, and discrimination: Another look. In C. N. Macrae, C. Stangor, & M. Hewstone (Eds.), *Stereotypes and stereotyping* (pp. 276-322). New York: Guilford Press.

Dovidio, J., ten Vergert, M., Stewart, T., Gaertner, S., Johnson, J., Esses, V. M., et al. (2004). Perspective and Prejudice: Antecedents and mediating mechanisms. *Personality and Social Psychology Bulletin, 30,* 1537-1549.

Esses, V. M., Dovidio, J. F., Jackson, L. M., & Armstrong, T. L., (2001). The immigration dilemma: The role of perceived group competition, ethnic prejudice, and national identity. *Journal of Social Issues, 57,* 389-412.

Festinger, L. (1954). A theory of social comparison processes. *Human Relations, 7,* 117-140.

Fiske, S. T. (1993). Controlling other people: The impact of power on stereotyping. *American Psychologist, 48,* 621-628.

Fiske, S. T. (1998). Stereotyping, prejudice, and discrimination. In D. Gilbert & S. T. Fiske (Eds.) *The handbook of social psychology* (Vol. 2, 4th ed., pp. 357-411). New York: McGraw-Hill.

Fiske, S. T. (2004). *Social beings: A core motives approach to social psychology.* New York: Wiley.

Fiske, S. T., Cuddy, A. J., Glick, P., & Xu, J. (2002). A model of (often mixed) stereotype content: Competence and warmth respectively follow from perceived status and competition. *Journal of Personality and Social Psychology, 82,* 878-902.

Gaertner, S. L., & Dovidio, J. F. (2005). Understanding and addressing contemporary racism: From aversive racism to the common ingroup identity model. *Journal of Social Issues, 61,* 615-639.

Galinsky, A. D., Greunfeld, D. H., & Magee, J. C. (2003). From power to action. *Journal of Personality and Social Psychology, 85,* 453-466.

Guinote, A., Judd, C. M., & Brauer, M. (2002). Effects of power on perceived and objective group variability: Evidence that more powerful groups are more variable. *Journal of Personality and Social Psychology, 82,* 708-721.

Halloway, R. (1974). *Primate aggression, territoriality, and xenophobia.* New York: Academic Press.

Hamilton, D. L. (1981). Stereotyping and intergroup behavior: Some thoughts on the cognitive approach. In D. L. Hamilton (Ed.), *Cognitive processes in stereotyping and intergroup behavior* (pp. 333-354). Hillsdale, NJ: Erlbaum.

Hardin, G. (1968). The tragedy of the commons. *Science, 162,* 1243-1248.

Heylighen, F., & Campbell, D. T. (1995). Selection of organization at the social level. *World Futures, 45,* 181-212.

Homans, G. C. (1974). *Social behavior: Its elementary forms.* New York: Harcourt, Brace, Jovanovich.

Jackson, P. I. (1989). *Minority group threat, crime, and policing: Social context and social control.* New York: Praeger.

Judge, P. G., & de Waal, F. B. M. (1994). Intergroup grooming relations between alpha females in a population of free-ranging rhesus macaques. *Folia Primatologica, 63,* 63-70.

Katz, D., & Braly, K. W. (1933). Racial stereotypes of 100 college students. *Journal of Abnormal and Social Psychology, 28,* 280-290.

Keltner, D., Gruenfeld, D. H., & Anderson, C. (2003). Power, approach, and inhibition. *Psychological Review, 110,* 265-284.

Kenny, D. A. (1994). *Interpersonal perception.* New York: Guilford Press.

Kenny, D. A., & Nasby, W. (1980). Splitting the reciprocity correlation. *Journal of Personality and Social Psychology, 38,* 249-256.

Leach, C. W., Spears, R., Branscombe, N. R., & Doosje, B. (2003). Malicious pleasure: Schadenfreude at the suffering of another group. *Journal of Personality and Social Psychology, 84,* 932-943.

LeVine, R. A., & Campbell, D. T. (1972). *Ethnocentrism: Theories of conflict, ethnic attitudes, and group behavior.* New York: Wiley.

Mackie, D. M., & Smith, E. R. (1998). Intergroup relations: Insights from a theoretically integrative approach. *Psychological Review, 105,* 499-529.

Mackie, D. M., Devos, T., & Smith, E. R. (2000). Intergroup emotions: Explaining offensive action tendencies in an intergroup context. *Journal of Personality and Social Psychology, 79,* 602-616.

Malloy, T. E., & Albright, L. (2001). Multiple and single interaction dyadic research designs: Conceptual and analytic issues. *Basic and Applied Social Psychology, 23,* 1-19.

Malloy, T. E., Albright, L., Diaz-Loving, R.. Dong, Q., & Lee, T. T. (2004). Agreement in personality judgments in non-overlapping social groups in collectivist cultures. *Personality and Social Psychology Bulletin, 30,* 106-117.

Malloy, T. E., Albright, L., Kenny, D. A., Agatstein, F., & Winquist, L. (1997). Interpersonal perception and metaperception in non-overlapping social groups. *Journal of Personality and Social Psychology, 72,* 390-398.

Malloy, T. E., Barcelos, S., Arruda, E., DeRosa, M., & Fonseca, C. (2005). Individual differences and cross-situational consistency of dyadic social behavior. *Journal of Personality and Social Psychology, 89,* 643-654.

McCauley, C., Worchel, S., Moghaddam, F., & Lee, Y.-T. (2004). In Y.-T. Lee, C. McCauley, F. Moghaddam, & S. Worchel (Eds.), Contact and identity in intergroup relations. In *The psychology of ethnic and cultural conflict. Psychological dimensions to war and peace* (pp. 309-326). Westport, CT: Praeger Publishers/Greenwood.

Miller, S., & Malloy, T. E. (2003). Interpersonal behavior, perception, and affect in status-discrepant dyads: Social interaction of gay and heterosexual men. *Psychology of Men and Masculinity, 4,* 121-135.

Mullen, B., & Hu, L. (1989). Perceptions of ingroup and outgroup variability: A meta-analysis integration. *Basic and Applied Social Psychology, 10,* 233-252.

Mullen, B., Brown, R., & Smith, C. (1992). Ingroup bias as a function of salience, relevance, and status: An integration. *European Journal of Social Psychology, 22,* 103-122.

Nadler, A., & Laviatan, I. (2006). Intergroup reconciliation: Effects of adversaries' expressions of empathy, responsibility, and recipients' trust. *Personality and Social Psychology Bulletin, 32,* 459-470.

Osborne, J. W. (2004). Identification with academics and violence in schools. *Review of General Psychology, 8,* 147-162.

Preuschoft, S., Wang, X., Filippo, A., de Waal, F. B. M. (2002). Reconciliation in captive chimpanzees: A reevaluation with controlled methods. *International Journal of Primatology, 23,* 29-50.

Perdue, C. W., Dovidio, J. F., Gurtman, M. B., & Tyler, R. B. (1990). "Us" and "them": Social categorization and the process of intergroup bias. *Journal of Personality and Social Psychology, 59,* 475-486.

Pettigrew, T. F. (1998). Intergroup contact theory. *Annual Review of Psychology, 49,* 65-85.

Pronin, E., Gilovich, T., & Ross, L. (2004). Objectivity in the eye of the beholder: Divergent perceptions of bias in self versus others. *Psychological Review, 111,* 781-799.

Pruitt, D. G. (1998). Social conflict. In D. T. Gilbert & S. T. Fiske (Eds.), *The handbook of social psychology,* (Vol. 2, 4th ed., pp. 504-553). Boston, MA: McGraw Hill.

Robinson, R. J., Keltner, D., Ward, A., & Ross, L. (1995). Actual versus assumed differences in construal: "Naïve realism" in intergroup perceptions and conflict. *Journal of Personality and Social Psychology, 68,* 404-417.

Ross, L., & Ward, A. (1996). Naïve realism in everyday life: Implications for social conflict and misunderstanding. In T. Brown, E. S. Reed, & E. Turiel (Eds.), *Values and knowledge: The jean piaget symposium series* (pp. 103-135). Hillsdale, NJ: Erlbaum.

Searle, S. R., Casella, G., & McCulloch, C. E. (1992). *Variance components.* New York: Wiley.

Sherif, M. (1966). *Group conflict and co-operation: Their social psychology.* London: Routledge & Kegan Paul.

Sherif, M., Harvery, O. J., White, B. J., Hood, W. R., & Sherif, C. W. (1961). *Intergroup cooperation and competition: The Robbers Cave experiment.* Norman, OK: University Book Exchange.

Sherif, M., & Sherif, C. W. (1979). Research on intergroup relations. In W. G. Austin & S. Worchel (Eds.), *The social psychology of intergroup relations* (pp. 7-18). Monterey, CA: Brooks/Cole.

Sidanius, J., & Pratto, F. (2001). *Social dominance.* Cambridge: Cambridge University Press.

Smith, E. R. (1993). Social identity and social emotions: Toward new conceptualizations of prejudice. In D. M. Mackie & D. L. Hamilton (Eds.), *Affect, cognition, and stereotyping: Interactive processes in group perception* (pp. 297-315). San Diego, CA: Academic Press.

Staub, E. (1996). Moral exclusion, personal goal theory, and extreme destructiveness. *Journal of Social Issues, 46,* 47-64.

Steele, C. (1997). A threat in the air: How stereotypes shape intellectual identity and performance. *American Psychologist, 52,* 613-629.

Stephan, W. G. (1985). Intergroup relations. In G. Lindzey & E. Aronson (Eds.), *The handbook of social psychology* (3rd ed., Vol. 2, pp. 599-658). New York: Random House.

Stephan, W. G., & Stephan, C. W. (2000). An integrated threat theory of prejudice. In S. Oskamp (Ed.), *Reducing prejudice and discrimination* (pp. 23-46). Hillsdale, NJ: Erlbaum.

Sumner, W. (1906). *The folkways.* Boston: Ginn & Company.

Tajfel, H. (1978). *Differentiation between social groups: Studies in the social psychology of intergroup relations.* New York: Academic Press.

Tajfel, H. (Ed.), (1982). *Social identity and intergroup relations.* Cambridge, England: Cambridge University Press.

Tajfel, H., & Turner, J. (1979). An integrative theory of intergroup conflict. In W. G. Austin & S. Worchel (Eds.), *The social psychology of intergroup relations* (pp. 33-46). Monterey, CA: Brooks/Cole.

Taylor, S. E., & Brown, J. D. (1988). Illusion and well-being: A social psychological perspective on mental health. *Psychological Bulletin, 103,* 193-210.

Turner, J. C. (1982). Towards a cognitive redefinition of the social group. In H. Tajfel (Ed.), *Social identity and intergroup relations* (pp. 15-40). Cambridge: Cambridge University Press.

Turner, J. C. (1987). *Rediscovering the social group: A self-categorization theory.* Cambridge, MA: Blackwell.

Weaver, A., & de Waal, F. B. M. (2003). The mother-offspring relationship as a template in social development: Reconciliation in captive brown capuchins (cebus apella). *Journal of Comparative Psychology, 117,* 101-110.

Wohl, M. J. A., & Branscombe, N. R. (2005). Forgiveness and collective guilt assignment to historical perpetrator groups depend on level of social category inclusiveness. *Journal of Personality and Social Psychology, 88,* 288-303.

Part IV

Programs to Promote Intergroup Reconciliation

CHAPTER 16

The Road to Reconciliation

WALTER G. STEPHAN

I have spent a considerable portion of my career studying the causes and consequences of prejudice, as well as techniques to counteract prejudice. This experience has given me a keen appreciation of how difficult it is to change prejudice, even though we understand a great deal about its causes. When I think about the problems facing people who wish to promote intergroup reconciliation, the challenge seems even more daunting than the one facing those who would overcome prejudice. This is so because reconciliation is a much higher goal than prejudice reduction and the types of intergroup conflicts for which it is most needed are much more severe than those commonly confronted by people attempting to reduce intergroup prejudice. Fortunately, we have now begun to travel the difficult road to understanding reconciliation and helping groups to achieve it.

In this chapter, I discuss the goals of reconciliation at the societal and individual level, the antecedent conditions that make reconciliation so difficult, the intervention techniques we currently have available to address reconciliation, some of the processes by which these techniques work, the societal context variables that can affect the success of reconciliation interventions, and the roles that psychologists can play in this process. Although I focus extensively on the problems that confront those who would promote reconciliation, I do not wish my message to be read as discouraging such attempts. Understanding the nature of the obstacles to reconciliation can facilitate the process of finding means to overcome them. I hope that readers will come away with a better appreciation of the problems that need to be dealt with if attempts at reconciliation are to be effective.

It is impossible to write a chapter on this topic without being influenced by one's own background and biases. The ones that I am most concerned about are the biases created by my own Western cultural background and my training in social psychology. Readers should be aware that the concepts, theories, and techniques discussed here may not apply across cultures and I am undoubtedly missing valuable contributions that other disciplines have to offer students of reconciliation. My comments are directed at the most severe kinds of intergroup conflicts, those that are protracted and involve a history of violence between groups within a nation state, However, much of what I have to say would apply equally well to less severe intergroup conflicts and to protracted internation conflicts.

Defining the Goals of Reconciliation

Perhaps the first issue to be addressed in any attempt at intergroup reconciliation is the problem of deciding what the goals of reconciliation are in a particular context. The second issue is to determine what means exist to achieve these goals. Basically, reconciliation can occur at two levels—the societal level and the individual level, although there is extensive feedback between them.

Societal Level Reconciliation

The fundamental goal of societal level reconciliation is to renew a lapsed social contract—that is, the implicit agreement between the governed and the state concerning the rights and obligations of each. In functioning societies, citizens agree to give up some freedoms and abide by the laws of the state (i.e., to be governed) in exchange for certain rights and the protection of the state. In societies suffering from protracted intergroup conflict, people have lost faith in their government's capacity to protect them and their rights and they cease adhering to the laws. Renewing the social contract between citizens and the state involves repairing the fundamental institutions of a functioning society. The social institutions that are potentially involved at this level include: the government, the judicial system, the educational system, the mass media, economic institutions (banks, large and small industries), religious institutions, political parties, government agencies (health care, education, social welfare agencies, etc.), as well as nongovernmental organizations (charities, activist organizations, etc.) and other community services that meet the basic needs of the society.

From a societal perspective, it is the community itself that needs to be healed and this task often involves issues that are largely symbolic, such as the language that leaders use to frame the conflict and the use of group symbols. Public displays of group symbols that can incite violence, such as flags, may need to be curtailed. More generally, the symbolic landscape needs to be reengineered to support peace and reconciliation through such actions as the creation of monuments to those who died in the conflict and billboards or other public displays that promote coexistence. People also need to have symbols that lead them toward a more peaceful future. Social norms and roles may need to be reconfigured to place a greater emphasis on inclusiveness and equality, especially those roles that involve extensive intergroup contacts such as those in health care, social welfare, government agencies, education, and other service professions.

The means available to move groups toward societal reconciliation typically start with some type of treaty or other formal agreement to cease hostilities. Because basic human rights have to be protected and security issues are of paramount importance in the aftermath of conflict, laws may need to be enacted to prevent violence, discrimination, and exclusionary policies. In many societies, it may also be necessary to take affirmative actions to ensure the representation of all groups in employment, government, and educational settings. In addition, techniques that are specifically designed to promote reconciliation can be employed. These may include the creation of "truth and reconciliation commissions," establishing high profile committees to investigate the conflict, the prosecution of crimes against humanity, offering amnesty to common combatants, and reparations programs for victims. Media campaigns can be initiated that are aimed at keeping the public better informed and preventing future incidents of intergroup violence from getting out of control. Societal level attempts at reconciliation may also include the establishment of high-level community councils or workshops where the leadership of the conflicting groups meet to discuss future steps toward reconciliation. The arts and entertainment sectors have a special role to play in reconciliation. The arts can offer a deeper understanding of the conflict, and both the arts and the entertainment industry can bring people from the conflicting groups together to share positive experiences.

Leaders of both groups can come together to renounce violence, denounce hate groups, and otherwise model civil public discourse between groups. They may also establish a set of mutually verifiable future steps toward intergroup peace. Leaders may also be in a position to seek assistance from international aid agencies and foundations that can provide expertise and funding for reconciliation efforts. The power of leaders to make both real and symbolic gestures that further the goals of reconciliation cannot be underestimated. They can create an ethos of peace that will set the tone for their entire society. Similarly, they can try to counteract the *culture of conflict* (Bar-Tal, 2004) that is so often created during protracted conflicts. Cultures of conflict are associated with the creation of subgroups with vested interests in maintaining conflict. To move toward reconciliation, these groups need to be marginalized, coopted, or defused (and ultimately disarmed) if reconciliation efforts are to succeed. It seems clear that at the societal level, reconciliation requires courageous and visionary leaders who are dedicated to repairing the dysfunctional intergroup relations created by protracted conflict.

Psychologists have had only limited experience in helping to promote societal reconciliation. However, to aid them in their efforts to promote reconciliation there are case histories of the attempts that have been made in earlier conflicts that are worth studying with great care. These include documentation of reconciliation programs in South Africa, Northern Ireland, Rwanda, Peru, Chile, and Richmond, Virginia, among others.

Individual Level Reconciliation

As important as societal level reconciliation is, most of the means of achieving societal level reconciliation are beyond the scope of psychology, which is better suited to addressing individual level reconciliation. The overall goal at the individual level is to alleviate the suffering that people have experienced during the conflict and provide them with the will and the means to move forward toward peaceful coexistence.

A number of specific steps can be taken to achieve these overall goals. Basic psychological needs for recognition, respect, and acceptance, as well as feelings security need to be met (Burton, 1986). In particular, people should be encouraged to take pride in their own identities, but not at the cost of denigrating out-groups. At least a minimum level of intergroup trust must also be created (Bar-On & Kassem, 2004). Reducing the levels of destructive negative emotions aroused by the conflict (e.g., hatred, anger, fear, guilt,) is also an important goal. Similarly, it is important to reduce stress levels. Forgiveness, repentance, and atonement should be promoted. In addition, people may need help to process their grief.

Attempts also need to be made to address the feelings of injustice and unfairness that are pervasive during and after protracted conflicts. Efforts should be made to redress individual grievances created during the conflict and to create closure on the events of the past. Efforts should be made to foster hope in a shared future involving common goals and a recognition of a mutually shared humanity. Opportunities should be made available to resolve future conflicts between individual members of different groups (e.g., through mediation centers). Ongoing programs need to be adopted that will reduce prejudice, stereotyping, and other intergroup misperceptions. These programs should also improve intergroup understanding, promote intergroup acceptance, and create viable patterns of coexistence. These programs will be discussed in a later section of this chapter.

For both societal and individual level reconciliation efforts, some attention must also be devoted to deciding who is most in need of reconciliation efforts, since the resources available to promote reconciliation are likely to be limited. To pursue these goals, it is necessary to understand the existing conditions that prevail during the terminal phases of a protracted intergroup conflict.

Conditions Prevailing Prior to Reconciliation Efforts

As is the case with the goals of reconciliation, it is necessary to take into consideration both the prevailing societal conditions and the prevailing individual (psychological) conditions.

Societal Conditions

Protracted conflicts are those that have raged out of control and left a path of destruction in their wake. The conflicts have usually been violent, often intensely so, with the consequence that there have been deaths and injuries. Frequently there are humanitarian crises that result from protracted conflicts and the first order of business before reconciliation can even begin is to address such problems as starvation, disease, and homelessness. There may also be refugees in need of assistance, if the fighting has led people to attempt to escape it. In large-scale protracted conflicts, the infrastructure of the society may also have been damaged (roads, bridges, electric, and water systems, etc.). Even if formal peace treaties or other types of agreements have been signed (e.g., cease fires), lawlessness and persistent intergroup violence may create problems. As noted earlier, fundamental social institutions including the government, judiciary, education system, economic institutions (e.g., banks, food distribution), health system, and so forth may be functioning poorly or not at all. Basically, the social structure of societies characterized by protracted intergroup conflicts tends to be compromised, often severely. All attempts at reconciliation in such societies take place against the backdrop of these societal problems.

Psychological Conditions

The psychological damage done by protracted intergroup conflicts is often no less severe than the societal damage done by the conflict. First and foremost, there are the ravaged psyches of the members of the groups involved who are dealing with the loss of loved ones, as well as their own physical pain, trauma, and suffering. They may be experiencing a wide range of negative emotions including rage, anger, fear, helplessness, humiliation, loathing, guilt, defensiveness, grief, and too many more. Many members of these groups are likely to be suffering from varying degrees of posttraumatic stress disorder or otherwise displaying the symptoms of prolonged stress (anxiety, psychophysiological symptoms, depression, etc.). People involved in such conflicts are apt to feel like they are under constant threat and they may feel insecure and vulnerable.

In most conflicts, there will be victims and perpetrators on both sides. The perpetrators will be in a position of defensively having to justify their actions, although in many cases their actions will have caused them to feel guilty and ashamed of behaviors that violate their own moral codes. The victims have their own physical and mental suffering to contend with and they, too, may feel guilty—in this case for surviving. In some instances, they will wonder what they have done to bring their woes upon them. Both victims and perpetrators may be reluctant to disclose their experiences to others (as many Holocaust survivors were with their own children, Bar-On & Kassem, 2004) and this may hinder reconciliation efforts. Noncombatants may *blind* themselves to the more heinous behaviors of members of their own group and deny any culpability for participating in a social system that made these behaviors possible (as many Germans did during World War II).

At a more cognitive level, members of both groups may experience an acute sense of injustice. Members of both groups will also perceive that their group has been delegitimized by other group. They may lack faith in their societies and be distrustful of all others, including people who seek to reconcile the conflicting groups. Their attitudes toward the other group will verge on hatred and out-group stereotypes will be intensely negative and polarized. The other group will probably be viewed as highly homogeneous. The in-group will be maximally differentiated from the out-group and distinctions between groups will overwhelmingly favor the in-group. As a result, most intergroup interactions will be category-based, meaning that people will view others primarily in terms of whether they belong to the in-group or the out-group. In fact, members of the out-group will most likely be viewed as less than human. This dehumanization of members of the other group may be so profound that they are excluded from the moral universe of the in-group, thus permitting the most inhumane of crimes to be committed against them without guilt or remorse. The in-group will almost invariably consider itself to be morally superior to the out-group.

The thinking of the in-group about the out-group will be subject to a host of distortions. Out-groups are likely to be blamed for negative acts, ignoring the situational pressures that may exist. Conversely, they are unlikely to receive credit for their positive acts and these acts are less likely to be remembered than the negative ones (Ybarra, Stephan, & Schaberg, 2000). This leads to a view of the other group as unremittingly negative in their traits and behavior. Counteracting these negative views is difficult. Research indicates that in-group members need more contrary information to change negative views of the out-group than they would to change similarly negative views of the in-group (Ybarra, Stephan, Schaberg, & Lawrence, 2003). People are also less likely to accurately process information that contradicts their views of the out-group. Expecting the worst of out-group members predisposes in-group to behave negatively toward them, thereby increasing the chances that the out-group will confirm the negative expectations held about them (Snyder, 1992). Thinking about the out-group is also likely to be simplified and concrete (Maass, Salvi, Arcuri, & Semin, 1989). The differences in core values between the groups will most likely be exaggerated and prevent people from perceiving values the groups hold in common (Chambers, Baron, & Inman, 2006).

Given the terrible societal and psychological conditions that prevail in the aftermath of protracted conflicts, it is important to try to understand the techniques and psychological processes that may be involved in bringing reconciliation about. I start by outlining some of the intergroup relations programs and techniques that are currently available and then discuss some of the psychological processes that appear to be relevant to reconciliation efforts.

Intergroup Relations, Programs, and Techniques

Many of the programs developed in the United States and other countries to improve intergroup relations are relevant to reconciliation, but most would have to be substantially modified to address the issues of reconciliation. The psychological conditions just reviewed indicate that the intergroup relations have deteriorated during the conflict to a condition that is far worse than conditions prevailing in functioning multiethnic societies. In addition, the goals of reconciliation are qualitatively different from improving intergroup relations in stable, multiethnic societies and the programs designed to address reconciliation must be correspondingly different. I discuss four basic types of intergroup relations programs and techniques that could be adapted for use in reconciliation efforts: enlightenment programs, contact programs, skill-based programs, and healing and problem-solving programs.

Enlightenment Programs

These programs are based on the idea that ignorance is a crucial component of negative intergroup relations. In one form or another, all of these programs assume that providing information about the out-group's values, norms, beliefs, practices, and experiences will undercut negative attitudes, stereotypes, and discrimination (Dovidio, Gaertner, et al., 2004). These are all basically educational programs and rely to some extent on didactic approaches to present information about out-groups. In addition, most rely extensively on simulations, role-playing, and other interactive exercises.

Perhaps the most widely used enlightenment program is multicultural education (Banks, 1973, 2002). These programs are currently popular in diverse democratic societies and they may be difficult to implement during the initial phases of reconciliation efforts when educational institutions may not be functioning effectively. These programs focus on the history of the various groups in a society and, in doing so they ensure that minority perspectives are well represented. They aim to improve intergroup relations by providing students with the knowledge, attitudes, and skills needed to participate in the social, civic, and cultural life of a diverse society (Banks, 1997). They also strive to increase students' identification with their own racial, ethnic, religious, and cultural groups. Multicultural education, and other enlightenment programs, are limited to school settings and require functioning educational systems and trained teachers to be effective. They are most often employed with middle school students, although programs exist for both younger and older students. In many societies, multicultural education would require new curriculum materials, since the history of intergroup relations in most societies is taught from the perspective of the dominant group. Educational programs such as multicultural education are an investment in a more peaceful future. There may be some short-term benefits from such programs, but the real gains are realized over time.

Another enlightenment program that is primarily school-based is moral education. These programs are often based on Kohlberg's theories of moral development (Kohlberg, 1969, 1981). They usually teach moral reasoning, most often through the examination of moral dilemmas and their implications. Some moral education programs emphasize moral discourse and attempt to inculcate respect and interpersonal sensitivity, as well as promote tolerance and understanding of others (Battistich, Solomon, Watson, Solomon, & Schaps, 1989; Fine, 1995; Oser, 1985; Schulz, Barr, & Selman, 2001). Moral education programs could serve some of the goals of reconciliation by emphasizing morality, respect, tolerance, and justice. They are most likely to be effective for middle and high school level students who have sufficient mental maturity to process moral issues. They will inevitably bring up complex issues related to the recent conflict that may be emotionally intense and morally complex. It is likely that they can only be conducted by teachers who are well trained in handling such difficult discussions.

An enlightenment program for adults that can be implemented in many societies that have suffered protracted conflicts is diversity training. These programs are generally conducted in business organizations (Stephan & Stephan, 2001, 2004). Diversity training typically encourages participants to value the differences among racial, ethnic, and cultural groups. Some diversity programs also attempt to promote changes in the structure and climate of the organizations in which they are conducted to make them more fair and open. For example, the Xerox Corporation has a program that not only trains individuals to value diversity, but also includes changes in recruitment practices, the creation of caucus groups for minority employees, and new performance criteria that emphasize dealing with a diverse workforce and achieving affirmative action goals (Sessa, 1992). Diversity training programs use both didactic (e.g., lectures, readings) and interactive techniques (e.g., role-playing, simulation games). They generally provide information on the various groups present in a given work environment, along with information on laws relevant to intergroup relations in organizational contexts (e.g., affirmative action, sexual harassment). As they are currently practiced, most diversity programs tend to be rather brief in duration, but there is no reason they could not be longer. In societies striving for reconciliation, these programs may be especially useful in government organizations.

Programs developed to promote cross-cultural understanding may be relevant to protracted conflicts that involve different ethnic or cultural groups. These programs are intended to alleviate the problems of intercultural misunderstandings, stereotyping, biased attributions, and fear. They accomplish this task by teaching interpersonal relations skills, enhancing understanding of the other group, and improving the accuracy of intercultural perceptions (Brislin & Yoshida, 1994). These programs are expected to lead to an increased capacity to work and live with people from other cultural groups and reduce the stress of intercultural interactions. An operating assumption of these programs is that it is the differences between groups that are most likely to cause conflicts, not the similarities. Thus, these programs focus on understanding group differences in values, beliefs, norms, roles, and behaviors. The group differences are presented in a nonevaluative manner. These programs tend to be highly interactive involving role-plays, simulation games, and discussions of critical intercultural incidents, although some information is presented through readings and didactic presentations. They seek to help people understand the thoughts and behaviors of out-group members and to see the world from their perspective. Cross-cultural training programs have been employed with students, refugees, technical assistants, government advisers, diplomats, social service providers, and businesspeople (Brislin & Yoshida, 1994). Although they have been used primarily with adults, there is no reason why this basic approach could not be used with younger people.

Contact Programs

A number of intergroup relations programs have been created that employ intergroup contact in controlled settings. Intergroup dialogues provide one example of such programs (Gurin, Peng, Lopez, & Nagda, 1999). Intergroup dialogue programs typically involve a series of face-to-face discussions and experiential exercises among members of two groups, facilitated by trainers. Although most dialogues have been conducted in academic settings, they can also be conducted in work, government, and community settings. The goals of these dialogues are to increase intergroup understanding and provide participants with the skills to interact across group boundaries. Unlike most other intergroup relations programs, conflict is often brought out into the open and discussed. Participants are encouraged to express their emotions and discuss their reactions to prejudice, stereotyping, discrimination, and conflict.

In academic settings, dialogue groups usually involve 10-20 participants (Nagda, Zuniga, & Sevig, 1995). The participants are drawn equally from two groups that have a history of conflict. The dialogue groups meet under the direction of trained facilitators from each group whose task is to guide the discussions and help the participants adhere to norms that are conducive to a productive exchange of views (Nagda et al., 1999). The facilitators emphasize honesty and openness and expect participants to respect one another and be nonjudgmental. They encourage participants to help members of the other group understand their perspective, rather than trying to win over the other side, as in a debate. In the course of the dialogues, participants come to value the opinions and welfare of people who differ from them and they learn about the common values that are shared between groups. Thus, intergroup dialogues may be a useful tool to address reconciliation, if the members of the two groups are willing to meet in structured small group contexts. They may be difficult to use with young people (below the age of 15 or so) because they may have difficulty observing the ground rules of productive dialogues.

Another type of program that involves intergroup contact is cooperative learning. Intergroup cooperative learning programs have been widely used in the United States and elsewhere to improve intergroup relations. They may be especially useful in integrated school settings where it is considered ill-advised to have students focus directly on intergroup relations issues because they are too volatile. In these programs, intergroup contact occurs in small learning groups in which the task and reward structure require face-to-face interaction and interdependence (Aronson, Blaney, Stephan, Sikes, & Snapp, 1978; Blaney, Stephan, Rosenfield, Aronson, & Sikes, 1977; DeVries, Edwards, & Slavin, 1978; Johnson & Johnson, 1992; Weigel, Wiser, & Cook, 1975). The students can only reach their individual academic goals by working together across group lines. The content of these programs consists of the same materials that comprise the traditional curricula, but they are presented in a new format. In one version of this approach, the materials are divided up into as many segments as there are students in the group and each student is responsible for teaching his or her portion of the materials to the other students (Aronson et al., 1978). The teachers facilitate the work of the learning teams. Both the students and the teachers must be trained to adopt their new roles. Similar to other techniques used in the schools, this program is an investment in the future. Its use will be limited in societies where the contending groups attend separate schools.

An interesting contact-based program centers around a community approach to the improvement of educational programs in a mixed Jewish-Arab city in Israel (Hertz-Lazarowitz, 2004). This project involved work in the schools to improve children's achievement, work with parents to promote literacy and coexistence, and work with principals and political leaders from both groups. The in-school program employed cooperative learning groups. One component of the parents program employed Jewish-Arab workshops led by facilitators from both groups. These workshops focused on intergroup relations issues as well as developing a joint educational plan for the city. The principals and community leader group became an advocacy group for education change and worked together to obtain more resources for the schools. This is just one of dozens of coexistence programs that were implemented in Israel between the first and second Palestinian intifadas (Hertz-Lazarowitz, Zelniker, Stephan, & Stephan, 2004).

Skill-Based Programs

Some intergroup relations programs are designed to teach skills that promote positive intergroup relations. For example, many conflict resolution programs are designed to help members of conflicting groups to resolve intergroup disputes in community and school settings (Fisher, 1990). Mediation, negotiation, and third party consultation provide examples of the techniques that are taught in these programs. The goals of these techniques are to lessen or resolve interpersonal conflicts in a peaceful manner. In some programs, the participants are taught mediation skills they can use to deal with their own conflicts or in mediating conflicts between others (Johnson & Johnson, 1996). The approach to teaching is usually highly interactive, involving practicing and role-playing conflict resolution. These programs have been employed with people of all ages. Most of the programs that currently exist have not been specifically oriented toward resolving intergroup conflicts, but there is no reason that they could not be adapted for such purposes. Adapting these programs for use in intergroup conflicts would require teaching the participants to take into consideration group-related history and characteristics that would influence the groups' approaches to intergroup conflicts. In communities working toward reconciliation, it may be valuable to create conflict resolution centers or mediation centers as a means of preventing intergroup conflicts from escalating into larger conflicts.

Healing and Problem-Solving Programs

Healing programs are designed to address the emotional trauma and needs of people affected by protracted conflicts, while problem-solving programs are more oriented toward healing the communities affected by protracted conflicts. A relatively recent approach to healing involves working through collective trauma by sharing narratives in small group settings involving members of the affected groups (Bar-On & Kassem, 2004; Staub, this volume). One example of this approach was conducted in Israel between Jews and Israeli Arabs (Bar-On & Kassem, 2004). College students from both groups met together over the course of a year to share stories about the traumas their families had experienced during the ongoing conflict between their groups. The processing of these participants' feelings in response to the stories was facilitated by two leaders, one from each group. Telling these stories provided the students with an opportunity to work through their unresolved pain and anger. The storytelling technique created empathy for the other group and fostered mutual trust and respect among the participants. The ultimate goal of the program was to help the participants to learn to come to terms with the traumatic experiences suffered by their group. These programs have been conducted primarily with adults and it is not clear if they would be effective with people younger than 18 or so.

A related program that has been traditionally employed to assist in resolving conflicts and finding solutions to intergroup problems could be adapted for use in reconciliation efforts. This approach, known as problem-solving groups, is aimed at participants who occupy positions of power and influence in their respective groups (e.g., government advisors, journalists, business leaders, scholars) (Fisher, 1990; Kelman & Cohen, 1986). When it is possible, the participants are brought together on neutral ground. The discussions are facilitated by impartial leaders who are well acquainted with the conflict, but who are not members of either group. The workshops are usually short, but intense. The facilitators establish the ground rules, set the agenda, and promote constructive discussion. They try to foster a safe environment so participants can express themselves openly. They encourage an analytic approach to the conflict and the participants urged to try to understand the perspective of the other group. Considerable time is spent on brainstorming creative solutions to the conflict. It is hoped that the participants will carry these ideas back to policy makers. For use in reconciliation efforts, the participants would need to be more oriented toward finding creative ways to promote reconciliation, rather than focusing on resolving the conflict itself.

Cyberspace

There are a growing number of websites that have been created to improve intergroup relations (e.g., the Southern Poverty Law Center's website). There is only a limited literature on the use of the worldwide web to promote intergroup relations, but it would seem to offer rich possibilities that should be explored (Gorski, 2004). For instance, the multicultural pavilion (www.edchange.org/multicultural) provides resources about multicultural education, creates a forum for the exchange of ideas, contains a social justice news service, and provides ideas for curriculum reform, among other things.

Although the programs just reviewed may all be relevant to reconciliation to a greater or lesser extent, there is a pressing need for new types of programs that address the full range of consequences of intractable, violent conflicts and that seek to fulfill the many goals of reconciliation. These programs should be designed to accomplish specific goals, by marrying the psychological processes covered in the next section to the particular techniques that lead to change. There is also a need to evaluate the programs that are conducted in order to determine what works, under what conditions, and why. We need to understand both the short- and long-term outcomes of these programs. As important as it is to understand what works, it is just as important to understand what does not work so that time, effort, and resources are not wasted on programs that do not advance reconciliation. The results of these evaluations need to be widely published and disseminated both in professional journals and in more publicly accessible media.

All of the programs described in the earlier section depend for their success on psychological change processes. These processes have been the subject of considerable theorizing and research. Understanding them is crucial to improving existing techniques and creating new ones.

Psychological Processes Involved in Reconciliation

There are three fundamental domains of psychological processes involved in achieving intergroup reconciliation: affective, cognitive, and behavioral processes. Although this distinction is useful for analytical purposes, these processes interact with one another in everyday life.

Affective Processes

Anxiety and perceptions of threat are pervasive conditions in the wake of protracted conflict. Research indicates that anxiety and threat lead to negative emotions and negative attitudes toward out-groups (Stephan & Renfro, 2002; Stephan & Stephan, 2000). Reducing feelings of anxiety and threat would seem to be essential if reconciliation is to be achieved. Threat may be reduced by providing accurate information about the out-group. Face-to-face contact under favorable conditions can also reduce feelings of threat.

A second affective process that can play a crucial role in reconciliation is emotional empathy. The type of emotional empathy most relevant to reconciliation is the capacity to feel the pain and suffering of the out-group as one's own. Empathizing with the out-group can lead to a concern about their welfare and more positive feelings and attitudes toward them (Batson et al., 1997; Dovidio, ten Vergert, et al., 2004; Stephan & Finlay, 1999; Stephan et al., 2005). Emotional empathy may also counteract the tendency to blame the other side for the suffering the in-group has experienced (Finlay & Stephan, 2000). Emotional empathy can be induced through mass media presentations of the experiences of both groups and at a more personal level through dialogues and exercises such as role-playing and simulation games.

A third process that is primarily affective in nature involves making people aware of the discrepancies between their values and their behavior (Grube, Mayton, & Ball-Rokeach, 1994). When people have behaved in ways that violate their fundamental morals and values, as they most certainly do during protracted conflicts, it may be possible to motivate them to change their attitudes and behavior by making them aware of the discrepancies between their behavior and their values. The danger here is that people may respond to these discrepancies by justifying their behavior, but under the right conditions, the distress elicited by becoming aware of these discrepancies can lead people to change their behaviors and their attitudes toward the other group to be more in accord with their morals and values. If people who are experiencing value/behavior discrepancies due to their past behavior toward the out-group can be helped to see that they can change their future behavior and attitudes to be consistent with their values, they can reduce the discomfort they are experiencing over their prior behavior, rather than simply justifying it.

A fourth affective process derives from social learning theory and emphasizes the learned associations between objects and emotions, including associations between social groups and affective responses to them (Bandura, 1986). In protracted conflicts, people have learned to link the out-group with negative affect through direct experience, socialization, and exposure to the media. As a consequence, the out-group is feared, disliked, and avoided. It may be possible to modify the associations between out-groups and negative affect by providing group members with positive experiences and information about out-groups. Contact settings are the most likely type of situation for these positive associations to be fostered.

A related process involves feelings of compunction. People who believe that stereotyping is wrong experience guilt or self-criticism (compunction) when they apply stereotypes to out-groups (Devine, 1989, Devine, Plant & Buswell, 2000; Devine, Monteith, Zuwerink, & Elliot, 1991). People who are motivated to change their reliance on stereotypes can learn to put self-regulatory processes into effect that lead to the suppression of such stereotypes (Monteith, 1993; Monteith, Zuwerink, & Devine, 1994). Unfortunately, there is some evidence that people who are high in prejudice, and who may therefore not be motivated to change their attitudes, may respond to attempts to make them feel guilty with increased anger toward the out-group. Thus, invoking compunction is something that must be done with great care. Certainly, in the aftermath of protracted conflicts, people can be encouraged to adopt nonprejudiced norms and replace their stereotypes with nonbiased responses (see Devine, Plant, & Buswell, 2000). The mass media can play a role in stimulating such changes, as can the leaders of both groups, but this type of information is probably best introduced in educational settings or small group dialogues and workshops.

Closely linked to the idea of compunction is the notion of collective guilt, which involves the perception that the in-group bears some responsibility for the suffering of the out-group (Branscombe, Doosje, & McGarty, 2002). Collective guilt can lead to attempts to repair the harm to the out-group, but it is likely that it is a volatile emotion and that members of both groups may resist taking any collective responsibility for the negative aspects of the past behavior of their in-group. Another related idea is moral outrage or anger at the behavior of the in-group, which has been shown to reduce prejudice in laboratory studies (Dovidio, ten Vergert et al., 2004; Finlay & Stephan, 2000). Both emotions may be elicited in dialogue settings where people learn about the suffering inflicted on the out-group by their own group, but they may also be activated by simply learning about the injustices committed by the in-group from credible sources.

Cognitive Processes

Creating cognitive empathy can also result in prejudice reduction (Stephan & Finlay, 1999). Individuals experience cognitive empathy when they take the role of another and view the world from that person's perspective. Cognitive empathy can be promoted during reconciliation by helping people acquire knowledge about the out-group, in particular their worldviews and their practices, norms, and values. It may also help people to learn about the way the out-group views the in-group. Again, the mass media can play a role in conveying this type of information, but it can also be encouraged in the schools or in small group dialogues and workshops.

Protracted conflicts almost certainly lead people from both group to view the out-group as being very dissimilar from the in-group in ways that are integral to group identity. Changing these beliefs should lead to improvements in intergroup relations. Considerable evidence indicates that perceiving others as similar to the self increases liking for them (Byrne, 1971; Rokeach, Smith, & Evans, 1960). Thus, the goals of reconciliation may be furthered by providing information indicating that the in-group and the out-group are similar in fundamental ways. Again, the mass media and educational institutions seem ideally suited to provide this type of information.

The polarization of intergroup perceptions that characterizes intergroup conflict leads people to view others first and foremost in terms of their group identities. If people can be induced to interact with members of other groups in terms of their individual identities, rather than their group identities, it can undermine the tendency to make such sharp distinctions between groups (Brewer & Miller, 1984; Dovidio, Gaertner, Isen, Rust, & Guerra, 1998; Miller,

Brewer, & Edwards, 1985). When the salience of group identities is reduced, people come to know one another as individuals. This process of personalizing out-group members can probably best be accomplished in one-on-one inter-actions or in small groups where positive individualized contact is possible. These interactions break down monolithic perceptions of the out-group by providing in-group members with accurate information about individual out-group members as well as information on the heterogeneity of out-group members. In highly factionalized societies, such as those that have experienced protracted conflict, such interactions rarely occur naturally and instead must be actively promoted in work, education, and recreational settings.

The tendency to interact with others solely in terms of one set of group iden-tities can be undercut by reminding people that there are multiple social cat-egories to which they belong and that many of them intersect in complex ways with the identities of out-group members (Brewer, 2000; Dovidio et al., 1998; Dovidio, Kawakami, & Gaertner, 2000; Hewstone, Islam, & Judd, 1993). Thus, prejudice toward a specific out-group can be undermined if people are made aware of other important crosscutting in-group-out-group categories such as age, sex, social class, interests, social and work roles. Becoming aware of multiple crosscutting identities blurs the distinctions between in-group and out-group. These lessons are probably best learned in small group contexts when conscious efforts can be made to help people become aware of their multiple identities.

Another effective way of reducing a heavy reliance on in-group and out-group categories is of help members of both groups to think of themselves as members of one superordinate group (Gaertner, Dovidio, Nier, Ward, & Banker, 1999; Gaertner, Mann, Murrell, & Dovidio, 1989; Sherif, 1966). Such superordinate categories as the community, the nation state, a unifying religion, or humanity itself can improve intergroup relations. The former out-group is perceived to be part of a larger, all encompassing in-group. In educational and work settings members of different group can be encouraged to identify with the school or the company. Creating a superordinate identity does not mean that former group identities are lost, only that a unifying identity has been introduced (Gaertner, Rust, Dovidio, Bachman, & Anastasio, 1994).

The transition to new superordinate identities takes time. It may begin with personalizing out-group members by coming to know them as individuals. The positive attitudes created as a result of such contacts can generalize to the out-group as a whole leading to more positive evaluations of the out-group itself. The positive appraisals of the out-group may then facilitate the process of seeing the out-group as part of a superordinate group (Hewstone, 1996; Hewstone & Brown, 1986; Pettigrew, 1998). Because these processes build on one another over time, they are probably best fostered in contexts where ongoing contact is common, such as in school and work settings.

Protracted conflicts often involve biased reporting about the other group such that misinformation and negative stereotypes abound. Providing accurate information about the out-group addresses one of the primary causes of negative intergroup perceptions, namely, ignorance (Stephan & Stephan, 1984). Information about the similarity of the groups, the variability within groups, the out-group members' motives for doing the things they do, and their personal lives can begin to undo the distorted perceptions created by the conflict. It is particularly difficult to counteract negative stereotypes. Studies show that negative out-group stereotypes can be weakened if people are encouraged to pay close attention to information that contradicts their stereotypes and they then attribute the causes of the disconfirming behaviors to internal factors (Crocker, Hannah, & Weber, 1983; Mackie, Allison, Worth, & Asuncion, 1992). It helps if multiple members of the out-group are presented as contradicting the stereotype across a variety of settings so that it is difficult to explain away the disconfirming information (Rothbart & John, 1985). The mass media are well positioned to provide this kind of information. In the schools, multicultural education classes can provide accurate information on all of the groups in a given society. This type of information can also be acquired in face-to-face interaction, particularly if that interaction involves mutual interdependence (cooperation) since that seems to encourage accurate perceptions of others (Fiske, 2000; Fiske & Neuberg, 1990).

Behavioral Processes

A long line of research provides evidence that intergroup contact can improve intergroup relations under certain conditions. Chief among these conditions are equal status in the contact situation, cooperation in pursuit of common goals, a perception of common interests and common humanity, and support from authority figures (Allport, 1954; Amir, 1976; Pettigrew, 1971). However, in an extensive review of the evidence on the effects of contact, it was found that increasing levels of intergroup contact can improve intergroup relations, even in the absence of these optimal conditions (Pettigrew & Tropp, 2000). Although the optimal circumstances for contact are unlikely to occur naturally with any great frequency in the aftermath of protracted conflicts, they can be encouraged in work settings and the schools. A variety of intergroup relations programs, such as those relying on cooperative learning and dialogue groups, create these conditions (Slavin, 1995; Stephan & Stephan, 2001).

If people find their interactions with out-group members to be rewarding, they are likely to change their behavior and attitudes toward them. Incentive structures can be set up in work settings and the schools to promote positive intergroup interactions. Incentives can also be used with community programs that are designed to bring members of the two conflicting groups together for interactions that are rewarding, including sporting and entertainment events. Similarly, people are influenced by the models to whom they are exposed. Business and government leaders, as well as teachers and administrators, can publicly model positive intergroup relations.

Learning about members of the other group in face-to-face interactions can be a powerful tool to improve intergroup relations. Such interactions provide opportunities for self-disclosures that can activate empathy. Mutual self-disclosures can create an atmosphere of trust (Derlega, Metts, Petronio, & Margulis, 1993). The positive effects are likely to be enhanced if the self-disclosures occur in structured contexts where rules of civil discourse prevail and where they are modeled by facilitators. These types of interactions characterize dialogue groups (Gurin et al., 1999). One study of self-disclosures in the context of multicultural education programs found that they enhanced in-group identity and acceptance of out-group identity (Davidman, 1995). In fact, many of the characteristics of multicultural education programs, such as their duration, openness of communication, informality, and use of interactive exercises, foster a climate in which self-disclosure can become more intimate and thereby improve intergroup relations. The timing of self-disclosures is important even in everyday social relations (Derlega et al., 1993), but it takes on added significant in relations between members of groups that have been in conflict. Too much self-disclosure too early in new intergroup relationships, particularly about painful issues, may not be beneficial.

We are now in a position to design programs for use in reconciliation efforts that are specifically created to capitalize on our knowledge of some of the key psychological processes involved in improving intergroup relations. In addition, the techniques that have been developed in earlier programs can be refined for application to reconciliation efforts by incorporating psychological processes known to promote change. Nonetheless, we need more research into the psychological processes specifically involved in reconciliation. We also need more comprehensive theories of the reconciliation process itself. For instance, it seems likely that there is a time course for reconciliation, but little is known about its properties. Clearly, efforts at processing grief, pain, anger, and hatred must precede efforts directed at forgiveness, but the role and timing of more cognitive processes and intergroup contact and how they relate to more affective processes is yet to be understood. The timing of specific interventions is just one example of a range of intervention issues that must be considered when planning reconciliation efforts. The next section reviews some other intervention issues.

Intervention Issues

Adding to the complexity of achieving reconciliation is the fact that there can be no recipe that fits all situations. Reconciliation strategies have to be tailored to the specific context in which the protracted conflict has occurred. The programs that are needed depend on the context. What are the cultural differences among the groups in conflict? What is the nature of the conflict (religious, ethnic, political, territorial, resource based, etc.)? How is it construed by the different groups? What is the history of the conflict? How protracted and how intense was the conflict? Were atrocities committed? Are there humanitarian crises that must be addressed immediately? With these and other background issues in mind, decisions must be made about how to intervene in a particular conflict. Who will conduct the interventions? In what contexts will they be conducted (schools, community settings, work settings, government agencies, etc.)? To what degree will the mass media be involved in reconciliation efforts?

Decisions about intervention issues depend to a significant degree on the resources available to address reconciliation. The motivation of the two sides to engage in reconciliation is another factor that must be considered. Where can the greatest impact be achieved in a particular social system and what parts of the system are most receptive to reconciliation efforts? If efforts will be made to reach various age groups, psychological development issues must be taken into consideration for the programs suited to adults are unlikely to be suited to children. Reconciliation must be seen as a long-term process. A special emphasis must be placed on young people to break the cycle of violence.

In addition, the relative size of the groups and the existing asymmetries in power must be taken into consideration. Situations in which the groups are of more or less equivalent size and power may be amenable to a wider range of interventions than those where size or power asymmetries exist. The preexisting and current governmental structures (democratic, authoritarian, military rule, dictatorship, etc.) may also influence attempts at reconciliation. Internal factions within the primary groups involved in the conflict will most likely impede attempts at reconciliation by creating multiple stakeholders with divergent viewpoints and goals. Subgroups that are deeply disaffected from the major parties to the conflict will pose particular problems. Finally, different contexts may be characterized by different levels and types of resistance to reconciliation that will have a powerful effect on reconciliation efforts. One or both groups may resist reconciliation efforts particularly if they believe they have something to lose (e.g., power) in the process. Similarly, some individuals in both groups may resist reconciliation efforts, while others support them.

Roles for Psychologists

There are many roles that psychologists can play in the reconciliation process. They may be able to chart the state of intergroup relations at the end of a protracted conflict and make recommendations concerning programs that may be best suited to local circumstances. They can provide advice on social policy to leaders in government and the private sector. They can help to develop new interventions, as well assisting in the implementation of more established reconciliation interventions. They can train facilitators for these interventions and they can evaluate their effectiveness. They can also help to develop theories about the reconciliation process and its components and they can conduct basic research into the psychological processes involved in reconciliation.

Concluding Comments

Our understanding of how to bring about intergroup reconciliation is in its infancy. The stakes are high and the need is pressing, for there are few signs that intergroup violence and warfare are fading from the international scene. Fortunately, we have never been better equipped to undertake these challenges and there are great number of people who are dedicated to making intergroup reconciliation possible. It is in all our interests for them to succeed.

References

Allport, G. W. (1954). *The nature of prejudice*. Cambridge, MA: Addison-Wesley.

Amir, Y. (1976). The role of intergroup contact in change of prejudice and race relations. In P. Katz & D. A. Taylor (Eds.), *Towards the elimination of racism* (pp. 245-308). New York: Pergamon.

Aronson, E., Blaney, N., Stephan, C., Sikes, J., & Snapp, M. (1978). *The jigsaw classroom*. Beverly Hills, CA: Sage.

Bandura, A. (1986). *The social foundations of thought and action*. Englewood Cliffs, NJ: Prentice-Hall.

Banks, J. A. (1973). *Teaching ethnic studies: Concepts and strategies*. Washington, DC: National Council for the Social Studies.

Banks, J. A. (1997). *Educating citizens in a multicultural society*. New York: Teachers College Press.

Banks, J. A. (2002). *An introduction to multicultural education* (3rd ed.). Boston, MA: Allyn & Bacon.

Bar-On, D., & Kassem, F. (2004). Storytelling as a way to work through intractable conflicts: The German-Jewish experience and its relevance to the Palestinian-Israeli context. *Journal of Social Issues, 60,* 289-306.

Bar-Tal, D. (2004). Nature, rationale, and effectiveness of education for co-existence. *Journal of Social Issues, 60,* 253-272.

Batson, C. D., Polycarpou, M. P., Harmon-Jones, E., Imhoff, H. J., Mitchener, E. C., Bednar, L. L., et al. (1997). Empathy and attitudes: Can feeling for a member of a stigmatized group improve feelings toward the group? *Journal of Personality and Social Psychology, 72,* 105-118.

Battistich, V., Solomon, D., Watson, M., Solomon, J., & Schaps, E. (1989). Effects of an elementary school program to enhance prosocial behavior on children's cognitive-social problem-solving skills and strategies. *Journal of Applied Developmental Psychology, 10,* 147-169.

Blaney, N., Stephan, C., Rosenfield, D., Aronson, E., & Sikes, J. (1977). Interdependence in the classroom: A field study. *Journal of Educational Psychology, 69,* 121-128.

Branscombe, N., Doosje, B., & McGarty, C. (2002). Antecedents and consequences of collective guilt. In D. M. Mackie & E. R. Smith (Eds.), *From prejudice to intergroup emotions: Differentiated reactions to social groups* (pp. 49-66). Philadelphia, PA: Psychology Press.

Brewer, M. B. (2000). Reducing prejudice through cross-categorization: Effects of multiple social identities. In S. Oskamp (Ed.), *Reducing prejudice and discrimination* (pp. 165-183). Mahwah, NJ: Lawrence Erlbaum.

Brewer, M. B., & Miller, N. (1984). Beyond the contact hypothesis: Theoretical perspectives on desegregation. In N. Miller & M. B. Brewer (Eds.), *Groups in contact: The psychology of desegregation* (pp. 281-302). New York: Academic Press.

Brislin, R., & Yoshida, T. (Eds.) (1994). *Intercultural communication training: An introduction.* Thousand Oaks, CA: Sage.

Burton, J. W. (1986). The procedures of conflict resolution. In A. E. Azar & J. W. Burton (Eds.), *International conflict resolution: Theory and practice* (pp. 92-116). Boulder, CO: Lynne Reiner Publishers.

Byrne, D. (1971). *The attraction paradigm.* New York: Academic Press.

Chambers, J. R., Baron, R. S., & Inman, M. L. (2006). Misperceptions of intergroup conflict. *Psychological Science, 17,* 38-44.

Crocker, J., Hannah, D. B., & Weber, R. (1983). Person memory and causal attributions. *Journal of Personality and Social Psychology, 44,* 55-66.

Davidman, L. (1995). Multicultural education: A movement in search of meaning and positive connections. *Multicultural Education, 2,* 8-12.

Derlega, V. J., Metts, S., Petronio, S., & Margulis, S. T. (1993). *Self-disclosure.* Newbury Park, CA: Sage.

Devine, P. (1989). Stereotypes and prejudice: Their automatic and controlled components. *Journal of Personality and Social Psychology, 56,* 5-18.

Devine, P. G., Monteith, M. J., Zuwerink, J. R., & Elliot, A. J. (1991). Prejudice with and without compunction. *Journal of Personality and Social Psychology, 60,* 817-830.

Devine, P. G., Plant, E. A., & Buswell, B. N. (2000). Breaking the prejudice habit: Progress an obstacles. In S. Oskamp (Ed.), *Reducing prejudice and discrimination* (pp. 185-208). Hillsdale, NJ: Erlbaum.

DeVries, D. L., Edwards, K. J., & Slavin, R. E. (1978). Biracial learning teams and race relations in the classroom: Four field experiments on Teams-Games-Tournaments. *Journal of Educational Psychology, 70,* 356-362.

Dovidio, J. F., Brigham, J. C., Johnson, B. T., & Gaertner, S. (1996). Stereotyping, prejudice, and discrimination: Another look. In C. N. Macrae, C. Stangor, & M. Hewstone (Eds.), *Stereotypes and stereotyping* (pp. 276-319). New York: Guilford.

Dovidio, J. F., Gaertner, S. L., Isen, A. M., Rust, M., & Guerra, P. (1998). Positive affect, cognition, and the reduction of intergroup bias. In C. Sedikides, J. Schopler, & C. A. Insko (Eds.), *Intergroup cognition and intergroup behavior* (pp. 337-366). Mahwah, NJ: Lawrence Erlbaum.

Dovidio, J. F., Gaertner, S. L., Stewart, T. L., Esses, V. M., ten Vergert, M., & Hodson, G. (2004). From intervention to outcome: Processes in the reduction of bias (pp. 243-265). In W. G. Stephan & W. P. Vogt (Eds.), *Learning together: Intergroup relations programs.* New York: Teachers College Press.

Dovidio, J. F., Kawakami, K., & Gaertner, S. L. (2000). Reducing contemporary prejudice: Combating explicit and implicit bias at the individual and intergroup level. In S. Oskamp (Ed.), *Reducing prejudice and discrimination* (pp. 137-163). Mahwah, NJ: Lawrence Erlbaum.

Dovidio, J. F., ten Vergert, M., Stewart, T. L., Gaertner, S. L., Johnson, J. D., Esses, V. M., et al. (2004). Perspective and prejudice: Antecedents and mediating mechanisms. *Personality and Social Psychology Bulletin, 30,* 1537-1549.

Fine, M. (1995). *Habits of the mind: Struggling over values in America's classrooms.* San Francisco, CA: Jossey-Bass.

Finlay, K. A., & Stephan, W. G. (2000). Reducing prejudice: The effects of empathy on intergroup attitudes. *Journal of Applied Social Psychology, 30,* 1722-1736.

Fisher, R. J. (1990). *The social psychology of intergroup and international conflict resolution.* New York: Springer-Verlag.

Fiske, S. T. (2000). Interdependence and the reduction of prejudice. In S. Oskamp (Ed.), *Reducing prejudice and discrimination* (pp. 115-136). Thousand Oaks, CA: Sage.

Fiske, S. T., & Neuberg, S. L. (1990). A continuum model of impression formation, from category-based to individuating processes: Influences of information and motivation on attention and interpretation. In M. P. Zanna (Ed.), *Advances in experimental social psychology* (Vol. 23, pp. 1-74). New York: Academic Press.

Gaertner, S. L., Dovidio, J. F., Nier, J. A., Ward, C. M., & Banker, B. S. (1999). Across cultural divides: The value of superordinate identity. In D. A. Prentice & D. T. Miller (Eds.), *Cultural divides: Understanding and overcoming group conflict* (pp. 173-212). New York: Russell Sage Foundation.

Gaertner, S. L., Mann, J., Murrell, A., & Dovidio, J. F. (1989). Reducing intergroup bias: The benefits of recategorization. *Journal of Personality and Social Psychology, 57*, 239-249.

Gaertner, S. L., Rust, M. C., Dovidio, J. F., Bachman, B. A., & Anastasio, P. A. (1994). The contact hypothesis: The role of a common ingroup identity on reducing intergroup bias. *Small Group Research, 25*, 224-249.

Gorski, P. (2004). *Multicultural education and the internet* (2nd ed.). Boston, CA: McGraw-Hill.

Grube, J. W., Mayton, D. M., & Ball-Rokeach, S. J. (1994). Inducing change in values, attitudes, and behaviors: Belief system theory and the method of value self-confrontation. *Journal of Social Issues, 50*, 153-173.

Gurin, P., Peng, T., Lopez, G., & Nagda, B. R. (1999). Context, identity, and intergroup relations. In D. Prentice & D. Miller (Eds.), *Cultural divides: The social psychology of intergroup contact* (pp. 133-170). New York: Russell Sage Foundation.

Hertz-Lazarowitz, R. (2004). Existence and coexistence in acre: The power of educational reform. *Journal of Social Issues, 60*, 357-371.

Hertz-Lazarowitz, R., Zelniker, T., Stephan, C. W., & Stephan, W. G. (Eds.) (2004). Improving Arab-Jewish relations in Israel: Theory and practice in coexistence education programs [Special issue]. *Journal of Social Issues, 60*.

Hewstone, M. (1996). Contact and categorization. In C. N. Macrae, C. Stangor, & M. Hewstone (Eds.), *Foundations of stereotypes and stereotyping* (pp. 323-368). New York: Guilford.

Hewstone, M., & Brown, R. (1986). Contact is not enough: An intergroup perspective on the contact hypothesis. In M. Hewstone & R. Brown (Eds.), *Contact and conflict in intergroup encounters* (pp. 1-44). Oxford, UK: Basil Blackwell.

Hewstone, M., Islam, M. R., & Judd, C. M. (1993). Models of cross categorization and intergroup relations. *Journal of Personality and Social Psychology, 64*, 779-793.

Johnson, D. W., & Johnson, R. T. (1992). Positive interdependence: Key to effective cooperation. In R. Hertz-Lazarowitz & N. Miller (Eds.), *Interaction in cooperative groups* (pp. 174-199). New York: Cambridge University Press.

Johnson, D. W., & Johnson, R. T. (1996). Conflict resolution and peer mediation programs in elementary and secondary schools: A review of the research. *Review of Educational Research, 66*, 459-506.

Kelman, H. C., & Cohen, S. P. (1986). Resolution of international conflict: An interactional approach. In S. Worchel & W. G. Austin (Eds.), *Psychology of intergroup relations* (pp. 323-342). Chicago, IL: Nelson Hall.

Kohlberg, L. (1969). Stage and sequence: The cognitive developmental approach to socialization. In D. A. Goslin (Ed.), *Handbook of socialization theory and research*. Chicago: Rand McNally.

Kohlberg, L. (1981). *Essays on moral development*. New York: Harper and Row.

Maass, A., Salvi, D., Arcuri, L., & Semin, G. (1989). Language use in intergroup contexts: The linguistic intergroup bias. *Journal of Personality and Social Psychology, 57*, 981-993.

Mackie, D. M., Allison, S. T., Worth, L. T., & Asuncion, A. G. (1992). Social decision making processes: The generalization of outcome-biased counter-stereotypic inferences. *Journal of Experimental Social Psychology, 28,* 23-42.

Miller, N., Brewer, M. B., & Edwards, K. (1985). Cooperative interaction in desegregated settings: A laboratory analogue. *Journal of Social Issues, 41,* 63-81.

Monteith, M. J. (1993). Self-regulation of prejudiced responses: Implications for progress in prejudice-reduction efforts. *Journal of Personality and Social Psychology, 65,* 469-485.

Monteith, M. J., Zuwerink, J. R., & Devine, P. G. (1994). Prejudice and prejudice reduction: Classic challenges, contemporary approaches. In P. G. Devine, D. L. Hamilton, & T. M. Ostrom (Eds.), *Social cognition: Impact on social psychology* (pp. 324-346). San Diego, CA: Academic Press.

Nagda, B. A., Spearmon, N. A., Holley, L. C., Harding, S., Balassone, M. L., Moise-Swanson, D., et al. (1999). Intergroup dialogues: An innovative approach to teaching about diversity and justice in social work programs. *Journal of Social Work and Education, 35,* 433-449.

Nagda, B. A., Zuniga, X., & Sevig, T. (1995). Bridging differences through peer facilitated intergroup dialogues. In S. Hatcher (Ed.), *Peer programs on a college campus: Theory, training and voices of the peers* (pp. 378-414). San Diego, CA: New Resources.

Oser, F. K. (1985). Moral education and values education: The discourse perspective. In M. C. Wittrock (Ed.), *Handbook of research on teaching* (3rd ed.). New York: Macmillan.

Pettigrew, T. F. (1971). *Racially separate or together?* New York: McGraw-Hill.

Pettigrew, T. F. (1998). Intergroup contact theory. *Annual Review of Psychology, 49,* 65-85.

Pettigrew, T. F., & Tropp, L. R. (2000). Does intergroup contact reduce prejudice: Recent meta-analytic findings. In S. Oskamp (Ed.), *Reducing prejudice and discrimination* (pp. 93-114). Mahwah, NJ: Erlbaum.

Rokeach, M., Smith, P. W., & Evans, R. I. (1960). Two kinds of prejudice or one. In M. Rokeach (Ed.), *The open and closed mind* (pp. 132-168). New York: Basic Books.

Rothbart, M., & John, O. P. (1985). Social categorization and behavioral episodes: A cognitive analysis and the effects of intergroup contact. *Journal of Social Issues, 41,* 81-104.

Schulz, L. H., Barr, D. J., & Selman, R. L. (2001). The value of a developmental approach to evaluating character development programs: An outcome study of Facing History and Ourselves. *Journal of Moral Education, 30,* 3-27.

Sessa, W. I. (1992). Managing diversity at the Xerox corporation: Balanced workforce goals and caucus groups. In S. E. Jackson & Associates (Eds.), *Diversity in the workforce* (pp. 37-64). New York: Guilford.

Sherif, M. (1966). *In common predicament: Social psychology of intergroup conflict and cooperation.* London: Routledge and Kegan Paul.

Slavin, R. E. (1995). *Cooperative learning: Theory, research, and practice* (2nd ed.). Boston: Allyn & Bacon.

Snyder, M. (1992). Motivational foundations of behavioral confirmation. In M. Zanna (Ed.), *Advances in experimental social psychology* (Vol. 25, pp. 67-114). Orlando, FL: Academic Press.

Stephan, C. W., & Stephan, W. G. (2004). Intergroup relations in multicultural education programs. In J. A. Banks & C. McGee-Banks (Eds.), *Handbook of research on multicultural education* (2nd ed.). New York: Jossey-Bass.

Stephan, W. G., & Finlay, K. A. (1999). The role of empathy in improving intergroup relations. *Journal of Social Issues, 55,* 729-744.

Stephan, W. G., & Renfro, C. L. (2002). The role of threats in intergroup relations. In D. Mackie & E. R. Smith (Eds.), *From prejudice to intergroup emotions* (pp. 191-208). New York: Psychology Press.

Stephan, W. G., Renfro, C. L., Esses, V. M., Stephan, C. W., & Martin, T. (2005). The effects of feeling threatened on attitudes toward immigrants. *International Journal of Intercultural Relations. 29,* 1-19.

Stephan, W. G., & Stephan, C. W. (1984). The role of ignorance in intergroup relations. In N. Miller & M. B. Brewer (Eds.), *Groups in contact: The psychology of desegregation* (pp. 229-257). New York: Academic Press.

Stephan, W. G., & Stephan, C. W. (2000). An integrated threat theory of prejudice. In S. Oskamp (Ed.), *Reducing prejudice and discrimination* (pp. 225-246). Hillsdale, NJ: Erlbaum.

Stephan, W. G., & Stephan, C. W. (2001). *Improving intergroup relations.* Thousand Oaks, CA: Sage.

Weigel, R. H., Wiser, P. L., & Cook, S. W. (1975). The impact of cooperative learning experiences on cross-ethnic relations and helping. *Journal of Social Issues, 31,* 219-244.

Ybarra, O., Stephan, W. G., & Schaberg, L. (2000). Misanthropic memory for the behavior of group members. *Personality and Social Psychology Bulletin, 26,* 1515-1525.

Ybarra, O., Stephan, W. G., Schaberg, L., & Lawrence, J. S. (2003). The stereotype disconfirmability bias. *Journal of Applied Social Psychology, 33,* 2630-2646.

CHAPTER 17

Promoting Reconciliation After Genocide and Mass Killing in Rwanda—And Other Postconflict Settings: Understanding the Roots of Violence, Healing, Shared History, and General Principles

Ervin Staub

In the aftermath of genocide, mass killing, or intractable—persistent and violent—conflict between groups, how can members of these groups continue to live together and build a nonviolent future.[1] How can they create reasonably harmonious relations? Increasingly, research and observations have shown that when violent conflicts end, even if they end by a peace agreement—rather than one party defeating another as in Rwanda, which will be a focus of this chapter—violence is likely to recur (de la Rey, 2001; Lederach, 1997). The peace agreement may not fit the interests of all the segments of the population or elites. Even more importantly, the end to the violence is not likely to change the hostility that gave rise to violence in the first place, and has become more intense in the course of and as a result of the violence.

I will describe here an approach my associates and I have developed to promote reconciliation between Tutsis and Hutus in the aftermath of the horrific genocide in

Rwanda (Staub & Pearlman, 2001, 2006; Staub, Pearlman, Gubin, & Hagengimana, 2005). We believe this approach is widely applicable in postconflict settings. I will describe the approach, the research we have conducted to evaluate it, and the varied uses of it, or of aspects of it, in the course of our work in Rwanda. I will describe the use of the approach in seminars/workshops/trainings with people in the community, with journalists, with national leaders, with community leaders, and in weekly and monthly radio programs. My purpose is to advance both theory and practice. To fulfill the former purpose I will stress the importance of both healing after group violence, and understanding the roots of violence as avenues to the prevention of new violence and to reconciliation. As a background, before I describe our approach, I will briefly discuss general principles of reconciliation.

Reconciliation is a change in attitudes and behaviors toward the other group. We define it as *mutual* acceptance by members of groups of each other, and the processes and structures that lead to or maintain that acceptance (Staub & Pearlman, 2001). Reconciliation implies that victims and perpetrators do not see the past as defining the future. They come to accept and see the humanity of one another and see the possibility of a constructive relationship. However, while the essence of reconciliation is a changed psychological orientation toward the other, political and social processes, and structures and institutions that serve reconciliation are important both to promote it, and to solidify and maintain the progressively evolving psychological changes that result from it. Our definition is consistent with others', for example, Kriesberg's (1998), which focus on the relationship between parties. It is consistent in content but different in approach from the definition of Broneus (2003), who includes not only changes in attitude and behavior between parties, but also processes important in bringing them about (e.g., mutual acknowledgment of past suffering) in the definition of reconciliation.

Following great violence, reconciliation is a difficult, long-term process (Staub & Bar-Tal, 2003). Theory, research, and practice are in their early phases, and it is an important challenge to develop effective procedures that promote reconciliation. Since in many postconflict settings hostile groups continue to live next to or intermixed with each other, it is also important to explore ways to speed up reconciliation.

The Impact of Violence on Survivors, Perpetrators, and Passive Bystanders

Genocide and mass killing—the latter often an aspect of intractable conflict, lasting conflict that resists resolution and is violent—deeply affect survivors, their perception of themselves and of the world. Being the victims of such violence makes people see the world as dangerous, and makes them feel diminished and vulnerable (Staub, 1998). Victimization may give rise to trauma symptoms, and disrupt survivors' worldview, identity, and relationships to people (McCann & Pearlman, 1990; Pearlman & Saakvitne, 1995). Since identity is rooted in part in-group membership (Tajfel, 1982), even members of the victim group who were not present when the genocide was perpetrated may be greatly traumatized (Staub, 1998). In Rwanda, this means *returnees*, mainly children of Tutsi refugees from earlier violence who came back from neighboring countries after the genocide to devastated families and community. Since they now rule the country, the impact of the genocide on them (and the earlier experiences of their families who fled Rwanda in response to mass killings and were refugees in other countries) is likely to have significant political consequences.

The psychological consequences of victimization include great sensitivity to threat (Herman, 1992; Staub, 1998). When new conflict arises, this makes it more difficult for survivors to balance their own needs and the needs and concerns of others. Without corrective experiences that help in psychological recovery, they may believe that they need to forcefully defend themselves even when violent self-defense is not necessary. In response to new threat or conflict, they may strike out, in the process becoming perpetrators (Staub, 1998; Staub & Pearlman, 2006; Volkan, 1997). Healing from psychological wounds is important both to prevent such defensive violence and to enhance the openness of the group for reconciliation.

Perpetrators also carry psychological wounds. At times, their earlier woundedness is one source of their violence (Mamdani, 2002). In addition, to engage in their violent actions, perpetrators have to distance themselves from their victims, so that they see their humanity less and feel less empathy, which is likely to generalize to other human beings. This may partly explain why violence by one group toward another tends to spread to other victims as well (Staub, 1989). Recent research shows that people who engage in varied forms of violence against others are psychologically wounded by their actions (MacNair, 2002; Rhodes, Allen, Nowinski, & Cillessen, 2002). Passive bystanders, members of the perpetrator group who have witnessed the evolution of hostility, discrimination, and increasing violence that usually precedes genocide or mass killing, are likely to be also deeply affected. To reduce their empathic suffering and maintain their sense of connection to their own group, which is perpetrating this violence, they progressively distance themselves from victims, in part by increasingly devaluing them (Staub, 1989).

The extent, moral meaning, and nature of psychological woundedness of these different groups is obviously different. However, addressing the woundedness of all of them is important to promote reconciliation. When violence ends, both perpetrators and passive members of a perpetrator group tend to go into a defensive stance, without empathy for their victims and without the willingness to assume responsibility for their own or their group's actions (Staub & Pearlman, 2001, 2006). Addressing their woundedness may diminish their defensiveness and increase their openness to and capacity for reconciliation. Together with other processes of reconciliation it may enable them to see the humanity of the victims, to feel empathy, regret, and sorrow, and to become capable of apology, which is important for both forgiveness and reconciliation (Staub, 2005a). In summary, healing by deeply wounded survivors, as well as by perpetrators and passive members of a perpetrator group who are also wounded, respectively by their violence and passivity, seem important requirements of and contributors to reconciliation (see also Montville, 1993).

Genocide in Rwanda

Starting in April 7, 1994, over a 100-day period, Hutus killed about 700,000 Tutsis, as well as about 50,000 Hutus who were politically moderate or regarded as enemies for historical reasons. The division between the groups had a long history. The Tutsis were dominant already before colonial rule. The Belgian colonizers elevated the Tutsis and had them rule in their behalf, increasing their dominance over Hutus. In 1959, there was a Hutu revolt, with about 50,000 Tutsis killed. From then on, continuing after independence in 1962, the Hutus ruled the country. The Tutsis suffered discrimination and periodic mass killings. In 1990, a primarily Tutsi military group, many of them children of Tutsis refugees from earlier violence, the Rwandan Patriotic Army (RPA), entered from Uganda. A civil war began. In 1993, after a cease-fire, the Arusha accords were signed, an agreement to establish a shared government. In 1994, the President's plane was shot down, and the genocide immediately began. The perpetrators in this government-organized violence included members of the military, young men organized into paramilitary groups, and ordinary people including neighbors and even family members in mixed families (des Forges, 1999; Mamdani, 2002). The community of nations watched while about 10,000 Tutsis a day were killed. The genocide ended when the RPA defeated the government army and took over the government.

Since then, the power has been in the hands of the minority Tutsis. The government has been promoting the idea of unity and reconciliation among Rwandese and has taken active steps to promote reconciliation. However, over the years the government has been increasingly intolerant of *divisionism*, at time applying the term, and also the more extreme accusation of propagating genocidal ideology, to individuals and groups it sees as potential opposition.

The political context and societal processes affect reconciliation, and impact the kind of reconciliation efforts we have been engaged in. However, in Rwanda some processes continue to promote reconciliation, for example, the absence of discrimination in education.

Conceptual Elements and Practical Avenues in Reconciliation: A Brief Overview

I will review some elements of reconciliation that have been emphasized in the literature. These elements are conceptually/psychologically compelling, but as yet with limited evidence of their effects.

Two important elements are *truth and justice* (Gibson, 2004; Proceedings, 2002). Anyone who has worked with survivors of genocide or engaged with groups that have survived genocide (e.g., Hovannisian, 2003) will know that survivors desperately want to have the truth of what was done to them be established and their suffering acknowledged. Acknowledgement, especially when it is empathic, is healing. When the world (other groups, one's society, other countries, the international community) acknowledge and condemn victimization of a group of people, this says that such violence is unacceptable. It tells survivors that the moral order is being reinstated and helps them feel safer. Truth and the acknowledgment of suffering may enhance diminished personal and group identity, by showing that the victims are innocent and not to be blamed for their victimization. Acknowledgment from the perpetrator group of their actions, expressions of regret and empathy, are of special importance to survivors. Unfortunately, as I have noted, perpetrators usually continue to justify their actions and to devalue and blame their victims. Healing by them may lessen their defensiveness. While truth is sometimes simple, in that violence is completely one-sided, it is often complex. In Rwanda, the genocide, according to most observers, was one sided. But Hutus refer to their *slavery* before 1959 (Staub, 2006), and also to violence against civilians by the RPA during the civil war (desForges, 1999), and subsequent violence against Hutus, for example, against refugees in Zaire, now the Congo (Mamdani, 2002). After conflict, groups tend to focus on their own suffering and blame the other. Reconciliation requires acknowledgment of suffering by both sides, even when substantially unequal. However, creating a mutually acceptable, shared history is extremely difficult (see below).

The importance of justice for reconciliation has also received substantial attention (Byrne, 2004; Gibson, 2004; Proceedings, 2002). Truth is a prerequisite for justice. Some regard justice as punishment as important for stopping future perpetrators, which it may or may not accomplish. However, survivors of genocide probably also desperately want and need justice as a form of acknowledgement and to recreate a moral order. Justice can take varied forms, such as punishment (retributive), compensation, or perpetrators and their group making a positive contribution to building society (restorative). Just societal procedural (procedural justice) may be especially important (Tyler & Smith, 1998).

Firm empirical evidence about the role of truth is limited as yet (but see Gibson, 2004). However, the absence of truth and justice seems to make it difficult for survivors to heal, look into the future, and move on psychologically. The Armenian community has greatly struggled with the absence of acknowledgment of the Turkish genocide against them, both by Turkey, and as a result of pressure by Turkey, which has used its political and financial influence on other countries, also by other nations of the world. A great deal of the Armenian community's energy has focused on engaging with the issue of the denial of the genocide (Hovannisian, 2003). When acknowledgment and justice are not forthcoming, a community may need to create internal healing processes (Staub, 2003a).

While the justice discussed in relation to reconciliation usually refers to justice following wrongdoing by a group and its members in the course of violence against the other group, justice in terms of fair, equitable relations among members of a society is also very important. In Northern Ireland, the possibility of resolving the conflict between Catholics and Protestants greatly increased by the improvement of economic and educational circumstances of and opportunities for the Catholic minority (Cairns & Darby, 1998).

Another significant element in promoting reconciliation is *contact*, especially deep engagement by people belonging to hostile groups. Social-psychological theories of contact are highly relevant here. Meta-analysis of a large body of research on contact shows that it has positive effects (Pettigrew & Tropp, 2006). While research has shown that superficial contact, people living in the same area, does not help to overcome devaluation and prejudice, even that can have positive effects by making deeper contact possible (Tausch, Kenworthy, & Hewstone, 2006). People from different groups working together for shared goals can be especially valuable. In three cities in India where instigating events did not lead to violence, Hindus and Muslims belonging to and committed to the same organizations have been able to work together and act in response to instigating events in ways that prevented the flare up of violence. In contrast, in three cities where similar conditions did lead to violence, such organizations did not exist (Varshney, 2002).

Forgiveness has also been proposed as important for reconciliation (Helmick & Petersen, 2001; Staub & Bar-Tal, 2003). Both theory and research with individuals suggest that forgiveness, letting go of hostility, anger, and the desire for revenge, and developing a more positive attitude toward a harmdoer can ease the suffering of those who have been harmed (see Worthington, 2005). An important difference between forgiveness and reconciliation is that the former is one sided, the latter mutual. Anecdotal information in Rwanda suggests that forgiveness by a survivor may lead to expressions of regret and apology by perpetrators. However, forgiveness is usually *facilitated* by expressions of regret and apology. Without them, after one group victimized another, with the groups continuing to live together, forgiveness can be problematic, maintaining or even enhancing the imbalance that the harmdoing has created between victims and perpetrators (Staub, 2005a).

A great deal of practical intervention to promote reconciliation is in the tradition of *conflict resolution* approaches (see Kelman & Fisher, 2003), involving dialog between members of the group who are parties to the conflict, often between influential members of these groups. Dialog groups can have different goals, from overcoming hostility and developing more positive attitudes, to identifying and working to resolve conflict, both material and psychological, to resolving practical problems in coexistence (Kelman & Fisher, 2003; Kriesberg, 1998; Volkan, 1998). Contact, significant engagement in working for shared goals, is an aspect of this process. However, whatever the goal, to be able to work together, participants need to move from blaming and anger, to some degree of empathy with each other, and the ability to accept some responsibility for their own group's actions. It is hoped and assumed that changes in participants will be transmitted to other people.

In describing our work, I will discuss further the role of healing and discuss the creation of a shared history of the past, in place of conflicting views of the past that can generate new violence.

The Role of Psychology and Structure

Our definition of reconciliation focuses on psychological elements—which we see as central and essential. However, societal structures have a great deal to do with promoting and maintaining reconciliation. By psychological elements, I mean people's perceptions, interpretations, evaluations, and attitudes (in relation to past and current events, other people and groups, current policies and practices), the resulting emotions, as well as affects associated with their own and their group's past history and expectations of the future. By structure, I mean policies and practices, the nature of institutions. Equality or equity that policies and institutions promote and create, in the education of children belonging to different groups, in access to jobs, in opportunities for contact, in the application of the justice system, in access by members of different groups to the public arena, make reconciliation easier and more likely (Cairns & Darby, 1998).

Our interventions focused on psychological change. However, we hoped that our work over time would have a progressively expanding influence, as we combine a bottom-up approach, training people who work with groups in the community and creating radio programs that reach much of the population, and a top-down approach, working with members of the media, community leaders and national leaders, who can exert wide ranging influence on people and can shape policies and institutions. This was a progressively developing vision, as in the course of our work new possibilities became available to us.

An Approach to Healing and Reconciliation

We (see Staub & Pearlman, 2006) have developed an approach to reconciliation that we used with varied groups in Rwanda, ranging from the level of the community to national leaders. The approach is based in part on our own research and theories about the origins and prevention of genocide (Staub, 1989, 1996, 1998, 1999, 2003b), informed also by others' work on genocide (for reviews of work on genocide see Chorbajian & Shirinian, 1999; Totten, Parsons, & Charny, 1997) as well as by work on reconciliation (see Staub & Pearlman, 2001; Staub & Bar-Tal, 2003). It is also based on our work on trauma and healing (McCann & Pearlman, 1990; Pearlman & Saakvitne, 1995; Saakvitne, Gamble, Pearlman, & Lev, 2000; Staub, 1998) as well as the work by others on complex trauma (Allen, 2001; Esterling, L'Abate, Murray, & Pennebaker, 1999; Herman, 1992). I will review the central procedures of the approach in the context of describing our first project. In describing subsequent projects, I will indicate the further evolution of our interventions.

The approach focuses on psychological education, with experiential elements. In this approach participants, members of antagonistic groups, in our work in Rwanda Tutsi survivors of the genocide and Hutus who themselves were not perpetrators, receive information relevant to their experiences and engage in extensive discussion of this information (however, the radio project also targeted prisoners accused of perpetrating the genocide). They do not engage in dialog around the events of the past, about who inflicted harm on whom, about the feelings they have toward each other. Thus, the *process* is less emotionally charged than in conflict resolution dialogs.

The primary aims of our interventions were to prevent new violence and promote reconciliation. These aims are served by procedures to help people heal and to promote a more positive orientation by members of the groups toward each other. We provided information about the influences that lead to genocide, about the psychological consequences of victimization on people and avenues to healing, about the role of basic human needs—their frustration, and their constructive fulfillment. Participants in our first projects also shared their experiences during the genocide. These activities were expected to have the following effects:

- Reduce trauma, and thereby reduce feelings of vulnerability, and strengthen identity diminished by being either the victims of violence, or members of a group that perpetrated violence which the world strongly disapproves of (Nadler, 2003). We expected these changes to increase feelings of security and in turn create some degree of openness to the other group and thereby make the beginning of reconciliation possible.
- Create understanding of the varied influences that had affected perpetrators and thereby reduce the negative orientation to perpetrators among survivors, and reduce the defensiveness of perpetrators and thereby also their negative orientation toward the victim group. This would further increase the possibility of engagement with the other and with activities that promote reconciliation.
- Make people more resistant to both the conditions and leaders that instigate violence, thereby reducing the likelihood of new violence.
- Provide people with knowledge of what is required to prevent violence and promote positive groups relations, and empower them to take appropriate action by responding to events (as *active bystanders*) and addressing the conditions and cultural characteristics that produce violence.

When we arrived in Rwanda, we were planning to hire people to work for us, train them to do an intervention and then conduct a study to evaluate its impact on groups in the community. However, faced with the evident tremendous need in Rwanda—many people on the streets with faces that seemed frozen in pain, and in a culture where people are legendary for not showing and sharing their feelings everybody telling us the horrors they have experienced—we revised our plans shortly after our arrival. We decided to work with people from local organizations, who then can continue to use the approach, if it proves effective, in their work with groups in the community.

It was important to focus on groups, even in promoting healing and much more to promote reconciliation. One reason is that in a country of eight million people, everyone was affected. In addition, the violence in Rwanda was a communal event. Rwanda is a communal culture; so healing in groups is likely to be more effective (Herman, 1992; see Staub & Pearlman, 2006; Wessells & Monteiro, 2001). Further, one of the consequences of victimization is disconnection from other people (Saakvitne et al., 2000), and group healing can help people reconnect with others. Finally, reconciliation after mass violence is primarily a group, not an individual, issue.

In this first project we trained 35 people, both Hutus and Tutsis, who worked for varied local organizations that worked with groups in the community. The 2-week long seminar/workshop included brief psycho-educational lectures with extensive large- and small-group discussions after each lecture, and experiential components that included both people in small groups talking about their experiences during the genocide, and developing ways to use the information and experience in the seminar in their own work. The training had five elements.

Understanding the Effects of Trauma and Victimization and Avenues to Healing

Understanding psychological trauma, especially *awareness* of the symptoms that result (American Psychiatric Association, 1994) and of the profound effects of traumatic experiences on creating vulnerability and diminishing the self, on perceptions of other people and the world as dangerous, and in damaging spirituality, can contribute to healing (Allen, 2001; Rosenbloom & Williams, 1999; Saakvitne et al., 2000; Staub, 1998). The seminar aimed to help people understand the behavioral, cognitive, emotional, interpersonal, spiritual, and physiological squeal of violence. Realizing that the way one has changed, and other people have changed, is the normal consequence of extraordinary, painful experiences can ease distress, strengthen the self, and increase feelings of security. These in turn create greater openness to members of an antagonistic group.

Providing people with information about avenues to recovery is also important (Saakvitne et al., 2000). One of these avenues is people talking about their painful experiences. This can help overcome the avoidance that maintains trauma symptoms (Foa, Keane, & Friedman, 2000). While there is some disagreement about the need for survivors to talk about their traumatic experiences (Bonnano, Noll, Putnam, O'Neill, & Trickett, 2003), the preponderance of clinical and empirical evidence suggests that doing so is helpful for most survivors (Pennebaker, 2000). To generate community healing, we promoted understanding of the ways people in the community can help each other, by empathic listening and in other ways. All of our trainings (and our radio programs—see below), encouraged person-to-person healing in the community, promoting awareness, understanding, and sensitivity to other people (our radio field research found that traumatized people in Rwanda have traditionally been seen as crazy) and attempting to empower people to acknowledge each others' suffering and provide support.

Understanding the Origins of Genocide and Mass Killing

People often see genocide as incomprehensible evil, and their own suffering as unique. Learning about similar ways that others have suffered and examining the psychological and social roots or influences leading to such violence can help people see their common humanity with others. It can mitigate negative attitudes toward oneself. Understanding the influences that have affected and shaped the actions of perpetrators and passive bystanders can also mitigate negative attitudes toward them, helping victims see them as human beings, in spite of their horrible actions or their passivity. This should make reconciliation with members of a perpetrator group more possible. Understanding of the influences on themselves can also ease the defensiveness of perpetrators and passive bystanders. We hypothesized that exploration of the influences that lead to genocide would contribute to healing and to a more positive orientation by members of the two groups toward each other.

According to the conception, difficult life conditions, such as severe economic problems, political chaos, great social/cultural changes, as well as persistent groups conflict, are starting points for violence. They frustrate universal human needs (see below). Groups tend to respond to such instigating conditions by scapegoating some group and creating destructive ideologies—visions hopeful for the group but identifying enemies who must be destroyed to fulfill the vision. Devaluation of members of some group, unhealed wounds from past victimization and trauma, excessive respect for authority and the absence of pluralism are societal/cultural characteristics that make it probable that instigation is followed by the evolution of increasing violence. The passivity of bystanders allows this evolution to unfold. In our lectures about the origins of genocide we did not discuss how these influences apply to Rwanda (see Staub, 1999, for such an extension to Rwanda). Instead, we presented the concepts, applied them to the analyses of other genocides (Staub, 1989, 1996, 2003b), and asked participants to apply them to Rwanda.

With the exception of national leaders, who in the end asked us to apply the conception to Rwanda (Staub & Pearlman, 2002), every group eagerly did this, and together with the leaders found the conception highly applicable. The leaders were hindered by their new ideology of unity, which proclaimed that there are no Hutus and Tutsis in Rwanda. In this view the differentiation between these groups was not real but created by colonialists. In spite of the recent genocide, the leaders said that if there were no groups, they could not have devalued each other—one of the elements that in most conceptions is a central contributor to genocide. In the course of subsequent discussion, we came to agree that while there may be no biological differences between Hutus and Tutsis, there have been psychological and social differences.

Understanding Basic Psychological Needs

Basic, universal psychological needs (see Staub, 1989, 2003b) have a role in genocide, trauma, and healing. Understanding these needs and their functions would, therefore, have significant value. Basic psychological needs on which we focused, which we found important in our previous work, include security or safety, positive identity and esteem, feelings of effectiveness and control, trust and positive connections to other people, a comprehension of reality and of one's own place in the world, and transcendence (or spiritual needs; McCann & Pearlman, 1990; Pearlman & Saakvitne, 1995; Saakvitne et al., 2000; Staub, 1989, 1996, 2003b). First, the frustration of basic psychological needs by social conditions is one cause of groups turning against other groups (Burton, 1990; Kelman, 1990; Staub, 1989). It tends to give rise to scapegoating and the creation of destructive ideologies. Second, traumatic experiences frustrate or disrupt basic needs (McCann & Pearlman, 1990; Pearlman, 2003). Third, healing promotes the fulfillment of these needs (Staub, 2005b). It helps people feel safer, strengthens identity, helps people reconnect with others, and so on.

Making sense of and developing a story about their experiences, and creating meaning out of them, have been identified as important contributors to healing from trauma (Herman, 1992; Pennebacker, 2000). The conceptions of the origins of genocide and of basic needs and their functions can be important tools for both survivors and members of a perpetrator group to develop a meaningful story of their experience—and in that process help fulfill varied needs, including the need for a comprehension of reality.

Engagement With Experience

During the second week of the seminar, after people knew each other and were comfortable with each other, we had them talk about their experiences during the genocide. We discussed the importance of empathic responding to others' experiences, and provided demonstrations of less and more empathic responses: lack of response, inappropriate responses such as offering advice or immediately beginning to tell one's own story, as well as listening and support.

In small groups, participants then told their stories, and often cried with each other in this process.

Since the genocide was perpetrated by Hutus, with the Tutsis now in power, it is not surprising that although Hutus actively participated in the seminar, they did not tell the *stories* of their experiences during the genocide. Hearing the painful stories of Tutsis—stories that focused on what happened to the victims, only infrequently mentioning perpetrators—led, however, to the empathic participation of Hutus, which may have helped Tutsis (Jordan, Walker, & Hartling, 2004).

Integration

The participants in the training worked in organizations that varied in the way they worked with groups in the community. Some of them helped people who did agricultural work together to build community. Other groups met to promote healing. Some organizations had a religious orientation, others secular. A final aspect of the training was to help participants *integrate* the material from the training with their usual (*traditional*) approach in working with groups. We helped them conceptualize and practice how they would use information about the origins of genocide, basic needs, and so on, as part of whatever activities their groups engaged in—for example, in groups that used religious writings to promote healing, with the texts and discussion they would normally use.

Evaluating the Effects of the Approach With Community Groups: A Field Study

While there has been a great deal of research on the effects of contact between members of different groups in overcoming prejudice or devaluation (Pettigrew & Tropp, 2006), the evaluation of interventions to reduce conflict between groups has been mostly informal, anecdotal, rather than systematic research (Ross & Rothman, 1999). We conducted a field study to assess the impact of our intervention—not on the people in our seminar, but one step removed, on members of community groups that the people we trained subsequently facilitated.

With the help of the organizations whose staff has participated in the project, and with the help of a Rwandan associate and research assistants, we set up community groups comparable to the type of groups our facilitators have worked with in the past (Staub et al., 2005). These again were mixed groups,

Tutsi and Hutu, their members people in the countryside, including survivors, women who were raped, a cross-section of the population in Rwanda.

We set up three treatment conditions, each including an equal number of different types of subgroups: community versus healing groups, with secular versus religious orientation. This provided a three by two by two design: here I will report the main findings only, the effects of treatments (see Staub et al., 2005). In one treatment condition, the *integrated groups*, facilitators we have trained (who integrated our approach and their traditional approach) worked with these newly created groups. In another treatment condition, the *traditional groups*, facilitators from the same organization whom we did not train worked with newly created community groups. The participants met for 3 hours, twice a week, for 3 weeks. Observers recorded the actual practices of the facilitators. The facilitators did use the varied elements of our approach, although in somewhat varying proportions.

Measures of trauma (traumatic experiences, symptoms, trauma-related beliefs), and a measure we developed for this study that we named *orientation to the other*, were administered to participants before their participation, immediately afterward, and 2 months later. In *control groups* (whose membership was selected by the same organizations and the same way as of the groups in the other two conditions), participants received no training, but had the same measures administered to them at about the same time as in the two treatment groups (Staub et al., 2005).

We found that trauma symptoms decreased in the integrated groups, led by the facilitators who participated in our seminar, both over time and in comparison to the other groups. Symptoms increased slightly (not significantly) in both the traditional and control groups (Figure 17.1). The figures show the results for Tutsi participants. We did separate analysis of Tutsis and the whole group, which provided similar result. The number of Hutus in the sample was smaller, and while *t*-tests indicated the same effects as for Tutsis, we did not perform an analysis of variance on the Hutu only date (see Staub et al., 2005). We also found an increase in positive orientation by the two groups toward each group in the integrated groups, both over time and in comparison to the other treatment groups (Figure 17.2). The elements of this positive orientation included (a) seeing the genocide as having complex origins (rather than simply resulting from the evil nature of the perpetrators, or bad leaders), (b) expressing willingness to work with the other group for important goals (e.g., a better future), and indicating awareness that not all Hutus were the same and some resisted the genocide and some saved lives, and (c) expressing willingness to forgive the other group if its members acknowledged what they did and apologized for the group's actions—which we named conditional forgiveness (Staub et al., 2005). The orientation to the other measure might also be interpreted as an indicator

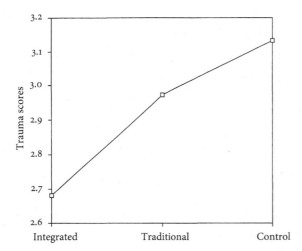

FIGURE 17.1. Covariance analysis of Tutsi participants' trauma scores 2 months postintervention. Covariates: trauma scores and traumatic experiences, both at Time 1. Reprinted from Staub et al. (2005). *Journal of Social and Clinical Psychology, 24*, 297-334.

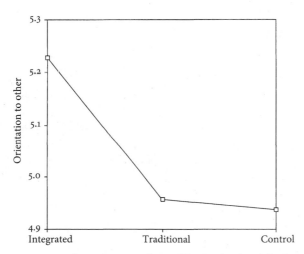

FIGURE 17.2. Covariance analysis of Tutsi participants' other orientation (or readiness to reconcile) scores 2 months postintervention. Covariates: other orientation scores and traumatic experiences, both at Time 1. Reprinted from Staub et al. (2005). *Journal of Social and Clinical Psychology, 24*, 297-334.

of readiness to reconcile. While some of the items would have different meaning for Tutsis and Hutus, the treatment had similar impact on them.

Although we were unable to evaluate in this study the effects of specific components of the intervention, our observations in the course of the training suggested that the information about the origins of genocide—which we regard as a new tool in promoting healing and reconciliation and therefore especially important to learn about—had striking effects. Some participants expressed the realization that they were not outside history and human experience, and the genocide in Rwanda was not God's punishment. Participants seemed to feel *rehumanized* by the understanding that what happened in their society is a human, albeit horrific, process. They came to regard the influences that lead to genocide as understandable, and therefore action to prevent future violence possible. By connecting the conception and examples from other genocides to their own experience in Rwanda, participants seemed to gain what I regard as an *experiential understanding* of the roots of the genocide—knowledge that is strengthened and confirmed by one's own experience.

In summary, relatively limited participation in groups led by facilitators who participated in our 2-week long seminar contributed to both healing, as measured by the reduction in trauma symptoms, and to a more positive attitude by Hutus and Tutsis toward each other. We used elements of this approach, and further developments of it, in subsequent work.

Working With National Leaders

We conducted two seminars with national leaders. A 4-day seminar in 2001 included about 25 government ministers, members of the supreme court, heads of national commissions (electoral, constitutional), the heads of the national prison system and of the main Kigali prison, an advisor to the president, leaders of religious organizations, and commissioners of the National Unity and Reconciliation Commission that helped us organize these and other seminars/workshops (Staub & Pearlman, 2002). We conducted a 1-day seminar in 2003 with 69 national leaders—leaders like those in the first seminar, as well as members of the parliament and leaders of the various parties.

We discussed the psychological impact of violence on people. We extended the discussion of the origins of group violence, focusing on prevention as well. Using a table we showed some of the influences that contribute to genocide as one endpoint of dimensions on the left side of the table, and the opposing influences that can prevent the evolution of violence as the other endpoint on the right side of the table (Staub, 2006). Devaluation of the other, past victimization and psychological woundedness, a monolithic society, and very strong respect for authority contribute to violence: Humanizing the other group, healing group psychological wounds, and promoting moderate respect for authority and pluralism help prevent violence. The group members identified and discussed government policies and practices from the standpoint of these dimensions. For example, they discussed how new decentralization policies might diminish people's orientation to and obedience to authority. They considered what might be the impact, in terms of the above dimensions, and elements of reconciliation I discussed earlier such as truth, justice, and contact, of providing special help to needy survivors of the genocide, but given highly limited resources, not to needy Hutus. The leaders considered what they could do to shape policies and practices so that they would reduce the likelihood of future violence.

Creating a Shared History

We also engaged the group in discussing the creation of a shared history. Increasingly, coming to a shared view of history has been recognized as an important aspect of reconciliation (Bar-Tal, 2002; Cairns & Roe, 2002; Penal Reform International, 2004; Staub & Bar-Tal, 2003; Willis, 1965). Groups that have engaged in violence against each other tend to have conflicting views of the reasons for the violence, usually blaming each other, which makes renewed conflict more likely. While some people in the group argued that history is objective, that there is only one correct factual account of events, predominantly the group recognized that there can be different perspectives on historical events and that it was important to create a shared view of history. As part of small group discussions in the 2001 seminar, a group of prominent leaders proposed a variety of ideas for how to create such a history, like each group taking the role of the other in describing history, and the recognition of earlier peaceful coexistence. However, in the end many participants expressed skepticism that it would be possible to create such a history at this time, in light of the feelings generated by the recent genocide.

In our subsequent seminars/workshops, we began to use, in an informal manner, *understanding the roots of violence* as an avenue to the creation of a shared history. By bringing understanding to how particular historical events and actions came about, we hoped to help people acknowledge their own group's blameworthy actions and begin to accept the other group in spite of its blameworthy actions.

For example, in the second leaders' seminar, one of the participants referred to the *genocide* in 1959. At that time, there was a Hutu uprising against Tutsi rule, with about 50,000 Tutsis killed. With regard to the actions of Tutsis before

411

1959, and the violence by Hutus toward Tutsis in 1959, and violent repression of Tutsis after 1959, we offered the following explanation:

> The Tutsis have long been dominant in Rwandan society. The Belgians, after they took over the country, ordered a reexamination of "race policies." The first expression of this was a "White Paper" on the relation between the races in Rwanda written by (white) church leaders in 1916 (Mamdani, 2002), identifying the Tutsis as a different and superior race. After this the Belgians intensified the differences between the Tutsis and Hutus. They elevated the Tutsis, had them rule in their behalf, greatly intensifying Tutsi dominance. They gave them more power and privilege, and boosted them psychologically as they emphasized their intelligence, physical attractiveness and similarity to Europeans. In contrast, they diminished the Hutus psychologically and in terms of their position in society and material well being. (des Forges, 1999; Mamdani, 2002)
>
> These actions by the powerful colonial rulers, given the preexisting divisions and a highly authority oriented society, would have been psychologically nearly impossible to resist by those so elevated. The resulting persistent injustice in social arrangements gave rise to the revolution and mass killing in 1959. The discrimination and violence against Tutsis under the Hutu rule that followed can be understood as the outcome of the psychological woundedness, fear and anger of Hutus. However, the policies and practices of Hutus after 1959 both created new, grave injustice, and interfered with healing by Hutus, further wounding them instead, and maintaining the focus on their chosen trauma. (The concept of chosen trauma was proposed by Vamik Volkan, e.g. 1997, to describe the focus of a group on a historical trauma and the psychological and behavioral consequences of that focus.)

These and other efforts to use the *understanding approach* to create a shared, mutually acceptable history were surprisingly well received. Our use of this approach was experimental and ad hoc, but its seeming effectiveness makes it desirable to test its systematic use in helping groups develop a shared history.

Working With Journalists/the Media and With Community Leaders

We conducted a number of seminars/workshops with members of the media and community leaders. Here again, the focus has been understanding the roots of violence between groups and the impact of violence on people, the psychological wounds violence creates, and avenues to healing. People in the media can make violence more or less likely by the way they write about the members of different groups, about conflict between groups, about relationships between people belonging to different groups and about social and political issues involving group relations. They can humanize or devalue people belonging to different groups. As in Rwanda, where leading up to the genocide, radio and other media were infused with hate against Tutsis, they can create devaluation and propagate destructive ideologies. Or as in Macedonia, where journalists belonging to different ethnic groups joined in interviewing families belonging to these groups and wrote joint articles about their lives, which were then published in the newspapers of each group, they can show the humanity of members of each group and promote harmonious relations (Manoff, 1996). Individuals who have leadership roles within their communities can have similar positive or negative influence. In our work, such people included advocates for survivors of the genocide, gacaca judges, directors of hospitals, and varied individuals who in some ways were intermediaries between the government and local communities.

One of the issues that we addressed in these seminars was the potential effects of the gacaca and ways of addressing them. The gacaca is a community justice system that was created to deal with the approximately 120,000 people who were in jail, accused of being perpetrators of the genocide, in a country where the justice system was completely destroyed in the genocide. About 250,000 people were elected to act as judges in gacaca courts in groups of 19, as well as to serve as administrative personnel. About 10,000 gacaca courts were created. Later the number of judges to serve in each court was reduced (Honeyman et al., 2004; Staub, 2004).

The purpose of the gacaca was to establish what has happened and to punish perpetrators, and through truth and justice contribute to reconciliation. The proceedings of the gacaca courts are public events, which the members of the community in each location are expected to attend. However, there were intense concerns by leaders in Rwanda that as people gave testimony about what happened during the genocide, not only witnesses but also people in attendance will be retraumatized, and some, like children too young to remember events, will be newly traumatized. My associates and I were also greatly concerned that as Tutsis hear descriptions of the horrible violence against them, they will feel renewed anger. And that as Hutus who may not have participated in violence hear repeatedly the horrible actions by members of their group, they will feel personally accused and respond with hostility and anger (Staub, 2004; Staub & Pearlman, 2006).

For these reasons part of the focus of our work was to discuss what community leaders and journalists can do to help mitigate these consequences. We

413

stressed support that community members can provide each other, by their presence, empathic listening, and other ways. We stressed again how understanding the roots of violence may help in modulating thoughts and feelings, specifically how an *understanding orientation* in listening to and even in providing testimonies in front of the gacaca may lessen retramautization and anger.

We applied the understanding of general societal processes to the level of individual perpetrators. We discussed, for example, the psychological and behavioral evolution of a member of the Interahamwe, militia groups composed of young men who did a great deal of the killings (des Forges, 1999). We looked at how the societal processes that led to the genocide played themselves out in directly affecting these young men—for example, their exposure to the devaluation of Tutsis both in the society in general, and by the leaders of the Interahamwe in particular (see Staub, 2006).

The Radio/Communication Project

We were frequently asked in the course of our seminars and workshops to expand the reach of our work. In 2001, after our first seminar with national leaders, the general secretary of the ruling party (now foreign minister) and the then justice minister specifically asked us to do so. We then initiated radio programs. Radio is the primary media that people have access to in Rwanda. While not every person has a radio, every village has radios and people listen together. In 2001, we invited a producer and his organization, LaBenevolencija, located in Amsterdam, to work with us to create radio programs that would communicate our approach to reconciliation to the larger community. We developed two types of programs.

One of them is a radio drama, the story of two neighboring villages, called Musekeweya—New Dawn. The story is about conflict and violence between the villages, but also about love stories, friendships, and family relations. We developed communication objectives, which summarize the elements of the approach I have described (see Table 17.1). These were to be embedded in the radio drama: the influences that lead to violence or can prevent violence, the traumatic impact of violence, healing and how people can help each other heal, the behavior of leaders, followers, and passive and active bystanders. We developed an overall storyline. Rwandese writers trained in the approach write the weekly episodes, with material based on the communication objectives embedded in the episodes. The episodes are translated into English, edited (by Laurie Perlman, Ervin Staub, and other staff of the project), and then revised in the local language, Kinyarwanda.

TABLE 17.1 Examples of Communications Objectives

Message: "The Healing of Psychological Wounds Helps People Live More Satisfying Lives and Makes Unnecessary Defensive Violence Less Likely."
Prevention Objective: Healing of Past Wounds
    The listener is aware of the importance of healing and of participating in and promoting the healing process as a way of lessening vulnerability, changing the perception of the world as a dangerous place, and diminishing the resulting potential for unnecessary violence that the actors perceive as self-protective

Message: "Passivity Facilitates the Evolution of Harm Doing Whereas Actions by People Inhibit It."
Understanding Objective: Passive Bystanders
    The listener will understand that passivity in face of harmful actions encourages perpetrators
Prevention Objective: Positive Bystanders
    Listeners will be able to cite the actions that make someone a positive bystander
    Listeners will understand that acting as a positive bystander is important to stop the evolution of increasing violence that may end in genocide

Message: "Varied Perspectives, Open Communication and Moderate Respect for Authority in a Society Make the Evolution of Violence Less Likely."
Understanding Objective: Uncritical Respect for Authority
    Listeners will know the danger of not critically evaluating the words and actions of authority
Prevention Objective: Moderate Respect for Authority
    Listeners will know the importance of examining and evaluating the words and actions of authority
Prevention Objective: Pluralism
    The listener will understand the importance of respecting, expressing, and encouraging multiple perspectives
    The listener will respect, express, and encourage multiple perspectives

This radio drama began twice-weekly broadcasts in May 2004. A survey of general radio listening habits in mid-2005 found that in a country where over 90% of the population listens to the radio, the major media outlet, 89% of the women and 92% of the men who listen to radio listen to this program. Data collection in a large study to evaluate the initial impact of this program—the knowledge that results from it and the cognitive and behavioral effects of it (Paluck, 2007; Staub, Pearlman, Weiss & Hoek, 2007) was completed in 2005. Since changes resulting from radio programs take time, further evaluation has been conducted in 2006 and is planned in 2007. Initial results from 2005 indicate changes in both attitudes and behavior. After a little over a year, those who listened to the radio drama, in comparison to those who listened to a different program at the same time in a controlled setting:

- Believe more in the importance of trust
- Report increased trust in their communities

- Understand the importance of being an *active bystander*
- Believe in collaboration and deep contact between various social groups
- Understand the importance of talking for trauma healing

(*LeBenevolencija Newsletter*, January 2006).

They also show behavioral differences. At the end of the study, both treatment group participants and control group participants, who listened to an alternative program during the year, received tapes of the first year programs, together with an audio cassette. In this unobtrusive measure, treatment participants in 10 different locations in the country extensively discussed who will be in charge of the tapes and the cassette and decided that it will be the participants themselves. In the control group, with very little or no discussion they decided to give these materials to the local authority to be in charge of. The behavior of the treatment participants was in line with two of the aims of the program: supporting pluralism and in a very authority-oriented culture moderating respect for authority (Paluck, 2007; Staub et al., 2007).

A second program, a monthly program that began to broadcast in September 2004 is a straightforward informational/journalistic program. In this, the elements of the approach are laid out, with the participation of local commentators, both experts and citizens with relevant experience. In January 2005, this radio drama also began to be broadcast in Burudi, which has the same language and where there has also been a great deal of violence between Tutsis and Hutus—although here, the Tutsis, who remained in power, were the primary perpetrators. In 2006, new programs of both kinds were created for Burundi, and for the Eastern Congo, where since about 1995 over three million people have died due to violence and its side effects, disease and hunger. In developing the programs for the Congo, elements of the theory especially relevant to a highly complex conflict situation and application of the theory to such a situation were guiding principles (Staub et al., 2007).

Concluding Thoughts

We have focused in our approach on psychological education that creates knowledge, develops genuine understanding, and can change feelings and lead to action. The content of the information we provided was about the impact of violence on people and avenues to healing, especially person-to-person healing, and about the influences the lead to violence between groups and their implications for prevention. Our primary aims were to promote healing on both the individual level and, through people we trained to be trainers in our approach and through the activities journalists, community and national leaders, and radio programs also on the societal level; to promote a more positive orientation by Hutus and Tutsis toward each other; and to promote awareness of the importance of and ways to begin to create a shared view of history. These activities and processes can humanize both the self and the other, increase safety by helping people realize (through healing) that the present is not the past, and create a shared understanding of both the roots of genocide and of past history that makes it possible for people to engage with each other in ways that can further promote reconciliation.

Research, theory, and practices to promote reconciliation are in their initial stages of development. They are of tremendous importance, especially because of the overlap in the processes and practices involved in the prevention of violence after and *before* significant violence between groups. Research and the development of practice cannot simply take place in universities. To develop a science of reconciliation interventions in the real would ought to be further explored in laboratory settings, while principles and practices developed in analog research conducted in the laboratory, usually with individuals or at best small groups, must be applied and studied in real world settings.

It is of great importance to develop general principles of process and practice/intervention, such as healing, shared history, the importance of truth, and the role of understanding. However, whether they apply to particular settings given the idiosyncratic characteristics of groups, their culture, political processes, and past relations must be carefully considered before practices are introduced, and evaluated after they have been introduced. This applies to our work as well. While understanding the roots of violence and its implications for prevention seems relevant to many and varied situations, the extent and limits of this applicability must be evaluated.

The circumstances under which prevention and reconciliation are needed vary tremendously, from before mass violence, for example, in a setting like the Netherlands, where violence-producing conditions exist to a moderate degree and there has been limited violence between Muslims and the local Dutch population (Staub, 2007), to the aftermath of a genocide. Procedures have to be adapted to each setting, with the proper combination of universal elements and uniqueness required by the characteristics of the setting.

Note

1. This chapter draws on and extends our previous articles and book chapters on reconciliation, including the description of the approach we have developed and used in Rwanda (see Staub, 2006; Staub et al., 2005; Staub & Pearlman, 2001, 2006).

References

Allen, J. G. (2001). *Traumatic relationships and serious mental disorders.* West Sussex: John Wiley & Sons Ltd.

American Psychiatric Association. (1994). *Diagnostic and statistical manual of mental disorders* (4th ed.). Washington, DC: Author.

Bar-Tal, D. (2002). Collective memory of physical violence: Its contribution to the culture of violence. In E. Cairns & M. D. Roe (Eds.), *Memories in conflict.* London: Macmillan.

Broneus, K. (2003). *Reconciliation—Theory and practice for development cooperation.* Stockholm: Swedish International Development Cooperation Agency.

Byrne, C. (2004). Benefit of burden: Victims' reflections on TRC participation. *Peace and Conflict: Journal of Peace Psychology, 10*(3), 237-256.

Bonnano, G., Noll, J., Putnam, F., O'Neill, M., & Trickett, P. K. (2003). Predicting the willingness to disclose childhood sexual abuse from measures of repressive coping and dissociative tendencies. *Child Maltreatment, 8,* 302-318.

Burton, J. W. (1990). *Conflict: Resolution and prevention.* New York: St. Martin's Press.

Cairns, E., & Darby, J. (1998). Conflict in Northern Ireland. *American Psychologist, 53,* 754-776.

Cairns, E., & Roe, M. D. (2002). *Memories in conflict.* London: Macmillan.

Chorbajian, L., & Shirinian, G. (1999). *Studies in comparative genocide.* New York: St. Martin's Press.

De la Rey, C. (2001). Reconciliation in divided societies. In D. J. Christie, R. V. Wagner, & D. D. Winter (Eds.), *Peace, conflict, and violence: Peace psychology for the 21st century* (pp. 251-261). Upper Saddler River, NJ: Prentice Hall.

Des Forges, A. (1999). *Leave none to tell the story: Genocide in Rwanda.* New York: Human Rights Watch.

Esterling, B. A., L'Abate, L., Murray, E. J., & Pennebaker, J. W. (1999). Empirical foundations for writing in prevention and psychotherapy: Mental and physical health outcomes. *Clinical Psychology Review, 19,* 79-96.

Foa, E. B., Keane, T. M., & Friedman, M. J. (Eds.). (2000). *Effective treatments for PTSD: Practice guidelines from the International Society for Traumatic Stress Studies.* New York: Guilford Press.

Gibson, J. L. (2004). *Overcoming apartheid: Can truth reconcile a divided nation?* New York: Russell Sage Foundation.

Helmick, S. J., & Petersen, R. L. (Eds.). (2001). *Forgiveness and reconciliation: Religion, public policy and conflict transformation* (pp. 195-217). Radnor, PA: Templeton Foundation Press.

Herman, J. (1992). *Trauma and recovery: The aftermath of violence from domestic abuse to political terror.* New York: Basic Books.

Honeyman, C., Hudami, S., Tiruneh, A., Hierta, J., Chirayath., L., Iliff, A., et al. (2004). Establishing collective norms: Potentials for participatory justice in Rwanda. *Peace and Conflict: Journal of Peace Psychology, 10,* 1-24.

Hovannisian, R. (Ed.). (2003). *Looking backward, moving forward.* New Brunswick, NJ: Transaction Publishers.

Jordan, J. V., Walker, M., & Hartling, L. M. (Eds.). (2004). *The complexity of connection: Writings from the Jean Baker Miller training institute.* New York: Guilford Publications.

Kelman, H. C. (1990). Applying a human needs perspective to the practice of conflict resolution: The Israeli-Palestinian case. In J. Burton (Ed.), *Conflict: Human needs theory.* New York: St. Martin's Press.

Kelman, H. C. & Fisher, R. J. (2003). Conflict analysis and resolution. In D. Sears, L. Huddy, & R. Jervis (Eds.). *Political Psychology* (pp. 315-357). Oxford: Oxford University Press.

Kriesberg, L. (1998). Coexistence and the reconciliation of communal conflicts. In E. Weiner (Ed.), *The handbook of interethnic coexistence* (pp. 182-198). New York: Continuum.

Lederach, J. P. (1997). *Building peace: Sustainable reconciliation in divided societies.* Washington, DC: United States Institute of Peace Press.

MacNair, R. M. (2002). *Perpetration-induced traumatic stress: The psychological consequences of killing.* Westport, CT: Praeger Publishers/Greenwood Publishing Group, Inc.

Mamdani, M. (2002). *When victims become killers.* Princeton: Princeton University Press.

Manoff, R. (1996). *The mass media and social violence: Is there a role for the media in preventing and moderating ethnic, national, and religious conflict?* Unpublished manuscript, Center for War, Peace, and News Media, Department of Journalism and Mass Communication, New York University, New York.

McCann, I. L., & Pearlman, L. A. (1990). *Psychological trauma and the adult survivor: Theory, therapy, and transformation.* New York: Brunner/Mazel.

Montville, J. V. (1993). The healing function in political conflict resolution. In D. J. D. Sandole & H. Van der Merve (Eds.), *Conflict resolution theory and practice: Integration and application.* Manchester, England: Manchester University Press.

Nadler, A. (2003). *Opening comments on the Social Psychology of Reconciliation.* Presentation at the conference on Social Psychology of Reconciliation: Moving from violent confrontation to peaceful coexistence, University of Connecticut, Storrs.

Paluck, E. L. (2007). *Reconciling intergroup prejudice and violence with the mass media: A field experiment in Rwanda.* Unpublished doctoral dissertation, Yale University, New Haven, CT.

Pearlman, L. A. (2003). *Trauma and attachment belief scale manual.* Los Angeles: Western Psychological Services.

Pearlman, L. A., & Saakvitne, K. W. (1995). *Trauma and the therapist: Countertransference and vicarious traumatization in the treatment of incest survivors.* New York: W.W. Norton.

Penal Reform International. (2004, May). *Research report on the Gacaca VI: From camp to hill, the reintegration of released prisoners.* PRI Rwanda, BP 370, Kigali, Rwanda.

Pennebaker, J. W. (2000). The effects of traumatic disclosure on physical and mental health: The values of writing and talking about upsetting events. In J. M. Violanti, D. Paton, & C. Dunning (Eds.), *Posttraumatic stress intervention.* Springfield, IL: Charles Thomas Publisher.

Pettigrew, T. F., & Tropp, L. R. (2006). A meta-analytic test of intergroup contact theory. *Journal of Personality and Social Psychology, 90,* 751-783.

Proceedings of Stockholm International Forum on Truth, Justice and Reconciliation, 2002.

Rhodes, G., Allen, G. J., Nowinski, J., & Cillessen, A. (2002). The violent socialization scale: Development and initial validation. In J. Ulmer & L. Athens (Eds.), *Violent acts and violentization: Assessing, applying, and developing Lonnie Athens' theories* (Vol. 4, pp. 125-144). Amsterdam: Elsevier Science Ltd.

Rosenbloom, D. J., & Williams, M. B. (1999). *Life after trauma.* New York: Guilford.

Ross, M. H., & Rothman, J. (1999). *Theory and practice in ethnic conflict management: Theorizing success and failure.* New York: Macmillian.

Saakvitne, K. W., Gamble, S. G., Pearlman, L. A., & Lev, B. T. (2000). *Risking connection: A training curriculum for working with survivors of childhood abuse.* Lutherville, MD: Sidran Foundation & Press.

Staub, E. (1989). *The roots of evil: The origins of genocide and other group violence.* New York: Cambridge University Press.

Staub, E. (1996). The cultural-societal roots of violence: The examples of genocidal violence and of contemporary youth violence in the United States. *American Psychologist, 51,* 17-132.

Staub, E. (1998). Breaking the cycle of genocidal violence: Healing and reconciliation. In J. Harvey (Ed.), *Perspectives on loss* (pp. 231-241). Washington, DC: Taylor & Francis.

Staub, E. (1999). The origins and prevention of genocide, mass killing and other collective violence. *Peace and Conflict: Journal of Peace Psychology, 5,* 303-337.

Staub, E. (2003a). Healing and reconciliation. In R. Hovannisian (Ed.), *Looking backward, moving forward* (pp. 263-274). New Brunswick, NJ: Transaction Publishers.

Staub, E. (2003b). *The psychology of good and evil: Why children, adults and groups help and harm others.* New York: Cambridge University Press.

Staub, E. (2004). Justice, healing and reconciliation: How the people's courts in Rwanda can promote them. *Peace and Conflict: The Journal of Peace Psychology, 10,* 25-31.

Staub, E. (2005a). Constructive and destructive forms of forgiveness and reconciliation after genocide and mass killing. In E. Worthington (Ed.) *Handbook of forgiveness* (pp. 443-461). New York: Brunner-Routledge.

Staub, E. (2005b). The roots of goodness: The fulfillment of basic human needs and the development of caring, helping and nonaggression, inclusive caring, moral courage, active bystandership, and altruism born of suffering. In G. Carlo & C. Edwards (Eds.), *Moral motivation across the life span* (pp. 33-73). Nebraska Symposium on Motivation. Lincoln, NE: Nebraska University Press.

Staub, E. (2006). Reconciliation after genocide, mass killing or intractable conflict: Understanding the roots of violence, psychological recovery and steps toward a general theory. *Political Psychology, 27*(6), 867-895.

Staub, E. (2007). Preventing violence and terrorism and promoting positive relations between Dutch and Muslim communities in Amsterdam. *Peace and Conflict: Journal of Peace Psychology, 13*(3), 333-361.

Staub, E., & Bar-Tal, D. (2003). Genocide, mass killing and intractable conflict: Roots, evolution, prevention and reconciliation. In D. Sears, L. Huddy, & R. Jarvis (Eds.), *Handbook of political psychology* (pp. 710-755). New York: Oxford University Press.

Staub, E., & Pearlman, L. A. (2001). Healing, reconciliation, and forgiving after genocide and other collective violence. In S. J. Helmick & R. L. Petersen (Eds.), *Forgiveness and reconciliation: Religion, public policy and conflict transformation* (pp. 195 217). Radnor, PA: Templeton Foundation Press.

Staub, E., & Pearlman, L. A. (2002). *Facilitators' summary of observations and recommendations from leaders seminar.* Retrieved from www.heal-reconcile-rwanda.org

Staub, E., & Pearlman, L. A. (2006). Advancing healing and reconciliation. In L. Barbanol & R. Sternberg (Eds.), *Psychological interventions in times of crisis* (pp. 213-245). New York: Springer-Verlag.

Staub, E., Pearlman, L. A., Gubin, A., & Hagengimana, A. (2005). Healing, reconciliation, and the prevention of violence after genocide or mass killing: An intervention and its experimental evaluation in Rwanda. *Journal of Clinical and Social Psychology, 24,* 297-334.

Staub, E., Pearlman, L. A., Weiss, G., & van Hoeak, A. (2007). *Public education through radio to prevent violence, promote trauma healing and reconciliation, and build peace in Rwanda and the Congo.* Unpublished manuscript, Department of Psychology, University of Massachusetts, Amherst.

Tajfel, H. (1982). Social psychology of intergroup relations. *Annual Review of Psychology, 33,* 1-39.

Tausch, N., Kenworthy, J., & Hewstone, M. (2006). Intergroup contact and the improvement of intergroup relations. In M. Fitzduff & C. E. Stout (Eds.), *The psychology of resolving global conflicts: From war to peace* (Vol. 2). Group and social factors. Westport, CT: Praeger.

Totten, S., Parsons, W. S., & Charny, I. W. (Eds.). (1997). *Century of genocide*. New York: Garland Publishing.

Tyler, T. R., & Smith, H. J. (1998). Social justice and social movements. In D. T. Gilbert, S. T. Fiske, & G. Lindzey (Eds.), *Handbook of social psychology* (4th ed., Vol. 2, pp. 595-629). New York: McGraw-Hill.

Varshney, A. (2002). *Ethnic conflict and civic life: Hindus and Muslims in India*. New Haven, CT: Yale University Press.

Volkan, V. (1997). *Blood lines: From ethnic pride to ethnic terrorism*. New York: Farrar, Straus and Giroux.

Volkan, V. D. (1998). Tree model: Psychopolitical dialogues and the promotion of coexistence. In E. Weiner (Ed.), *The handbook of interethnic coexistence*. New York: Continuum.

Wessells, M., & Monteiro, C. (2001). Psychosocial intervention and post-war reconstruction in Angola: Interweaving western and traditional approaches. In D. J. Christie, R. V. Wagner, & D. D. Winter (Eds.), *Peace, conflict and violence: Peace psychology for the 21st century* (pp. 262-275). Upper Saddler River, NJ: Prentice Hall.

Willis, F. R. (1965). *France, Germany, and the New Europe, 1945-1963*. Palo Alto: Stanford University Press.

Worthington, E. (Ed.). (2005). *Handbook of forgiveness*. New York: Brunner-Routledge.

CHAPTER 18

Between Conflict and Reconciliation: Toward a Theory of Peaceful Coexistence

Stephen Worchel and Dawna K. Coutant

The only thing to fear is fear itself.

—*Franklin D. Roosevelt*

Few topics in social psychology excite students' interest as much as intergroup relations. They are captivated by descriptions of the confrontations between the Eagles and Rattlers at Sherif's Robbers Cave (Sherif, Harvey, White, Hood, & Sherif, 1961) and the elegant logic of social identity theory (Tajfel & Turner, 1979) that relates groups to individual identity. But they are also quick to identify the disconnect between the research and current global conditions: "If social psychologists know so much about the intergroup hostility, why is this hatred so common throughout the world?"

Whether one looks at the Middle East, Balkans, Spain, Fiji, Ireland, and the United States, one finds violent conflict between groups. These conflicts are noteworthy not only because of the level of violence and cruelty, but also because of their persistence. Although the individual combatants may change from generation to generation, the participating groups remain the same. These groups are typically ethnic or cultural groups that are characterized by their endurance (long history and expectation of future existence) and the fact that group membership is permanent (individual born into the group and is always a member of the group).

Existing theories do not comfortably explain why conflict between these groups often becomes chronic and stubbornly resists resolution. Given the destructiveness and suffering that occurs in these conflicts, it is imperative to develop a better understanding of the causes and possible cures of persistent confrontation between enduring groups. We suggest that a combination of unique factors conspire to maintain these conflicts over generations and make them resistant to change. We also propose that a critical step in dealing with these conflicts involves achieving peaceful coexistence between these groups. Our goals in this chapter are to explore the factors that cause and nurture intractable conflict between enduring groups, examine the implications of a focus on peaceful coexistence, and relate this perspective to theories of conflict resolution and reconciliation. Our ultimate aim is to address the question about why ethnic and cultural conflict is so prevalent and persistent and suggest approaches to improve intergroup relations. In supporting our position we will draw on our observations and research on *peace* programs involving ethnic groups consumed by intractable conflict, groups involving immigrants and hosts, and ethnic groups living on the island of Hawaii.

Lighting the Fuse: Causes of Intergroup Hatred and Conflict

To begin the journey toward coexistence, it is important to understand the forces working against this relationship. Social psychology offers two general theories to explain the animosity between groups. Realistic conflict theory (Sherif, 1966) suggests that competition for scarce resources ignites the fires of conflict and hatred. The competitive contests between the newly established groups at Robber's Cave (Sherif et al., 1961) demonstrate the possible negative effects of competition.

Social identity theory (Tajfel & Turner, 1979) and social categorization theory (Turner, 1985) offer a different perspective. They suggest that groups comprise a critical component of an individual's identity (his/her social identity). Because individuals covet positive self-identities, they are motivated to join positive groups and/or advantage their in-group while discriminating against out-groups. Out-groups are disliked because they threaten the individual's positive identity. Groups, in a sense, are the clothes that cloak one's identity, and the identity can be improved by changing groups, reconstituting the social world into different groupings, or by enhancing (relatively) one's in-group.

These theories have received wide support and have been valuable for understanding the causes of hostility between many groups. But in giving them their due, it is important to remember their rather humble beginnings. Realistic conflict theory developed from a paradigm that involved constituting groups of individuals who initially shared many common characteristics. After the groups are formed, competition is introduced into a situation. Factors such as the nature of the group, its history, its culture, and its meaning for the individual are effectively excluded. The methodological foundation of social identity theory is even more refined. The minimal group paradigm (Tajfel, 1970) involved developing cognitive categories linking individuals by real or imaginary characteristics. Not only are factors such as group history and culture uninvited, but actual interaction between group members is not necessary. However, the meaning of the group for the individual's identity takes center stage.

These approaches are methodologically elegant because they allow an examination of the most basic conditions that can lead to group hostility. However, we suggest that reliance on these paradigms may mask factors that are critical to the development of intergroup hostility in some very important situations. In order to illustrate this point, let's move the setting from the foothills of Oklahoma (Robber's Cave) to the woods of Maine where each summer since 1991 adolescents from groups involved in violent and protracted conflict (Middle East, South Asia, Balkans, Cyprus) have gathered at the Seeds of Peace International Camp (Wallach, 2000). Participants live together for 2-3 weeks, engage in typical camp activities (swimming, arts and crafts, sporting events), and discuss the conflict in their regions. This camp is a prototype of countless peace programs from around the world that aim to promote peace in regions of violent conflict (see Cannon, 2003; Maoz, 2000). The programs differ in duration, specific activities, and participants (immigrants/host, majority/minority, international tension), but in all cases the participants represent different cultural and ethnic groups.

We have spent the last 10 years working with several programs and our observations along with those reported in the literature (Maoz, 2000; Wallach, 2000) raise several points that relate to the causes of persistent intergroup hatred. One critical issue concerns the nature of the group or category. Membership in most groups to which people belong is *voluntary* (e.g., chosen) and *temporary*. Individuals can choose to leave the group or join other groups. For example, a colleague recently announced that after 20 years as a social psychologist, she now considered herself to be an organizational psychologist. However, there are a few groups into which we are born (religious, nationality, economic status). In some of these cases, we can renounce our membership in these groups; we can convert from one religion to another or adopt another nationality. But our membership in some groups is permanent, and we can neither choose to leave the group nor can the group exclude us. Our ethnicity is one example of this type of group (Verkuyten, 2005). We are born into our ethnic group, and although its salience may vary, we will always be a member of the ethnic group. Ethnic groups are generally defined by language, culture, history, homeland, physical characteristics, and *blood line* (biological heritage). A critical component of these groups is their *history* and *future endurance*. Ethnic groups, for example, have a history of data, myths, and recollection that describes their beginning and justifies their existence (Worchel, 1999). They typically have a homeland or place of origin that has a spiritual quality for the group. It would be unthinkable to sell or barter away any part of this homeland. The future of the group is equally important. Not only will the individual always be part of this group, but his/her children and their children will be members of this group. For example, in countless discussion sessions at the Seeds of Peace camp, participants recount the Old Testament to justify the existence of the Jews or Palestinians in Israel and make passionate announcements about protecting the land and the group for unborn children and grandchildren.

Although it is tempting to consider these groups within a social identity framework, a unique quality creeps into the calculus. Social identity theory views the group as a component of the individual identity. However, in the case of these enduring groups, the focus shifts from the individual to the group. The group is not so much a component of the individual's identity as the individual is a part of (and protector of) the group identity. For example, Worchel, Webb, and Hills (1987) collected responses on the Cantril Self Anchoring Scale (1965) from respondents in New Zealand, border region of Texas, China, and prewar Yugoslavia. A typical response to questions about hopes and fears was "I don't care much about myself, but it is important that I protect the Maori culture so that it will be strong in the future. I worry that the Maori language and customs, even the Maori people, will be gone in the next 100 years."

A second point of departure between the intractable conflicts and those focused on the present situation involves the *nature of the conflict*. In many cases, conflict is viewed as disagreement(s) between groups, often over resources (realistic conflict theory). The disagreement is relatively contemporary and the aggrieved parties are present. Social identity theory expanded the territory in pointing out that the roots of intergroup conflict are concern for individual identity arising from the simple demarcation of groups or categories. However, our observations and the literature on intractable conflicts (Bar-Tal, 2001) reveal some very different characteristics. First, there is the issue of *history*. The root of conflict is often generations in the past. Ethnic groups often make historical claims based on a one-sided interpretation of events, but which are interpreted as fact. For example, many Palestinians recount that the Jews came to Israel in the 1940s and kicked out the Arabs, while Jews trace their presence in the region to the time of Abraham. Similarly, present day conflicts about Hawaiian sovereignty are rooted in perceptions that missionaries came to Hawaii in the 1860s and stole Hawaiian land. The immediate conflict may involve discrimination or land, but the latent causes are buried deep in the past. Settling present differences may temporarily cool passions, but the underlying historical causes remain. History not only defines the group, but it is also the heart of the conflict. The role of history is not given sufficient credence in many explanations for intergroup conflict. And, as we will explain in the next section, the challenge of addressing past grievances of individuals long dead presents a conundrum for conflict resolution. Positive feelings for the out-group are likely to be accompanied by guilt as the in-group member remembers, or is reminded of, past conflicts.

Concern for *group security* (indeed, group existence) has a prominent place in intractable conflict. History demonstrates that the out-group is a threat to the security and existence of the in-group. An acre of barren land or the right to speak one's native language assumes vital importance in the relation between groups because they symbolize the right of the group to exist. Compromise on these issues is tantamount to compromising group security and safety. Any sacrifice of security in the present has negative implications for the group's future existence. Israel has repeatedly demanded that its Arab neighbors guarantee its right to exist before any further negotiations take place. Bar-Tal (1990a) presents a similar analysis in his examination of delegitimization. Compromise delegitimizes the right of the group to exist or be treated fairly.

Herein hides the culprit in violent conflict between enduring groups such as ethnic groups. The underlying characteristic of ethnic (and to a lesser extent, international) conflict is fear (Bar-Tal, 2001; Greenland & Brown, 1999; Jarymowicz & Bar-Tal, 2005). The fear is not simply general anxiety (Smith, 1993; Stephan & Stephan, 1985). It involves a real or perceived threat that the out-group will destroy the in-group. The fear is not about the individual and his/her position or life, but rather it focuses on the existence and security of the in-group, now and in the future. Worchel and Coutant (2004) found high fear of the out-group in campers entering peace programs. For example, one camper observed: "The Israelis want to destroy the Palestinians and our way of life. Palestinians as a people will cease to exist." In another case, a Hawaiian responded, "The Hawaiian language, culture, and way of life will disappear if we do not take a stand now." Responses to other types of conflicts typically include anger and hostility, but not fear (Brewer & Brown, 1998).

The consequences of fear on intergroup conflict are profound and pervasive. Fear dominates and controls thinking. Bar-Tal (2001) observes, "Societies involved in intractable conflict tend to be dominated by a collective fear orientation." Fear sensitizes attention to threatening cues; it gives priority to processing information about potential threats (LeDoux, 1996). Fear leads individuals to interpret ambiguous information or events as negative and threatening. Once fear invades an individual or group, there is a need to justify that fear. No group wants to feel that it is experiencing unreasonable or unfounded fear. Fear may not be reasoned, but there is a need to make it appear reasonable. The fear of the out-group can best be justified by enhancing the danger posed by the out-group. Enhancing the danger, however, not only justifies existing fear, but it also becomes the stimulus for higher levels of fear (Wilder, 1993). It is important to realize that the basis for the present fear may be clearly justifiable. However, the level of fear may be greatly exaggerated when placed in a historical context.

Associated with these evil portrayals of the out-group are perceptions of out-group homogeneity (Figure 18.1). Individuals who fear the out-group fail to differentiate between members of the out-group (Wilder & Shapiro, 1989) and view *them* as dangerous and evil. "It (Arab) is like a curse in slang Hebrew. When someone plays some sport badly, the other ones say, you play like an 'Arab'" (Wallach, 2000, p. 38). Fear of specific groups becomes chronic and is adopted into the group's history (Covell, 1996). Analyses of Israeli society (Bar-Gal, 1993; Yaoz, 1980) suggest that fear invades every pore of society (politics, literature, school books, media, and religion). The present Middle East conflict is interpreted against the framework of the Holocaust and thousands of years of persecution of Jews. Present and the past emotions easily merge and become indistinguishable, an effect that is not possible in conflict between new or ad hoc groups.

Perceptions of out-group homogeneity		Perceptions of out-group homogeneity
Out-group threat to in-group existence		Out-group threat to in-group existence
Leadership emphasizes out-group threat		Leadership emphasizes out-group threat
Threat to personal well-being	→ Fear →	Threat to personal well-being
Threat to in-group security and identity		Threat to in-group security and identity
Focus on intergroup differences		Focus on intergroup differences
Narrow focus of attention		Narrow focus of attention
High emotional arousal		High emotional arousal

FIGURE 18.1. The cycle of fear in intergroup relations.

Fear also affects group dynamics. Fear leads people to affiliate and communicate with similar others (Schachter, 1959). Terror management theory (Greenberg, Solomon, & Pyszcynski, 1997) argues that when people are confronted with their own demise, group membership and identity become more salient. And shared fear (collective fear) increases group cohesiveness, acceptance of centralized leadership, conformity, and rejection of deviants (Worchel, Coutant-Sassic, & Grossman, 1992). Increased group cohesiveness laced with high fear nurtures hostility toward the out-group (Stephan, 1985; Worchel, Coutant-Sassic, & Wong, 1993). Both psychological (Newcomb, 1947) and group forces motivate individuals to avoid contact with out-group members (Figure 18.2).

It is tempting to lament the effects of fear. However, its effects are often functional to both the individual and group. Fear "is an evolutionary safeguard that ensures survival in view of potential threats and dangers" (Bar-Tal, 2001, p. 605). From the group's perspective, fear maintains loyalty to the group and solidifies the position of leaders. Fear of the out-group, not love of the in-group, is often the glue that binds people together and allows the group to maintain its identity. Group members are frequently reminded of the danger of the out-group. "In every generation they rise up to destroy us, and we must remember that this could happen in the future" (Rabin, 1987, cited by Bar-Tal, 2001, p. 617).

The bottom line is that the conflict that occurs between these enduring groups often has causes that are distinct from those found in the conflict between temporary or ad hoc groups. We do not mean to imply that all ethnic, or enduring, group conflicts are intractable. However, once violence and

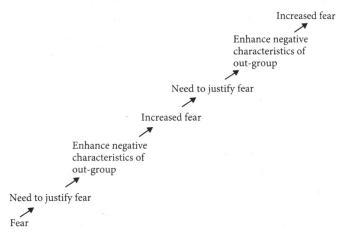

FIGURE 18.2. Escalation of fear in intergroup relations.

threat perception become historically ingrained in an ethnic group's history and myth, there is a high likelihood of that conflict becoming intractable. This point needs to be recognized in theories of intergroup relations. More importantly, this difference helps explain why conflict between enduring groups is often intractable, and why reconciliation and conflict resolution are so elusive.

Toward Tolerance and Coexistence

The literature on the *resolution* of intergroup conflict is both long and broad. Allport (1954) blazed the trail by suggesting that contact between groups is a necessary condition to begin the resolution process. Research (Pettigrew, 1997; Stephan, 1985) has generally supported the *contact hypothesis*, but there have been important modifications. Amir (1969) argued that the contact must occur in a setting in which both groups have equal status. Sherif et al. (1961) demonstrated that the contact must involve repeated incidents of cooperation toward superordinate goals. Worchel, Andreoli, and Folger (1977) found that cooperation reduces conflict only when the efforts are successful.

Pettigrew (1997) suggested that contact can be the basis for forming friendships across group lines, and this attraction can be generalized to the groups. Other explanations for the influence of contact are based on social identity theory suggesting that reducing the prominence of the line that separates groups should reduce intergroup hostility. There are two approaches toward this end. One involves emphasizing the commonality between the groups, and creating (cognitively) one *supergroup* that incorporates the members of both groups. *Recategorization* results when contact emphasizes characteristics shared by all individuals (Gaertner, Dovidio, & Bachman, 1996). Many peace programs, for example, require participants to wear the same uniform, speak a common language, and/or refer to themselves with a common name (e.g., *Seeds* in the Seeds of Peace camp) to create a new *supergroup*. A second *cognitive* process is decategorization, *which* involves eliminating group distinction and viewing each person as an individual (Bettencourt, Brewer, Croak, & Miller, 1992; Brewer & Miller, 1984).

There is clear logic to these explanations, and each approach has supporting research (Gaertner, Mann, Murrell, & Dovidio, 1989). However, we suggest that these perspectives are best applied to ad hoc groups that are not central to individual identity. There are several reasons why these approaches may have limited value in dealing with conflict involving enduring groups, such as ethnic groups, in which membership is permanent and the group is central to personal identity.

Achieving Intergroup Contact

There is a Cajun saying that dental hygiene is good for the alligator, but how do you get the alligator to brush its teeth. A similar statement might apply to cooperative contact and intergroup hostility; contact might be beneficial for the groups but how does one get the groups to engage in cooperative contact. The answer is relatively simple in the laboratory where the participants are controlled by the experimenter. However, the situation is very different with ethnic, cultural, or religious groups engaged in protracted violent conflict. In these cases, the individuals hate and fear each other. The in-group often prohibits unapproved cooperation with the enemy. Indeed, participants in peace programs and camps often state that they are concerned about how they will be treated when they return home, and report being shunned or scolded for engaging in contact with the out-group.

For this reason, we stress the point made by Pettigrew (1998) that intergroup contact must be promoted and supported by recognized in-group leaders. Many peace programs invite in-group leaders to help select participants and require the in-group to send observers (adult) to accompany the participants. Their presence sanctions the contact and these observers help publicize the contact to other group members. However, even with steps, it is important to recognize that contact and the friendships across groups do not necessarily address the critical component of conflict: fear for the security of the in-group. This explains why neighbors, even husbands and wives, can become bitter enemies in ethnic conflicts (Worchel, 1999).

A Passing Fancy?

Recategorization and decategorization may be effective in reducing conflict when change in real or perceived category membership is possible. The Eagles and Rattlers can shed their separate identities because their conflict is confined to the camp experience, and that experience will soon end. However, the African Americans cannot escape this identity, either physically or psychologically. Not only do physical constraints and the group's ever present role in personal identity work against adopting a new identity, but when the individual returns to his/her home, others will quickly remind him/her of group identity. Ethnic identity is the lens through which relations with members of *certain* other groups are interpreted and evaluated, and members of one's in-group will remind an individual to wear his/her glasses. The Jew will always remember, and be reminded of the Holocaust, especially when interacting with Germans.

It is difficult to conceive of a situation that could motivate an individual to reduce the importance of a component that is so core to personal identity. However, even if this could be achieved, the effect on intergroup conflict should be muted, transitory, and largely confined to the specific contact situation (Hornsey & Hogg, 2000a, 2000b). For the most part, social psychology is a science of the here and now (McGrath & Tschan, 2004). Dependent measures are generally collected shortly after the manipulation of the independent variable. The typical study on conflict resolution examines only the immediate effects of contact, cooperation, and recategorization (Brewer & Brown, 1998; Stephan & Stephan, 2001). Research evaluating programs of intergroup contact generally collect measures of impact at the end of the program. It is obviously important to determine how individuals feel after contact with out-group members, but care must be taken about generalizing to long-term consequences. Malhorta and Liyanage (2003) examined the impact of a 4-day peace camp that brought together Tamil and Sinhalese adolescents. Measures taken 1 year after participation showed that the only enduring effect was that participants empathized more with the out-group than did nonparticipants. There were no long-term differences between participants and nonparticipants on measures of trust of the out-group and social distance (recategorization). Our research on peace programs found that increased attraction for and more positive stereotypes of the out-group did not endure beyond the program setting. However, the program did have lasting impact on self-esteem and self-efficacy, fear of the out-group and perception of out-group homogeneity. We suggest that cognitive reorganization of group categories will most likely have positive effects when the conflict involves ad hoc groups with no history and no expectations of future existence. In the case of more enduring groups, such as ethnic groups, the effect will be of short duration, often limited to the immediate contact situation.

To what end? Before going further, one more issue needs to be raised. Investigators of conflict resolution have employed a wide variety of measures to chart the thawing of intergroup conflict. These measures include assigning imaginary points, evaluating out-group performance, attraction, formation of friends, intergroup helping or cooperation, trust of the out-group, and perception of in-group and out-group. Nadler and Liviatan (2004) emphasized that trust, feelings of power, control and *moral worthiness* are outcomes of reconciliation. The aim of many peace programs is very clear, although not necessarily clearly reasoned. These programs want/expect dramatic change in attraction across group boundaries, cooperation, and positive stereotypes of the out-group. For example, Cornerstone International Youth Camp states that its aims are to get participants to "think globally and build global friendships"; the Middle East Camp for Children (Seattle) states that "We hope that through the week that the children, teenagers, and adults will take another step toward peace through friendship and knowledge."

This variety of measures provides a broad examination of the relationship between groups, but it raises several theoretical issues. At the most elementary level, the cafeteria of dependent measures suggests a conceptual fuzziness. Does *conflict resolution* imply intergroup attraction or does it simply involve agreement over a resource disagreement? Nadler and Liviatan (2004) suggest that conflict resolution is best reflected in agreements over resources, while reconciliation is best gauged by emotional responses. How do these various responses relate (or should relate) to each other? For example, does attraction necessarily accompany reduced discrimination and more equal distribution of resources? It is equally unclear whether some outcomes are the direct products of specific processes (Wright & Taylor, 2005). For example, could attraction be the product of decategorization while trust and compromise follow recategorization? Finally, there is the pesky question of whether some responses are more durable than others.

The plethora of dependent variables is both a blessing and curse for the field of intergroup relations. On one hand, it demonstrates the range of behaviors and emotions involved in intergroup relations, and suggests a host of new research issues for the field. On the other hand, the variety of measures demands greater conceptual clarity in the theories and research. The broad label of *conflict resolution* may not adequately describe efforts to improve the relationship between groups. To this end, a case has been made for considering reconciliation as a process that is distinct, but related to conflict resolution (Minow, 1998; Nadler & Liviatan, 2004). We propose that the process for achieving peaceful coexistence also should be examined in this framework. In the next section, we will make the case for acceptance as a distinct process by suggesting that hatred and conflict between enduring groups with permanent membership (e.g., ethnic groups) have unique causes that require unique solutions. We also suggest that a state of peaceful coexistence is defined by specific outcomes that are directly related to the causal factors of conflict and are durable over time.

A Model of Peaceful Coexistence Between Enduring Groups

Our starting point is a focus on groups that are enduring (have a history and expectations for future existence) in which group membership is permanent or relatively permanent. An example of this type of group is the ethnic group, although religious and national groups may also fit the category. We are also most concerned with conflicts that can be viewed as intractable and violent. We adopt this focus because these types of conflicts are among the most destructive and violent, and efforts to improve intergroup relations in these situations often prove ineffective, especially in the long run. Further, these conflicts and the groups involved are not easily handled by existing theories of intergroup relations.

Our approach builds on recent discussions of reconciliation (Nadler & Saguy, 2004; Scheff, 1994) that recognize the role of past events in present conflicts, and the importance of dealing with emotions engendered by conflict. Nadler (2002) has suggested two types of reconciliation processes: socioemotional processes, which involve a specific act, such as an apology, and forgiveness exchange, which allows the immediate halting of the cycle of negative emotions associated with conflict. This release of pent up emotions theoretically then allows conflict parties to build trust. Instrumental reconciliation, on the other hand, also focuses on both parties building trust, but in a more gradual manner than socioemotional processes. Thus, instrumental reconciliation is a product of measured, incremental steps, which allows parties in conflict to reduce animosity and build trust.

Our model departs from the work on reconciliation, particularly socioemotional reconciliation at two important conceptual junctures. The reconciliation process often adopts a perspective that involves perpetrators apologizing for past transgressions and victims forgiving these transgressions. Our observations of discussion groups involved in intractable conflict reveals that both sides are firmly convinced that their group is the victim. Endless debates often revolve around which side has suffered the greatest wrong. Worchel (1999) points out that it is difficult to identify a single example of a war in which one side admits that it is the aggressor. Apology implies accepting the role as perpetrator. In addition, discussion of past sufferings (victimization) often heightens tensions and increases the fear of the out-group. Second, it is unclear whether forgiveness involves forgiving present group members for transgressions of ancestors or forgiving the ancestors for their own actions. Our observations suggest that when apologies are offered, they are done so with the aim of extracting repricol apologies, not forgiveness. The apology implies that past actions will not be repeated, and this reduces fear over group security. Reconciliation and forgiveness may be long-term consequences that follow the establishment of peaceful coexistence. Hence, any effort to distinguish victim from perpetrator or separate apology from forgiveness can quickly become the source of additional conflict.

Instrumental reconciliation is more closely related to our model in that it requires a dynamic approach with a recognition of the concept of time. But the concept of instrumental reconciliation focuses primarily on trust as the sole product. Our model suggests there are competing pressures and concerns involved in intractable conflicts and although trust may help soothe the waters, there are other issues that must be addressed to achieve peaceful coexistence. With these points in mind, let us present our perspective on achieving peaceful coexistence between enduring groups.

On the causal side of the equation, we suggest that the root of hatred and violence between enduring groups is concern about in-group security. The out-group is identified as a threat to in-group security, and collective fear of the out-group arises as a result of this view. The precipitating incident may be competition over scarce resources or events internal to the in-group (e.g., economic difficulties or rumors about the out-group's aggressive intentions). Regardless of the proximate cause, the foundation for fear rests in the historical past of the in-group and/or its collective beliefs (Bar-Tal, 1990b). The combination of history, concern about group security, and fear initiate efforts to justify the fear and concern by enhancing the negative characteristics of the out-group. Historical relations with certain out-groups increase both the intensity and breadth of fear experienced from a present conflict. This factor explains why a conflict, even intense conflict, between groups without a history of hatred may be resolved rather quickly, while conflict, even seemingly minor or localized, between groups with a history of confrontation often expand and resist resolution or reconciliation. Escalating fear increases the perception of the out-group as homogeneous and united in its intention to destroy the in-group. These processes are fed by internal group dynamics that pressure individuals to adopt the prevailing group attitudes and emotions and to avoid unsanctioned contact with out-group members.

Effort to reduce the violence and hostility must directly address these causal factors. Intergroup contact *may* have a positive impact, but several conditions (beyond those identified in earlier studies) must be met in order to achieve a lasting impact. The contact must be sanctioned and approved by respected in-group parties and leaders. Approval can be demonstrated by having group leaders involved in the selection of contact participants, acknowledging the legitimacy of the contact, and/or contributing resources. The contact must be perceived as a means of enhancing group identity and promoting group security. Emphasis on goals such as promoting understanding of the out-group or cooperation will create reluctance to engage in contact unless it is clear that in-group identity and security will be respected. Accepting the right of the group to exist can be achieved through seemingly small, often symbolic, gestures. For example, discussion groups in peace programs are specifically identified as *coexistence* meetings rather reconciliation or compromise sessions. The *coexistence* label implies the right of each group to exist. Respect for group identity is often recognized in programs by allowing the groups to hold their own religious services (open to others), present their culture (e.g., *Culture Night* at Seeds of Peace), or hold in-group meetings. This perspective is captured in the Hewstone and Brown (1986) mutual-differentiation model that counters the decategorization approach by suggesting that in some cases conflict resolution must be built on making in-group identity salient and secure.

Efforts to improve the relations between groups should emphasize peaceful coexistence rather than attraction or improving stereotypes. Intergroup attraction is fickle and given that groups/categories will continue to exist, in-group favoritism will continue to exist. Accepting that different groups can coexist, even cooperate, without threatening each other's security does not require affection or positive stereotypes. Further, Worchel and Rothgerber (1997) argued that stereotypes of and attraction for the out-group are deeply rooted within the in-group (e.g., collective beliefs), and not easily changed at the individual level. Peaceful coexistence may be a precondition for intergroup attraction, but attraction does not guarantee peaceful coexistence.

Peaceful coexistence has several components. One involves emotion. Specifically, fear of the out-group must be reduced. Changing fear to curiosity about the out-group can be achieved by *emphasizing group and personal security and demystifying cultural practices of the out-group*. To reduce fear, contact can be arranged whereby in-group members visit the homes of out-group members, observe their religious ceremonies, hear their history, and visit their schools. These activities do not ignore group differences, but humanize the out-group and demonstrate that these differences are not necessarily a threat to in-group security. It is important to realize that fear reduction efforts must also include opinion leaders in the media, education agencies, textbooks, and politicians (Raviv, Oppenheimer, & Bar-Tal, 1999). Regardless of the specific approach, efforts to achieve peaceful coexistence must focus on reducing fear of the out-group.

Cognition is also an important component. Fear and conflict exacerbate tendencies to view the out-group as homogeneous and evil. Individuals have *data* based on history and group beliefs that the out-group dislikes and mistreats the in-group. A critical step toward peaceful coexistence involves developing the perception that *the out-group, like the in-group, is heterogeneous* and composed of individuals with different views, life styles, and desires. The process requires humanizing the out-group (*the enemy has a face*) while still respecting integrity of group boundaries. A second important cognition is *acceptance of the position that group differences do not necessarily result in conflict and violence*. This position includes tolerance of intergroup differences (Seeds of Peace, 2000) and acceptance that these differences are not necessarily threats to in-group security. Thomas and Ely (1996) report that many businesses are attempting to promote tolerance of diversity by emphasizing how difference enriches the organization. Finally, peaceful coexistence entails *enhanced perceptions of self-esteem and self-efficacy.* Buddhist philosophy argues that one cannot accept others until one accepts oneself (Kraft, 1992). Participation in violence is often common among those who feel personally insecure and strive for acceptance by their own group (Wright & Taylor, 2005).

The third component of peaceful coexistence is behavioral. Intractable conflicts are often accompanied by discriminatory and/or avoidant behavior patterns that become routine, and, like habits, they remain long after the conflict has diminished. Cognitive dissonance theory (Festinger, 1957) supports the wisdom of popular slogan practice kindness in suggesting that attitude change often follows behavior change. Behaviors associated with peaceful coexistence include exploration, engaging in both cooperation and competition without resorting to violence, and adopting a problem-solving approach to conflict.

Studying the Impact of Peace Programs

Although it was tempting to set up a study of our model, we found that countless studies were being unwittingly conducted each year around the world. Unfortunately very few of these studies collected systematic data. Each year there are dozens of peace programs with flowery names such as Seeds of Peace, Youth Reconciliation Initiative, and Initiative for Peace taking place in numerous countries. The programs have many of the components that, according to our model, should bring about peaceful coexistence (Figure 18.3). The programs bring together individuals from ethnic groups that are engaged in protracted, often violent, conflict. Although there is considerable variation in duration, context, and participants, all of the programs involve contact and communication between members of the different groups. Contact occurs in a variety of settings including discussion groups (coexistence sessions) and enjoyable activities involving cooperation (athletic contests, arts and crafts, dances). Group identity is maintained by allowing religious services, culture presentations, and in-group meetings. Participants, often teenagers, are chosen by their governments, religious groups, or educational leaders. Often the groups are accompanied by adults from their own regions. Most, but not all, of the programs involved participants living together in mixed-group settings.

We are presently involved in a study of several programs to examine the short- and long-term impact of the programs. Although data are still being

Cognition
In-group identity and security
Recognition of out-group existence
Positive attitude toward multiple group condition
Recognition and acceptance of in-group–out-group differences
Attitude of peaceful coexistence (tolerance)
Personal security and self-efficacy
Focus on the future

Behavior
Open to intergroup contact
Willing to cooperate
Peaceful competition
Exploration of characteristics of out-group
Friendship
Identification of common problems
Involvement with in-group

Emotion
Low fear
Hopeful

Motivation
Curiosity
Approach differences (rather than avoid)
Exploration

Not Necessarily
Attraction/liking
Positive stereotypes
Absence of stereotypes
Similarity with out-group (recategorization)

FIGURE 18.3.
Characteristics of
peaceful coexistence.

collected, the results of a pilot study involving one program are relevant to the present discussion. The program was a 3-week summer camp in Maine. Participants came from the Middle East and Balkans. Our pilot data came from 62 participants (Israeli, Palestinian, Croatian, Serbian, and Bosnian youth ages 14-16) who responded to questionnaires at the beginning of the camp and on the last day. Long-term data involve 18 participants who were examined 2-4 years after involvement in the program.

A questionnaire was designed to measure variables related to theories of conflict resolution, reconciliation, and the model of peaceful coexistence. These measures included in-group/out-group attraction, perceptions of the in-group and out-group (group homogeneity and stereotypes), perceived group security, perceptions of the conflict (blame, probable outcome), emotions (including fear, happiness, hope), Cantril Self Anchoring Scale, and ratings of the camp activities. In addition, self-esteem and self-efficacy were measured. Finally, demographic data and self-reports of involvement (school, social activities, religious attendance, etc.) with the in-group were collected. In addition, interviews were conducted with several of the respondents. A small control group of Israeli and Palestinian was included.

Space permits only a brief overview of the results. Looking first at the immediate impact of the programs (before-immediately after), the results support the broad value of intergroup contact. The preparticipation responses indicated that the out-group was disliked, seen as possessing negative traits (stereotype), perceived as very homogeneous, and portrayed as being the party largely responsible for the conflict. The *immediately after* data revealed that attraction for the out-group increased and out-group stereotypes became more positive. The out-group was perceived as more heterogeneous, and participants expressed less fear of the out-group and greater hope that the conflict/confrontation would be resolved. At the same time, attraction and positive perceptions of the in-group decreased (before-after) and the in-group was also viewed as more heterogeneous. Further, greater blame was placed on the in-group for causing and perpetuating the conflict (before-after), but most relevant to theories on reconciliation, there was no decrease in the blame of the out-group for the conflict. There was, however, no discernable tendency to increase the perceived similarity between the groups. Finally, self-esteem and self-efficacy became more positive, and evaluations of the camp were overwhelmingly positive. Neither age nor sex of respondent influenced the results. However, the changes were more pronounced in participants from the stronger groups (Israelis, Croats, Serbs) than in the weaker groups (Palestinians, Bosniaks).

The long-term follow-up data, however, revealed a different pattern. The only lasting effects were found in the increased perceptions of both in-group and out-group heterogeneity, reduced fear of the out-group, increased tendency to view the in-group as contributing to the conflict, and elevated self-esteem and self-efficacy. There were no differences (before-long term) in attraction for the in-group or out-group stereotypes (with the exception of *dangerous*), or anticipation that the conflict would soon end. Evaluations of the contact program were more negative in the long-term ratings than immediately after the program. Participants saw their own future as decidedly more positive than the future of their group, but the group's future was viewed more positively in the long-term ratings than in the *before* responses (Self Anchoring Scale).

Without going too far with these preliminary data, there are some interesting trends, that if supported by further research, relate to the present discussion on peaceful coexistence. Most importantly, there were clear differences between immediate and long-term impact of the programs. Increases in attraction and positive stereotyping of the out-group disappear over time, while reduced fear of the out-group, increased perceptions of out-group heterogeneity, and enhanced self-esteem and self-efficacy remain even after 2-4 years. These lasting effects were the ones (emotional, cognitive) that we have argued are indicative of an acceptance of peaceful coexistence. In the more comprehensive study, we are examining the behavioral component of the model to determine whether participants increase their interaction and communication with the out-group. One other lasting effect is worth noting. Although participants continued to place blame for the conflict on the out-group (both immediate and long term), there was a clear tendency in both immediate and long-term responses to report that their in-group also shared responsibility for the conflict. Although these data do not suggest that the out-group is viewed as a victim or that an apology is offered, they may indicate a willingness to accept both sides as perpetrators of hostilities. This change in perceptions may indicate a willingness to engage in reciprocal apologies, a possible step toward reconciliation.

Some Closing Comments

We view our focus on peaceful coexistence as being both distinct and, at the same time, closely related to existing theories of conflict resolution and reconciliation. It is distinct from the conflict resolution approach because of the emphases on the permanence of groups and group history, the role of fear and concern for group security as the foundation of intractable conflict, and the emphasis on establishing peaceful coexistence. Our approach is distinct from theories of reconciliation and forgiveness (Govier, 2002; Nadler & Liviatan, 2004; Staub & Pearlman, 2001) because it avoids delineating perpetrator and victim, and it does not deal with the conceptually difficult concepts of apology and forgiveness. Our experience has shown that enduring groups involved in intractable conflicts have little desire to reconcile differences with the out-group or view the out-group as a victim. Apology for the acts of ancestors is viewed as hearsay that besmirches the reputation of those ancestors who often stand as heroes of the in-group.

Another point of departure is that conflict resolution and reconciliation can be viewed as end-states or solutions to difficulties in the relationship between groups. It is unclear what occurs after resolution and reconciliation are reached. Our presentation of peaceful coexistence is that it is an ongoing process that must be constantly nurtured and supported. Peaceful coexistence is not a cure to intergroup problems such as conflict and confrontation, but rather a condition that allows groups to exist and interact with each other. This difference is somewhat anticipated by Nadler's (2002) division of reconciliation into socioemotional and instrumental approaches. Socioemotional reconciliation is an end state that is achieved when apology is followed by forgiveness. However, instrumental reconciliation, like peaceful coexistence, is a long process that involves contact, cooperation, acceptance, and understanding that creates conditions for conflict resolution and socio-emotional reconciliation.

Despite these differences, our approach is very closely related to these other perspectives. On the surface, many of the points that we emphasize are already being incorporated into existing theories. For example, several investigators (Hornsey & Hogg, 2000b) have recognized that protecting the identity of the in-group may be necessary to deal with some types of conflict, but they have not clearly defined the conditions that are most conducive to this approach. And to be fair to the reconciliation literature, investigators have explicitly pointed out the difficulties of designating victim and perpetrator (Nadler & Liviatan, 2004). There is, then, already convergence in approaches to conflict. However, the relation between the peaceful coexistence and other perspectives on conflict resolution runs even deeper. A perplexing question that dogs the literature on intergroup relations is *why groups in conflict should have any interest in reconciliation or conflict resolution.* Why should a group wish to apologize or forgive an enemy, especially in the case of intractable conflicts when group structure and history is related to the conflict? And a related question involves how to entice enemies to engage in cooperative contact. Our answer to these questions comes from the perspective that peaceful coexistence enhances in-group security and reduces fear. We suggest that these goals can be used to encourage enemies to engage in contact and tolerate differences. The challenge is to demonstrate that peaceful coexistence will satisfy these goals without threatening group identity. We, therefore, suggest that the road toward lasting conflict resolution and reconciliation passes through the establishment of peaceful coexistence. Hence peaceful coexistence may be viewed as a goal for reducing intergroup violence and a precondition for reconciliation and conflict resolution.

We, therefore, propose that investigators focus on creating a paradigm that recognizes the unique characteristics of conflicts between enduring groups, such as ethnic groups. The approach should incorporate the role of history, concern for group security, and fear of the out-group as factors leading to entrenched hatred, and examine the long term, as well as short-term, effects of conflict resolution. General theories should also explicate the relationship between peaceful coexistence, conflict resolution, and reconciliation, and embrace the position that the causes of conflict and the path toward resolution may vary depending on the situation and characteristics of the protagonists.

In closing, we would like to make two points. First, our experience with *peace programs* revealed that the social landscape is populated with opportunities to study conflict between enduring groups. The programs are wonderfully varied, a situation that offers the opportunity to study a wide range of variables and to test for generalizability of results. These programs are a candy shop for investigators with nearly every conceivable variable already being manipulated. Given this situation, it is somewhat surprising to find relatively little interaction between the academic theory and research and the applied programs. Our experience revealed several possible reasons for this divide. From the applied side, there is often a suspicion of academic research that may be viewed as being designed to uncover flaws in the programs without offering concrete suggestions in return. Program funding, whether from private sources or public ones, is often dependent on demonstrating positive outcomes. From the academic side, the programs are often viewed as a methodological quagmire lacking experimental control, random selection of participants, and a lack of theoretical basis for specific activities. These different perspectives cannot be ignored, but they should not be viewed as insurmountable obstacles for building bridges and dialogue between the two sides that can greatly enrich and expand both.

The second point echoes Benjamin Franklin's advice, "an ounce of prevention is worth a pound of cure." Intergroup conflict is notoriously resistant to change once it becomes violent. Fear feeds upon itself; hostility and hatred become ingrained in the history of groups. Although efforts at identifying approaches to reducing intergroup hostility are of great value, equal, if not more, attention should be directed toward the prevention of intergroup hatred. Efforts toward this goal are likely to be far more effective and successful than attempts to reduce intractable hatred and conflict. Social psychology research has identified many of the conditions that are likely to lead to violence between enduring groups. These precipitating conditions include fear, competition, internal threats to in-group security and identity (poverty, change), and uncertainty. The world is filled with examples of "violent conflict in the making." For example, many European countries are experiencing rapid increases in the influx of immigrants, setting the stage for conflicts between immigrant and host groups. In many locations such as Hawaii, Australia, New Zealand, and Fiji, indigenous groups are seeking to recapture their identities, thereby sowing the seeds for confrontation with other groups in the regions. Indeed, the greatest value of social-psychological theories of intergroup relations may be in serving as an early warning system to guide prevention rather than suggesting ways to deal with victims.

References

Allport, G. W. (1954). *The nature of prejudice*. Cambridge: Addison-Wesley.

Amir, Y. (1969). Contact hypothesis in ethnic relations. *Psychological Bulletin, 71*, 319-342.

Bar-Gal, Y. (1993). *Homeland and geography in a hundred years of Zionist education.* Tel Aviv: Ovid.

Bar-Tal, D. (1990a). Causes and consequences of delegitimization: Models of conflict and ethnocentrism. *Journal of Social Issues, 46,* 65-81.

Bar-Tal, D. (1990b). *Group beliefs.* New York: Springer-Verlag.

Bar-Tal, D. (2001). Why does fear override hope in societies engulfed by intractable conflicts, as it does in the Israeli society? *Political Psychology, 22,* 601-627.

Bettencourt, B., Brewer, M., Croak, M., & Miller, N. (1992). Cooperation and reduction of intergroup bias: The role of reward structure and social orientation. *Journal of Experimental Social Psychology, 28,* 630-659.

Brewer, M., & Brown, R. (1998). Intergroup relations. In D. Gilbert, S. Fiske, & G. Lindzey (Eds.), *The handbook of social psychology* (4th ed., pp. 554-594). New York: McGraw Hill.

Brewer, M., & Miller, N. (1984). Beyond the contact hypothesis: Theoretical perspectives on desegregation. In N. Miller & M. Brewer (Eds.), *Groups in contact: The psychology of desegregation* (pp. 281-302). London: Academic Press.

Cannon, M. (2003). *Youthcruise 4.* Unpublished paper from Irish Peace Institute.

Cantril, H. (1965). *The pattern of human concerns.* New Brunswick, NJ: Rutgers University Press.

Covell, K. (1996). Adolescents' attitudes toward international conflict: A cross-national comparison. *International Journal of Behavioral Development, 19,* 871-883.

Festinger, L. (1957). *A theory of cognitive dissonance.* Palo Alto, CA: Stanford Press.

Gaertner, S., Dovidio, J., & Bachman, B. (1996). Revisiting the contact hypothcsis: The introduction of a common group identity. *International Journal of Intercultural Relations, 20,* 271-290.

Gaertner, S., Mann, J., Murrell, A., & Dovidio, J. (1989). Reducing intergroup bias: the benefits of recategorization. *Journal of Personality and Social Psychology, 57,* 239-249.

Govier, T. (2002). *Forgiveness and revenge.* New York: Routledge.

Greenberg, J., Solomon, M., & Pyszcynski, T. (1997). Terror management theory o self-esteem and cultural world view: Empirical assessment and conceptual refinement. In M. Zanna (Ed.), *Advances in experimental social psychology.* New York: Academic Press.

Greenland, K., & Brown, R. (1999). Categorization and intergroup anxiety in contact between British and Japanese nationals. *European Journal of Social Psychology, 29,* 503-521.

Hewstone, M., & Brown, R. (1986). Contact is not enough: An intergroup perspective on the "contact hypothesis." In M. Hewstone & R. Brown (Eds.), *Contact and conflict in encounters* (pp. 1-44). Oxford: Blackwell.

Hornsey, M., & Hogg, M. (2000a). Assimilation and diversity: An integrative model of subgroup relations. *Personality and Social Psychology Review, 4,* 143-156.

Hornsey, M., & Hogg, M. (2000b). Subgroup relations: A comparison of mutual intergroup differentiation and common identity models of prejudice reduction. *Personality and Social Psychology Bulletin, 26,* 241-256.

Jarymowicz, M., & Bar-Tal, D. (2005). The dominance of fear over hope in the life of individuals and collectives. *Unpublished paper University of Warsaw, Warsaw, Poland and University of Tel Aviv, Tel Aviv, Israel.*

Kraft, K. (1992). Prospects of socially engaged Buddhism. In K. Kraft (Ed.), *Inner peace, world peace: Essays on Buddhism and nonviolence.* Albany: SUNY Press.

LeDoux, J. (1996). *The emotional brain: The mysterious underpinnings of emotional life.* New York: Touchstone.

Malhorta, D., & Liyanage, S. (2003). *Assessing the long-term impact of "peace camps" on youth attitudes and behaviors: The case of ethno-political conflict in Sri Lanka.* Social Science Research Network: Harvard NOM Research Paper No. 03-24.

McGrath, J., & Tschan, F. (2004). *Temporal matters.* Washington, DC: American Psychological Association.

Minow, M. (1998). *Between vengeance and forgiveness: Facing history after genocide and mass violence.* Boston, MA: Beacon Press.

Maoz, I. (2000). An experiment in peace: Reconciliation-aimed workshops on Jewish-Israeli and Palestinian youth. *Journal of Peace Research, 37,* 721-736.

Nadler, A. (2002). Social-psychological analysis of reconciliation: Instrumental and Socio-emotional routes to reconciliation. In G. Salomon & B. Nevo (Eds.), *Peace education worldwide: The concept, underlying principles, the research.* Mawheh, NJ: Erlbaum.

Nadler, A., & Liviatan, I. (2004). Inter-group reconciliation: Theoretical analysis and empirical findings. In N. R. Branscombe & B Doosje (Eds.), *Collective guilt: International perspectives.* New York: Cambridge University Press.

Nadler, A., & Saguy, T. (2004). Trust building and reconciliation between adversarial groups: A social psychological perspective. In H. Langholtz & C. Stout (Eds.), *The psychology of diplomacy* (pp. 29-46). New York: Praeger.

Newcomb, T. (1947). Autistic hostility and social reality. *Human Relations, 1,* 69-86.

Pettigrew, T. (1997). Generalized intergroup contact effects on prejudice. *Personality and Social Psychology Bulletin, 23,* 173-185.

Pettigrew, T. (1998). Intergroup contact theory. *Annual Review of Psychology, 49,* 65-85.

Raviv, A., Oppenheimer, L., & Bar-Tal, D. (1999). *How children understand war and peace.* San Francisco, CA: Jossey Bass.

Schachter, S. (1959). *The psychology of affiliation.* Palo Alto, CA: Stanford University.

Scheff, T. (1994). *Bloody revenge: Emotions, nationalism, and war.* Boulder: Westview.

Seeds of Peace (2000). *Rewriting the grammar of coexistence: Teaching tolerance in the classroom.* New York: Seeds of Peace.

Sherif, M. (1966). *Group conflict and co-operation: Their social psychology.* London: Routledge & Kegan Paul.

Sherif, M., Harvey, O., White, B., Hood, W., & Sherif, C. (1961). *Intergroup conflict and cooperation: The Robber's Cave experiment.* Norman, OK: University of Oklahoma.

Smith, E. (1993). Social identity and social emotions. In D. Mackie & D. Hamilton (Eds.), *Affect, cognition and stereotyping: Interactive processes in group perception* (pp. 297-315). San Diego: Academic Press.

Staub, E., & Pearlman, L. (2001). Healing, reconciliation, and forgiving after genocide and other collective violence. In S. Helmick & R. Peterson (Eds.), *Forgiveness and reconciliation* (pp. 195-217). Radnor, PA: Templeton Foundation Press.

Stephan, W. (1985). Intergroup relations. In G. Lindzey & E. Aronson (Eds.), *The handbook of social psychology* (3rd ed., Vol. 2, pp. 599-658). New York: Random House.

Stephan, W., & Stephan, C. (1985). Intergroup anxiety. *Journal of Social Issues, 41,* 157-175.

Stephan, W., & Stephan, C. (2001). *Improving intergroup relations.* Thousand Oaks, CA: Sage.

Tajfel, H. (1970). Experiments in intergroup discrimination. *Scientific American, 223,* 96-102.

Tajfel, H., & Turner, J. (1979). An integrative theory of intergroup conflict. In W. Austin & S. Worchel (Eds.), *The social psychology of intergroup relations* (pp. 33-47). Monterey, CA: Brooks/Cole.

Thomas, D., & Ely, R. (1996). Making differences matter: A new paradigm for managing diversity. *Harvard Business Review, September-October,* 79-90.

Turner, J. C. (1985). Social categorization and self-concept: A social cognitive theory of group behavior. In E. Lawler (Ed.), *Advances in group processes* (Vol. 2, pp. 71-122). Greenwich, CT: JAI Press.

Verkuyten, M. (2005). *The social psychology of ethnic identity.* East Sussex: Psychology Press.

Wallach, J. (2000). *The enemy has a face: The Seeds of Peace Experience.* Washington, DC: United States Peace Institute.

Wilder, D. (1993). The role of anxiety in facilitating stereotypic judgment of outgroup behavior. In D. Mackie & D. Hamilton (Eds.), *Affect, cognition, and stereo-typing: Interactive processes in group perception* (pp. 87-109). San Diego: Academic Press.

Wilder, D., & Shapiro, P. (1989). Effects of anxiety on impression formation in a group context: An anxiety-assimilation hypothesis. *Journal of Experimental Social Psychology, 25,* 481-499.

Worchel, S. (1999). *Written in blood: Ethnic identity and the search for human harmony.* New York: Worth.

Worchel, S., Andreoli, V., & Folger, R. (1977). Intergroup cooperation and intergroup attraction: The effect of previous interaction and outcome of combined effort. *Journal of Experimental Social Psychology, 13,* 131-140.

Worchel, S., & Coutant, D. (2004). *Sowing the seeds of peace in ethnic conflicts: The potential of interactive camps for reducing and preventing ethnic violence.* Paper presented at War and Peace: Social psychological approaches to armed conflicts and humanitarian issues. Geneva: Switzerland (Proceeding).

Worchel, S., Coutant-Sassic, D., & Grossman, M. (1992). A developmental approach to group dynamics: A model and illustrative research. In S. Worchel, W. Wood, & J. Simpson (Eds.), *Group process and productivity.* Newbury Park, CA: Sage.

Worchel, S., Coutant-Sassic, D., & Wong, F. (1993). Toward a more balanced view of conflict: There is a positive side. In S. Worchel & J. Simpson (Eds.), *Conflict between people and groups*. Chicago, IL: Nelson-Hall.

Worchel, S., & Rothgerber, H. (1997). Changing the stereotype of the stereotype. In R. Spears, P. Oakes, N. Ellemers, & S. Haslam (Eds.), *The social psychology of stereotyping and group life*. Oxford: Blackwell.

Worchel, S., Webb, W., & Hills, M. (1987). *Cross-cultural variation in social identity formation*. Unpublished manuscript, Texas A&M University: College Station, TX.

Wright, S., & Taylor, D. (2005). The social psychology of cultural diversity: social stereotyping, prejudice, and discrimination. In M. Hogg & J. Cooper (Eds.), *The Sage handbook of social psychology* (pp. 432-457). London: Sage.

Yaoz, H. (1980). *Holocaust stories in Hebrew literature as historical and transhistorial fiction*. Tel Aviv: Akad.

CHAPTER 19

Help as a Vehicle to Reconciliation, With Particular Reference to Help for Extreme Health Needs

JEFFREY D. FISHER, ARIE NADLER, JESSICA S. LITTLE, AND TAMAR SAGUY

The issue of what occurs when individuals, groups, or nations with adversarial relations initially attempt to act favorably toward one another has been considered infrequently in the literature. It is an intriguing problem and one at the very heart of the success or failure of early attempts at reconciliation. Charles Osgood (1962) considered this issue in his "graduated reductions in tension" (GRIT) proposal and argued that it may be possible for one side in a conflict to engage in a unilateral positive act and for this act to elicit a reciprocal positive act from its adversary. Others (e.g., Reeder, Pryor, Wohl, & Griswell, 2005; Robinson, Keltner, Ward, & Ross, 1995; Ross & Ward, 1996) argue more pessimistically that an initial favorable act by an adversary is likely to be misconstrued to be consistent with preexisting negative relations between the two parties and is unlikely to elicit a favorable response.

The present chapter will consider this issue, giving special attention to programs providing aid to deal with extreme health needs occasioned by the global HIV/AIDS pandemic (e.g., help with the provision of life-saving antiretroviral drugs; help in designing, implementing, or evaluating HIV risk reduction programs). Nevertheless, our discussion is relevant to other contexts in which a party (e.g., group or nation) with preexisting negative relations with a party with lesser resources provides help to that party, at least in part in the hope that it will be a step toward better relations (e.g., reconciliation).

To date, more than 65 million people worldwide have been infected with HIV (UNAIDS, 2006) and 25 million have died from AIDS (UNAIDS, 2006). In sub-Saharan Africa, 24.5 million individuals are infected and more than 17 million have died (UNAIDS, 2006). Fortunately, since the mid-90s, in the United States and other industrialized nations, due to the discovery and dissemination of antiretroviral drugs (ARVs), HIV has become more a chronic illness than an inevitable death sentence. Nevertheless, globally, ARVs are available to only about one in five who need them, and in impoverished nations, they reach a much smaller percentage of needy individuals (UNAIDS, 2006).

These statistics have elicited worldwide consternation and horror and have occasioned attempts by nations (e.g., the United States, Canada, the Netherlands, Norway, the United Kingdom), other international entities (e.g., the United Nations), and large corporations (e.g., international drug manufacturers) to provide assistance to countries suffering from HIV. Sometimes the donor and the recipient have had a history of poor relations and the donation of assistance is an attempt, in part, to improve them. The United States' relations with many African nations hard hit by HIV has historically been characterized by indifference and at times repression and injustice (e.g., Browne, 1986; Clough, 1992; Rothchild, 2002; Schraeder, 1994). Moreover, early U.S. HIV assistance to Africa may not have contributed optimally to changing problematic relations. According to some accounts, the U.S. President's Emergency Plan for AIDS Relief (PEPFAR) did not sufficiently consult officials in Mozambique, Uganda, Rwanda, and other nations before designating them PEPFAR beneficiaries. Nor did the United States adequately take into account the countries' healthcare infrastructures and their own plans to combat HIV in designing its assistance (The End of the Beginning? 2004; Sontag, 2004).

While PEPFAR has saved many lives, it has had characteristics that elicit negative responses from recipients (e.g., not providing broad funding for cheaper, more sustainable, generic ARVs; underemphasizing condom use while overemphasizing abstinence and "being faithful"—Office of the U.S. Global AIDS Coordinator, 2004; President's Emergency Plan for AIDS Relief, 2004). Help that is tailored to the recipient's needs and that is consistent with their plans, policies, and traditions elicits more favorable reactions than help given without attending sufficiently to these elements (e.g., Fisher, Nadler, & Whitcher-Alagna, 1982; Nadler & Fisher, 1986).

In addition to relations between nations (e.g., the United States and African countries), relations between multinational drug companies and African nations have been troubled throughout the HIV epidemic (e.g., due to high prices of HIV drugs, restrictions on cheaper generic drugs, and other factors; Horton, 2000; von Schoen-Angerer, Wilson, Ford, & Kasper, 2001). While donors (e.g., nations or pharmaceutical corporations) who have begun to provide free or lower price ARVs are interested in eliciting favorable recipient reactions and often use donations to further a reconciliation process *and* to improve the health of nations impacted by HIV, the responses to such aid have been variable (e.g., The End of the Beginning? 2004; Sontag, 2004). This is probably caused by negative preexisting relations and by characteristics of the assistance program itself (e.g., the extent to which the donor and the recipient nation collaboratively designed it and the extent to which it met the recipient nation's needs).

Complementing *unilateral* forms of aid (e.g., help from one nation to another; help from a drug company to a nation), *multilateral* attempts at HIV-related assistance have been undertaken (e.g., by the United Nations). Here, some potential negative recipient reactions are obviated because previous donor-recipient relations are often better and because the relative inferiority of the recipient to the donor is blunted since the recipient is part of the donating body (Fisher et al., 1982). Moreover, compared with some initial unilateral, nation-based, assistance programs, multilateral (e.g., United Nations-based) programs better anticipated the recipient's needs, included them in consultations, and fit programs better into the local ecology (The End of the Beginning? 2004; Sontag, 2004; WHO/UNAIDS, 2004).

This chapter considers attempts to provide assistance with health emergencies to nations with whom there have been adverse relations as a metaphor for attempts to provide aid in related contexts (e.g., help with technology or agriculture; humanitarian assistance for natural disasters). Our discussion is relevant to any type of aid motivated, in part, to promote goodwill or reconciliation between the helper and recipient. The results of such aid in terms of improving—or in "backfiring," and further impairing relations between the parties—will be critical in either facilitating reconciliation or promoting a downward spiral in the relationship. We attempt to outline in conceptual and empirical terms the conditions under which aid may serve as a first powerful step in a reconciliation process, or when it may "backfire," promoting additional conflict. In this process, we suggest that characteristics of the groups involved (e.g., their relative levels of power), preexisting intergroup relations, and the characteristics of the help itself (e.g., whether it promotes autonomy or furthers dependency) need to be considered for a conceptually coherent approach to this critical question.

The analysis which we will forward emphasizes processes of *instrumental* (Nadler & Saguy, 2004) rather than *socio-emotional* (Nadler, 2002; Nadler & Schnabel, this volume) reconciliation. Processes of instrumental reconciliation consist of attempts to improve perceptions of an adversary, enhance trust felt toward them, and ultimately, the relations with them, through meaningful positive gestures toward them. These gestures may be enacted unilaterally by one of the parties (termed "trust building measures," Osgood, 1962) or enacted reciprocally and over time (termed "peace building" efforts, Lederach, 1997). Instrumental reconciliation may be contrasted with socio-emotional reconciliation, which attempts to affect change in the *identities* of each of the parties by addressing the pain and humiliation that they may have caused each other during their conflict. A major tool of socio-emotional reconciliation is the "apology-forgiveness" cycle, discussed in this volume (see chapter by Nadler & Schnabel).

The first two authors' initial attempt to address the issue of reconciliation was early in our careers—over 30 years ago—as graduate students at Purdue University. It comprised one of the first published experimental studies on intergroup helping involving medical assistance in the context of a preexisting favorable or unfavorable donor-recipient relationship. In this work, we tested competing predictions on the effects of aid from an "enemy" in the context of a medical emergency. Would such help be perceived favorably and have the potential to elicit reciprocal positive acts, consistent with Osgood's GRIT proposal (described earlier) and work by Amatai Etzioni (Etzioni, 1967) or would it be misconstrued and viewed as a malevolent gesture (e.g., Reeder et al., 2005; Robinson et al., 1995; Ross & Ward, 1996)? The latter could be predicted on conceptual grounds, and is consistent with findings by Gergen and Gergen (1971, 1974) that the preexisting donor-recipient relationship often predicts the favorability of recipient reactions to aid.

Because it is difficult to test, experimentally, the effects of the preexisting donor-recipient relationship on reactions to humanitarian aid in the "real world," we employed a highly impactful experimental simulation, the "Tactical and Negotiations Game" (Streufert, Kliger, Castore, & Driver, 1967), in which participants role-played decision makers for one side in an international conflict. They had responsibility for military, economic, intelligence, and negotiation functions for a nation involved in a limited war and were led to believe they were playing against another nation. The simulation began with participants reading a manual on the history of the conflict (the "Shamba" conflict) and their nation's role in it. In the manual, it was mentioned that a disease called "Menesitis" had broken out in Shamba in the past, had killed or crippled many individuals, and that a neutral party in the conflict, the Mandero Research Center, was working to find a cure.

The simulation proceeded with several hours of interactions in which players received military, intelligence, and economic information about the progression of the conflict, and which established a credible enemy and ally, each represented by a group of players. At one point, it was announced that the Madero Research Center had developed a Menesitis vaccine but that production would be slow and insufficient for a serious disease outbreak. While this was incidental to participants' primary concerns at the time, participants were later informed that their military and civilian populations had become heavily impacted by the disease, and their troops were asking to be relieved of duty. The team then received an offer of 3,000 units of vaccine from a country that was their enemy or ally, and we measured reactions to humanitarian medical aid from either party. We observed that participants were more likely to attribute ulterior motives to aid from an enemy than an ally and perceived it to reflect less sacrifice and to be of lower value than help from an ally (Nadler, Fisher, & Streufert, 1974). This suggests that preexisting relations may indeed color perceptions of humanitarian aid intended by donors as an initial step in a reconciliation process.

Over the past 30 years, social and health psychology have provided new conceptual and empirical insights into why an initial positive act by a conflicting party may not have the desired effect and on how to provide aid to foster favorable short- and long-term responses and reconciliation. This work includes theory and research on intergroup helping (e.g., Nadler, 2002; Nadler & Halabi, 2006), on recipient reactions to help (e.g., Fisher et al., 1982; Nadler & Fisher, 1986), and on reconciliation (e.g., Nadler & Saguy, 2004). Collectively, this body of research helps define the conditions under which aid from a group with which one has had adversarial relations will be *psychologically acceptable* to the recipient. Unless this occurs, aid is unlikely to elicit favorable recipient responses and promote reconciliation.

In addition to being psychologically acceptable, help must often be *effective at promoting long-term recipient self-sufficiency, or autonomy,* to facilitate favorable recipient responses and reconciliation. Aid that promotes autonomy is strongly preferred by recipients who have had previous conflict with, and have lower status than, their donors (e.g., Nadler, 2002; Nadler & Halabi, 2006). For aid to promote autonomy, in addition to providing the recipient with an objective resource (e.g., condoms or ARVs), it must include elements facilitating long-term self-sufficiency in its effective use. Recent theory and research by Fisher and associates on helping interventions that promote recipient autonomy-oriented behavior change has much to offer in this context (Fisher & Fisher, 1992, 2002). Application of such conceptualizations makes it possible for the recipient to utilize the aid they receive over the long-term in order to obviate the need state that initially made help necessary.

Making Help Psychologically Acceptable

Several models highlight the conditions under which help will be psychologically acceptable to a recipient group. Nadler and affiliates' model of intergroup helping (Nadler, 2002; Nadler & Halabi, 2006), which is based on past work on helping relations and social identity process, highlights the role of *social inequality* in determining reactions to intergroup helping. A helping context may make salient information about the donor group (e.g., their power or motives), the recipient group (e.g., their relative failure or inferiority), and the donor-recipient relationship (e.g., the relative status of the two groups and its legitimacy). Nadler's model assumes that reactions to intergroup helping (e.g., help between nations or between drug companies and nations) depends importantly on (a) the perceived *legitimacy* and *stability* of the status differences between the groups (in social identity theory terms, the degree of *security* in the status relations between the groups), and (b) on whether the help is oriented toward the recipient's ultimate *autonomy* or its *dependency* (Nadler, 1997, 1998).

Social identity theory tells us that if the lower power entity perceives the status differential between groups to be *illegitimate* or *unstable,* they will likely challenge it by taking measures to gain equality (Tajfel & Turner, 1986). In a helping context, for example, the low power group may limit the amount of help they receive and its duration (e.g., rejecting help offered without first being requested; expressing a strong preference for help that promotes long-term autonomy vs. dependency) (see *left* box in Figure 19.1). This state of affairs (i.e., perceived illegitimacy and instability of lower status) may characterize relations between poor nations hard hit by HIV (e.g., African nations) and potential donors (e.g., the United States and/or multinational drug companies). Both potential donors had ARVs available yet did *not* make them available to poor nations in a potentially sustainable way until relatively recently. The United States may be perceived as having attended to the needs of its own citizens and the profits of its pharmaceutical companies before making ARVs available to others and the pharmaceutical companies as maximizing profits before distributing drugs free or at lower cost. Both entities have also been perceived at times by needy countries as actively thwarting their attempts to acquire ARVs by defending patent laws against generics and other actions (Baker, 2006). Some would argue that recent changes in policies are "too little, too late" and were occasioned, in part, by protests and worldwide indignation that occurred long before they became interested in helping (Betraying Africa's priorities: A short analysis of U.S. policies on HIV/AIDS in Africa, 2006). For these reasons, the powerful entity's "advantage" may not be perceived as legitimate by nations without early access to ARVs.

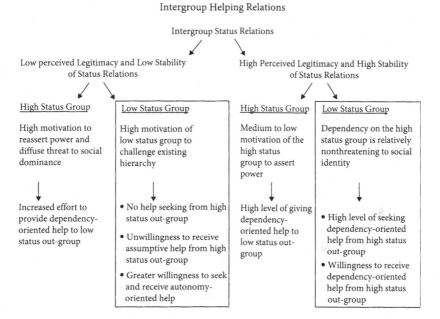

FIGURE 19.1. Intergroup helping relations as affected by perceived legitimacy and stability of power relations between groups. From "Inter-group helping relations as power relations: Maintaining or challenging social dominance between groups through helping," by A. Nadler, 2002, *Journal of Social Issues, 58*, 487-502. Copyright 2002 by Blackwell Publishing. Reprinted with permission.

The type of help that may be preferred by the lower status (recipient) nation under these circumstances is *autonomy-oriented* rather than *dependency-oriented* aid (Nadler, 1997, 1998) (see box at the *left* side of Figure 19.1). Autonomy-oriented help can assist the recipient to ultimately become self-sufficient—it is analogous to providing a hungry person with a fishing rod versus merely giving them a fish to eat. Psychologically, the provision of such help implies that the donor views the recipient group as possessing the self-efficacy to become independent and self-reliant, if given the appropriate tools. From a social identity perspective, such help can reduce the disparity between the two groups and promote a positive social identity in the recipient. Ultimately, it can facilitate changes in status that promote respect for the recipient by *both* the recipient and the donor.

Under these conditions (i.e., low perceived legitimacy and instability of status differences), the high status donor and the lower status recipient will have very different needs and preferences (Nadler & Halabi, 2006). Contrary to the low status recipient, who will find autonomy-oriented help most psychologically acceptable and who is attempting to challenge the existing status hierarchy, under challenge the high status donor may be motivated to reassert power and to diffuse the threat to social dominance. This may result in efforts to provide dependency as opposed to autonomy-oriented help to the low status group (see the *left most column* of Figure 19.1). In effect, the type of help that may be most likely to be provided for HIV-related issues (i.e., dependency-oriented help) may be the *least* likely to promote optimal recipient reactions and reconciliation. Some analyses of the context in which HIV-related aid has been provided by the U.S. government and the pharmaceutical industry support this assertion (Africa Action, 2006; Baker, 2006). For example, early U.S. government programs to provide ARVs (under the PEPFAR program) involved expensive "brand name" drugs made by U.S. manufacturers, rather than much less costly generics. For recipient nations concerned with ultimately achieving autonomy, lower cost generics are much more sustainable over the long-term and more easily scalable to saving larger numbers of patient's lives. Before the requirement for using only "brand name" drugs was modified, it elicited quite negative reactions from some PEPFAR recipients.

If, on the other hand, the low status recipient group perceives intergroup power differences to be more *stable* and *legitimate,* they will find dependency on the high status group less threatening to social identity and will be apt to seek help or to accept it if offered, even if it is dependency-oriented (see the box on the *right* side of Figure 19.1). Note that under such conditions the donor is quite willing to provide the recipient with a type of help with which they are comfortable (see the column immediately to the *left* of this box). This characterizes *colonial* relations between nations—when inequality is perceived as stable and legitimate—but is *not,* generally, likely to be the case today for relations between African nations and donors of HIV-related assistance. Dependency-oriented help, in providing the complete (short-term) solution to the problem, asserts that the recipient is unable to contribute to resolving their need state, reinforces their dependency, and maintains the social status disparity between the groups.

In the model depicted in Figure 19.1, although altruism is certainly possible, help by the high power group may be motivated, at least in part, by a desire to assert and maintain power. For this reason, high status groups may be disposed to giving dependency- as opposed to autonomy-oriented help. This is especially likely when the lower status group challenges the higher power group's legitimacy. *In effect, the type of help most likely to be given may be precisely the type that will not be received well by a lower status group that views the high status group's power as unstable and illegitimate.*[1]

This model points to a fundamental potential problem in humanitarian assistance involving the provision of ARVs from powerful nations or large pharmaceuticals to less powerful countries suffering from HIV. We are arguing that in the typical case of ARV assistance from a powerful nation or multinational drug company there will be low perceived legitimacy and stability of donor-recipient power relations that could set up a conflict of interests between the parties. The donor will be likely to offer dependency-oriented help to serve his or her psychological/social identity needs and the recipient will be likely to eschew such help for his or her psychological/social identity needs. Unfortunately, under these conditions, high status donors are unlikely to be amenable to the recipient's concerns, since they may be motivated to reassert their dominance.

To mitigate the threat associated with such help, the recipient may attempt to change dependency- to autonomy-oriented help. One way to achieve autonomy-oriented aid would be for the recipient and donor to negotiate the conditions under which the aid is given (which, unfortunately, the high power party may be unlikely to agree to). Research has shown that when the conditions associated with help are jointly conceived by the donor and recipient, following some initial discomfort, both parties are quite satisfied with the transaction and help is very effective at increasing long-term recipient autonomy (Fisher, Cornman, Norton, & Fisher, 2006; Fisher, Cornman, Osborn, Amico, Fisher, & Friedland, 2004; Fisher, Fisher, Cornman, Amico, Bryan & Friedland, 2006). Another way to make help acceptable to recipients would be for them to identify ways to reciprocate to the donor at some point in time (e.g., Fisher et al., 1982; Greenberg, 1980; Worchel, Wang, & Scheltema, 1989). This might involve providing future, reciprocal assistance in a realm in which the recipient has special expertise or resources.

A third means that could make help acceptable to the recipient and the donor would be to reframe the helping context as one in which *both* are making a substantial contribution; this would help equalize their power. There could be an acknowledgement that the donor's contribution (e.g., providing ARVs) is a necessary but *not* a sufficient condition for the recipient's health to improve. In effect, the donor is providing a critical resource, ARVs, but taking them regularly, *adherence*, which must be 95% or greater, a huge task to sustain over time (Fisher, Fisher, Amico, & Harmon, 2006), and which involves substantial autonomy-oriented behavior change, is the recipient's responsibility. In this context and others, both donor and recipient must, collaboratively, make a substantial commitment to the process for aid to have beneficial long-term outcomes for each (Fisher, et al., 2006). If both work together, similar to Aronson's "jigsaw technique" (Aronson, Blaney, Stephan, Sikes, & Snapp, 1978) they succeed; if either fails to commit, both fail.

Unfortunately, a recipient can deal less constructively than in the examples depicted above with help from a donor whose greater status is perceived to be illegitimate. For example, a recipient might deny the need for help, which is, in fact, necessary. South African officials initially maintained, in the context of limited international offers of assistance with ARVs and lack of local capacity to produce them, that AIDS was caused by poverty and malnutrition rather than HIV and that ARVs were toxic (Boyle, 2001). (While AIDS is a disease of poverty and social disorganization, poverty is not, of course, the biological cause of AIDS). If HIV does not cause AIDS and ARVs are toxic, there is little need for help in obtaining such drugs. When South Africa became able to manufacture inexpensive generic versions of some ARVs themselves (von Schoen-Angerer et al., 2001), and when multinational drug companies and other nations were willing to "forgive" the patent violations involved in this form of autonomous self-help (i.e., local production of generic versions of the drugs), ARVs began to be officially more accepted in South Africa (Horton, 2000).

Clearly, when status legitimacy is threatened, autonomy-oriented help is preferred by recipients and dependency-oriented help may be preferred by donors. Nevertheless, we argue that dependency-oriented help is *not* ultimately the best type of aid for donors to offer if their motives involve concerns about improving relations with the recipient group. It is clear that such help, which maintains the status quo, is not psychologically acceptable to recipients who view the donor's superior status as illegitimate and unstable. Moreover, when status differences between two groups in conflict are illegitimate and unstable (i.e., insecure, in terms of social identity theory), true long-term reconciliation often cannot occur without real movement toward addressing the differential status between the groups (Lederach, 1997; see chapter by Malloy in this volume). Autonomy-oriented aid can play a very critical role in this regard; indeed, it may be the only type of help that can foster reconciliation in this situation. Note, in contrast, that *dependency*-oriented aid can foster reconciliation following conflict between different status groups that view their inequity as legitimate and unstable.

While autonomy-oriented help is often preferred by recipients, and may be a *precondition* to reconciliation, it is a necessary but *not* a sufficient condition for reconciliation. *When the donor's greater power is viewed as unstable and illegitimate, aid will lead to long-term positive reactions and reconciliation only if it is both autonomy-oriented and does, in fact, ultimately lead to recipient autonomy.* This type of aid is effective and efficient, and ultimately changes the status of the donor and the recipient, consistent with the recipient's motivation to challenge the existing hierarchy (see box on *left* side of Figure 19.1). It also enhances the recipient's social identity and, ultimately, the donor's respect for them, which is critical to reconciliation (see chapter by Janoff-Bulman and werther in this volume). Autonomy-oriented aid that does *not* actually lead to long-term autonomy (e.g., analogous to giving a nation farming equipment and seeds without instruction in how to use them and support for the behavior change involved in transitioning from other activities to farming) will ultimately elicit negative responses from both the donor (e.g., disrespect and derogation of the recipient) and the recipient (e.g., further threat to social identity and esteem; derogation of the donor) and will not serve reconciliation.

Thus far in this chapter, we have proposed a model of effective and efficient helping and a model of helping that can foster reconciliation, and they often require the same conditions. Previous models of helping and recipient reactions to aid, including our earlier work (e.g., Fisher et al., 1982; Nadler & Fisher, 1986) and more recent work on intergroup helping (Nadler, 2002; Nadler & Halabi, 2006), focus mostly on recipient preferences for aid in different contexts, on help-seeking (Nadler, 1991; Wills & DePaulo, 1993), and on types of aid that elicit positive short-term responses to the donor and the help. In effect, they focus on the psychological acceptability of different types of aid. These conceptualizations have *not* focused sufficiently on the critical issue of the long-term efficacy of aid (i.e., the extent to which it actually promotes recipient self-sufficiency and autonomy).

We contend that for autonomy-oriented help to actually lead to true long-term autonomy requires *behavior change* by the recipient. The models of helping we have discussed thus far do not describe the necessary and sufficient conditions for recipient behavior change from a dependent to a more independent, self-reliant state. We believe such an outcome requires the receipt of autonomy-oriented aid that *can* support self-sufficiency (e.g., a fishing rod vs. a fish; seeds and gardening equipment vs. a salad), but autonomy-oriented help, in its objective form, does not ensure self-sufficiency (e.g., being able to fish, in an autonomous fashion, over time to provide oneself with sustenance). Models of *behavior change*, to be described below, specify what is necessary for aid to be behaviorally effective (i.e., for it to actually promote long-term self-sufficiency). Unless aid promotes long-term autonomous behavior change, it is often not an efficient use of resources. Resources expended in the service of long-term autonomy are much more cost-effective than those expended in the service of dependency.

Our early theorizing on recipient reactions to aid (Fisher et al., 1982; Nadler & Fisher, 1986) emphasized the notion of "self-help," which is a behavioral reaction to help received under specifiable conditions. Self-help is associated with short-term striving for independence and self-reliance. Nevertheless, this early work failed to specify the full set of help-related conditions needed for *long-term* recipient self-reliance. This is at the center of health-related models of behavior change (specifically, the information-motivation-behavioral skills [IMB] model, Fisher & Fisher, 1992, to be reviewed herein). The inclusion of this model in a conceptual map that begins with the receipt of help from an out-group, continues with behavior change in the direction of long-term self-sufficiency and ends in greater equality between donor and recipient groups provides a fuller account of intergroup assistance as a vehicle to instrumental reconciliation.

Help That Effectively Promotes Behavior Change

Help that encourages behavior change enabling autonomy must involve the exchange of some objective good (e.g., ARVs, condoms, fishing rods, tractors) accompanied by other elements that ensure the use of these goods to promote long-term autonomy. The donation and receipt of ARVs, condoms, fishing rods, or tractors does not ensure the long-term use of these objects in a beneficial way. One may take ARVs or use condoms regularly or sporadically, the latter with potentially disastrous results (If one does not take prescribed ARVs fully 95% of the time, one may develop treatment-resistant strains of HIV such that ARVs will not benefit them—Fisher, Fisher, Cornman, et al., 2006). In effect, for aid to lead to autonomy *and* have the potential to foster reconciliation a donor must give autonomy-oriented aid *and* facilitate behavior change to ensure its consistent, long-term use to promote self-sufficiency, which alleviates the need state that provoked aid.

Models of behavior change, such as the IMB model (Fisher & Fisher, 1992, 2000), the Fishbein-Ajzen model (Ajzen & Fishbein, 1980), the social cognitive theory (Bandura, 1997), and others are critical at this juncture. In their earlier work on helping relations, Fisher and Nadler (Fisher et al., 1982; Nadler & Fisher, 1986) argued that self-threat associated with the helping transaction (which increases motivation for self-sufficiency) was associated with the practice of *short-term* self-help behavior and autonomy. We argue here, based on well-validated models of behavior change, that for autonomy-oriented aid to actually promote *long-term* autonomy, it must be accompanied by an intervention with a more extensive set of conceptually related behavior change elements (Fisher et al., 1996, Fisher, Fisher, Cornman, et al., 2006).

The IMB model of behavior change (Fisher & Fisher, 1992, 1993, 2000, 2002) has been used to promote long-term autonomy-oriented behavior change in aid recipients in several domains. It has been extensively validated in over a decade and a half of correlational and experimental research with diverse populations (Fisher & Fisher, 2000). The model asserts that if a donor has given a recipient a critical resource (e.g., ARVs, condoms, farming equipment), three additional elements are needed to elicit long-term, autonomy-oriented, behavior change (i.e., the independent use of the resource to alleviate a need state) (see Figure 19.2). A first prerequisite is *information* that is behaviorally relevant to using the resource in an independent fashion. A second critical element, autonomy-related *motivation*, influences whether individuals will use what

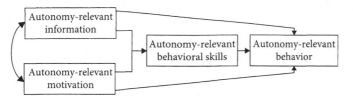

FIGURE 19.2. The information-motivation-behavioral skills (IMB) model of autonomy-relevant behavior change.

they know about the resource to practice autonomous behavior. Motivation is fostered by favorable attitudes toward the resource and social normative support for its long-term, independent use. It may also be fostered by self-threat associated with previous helping transactions with the donor, since this may promote long-term recipient efforts at self-reliance. Finally, one must possess the requisite *behavioral skills* (i.e., a repertoire of the skilled behaviors needed to perform the acts required for sustained use of the resource over time), e.g., for taking ARVs regularly or for farming for a living over time, and even under difficult circumstances. For example, to take ARVs regularly, one must have the ability to remind oneself to take them on time, every time, and to ensure that one always has their medications with them, despite the complexities of daily life.

The IMB model specifies the causal relations between its information, motivation, and behavioral skills constructs. It assumes that autonomy-relevant information and motivation work primarily through autonomy-oriented behavioral skills to influence autonomy-relevant behavior (see Figure 19.2). Thus, the effects of autonomy-relevant information and motivation are expressed as a result of the application of behavioral skills to the initiation and maintenance of autonomy-relevant behavior. The model also specifies that autonomy-relevant information and motivation may have direct effects on autonomy-relevant behavior when complex or novel behavioral skills are *not* necessary to effect such behavior. Finally, information and motivation are regarded as generally independent constructs in that well-informed individuals are not necessarily highly motivated to practice autonomy-relevant behavior and highly motivated individuals are not always well informed about it. These relationships have been consistently supported in almost 20 years of model testing research (Fisher & Fisher, 2000, 2002).

In terms of the IMB model, a group must receive *two* complementary interventions to practice sustained autonomous behavior in a given domain. In addition to the provision of the *objective resources* (e.g., condoms, ARVs) that are necessary but not sufficient for long-term behavior change (e.g., long-term practice of safer sex; taking ARVs regularly), a group must receive a *behavior change intervention.* This must contain the requisite information, motivation, and behavioral skills content for them to become autonomous in the sustained use of condoms or ARVs. For example, to practice safer sex over time, in addition to possessing condoms, one must have information (e.g., about how HIV is transmitted and prevented), motivation (e.g., positive attitudes toward condoms and social support for their use), and behavioral skills (e.g., ability to put on a condom properly, to negotiate safer sex with an unwilling partner) (Fisher et al., 2002; Fisher, Fisher, Cornman, et al., 2006). In effect, the IMB model asserts that long-term autonomous practice of a new behavior requires more than the objective means to perform it (e.g., condom, ARVs), which may be relatively easily provided by a donor. It requires behavior change, which necessitates imparting the critical information, motivation, and behavioral skills elements necessary for the long-term autonomous practice of the behavior (see Figure 19.2).

The assertion that helping interventions must provide access to an objective good (e.g., access to condoms, ARVs) *and* intervention components which convey critical information, motivation, and behavioral skills elements concerning its independent use to promote long-term autonomous behavior change has been confirmed in large-scale, randomized controlled, experimental studies (e.g., Fisher et al., 1996, 2002, 2006). In our Options Project intervention, HIV-infected patients with access to condoms were assigned to a no treatment control group or to a physician-initiated intervention containing information, motivation, and behavioral skills content to encourage patients' self-directed condom use over time. In the control group (access to condoms, but no intervention to promote their autonomous long-term use), patients exhibited relatively high rates of risky sexual behavior that could infect others with HIV and that increased over time. In contrast, in the experimental group (access to condoms *and* an IMB model-based intervention to encourage long-term self-directed condom use), risky sexual behavior decreased dramatically from approximately 7.5 risky acts per participant at the baseline interval to about 1.5 risky acts per participant at follow-up (Fisher et al., 2006). This may have helped prevent our HIV-positive participants' sexual partners from becoming infected with HIV.

Our Options Project physician-initiated intervention was performed in a medical setting with patients who were HIV-infected. Helping interventions between doctors and patients typically involve significant status differences between the parties that are viewed as legitimate. The physician has definitively higher status and often tells the patient what to do. The patient relies on the physician to help, or in some cases, to "cure" them (i.e., the physician provides dependency-oriented help). In order to be successful, our Options intervention had to change this context. To promote long-term self-directed condom use or ARV adherence by patients, an autonomy-oriented helping intervention is necessary. We had to provide the patient with the information, motivation, and behavioral skills to use condoms consistently, on their own, and in the context of countervailing influences in everyday life (e.g., partners who do not want to use condoms).

We have found that creating and gaining acceptance for interventions that are autonomy-oriented in a context in which they are typically dependency-oriented, such as the medical context, requires collaboration between the parties in the intervention design phase. Based on preliminary focus group data collected in designing Options, we found that HIV-infected patients would be willing to talk to their doctors about their HIV risk and prevention behavior if the doctors would treat them more as equals, and not be evaluative, during the discussion. In these conversations, patients wanted to be considered the "experts" on the dynamics of their risk behavior and wanted to work with the physicians on how they might collaborate to change it. Patients clearly wanted physicians to "help them to help themselves" (Fisher et al., 2004).

On the other hand, physicians were aware of their patients' risky behavior, wanted to assist them to change it, but felt that they had little time and had not been trained in behavior change in medical school. They felt if they could be taught some brief but effective behavior change techniques to use, they would be willing to engage in safer sex interventions with patients, should patients be willing (Fisher et al., 2004). We designed the Options intervention based on the joint needs of the stakeholders (i.e., the providers and the patients). By taking both stakeholders' needs into account, we were able to "negotiate" the design of a helping intervention involving the provision of autonomy-oriented aid in a context in which dependency-oriented aid was typically given. The resulting intervention was psychologically acceptable to both parties, and, as indicated above, was highly effective at changing behavior and maintaining behavior change. We have recently applied this process of collaborative design of helping interventions by donor and recipient stakeholders (Fisher et al., 2006) to the design and implementation of helping interventions in other contexts.

Convincing Donors to "Do the Right Thing"

Although the desire to sustain an advantaged position may sometimes constitute a barrier to a donor's provision of autonomy-oriented help, theory and research on the psychology of advantaged groups can provide additional insights into how donors may be induced to do just that. One line of research derived from the Common Ingroup Identity model (Gaertner & Dovidio, 2000; see also Dovidio et al., in this volume) suggests that when members of donor and recipient groups can come to conceive of themselves as part of a single, inclusive category, positive attitudes formerly directed solely toward the in-group become redirected toward the new shared entity. Further, recategorization can promote perceptions of similarity and common fate, which give rise to feelings of belonging to a common group (Hornstein, 1976). In turn, this sense of common identity leads to more positive behaviors, including willingness to provide help, *particularly* under conditions of threat (Dovidio et al., 1997; Flippen, Hornstein, Siegal, & Weitzman, 1996).

Applying these principles to the present context, if donors (e.g., nations, multinational drug companies, and others) can be induced, even under challenge, to hold a shared identity with the recipient group, types of help that were formerly unacceptable to them may become acceptable. Thus, when the context of intergroup helping is framed as helping "other human beings" or "people throughout the world affected by HIV" rather than different nations or entities, true autonomy-oriented help could become easier for donors to provide. Further, stressing that *everyone* can be infected by HIV and that the epidemic crosses borders and continents can help induce a sense of a shared fate between recipients and donors. In this way, the sense of intergroup threat can be reduced so that donors may be less concerned with losing their general advantage over less fortunate groups, through the perception of a joint "enemy."

Another process through which members of advantaged groups may be influenced to provide recipient groups with true autonomy-oriented help involves raising concerns about justice and morality vis-à-vis the other group within potential donors. Invoking principles of fairness, equity, and legitimacy has been shown to motivate people to behave in ways that benefit others even at a perceived cost to their group (Montada, 1996; Taylor, 1990). For example, research demonstrates that perceiving one's group's advantage over another as illegitimate increases the dominant group's support for providing compensation to the weaker group and for making a collective apology to them (e.g., Iyer, Leach & Crosby, 2003). When confronted with the illegitimate aspects of social inequality, members of advantaged groups may become willing to recognize their relative advantage in power and to discuss ways to change the *status quo* (Saguy, Pratto, Dovidio, & Nadler, in press), including the provision of autonomy-oriented help.

In effect, the general need to view one's group as just and moral can be directed toward influencing donors to act in a way that serves the recipient's needs. Efforts to raise justice concerns can involve disseminating information to the donor group regarding the justice-related costs of dependency-oriented aid and the benefits of autonomy-oriented help. Donors can be informed about the long-term consequences of receiving each type of help for the recipient and about recipients' strong preference for autonomy-oriented aid, stressing the power and potential responsibility of the donor to deliver it. Acknowledging, rather than obscuring, the power dynamics that surround the donor-recipient helping context can serve to raise awareness of issues of justice, morality, and responsibility, which in turn may motivate donors to "do the right thing."

In sum, to influence donors to provide the type of help that will be most likely to be beneficial to both parties in the long-run, principles of shared identity and fairness should be emphasized. Promoting these principles can potentially facilitate the donor's realization that the long-term cost-benefit ratio of giving true autonomy-oriented aid is much greater than of giving dependency-oriented aid.

Summary

Assistance with extreme health needs may frequently be problematic for donor and recipient. Members of low status groups, including nations that need assistance due to the global HIV pandemic, often view their lower status as illegitimate and unstable and prefer not to seek or receive dependency-oriented assistance from the high status group. Low status groups are highly motivated to change their social status by taking direct actions to address the inequity, and accepting dependency oriented-help is inconsistent with this aim. The work reviewed in this chapter discusses the dynamics of this type of helping context and suggests ways to harness and change them for the mutual benefit of the donor, the recipient, and the reconciliation process. It is proposed that in the long-term, the provision of autonomy-oriented help accompanied by an intervention to facilitate true recipient autonomy will best serve the recipient, the donor, and the cause of reconciliation.

Note

1. The model does not assert that intergroup helping relations are completely dominated by status concerns. Oftentimes intergroup helping reflects true concern and empathy with the plight of members of the out-group. Yet, in order to fully understand the dynamics of intergroup helping and avoid pitfalls that may be associated with it, one needs to consider the status-related dimensions of intergroup helping. This is especially so in the

present analysis that focuses on a social interaction between socially and economically advantaged helpers (i.e., the US government; pharmaceutical companies) and socially and economically disadvantaged recipients (e.g., HIV-stricken nations in Africa).

References

Ajzen, I., & Fishbein, M. (1980). *Understanding attitudes and predicting social behavior.* Englewood Cliffs, NJ: Prentice-Hall.

Aronson, E., Blaney, N., Stephan, C., Sikes, J., & Snapp, M. (1978). *The jigsaw classroom.* Beverly Hills, CA: Sage Publications.

Baker, B. (2006). *Between the lines: GAO report on PEPFAR prevention programs: U.S. abstinence/being faithful-only programs produce stigma and death.* Retrieved July 8, 2006, from Health Global Access Project website: http://www.healthgap.org/camp/pepfar.html

Bandura, A. (1997). *Self-efficacy: The exercise of control.* New York: W. H. Freeman & Company.

Betraying Africa's priorities: A short analysis of U.S. policies on HIV/AIDS in Africa. (2006). Africa Action. Retrieved June 4, 2006, from http://www.africaaction.org/newsroom/index.php?op=read&documentid=1879&type=15&issues=1

Boyle, B. (2001, March 22). *South Africa's Mbeki says panel to question AIDS tests* (Reuters). Retrieved August 7, 2006, from http://campaignfortruth.com/latestnews/Mbeki230301.htm

Browne, R. S. (1986). United States and economic policies toward Africa. In E. P. Skinner (Ed.), *Beyond constructive engagement: United States foreign policy toward Africa* (pp. 1-24). New York: Paragon House Publishers.

Clough, M. (1992). *Free at last? U.S. policy toward Africa and the end of the Cold War.* New York: Council on Foreign Relations Press.

Dovidio, J. F., Gaertner, S. L., Validzic, A., Matoka, K., Johnson, B., & Frazier, S. (1997). Extending the benefits of recategorization: Evaluations, self-disclosure, and helping. *Journal of Experimental Social Psychology, 33,* 401-420.

The end of the beginning? (2004, July 15). *The Economist.* Retrieved October 1, 2004, from http://www.economist.com/PrinterFriendly.cfm?Story_ID=2921425

Etzioni, A. (1967). The Kennedy experiment. *The Western Political Quarterly, 20,*361-380.

Fisher, J. D., Cornman, D. H., Norton, W. E., & Fisher, W. A. (2006). Involving behavioral scientists, health care providers, and HIV-infected patients as collaborators in theory-based HIV prevention and antiretroviral adherence interventions. *Journal of Acquired Immune Deficiency Syndromes, 43,* S10-S17.

Fisher, J. D., Cornman, D. H., Osborn, C. Y., Amico, K. R., Fisher, W. A., & Friedland, G. H. (2004). Clinician-initiated HIV risk reduction intervention for HIV-positive persons: Formative research, acceptability, and fidelity of the Options Project. *Journal of Acquired Immune Deficiency Syndromes, 37*(2), 78-87.

Fisher, J. D., & Fisher, W. A. (1992). Changing AIDS-risk behavior. *Psychological Bulletin, 111*, 455-474.

Fisher, J. D., & Fisher, W. A. (2000). Theoretical approaches to individual-level change in HIV risk behavior. In J. Peterson & R. DiClemente (Eds.), *HIV prevention handbook* (pp. 3-55). New York: Kluwer Academic/Plenum Press.

Fisher, J. D., & Fisher, W. A. (2002). The information-motivation-behavioral skills model. In R. DiClemente, R. Crosby, & M. Kegler (Eds.), *Emerging theories in health promotion practice and research* (pp. 40-70). San Francisco: Jossey Bass Publishers.

Fisher, J. D., Fisher, W. A., Amico, K. R., & Harman, J. J. (2006). An information-motivation-behavioral skills model of adherence to antiretroviral therapy. *Health Psychology, 25*(4), 462-473.

Fisher, J. D., Fisher, W. A., Bryan, A. D., & Misovich, S. J. (2002). Information-motivation-behavioral skills model-based HIV risk behavior change intervention for inner-city high school youth. *Health Psychology, 21*(2), 177-186.

Fisher, J. D., Fisher, W. A., Cornman, D. H., Amico, K. R., Bryan, A., & Friedland, G. H. (2006). Clinician-delivered intervention during routing clinical care reduces unprotected sexual behavior among HIV-infected patients. *Journal of Acquired Immune Deficiency Syndromes, 41*(1), 44-52.

Fisher, J. D., Fisher, W. A., Misovich, S. J., Kimble, D. L., & Malloy, T. E. (1996). Changing AIDS risk behavior: Effects of an intervention emphasizing AIDS risk reduction information, motivation, and behavioral skills in a college student population. *Health Psychology, 15*(2), 114-123.

Fisher, J. D., Nadler, A., & Whitcher-Alagna, S. (1982). Recipient reactions to aid. *Psychological Bulletin, 91*, 27-54.

Fisher, W. A., & Fisher, J. D. (1993). Understanding and promoting AIDS preventive behavior: A conceptual model and educational tools. *The Canadian Journal of Human Sexuality, 1*, 99-106.

Flippen, A. R., Hornstein, H. A., Siegal, W. E., & Weitzman, E. A. (1996). A comparison of similarity and interdependence as triggers for ingroup formation. *Personality and Social Psychology Bulletin, 22*, 882-893.

Gaertner, S. L., & Dovidio, J. F. (2000). *Reducing intergroup bias: The common ingroup identity model*. Philadelphia: Psychology Press.

Gergen, K. J., & Gergen, M. (1971). International assistance from a psychological perspective. In G. W. Keeton & G. Schwarzenberger (Eds.), *Yearbook of World affairs* (pp. 87-103). London: Institute of World Affairs.

Gergen, K. J., & Gergen, M. (1974). Understanding foreign assistance through public opinion. In G. W. Keeton & G. Schwarzenberger (Eds.), *Yearbook of World affairs* (pp. 125-140). London: Institute of World Affairs.

Greenberg, M. S. (1980). A theory of indebtedness. In K. Gergen, M. S. Greenberg, & R. Willis (Eds.), *Social exchange: Advances in theory and research* (pp. 3-26). New York: Plenum Press.

Hornstein, H. A. (1976). *Cruelty and kindness: A new look at aggression and altruism.* Englewood Cliffs, NJ: Prentice-Hall.

Horton, R. (2000). African AIDS beyond Mbeki: Tripping into anarchy. *The Lancet, 356*(9241), 1541-1543.

Iyer, A., Leach, C. W., & Crosby, F. J. (2003). White guilt and racial compensation: The benefits and limits of self-focus. *Personality and Social Psychology Bulletin, 29*(1), 117-129.

Lederach, J. P. (1997). *Building peace: Sustainable reconciliation in divided societies.* Washington, DC: U.S. Institute of Peace.

Montada, L. (1996). Trade-offs between justice and self-interest. In L. Montada & M. J. Lerner (Eds.), *Current societal concerns about justice* (pp. 259-274). New York: Plenum Press.

Nadler, A. (1991). Help seeking behavior: Psychological costs and instrumental benefits. In M. S. Clark (Ed.), *Review of personality and social psychology* (Vol. 12, pp. 290-312). New York: Sage.

Nadler, A. (1997). Autonomous and dependent help-seeking: Personality characteristics and the seeking of help. In B. Sarason, I. Sarason, & R. G. Pierce (Eds.), *Handbook of personality and social support* (pp. 258-302). New York: Plenum.

Nadler, A. (1998). Esteem, relationships and achievement explanations of help seeking behavior. In S. A. Karabenick (Ed.), *Strategic help seeking: Implications for learning and teaching* (pp. 61-96). Hillsdale, NJ: Erlbaum.

Nadler, A. (2002). Inter-group helping relations as power relations: Maintaining or challenging social dominance between groups through helping. *Journal of Social Issues, 58*(3), 487-502.

Nadler, A., & Fisher, J. D. (1986). The role of threat to self-esteem and perceived control in recipient reaction to help: Theory development and empirical validation. In L. Berkowitz (Ed.), *Advances in experimental social psychology* (Vol. 19, pp. 81-124). New York: Academic Press.

Nadler, A., Fisher, J. D., & Streufert, S. (1974). The donor's dilemma: Recipient's reactions to aid from friend or foe. *Journal of Applied Social Psychology, 4*(3), 275-285.

Nadler, A., & Halabi, S. (2006). Intergroup helping as status relations: Effects of status stability, identification, and type of help on receptivity to high-status group's help. *Journal of Personality and Social Psychology, 91*(1), 97-110.

Nadler, A., & Saguy, T. (2004). Reconciliation between nations: Overcoming emotional deterrents to ending conflicts between groups. In H. Langholtz & C. E. Stout (Eds.), *The psychology of diplomacy* (pp. 29-46). New York: Praeger.

Office of the U.S. Global AIDS Coordinator. (2004). *The President's emergency plan for AIDS relief: U.S. five-year global HIV/AIDS strategy.* Retrieved October 1, 2004, from http://www.state.gov/s/gac/plan/c11652.htm

Osgood, C. E. (1962). *An alternative to war or surrender.* Urbana, IL: University of Illinois Press.

President's Emergency Plan for AIDS Relief. (2004). *Inter-agency emergency plan annual program statement US government mission to South Africa.* Annual Program Statement 674-06-002. Retrieved September 2, 2004, from http://usembassy.state.gov/posts/sf1/wwwfa:1b.pdf

Reeder, G. D., Pryor, J. B., Wohl, M. J., & Griswell, M. L. (2005). On attributing negative motives to others who disagree with our opinions. *Personality and Social Psychology Bulletin, 31,* 1498-1510.

Robinson, R., Keltner, D., Ward, A., & Ross, L. (1995). Actual versus assumed differences in construal: "Naïve realism" in intergroup perception and conflict. *Journal of Personality and Social Psychology, 68,* 404-417.

Ross, L., & Ward, A. (1996). Naïve realism in every day life: Implications for social conflict and misunderstanding. In T. Brown, E. S. Reed., & E. Turiel (Eds.), *Values and knowledge* (pp. 103-135). Hillsdale, NJ: Erlbaum.

Rothchild, D. (2002). The United States and Africa: Power with limited influence. In R. J. Lieber (Ed.), *Eagle rules? Foreign policy and American primacy in the twenty-first century* (pp. 214-339). Upper Saddle River, NJ: Pearson Education, Inc.

Saguy, T., Pratto, F., Dovidio, J. F., & Nadler, A. (in press). Talking about power: Group power and the desired content of intergroup interactions. In S. Demoulin, J. P. Leyens, J. F. Dovidio (Eds.), *Intergroup misunderstandings: Impact of divergent social realities.* Washington, DC: Psychology Press.

Schraeder, P. J. (1994). *United States foreign policy toward Africa: Incrementalism, crisis and change.* Cambridge: Cambridge University Press.

Sontag, D. (2004, July 14). Early tests for U.S. in its global fight on AIDS. *The New York Times.* Retrieved October 1, 2004, from http://www.nytimes.com/2004/07/14/health/14aids.html?ex=1098417600&en=f0c68fe501543efa&ei=5070&ei=5070?oref=login

Streufert, S., Kliger, S. C., Castore, C. H., & Driver, M. J. (1967). A tactical and negotiations game for analysis of decision integration across decision areas. *Psychological Reports, 20,* 155-157.

Tajfel, H., & Turner, J. C. (1986). The social identity theory of intergroup behavior. In S. Worchel & W. G. Austin (Eds.), *The psychology of intergroup relations* (pp. 7-24). Chicago: Nelson-Hall.

Taylor, T. R. (1990). Justice, self-interest and the legitimacy of legal and political authority. In J. J. Mansbridge (Ed.), *Beyond self-interest* (pp. 171-179). Chicago: The University of Chicago Press.

UNAIDS. (2006, May). *06 Report on the global AIDS epidemic: Executive summary.* Retrieved June 4, 2006, from UNAIDS website: http://www.unaids.org/en/HIV_data/2006GlobalReport/default.asp

von Schoen-Angerer, T., Wilson, D., Ford, N., & Kasper, T. (2001). Access and activism: The ethics of providing antiretroviral therapy in developing countries. *AIDS, 15*(5), 81-90.

WHO/UNAIDS. (2004, December). *Treat 3 million by 2005 progress report*. Retrieved February 12, 2005, from World Health Organization website: http://www.who. int/3by5/progressreport05/en/

Wills, T. A., & DePaulo, B. M. (1993). Interpersonal analysis of the help-seeking process. In C. R. Snyder & D. R. Forsyth (Eds.), *Handbook of social and clinical psychology* (pp. 350-375). New York: Pergamon.

Worchel, S. W., Wang, F. Y., & Scheltema, K. E. (1989). Improving intergroup relations: Comparative effects of anticipated cooperation and helping on attraction for an aid-giver. *Social Psychology Quarterly, 52*(3), 213-219.

Part V

Intergroup Reconciliation:
An Overall View

CHAPTER 20

Reconciliation After Destructive Intergroup Conflict

MORTON DEUTSCH

Types of Relations Among Groups

The focus of this book, on reconciliation after destructive intergroup conflict, may lead the reader to the mistaken view that intergroup relations are primarily competitive or destructive. This is certainly not the case. Although I have not done any census of intergroup relations, a little reflection makes it evident that most groups have no relation with one another; they are independent of one another. Thus, I am a member of the Accabonac Tennis Club and a book club. These two groups have no relations apart from my membership in both. There are many more groups that are completely independent without even any common membership, for example, a soccer team in Argentina and a kindergarten class in Germany.

Most groups have no relation to one another, apart from being human beings who exist on the same planet (and possibly in the same nation or locality). There are, of course, many groups who have, much more directly, interdependent or dependent relations with one another. The type of interdependency between groups varies along several dimensions, which include cooperative-competitive, equal-unequal, importance of the relationship, duration of the relationship, and substantive focus of the relationship. (For further discussion of dimensions of interdependence, see Deutsch, 1985; Hofstede, 1980.)

The focus in this book is on interdependent intergroup relations that have been competitive and destructive, of considerable duration, usually between groups of unequal power, involved in conflict about issues such as justice-injustice, control of land and other resources, political and economic power, identity, status, security, and respect. The term "in-group" refers to members of one's own group and "out-group" refers to members of other groups with whom one is competitively interdependent or who is used as a comparison group.

It is well to recognize that most interdependent group relations are not mainly competitive or destructive; assuming that they are leads to undue pessimism about intergroup relations. Most groups are part of larger systems—a university, an industrial organization, a hospital, an army, or a nation. If these larger systems are to be effective enough to survive and thrive, the groups of which they are composed must be mainly cooperative even though some aspects of their relations are competitive. Usually, they are cooperative because of their common superordinate goal, that is, survival of the larger system of which they are a component. In many of the chapters in this book, this is recognized by the emphasis on the importance of developing superordinate goals as part of the process of reconciliation between groups that have been engaged in a bitter destructive conflict.

I note that my discussion in the following sections of this chapter is meant to be quite general. I have sought to present my views about conflict so that they are applicable to conflict between groups of various sorts and sizes—between families, between groups within a community, between tribes, between ethnic groups, and between nations—as well as to interpersonal conflict. In doing so, I have ignored many of the differences that exist when the conflict is between different types of groups. My emphasis is on the similarities across different types of groups, rather than the differences, so that the reader may have a general framework for thinking about intergroup conflict. This framework needs to be supplemented and enriched by specific particularities when considering any actual conflict.

Constructive and Destructive Processes Involved in Intergroup Conflict

In my book *The Resolution of Conflict: Constructive and Destructive Processes* (Deutsch, 1973), I presented a detailed characterization of the nature of such processes. The main point that I made was that a constructive process of resolving conflict is similar to a cooperative process of solving a mutual problem, the conflict being the mutual problem. In contrast, a destructive process is like a competitive struggle to win the conflict. Below, I summarize the main features of these two types of processes.

Cooperative relations (whether within or between groups), as compared with competitive ones, show more of the following positive characteristics:

1. Effective communication is exhibited. Ideas are communicated and members of the different groups are attentive to one another, accepting of the ideas of the others, and influenced by them. They have fewer difficulties in communicating with or understanding others.

2. Friendliness, helpfulness, respect, and less obstructiveness are expressed in their discussions. Members of the cooperating groups also are more satisfied with the relationship between the groups and their solutions as well as being favorably impressed by the contributions of the other group's members. In addition, members of the cooperating groups rate themselves high in desire to win the respect of their colleagues and in a sense of obligation to the others.

3. The members of each group expect to be treated fairly by the other and feel obligated to treat the other fairly. In their relations to one another, justice is an important value.

4. Coordination of effort, division of labor, orientation to task achievement, orderliness in discussion, and high productivity are manifested in the cooperating groups (if the solution of the conflict requires effective communication, coordination of effort, division of labor, or sharing of resources).

5. Feeling of agreement with the ideas of others and a sense of basic similarity in beliefs and values, as well as confidence in one's own ideas and in the value that other members attach to those ideas, are obtained in the cooperating groups.

6. Recognizing and respecting the others by being responsive to the other's needs.

7. Willingness to enhance the other's power (e.g., the knowledge, skills, resources and so on) to accomplish the other's goals increases. As the other group's capabilities are strengthened, you are strengthened; they are of value to you as well as to the other. Similarly, the other is enhanced from your enhancement and benefits from your growing capabilities and power.

8. Attempts to influence the other rely on persuasion and positive inducements.

9. Defining conflicting interests as a mutual problem to be solved by collaborative effort facilitates recognizing the legitimacy of each other's

interests and the necessity to search for a solution responsive to the needs of all. It tends to limit rather than expand the scope of conflicting interests.

In contrast, a competitive process has the opposite effects:

1. Communication is impaired as the conflicting parties seek to gain advantage by misleading the other through use of false promises, ingratiation tactics, and disinformation. It is reduced and seen as futile as they recognize that they cannot trust one another's communications to be honest or informative.
2. Obstructiveness and lack of helpfulness lead to mutual negative attitudes and suspicion of each other's intentions. One's perceptions of the other tend to focus on the other's negative qualities and ignore the positive.
3. Fairness to the other is not valued. Each group is willing to exploit or harm the other to advantage themselves.
4. The parties to the process are unable to divide their work, duplicating one another's efforts such that they become mirror images; if they do divide the work, they feel the need to check continuously what the other is doing.
5. The repeated experience of disagreement and critical rejection of ideas reduces confidence in oneself as well as the other.
6. Attempts to influence the other often involve threats, coercion, or false promises.
7. The conflicting parties seek to enhance their own power and to reduce the power of the other. Any increase in the power of the other is seen as threatening to oneself and one's group.
8. The competitive process stimulates the view that the solution of a conflict can be imposed only by one side on the other, which in turn leads to using coercive tactics such as psychological as well as physical threats and violence. It tends to expand the scope of the issues in conflict as each side seeks superiority in power and legitimacy. The conflict becomes a power struggle or a matter of moral principle and is no longer confined to a specific issue at a given time and place. Escalating the conflict increases its motivational significance to the participants and may make a limited defeat less acceptable and more humiliating than a mutual disaster.
9. As the conflict escalates, it perpetuates itself by such processes as autistic hostility, self-fulfilling prophecies, and unwilling commitments. *Autistic hostility* involves breaking off contact and communication with

the other; the result is that the hostility is perpetuated because one has no opportunity to learn that it may be based on misunderstandings or misjudgments nor to learn whether the other has changed for the better.

Self-fulfilling prophecies are those wherein you engage in hostile behavior toward another because of a false assumption that the other has done or is preparing to do something harmful to you; your false assumption comes true when it leads you to engage in hostile behavior that then provokes the other to react in a manner hostile to you. The dynamics of an escalating, destructive conflict have the inherent quality of a folie à deux, in which the self-fulfilling prophecies of each side mutually reinforce one another. Consequently, both sides are right to think that the other is provocative, untrustworthy, and malevolent. Each side, however, tends to be blind to how it as well as the other have contributed to this malignant process.

In the case of *unwitting commitments*, during the course of escalating conflict, the parties not only overcommit to rigid positions, but also may unwittingly commit to negative attitudes and perceptions, beliefs, stereotypes of the other, defenses against the other's expected attacks, and investments involved in carrying out their conflictual activities. Thus, during an escalated conflict, a person (a group, a nation) may commit to the view that the other is an evil enemy, the belief that the other is out to take advantage of oneself (one's group, nation), the conviction that one has to be constantly vigilant and ready to defend against the danger the other poses to one's vital interests, and also invest in the means of defending oneself as well as attacking the other (Deutsch & Collins, 1951; Wright Evans & Deutsch, 1962). After a protracted conflict, it is hard to give up a grudge, to disarm without feeling vulnerable, as well as to give up the emotional charge associated with being mobilized and vigilant in relation to the conflict.

The Development of Destructive Conflicts

Several of the preceding chapters in this book have referred to "Deutsch's crude law of social relations": the characteristic processes and effects elicited by a given type of social relationship also tend to elicit that type of social relationship (Deutsch, 1949).

Thus, cooperation induces and is induced by perceived similarity in beliefs and attitudes, readiness to be helpful, openness in communication, trusting and friendly attitudes, sensitivity to common interests, and de-emphasis of opposed interests, orientation toward enhancing each other's mutual power rather than power differences and so on. Similarly, competition induces and is induced by use of tactics of coercion, threat, or deception; attempts to enhance the power differences between oneself and the other; poor communication; minimization of the awareness of similarities in values and increased sensitivity to opposed interests; suspicious and hostile attitudes; the importance, rigidity, and size of issues in conflict; and so on.

In other words, if one has systematic knowledge of the effects of cooperative and competitive processes, one has systematic knowledge of the conditions that typically give rise to such processes and by extension to the conditions that affect whether a conflict takes a constructive or destructive course. My early theory of cooperation and competition is a theory of the effects of cooperative and competitive processes. Hence, from the crude law of social relations it follows that this theory brings insight into the conditions that give rise to cooperative and competitive processes. The crude law further suggests that enhancement of any correlate of cooperation (e.g., trusting and friendly attitudes) would enhance its other correlates (e.g., an orientation to enhancing one another's power). Similarly for competition, as any of its correlates are enhanced, this would lead to the enhancement of its other correlates.

My "crude law" would suggest that a competitive, destructive conflict would develop and endure, becoming an intractable conflict (see Coleman, Vallacher, Nowak, & Bui-Wrzosinska, 2007; Coleman, 2003, 2004, 2006, Deutsch, Coleman, & Marcus, 2006; Deutsch & Coleman, 2000 for a comprehensive discussion of intractable conflicts), if the issues in conflict are or become of central importance to the parties involved and if such a conflict does not occur in a context of strong cooperative relations between the parties in conflict. There is evidence from research on primates and children (Pellegrini & Roseth, 2006) as well as from observations of marital conflict that a flare-up of destructive conflict is often followed by reconciliation if the relationship is otherwise cooperative.

My crude law suggests that a destructive conflict can be initiated by many different causes:

1. Poor communication, which leads one to believe, mistakenly, that the other is preparing to take harmful, unjust actions or has initiated such actions, which threaten one's security, power, well-being, resources, reputation, or identity. A history of destructive intergroup conflict with the other predisposing one to such misunderstandings when there is little or poor communication between the groups.
2. Of course, accurate perceptions of the other's preparations for harmful, unjust actions is likely to lead to destructive conflict unless there are

respected and powerful third parties who can successfully intervene to prevent, limit, or mediate such conflicts.

3. The feeling of being treated unjustly, of being exploited and humiliated by the other (more powerful group) often create humiliation (Lindner, 2006), rage, and a desire for revenge (in members of the less powerful group), which may lead to acts of violence against the perceived oppressor and humiliator. This, in turn, can stimulate fear and indignation in members of the more powerful group and lead to strong actions of counterviolence by them to intimidate and deter the rebellious and violent actions of the oppressed group.

4. Competition for superior rights to land, resources (e.g., oil, water, food, precious metals), power, status, or achievement that cannot be shared equitably is often the instigation of destructive conflict. This is especially the case when the claim to superiority is central to one's identity and esteem.

5. Negative stereotypes and attitudes as well as distrust of the other can be the initiators as well as the effects of destructive conflict. The history of past destructive conflicts and injustices is kept salient by the way history is taught in schools, by family legends, by the songs, stories, and art in one's group. The negative attitudes generated by frequent exposure to this history can magnify a minor incident so that it comes to be symbolically central to one's identity and, hence, an instigator to major, destructive conflict.

Most protracted, intractable conflicts—no matter how they are initiated—come to have all of the characteristics described in the above points.

Forgiveness and Reconciliation

After protracted, violent conflicts in which the conflicting parties have inflicted grievous harm (humiliation, destruction of property, torture, assault, rape, murder) on one another, the conflicting parties may still have to live and work together in the same communities. This is often the case in civil wars, ethnic and religious conflicts, gang wars, and even family disputes that have taken a destructive course. Consider the slaughter that has taken place between Hutus and Tutsis in Rwanda and Burundi (Staub, this volume; chapter 17); between blacks and whites in South Africa; between the "Bloods" and "Crips" of Los Angeles; between the Protestants and Catholics in Northern Ireland; and among Serbs, Croats, and Muslims in Bosnia. Is it possible for forgiveness and reconciliation to occur? If so, what fosters these processes?

There are many meanings of forgiveness in the extensive and growing literature concerned with this topic. I shall use the term to mean giving up the rage, the desire for vengeance, and a grudge toward those who have inflicted grievous harm on you, your loved ones, or the groups with whom you identify. It also implies willingness to accept the other into one's moral community so that he or she is entitled to care and justice. As Borris (2003) has pointed out, it does not mean you have to forget the evil that has been done, condone it, or abolish punishment for it. However, it implies that the punishment should conform to the canons of justice and be directed toward the goal of reforming the harmdoer so that he or she can become a moral participant in the community.

There has been rich discussion in the psychological and religious literature of the importance of forgiveness to psychological and spiritual healing as well as to reconciliation (see Minow, 1998; Shriver, 1995). Forgiveness is, of course, not to be expected in the immediate aftermath of torture, rape, or assault. It is unlikely, as well as psychologically harmful, until one is able to be in touch with the rage, fear, guilt, humiliation, hurt, and pain that has been stored inside. But nursing hate as well as "competition for victimhood" between the conflicting parties keeps the injury alive and active in the present instead of permitting it to take its proper place in the past. Doing so consumes psychological resources and energy that are more appropriately directed to the present and future. Although forgiveness of the other may not be necessary for self-healing, it seems to be very helpful, as well as an important ingredient in the process of reconciliation.

A well-developed psychological and psychiatric literature deals with posttraumatic stress disorder (PTSD). Treatment of PTSD (Basoglu, 1992; Foa, Keane, & Friedman, 2000; Ochberg, 1988) essentially (a) gives the stressed individual a supportive, safe, and secure environment; (b) an environment in which he or she can be helped to reexperience in a modulated fashion, the vulnerability, helplessness, fear, rage, humiliation, guilt, and other emotions associated with the grievous harm (medication may be useful in limiting the intensity of the emotions being relived); (c) this reliving would help him or her identify the past circumstances and contexts in which the harm occurred and distinguish current realities from past realities; (d) this would help him or her understand the reasons for his or her emotional reactions to the traumatic events and the appropriateness of his or her reactions; (e) it would help him or her acquire the skills, attitudes, knowledge, and social support that make him or her less vulnerable and powerless; and (f) it would help him or her develop an everyday life characterized by meaningful, enjoyable, and supportive relations in his or her family, work, and community.

The PTSD treatment just described is very appropriate for individuals suffering from this disorder. However, when many members of a group have developed this disorder as a result of destructive intergroup conflict, it requires considerable supplementation. This entails work with the relations that exist among the members of the in-groups and the relations between the groups that were involved in the destructive conflict. As Kantowitz (2006, p. 1) has stated: "Current models of trauma individualize, pathologize and decontextualize this phenomenon." I do not have the space here to more than suggest what needs to be done. At the communal level, the chaos, the displacement and physical destruction, the poverty, the unemployment, and the continued social focusing on victimhood are some of the issues that must be addressed. At the intergroup level, constructive dialogue between representatives of the two groups is required, which enables both sides of a destructive conflict to come to an understanding of the conflict and its dynamics as well as its history and to learn that similar conflicts have occurred elsewhere (Staub, this volume; chapter 17). Their dialogue must deal not only with the past but also with issues relating to their present and future. (The chapters by Kelman and Staub in this volume are most relevant to the foregoing.)

Forgiveness and reconciliation may be difficult to achieve at more than a superficial level unless the posttraumatic stress is substantially relieved. Even so, it is well to recognize that the processes involved in forgiveness and reconciliation may also play an important role in relieving PTSD. The causal arrow is multidirectional; progress in "forgiveness" or "reconciliation" or posttraumatic stress reduction facilitates progress in the other two.

There are two distinct but interrelated approaches to developing forgiveness. One centers on the victims and the other on the relationship between the victims and the harmdoers. The focus on the victim, in addition to providing some relief from PTSD, seeks to help the victim recognize the human qualities common to victim and victimizer. In effect, various methods and exercises are employed to enable the victim to recognize the bad as well as good aspects of herself and her group, that she has "sinful" as well as "divine" capabilities and tendencies. In other words, one helps the victim become aware of herself as a total person—with no need to deny her own fallibility and imperfections—whose lifelong experiences in her family, schools, communities, ethnic and religious groups, and workplaces have played a key role in determining her own personality and behavior. As the victim comes to accept her own moral fallibility, she is likely to accept the fallibility of the harmdoer as well and to perceive both the good and the bad in the other.

Both victims and harmdoers are often quite moral toward those they include in their own moral community but grossly immoral to those excluded. Thus, Adolf Eichmann, who efficiently organized the mass murder of Jews for the Nazis, was considered a good family man. The New England captains of the slave ships, who transported African slaves to the Americas under the most abominable conditions, were often deacons of their local churches. The white settlers of the United States, who took possession of land occupied by Native Americans and killed those who resisted, were viewed as courageous and moral within their own communities.

Recognition of the good and bad potential in all humans, the self as well as the other, facilitates the victim's forgiveness of the harmdoer. But it may not be enough. Quite often, forgiveness also requires interaction between the victim and harmdoer to establish the conditions needed for forgiving. This interaction sometimes takes the form of negotiation between the victim and harmdoer. A third party representing the community (such as a mediator or judge) usually facilitates the negotiation and sets the terms if the harmdoer and victim cannot reach an agreement. It is interesting to note that in courts, such negotiations are, sometimes, required in criminal cases before the judge sentences the convicted criminal.

Obviously, the terms of an agreement for forgiveness vary as a function of the nature and severity of the harm as well as the relationship between the victim and harmdoer. The victim may seek full confession, sincere apology, contrition, restitution, compensation, and self-abasement or self-reform from the harmdoer. (For an excellent discussion of apology and other related issues, see Lazare, 2004.) The victim may also seek some form of punishment and incarceration for the harmdoer. Forgiveness is most likely if the harmdoer and the victim accept the conditions, whatever they may be.

Reconciliation goes beyond forgiveness in that it not only accepts the other into one's moral community but also establishes or reestablishes a positive, cooperative relationship among the individuals and groups estranged by the harms they have inflicted on one another. Borris (2003) has indicated, "Reconciliation is the end of a process that forgiveness begins."

Earlier, I discussed in detail some of the factors involved in initiating and maintaining cooperative relations; that discussion is relevant to the process of reconciliation. Here, I wish to consider briefly some of the special issues relating to establishing cooperative relations after a destructive conflict. Below, I outline a number of basic principles:

1. *Mutual security.* After a bitter conflict, each side tends to be concerned with its own security, without adequate recognition that neither side can attain security unless the other side also feels secure. Real security requires that both sides have as their goal mutual security. If weapons have been involved in the prior conflict, mutually verifiable disarmament and arms control are important components of mutual security.

   After violent conflict, fear that the other will violate an agreement to cease hostilities and will engage in violence again is slow to disappear.

The intervention of powerful and respected third parties is often necessary to create confidence that the cessation of violence will be observed by both of the conflicting parties.

2. *Mutual respect.* Just as true security from physical danger requires mutual cooperation, so does security from psychological harm and humiliation (Lindner, 2006). Each side must treat the other with the respect, courtesy, politeness, and consideration normatively expected in civil society. Insult, humiliation, and inconsiderateness by one side usually lead to reciprocation by the other and decreased physical and psychological security.

Mutual respect requires the belief that justice will be established in the relations between the conflicting parties. Doing so will involve the elimination of superiority-inferiority in rights and privileges as well as elimination of exploitation in the relations between the conflicting groups.

3. *Humanization of the other.* During bitter conflict, each side tends to develop negative stereotypes of and dehumanize the other, which justifies images of the other as an evil enemy (Oppenheimer, 2006). There is much need for both sides to experience one another in everyday contexts as parents, homemakers, schoolchildren, teachers, and merchants, which enables them to see one another as human beings who are more like themselves than not. Problem-solving workshops and dialogue groups along the lines described by Burton (1969, 1987) and Kelman (1972) are also valuable in overcoming dehumanization of one another.

4. *Economic security.* Basic supplies of food, shelter, and medical care are often seriously impaired during violent conflict. This lack of these basics must be addressed expeditiously if reconciliation is to be possible.

5. *Education and the media.* During a protracted, bitter conflict, the educational system as well as the media within each of the conflicting parties is often warped so that the in-group members are taught to view the out-group as an evil enemy and to consider their own heroes to be those who are most effective in destroying the enemy. A lasting reconciliation will require transformations in the educational system and the media within each group to achieve three objectives: (a) a nonpartisan view of the conflict and its history which is understood and essentially agreed upon by both parties (see Staub, this volume; chapter 17); (b) providing knowledge and support for nonviolent constructive methods of conflict resolution; and (c) developing a positive image of the peace-makers and of peaceable persons.

6. *Fair rules for managing conflict.* Even if a tentative reconciliation has begun, new conflicts inevitably occur—over the distribution of scarce

resources, procedures, and values as well as perceived nonadherence to the terms of prior agreements. It is important to anticipate that such conflicts will occur and to develop beforehand the fair rules or laws, experts (such as mediators, arbitrators, conflict resolvers), institutions (such as courts), and other resources (such as neutral peace-keepers) for managing such conflicts constructively and justly.

7. *Curbing the extremists on both sides.* During a protracted and bitter conflict, each side tends to produce extremists committed to the processes of the destructive conflict as well as to its continuation. Attaining some of their initial goals may be less satisfying than continuing to inflict damage on the other. It is well to recognize that extremists stimulate extremism on both sides; it is an unwitting cooperation to keep the destructive conflict going by the extremists on each side. The parties need to cooperate in curbing extremism on their own side and in restraining actions that stimulate and justify extremist elements on the other side. This is often difficult to do. Extremists will seek to provoke the other to engage in a destructive counteraction in the expectation that their counter-response will justify the negative view of the other as an evil enemy with whom one cannot have peaceful, cooperative relations. In so doing, they will also try to discredit the moderates in their group as weak appeasers who are helping the enemy.

8. *Gradual development of mutual trust and cooperation.* It takes repeated experience of successful, varied, mutually beneficial cooperation to develop a solid basis for mutual trust between former enemies. In the early stages of reconciliation, when trust is required for cooperation, the former enemies may be willing to trust a third party (who agrees to serve as a monitor, inspector, or guarantor of any cooperative arrangement) but not yet willing to trust one another if there is a risk of the other failing to reciprocate cooperation. Also in the early stages, it is especially important that cooperative endeavors be successful. This requires careful selection of the opportunities and tasks for cooperation so that they are clearly achievable as well as meaningful and significant. As many chapters in this book have indicated, the development of superordinate goals (such as building a bridge, a school, or a hospital that would benefit both groups) is often an excellent way to develop cooperation.

I also suggest that it would be particularly useful to create cross-cutting groups whose members have common identities as well as the identities arising from their memberships in the reconciling conflicting groups. Here, for example, I am referring to such groups as health care workers, from both sides, working together to treat patients and to prevent diseases;

as construction workers, from both sides, working together to repair roads and bridges, and build houses; as educators working to develop joint curricula; and as law-makers working together to develop fair laws and institutions. Many other types of cross-cutting, cooperative groups could be listed. In the initial stage of the development of such groups, it would undoubtedly be helpful if such groups had respected third party facilitators who could help with the development of the cooperative process and with the substantive issues (e.g., health care) on which the group will be working. Levine and Campbell (1972) documented that destructive intergroup conflict is more conducive in pyramidal-segmentary social structures within a society than the cross-cutting structures proposed here.

Concluding Thoughts

After bitter destructive conflict, it can be expected that reconciliation will be achieved, if at all, after a slow process with many setbacks as well as advances. The continuous and persistent help and encouragement of powerful and respected third parties is often necessary to keep the reconciliation process moving forward and to prevent its derailment by extremists, misunderstandings, or harmful actions by either of the conflicting parties. The help and encouragement must be multifaceted. It must deal, justly, not only with the social psychological issues addressed so well in this volume, but also, justly, with such institutions as the economic, political, legal, educational, health care, and security, whose effective functioning is necessary for a sustained reconciliation.

Unfortunately, currently there is limited availability and willingness of powerful and respected third parties to offer the help that is needed to achieve reconciliation after bitter civil or international strife. I suggest that there is much need to develop stronger and more effective institutions within the United Nations, as well as in regional organizations, that can intervene in violent conflicts to bring about a cessation of hostilities and to facilitate a process of reconciliation. Such institutions could also function to develop ways to prevent potential violent conflict by early intervention when signs of a potentially dangerous conflict appear. The intervention can take the forms suggested in many of the chapters in this book.

Efforts to further reconciliation after bitter, violent conflict are important, but even more important is the prevention of such conflicts. As is true for many diseases, the prevention of the "social disease" of destructive conflict is easier and more effective than its treatment and remediation. Peck (1998), in a chapter on preventive diplomacy, has described how new regional conflict resolution centers (established under the auspices and direction of the United Nations) could provide preventive educational, mediation, and early warning signs that could deter the development of bitter, destructive conflict. And I (Deutsch, 1994, 2006a, 2006b, 2006c) have articulated a somewhat utopian proposal for what the United Nations, as well as the various institutions of national societies, could do to prevent destructive conflicts. These papers are suggestive efforts related to prevention that need considerably more work by many more scholars and practitioners in the field of conflict resolution.

References

Basoglu, M. (Ed.). (1992). *Torture and its consequences: Current treatment approaches.* Cambridge, England: Cambridge University Press.

Borris, E. (2003). *The healing power of forgiveness.* Occasional Paper, Number 10, Institute for Multi-Track Diplomacy, Arlington, VA.

Burton, J. W. (1969). *Conflict communication: The use of controlled communication in international relations.* London: Macmillan.

Burton, J. W. (1987). *Resolving deep-rooted conflicts: A handbook.* Lanham, MD: University Press of America.

Coleman, P. T. (2003). Characteristics of protracted, intractable conflict: Toward the development of a meta-framework—I. *Peace and Conflict: Journal of Peace Psychology, 9*(1), 1-37.

Coleman, P. T. (2004). Paradigmatic framing of protracted, intractable conflict: Toward the development of a meta-framework—II. *Peace and Conflict: Journal of Peace Psychology, 10*(3), 197-235.

Coleman, P. T. (2006). Conflict, complexity and change: A meta-framework for addressing protracted, intractable conflicts—III. *Peace and Conflict: Journal of Peace Psychology, 12*(4), 325-348.

Coleman, P. T., Vallacher, R., Nowak, A., & Bui-Wrzosinska, L. (2007). Intractable conflict as an attractor: Presenting a dynamical model of conflict, escalation, and intractability. *American Behavioral Scientist, 50*(11), 1454-1475.

Deutsch, M. (1949). A theory of cooperation and competition. *Human Relations, 2,* 129-231.

Deutsch, M. (1973). *The resolution of conflict: Constructive and destructive processes.* New Haven, CT: Yale University Press.

Deutsch, M. (1985). *Distributive justice.* New Haven, CT: Yale University Press.

Deutsch, M. (1994). Constructive conflict management for the world today. *The International Journal of Conflict Management, 5*(2), 111-129.

Deutsch, M. (2006a). Mediation and difficult conflicts. In M. Herrman (Ed.), *Handbook of mediation* (pp. 353-373). Malden, MA: Blackwell Publishing.

Deutsch, M. (2006b).The interplay between internal and external conflict. In A. Schneider & C. Honeyman (Eds.), *The negotiators fieldbook* (pp. 231-238). Washington, DC: American Bar Association.

Deutsch, M. (2006c). A framework for thinking about oppression and its change. *Social Justice Research, 19,* 7-41.

Deutsch, M., & Coleman, P. T. (Eds.). (2000). *The handbook of conflict resolution: Theory and practice.* San Francisco: Jossey-Bass.

Deutsch, M., Coleman, P. T., & Marcus, E. (Eds.). (2006). *The handbook of conflict resolution: Theory and practice* (2nd ed.). San Francisco: Jossey-Bass.

Deutsch, M., & Collins, M. E. (1951). *Interracial housing.* Minneapolis, MN: University of Minnesota Press.

Foa, E. B., Keane, T. M., & Friedman, M. J. (2000). *Effective treatment for PTSD: Practice guidelines from the International Society for Traumatic Stress Studies.* New York: Guilford Press.

Hofstede, G. G. (1980). *Cultures consequences: International differences in work-related value.* Thousand Oaks, CA: Sage.

Kantowitz, R. (2006). *Healing systems: A multi-level social psychological model of trauma in Guatemala.* Doctoral dissertation, Graduate School of Arts and Sciences, Columbia University, New York.

Kelman, H. C. (1972). The problem-solving workshop in conflict resolution. In R. L. Merritt (Ed.), *Communication in international politics* (pp. 168-203). Urbana, IL: University of Illinois Press.

Lazare, A. (2004). *On apology.* New York: Oxford University Press.

Levine, R. A., & Campbell, D. T. (1972). *Ethnocentrism: Theories of conflict, ethnic attitudes and group behavior.* New York: Wiley.

Lindner, E. (2006). *Making enemies: Humiliation and international conflict.* Westport, CT: Praeger Security International.

Minow, M. (1998). Between vengeance and forgiveness: South Africa's truth and reconciliation commission. *Negotiation Journal, 14,* 319-356.

Ochberg, F. (1988). *Post-traumatic therapy and victims of violence.* New York: Brunner/ Mazel.

Oppenheimer, L. (2006). The development of enemy images: A theoretical contribution. *Peace and Conflict: Journal of Peace Psychology, 12*(3), 269-292.

Peck, C. (1998). *Sustainable peace: The role of the UN and regional organizations in preventing conflict* (pp. 68-98). Lanham, MD: Rowman & Littlefield.

Pellegrini, A. D., & Roseth, C. J. (2006). Relational aggression and relationships in preschoolers: A discussion of methods, gender, and function. *Journal of Applied Developmental Psychology, 27,* 269-276.

Shriver, D. W., Jr. (1995). *An ethic for enemies: Forgiveness in politics.* New York: Oxford University Press.

Wright, Q., Evans, M. E., & Deutsch, M. (Eds.). (1962). *Preventing World War III: Some proposals.* New York: Simon & Schuster.

INDEX

Achieved status, 150

Acknowledgments, 399

of responsibility, in reconciliation
process, 29

Affect-consistency hypothesis, 308

Affective processes, involved in
reconciliation, 382-384

African Americans, 83, 91, 118-119, 124-125,
129, 231

expression of self-esteem, 120

form of social consciousness, 236

perceptions of intergroup contact on
campus, 240

America's integrity, 118

Anxiety-reduction motivations, 127

Anxious expectation, of rejection, 174

Apologies, role on the reduction of
interpersonal conflict, 39-40

Apology-forgiveness cycle, 25

as an act of social exchange, 48

victims vs perpetrators, 42

Arusha accords, 398

Assimilation, 237, 240

Aussöhnung, 16

Authoritarian personality theory, 121

personality trait authoritarianism, 259

Behavioral processes, involved in
reconciliation, 386-387

Belfast Agreement, 200-201

Belongingness, 120-122

after having harmed another
group, 133-134

when harmed by another, 129-130

Bereaved Families Forum, 278

Berry's adaptation strategies, 238

*Beyond Reason: Using Emotions as
You Negotiate*, 39

Black Pride, 129

Blame schema, 64

Bohr's principle of complementarity, 276

Cantril Self Anchoring Scale, 426

Categorical respect, 147-149

Coexistence meetings, 435

Cognitive empathy, 384

Cognitive processes, involved in
reconciliation, 384-386

Collective guilt, 79-80, 384

Collective identity and conflict
settlement, 24

Collective self-esteem, 128-129

Colorblind ideology, 236

Common In-group Identity Model, 234-239, 261-262
Community membership, 105-106
Compassion for oneself, 187
Competence, 151-154
Competitive victimhood, 102
Confirmatory standards, 78
Conflict, perspectives of, 38-40, 85-86
Conflict fatigue, 98
Conflict settlement and resolution, 22-24, 40-41, 433
    application of negotiating process, 22
    conflict resolution as a process of peacemaking, 23-24
    as instrumental reconciliation, 23
    interactive problem-solving framework, 23
    possibilities for sports, 289-290
    public support in, 22
    role of third parties, 22
Confronting history, for reconciliation process, 28-29
Contact Hypothesis, 233, 235, 260, 430
    Revised Contact Hypothesis, 233, 235, 260
Contact programs, for reconciliation efforts, 378-379
Contingent respect, 149-151
Cooperative activities, in reconciliation process, 29-30
    cooperative experiences, 278-279
    we-ness of, 278
Cross-cultural training programs, 378
Cross-group friendships, 161
crude law of social relations, 153, 161
Culture of conflict, 372
Culture of honor, 131-132, 134
Custer's last stand, 132-133
Cyberspace-based programs and techniques, for reconciliation efforts, 381-382

Decategorization, 234-235, 260-266, 431
The Decent Society, 151
Dehumanization, 65-66, 311-312, 375
Delegitimization, 427
Desired image triggers, 175-176
Destructive intergroup conflict. *See* Violent conflict
Devalued identity, 180-182
Discrimination, between groups:
    according to social identity theory, 320-322
    determinist accounts:
        based on social identity theory, 325-326
        based on status functions, 326-328
        minimal group paradigm, 323-325
        role of social stereotypes, 328-329
        of self-categorization theorists, 328-329
    effect of in-group bias or hostility between groups, 322-323
    legitimacy and:
        emotion-based prejudice, 333-335
        group discrimination, 331-333
        justice judgments, 335-337
        social stereotyping, 331
Disrespect. *See* Respect
Dissonance theory, 123
Distributive bargaining, 38
Diversity training programs, 377
Dual identity, 238, 240-241
    and the Mutual Intergroup Differentiation Model, 263-265
Dutch cultural identity, 238

Economic security, 481
Ecosystem motivations, 183-185
Ego-defense, 177-178
Egosystem motivational dynamics:
    desired image, 175-176
    downward spirals of, 178-183
    driving idea, 174

ego-defense, 177-178
unconscious goal, 175
upward spirals of, 185-187
Emotional empathy, 382
Emotional justice, 28
Emotion-based prejudice, 333-335
Empathy, 106, 156, 186-187, 382
Encounter Point, 278-279, 281
Enemy images, 155-156
Enlightenment programs, for
reconciliation efforts, 376-378
Essentialism, 309-310
Ethnic groups, 426-427
Ethnic identity, 431
Existential anxiety, 121

Fair rules, for managing conflict,
481-482
Fear, *428, 429*
of the out-group, 429
Forgiveness, 66-67, 400-401
in the face of a perpetrator's remorse, 69
as a focus of peace-building work, 63
interpersonal, as predictor of
reconciliation, 100-102, 200
empathy, 106-107
evaluation of past violence, 107-109
group identification, 105-106
self-conscious emotions of collective
guilt and collective shame, 109-110
intervention, 62-63
language of, in the context of
interpersonal conflict, 63
and reconciliation, 477-483
research on, 62-64
story of the "Mothers of the Gugulethu
Seven", 67-69
Forgiveness model, of intergroup
reconciliation, 44-45
Fundamental institutions, of a
functioning society, 370-371, 373
Future justice, 28

Gender stereotypes, 171-172
Genocidal campaigns, 37
German conquest of Poland, 128
*Getting to Yes: Negotiating Agreement
Without Giving In*, 39
Good Friday Agreement, 98
Good side/bad side portrayals, in
intergroup conflicts, 133
"graduated reductions in tension" (GRIT)
proposal, 447, 450
Granovetter's principle, 280
Group cohesiveness, 276
Group discrimination, 331-333
Group homogeneity, 309-310
Group identification, 87-89, 106, 160-161,
164n, 228-229
Group membership, 77
Guerilla warfare, 133
Guilt:
categorization-based justice model,
79, 82-83
collective guilt, in intergroup
relations, 79-80, 91
effect of level-specific standards on, 89
human sex differences in perceptions
of, 81
legitimacy-supported condition
vs legitimacy-undermined
condition, 81-82
role of justice and violations of
moral standards in the
experience of, 81-82

Hawaiian sovereignty, 427
Healing and problem-solving programs,
for reconciliation efforts, 380-381
High-status groups, 304, 308
HIV/AIDS pandemic:
issue of reconciliation, between the
helper and recipient, 449-451
Nadler and affiliates' model of
intergroup helping:

HIV/AIDS pandemic (*continued*)
    assumptions, 452
    legitimacy and stability of the
      status, 452-458
    models of behavior change, 458-461
    statistics, 447-448
    unilateral forms of aid, 448-449
    donors position, 461-463
Humanization, 481
Hutu genocide, of the Tutsis, 132

Image Theory of Emotions, 306-307
Immorality, 154
Implicit Association Test (IAT), 218
In-group and out-group members, 65-66,
    78. *See also* Residual negative
    affect; Respect
    attributions of morality, 153
    decategorization and
      recategorization, 234-235
    degree of conflict, 85-86
    degree of identification with one's
      in-group, 87-89, 229
    evil portrayals of the out-group, 428
    extent of cooperative and friendly
      contact, 86-87
    guilt experiences, 81
    humanitarianism, 85
    implications of standard shifting
      processes for reconciliation, 90-92
    judging the injustice of the, 82-83
    out-group delegitimization, 154-156
    perceived differences, 174
    perceived similarity, 84-85
    perception of injustice, 81-82
    perceptions of morality, 153
    prototypicality, 85
    social categorization, 257-258
    thinking of the in-group about the
      out-group, 375
In-group favoritism, 231, 436
Individual-group discontinuity effect, 230

Individual-group interface, 277
Individual level reconciliation, 372-373
Infrahumanization, 208, 311, 322
Instrumental reconciliation, 41, 434-435
    change in relations, 43
    nature of change, 43
    process of, 42-45
    vs socioemotional reconciliation,
      44-45
    target of change in, 43
    temporal focus of the process
      of change, 43-44
Integrative bargaining, 38
Intergroup anxiety, 307-308
Intergroup competition, 229-231
Intergroup conflict, 118
    causes of, 424-429
    constructive and destructive
      processes, 472-475
    and legitimacy, 337-339
    naive realism theory, 310-311
    in Northern Ireland:
      limitations of the study, 217-218
      religious segregation, 202-206
      sectarianism, 201-202
      study of intergroup forgiveness,
        206-210
      study of intergroup trust, 211-217
    Pinochet regime in Chile, 103-104
    psychological perspectives on
      bias and, 256
    resolution, 6, 312
    role of competition, 303
    study at Robbers Cave State Park in
      Oklahoma, 230-231, 258, 286
    violent conflict between the Catholic
      and the Protestant communities in
      Northern Ireland, 103, 128, 130
Intergroup contact, 233-234, 431
    across sectarian divide, 203-206
    role in creation of common
      identity, 235-236

Intergroup cooperative learning
    programs, 379
Intergroup dialogue programs, 378
Intergroup emotions:
  image theory of, 306-307
  Stereotype Content Model, 305-306
Intergroup forgiveness, in the context of
    Northern Ireland:
  experimental study of, 209-210
  and reconciliation, 210
  survey research on, 207-209
  theoretical background, 206-207
Intergroup hatred, 424-429
Intergroup reconciliation:
  vs conflict resolution, 6
  defined, 39
  implications of standard shifting
      processes for, 90-92
  instrumental reconciliation, 6
  interpersonal forgiveness as
      predictor of, 100-102
    empathy, 106-107
    evaluation of past violence, 107-109
    group identification, 105-106
    self-conscious emotions of collective
        guilt and collective shame,
        109-110
  model of peaceful coexistence between
      enduring groups, 433-437
  peace programs, 437-440
  perception of injustice, 89-90
  processes in, 234-235
  role of belongingness, 122
  role of competitive processes, 102
  role of tolerance and coexistence,
      430-433
  socio-psychological predictors, 98-100
  socioemotional reconciliation, 7
  sociopolitical and social-psychological
      background, 3-5
Intergroup relations. *See also* Intergroup
    conflict

  adaptation strategies for, 237-238
  continuum of, 345-346
  egosystem motivational dynamics. *See*
      Egosystem motivational dynamics
  fear in, *428, 437*
  implications of identity needs for
      reconciliation, 127-135
  majority- and minority-group members:
    preferences, 237-238
    and representations, 239-240
    roles of threat and trust, 240-243
  psychological processes promoting bias:
    intergroup competition, 229-231
    intergroup threat and distrust,
        231-233
    interventions to reduce bias, 233-236
    social categorization and group
        identification, 228-229
  roles of threat and trust, 240-243
  social needs relevant to:
    belongingness, 120-122
    distinctions and conflicts among the
        basic needs, 126-127
    self-esteem, 119-120
    self-integrity, 122-126
Intergroup Relations Model (IRM):
  cognition-affect-behavior mediational
      model, 350-351
  componential structure of reciprocal
      intergroup relations, 353-354
  differences with other models,
      351-352
  features of, 351
  perceived equality and
      inequality of opportunity for
      resource attainment, 352-353
  power, reciprocity, and a reconciliation
      attempt, 357-359
  psychological interpretation of the
      variance components in intergroup
      responses, 354-357
Intergroup Schadenfreude, 333-335

Intergroup social identity, 284

Intergroup threat and distrust, 231-333, 258-259

Intergroup trust, in the context of Northern Ireland:

experimental studies, 212-214

and reconciliation, 216-217

survey research, 214-216

theoretical background, 211-212

International conflicts, 38, 44

role of emotions in, 46

Interpersonal friendships, 267-268

Interracial prejudice and mistrust, in U. S., 231-232

Intragroup social identity, 284

Intrasocietal conflicts, 44

Israeli-Palestinian case, settlement and resolution of conflict, 17, 28, 124

Camp David 2000 peace discussions, 51

different aspect of we-ness, 278

and essence of teamness, 289-290

exchange of the letters of mutual recognition, 17

functions of trust, 285-287

instrumental reconciliation, 42-43

modeling group processes with a complex dynamical systems (CDS) approach, 279-280

needs-based model of reconciliation, 51-52

negation of the other, 26

Oslo accord, 17-18

"people-to-people" programs, 43

problem-solving workshops, 18

processes of socioemotional reconciliation, 51

psychological roots of terrorism, 288

reconciliation. *See* Reconciliation

Jewish-Arab workshops, 379

Justice judgments, 335-337

Kant's case of human community, 147

Kelman's conflict-resolution workshops, 277, 291-292

Kohlberg's theories of moral development, 376-377

Legitimacy constraint, 334

Legitimizing myths, 339

Lewin's group decision-making paradigm, 285-286

Low-status competing groups, 306

Male stereotypic domain, 337

Mandela, Nelson, 160

Marginalization, 237

Moral education, for reconciliation efforts, 377

Moral worthiness, 432

Morality, 151-154

Mortality salience, 121

Multicultural education, for reconciliation efforts, 376, 386-387

Multiethnic societies, 376

Musekeweya—New Dawn, 414-416

Mutual Intergroup Differentiation Model, 263-265

Mutual negation, of the other's identity, 24

Mutual respect, 481

Mutual security, 480-481

Mutual trust and mutual acceptance, 16

9/11 attack, 128-129, 131

Naive realism, 310-311

Nash Equilibrium problem, 281-282

Needs-based model, of reconciliation:

effects of intergroup apologies, 51

perpetrators' ratings of moral image, 49-50

readiness to reconcile, 52

victims experiences of threat, 49

victims' reactions to victimization, 49

victims' readiness to reconcile, 50
victims' sense of power, 51
Negative identity elements, 25
Negative out-group attitudes, 269
Negative perceptions and emotions, 65
Northern Irish conflict. *See*
    Intergroup conflict

Optimal Distinctiveness Theory, 263
Osgood's GRIT proposal, 42
Oslo Peace Accord, 268

Palestine Liberation Organization
    (PLO), 17
Peace building process, 42-43
Peaceful coexistence, 433-437
Perceived legitimacy, of group power and
    status, 308-309
Perceived social status, 304
Perpetrators, 46-47, 397
  act of social exchange with
    victims, 47
  as moral actors, 47
Personalization, 260-261
Personalization Model, 260
Pervasive cultural messages, 172
Pettigrew's Reformulated Contact
    Theory, 266
Posttraumatic stress disorder (PTSD)
    treatment, 478-479
Power, 302-305
Prison abuse scandals, in Iraq and
    Cuba, 135, 147
Procedural justice, 28, 149, 336-337
Programs and techniques, for
    reconciliation efforts:
  contact programs, 378-379
  cyberspace promotions, 381-382
  enlightenment programs, 376-378
  healing and problem-solving
    programs, 380-381
  skill-based programs, 380

Prototypicality, 85
Psychological needs perspective, of
    conflict, 38-40
Psychological processes:
  conditions, prior to reconciliation,
    374-375
  involved in reconciliation:
    affective processes, 382-384
    behavioral processes, 386-387
    cognitive processes, 384-386
Public support, in conflict settlement, 22

Realist perspective, of conflict, 38-40
Realistic conflict theory, 424-425
Recategorization, 234-235, 261-266, 431
Reconciliation, 24-27, 278-279. *See also*
    Conflict settlement and resolution;
    Intergroup reconciliation
  application of interpersonal
    forgiveness, 70
  barriers to, 294-296
  based on the achievement of a
    "fragile we", 284-285
  basic constructs in:
    ethnocentrism, 347-348
    intragroup and intergroup
      affect, 349-350
    perceived equality of opportunity for
      resource attainment, 348-349
    shared social consensus, 348
  bottom-up intergroup process,
    291-292
  categorization models for
    promoting, 259-260
  changes in reciprocal responses of
    groups, 346-347
  combination intra- and intergroup
    reconciliation processes, 292-293
  conceptual model of:
    compliance, 19-20
    identification, 20
    internalization, 20

Reconciliation (*continued*)
    social influence, 21
    types of political orientation, 20-21
    conditions for:
        acknowledgments of
           responsibility, 29
        confronting history and coming to
           terms with the truth, 28-29
        establishment of cooperative
           activities, 29-30
        moral considerations, 28
        mutual acknowledgment, 27
        using needs, 135-137
    vs conflict resolution, 18
    connotation, 15-16, 200
    dealing with threats of victimhood
        and guilt:
        needs-based model of
           reconciliation, 47-53
        unilateral actions, 46-47
    defined, 41, 396
    and forgiveness, 477-483
    in German foreign policy, 16
    Germany's relations with Europe,
        16-17
    goal of, 44
        individual level reconciliation,
           372-373
        psychological conditions
           prior to, 374-375
        societal conditions prior to, 373-374
        societal level reconciliation, 370-372
    as a goal of conflict resolution, 17-18
    identity change in, 24, 40
        dilemma of, 26
        negation of the other, 26-27
        process of internalization, 25
        socioemotional reconciliation, 24-25
    implications of identity needs for:
        belongingness after having harmed
           another group, 133-134
        belongingness when harmed by
           another, 129-130
        self-esteem after having harmed
           another group, 132-133
        self-esteem when harmed by
           another, 127-129
        self-integrity after having harmed
           another group, 134-135
        self-integrity when harmed by
           another, 130-132
    intervention issues, 388
    models of, 282-283
    Op-Ed report, 295-296
    for Palestinians and Israelis, 160
    paths to reconciliation, 40-44
    programs and techniques:
        contact programs, 378-379
        cyberspace promotions, 381-382
        enlightenment programs, 376-378
        healing and problem-solving
           programs, 380-381
        skill-based programs, 380
    psychological processes involved in:
        affective processes, 382-384
        behavioral processes, 386-387
        cognitive processes, 384-386
    "realist" and the "psychological needs"
        perspectives, 38-40
    as a reciprocal process of individual and
        group-level change, 283-284
    reconciliation as a precondition for
        negotiation, 18
    role of respect, 159-164
    role of trustworthy relations, 41
    roles of psychologists, 389
    significance of mutual acceptance, 16
    in South Africa, 160
    strategies for peace, 281-282
    tipping points, 290-291
    between two nations, challenges, 162
    value of one's social identity, 288

Rejection sensitivity, 174
Residual negative affect:
  contribution of group homogeneity and
    essentialism, 309-310
  dehumanization, 311-312
  intergroup anxiety, 307-308
  naive realism, 310-311
  perceived legitimacy, of group power
    and status, 308-309
  and power, 302-303
  and social status, 304-305
Respect:
  basis for evaluations of, 151-154
  categorical, 147-149
  contingent, 149-151
  disrespect and delegitimization,
    154-156
  implications for reconciliation, 159-164
  intragroup disrespect, 157-159
  intrasocietal patterns of disrespect, 157
  primary elements of appraisals, 151-154
Respect ritual, 162-163
Revenge, psychologically positive
  aspect of, 46-47
Rwandan genocide, 39, 130, 132, 135
  approach to reconciliation:
    aim of, 403
    empathic responding,
      significance of, 406-407
    evaluation of, field study, 407-410
    integration of materials with
      participants, 407
    psychological education, 402
    Radio/Communication Project,
      414-416
    understanding basic psychological
      needs, 406
    understanding effects of trauma and
      victimization, 404-405
    understanding origin of genocide and
      mass killing, 405-406

    working with national leaders,
      410-412
    working with the media and
      community leaders, 412-414
  background, 398-399
  conceptual elements and practical
    avenues in reconciliation, 399-401
  role of psychology and structure,
    401-402

Safe space, 186
Schachter's affiliation principle, 281
Sectarianism, 200
  background of, in Northern
    Ireland, 201-202
Seeds of Peace Program, 437
Self-affirmation theory, 123
Self-categorization theory, 234, 257, 259
Self-disclosures, 387
Self-discrepancy theory, 123
Self-esteem, 119-120, 234
  after having harmed another
    group, 132-133
  when harmed by another, 127-129
Self-handicapping behavior, 173
Self-integrity, 122-126
  after having harmed another
    group, 134-135
  negative effects on intergroup
    relations, 123-124
  when harmed by another, 130-132
Sherif's Robbers Cave paradigm, 230-231,
  258, 281-282, 286, 423-424
Signaling model, of intergroup
  reconciliation, 44-45
Skill-based programs, for reconciliation
  efforts, 380
Social behavior, in category-based
  interactions, 260
Social categorization, 228-229,
  257-258, 260

Social categorization theory, 424
Social expectation, 276
Social identity, 126, 259, 288
Social identity theory, 65, 234, 257, 259,
     276, 304, 424, 426
Social learned helplessness, 287
Social needs, relevant to intergroup
     relations:
  belongingness, 120-122
  distinctions and conflicts among the
     basic needs, 126-127
  implications of identity needs for
     reconciliation:
     belongingness after having harmed
        another group, 133-134
     belongingness when harmed by
        another, 129-130
     self-esteem after having harmed
        another group, 132-133
     self-esteem when harmed by
        another, 127-129
     self-integrity after having harmed
        another group, 134-135
     self-integrity when harmed by
        another, 130-132
  self-esteem, 119-120
  self-integrity, 122-126
Social psychology, 3
Social reality constraints, on
     stereotypes, 331
Social stereotypes, of a group, 178,
     328-329, 331
Societal conditions, prior to
     reconciliation, 373-374
Societal level reconciliation, 370-372
Socioemotional processes, 434
Socioemotional reconciliation, 24-25,
     41, 434
  change in relations, 43
  conditions of "double victimhood", 53
  goal of, 44
  vs instrumental reconciliation, 44-45

  nature of change, 43
  process of, 42, 45
  target of change in, 43
  temporal focus of the process of
     change, 43-44
The Souls of Black Folk, 236
Southern Poverty Law Center's website, 381
Status, 308
Stereotype Content Model
     (SCM), 305-306
Storytelling technique, 380
Substantive justice, 28

Teamness and reconciliation, 289-290
Terror management theory, 121, 429
Theory of infrahumanization,
     208-209
A Theory of Justice, 144
Third parties, in conflict resolution,
     17, 22
Threats, 38
  and authoritarianism, 121
  ego, 173
  to individuals' self-esteem, 120
  intergroup, 258-259
  realistic, 205
  symbolic, 205, 258, 261
  unilateral removal of, 46-47
  Zionism, 118
Tony Blair's declaration, in 2004, 128
Transcendent identity, 264
Transgenerational revenge-based
     violence, 64
Trauma:
  collective, 65
  consequences of, 66
  emotions associated with, 64
  intrapsychic dimensions of, 66
  past, 64
  phenomenon of reenactment, 64-65
  unfinished business of, 66
Trust, 482

Trustworthy relations, 41, 278-279.
  See also Intergroup trust, in the
  context of Northern Ireland
interracial prejudice and mistrust,
  in U. S., 231-232
Truth and Reconciliation Commission,
  South Africa, 15, 39, 42, 162
  establishment of, 59-62
  research on forgiveness, 62-64
Turkish genocide, 400
Tutu, Desmond, 160

Unconscious goal, 175
Underlying conflict, defined, 302
Uneasy coalition, 278
Unilateral actions, against threats,
  46-47
Unilateral gestures, significance of, 162
United Nation Universal Declaration of
  Human Rights, 148-149
Universal stereotype, 155
Unprecedented evil, 131
U.S. President's Emergency Plan for
  AIDS Relief (PEPFAR), 448

Versöhnung, 16
Victimization, 397, 434
Victims:
  categorization of, 78-79
    factors affecting, 85-89
    self-categorization, 83
    social categorization, 84-85

feelings of:
  humiliation, 46
  role of revenge, 47
  tactic of social distancing, 47
victimized out-group's perspective and
  reconciliation, 80
Vietnam antiwar movement, 280
Violent conflict, 80, 159, 200
  between the Catholic and the Protestant
    communities in Northern
    Ireland, 103, 128, 130
  development of destructive
    conflicts, 475-477
  establishing cooperative relations
    after, 480-483
  forgiveness and reconciliation, 477-483
  between Hindus and Muslims
    in India, 165n
  impact on survivors, perpetrators and
    passive bystanders, 396-398

Warfare, nature of, 15-16
Well-being, 234
White Americans, 83, 91, 124, 231
  form of social consciousness, 236
  perceptions of intergroup contact on
    campus, 240
Women job applicants and tenure candidates,
  discrimination of, 171-172

Youth Reconciliation Initiative and
  Initiative for Peace, 437